Robert Ferber

P. J. Verdoorn

RESEARCH METHODS IN
Economics & Business

The Macmillan Company | NEW YORK

Library of Congress catalog card number: 62–7080

The Macmillan Company, New York
Collier-Macmillan Canada, Ltd., Toronto, Ontario

Printed in the United States of America

Preface

THE INCREASINGLY complex nature of business and government has not only focused attention on the uses of research in solving operational problems but also has given rise to a greater variety of problems for research to solve. The result has been a greatly expanded role of research in the several fields of applied economics, whether related to business or to the economy as a whole.

One important consequence of this expansion of research activities is the growing similarity between the approaches used to solve business, and particularly marketing, problems of the single firm, and those used for the economic analysis of aggregates. This increased similarity is no doubt also brought about by the more widespread realization of the interdependence between the firm and the economy. In part, it is also due to the related tendency of these two main fields of application to overlap each other. Problems handled by a marketing research department in one company, for instance, are often handled by the economic research department in another company. This is particularly so for problems related to sales forecasting, price policies, inventory control, and even for distribution methods. A third factor is the growing awareness of the value of methods previously used largely in one particular area to solve other types of problems as well. Thus, consumer surveys have found wide favor among business-cycle specialists for purposes of forecasting, whereas time-series analyses are used much more frequently by business analysts to solve demand problems.

At the same time, the expansion of applied economic research has been accompanied by the introduction of new techniques and means of approach. Some of these, such as motivation research, operations research, and business cycle models have been developed specifically to solve problems of an economic nature, while others, such as factor analysis and scaling methods, have originated in other disciplines.

v

All in all, it is apparent that, as a consequence of these developments, the techniques at the disposal of a research worker in any field of applied economics are extremely varied. Thus, there would seem to be a considerable need for a book to bring these techniques together, to explain how they can be applied to research problems, and to discuss their relative merits in particular situations. This, essentially, is the purpose of the present volume. It seeks to provide in a more or less logical manner a general outline of the organization of research operations, an exposition of the main approaches to research problems as well as descriptions of specific research techniques and the relative merits of each. Apart from this, illustrative examples of the application of these methods to solve various business and economic problems are given, whereas the two last chapters present a down-to-earth discussion of the manner in which different approaches and techniques can be coordinated in business research.

The general approach followed in the present book runs closely parallel to that used in a Dutch textbook on market research by the second author: *Grondslagen en Techniek der Marktanalyse* (Leiden, 1950). Thanks to the generosity of the publisher, H. E. Stenfert Kroese's Uitgevers-Maatschappij N.V., much material of the Dutch text could be adapted to the needs of the present volume.

The book is intended basically for three categories of people:

1. As a text for a research methods course taught at the senior or graduate level.
2. As a reference manual for students struggling to write a master's or Ph.D. thesis, many of whom have great difficulty in knowing what methods are available for different purposes.
3. As a reference manual for researchers in business and industry on methods that can be used in different situations.

This book is not a statistics text, though a knowledge of elementary statistics—and some background in marketing or economics—is a prerequisite to its use. Rather, the book seeks to provide the reader with an overall perspective of research-problem organization and of means of solving research problems. Exercises are included for the benefit of those who would like some practice in the use of various techniques, though for complete mastery of the technical aspects the reader will have to refer to the many more specialized books mentioned in footnotes and at the end of chapters. Moreover, to give the reader familiarity with the various systems of notation as currently used for different purposes, different types of notation have been used throughout this book.

We should like to express our appreciation to A. P. Barten and L. M. Koyck of the Rotterdam School of Economics for reading various parts of Chapters 7 and 8, to Marvin Frankel of the University of Illinois for reading

Chapter 10, and to Marianne A. Ferber for going through the entire volume, and for the many helpful suggestions that these people have provided. We are also indebted to the following individuals and organizations for permission to reproduce various material in this book:

American Sociological Review
Bureau of the Budget
Centraal Planbureau, The Hague, Netherlands
Educational and Psychological Movement, Durham, North Carolina
Harvard University Press
W. W. Heusner
Louis Guttman
Iowa State University Press
Journal of Applied Psychology
Journal of Marketing
Journal of the American Statistical Association
McGraw-Hill Book Company
North Holland Publishing Company
George W. Snedecor
Alfred Politz
H. E. Stenfert Kroese N.V.
Tide Magazine

We are also indebted to Professor Sir Ronald A. Fisher, F.R.S., Cambridge, and Messrs. Oliver & Boyd Ltd., Edinburgh, for permission to reprint a table from their book *Statistical Methods for Research Workers*.

It is perhaps needless to note that in the final analysis we alone are responsible for the content and organization of this book and stand ready to face up to (or dodge, as the case may be) any criticisms resulting therefrom.

Robert Ferber
P. J. Verdoorn

Table of Contents

ix

Figures

Tables

| Part One | A SYSTEMATIC APPROACH |

THE ADVANTAGES OF A SYSTEMATIC APPROACH TO RESEARCH PROBLEMS are many. Such an approach contributes to greater accuracy and a more orderly approach in handling research problems. In a research department it also promotes better organization for research and aids in quicker and more efficient solution of research problems. Greater validity is also engendered, since alternative approaches are then not easily overlooked. At the same time, systematization can be overdone, for no two research problems are exactly alike, and a certain amount of flexibility in operations (and in one's attitude) is highly desirable.

The two chapters that follow illustrate the systematic approach to marketing and economic research. The first chapter presents an overall view of the different types of research problems in these areas, while the second suggests a systematic approach to the solution of these problems.

1

1 | Research as a Tool of Economic Policy

1.1. IN GOVERNMENT

ONE CONDITION for the success of a government in any free society is its ability to anticipate needs and desires in those fields where it has been entrusted with responsibility. At the same time, however, it must also anticipate whether or not the possible means of satisfying those needs will be adequate. If demand and supply appear to be about equal, a state of balance is in prospect and the government is in a fortunate position, indeed. But if this is not the case, corrective action is needed, and if it is not taken quickly enough or is not in the right direction, the party in power might well be faced with serious difficulties. In either case, research is indicated, for one thing to ascertain the current state of affairs, and for another to reveal future prospects and what corrective action, if any, may be needed.

Research provides the basis for nearly all government policies in our economic system. Thus, the government's budget rests in part on an analysis of the needs and desires of the people and on the availability of revenues to meet these needs. Each gives rise to numerous major problems in itself. Needs, for example, cover a host of things—schools, hospitals, health, roads, public safety, recreational facilities, conservation, etc. Each of these needs has to be considered separately, and even broken down further before it can be put into manageable form. Thus, in the case of schools, questions have to be asked about school attendance by area, and by grades within areas, before any reliable estimates of classroom space can be made. Although this is an easier problem than most—because the school-age population is known several years in advance—continual research is nevertheless needed on factors like population migration, drop-outs from school (especially from high schools), the supply of teachers, teaching facilities, and related matters.

3

Then, needs have to be translated into costs. This means predicting prices one or two years in advance, a highly risky task.

Even more difficult is the estimation of probable government revenues. Given the structure of tax rates, there still remain to be predicted the level of sales of the many commodities subject to excise taxes, the distribution of individuals by income level, a similar distribution for corporate and for non-corporate business, as well as revenue from a host of other sources—tariffs, licenses, fees, etc. This involves the prediction of business conditions, as most of these factors are governed by the level of business activity. Even when this series of steps has been taken, the government budget is by no means complete. Then the cost of the needs has to be equated to probable revenues and the inevitable discrepancy eliminated. Here we move directly into policy formation, a field where research is as badly needed as anywhere.

Whether the researcher should participate in policy decisions is a debatable point, since decision-making itself is not a part of research. Not debatable, however, is the need for research to devise alternative policies and to examine the consequences of each of these alternatives in order to facilitate the decision of the policy maker. Before a rise in, say, the excise tax on gasoline can be recommended intelligently, the probable effect of this increase on the industry, and on related industries such as auto servicing, has to be examined and quantified, if possible. The implications of high tariffs, of an increase in postal rates, of tax reductions, and of any other proposed changes have to be carefully weighed in advance. Even the implications of "no change" have to be examined. Thus, if a recession appears probable, can the government afford to leave tax rates for the next fiscal year at current levels? With the increasing number of aged living on fixed pensions, what is the consequence of keeping old-age assistance at the same levels if prices are moving up?

Clearly, preparation of a government's budget takes in many different research problems. Yet, preparing the budget is only one facet of the government's economic operations. Equally important is the enactment of programs for dealing with all phases of the country's existence. Most of these programs will touch on economic conditions in one way or another. The plight of the farmer, the problems of both big and small business, working conditions, collective bargaining practices, even the size and nature of the military forces are matters requiring research on economic and marketing conditions for the preparation of well-conceived programs. Thus, one of the most fundamental problems of all is the allocation of the nation's resources between defense expenditures and civilian, presumably more productive, expenditures; and, for defense expenditures, a choice must be made between outlays for a strong current military force and outlays for development of new weapons years ahead. Economic as well as military considerations have to be taken into account in arriving at these decisions. Poor economic judgment can wreck a nation as easily as poor military judgment. If a government devotes most of its resources to maintaining a strong military force and neglects the other needs of its citizens, the resulting discontent can well endanger the stability of the country.

Another major function of research in government is collecting information on the economic and social structure of the nation. This includes the size and characteristics of the population, the income and income distribution of the people, sources and types of income payments, production of goods and services, employment and unemployment, consumption-saving patterns, business sales and inventories, prices and price movements, natural resources and their use (and depletion), foreign trade, banking transactions, money in circulation, transactions in stock and commodity markets, and all the other many aspects of economic life. This information tells the government what is happening in the economy and what changes are taking place. It gives a picture of the characteristics of the economy, and an insight into the mechanisms by which the system operates. In addition, these data are indispensable in evaluating the probable impact of planned changes in the system and in predicting future trends. Many of these data are at least as important to business for market and economic analysis of industry conditions as they are to government. Yet no single firm is in a position to compile by itself even the most crucial data required for these purposes.

Collecting these data is by no means a routine task. It involves a variety of research problems. Some of these are problems of concept and definition. Others arise from sampling difficulties because getting this information from all people in the country is invariably too expensive as well as too impractical. Hence, most governments maintain large staffs of research technicians purely to work on data-collection problems.

1.1.1. Three Distinct Phases

In effect, research as a tool of sound economic policy has three distinct phases of operation, as the foregoing material makes clear. First is the *investigation of economic structure*, the continual compilation of facts about the size and nature of the economic system. Without such data, economic policy can hardly be formulated on a sound basis (though the availability of these data does not, of course, ensure the soundness of economic policy). A more comprehensive discussion of this still somewhat vague concept "economic structure" and its relation to economic policy will be given in Sec. 4.1.

The second phase is *diagnosis*, namely, the description through the data of events that are taking place and the analysis of the forces underlying these events. Much of this is description of day-to-day developments in the economic system, such as changes in population, in employment, in prices, etc. Knowledge of these changes, and an explanation of how they come about, is indispensable to government administration as well as to business policy.

The third phase, which generally operates concurrently with the second, is *prognosis*—the prediction of future developments. In many ways, prognosis is the most difficult as well as the most fascinating of the three phases. It superimposes the forecast on top of the diagnosis of economic events and their causes. Techniques in this area are as yet rather primitive. Consequently, research is all the more necessary because effective government policies depend on successful prognostications.

It is useful to distinguish between two different kinds of prognosis. On the one hand, we have the "forecast proper," i.e., a prognosis of the future course of the economy if the government adheres to its current policy. Such a forecast will show whether it is desirable to make a change in policy in the near future, or even whether such a change is inevitable. On the other hand, a forecast can be made of the effects of a specific change in policy. To judge the desirability of the change, its estimated effects have to be superimposed upon the forecast proper.

Actually, considerable progress through research has been made in the latter type of prognosis, namely, in the evaluation of the effects on the economy of particular changes in government policy. Thus, if a rise in tariff barriers is advocated as a means of improving conditions in certain industries, it is generally possible to gauge in advance the effect on these industries, and on the economy generally, of such a move. It is also possible to estimate with fair reliability the extent to which sales of foreign products will be reduced in this country for given increases in tariff rates. The same is true of the effect on the money market of an increase in Federal Reserve bank rediscount rates; of the variation in product sales and government revenue with given changes in excise rates; of the effect of an increase in the Federal minimum wage on labor income and wage structures; etc. Prognosis is not accurate in all such problems, particularly where market conditions shift in some unforeseen manner. This was the case, for example, with certain aspects of the government materials stockpiling program in the early 1950's, when civilian demand for some materials was so greatly increased by growing prosperity that the government had to release part of its stockpile to relieve the pressure on prices.

On the whole, prognosis of effects of short-run changes in government policy has good chances of success. The other type of prognosis, the forecast proper, requires a prediction of business fluctuations as well as of other trends. Though theoretical studies in this area are numerous,[1] their applica-

---

[1] As an example of annual forecasts of this type, see KLEIN, LAWRENCE, R., and A. S. GOLDBERGER, *An Econometric Model of the United States, 1929–1952*, Chapters 5 and 6. For a framework for long-term estimates, see VERDOORN, P. J., "Complementarity and Long Range Projections," *Econometrica*, October, 1956, pp. 429–450.

tion is still pretty much in the realm of art. Short-run forecasts can be made with fair accuracy, if only because economic magnitudes do not change appreciably in a brief period of time anyway, but forecasts of conditions a year or more in advance are still bound to be inaccurate to a certain extent. Nevertheless, this inaccuracy does not necessarily obviate the usefulness of predicting consequences of policy changes. A government is bound to undertake a policy change occasionally under the pressure of present conditions and expected short-term future developments. A forecast will give a more accurate knowledge of the direction and probable intensity of the effects of that change. This will considerably reduce the uncertainty about the desirability of the policy change, even if the forecast of conditions without such a change is inaccurate.

In actual operation, the investigation of economic structure, diagnosis and prognosis are rarely distinguished as three different phases of research. From an organizational point of view, it makes more sense to set up the work by subject matter with one administrative unit encompassing not only forecasting but also diagnosis and some or all of the necessary structural research (though part of the latter may be delegated to one or more specialized agencies). Yet, from the point of view of research methodology and organization, we shall see in later chapters that these are highly useful distinctions.

1.2. IN BUSINESS

As it does with the government, ability to anticipate demand and supply underlies the success of nearly all business enterprise. In business, however, demand and market factors are the more important. Given knowledge of future demand, it is generally not difficult for an individual firm, or even an entire industry, to adjust its supply schedule within the limits of its projected total capacity. Since production has to be geared to demand several weeks or even months in advance, and investments have to be planned even a full year or more before the desired expansion of output can be realized, it becomes important to ascertain not only current market demands but also what demand will be some time in advance. Because of this need, market analysis has become an integral tool of modern business policy.

The organization of any sizeable enterprise requires a certain amount of budgeting if unity of action is to be maintained among its many departments. This budgeting has to be all the more fully elaborated as the enterprise grows and its organization becomes more complicated. Here the basic function of market analysis comes to the fore.

The entire system of budgeting, which ultimately results in a projected profit and loss account, the so-called master budget, is based essentially on the sales estimates. Once probable sales have been estimated, efficient production and investment programs can be set up. Around these are grouped, in turn, the purchasing and financing plans. The enormous risks inherent in an erroneous anticipation of future sales logically follow from this key position of the sales estimates. This position is all the more important as the duration of the production and sales periods lengthen, thereby increasing the chance of incorrectly projected capacity.

The margin of error in sales forecasts can be reduced considerably if derived from sound economic and market analysis. This does not mean that sales forecasts without previous market analysis, in its technical sense, are worthless. The intuition of many successful entrepreneurs testifies that this is not always the case. But such intuition is a rare gift, and excessive preoccupations with other matters often makes it necessary for even those executives who possess it to delegate a large part of this prognosis to others less well equipped. The feeling of internal security of the executive created by his own intuition, rooted in long experience and knowledge of the "sphere" of the market, cannot be denied. Attempts can be made at convincing others of its correctness, but to prove it is an impossibility. Therefore what is more attractive than systematically applied market investigation as confirmation of one's own intuition? It is true that this touchstone is not able, either, to furnish proof concerning *ex ante* managements, but market analysis does give, owing to the methods it follows, an insight into the *most probable* course of future market conditions under closely defined circumstances.

In addition, efforts may be directed toward organizing production and marketing in such a manner as to minimize losses due to unexpected changes in sales. Such an approach requires also a considerable amount of factual data and analyses of company operations under different operating conditions.

From the foregoing, the following definition of market research may be offered, for operating purposes:

> Marketing research is the investigation of the structure and development of a market for the purpose of formulating efficient policies for purchasing, production and sales.

Thus the aim of market research is given.[2] Formulated in this way, the scope of market research is not restricted to selling but covers purchasing and production as well. The objectives of the firm will determine the concrete requirements to be met by efficient policy. The widely different objectives of firms necessarily influence the character of market research in each case.

---

[2] The term "market research" is restricted at times to research into markets and sales opportunities, whereas "marketing research" encompasses study of the entire scope of marketing activities. In this book, however, the two terms are used interchangeably.

Financing plans and the labor budget need not be mentioned separately in the definition, for insofar as they are causally connected with the sales and production programs, they immediately evolve from these programs. It would therefore be superfluous to include these areas in the definition unless the capital and labor markets were also to be included in the field of market analysis.

The above definition of market research also sets it apart from economic analysis and research which, again for operating purposes, may be said to involve, more broadly,

> the investigation of the nature and causes of wealth including the allocation of scarce resources to achieve given ends.

These definitions emphasize the relatively narrow objectives of marketing research compared with economic research. However, since the methods of approach and techniques used are almost identical in the two areas, marketing research can be considered as a particular application of economic research for business purposes, particularly from a problem-solving point of view.

1.2.1. Market Structure

Of basic importance to the firm is the structure of the market it serves—its size and characteristics, the nature of its customers and consumption patterns, the characteristics of its product in relation to competing products, sales and price fluctuations as business conditions vary, seasonal patterns, the firm's status relative to its competitors, etc. If the organization of the firm is not well adapted to the structure of the market, the result will be either too high a level of costs or too small a sales volume. Like the market, industry possesses lasting characteristics describing its typical structure. The lasting character of this structure is often strengthened by investments made in the past. Unforeseen changes in market structure can render these investments completely or partly worthless. This applies not only to investments proper but also to all those expenses that result from long-term undertakings or that for any other reason are relatively fixed. Examples are a large part of salary expenses, rents, those patent obligations which do not possess the character of royalties, and so on.

Anything that leads to fixed expenses should be adapted with great care to the existing market structure. For example, the firm's location, production capacity and sales organization should be adapted to the geographical structure of the purchase and sales markets. The number and purchasing power of the ultimate buyers, beside the technical characteristics of the product, decide whether sales should take place to order, in series or in mass production. In choosing between horizontal integration—the output of several products side by side—and vertical integration it is again the nature of purchasing and selling markets, together with technical factors, that are decisive. An erroneous choice of business structure renders the organizational set-up of the firm highly vulnerable. With horizontal integration, apart from making the organizational and technical structure of the firm too complicated and hence unmanageable, there is the danger of too unequal a distribution of cyclical risks. Applied in the right way, however, such integration reduces those risks. Yet, differentiation brings the danger of too great a dependance on suppliers of raw and auxiliary materials, should monopolistic tendencies be present on the purchasing market.

Market structure also affects the financial policy of the firm. The intensity of cyclical and seasonal fluctuations influences not only the allowable extent of outside financing but also the most economical division between long- and short-term credit.

Capital budgets and expansion are yet other areas in which a knowledge of market structure is crucial. Most important is the initial capital budget, drawn up at the time of the firm's establishment or its entry into a particular market. It is based, among others, on a detailed study of prevailing market conditions. With later budgets, alterations in the firm's organization may well be indicated by changed market conditions. However, such modifications can only be planned rationally through constant study of market structure.

A continued and ever-deepening investigation into market structure is therefore one of the most important conditions if an investment budget is to be justified from an economic point of view. This budget, which pictures the future investment policy of the enterprise, is based, as a matter of course, on long-term forecasts. The underlying structural investigations and study of trends prevent hasty decisions, influenced by momentary conditions. They also help liberate the enterprise from being unduly affected by the erratic whirl of day-to-day economic life.

1.2.2. Market Diagnosis

The task of market diagnosis is possibly less fascinating than that of prognosis but a good deal more topical than structural investigation. If prognosis necessarily provides debatable information on the most likely developments, and structural investigation, with its averages and elasticities, a factual picture of reality as represented by its more latent aspects, diagnosis explains day-to-day changes and serves as the basis for market development and policy formation.

Market diagnosis offers, apart from its explanatory function, the two-fold possibility of correcting and checking. *Correction* is possible insofar as continued market diagnosis enables management to revise its plans on short notice. Assume, for example, that within the framework of some budgeting system, annual plans are based on a prognosis as of December 31. It is quite likely that these plans have to be reviewed again the following May or June. Unexpected price changes and movements in business conditions or entirely new sales possibilities may have appeared by then. These would indicate need for revisions in the plan. This is a point that deserves considerable emphasis: a plan retains actual value only if and insofar as the suppositions on which the prognosis was based retain their validity.

On the other hand, correction of a plan already in operation is acceptable only if circumstances have in the meanwhile changed to such an extent that the original suppositions cannot be retained. Here again is one of those cases where replacement of the intuitive managerial approach to the market by systematic market investigations bears fruit. As soon as the "why" of an alteration in the plan of those concerned cannot be explained objectively, budgeting loses its educational character.

Clearly, therefore, one task of market diagnosis is to verify, at regular intervals within the plan period, the validity of the assumptions underlying these plans and to correct the latter accordingly.

The other checking task of market diagnosis is completely different in character. That task is not confronting reality with a formal (or informal) plan, but rather comparing the achievements of the enterprise in the recent past with the possibilities offered by that past. Did the sales correspond to what could reasonably have been expected? Were the purchases rightly timed? Was the price policy followed the most efficient one?

Systematically applied, market diagnosis provides, in principle, the opportunity of judging the efficiency of each act of management after some time has elapsed, of analysing operating results in relation to market developments, and of expressing the quantitative influence of business policy on this result.

But if market diagnosis is to supply more than a pile of reports, worth reading but seldom read, the enterprise should be organized so that the responsibility for each function can be pinned down. Furthermore, the consequences of each decision of management should be systematically and periodically recorded. Most efficient for this is a system of budgeting set up according to the typical requirements of the enterprise. Only this method offers a means of systematically checking both the achievements of all departments and the efficiency of policy decisions, on the basis of the objectively given possibilities during the period concerned. Thus a means of control arises not only over the efficiency of the production process proper, but also over the market decisions of management. The next major section, on the marketing audit, will discuss these operational techniques at greater length.

1.2.3. Market Prognosis

Without the two previous phases of investigation market prognosis is an impossibility. The influence of market prognosis on the several activities of the firm finds its starting point in the sales forecast. In its turn this forecast is decisive for the production, inventory and financing plans. This is also true for long-term investment plans. And only after some insight into future sales possibilities can the investment and financing plans be judged effectively and thought given to rational purchasing and inventory policy.

In the same way, with more thorough planning, costs and expense budgets will ultimately register the effect of the sales forecast. It is clear that a sales forecast must answer the following three main questions before a production program can be set:

1. What types (qualities) of each product will be sold?
2. How many in each category?
3. At what price?

Expected sales depend as much on quality as on price. Furthermore, the combination of list price, discounts and quantity determines expected gross revenue, just as quality and quantity are decisive in preparing cost estimates. Both costs and returns are the backbone of the master budget, which encompasses all other budgets with its projected profit and loss account.

The techniques used in market analysis differ in dealing with each of these three factors mentioned, and are partly dependent on the role each plays in the firm's policy.

For *quality*, it is a matter of following carefully the changes in tastes and habits of consumers and watching competition closely in order to cope with innovations as early as possible. In a period of business decline when purchasing power is decreasing, the consumer may well be content with lower-priced goods in order to balance his budget. The entrepreneur then has to keep ahead of this tendency in his sales program, for example, by introducing more acceptable articles in the lower price brackets. The task of the market analyst will thus be to supply necessary guides to technical research, to show how lower-priced articles can be made more attractive. With improving conditions, differences in quality come to the fore. Market research then has to show which features of the product are worth pushing with the consumer.

Market research is also important when a new product is brought on the market; what requirements should type, quantity and packaging meet in order to attain a profitable volume of sales?

It is especially with this kind of problem that so-called "qualitative market research" finds a fertile field of activity. Here more can be achieved with surveys than with secondary data. The slightest differences in preference can be fairly important, and may determine whether or not a product will pay for itself.

As far as *prices* are concerned, the correctness of existing prices has to be checked again with each new sales program. This check must cover both expected and already existing changes in purchasing power, as well as the price policy of competitors. The development of substitute products also requires careful watching in both respects. Sales of margarine, for example, are determined not only by its own price but also by that of butter and other substitutes containing fat.

Fixing future prices requires consideration of such matters as:

a) General price developments in the market concerned; how will competitors prices change given a change in business conditions?
b) The price pattern of competing products: a certain degree of substitution is nearly always possible.
c) The relations between sales and prices both of the firm and of competitors.
d) The relation between output and production costs; though this does not belong to market research proper, it is nevertheless decisive with regard to ultimate price policy.
e) Fluctuations in the wage level and raw material prices. For the latter, interaction with demand on the markets concerned has to be taken into account.

Only in a few cases will sample surveys bring something to light about these relations. Rather, here there is an important task for diagnostic market research. Thus, by using statistical data, the elasticity of demand can be estimated in many cases. Armed with this and similar key-indicators, the market analyst can recommend a proper pricing policy. He can indicate at which moment and how far prices will have to be altered in order to retain or increase sales or which price differentiations—for example, by group of customers, geographical areas and quantities—can improve net revenue.

Finally, as far as the estimate of the *quantities* to be sold is concerned, the foregoing clearly shows that sales estimates without price estimates are unthinkable. The same applies also to qualities. Only specific combinations of price, quality and quantity can be estimated. It is therefore a matter of arriving at the most favorable combination.

Once quantities have been fixed in this way, sales estimates can be prepared and used as starting points for further plans. It is not only the total volume of sales during the period concerned that is important but also its distribution over time. This is necessary so that the production plan will operate at minimum cost. Sometimes it will be possible to schedule production in such a way that production remains in harmony with sales. In other cases, one has to fall back on inventory adjustment, or even sometimes on temporary closing as the only solution. In order to weigh these alternatives intelligently, sales have to be accurately estimated at short intervals. The statistician will have to indicate the seasonal pattern, to estimate the most likely year-to-year trend, etc. Furthermore, by means of a survey, the possibilities of future changes in the seasonal pattern or structural changes in trends can be brought to light.

1.3. THE MARKETING AUDIT

The marketing audit comprises an overall evaluation of the marketing policies of the firm with the ultimate objective of formulating an improved marketing policy. This it seeks to do through evaluation of the present marketing position of the firm in relation to itself, other firms, competing products and industries, and trends in general, giving consideration to all the different facets of the firm's operations—the products, pricing, advertising and promotion, distribution channels, etc. Essentially, the marketing audit proceeds through three stages, namely:

1. Analysis of the present status of the firm—its objectives, its means of operation, its problems, management's outlook.
2. Investigation of the functional position of the firm in the market, i.e., the function this particular firm performs as distinguished from the functions performed by its competitors.
3. In the light of the information gathered in the preceding two stages, determine whether
    a) The firm's present market position can be improved by a change in policy, or
    b) a fundamental change in the markets served by the firm or in its objectives might be in order.

A more detailed review of each of these stages is provided below, whereas Chapter 11 is devoted to technical research aspects encountered with the audit.

1.3.1. Present Status

A firm generally wishes to realize a number of objectives, only one of which is the maximization of profits. The firm has at its disposal certain "instruments" for realizing these objectives, such as product quality, pricing, and advertising. The purpose of the marketing audit, in effect, is to indicate which combination of the marketing instruments will help the firm attain its objectives in the best possible way.

OBJECTIVES. That maximization of profits is only one of a number of objectives of the firm is especially true in the short run, for it is obviously foolish to maximize this year's profits at the expense of reduced future earnings.

From the short-run point of view, therefore (say, less than five years), a firm invariably has a number of subsidiary objectives among which are likely to be the following:

1. Retaining its present share in the market. If possible, this share should be increased even though current profits might decline.
2. Maintaining comfortable cash reserves, and above all ensuring that control of the firm does not fall into outside hands.
3. Pleasant employee relations.
4. Profits low enough to avoid attracting potential competition. From the point of view of long-run earnings, this might be considered a fundamental objective.
5. Maintaining and building good-will with customers, the industry, the community, etc.

As will readily be seen, each of these subsidiary objectives is not a goal in itself. Rather, they should be considered as limiting factors or restrictions on the maximization of current profits, with future earnings prospects not to be impaired.

Essentially, these limiting factors act as *boundary conditions*. Thus, from the point of view of discouraging potential competition, every possible policy might be acceptable provided that prices are kept below a certain level, say two dollars. This two dollars therefore sets the (upper) boundary to price policy: every price is acceptable as long as it does not exceed two dollars. The same reasoning can be applied to cash reserves or market share: they are not an end in themselves. Therefore, every policy is all right as long as liquidity position or market share are not impaired.

Apart from these subsidiary objectives, technical and organizational restraints act, too, as so many boundary conditions. Thus, output cannot be expanded beyond a certain capacity. Neither is it possible to change overnight the attitude of one's sales force. Therefore, in undertaking a marketing audit, all the objectives of the firm as well as its operational restraints must be explored and the latter defined explicitly. Hence, this preparatory stage in which the firm's problems are analyzed and suitable methods of approach devised can legitimately require a considerable portion of the time available for the entire investigation.

THE INSTRUMENTS. A marketing policy is implemented by five broad groups of instruments. These are:

1. Product, including quality
2. Price including discounts and credits
3. Selling and promotional effort
   a) salesmen's activities
   b) advertising

4. Distribution channels
5. Product line

None of these instruments is inflexible or fixed, for with each a large degree of substitution is possible. Thus, we can produce a product of mediocre quality and sell it at a high price with the aid of extensive advertising. A product can be sold with no advertising whatsoever but with sole reliance on salesmen (and good will), or it can be sold by a small sales force backed by large-scale advertising.

The best combination of instruments in one set of circumstances is not the best combination in other circumstances. A given combination of instruments, e.g., a price x for quality y supported by an advertising appropriation at level z, is expressed by the term *marketing mix*. Obviously, one particular "mix" may yield higher profits than another, but it does not follow *a priori* that maximum profits can be attained by one and only one marketing mix. However, it is clear that different marketing mixes can produce considerable variation in profits, and that, because of the possibility of substitution, reliance on only one set of instruments to the exclusion of others is liable to affect profits adversely.

The whole problem of devising a marketing policy, therefore, is to find the particular marketing mix that will maximize this year's profits without violating the several boundary conditions arising from the firm's other objectives and possibilities.

1.3.2. Functional Position

Investigation of the functional place of the firm in the market is designed to locate both the weak points and the strongholds in its market. It proceeds, in effect, to determine why people bought this firm's products rather than those of competing firms. The reasons why people buy one product and not another can be widely different. They may include price considerations, quality, service, reputation of the firm, convenience, and numerous others.

Detection of these reasons rests in large measure on sample surveys and on so-called qualitative market analysis. At the same time, "internal analysis," such as study of the firm's own data and discussions with salesmen, is not to be overlooked. These sources will often yield new hypotheses for investigation by surveys and can also be used as a sort of cross-check on the results of the surveys.

Also useful is economic analysis of the competitive structure of the market for the particular products and of the long-run outlook for the industry. Such an analysis helps place the findings on the firm's current position in proper perspective.

Relevant in this context is the concept of the marketing *asset*, i.e., the ultimate reason why one's competitive position on the market is in certain aspects better than that of others. Among such reasons may be location, patents, mass production, etc. It is the marketing assets that permit the firm to use its instruments in such a way as to secure a specific functional position. Thus, mass production facilities may lead to relatively low prices, leading in turn to consumer preference for the firm's product.

1.3.3. Possible Changes

The foregoing two stages have indicated, on the one hand, the boundary conditions for the firm's marketing policy and, on the other hand, the assets and liabilities of the firm in the market. With these data, we can proceed to investigate the possibilities for a better policy.

Such an analysis should follow a definite sequence, for a change in a firm's functional position will require as a rule time as well as money, e.g., new investments in the factory, a new advertising campaign, etc. One method of proceeding is as follows:

1. Investigate whether better exploitation of the existing market position is possible by a change in the marketing mix, without surpassing the boundary conditions. Thus, often it will be possible by a change in price or quality to sell more to existing customers. A change in the product line might achieve the same effect. This first step requires, therefore, a systematic check upon the efficiency of the marketing mix. It will show whether the marketing instruments are being used most effectively to meet the requirements of the existing functional position. (It may reveal, for example, that some expensive quality features of the product are irrelevant from the consumer's point of view, such as fine stitchings in work clothing.) If the audit is repeated periodically—say once a year—it will act as an automatic control on the adaptation of the firm to changes in the market—in consumer preferences, in the strategy of competitors, etc.
2. Investigate whether either an expansion or a total change of the functional position will give better results. Here again the possibilities will be limited by the boundary conditions. The danger of surpassing them is even greater than in the former case. This step will show, for example, whether it will be profitable to expand sales to other groups of buyers; whether a new line of products should be launched in order to assure a higher degree of brand loyalty; whether a substitute product should be added to the existing line; and whether a different channel of distribution should be considered, etc.

The techniques used in this analysis cover the whole range of market and economic research, and many will be presented in the following chapters. A simplified graphic approach to this problem is provided in the Supplement to this chapter.

Summarizing, the determinants of the firm's functional position may be set out schematically as follows:

Marketing assets

|

Instruments

|

Functions performed

|

Customers' preference

The question of how a given combination of instruments can be most effectively manipulated is governed—so far as the marketing aspect of the problem is concerned—by two "poles":

a) Existing or potential preference on the part of the customer.
b) The firm's ultimate assets (from the marketing point of view).

If a firm decides upon a certain functional position or, as the case may be, wants to make full use of its existing position, then clearly the thing to do when deciding how to change the use of one or more instruments is to take full advantage of already available marketing resources. Conversely, if we wish to judge the efficacy of a given marketing mix, the crucial question is whether the available resources, or assets, are adequately utilized with respect to the existing functional position of the firm. For example, is full use being made of existing distribution channels and display arrangements in promoting a new product line? Here we have a practical criterion for deciding in the first instance the relative merits of a given marketing mix.

In the preceding paragraph, however, the full emphasis is on the term "in the first instance." For not only the marketing aspects of the problem but also the firm's objectives and possibilities determine the extent to which the marketing mix is really efficient in the sense of being optimal. In addition to the functional position, therefore, the cost of production and the boundary conditions, as given by the limited possibilities and auxiliary objectives of the enterprise, should be taken into account.

The problem thereby assumes a somewhat complicated character. In practical cases its solution requires a more systematic method of investigation than that provided by the traditional procedures of market research.

This largely explains the need for a systematic marketing audit and the work started by some research agencies along these lines. The novel aspect of this audit of all marketing activities is not so much that new marketing research techniques are introduced. It is rather the systematic set-up of the entire investigation, which covers not only the existing and expected possibilities of the market but also, and simultaneously, the objectives and possibilities of the firm itself.

1.4. INCIDENTAL VS. SYSTEMATIC RESEARCH

Stress has been laid in the foregoing on the importance of systematically applied market analysis as a permanent part of the organization of the enterprise. Nevertheless, questions will arise, often more or less incidentally, that require investigation in an area not yet covered by the firm's continuous research. This can lead to overestimation of the importance of these incidental research assignments while the durable importance of market analysis as an integral part of an existing organization fades into the background. Particularly in the earlier days of market research, the situation was somewhat similar to that of the auditor who was "called in" to diagnose ailing administrations while the importance of a permanent check on administrative organization and results was realized only later. In the same manner, market analysis gives greatest benefit when it is a permanent part of the enterprise, for both market prognosis and periodic records based on the diagnosis. Only in this way can the firm be kept informed regularly of important market changes.

The work needed to keep diagnosis and prognosis up to date in the enterprise can be designated *systematic market research*, and investigations carried out as special assignments, *incidental research*. There is no need to stress that both kinds of research are mutually fruitful. This holds particularly if a marketing audit as described in the foregoing section is repeated annually or every other year as an integral part of systematic research. On the one hand, the audit as such stands to benefit from the earlier research, whether incidental or not. On the other hand, the audit, by encompassing all the instruments of the marketing mix, automatically highlights any additional research that may be needed. A major advantage of a periodically-repeated audit is, therefore, the possibility of replacing a series of consecutive, disjointed assignments, each carried out on a near-emergency basis, by a well-integrated, smoothly-scheduled research program.

| *Supplement* | The Problem of Marketing Strategy |
| *to Chapter 1*[3] | |

Basic considerations. An enterprise has at its disposal certain possibilities, each of which, however, is subject to certain limitations. In addition, the enterprise strives for a number of objectives. The most important of these is the maximization of present profits; to this, the other objectives act as so many side conditions. Both the possibilities and these side conditions set certain boundary conditions which, in the process of maximizing present profits, must not be exceeded. Finally, in its marketing policy, the enterprise can utilize a number of instruments for the purpose of realizing both its main and its auxiliary objectives.

The central problem of marketing theory, therefore, is how to combine the five instruments constituting the "marketing mix" in such a way as to ensure the highest possible present profits, taking into account the various boundary conditions, such as concern for future profits and limitation of available means.

Diminishing returns. Leaving these boundary conditions provisionally out of consideration, we get the picture of an enterprise with unlimited productive and financial possibilities. This enterprise knows only one objective: maximization of present profits. Taking the existing demand structure as given, the firm will then be subject to only one group of limitations, namely, those resulting from the sales potential of its market.

It then follows that each of the instruments, beyond a certain limit, will be subject to diminishing returns. This applies to price reductions, improvements of quality, the activity of the sales force, trade-channel discounts, advertising, and, in certain cases, to the extent of the product line.

Maximization rule. If only one instrument is changed, the others remaining unchanged, the following *maximum rule* applies:

It is irrational to raise the costs of an instrument if the increase in gross revenue does not offset the extra costs of the instrument itself plus the added costs of producing the additional volume of sales.

---

[3] Adapted from P. J. Verdoorn, "Marketing from the Producer's Point of View," *Journal of Marketing*, January, 1956, pp. 221–235.

The term "costs" has here been used in its wider meaning so that it covers also the sacrifice of gross revenue in case of a price reduction or a rise in the middlemen's discounts. Gross proceeds must then obviously be measured in constant prices.

Rule of choice. The fact that a given instrument has not exceeded this limit does not necessarily imply that it has been used rationally. Thus, if the salesmen's organization is inadequately developed, an irrationally large share of advertising will be necessary to realize a given marketing objective.

A correct combination in the *relative* use of the several instruments, however, may be achieved by applying a variant of the rule that weighted marginal revenues should be equated.[4] In its modified form, it may be called the *rule of choice:*

> A rise in the unit cost of a given instrument by one cent is to be preferred to that of other instruments, as long as it enables a greater increase of the quantity sold than would result either from lowering the price by one cent or from raising the unit costs of the other instruments by one cent.

The accuracy of this rule may be tested by comparing two alternative cases. In one of them the unit price is lowered by $1.00; advertising costs in the other case are raised by $1.00. Both measures are assumed to result in a 50 per cent increase of sales. According to the "rule of choice," therefore, an equal change in business results may be expected in both cases. This, in fact, is seen to be so in Table 1.1.[5]

Table 1.1

RULE OF CHOICE: LOWERED PRICE VERSUS INCREASED ADVERTISING

Item	Situation without price reduction or increased advertising	Price reduction	Increased advertising
Quantity sold	100,000	150,000	150,000
Price	$ 10.00	$ 9.00	$ 10.00
Advertising cost per unit	—	—	1.00
Variable costs per unit	5.00	5.00	5.00
Proceeds	1,000,000	1,350,000	1,500,000
Variable costs	500,000	750,000	750,000
Advertising	—	—	150,000
Constant costs	500,000	500,000	500,000
Net profit	—	100,000	100,000

General rule. In the absence of boundary conditions, we finally get as a general rule for the optimal composition of the marketing mix:[6]

---

[4] *Vide*, for example, A. L. BOWLEY, *The Mathematical Groundwork of Economics* (Oxford: Clarendon Press, 1924), p. 29; also J. M. HENDERSON and RICHARD QUANDT, *Microeconomic Theory* (N. Y.: McGraw-Hill, 1958), pp. 53–54.

[5] For a formal proof, see Appendix to Chapter 11.

[6] Cf. J. R. HICKS, *Value and Capital* (Oxford: Clarendon Press. 1939), p. 86.

Optimal combination of instruments has been attained when improvement in net profit is not possible either by a change in one of the instruments or by another combination.

Each of the instruments then satisfies the maximum rule given above.

Formal principles. Viewed formally, the basic principles of marketing policy do not deviate from the laws governing production. Total production should be increased to the point where marginal cost equals marginal revenue. In a material respect, however, there exists a definite difference. This is clear when the factors decisive to marginal cost are considered. If only production costs are taken into account while marketing costs are ignored, these factors are the prices of the production factors and what one might call the "technical coefficients" of the manufacturing process.

Where marketing costs are also reckoned with, the "demand coefficients" of the market form an additional element in the problem. For an increase of sales by one unit of product not only requires additional production costs but also extra marketing costs. The sum of these two has to satisfy the condition that it shall be a minimum. In other words, the point at issue is not marginal cost if all the factors of production and marketing instruments are changed proportionally but minimum marginal cost if every possible combination of factors of production and marketing instruments is taken into account. The question on which instruments the marginal cost of marketing will bear and the size of the total amount is decided by the sensitivity of demand with respect to quality improvement, advertising, salesmen's activity, etc.[7]

Complicating factors. Once these demand coefficients are known, the application of the rules given above no longer presents any difficulties. In order, however, to arrive at a realistic theory, it is necessary to recognize four complications that were neglected above.

1. The existence of *boundary conditions*, which have been explicity left out so far.
2. The fact that not all instruments are amenable to infinitesimal variations. This applies, first and foremost, to the quality of the product. An automobile, for example, may have either "rocket" drive or not. Something similar applies to the distribution channels and, in practice, also to the other instruments. Generally, the problem of *non-continuous substitution* arises as soon as qualitative criteria are changed.
3. The fact that certain marketing costs should be considered as *investments*. This occurs, among other things, in the case of advertising. There, the influence of marketing costs often will show a "distributed lag." Expenses incurred in the present period partly influence future profits.

---

[7] R. M. Shone, "Selling Costs," *Review of Economic Studies*, 1935, pp. 225–231. Cf. especially Hans Brems, *Product Equilibrium under Monopolistic Competition* (Cambridge: Harvard University Press, 1951), Chapter 5.

4. The fact that more than one product is marketed; that is, the problems connected with the fifth instrument, the firm's *product line.*

The theoretical aspects of the latter two complications touch upon the theory of production at least as much as upon the theory of marketing.[8] Let us, therefore, confine ourselves to the first two mentioned.

The problem of boundary conditions can, in principle, be solved either mathematically or graphically. For the mathematical method, reference should be made to Tinbergen's treatment of the problem of government economic policy.[9] The graphic method, however, is to be preferred for marketing policy because it is easier for the non-mathematical reader. In addition, it allows for the second complication, namely, non-continuous substitution possibilities.

Graphic method of approach. The complications of the product line and the existence of time lags have already been disregarded. Besides, the problem may be simplified even further by assuming the retail price to be given. Distribution-channel discounts will be considered as costs—which is, moreover, the most practical way of looking at it from the producer's point of view. Let us, to start with, also leave out the boundary conditions.

By simplifying the problem in this way, only three instruments remain to be dealt with: quality, sales promotion, and the choice of distribution channels. The question, then, is how these three instruments can be combined into the marketing mix that will ensure the maximum profit at the given retail price.

Let us now represent the situation graphically. The quantities to be marketed are plotted on the horizontal axis; gross revenue and total cost corresponding to these quantities, on the vertical axis. Revenue may then be represented in Fig. 1.1 by the straight line R going through the origin: price being given, revenue varies proportionately to total sales.

Total cost, however, is not only dependent upon the quantity sold but also on the composition of the marketing mix used to sell those quantities.

As already remarked, the instruments cannot in many cases be subjected to infinitesimal changes. But not more than one quantity sold and only one level of total cost correspond to a specific combination of instruments. In other words, any imaginable marketing mix can be represented by a single point in the diagram. This makes it possible to examine and find out—for example, on the basis of a given quality—the extent to which sales and total cost may vary with changes in the activities of' salesmen, in promotion, and/or in the choice of distribution channels. Admittedly, quality, too, is

---

[8] Cf. BREMS, *op. cit.*, Chapter 8. With regard to the product line: R. DORFMAN, *Applications of Linear Programming to the Theory of the Firm* (Berkeley: University of California Press, 1951).

[9] Cf. the two publications cited in the previous footnote.

a variable; but the same procedure may be followed for the different qualities that are within the scope of the firm's technical possibilities.

Fig. 1.1 pictures a case in which three different qualities have been studied,
shown respectively by squares, circles, and triangles. For each quality, a
number of realistic alternative suppositions have been made about sales
promotion and distribution channels, and the consequences for marketing
possibilities and total cost have been examined.

If this diagram is filled in as completely as possible—that is, for all possible
qualities and the corresponding combinations of sales promotion and distribution channels—it will obviously contain a much larger number of points.
But, since we are dealing in principle with non-continuous phenomena, a

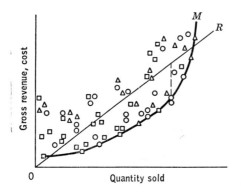

Fig. 1.1. *Determination of Most Profitable
Marketing Mix at a Given Price*

Source: P. J. Verdoorn, *op. cit.*

good many open places will, nevertheless, remain in the diagram. This means
that in practice no marketing mix corresponds to the combination of sales
and costs in question. For this reason, Brems—who has developed this
method of graphic representation—calls this diagram the "oasis and desert
map," the filled-in dots representing so many oases in the desert of technical
and practical impossibilities.[10]

The advantage of this method is that it enables one to determine realistically the *minimum-cost curve*, that is, the curve showing minimum cost for
each volume of sales at a given unit price. It is subject to the conditions that,
going from left to right,

   a) none of the points must appear below the curve; and
   b) the successive combinations forming part of the curve must show a continuous
       rising line of marginal cost.

This minimum-cost curve is shown as the broken line (*M*). It differs from the
traditional cost curve in that

---

[10] Brems, *op. cit.*, Chapter 5.

a) it is discontinuous; and

b) it allows for the fact that the volume of sales is dependent upon the composition of production as well as of marketing cost.

The marketing mix with which, at the given price, profits will be maximal is found by seeking the combination in which the distance between total cost and the gross revenue curve is greatest. If the minimum-cost curve had been continuous, marginal cost would at this point equal price. The optimal marketing mix, at a given price, therefore, is determined in the same way as in the case of perfect competition.

Price variable. To ascertain the influence of price changes, the "oasis and desert map" should be constructed for several prices. For each price,

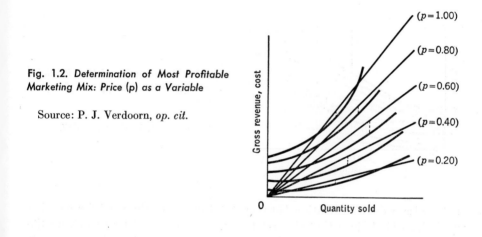

Fig. 1.2. Determination of Most Profitable Marketing Mix: Price (p) as a Variable

Source: P. J. Verdoorn, *op. cit.*

too, the corresponding minimum-cost curve can be determined. These minimum-cost curves can be incorporated into a recapitulation diagram, as shown in Fig. 1.2. The difference between this and the original "oasis and desert map" is that in Fig. 1.2 *each point already shows the minimal combination of cost at which a given quantity can be sold at a given price.* For each minimum-cost curve, the "mix" that will yield the largest profit is known. The best "mix" of all minimum-cost curves, therefore, may be found quite simply by comparing for the different curves the distances between the best "mix" and the corresponding points on the gross-revenue lines.

Introduction of boundary conditions. In this recapitulation diagram, it is also possible to represent the influence of the most important boundary conditions. If, for instance, market share is required to increase by a given percentage, then sales must increase from, say, 100 to at least 110. This desideratum can be expressed graphically in Fig. 1.3 by the line V_1 drawn perpendicularly on the abscissa at a sales figure of 110. All combinations to the left of this line fail to satisfy the condition that sales shall increase to 110 and can therefore be discarded.

If it is considered undesirable—from a competitive point of view—that the price should rise above, say, $0.80, then the combinations corresponding to the minimum-cost curve at a price of $0.80 also constitute a boundary. All combinations at a higher level then become unacceptable. For this reason, the minimum curve, 0.80, is shown in the diagram as a heavy curve (P).

As we have already seen, maintenance of liquidity gives rise to two boundary conditions, namely, one for investments and one for working capital. The former is the simpler of the two; it sets a limit to total sales. It is represented by the line V_2. The second boundary condition is more complicated. As long, however, as fixed cost remains unchanged, there is in every

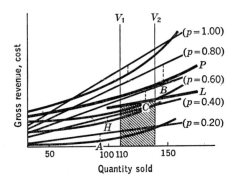

Fig. 1.3. Determination of Most Profitable Marketing Mix, Allowing for Boundary Conditions

Source: P. J. Verdoorn, *op. cit.*

enterprise a definite relation between total cost and the need for working capital. It is obvious that this relation may be changed by modifying the composition of total cost, that is, by a different choice of marketing mix. It nevertheless appears plausible that, as soon as investment and, with that, the amount of working capital are known, a ceiling figure for total cost can be calculated, at least tentatively. In the short run, this ceiling is dependent upon the possibility of raising short-term credits and, to a lesser degree, upon "plowing back" and, consequently, primarily upon total revenue. The maximum limit of total cost (the line L) will, therefore, show an upward slope.[11] It is important to note, however, that the two boundary conditions are interdependent: if V_2 is set higher, L will be lower, and vice versa.

Taking the boundary conditions into account, therefore, considerably limits the possibility of choice from all imaginable combinations—in fact, to the small shaded area in Fig. 1.3.

Assume H to represent the marketing mix that has been used by the firm

---

[11] Since the slope of the total-revenue curve varies proportionately with prices, the exact representation of liquidity as a limiting factor would be a bundle of rays.

up to the present moment. Then it is clear that its position might be improved considerably by switching the mix to B. B, in fact represents the *maximum maximorum* of profits. But then, it lies outside the possibilities of our firm. Although the required price is still within its reach—since B is situated exactly on the boundary condition P—two other boundary conditions originating from requirements of liquidity (V_2 and L) are violated. Neither is the combination A admissible. True, it guarantees a larger net profit than that of the past period, namely, that corresponding to the "mix" H, but the sales of combination A fail to reach the required level V_1.

In order to include all the side conditions set by the intermediary objectives of management, the choice of the mix is restricted to the points within the shaded area. Of all these points, C guarantees the highest level of present profits. At the same time, since no boundary conditions are violated, it is compatible with the intermediary objectives; that is, future profits will not be impaired unduly by a change from H to C.

The procedure described above will require modification according to the character of the problem studied and the nature of the accepted boundary conditions. In principle, however, it would seem to provide a practical starting point for a theory of marketing by the producer. It is especially important to note that the method allows for a symmetrical and simultaneous treatment of the different marketing instruments while taking into account the most frequently-occurring boundary conditions.

PROBLEMS

1. Discuss the different functions that marketing and economic research might perform in the management of an office furniture manufacturing firm.

2. What functions might a marketing audit perform in the management of a bank? What are the marketing instruments in this case? How are boundary limits for these instruments derived in this case?

3. *a*) What aspects of market structure might profitably be investigated by a newspaper?
   b) What questions of market diagnosis would be likely to arise as a result?

4. *a*) Outline the steps that might be covered in a marketing audit of a local lumber yard.
   b) By contrast, what would a marketing audit of a plywood manufacturer consist of?

5. How might the marketing audit approach be adapted to analyze the development of different sources of revenue for, say, the U. S. Internal Revenue Service?

6. A department store finds that its profits have declined although sales have risen. What sort of internal analysis might be undertaken to identify the causes? In what ways might this analysis have to be supplemented by other approaches?

7. In what ways would a knowledge of accounting and of management be of use in a marketing audit? Illustrate with reference to the marketing audit of a local lumber yard (Question 4a).

8. Integrate the three phases of research—market structure, diagnosis and prognosis—with the marketing audit. Illustrate with reference to the problems faced by an automobile manufacturer.

9. Discuss possible means of applying the method of selecting the best marketing mix, as outlined in the Supplement to this chapter, to the problem of selling U. S. Government savings bonds. Sketch the theoretical approach. What are the marketing instruments? What data would be required, how might they be collected, and what practical problems might be encountered in applying the method?

SELECTED REFERENCES

Research as a Tool of Policy

The nature of marketing and other business research and their application to business problems is discussed in almost all of the marketing research texts. Definitions of marketing research and illustrations of the applications of this research to business problems will be found in such publications as DAVID LUCK, H. G. WALES and D. F. TAYLOR, *Marketing Research* (New York: Prentice Hall, 1961) and in L. O. BROWN, *Marketing and Distribution Research* (Ronald Press, 1955). Perhaps the most practical of the lot is *Marketing Research Practice* edited by D. M. HOBART (Ronald Press, 1950) which presents numerous illustrations of how research helps to solve business problems.

Much more theoretical in its orientation is *Basic Methods of Marketing Research* (McGraw-Hill) by J. H. LORIE and H. V. ROBERTS, which contains an excellent discussion, in Chapters 3–5, of the role of scientific method in marketing research.

A methodical discussion of the role of research and particularly of model building in the formation of economic policy will be found in the book by J. TINBERGEN, *On the Theory of Economic Policy* (Amsterdam: North Holland Publishing Co., 1952). Further treatment of this subject with practical applications will be found in a later publication by TINBERGEN entitled *Economic Policy: Principles and Design* (Amsterdam: North Holland Publishing Co., 1956). In addition, a general discussion of the role of economic forecasting in policy formation is contained in Chapters 7 and 8 of *Economic Forecasts and Policy* by HANS THEIL (Amsterdam: North Holland Publishing Co., 1958).

The position of the economic adviser, particularly in his relation to the government and international organizations, is discussed by W. A. JÖHR and H. W. SINGER, *The Role of the Economist as Official Adviser* (London: Allen and Unwin, 1955).

The Marketing Audit

Relatively little has been written on the practical applications of the marketing audit since it was first proposed by WROE ALDERSON in his article: "The Marketing Audit and the Ad Budget" in the December, 1947, issue of *Industrial Marketing*.

The marketing audit as a means of co-ordinating marketing policies in different fields is discussed in the article by P. J. VERDOORN: "Marketing from the Producer's Point of View" in the January, 1956, issue of the *Journal of Marketing*, national quarterly publication of the American Marketing Association. Part of this article is reproduced in the Supplement to this chapter. The same subject is also treated by A. W. FREY in a pamphlet entitled *The Effective Marketing Mix* published in May, 1956 by the School of Business Administration of Dartmouth University. The emphasis in this publication is on bringing together all the different factors that might affect marketing efficiency and combining them into a program to achieve optimum results.

2 | Outline of Research Investigations

THIS CHAPTER provides a general review of the nature of research investigations—how they arise, how they are set up for working purposes, how to go about selecting a particular research method and applying it, and what to do with the results. Such a review is essential for a proper perspective of research methods in economics and business as well as for acquiring the knack of beginning a research study on the right foot—for many people the most difficult problem of all.

2.1. AN OPERATIONAL APPROACH

Although research studies can differ from one another in almost every respect imaginable, the same general steps lead to their solution. These steps can be outlined in various ways. The one we shall adopt is as follows:

1. Formulating the problem
2. Development of working hypotheses
3. Planning the study
4. Collecting and processing the data
5. Analysis and interpretation
6. Presentation of results

The general outline presented above can be adapted to any research investigation. In the remainder of this chapter we shall consider each of these steps in some detail. Before doing so, however, it should be noted that outlines of research investigations can be made up in as much detail as desired. Fig. 2.1 presents an example of a more detailed outline of the steps used to solve a typical consumer research problem involving a field survey. Similar outlines can be prepared for other types of problems, and in some cases it is, in fact, advisable to prepare a specific outline in advance.

2.2. FORMULATING THE PROBLEM

Careful detailing of the problem to be solved is a step frequently over-looked. This undoubtedly explains much of the perplexity encountered in a research operation. A usual approach is to take the original question posed to the researcher as the formulation of the problem and to set up techniques and procedures for throwing light on this question. Such an approach, how-ever, is not likely to produce definitive results because the question as origi-nally phrased is usually in broad, general terms and is not in a form suitable for testing.

For example, a question may be raised of "the effect of a particular excise tax on conditions in the industry concerned." Any attempt to solve the prob-lem by proceeding from this question to set up hypotheses and outline work-ing procedures will not provide a definitive answer because, as stated, the question is *not capable* of leading to definitive answers without years of work. In its original form, the question has a number of ambiguities, such as:

What is meant by "effect"—effect on sales, on production, on earnings or on something else?

Is consideration to be given to the effect on the industry as a whole or to the differential effect on the various firms in the industry?

What time period is involved? Effect over the past year or month? Cur-rent effects? Future possible effects?

What is meant by "conditions"? Prices? Earnings? Sales? Or something else, e.g., competitive position?

Which is the "industry concerned"? All the firms making the particular product? Firms that receive most of their revenue from that product or at least a certain minimum proportion? Or simply total sales of the product?

Not only do ambiguities such as these have to be resolved, but the feasi-bility of a particular solution has to be considered before a working formula-tion of the problem can be set up. Thus, it may be feasible to define the "industry" only in terms of total sales of the product because of the diffi-culty of segregating sales of this product from sales of related products by each firm; if only a restricted amount of data is available, it may be necessary to limit the "effect" to the past year, and so on. In this manner, the problem is restated in analytical "jargon." This not only has the advantage of leading to a clear, well-outlined problem but also helps overcome much of the re-searcher's initial confusion by establishing a closer connection between the problem at hand and the techniques that might be used in its solution. Thus, suppose the excise-tax problem is narrowed to "the determination of the influence of the tax on overall sales of the product in 1962." Stating the problem in this form makes it possible to focus attention on the theoretical questions involved and to look for an appropriate model for identifying the relationships that need investigation. From a theoretical point of view, sales and prices in any given year are a function of demand and supply. Superimposed is the influence of the excise tax, abolition of which therefore does not necessarily result in a price reduction of the same amount. (This would only be the case if the supply elasticity were infinite or if demand elasticity were zero.)

Hence, the really critical elements in the problem are the elasticities of demand and supply. Estimating these elasticities by means of regression analysis would be one approach (see Sec. 3.5). An alternative, and perhaps complementary, one would be a survey among consumers of their "price awareness" and another one among producers to ascertain supply flexibility. In either case, the initial "befuddlement" state is passed, and a good start would have been made toward a solution of the problem.

How does one go about formulating a problem? Essentially two distinct steps are involved—understanding the origin and nature of the problem, and then rephrasing it into meaningful terms from an analytical point of view.

2.2.1. Understanding the Problem

Perhaps the best way of understanding the problem is to discuss it with those who first raised it in order to find out how it originally came about and what considerations or objectives are involved in its possible solutions. Sometimes the motive for raising a problem is to seek recommendations for corrective action, for example, when sales have begun to decline. At other times, however, management may be seeking simply an explanation of a given phenomenon to aid in a more intelligent formulation of future policy. Thus, a researcher may be asked to evaluate the extent to which the firm's sales are related to general business conditions.

The more general the original statement of the problem, the more important are preliminary discussions about its nature. At times the real question may be entirely different from the one originally raised. For this there are several reasons, one being that in applied research an assignment generally stems from a provisional, but fragmentary, analysis of a particular problem. Thus, if sales are declining, management may suspect reduced appeal of its present product mix. It therefore authorizes a study of consumer preferences, although actually the introduction of a new distribution system is leading to slower deliveries and accounts for the sales drop.

Another reason occasionally encountered is that management does not deem it necessary, or desirable, to reveal the real problem. Thus, a researcher asked to investigate the effect of advertising on sales may discover that the reason for raising the problem at this particular time is that the firm has recently switched advertising agencies and some executives are becoming rather skeptical of the competence of the new agency. This information places the problem in a new light.

For reasons such as these, research is often much less efficient from a practical point of view than if the researcher had the opportunity to analyze more thoroughly the problem that originated the investigation.[1] The trend toward marketing audits can largely be explained by the fact that research based on too fragmentary knowledge of the original problem must often lead to inadequate recommendations.

Even if the problem is already well formulated—such as one of determining which of two alternative auto body styles consumers prefer—discussion can often produce useful information. In the case of the car body styles, where a survey would seem clearly indicated, these discussions can give the researcher a better insight into the practical aspects of the problem and aid him in devising a more effective survey. It may be, for example, that the manufacturer is hoping that his new body style will gain him more customers from the upper-income levels as well as retain his present market. In that case, a stratified sample design may well produce more efficient results.

With a dissertation being written on a subject proposed by one's thesis adviser, frequent discussion is highly advisable in order to assure a meeting of minds. Often the thesis adviser puts forth the problem in general terms and it is then up to the student to narrow it down and phrase the problem in operational terms.[2]

Discussion with colleagues is also highly advisable, particularly with those who have had experience in the same area or in working on similar problems. These discussions should encompass not only the formulation of the specific problem at hand but also general approaches to it, techniques that might be used, possible solutions, etc. The objective of such discussions is accordingly not only to pinpoint the problem but to secure leads and data toward a possible solution.

At the same time, all available literature has to be examined with two main purposes in mind—to find out what data and other material are available for operational purposes, and to examine studies on related problems to see how they were handled (and mishandled). Knowing what data are available often serves to narrow the problem itself as well as the techniques that

---

[1] BLANKENSHIP, A. B., "The Research Client As A Problem," in CHURCHMAN, ACKOFF and WAX, *Measurement of Consumer Interest*, University of Pennsylvania Press, pp. 16–20.

[2] Sometimes the thesis adviser will do this for him out of the kindness of his heart. In fact, the story is told of one thesis adviser, who had been unusually generous with his time in the past, who refused to advise a student on his thesis with the comment, "I'm sorry I can't work with you this year, but I just don't have time at present to write any more theses . . . "

might be used. Thus, the effect of assets on people's spending may well have to be narrowed to *liquid* assets if, as is presently the case, little data are available on other types of assets. Then again, the absence of comparable sets of observations rules out regression analysis as a method of approach.

Studies on related problems are mainly useful for indicating the types of difficulties that may be encountered in the present study and the possible analytical pitfalls. At times, however, they may also suggest useful, and even new, lines of approach to the present problem.

2.2.2. Rephrasing the Problem

With a thorough understanding of the nature and conditions of the problem, rephrasing it into analytical, or operational, terms is generally not difficult. The purpose of this rephrasing is, as indicated above, to put the problem in as specific terms as possible from an operational point of view and, if possible, in a form lending itself to the development of tentative hypotheses. Thus, the problem as originally posed might be:

"Why is productivity in the United States so much higher than in Great Britain?"

In this form, the question is much too general to be subjected to analysis.

Discussions about the problem, however, may narrow the question down to:

"What factors account for the higher labor productivity of U. S. manufacturing industries during 1950–59 relative to Great Britain's manufacturing industries?"

Further discussion might place the problem on yet more of an operational basis by narrowing it down perhaps as follows:

For each of 30 selected manufacturing industries
   1. To what extent did labor productivity in 1950–59 in the United States exceed that of the same industry in Great Britain?
   2. Assuming these 30 industries to represent productivity in each of the two countries, how does overall labor productivity in the two countries compare if the industries in each country are combined according to—
      a) the number of workers in each industry,
      b) "value added" in each industry.
   3. What factors would seem to account for the productivity differentials between the two countries by industries, and what is the relative importance of each factor?

Accompanying this formulation would be definitions of pertinent terms, in this case of "labor productivity," of the "value added" concept, and of the range of factors to be considered. At the same time, the researcher would have to check on whether the necessary data were available. Thus, if one of the industries happens to be one for which separate data are not available in one country or the other, another industry would have to be substituted. Then again the suitability of the time period has to be examined, in terms of the available data and its value in throwing light on the basic problem at hand. Might this particular period not have some strongly atypical events in it? In any case, might not a longer period of time be more appropriate for the purpose at hand? And so on.

It is also useful to examine the final formulation of the problem for the type of answers that might be obtained, and to make sure that the range of possible answers does bear directly on the problem as originally raised.

In effect, problem formulation often follows a sequential pattern: a number of formulations are set up, each formulation more specific than the last, each one phrased in more analytical terms, and each more realistic in terms of the available data and resources (a matter which we shall discuss shortly). The end result is a problem that is not only analytically meaningful but that also often points the way to means of solving it.

2.3. DEVELOPMENT OF WORKING HYPOTHESES

Theoretical analysis of a problem seldom points unambiguously in one direction. Usually alternative working hypotheses must be formulated. The latter serve two purposes. For one thing, they sharpen one's thinking on the subject and focus attention on the more important facets of the problem. Thus, one hypothesis that might be advanced in solving the labor productivity problem mentioned above is that, on the basis of theoretical considerations, the productivity differentials between the two countries are accounted for by a combination of only three factors, i.e., differences in (1) capital per worker, (2) size of total market, and (3) age distribution of plant and equipment. Whether or not these factors are the principal ones, this hypothesis immediately provides a starting point for the analysis, namely, it raises questions regarding the reasons and manner in which these factors might be pertinent, and whether it is plausible that no other relevant factors may exist. For this reason, it might be desirable to set up alternative hypotheses so that other possible explanations are not ignored.

Secondly, working hypotheses often show more clearly the methods of approach that might be used in the analysis. On the one hand, they pinpoint the type of data needed for the study, and then again the manner in which the hypotheses are stated can dictate what technique(s) should be employed.

Thus, the productivity hypothesis stated above points to the need for some method of comparing the importance of the factors mentioned in relation to others, either by simple comparisons of percentage changes or perhaps by a model of economic growth involving regression analysis.

To take another example, suppose the problem is why an election poll failed to predict the winner of an election. This is a problem that, even though well formulated, leaves one more or less at sea about how to start work on it. But if a series of alternative hypotheses, or possible explanations, is advanced, the problem and methods of attack come clearly into focus. Such hypotheses might include

a) atypicalness of the sample relative to the voting population,
b) faulty allocation of "undecided" replies among the candidates,
c) shift in voters' preferences between the time of the poll and the date of the election,
d) biased interviewing techniques.

Given these hypotheses, techniques for solving the problem readily suggest themselves.

How does one go about developing working hypotheses? The answer is by using much the same approach as in formulating the problem. In fact, information for both these steps, as well as later ones, is generally gathered at the same time. The sources for such information include the following:

1. Internal investigation—discussions with colleagues and superiors in the firm, or institution, about the problem, its origin, possible explanations and the objectives in seeking a solution. Also examination of firm records and other data within the firm for possible trends, peculiarities, and other clues.
2. External investigations—including discussions with colleagues in the field, examination of similar studies in the area or of studies on similar problems, and learning what secondary data may be available on the subject.
3. Exploratory personal investigation—this involves original field interviews on a limited scale with interested parties, with a few voters and interviewers on the voting problem, with factory managers in the United States and Great Britain (if your boss can be talked into sending you overseas!) on the productivity problem, etc. The purpose is to secure greater insight into the practical aspects of the problem, which often leads to valuable "hunches."

The last source is often most useful of all, for a hypothesis is nothing more than a formalized "hunch." Usually four to five interviews with the interested parties are sufficient, though if widely disparate views are obtained, more interviews may be deemed useful. Before undertaking these interviews, however, it is important to be well informed on the subject, if only to be able to direct queries with intelligence.

Essentially, therefore, working hypotheses arise as a result of *a priori* thinking about the subject, preliminary investigation of available data and material (including related studies), or advice and counsel of experts or interested parties. Like the formulation of the problem, such hypotheses are most useful when expressed in precise, clearly defined terms.

Occasionally, a problem will be encountered which won't need working hypotheses. This is particularly true of numerical estimation problems, such as, say, estimating the proportion of families covered by sickness insurance. As a general rule, however, specification of working hypotheses is another basic step in taking befuddlement out of research work (particularly in writing a thesis!).

2.3.1. Use of a Checklist

At some stage in exploring the nature of a problem and possible approaches to it, a checklist of marketing research functions can often prove useful. A number of such checklists are available, and one of them is reproduced as Fig. 2.2 on p. 38. The columns in this chart represent different problems encountered by the firm in its operations, while the rows indicate areas of exploration. The crosses in the body of the chart show which areas of study are likely to be of use in exploring a particular type of problem.

Not every area indicated may have to be explored in a particular problem, but research problems are generally enough alike that use of such a checklist will often point to areas worthy of exploration that might otherwise be overlooked. Needless to say, checklists are most useful for the beginning researcher, particularly when theory does not provide an adequate starting point.

2.4. PLANNING THE STUDY

A number of diverse steps are covered in the planning stage, for it is during this stage that procedures are devised, tested, and set up in final form, cost estimates are prepared, and operating schedules are made.

2.4.1. Selection of Method

If the problem has been phrased in clear, analytical terms and alternative hypotheses formulated, the range of methods that might be applied will have narrowed considerably. There will still be leeway, nevertheless, and at times the particular method to employ will not be too evident. For this reason, the

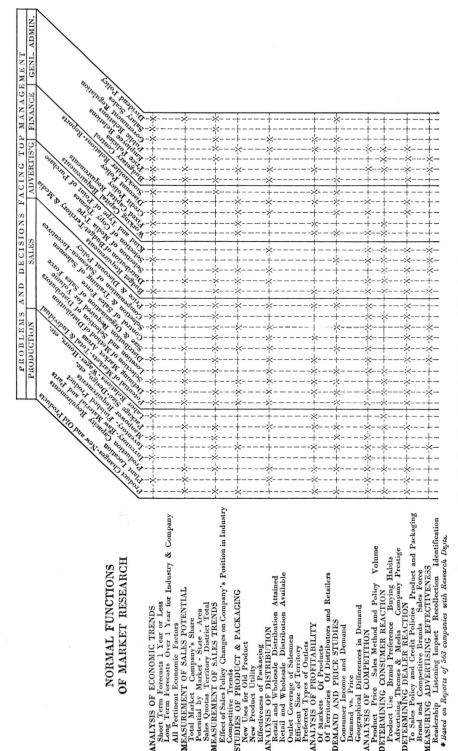

Fig. 2.2. Checklist of Marketing Research Functions*

* Source: Prepared by W. W. Heusner.

selection of the method to be followed is the next important step. It requires a thorough knowledge of the available data, a sharp insight into the potentialities of the different research techniques, as well as a good deal of originality.

Since the aim of research is to arrive at a solution for a given problem, the available data and the unknowns of the problem have to be related to each other to make a solution possible.[3]

From this point of view, research methods fall into three main categories. In the first category are those concerned with *collection of data;* they will be used where the data already available are not sufficient to arrive at the required solution. The second group consists of a set of statistical techniques for *establishing relationships* between the data and the unknowns. The third group is used to evaluate the *accuracy of the results* obtained. These techniques will show whether or not the solution is adequate from the statistical point of view. Since the techniques of this third group overlap to some extent those of the second, it is often convenient to refer to both as the analytical tools of research.

Thus, the problem of selecting a method is transformed to choice of data and to selecting appropriate techniques for establishing the required relationships. After that, the proper test for accuracy has to be selected. As a rule, the nature of the problem as well as the concrete working hypothesis developed will already determine to a great extent the choice of the data and the relationships. Nevertheless, a fair amount of leeway often remains, since the formulation of a working hypothesis, however complete, refers to the logical structure of the problem rather than to the concrete nature of the available data or to the specific form of the relationships needed in a given situation.

2.4.2. Collection of Data

Although considerable freedom of choice is present in the planning stage, it is important to note that the data cannot always be chosen independently of the relationships sought, and vice versa. Thus, if a producer is seeking to determine his share of the market of a consumers' good, it would be irrelevant from an analytical point of view whether the basis is:

$$market\ share = \frac{consumer\ purchases\ of\ own\ brand}{total\ consumer\ purchases}$$

or:

$$market\ share = \frac{retail\ sales\ of\ own\ brand}{total\ retail\ sales}$$

---

[3] For a formal treatment from the mathematical point of view, see G. POLYA, *How to Solve It. A New Aspect of Mathematical Method* (Princeton University Press, 1946).

Apart from sampling variations, the two relations will yield the same result. Hence, either the data secured by a consumer survey or those resulting from a store-audit may be used. If, on the contrary, the problem is to estimate the market share in total sales of *all* products by a specific category of drugstores—say, with an annual turnover between $50,000 and $100,000—the relationship required would not permit the use of consumer survey data.

With respect to the choice of the data, and of data-collection techniques, it is useful to distinguish between the following sources:

A. Data already available
  1. Government and other "official" statistics.
  2. Other published material, handbooks, periodicals.
  3. Non-published external reports (from university institutes, marketing research agencies, trade associations, etc.).
  4. Internal statistics and records of the firm itself. In the case of market research this is often a badly neglected source.
  5. Private information, e.g., from colleagues or firms in the same industry. Although information thus obtained is by no means necessarily exact, it sometimes provides at least an indication of the approximate value of an important "unknown" in the problem.

The major advantage of using data already available is the substantial savings in time and money. At the same time, it should be noted that such data may require laborious regrouping before they can be used to establish meaningful relationships. Foreign trade statistics and statistics taken from internal records often fall in this category.

B. Data not yet available

Two techniques may serve as a source of additional information:

1. *The survey method*, i.e., the use of sampling and questionnaire techniques in order to secure information from a selected number of respondents.

2. *The experiment*, i.e., the study of a process, such as the use and the buying or selling of a certain article, if that process has deliberately been designed for the purpose of obtaining information.[4] Product-testing and test markets are well-known applications.

Since in economic research, and particularly in market research, lack of appropriate data often proves the main stumbling block for an adequate solution, the important place taken by applications of the survey method is hardly surprising. This holds especially because the survey method is an extremely flexible tool of research and can be used for numerous purposes.

---

[4] See LORIE and ROBERTS, *Basic Methods of Marketing Research*, McGraw-Hill, 1951, Chapter 4.2.

Various techniques and applications of the survey method will be discussed in detail in Chapters 5 and 6.

2.4.3. Establishing Relationships

As has been shown in discussing the development of working hypotheses, the selection of relationships to be used is often facilitated by recourse to

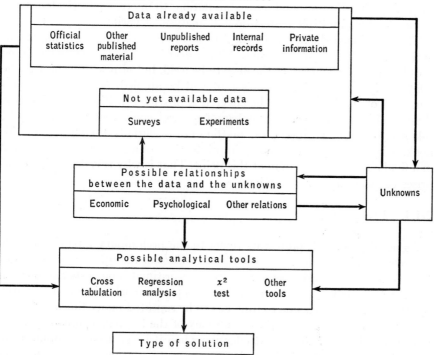

Fig. 2.3. *Fields Covered in the Planning Stage*

economic theory. Hence, in the three first sections of Chapter 4 attention will be given to the applications of economic theory to practical research. Similarly, Section 4 of Chapter 6 presents a psychological approach to market research.

To assume on purely theoretical grounds the existence of a number of relationships is one thing. However, to establish the same relations empirically by testing the hypotheses on the actual data and by measuring, where necessary, the numerical values of the parameters (such as elasticities) is quite another thing. Except in those cases where the relation concerned is a simple definition, e.g., where market share is the only unknown, more or less complicated techniques of statistical analysis will have to be used.

As an example, consider the productivity comparison between the United States and Great Britain. How can the contribution of each of the three factors to the differences in productivity be measured? How can we make sure that most probably these three and no others account for the greater part of the differences?

A number of useful analytical tools in economic and business research will be discussed in Chapter 3. As will be seen, they rank from the much-used frequency distribution and cross-tabulation to more sophisticated techniques, such as multiple regression and analysis of variance.

The selection of the method to be followed requires a number of important decisions by the research worker. A final decision is necessary not only on the character and sources of the data to be used, but also with respect to the relationships and statistical tools that will be applied. A schematic representation of the field thus to be covered is provided in Fig. 2.3. In making these decisions, however, a number of general considerations have to be taken into account. Since these matters are essentially the subject of this book, it is best to consider the appropriate place of a given research method in a final chapter rather than at this point. That is why this discussion comprises the last chapter of the book.

2.4.4. Pretesting

As usually defined, pretesting refers to the preliminary interviews made on a contemplated survey to test the soundness of the questionnaire and of the overall survey design as well as to secure estimates on costs and on such pertinent statistics as variances, means, etc. Similarly, in other research operations where the same routine has to be repeated many times, a pretest gives a valuable indicator of the efficiency of the large-scale operation.

In general, a pretest is most effective when it is set up as a miniature of the actual operation. Thus, in planning cross-tabulations, the adequacy of class limits can be tested by means of a small initial sample chosen at random. The adequacy of particular formulas can be tested in the same manner, e.g., whether zero or near-zero frequencies invalidate logarithms or reciprocals. Particularly if electronic computers are to be used, a preliminary "shadow operation" with a desk calculator using the same formulas can pinpoint sources of error or inconsistencies.

In the case of a survey, the pretest usually follows a well-established pattern. This means selecting, approaching, and interviewing a small sample in the same manner to be followed in the full-scale operation, and then analyzing the results in the light of the objectives of the study.

Do the replies provide the type of information needed for a solution to the problem? Are the respondents misinterpreting any of the questions? Is there difficulty in obtaining replies to particular questions? Do the original cost estimates seem reasonable? These are some of the questions that a pretest can answer. In addition, results obtained in a pretest can at times suggest new ideas or hypotheses worthy of further testing. The results can also be used at times on a "dry run" basis to test the soundness of the plans for coding, editing, and tabulating the data as well as the validity of assumptions underlying certain analytical techniques, e.g., lack of intercorrelation between the replies of families in the same block.

If a pretest indicates any changes of importance, a further pretest may be warranted of that particular step. Thus, the mere fact that the wording of a question originally misunderstood has been changed does not of itself ensure the clarity of the new form. A few interviews with the new question form are highly desirable.

Pretests are generally small, often involving less than a dozen interviews. They may be set up in a formal manner and cover the entire research operation, or they may seek to test one particular aspect of the study, such as the soundness of the questionnaire, in a more or less informal manner. Pretests are generally concentrated either on the most vital aspects of the study, such as the content of the questionnaire in a survey, or on aspects about which there may be little knowledge—costs, certain variances, etc.

2.4.5. Operating Schedules

Time and cost estimates are as much a part of a research operation as are methods and procedures. In part, this is because the latter can only be selected within the limitations of time, money, personnel, available facilities, and other resources. A knowledge of these limitations is an essential part of selection of the method, as discussed in Chapter 11. The other reason is that a planned schedule of operations leads to more efficient conduct of the study.

Scheduling also makes it easier to allocate different parts of an operation to various people and ensure smoothness of operations at the same time. However, scheduling is equally useful to an individual doing the entire task, like someone writing a thesis, for it allows him to judge the time and cost required for the study and, hence, its practicability. Particularly in individual projects, preparation of a schedule will often indicate that the amount of time and effort required for the project has been greatly underestimated.

A good way to prepare a schedule is to divide the project into its smallest operational parts—such as the various steps of a survey operation—and estimate cost and time needed for each step. Facilities needed at a particular stage in addition to those normally available should also be shown on the schedule opposite the particular step involved. An example of such a schedule

Table 2.1

OPERATING SCHEDULE FOR SURVEY OF MILK-BUYING HABITS

Item	Working days required	Expected date of completion	WAGES — Details	WAGES — Cost	OTHER EXPENSE — Details	OTHER EXPENSE — Cost	Total est. cost	ACTUAL COST — Wages	ACTUAL COST — Other exp.	ACTUAL COST — Total
Formulating problem										
Developing hypotheses	3	Oct. 16		—	Travel	$25	$25			
Planning										
Sample selection	2	Oct. 18	10 hrs. @ $1.50	15			15			
Interviewer selection and training (4 people)	1	Oct. 19	4 hrs. @ 1.50	6			6			
Questionnaire design and pretesting	3	Oct. 24	4 hrs. @ 1.50	6			6			
Printing & stationery	2	Oct. 26				40	40			
Collecting the data: 450 calls @ 3/hour to ensure at least 300 final interviews, plus expense	5	Nov. 2	150 hrs. @ 1.50	225	Travel: 500 mi. @ 8¢/mi. Misc. expense	40 20	285			
Editing and preparing punch cards	7	Nov. 13	50 hrs. @ 2.00 60 hrs. @ 1.00	100 60	Punch cards & misc.	5	165			
Tabulation	2	Nov. 15	16 hrs. @ 1.50	24	10 hrs. machine time @ $5/hr.	50	74			
Analysis and report-writing										
Statistical computations	3	Nov. 20	20 hrs. @ 1.50	30	Tab sheets & materials	5	35			
Report-writing and printing	5	Nov. 27	40 pages @ 25¢/page	10	Stationery Printing report	5 25	40			
SUBTOTAL	33			$476		$195	$691			
Supervisory expense, including analysis and report-writing			60 hrs. $15/hr.	900			900			
SUBTOTAL				$1,376		195	1,591			
Contingency allowance, 10 % of above							159			
SUBTOTAL							$1,750			
Overhead							875			
TOTAL							$2,625			

is shown in Table 2.1, as devised by a research organization for a survey of about 300 housewives on milk-buying habits in a middle western city.

Once prepared, these schedules should not be discarded after the relevant information has been copied. Rather, as shown in Table 2.1, the actual time and cost required for each step should be recorded next to the estimates. This procedure is not only useful for keeping track of expenses and of approaching deadlines but also can be of use as source material on which to base more reliable schedules on future studies.

A beginning researcher would be well advised to have his schedule checked by a more experienced person. The invariable tendency is to underestimate both time and costs, and it is only through experience that one gains a realistic perspective on these factors. Even experienced researchers often miss the mark, and it is partly for this reason and partly because unforeseen problems nearly always arise that many schedules carry a "contingency" item equal to 10 per cent or more of the accumulated total. Such a contingency item is shown in Table 2.1.

The general practice is to allow a good working margin in cases of uncertainty. It is better to overestimate and pleasantly surprise one's superior with a surplus than to underestimate and risk irritating those concerned by asking for more money or time after the study is well along.

2.5. COLLECTING AND PROCESSING THE DATA

Though usually considered as part of a survey operation, this is a stage encountered in every study involving empirical data. In fact, whenever a study is based largely on the collection and compilation of primary data, probably more time and effort will be expended on this activity than on any other.

Sometimes primary data will be collected by means of a survey, sometimes from company records or other source material. In either case, considerable care must be taken to ensure consistency of the methods used to obtain the data and overall comparability. In compiling primary data by some non-survey procedure, such consistency is best ensured by writing out all the concepts, definitions, and operating procedures to be used in the compilation process. Written instructions of this sort are indispensable when two or more people are doing the work, but they are also equally useful for an individual. These instructions are not only of aid in guarding against memory lapses while the data are compiled but also provide a ready source of information when the time comes to report the results of the study.

Much the same is true in processing secondary data, such as deflating dollar figures, eliminating seasonal variations, or adjusting two sets of data to make them comparable with each other. A written description of the procedures followed is highly useful on both an *ex ante* and *ex post* basis. The latter is particularly important if the entire investigation extends over a year or more, as is often the case. It may then prove difficult to recall the sources and processing methods that had been used in the early stages. In addition, a tabular representation is also advisable in making two sets of data comparable with each other, particularly when a number of steps are involved. Besides the aforementioned advantages, such a table has the additional advantage of indicating the effect on the data of each separate step in the adjustment. One example of a tabular representation showing the reconciliation of two sets of aggregate-savings estimates is presented in Table 2.2.

2.5.1. The Survey

Since collecting and processing the data are of special significance in a survey, a few remarks on their application to survey operations would seem appropriate. The main aspects of this work are precoding, editing, coding and tabulation.

Precoding is the process of placing code numbers directly on a questionnaire, as is illustrated in Fig. 2.4. Where this is feasible, it can be a major time-saver, speeding up the preparation of worksheet tables and eliminating the intermediate step of coding the replies on posting sheets. With machine tabulation, precoding enables punch cards to be made directly from the questionnaires. Precoding can also be used with semi-mechanical means of tabulation, some of which are described below, and even with hand tabulation.

It is important to note that precoding is advisable only if the answers can be classified in advance in clear-cut categories. Thus, questionnaires using mainly dichotomous or multiple-choice questions, or seeking numerical information, are most amenable to precoding. Projective techniques and depth interviews are least amenable to precoding. In any case, forcing replies into neat categories to facilitate precoding is most inadvisable. On questionnaires that combine questions easily precoded with those that are not, it is sometimes helpful to precode just the former and to make appropriate allowance for coding the other questions after the survey has been completed.

As a rule, precoding should be done unobtrusively. This is particularly true of mail questionnaires, where the respondent is likely to be confused by a profusion of numbers.

Editing and *coding* questionnaires for consistency, omissions and mistakes are essential phases of any survey operation, and should be completed before any tabulations are prepared. Editing is actually carried out in a number of different phases involving the following persons:

1. The interviewer—who should review his questionnaires for illegible writing and omissions.
2. The field supervisor—who should check the legibility and completeness of the questionnaires.

Table 2.2

RECONCILIATION OF ESTIMATES OF PERSONAL SAVING OF SECURITIES & EXCHANGE COMMISSION AND OF U. S. DEPARTMENT OF COMMERCE, 1957–59

(Billions of dollars)

Line	Item	1957	1958	1959
1	Gross investment in tangible assets	31.10	32.07	38.20
2	Nonfarm homes	15.59	16.44	20.34
3	Other construction and producers durable equipment	14.53	14.62	16.74
4	Noncorporate enterprises	8.09	7.45	9.01
5	Farm enterprises	3.97	4.44	4.88
6	Nonprofit institutions	2.47	2.73	2.85
7	Inventories of noncorporate enterprises	.98	1.02	1.11
8	Nonfarm	.22	−.02	.60
9	Farm	.76	1.04	.52
10	Depreciation	14.68	15.07	15.89
11	Nonfarm homes	4.70	4.93	5.25
12	Noncorporate nonfarm enterprises	5.53	5.60	5.90
13	Farm enterprises	3.89	3.96	4.12
14	Nonprofit institutions	.55	.58	.62
15	Net investment in tangible assets (lines (1)–(10))	16.42	17.01	22.31
16	Nonfarm homes	10.89	11.51	15.09
17	Other	5.53	5.50	7.21
18	Increases in financial assets[a]	23.10	25.74	31.06
19	Currency and bank deposits	4.93	10.26	3.54
20	Savings and loan association shares	5.21	6.46	7.28
21	Securities	4.96	.72	11.41
22	U. S. savings bonds	−1.91	−.52	−1.80
23	Other U. S. Government	1.56	−2.37	9.62
24	State and local government	2.24	1.24	2.49
25	Corporate and other	3.07	2.37	1.10
26	Private insurance and pension reserves	8.00	8.30	8.84
27	Increase in debt to corporations and financial intermediaries	15.39	21.24	30.05
28	Consumer debt	2.49	.43	6.07
29	Securities loans	−.07	.43	.17
30	Mortgage debt	9.64	12.54	16.37
31	On nonfarm homes	7.83	9.78	13.36
32	On noncorporate nonfarm enterprises	1.44	2.37	2.40
33	On farms	.37	.40	.61
34	Net trade debt of noncorporate nonfarm enterprises	1.34	4.06	1.61
35	Non-real-estate farm debt	.64	.94	1.07
36	Bank debt not elsewhere classified	1.35	2.83	4.76
37	Personal saving, SEC (lines (15) + (18) − (27))	24.14	21.51	23.32
38	Personal saving, Commerce[b]	23.63	24.38	23.43
39	Difference between lines (37) and (38)	.51	−2.87	−.12
40	Statistical discrepancy in the national income and product accounts	−.60	−1.66	−1.83
41	Alternative estimate of personal saving, Commerce (lines (38) + (40))	23.02	22.71	21.60
42	Difference between lines (37) and (41)	1.11	−1.21	1.71

[a] Excludes changes in government insurance and pension reserves, amounting to $3.19 billion in 1957; $0.63 billion in 1958; and $1.88 billion in 1959; and small amounts in Armed Forces leave bonds.

[b] Difference between personal disposable income and total consumption expenditures.

Source: *Survey of Current Business*, July 1960, p. 26.

3. The editor(s)—who should:
   a) Verify the internal consistency of the questionnaires wherever possible.
   b) Rectify errors and omissions.
   c) Ensure comparability between questionnaires.
   d) Determine the classifications to be used in the subsequent tabulations and analyses of the data.

In some instances the editor may also code the questionnaires, though on large surveys it is advisable to have coding done separately. In particular, preparation of codes, which is at times almost an art, is best done by the analyst himself.

Tabulation is a matter where some choice can often be exercised because of the large variety of tabulation methods available. On small-scale surveys (roughly 300 interviews or less), the traditional method of hand tabulation is generally still preferable. Hand tabulation is especially preferable when depth interviews, projective techniques, or many open-end questions are used, as other means of tabulation are hardly feasible in such cases. An ample supply of labor, a need for relatively few cross-tabulations, and no necessity for preserving records or later tabulations are also factors in favor of hand tabulation.

Mechanical tabulation is preferred under more or less opposite conditions —large-scale surveys, questions with answers easily classified into distinct categories, a great deal of cross-tabulation, and the likelihood of subsequent tabulations at some later stage, perhaps for comparison with other surveys. In addition, if much computation is required, tabulating the data on punch cards is often an intermediate step to carrying out the computations by data-processing machines, such as with electronic computers.

Most mechanical tabulation is undoubtedly done by putting the data on punch cards and then running the cards through IBM or Remington-Rand sorting and accounting machines. In addition, there are a number of semi-mechanical methods that are preferable under certain conditions. The *Key-sort* and *Findex* systems employ cards with holes punched in them; data can be recorded on them by connecting or breaking the holes. Such a procedure obviates the use of machines and permits tabulations to be made with a minimum of equipment or expenditure. These methods are most useful with studies using several hundred questionnaires where the information obtained on each is not too detailed or comprehensive.

2.6. ANALYSIS AND INTERPRETATION

Although the analytical methods to be used have undoubtedly been specified well in advance, and will not be discussed here, it is worthwhile to note some of the considerations that should be taken into account during this phase of the work in almost any study.

2.6.1. Reliability of the Data

Results can be no more sound than the data on which they are based. Yet, there is a common tendency to apply high-powered analytical methods to data of doubtful reliability and then to interpret the results in terms of the analytical techniques employed. From an analytical point of view, several precautions are indicated, as follows:

1. It is not wise to apply complex methods of analysis to data that are not very reliable in the first place. Also, in transforming such data, the danger of spurious accuracy must be avoided. Thus, if 16 out of 96 people borrowed to finance a certain purchase, the percentage should be represented as 17%, not as 16.67%.
2. Wherever a study is based on sample data collected by some probability method, the significance of the results should be evaluated against the sampling variation in the data. Often these variations will be large enough to cast considerable doubt on the validity of the findings. Even if data were collected by non-probability methods, it is often useful to apply sampling-error formulas as a rough approximation of sampling variations in the data—though this practice is frowned upon by most mathematical statisticians.
3. Whether or not the data are based on a sample, consideration should be given to the possible effect of biases or inaccuracies in the data on the type of results obtained. Precise numerical estimates are rarely possible, but reflection on the probable direction and plausible limits of such effects serves to place the findings in a better perspective.

2.6.2. Analyzing Data and Testing Hypotheses

The analytical requirements of an investigation depend largely upon the character of the problem to be solved. If an estimate of only one phenomenon is desired, such as the percentage of households using a certain product, the only analysis required is to determine whether the accuracy of the estimates satisfies the conditions of that assignment. As discussed later, however, comparison of this estimate with another estimate obtained independently is also desirable. Usually, the relationships implied are more complicated and less easily specified on an *a priori* basis. In such cases, it is useful to introduce one or more working hypotheses, and then the statistical testing of these hypotheses becomes an important element of statistical work. In many instances, moreover, the initial hypotheses may well have to be rephrased or broken down further in order to make them amenable to the statistical tests. Thus, the first hypothesis on the representativeness of the sample in the election poll problem on p. 36 might be rephrased as: "There is no significant difference between the distribution of the sample and that of the population with respect to party affiliation, family income, occupation, age, and education." The hypothesis is then ready for the statistical test, probably using chi-square analysis applied to each of the five characteristics in turn.

Next to the problem of accepting or rejecting certain hypotheses is that of quantifying those relationships embodied in the hypotheses that are acceptable. Thus, in the excise-tax example, the analyst has to estimate the decrease of consumption to be expected as a result of a given increase in prices.

This aspect of quantification may even be the dominating feature of the analysis, if the problem requires that the explanation of a certain phenomenon be as exhaustive as possible. In practice, problems of this kind are posed perhaps the more frequently: "Why is brand X preferred over brand Y?" "Why is productivity in one country higher than that in another?" "What were the factors governing the fluctuation in the volume of gross industrial investments during the period, 1919–1942?" In such cases, the analytical requirements of the problem are the more important, since it is not enough to establish the existence of one or more relationships between the data and the unknown; the choice of the relationships and the data should be such as to explain a reasonable part of the observed phenomenon.

The latter requirement, therefore, often necessitates a "feed-back" procedure from the analytical to the planning phase of the investigation. Apart from theoretical considerations, no particular rule for this procedure can be given. The researcher is best advised to cling to the device of the legendary sleuth:

"Arrange your facts and arrange your theories, and if some little fact does not fit in, be sure it will be significant."[5]

This approach, followed hitherto intuitively, has been more or less formalized in sociological research.[6] Known as "deviant case analysis," it supposes—quite rightly—that a separate and thoroughgoing analysis of observations that could not be explained by the hypothesis already accepted might bring to light the existence of a new, as yet unsuspected, relationship.

The indications resulting from a minute analysis of the observations mentioned are, of course, valuable, provided only that the general validity of the suggested new relationship can be established beyond reasonable doubt. The heuristic possibilities of paying close attention to deviant cases should therefore not be overlooked, for there might always be a chance of their leading

---

[5] Hercule Poirot as cited by AGATHA CHRISTIE.
[6] LAZARSFELD and ROSENBERG, ed., *The Language of Social Research*, 1955, Section II.C, "Deviant Case Analysis," pp. 167–175.

to a dependable working hypothesis. However, since indications obtained in this way tend to be unreliable, particularly if small samples are being analyzed, the method is—again rightly—not held in esteem by the mathematical statistician.

2.6.3. Computational Checks

All statistical manipulations have to be checked at least once, preferably by a different person each time but at least by a different routine. Built-in automatic checks are a great help, such as the Doolittle Solution for multiple regressions, but they do not obviate the need for supplementary checks all the same. People being what they are, considerable ingenuity has been shown in devising means of making mistakes even within the framework of an automatic check system. At best, such systems serve to check only certain types of operations, and rarely do they ensure the accuracy of an entire analysis.

2.6.4. Validation and Comparison of Results

Validation is the process of seeking independently-obtained data to check the accuracy of the survey data collected in the course of the project. This is a helpful thing to do in any survey operation. The difficulty is that validation is not often feasible because of lack of such other data. This is particularly so in a period of rapid change when U. S. Census data— the main source for validation—lose their applicability within a relatively short time.

Even where validation can be applied, the results are by no means foolproof. At best they indicate correspondence between the sample data tested and the other data. Since these are usually background data, they support the overall findings of the survey only to the extent that the findings are influenced by the particular characteristic tested. It is perhaps needless to note that validation is of no use when applied to characteristics used originally for planning the sample design.

A related step applicable to survey and non-survey projects alike is a comparison of the results obtained with those of similar studies in the past. Where such past studies exist, this step is essential to the interpretation of the present results, although they may have been already referred to in planning the project. If such past studies support the present findings, well and good—this provides so much more validity for the findings. If this is not the case, areas of disagreement should be noted and possible reasons for these differences suggested. It is much better for the researcher himself to do this than to allow someone to place him in an embarrassing position by doing it for him.

2.6.5. Generalizations

Everyone loves to draw generalizations, for the more sweeping such generalizations are, the more importance is likely to be attached to the study. Unfortunately, however, most research is not amenable to broad generalizations because the coverage is invariably restricted to a particular time, a particular area, and particular conditions. Such restrictions have to be specified and the results framed within their limits. However, one can attempt to extend the findings by relaxing these restrictions, and one can also indicate the type of modifications that might be needed if the results were broadened. This is best done separately, after the principal findings have been established.

Many types of generalizations do not meet the requirements of either theoretical statistics or formal logic. Examples are the application of findings beyond the range of the observations and identification of correlation with causation (more on this will be said later). Another major pitfall is the tendency to affirm that definite relationships exist on the basis of confirmation of particular hypotheses. Although negative results on a statistical test provide generally a strong basis for rejecting a hypothesis, positive results do not necessarily establish its validity for much the same reason that correlation does not establish causation. It is for this reason that such tests are best interpreted as "being in accord" with the hypothesis or as "not disproving it" rather than as "confirming the validity of the hypothesis."

2.7. PRESENTATION OF RESULTS

The results of a research investigation can be presented in a number of ways—a technical report for private consumption, a technical article or monograph, a popularized version, or oral presentation. Often two or more means are employed—a popular article or talk for the benefit of executives and others interested mainly in the findings and their implications for policy, and a technical report for colleagues in the general area or division. This is true of many theses too, where the object of the thesis is, at least in part, to impress the thesis adviser with a weighty report (literally as well as figuratively), while an attempt may be made to have the more significant results published as an article or monograph.

Which method(s) of presentation to employ in a particular study depends on the circumstances under which the study arose and the nature of the results. A technical report is indicated whenever a full written report of the study is desired, whether for record-keeping purposes or for public dissemination. If the results have policy implications or are likely to be of interest to those not primarily researchers, a popularized report will be prepared, supplemented perhaps by an oral presentation. Although the form of these various types of reports is discussed in some of the references at the end of this chapter, a few remarks on selected aspects of each are made below.

2.7.1. The Technical Report

The main emphasis in the technical report is on methods employed and assumptions made in the course of the study, and on a detailed presentation of the findings, including their limitations and supporting data. Nevertheless, simple presentation and ready availability of the findings remain an important consideration, for even many technical readers are often interested only in glancing over the report and acquiring a quick knowledge of the main findings. For this reason too, liberal use of charts and diagrams is desirable.

A general outline of a technical report might be as follows:

1. Summary of results—a brief review of the main findings, generally no longer than two or three pages.
2. Nature of the study—a description of the general objectives of the study (including perhaps how the study came about), the formulation of the problem in operational terms, the working hypotheses, the type of analysis and data required, etc.
3. Methods employed—covering not only the specific methods used but whatever compromises may have had to be made in applying the methods to the problem at hand and the limitations of the methods in these particular instances. In a sampling operation, this would include the details of the sample design—sample size, sample selection, type of sample (stratified, cluster, area), etc.
4. The data—a thorough discussion of the type of data employed, their sources, characteristics and limitations, particularly with regard to the purpose at hand. If secondary data are used, it is often advisable to examine the original sources to determine how the manner of collecting the data might affect their suitability to the problem at hand. If a survey was conducted, the manner in which the data were collected should be described in full. Response rates, validation, and the representativeness of the sample should also be discussed.
5. The analysis of the data and presentation of the findings of the study with supporting data in the form of tables and charts, together with a validation of results. This generally comprises the main body of the report, extending over several chapters.
6. Conclusions—a detailed summary of the findings and their limitations with an examination of their implications for the general problem studied as well as for possible policy decisions.

7. Bibliography of sources consulted.
8. Technical appendices—covering mathematical derivations, exposition or elaboration on particular techniques of analysis, and presentation of such data-collection forms as may have been used, questionnaires, covering letters, etc.
9. Supplementary tables—data not directly pertinent to the results derived but useful as background material.

The order of presentation of these sections will not always be the same nor will all these sections necessarily appear in any particular report. However, this outline does provide a general idea of the nature of this type of report.

2.7.2. The Popular Report

Here the emphasis is on simplicity and attractiveness. At the same time, the results and methods should not be oversimplified to the point of misrepresentation. Rather, simplification should be sought through clear writing, minimization of technical details (especially mathematics, the very sight of which gives most laymen the jitters), liberal use of charts and diagrams, emphasis on practical aspects and policy implications, and attractive layout —large print, uncrowded pages, many subheadings, even an occasional cartoon now and then.

An outline of a popular report might be as follows:

1. The findings and their implications—strong emphasis on the findings of most practical interest and on the implications of these findings from an operational point of view.
2. Recommendations for action—sometimes incorporated in the first part, this section makes positive recommendations for action on the basis of the findings of the study.
3. Objectives of the study—a general review of how the problem came about and the specific objectives of this project.
4. Methods employed—a brief, non-technical description of the methods and techniques used, including a short review of the data on which the study is based.
5. Results—the body of the report, presenting the results in clear, non-technical terms with liberal use of all sorts of illustrations.
6. Technical appendices—more detailed information on methods used, forms, etc.
7. Supplementary tables—additional tabular material pertinent to the objectives of the study but too formidable to be included in the body of the report.

The appendices in a popular report are often not too detailed or technical, especially if the report is aimed almost entirely at laymen. In that case, a technical report will undoubtedly be prepared also, and the reader of the popular report can be referred to it for the technical details.

At times, however, only one combination report will be prepared. If so, the aim generally will be to have the body of the report written on a popular level, with detailed methodological information relegated to the appendices.

2.7.3. Oral Presentation

Especially where certain policy recommendations are indicated by project results, oral presentation of results is likely to be the most effective means of explaining the implications of the findings and pointing out why a particular course of action would seem indicated. The big advantage of this approach is the opportunity it provides for give-and-take discussion, which generally leads to a better understanding of the findings and their implications than is otherwise possible. The main disadvantage is the lack of any permanent record, with the consequent tendency for the more awkward details to conveniently fade from people's memory before any action is taken. For this reason, a written report circulated before the oral presentation and referred to frequently during the discussions can be a very useful device.

In preparing an oral presentation, it is important to keep in mind that such presentations are most effective when supplemented by various visual-aid devices. Distributing a rough outline of the presentation together with a few pertinent tables and charts provides the listener with something to "hang onto," on which to focus his thinking. Use of slides, wall charts and blackboards is also likely to contribute to clarity and to reduction of boredom.

2.8. SUMMARY REMARKS

Although the foregoing steps are encountered in nearly every research operation, the degree of emphasis and amount of attention devoted to each step will naturally vary with the type of problem and with the resources available. The latter is a subject in itself, relating to the administration of research. Though not within the scope of this book, the subject is covered nevertheless in some of the references cited at the end of this chapter.

Experienced researchers will often run through these steps more or less instinctively, without distinguishing one from the other. Beginning researchers and thesis-writers, however, are well advised to consider each step deliberately and in writing. Doing this on a number of projects is the best way of developing a practical yet analytical approach to research problems.

PROBLEMS

1. Formulate the problem, develop working hypotheses, and suggest various approaches that might be used in each of the following situations:

   a) Why did U. S. farm prices weaken during 1952–55 while most other prices moved up?
   b) The sales of a farm implement manufacturer have been declining in one area while rising in others.
   c) A chemical firm wants to find out how best to market a newly-developed liquid window cleaner.
   d) An estimate is desired of the probable yield next year from a proposed new schedule of individual income tax rates.
   e) How does the quality of Russia's manufactured products compare with those of the United States?
   f) What is consumers' purchasing power likely to be five years from now?
   g) Can a published series on railroad shippers' expectations of their shipments one quarter ahead be of value to a particular railroad?
   h) Are low-priced brands of canned foods a serious threat to the so-called "quality" brands?
   i) A television manufacturer wants to develop new markets overseas.
   j) A magazine wants to estimate the size and characteristics of its audience.
   k) Is a newly developed plastic container for a consumer product better liked than the old glass container?
   l) In what sort of media should a men's shirt manufacturer advertise?
   m) How important is consumer credit to auto sales?

2. Describe what steps you would go through in planning the study for parts (a), (c), (e), (g), (h), (j), (k), and (m) of the preceding question.

3. Where would you obtain data for parts (a), (c), (d), (e), (i), and (m) of question 1?

4. Compare the validation problems in parts (e) and (j) of question 1. How would you handle each?

5. a) A hotel chain desires to engage in a long-run program of economic and marketing research to find out more about its potential customers and its outlook for the future. Outline the principal components of such a plan and the specific research objectives that might be investigated.
   b) Describe the administrative organization that you would recommend for this research program.

6. A panel study on consumer purchases of durable goods is to be undertaken by means of personal interviews every three months with about 400 families in a

particular metropolitan area. What administrative organization would be needed to run this operation?

7. In the previous problem, how might a pretest be conducted? What purposes might the pretest serve?

8. Outline an oral presentation to convince the management of an oil drilling machinery manufacturer of the value of a study of trends in demand for gas and oil. What sorts of charts and diagrams might be used?

SELECTED REFERENCES

Overall Research Design

Chapters 3–5 of *Basic Methods of Marketing Research* by LORIE and ROBERTS (McGraw-Hill, 1951) contain some excellent discussions of the application of scientific methods to research problems and of problem recognition and formulation.

Most of the book, *Cases and Problems in Marketing Research* by BLANKERTZ, FERBER and HOLLANDER (Ronald Press, 1962), is concerned with the various aspects of survey operations, and contains much working material on problem formulation, developing hypotheses, planning, and related matters.

Chapters 6–16 of *Marketing Research* by LUCK, WALES, and TAYLOR (Prentice-Hall, Inc., 1961) present some interesting discussions on the details of survey operations. The same subject is also discussed in Chapter 3 of *Statistical Techniques in Market Research* by FERBER (McGraw-Hill, 1949). *Marketing and Distribution Research* by L. O. BROWN (Ronald Press, 1955) also covers research design and organization as applied to marketing research.

Presentation of Results

Good references on report writing and on graphic presentation are invaluable aids to the research analyst. In the former case, we would recommend *Report Writing* by BALL and WILLIAMS (Ronald Press, 1955). This is a simply-written manual covering a wide range of business and technical reports with examples of actual presentations. A useful reference dealing with the sort of material that should be included in reports based on sample surveys is *The Preparation of Sampling Survey Reports* by the United Nations Statistical Office, 1950.

The Manual of Tabular Presentation by the U. S. Bureau of the Census (U. S. Government Printing Office, 1949) is a very good, reasonably-priced manual covering tabular organization in much detail. A readable though brief review of methods of graphic presentation is also provided in *Practical Rules for Graphic Presentation of Business Statistics* by SMART and ARNOLD (Ohio State University, Bureau of Business Research, 1951).

On the subject of charts and graphs, a very good reference manual on graphic presentation, discussing the mechanical as well as the creative aspects of the subject, is *Handbook of Graphic Presentation* by SCHMID (Ronald Press, 1954).

Research Administration

Perhaps because research administration is still more of an art than a science, relatively little has been published in this area that is likely to be of much practical use. Two useful monographs on organizational and administrative techniques of operating research departments in industry have been published by the National Industrial Conference Board under the title of *Organization for Market Research* (Studies in Business Policy, #12, 1945; #19, 1946). In addition, *Company Practices in Marketing Research* by Crisp (American Management Association, 1953) presents a summary of the research practices of 180 member companies of the American Management Association who responded to a mail survey on this subject conducted in 1952.

A thought-provoking article on the administrative problems encountered in international marketing communications research is "Some Problems in the Administration of International Communications Research" by FISKE and LOWENTHAL (*Public Opinion Quarterly*, Vol. 16, Summer, 1952, pp. 149–159).

An informative descriptive article on the organization and operation of a research department in an advertising agency is, "Operating a Research Department" by MAIN (*Advertising Agency*, Vol. 44, March, 1957, pp. 52ff.).

Part Two | FUNDAMENTALS OF ECONOMIC RESEARCH

Research methodology has many dimensions. three have already been discussed in Sec. 2.4.1-3: the collection of data, the establishing of relationships, and the evaluation of accuracy. Still another dimension is represented by the distinction between the analysis of data over time, *time-series analysis*, and the analysis of data at a single point of time, *cross-section analysis*.

Yet another dimension is encountered by considering the principal disciplines from which the leading analytical concepts or research techniques are borrowed. Thus, in the so-called *management sciences* the dominant role is played by applied mathematics; whereas in *motivation research* psychological methods come to the fore. As might be expected, however, most of the techniques covered in the following chapters derive primarily from economic theory, business economics, or statistics.

For expository reasons there is an advantage in starting the discussion of these various dimensions of research methodology with statistical techniques for establishing economic relationships, Chapter 3. These techniques are as necessary for the understanding of sampling methods and experimentation as they are for economic applications of time-series analysis or cross-section analysis. Familiarity with these techniques makes it easier to consider the distinctive contributions that the cross-section and time-series methods have to offer to economic and business research, the subject of Chapter 4. These fundamentals then serve as a basis for study of practical applications of these various approaches, which is the subject matter of the remaining parts of the book.

59

3 | Establishing and Quantifying Economic Relationships

A FULL REVIEW of the numerous techniques available for determining relationships in economics and business is outside the scope of any single chapter. Rather all that this chapter seeks to do is to survey the principal techniques and their advantages and limitations. No attempt is made to discuss each of these techniques thoroughly, for excellent, detailed treatments are already available in various statistical texts. Instead, the objective is to provide the reader with a general idea of their characteristics and uses.

From a technical, statistical point of view, this chapter covers a broad range—from simple frequency distributions to equation systems and factor analysis. This is as it should be, however, for, in establishing relationships, extremely simple techniques are used in some cases and elaborate ones in others. Before being able to make a choice, the researcher should be reasonably well acquainted with at least the principal possibilities, regardless of the difficulty of application.

Although techniques vary widely in complexity, it should be emphasized that in practice the relatively simple methods have proved the most fruitful. Such simple expedients as the preparation of frequency distributions, cross-tabulations and scatter diagrams not only serve as a useful start but often provide an adequate base for practical decisions. This is not to say that the more sophisticated techniques are of no value in practical work. Rather it is that the opportunities for practical application are fewer and, when present, require more specialized skill to be fully exploited.

3.1. FREQUENCY DISTRIBUTIONS

Because of their simplicity, frequency distributions are often derided as a tool of statistical analysis, if not overlooked altogether. Yet the fact remains

61

that frequency distributions can be a useful preliminary step where more complex techniques are to be used and, in many instances, represent the ultimate step of analysis as well. The latter is true if the underlying data are sufficiently unreliable to justify the use of other techniques or if the purpose of the analysis is simply to assess the degree of dispersion and concentration of a set of data.

Actually, frequency distributions are not such a simple tool of analysis as they may seem at first sight because of the many forms of distributions that are available. The simplest form is the so-called *absolute* frequency distribution, which is nothing more than the combination of the original observations into frequency classes. More useful for comparative purposes is the *relative* frequency distribution, which indicates what proportion of all the observations lies in a given range. Both types are illustrated in Table 3.1, which

Table 3.1
DISTRIBUTION OF U. S. INDIVIDUAL INCOME TAX RETURNS BY GROSS INCOME, 1958

Income	Number of returns (Absolute freq. dsn.) (000)	Per cent of returns (Relative freq. dsn.)
Under $1,000	7010	11.9%
$ 1,000– 1,999	7691	13.1
2,000– 2,999	7413	12.6
3,000– 3,999	7472	12.7
4,000– 4,999	7385	12.6
5,000– 5,999	6376	10.9
6,000– 6,999	4677	8.0
7,000– 9,999	6851	11.7
10,000– 14,999	2488	4.2
15,000– 19,999	588	1.0
20,000– 49,999	635	1.1
50,000– 99,999	92	.2
100,000–199,999	18	*
200,000 and over	5	*
TOTAL	58701	100.0%

* Less than .05 per cent
Source: *Statistics of Income for 1958, Preliminary Report,* U. S. Treasury Department, Internal Revenue Service, 1960, p. 11.

shows the distribution of individuals filing tax returns in 1958 by adjusted gross income classes (essentially income less allowable expenses incurred in earning income). The absolute distribution indicates how many people reported income in any given bracket, while the relative one shows the proportion of people in each bracket. The relative distribution also can be compared with similar distributions for earlier years to bring out what shifts may have taken place in the income distribution over time (assuming stability of tax laws, tax enforcement practices, etc.).

Table 3.1 also illustrates one means of avoiding overlapping class intervals (others are discussed in the references cited at the end of this chapter) as well as the use of unequal class intervals. Where the data permit, equal class intervals are usually preferred. However, many economic data show a rather uneven distribution, while at the same time the total range covered by the observations is considerable. This is often the case where money values are concerned. Unequal class intervals, therefore, as often as not prove more useful. This is particularly true because of the desirability of limiting the number of class intervals of the distribution to some manageable number, usually between 10 and 20. Some additional care has to be taken in using such distributions for analytical purposes, such as computing arithmetic means and standard deviations, but this is a minor consideration and not the bogey it is made out to be in many elementary statistics courses.

3.1.1. Types of Frequency Distributions

Frequency distributions are either *symmetrical* or *asymmetrical*. A distribution is symmetrical if its shape is the same on either side of the midpoint, in other words, if the same frequency is encountered on either side

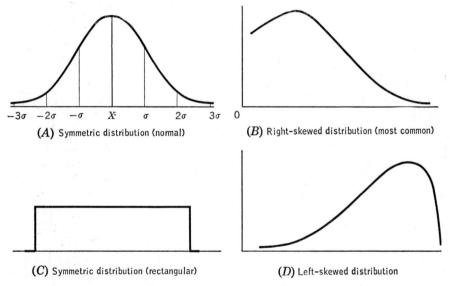

(*A*) Symmetric distribution (normal)

(*B*) Right-skewed distribution (most common)

(*C*) Symmetric distribution (rectangular)

(*D*) Left-skewed distribution

Fig. 3.1. *Types of Frequency Distributions*

of the distribution at any given distance from the midpoint. Otherwise the distribution is asymmetrical.

Various types of symmetrical and asymmetrical distributions are illustrated in Fig. 3.1. It is perhaps needless to note that, curiously enough, symmetrical distributions are practically nonexistent in economic and marketing work. Nevertheless, the symmetrical *normal distribution* plays a central role in analytical work because it possesses a number of useful properties and because many actual distributions are reasonably well approximated by it or can be made so by some simple transformation. As shown in Fig. 3.1A, the normal distribution is unimodal, tapering off symmetrically like a bell from both sides of the mode. It has the property that 68.27 per cent of the area under the curve is included within the range of the mean plus and minus one standard deviation, 95.45 per cent within two standard deviations of the mean, and practically all the area (99.75 per cent) within three standard deviations. If, therefore, a given set of observations shows this particular relative distribution, we may expect that their actual distribution can be approximated by the normal one. In addition, the other properties underlying the normal distribution are likely to hold as well. Conversely, the figures just given of 68.27 per cent, etc., are useful as a means of ascertaining for any set of observations the degree of approximation of the normal distribution.

In actual practice, right-skewed asymmetrical distributions are by far the most common type. This is because most economic magnitudes have lower limits, e.g., zero for incomes, but hardly any upper limit. As a result, most data or observations cluster around some midpoint, taper off sharply to the left to zero, but taper off only gradually to the right, as shown by Fig. 3.1B. The income distribution in Table 3.1 is a case in point.

The attribute underlying a frequency distribution can be either continuous, as money income per family, or discrete, such as the number of persons per family. In the latter case, the size classes are determined not by class intervals but by the actual numerical value of the variable (1 person, 2 persons, etc.). If the range covered by the numerical values is considerable, the size classes are often again determined by class limits, e.g., distribution of manufacturing firms by number of employees. From a theoretical point of view, however, these discrete distributions fall into a separate category, and a number of theoretical distributions are designed explicitly for discrete variables. Two such distributions play an important role in sampling analysis. One is the *binomial distribution*, which merges into the normal distribution as the sample size becomes increasingly large. The other is the *Poisson distribution*, which proves very useful when the chance of occurrence of a certain event determining the value of the variable is very small, such as the number of auto accidents per short time interval.

3.1.2. Descriptive Representation of Frequency Distributions

3.1.2.1. *Graphical.* Graphical representation of a frequency distribution is the simplest means of doing so, provides a broad visual picture of the

main characteristics of the distribution, and is at times preferable for analytical purposes as well.

For distributions that are sharply skewed to the right, as is the case with incomes and many other business magnitudes, the use of logarithms will often yield an approximately normal distribution, which has various advantages for analytical purposes. Panel A of Fig. 3.2 shows the effect of this

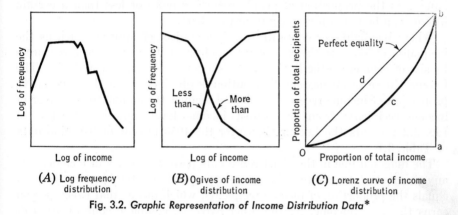

(*A*) Log frequency distribution   (*B*) Ogives of income distribution   (*C*) Lorenz curve of income distribution

Fig. 3.2. Graphic Representation of Income Distribution Data*

transformation on the income distribution data in Table 3.1; the result is now clearly much closer to a normal distribution, so close in fact that the use of properties of a normal distribution for approximation purposes may well be justified. (Whether or not it is justified can be tested by chi-square analysis, which is taken up at a later point.)

If the question is how many observations are above or below certain limits, *cumulative* frequency curves can be used. As the name implies, these curves show what number (or proportion) of observations lies beyond par-

---

DATA FOR FIG. 3-2A		DATA FOR FIG. 3-2B				DATA FOR FIG. 3-2C LORENZ CURVE OF INCOME DISTRIBUTION			
log of mid-point of each class	*log of frequency*	*Lower limit*	*Upper limit*	*Less than log f*	*More than log f*			*Proportion of income*	*Proportion of recipients*
2.0000	2.0000	2.0000~	3.0000	6.8457	85.5398	Under	1,000	1.2	11.9
2.6990	6.8457	3.0000≦	>3.3010	13.7317	78.6941	1,000 ~	1,999	5.3	25.0
3.1761	6.8860	3.3010≦	>3.4771	20.6017	71.8081	2,000 ~	2,999	11.8	37.6
3.3979	6.8700	3.4771≦	>3.6021	27.4751	64.9381	3,000 ~	3,999	21.0	50.3
3.5441	6.8734	3.6021≦	>3.6990	34.3435	58.0647	4,000 ~	4,999	32.7	62.9
3.6532	6.8684	3.6990≦	>3.7782	41.1480	51.1963	5,000	5,999	45.1	73.8
3.7404	6.8045	3.7782≦	>3.8451	47.8180	44.3918	6,000	6,999	55.8	81.8
3.8129	6.6700	3.8451≦	>4.0000	54.6538	37.7218	7,000	9,999	73.9	93.5
3.9031	6.8357	4.0000≦	>4.1761	61.0496	30.8860	10,000	14,999	84.9	97.7
4.0969	6.3959	4.1761≦	>4.3010	66.8190	24.4902	15,000	19,999	88.5	98.7
4.2430	5.7693	4.3010≦	>4.6990	72.6218	18.7208	20,000	49,999	96.3	99.8
4.5441	5.8028	4.6990≦	>5.0000	77.5855	12.9180	50,000	99,999	98.4	100.0
4.8215	4.9638	5.0000≦	>5.3010	81.8408	7.9542	100,000	199,999	99.2	100.0
5.1173	4.2553	5.3010≦	>6.699	85.5398	3.6990	200,000 ~ over		100.0	100.0
5.6021	3.6990								

ticular values of the variable. They are obtained by cumulating the original frequency distribution either from the lowest value upward or from the highest value downward, depending on the purpose for which the cumulative distribution is desired. Such distributions are sometimes known as *ogives*. Cumulative distributions of both types are shown in semi-logarithmic form in Panel B of Fig. 3.2. For approximation purposes, they can be quite handy, as the proportion of people reporting more or less than a certain income can be read off directly from the chart.

Where inequality or concentration is a subject of inquiry—such as the inequality of incomes, the concentration of production or financial resources by size of firm, etc.—the *Lorenz Curve* is a convenient graphical device. The Lorenz Curve of an income distribution is obtained when the cumulative proportion of income received is plotted against the cumulative number of income recipients from the lowest income levels upward. Panel C of Fig. 3.2 presents the Lorenz Curve for the 1958 income distribution data of Table 3.1.

The diagonal line in the chart represents perfect equality of incomes—at any given percentage of total income, the proportion of total income received equals the proportion of income recipients, which means that every person earns the same income. At the other extreme, complete concentration of income is represented by the discontinuous line, *oab*—one person receives all the income.

The position of the plotted distribution relative to these two extremes indicates the relative concentration of income. The closer this curve is to the diagonal line, the less concentrated is the distribution of income. This principle provides an easy means of evaluating which of two income distributions exhibits a lesser degree of concentration, namely, the one nearer the diagonal. Such an evaluation is, of course, only approximate,[1] but is nevertheless a useful tool of analysis except if the two distributions should intersect. But this is relatively rare.

Another measure of concentration applied primarily to incomes is the *Pareto Curve* and its associated slope. This curve is obtained when the number of income recipients with incomes greater than a given amount, y, is plotted against y on double-logarithmic paper. Theoretically, the curve turns out to be linear (the so-called *Pareto Law*), and on the basis of this assumption the slope of the curve, alpha, provides a numerical measure of income concentration. Alpha is always negative, and the higher the absolute value of alpha, the more concentrated is the distribution of income.

This is easily seen, since the average income of all people earning more

---

[1] Quantification is also possible, by defining concentration as the area between the curve and the diagonal relative to the total area under the diagonal, i.e., (Area *ocbd*)/ (Area *oabd*). The estimation of the numerator is not usually an easy task, however, and in practice such numerical estimates are almost never attempted.

than y is given by $\dfrac{\alpha}{\alpha - 1} y$.[2] If α increases from 1.5 to 2.0, this ratio declines from 3 to 2, and the concentration and in equality of income distribution have increased accordingly.

The "more-than" ogive in Panel *B* of Fig. 3.2 presents the Pareto curve for the 1958 income-distribution data and also one of the main shortcomings of this approach for measuring concentration—the assumption of linearity. Both at the lower and at the upper income levels linearity, at least for the U. S. income distribution, appears to be more the exception than the rule. Hence, insofar as obtaining a numerical measure of income concentration is concerned, this approach raises serious problems both of estimation and of interpretation. However, as a graphical representation of income concentration, the Pareto Curve remains very useful, particularly for comparative purposes.

3.1.2.2.   *Numerical.* For most practical work a frequency distribution is described numerically in two respects—central tendency and dispersion. Skewness and kurtosis (the relative degree of "peakedness") are the two other principal means of description, but except for theoretical work on the subject these types of measures are rarely used.

The arithmetic mean is still the most widely used measure of central tendency, although the median has been gaining increasing popularity for such sharply right-skewed distributions as that exemplified by the data in Table 3.1. For such skewed distributions, the mean's property of being influenced substantially by extreme (in this case, high) values is a serious shortcoming of the measure. The median, being the midpoint of the distribution, is of course not affected by the dispersion of the observations at the extremes and is, therefore, a more representative indicator of *central* tendency.[3] This is also true for the mode, the value with the maximum frequency. The mode, however, is at the other extreme; it is entirely unaffected by the dispersion of observations about the modal interval, so that the extent to which the mode reflects central tendency varies considerably with the dispersion of the distribution.

The standard deviation, the root mean square of the deviations of the observations about their mean, has become the almost universally accepted measure of absolute dispersion in economic and business analysis. Relative dispersion is measured by the ratio of the standard deviation to the mean, the coefficient of variation. The properties of the standard deviation as ap-

---

[2] See, for instance, R. G. D. ALLEN, *Mathematical Analysis for Economists* (London: Macmillan, 1947), pp. 407–408.

[3] Since the median is less affected by extreme observations, it is also more stable than the mean over time. For this reason, it is preferable to the latter for the computation of a price index when quality changes of the constituent parts underlie severe random fluctuations.

plied to the normal curve have already been discussed, and these properties
serve as the foundation for much practical sampling analysis. Even where
these properties are not applicable, the standard deviation is the invariably-
selected measure of dispersion, in part because people are so used to it and
in part because of various useful, algebraic characteristics.

At the same time, the use of the range—the difference between the highest
and lowest values—has also been increasing. This is largely due to the feasibility of using the range as a basis for estimating the standard deviation, a
procedure that is particularly useful and efficient for small samples.[4] Other
measures of dispersion are encountered infrequently, but it is useful to know
of their existence—the average deviation (the mean of the absolute deviations of the observations about their mean), the interquartile range (the
interval encompassing the middle 50 per cent of the observations), deciles,
and percentiles.

Turning to calculation procedures, it is worth noting that the mean and
the variance (the square of the standard deviation) represent the first two
moments of a distribution. The kth moment of a discrete distribution about
any arbitrary point, X_0, is defined as: $\sum_1^M f(X - X_0)^k \big/ N$, where X is the
various values of the variable under study, f is the frequency of each value of
X, the summation being over M distinct values of X. The mean of the distribution is the first moment of this distribution about zero, i.e., $X_0 = 0$,
$k = 1$:

$$\bar{X} = \frac{\Sigma f X}{N} \tag{3.1}$$

which can also be represented as:

$$\bar{X} = X_0 + \frac{\Sigma f X'}{N} \tag{3.2}$$

where X_0 is again any arbitrary value, and $X' = X - X_0$. If all class intervals are equal, X' can be replaced by $X'' = (X - X_0)/i$, where i is the width
of the interval, and the summation is then multiplied by i.[5]

The form (3.2) is easier to compute by hand, for X_0 can be taken as some
value near where $\bar{X}$ is suspected to be. Usually X_0 is taken as the midpoint
of an interval, so that X' reduces to relatively low integers. When machines
are available, as is usually the case, (3.1) is as easy as any other approach.

---

[4] For an example, see Sec. 5.2. Also, see W. E. DEMING, *Some Theory of Sampling;* and
ROBERT FERBER, *Statistical Techniques in Market Research,* Chapter 8.

[5] In the continuous case, the kth moment becomes: $\sum_1^N (X_i - X_0)^k \big/ N$, the summation
extending over all (N) values of X.

The variance is the second moment about the mean, i.e.:

$$\sigma^2 = \frac{\Sigma f(X - \bar{X})^2}{N} \tag{3.3}$$

which, for computational purposes, is better represented as:

$$\sigma^2 = \frac{\Sigma f X^2}{N} - \left(\frac{\Sigma f X}{N}\right)^2$$

the second term on the right being $\bar{X}^2$.

Higher moments are not encountered frequently in business and economic research, though it might be noted that the third moment about the mean reflects skewness and that the fourth moment about the mean reflects kurtosis.

The reader may care to verify for himself that the mean and standard deviation of the income-distribution data in Table 3.1 are \$4,829 and \$6,370, respectively.[6] The median would be a more suitable measure of central tendency than the mean, and the reader can verify that the value of the median is \$3,968, based on the usual formula:

$$Median = \begin{array}{c} Lower\ limit\ of \\ median\ class \\ interval \end{array} + \left(\begin{array}{c} Size\ of \\ median\ class \\ interval \end{array}\right) \left(\frac{\dfrac{N}{2} - \begin{array}{c} Total\ frequencies\ in \\ preceding\ intervals \end{array}}{\begin{array}{c} Number\ of\ frequencies\ in \\ median\ class\ interval \end{array}}\right)$$

3.1.3. The Constancy of Frequency Distributions

Apart from representing a series of data in an orderly fashion, as discussed above, frequency distributions may also serve as a basis for deriving some fundamental equation that describes the distribution of the phenomenon in general. Thus they pretend to be of more general validity, or even a "law." If, for example, a logarithmic transformation of a particular income distribution (e.g., annual wages paid out by a certain industry) brings it into line with a logarithmic normal distribution, the hypothesis can be suggested for further study that other income distributions of the same kind (e.g., annual wages in other years or industries) also possess the property of a logarithmic normal distribution.

If such a hypothesis can be proved approximately valid, the fundamental mathematical formula—in this case, the log-normal distribution—facilitates considerably the computational work required to arrive at certain conclusions. Hence, generalization to a given kind of distribution is important for many practical and theoretical purposes in business and economics.

---

[6] The midpoints of the intervals were taken as X for all but the highest three intervals. The midpoints of these intervals were estimated from the original data as \$66,300, \$131,500, and \$400,000, respectively.

Three qualifications are, however, in order. First, the general validity of a particular theoretical distribution is best established by testing it in a number of cases. Even then, the fundamental equation established is nothing more than an "empirical law," as long as it cannot be substantiated from a theoretical point of view. Pareto's famous law is a good example.

Secondly, although the same general mathematical formula may apply to a whole category of data, the numerical values of its parameters may differ from case to case. This is readily understandable, for the distribution of an economic variable at a given time and place is governed by prevailing institutions and economic conditions. However, this variability of the parameters implies that the application of the same general formula will yield conclusions that may differ substantially in different cases.

In the third place, since economic conditions as well as institutions change over time, the parameters of the same geographically or otherwise defined distribution tend to change over time. Thus, income concentration varies systematically with the business cycle, tending to decline in times of prosperity. The possibility of changes in parameters should, therefore, be taken into account if inferences are to be drawn on temporal changes.

Finally, in comparing different kinds of empirical distributions it is worth knowing that frequency distributions can be classified by various mathematical properties. The two most notable such classifications are the Pearsonian and the Gram-Charlier systems. (References are provided at the end of the chapter.)

3.2. CROSS-CLASSIFICATIONS

Cross-classifications of data can serve one of two purposes—to illustrate relationships that have already been established or to seek clues to relationships whose existence is a matter of speculation. Contrary to some popular belief, cross-classifications can be prepared equally well from continuous or discrete variables as from attributes. However, for purposes of detecting relationships between variables, especially continuous variables, scatter diagrams (taken up in the next section) are generally more useful.

Theoretically, cross-classifications can involve any number of variables or attributes. In practice, however, four or five variables are the maximum practical number for analytical purposes and only about two or three in a descriptive cross-classification. The latter should also have relatively few breakdowns of each variable, generally not more than four or five (and this is not a bad idea, either, when cross-classifications are prepared for throwing light on the general nature of relationships).

An example of a dichotomous two-way cross-classification is presented in Part A of Table 3.2. Presented in terms of actual numbers, it is clearly difficult to ascertain what relationship, if any, exists between stock ownership and income level. Parts *B* and *C* of the table illustrate two ways of bringing out this relationship, both ways based on percentage transformations. Converting each actual number into a percentage of the number of spending units at that particular income level, Part *B* of Table 3.2 shows how the proportion of people owning stock rises with income level; while representing

Table 3.2
STOCK OWNERSHIP OF U. S. SPENDING UNITS BY INCOME LEVEL, 1955

INCOME LEVEL	OWNING STOCK	NOT OWNING STOCK	TOTAL
	A. Number of spending units		
Under $3,000	40	948	988
$3,000–4,999	46	877	923
5,000–7,499	66	664	730
7,500–9,999	37	194	231
10,000 and over	86	161	247
TOTAL	275	2,844	3,119
	B. Per cent of total in given income level		
Under $3,000	4	96	100%
$3,000–4,999	5	95	100%
5,000–7,499	9	91	100%
7,500–9,999	16	84	100%
10,000 and over	35	65	100%
TOTAL	9	91	100%
	C. Per cent of total owning or not owning stock		
Under $3,000	15%	33%	32%
$3,000–4,999	17	31	30
5,000–7,499	24	23	23
7,500–9,999	13	7	7
10,000 and over	31	6	8
TOTAL	100%	100%	100%

Source: Survey reported in *Statistical Abstract of the United States, 1956*, p. 471.

each number as a percent of all those in the sample owning or not owning stock as the case may be, Part *C* of Table 3.2 shows that most owners of stock earn $5,000 per year or more whereas most non-owners are below this level of income. Thus, each means of representation is significant in itself, and the proper one(s) to use depends on the orientation of the analysis.

A more complicated cross-classification is shown in Table 3.3, which also illustrates how nature of debt, type of corporation, length of debt can be cross-tabulated against a continuous variable, time. Because of the complex classification, detection of relationships in Table 3.3 is harder than in Table 3.2.[7] At first glance, Table 3.3 might seem to be a hopeless

[7] Analytically, however, the problem is simplified in one respect because Table 3.3, being based on population data (at least, presumably), does not involve considerations of spurious relationships brought about by sampling variation, as does Table 3.2.

jumble of figures, but that is understandable, for interpreting a table presented more or less in the abstract is much more difficult than when the table is examined with a specific objective in mind.

Table 3.3
GROSS AND NET CORPORATE DEBT BY TYPE OF CORPORATION AND OF DEBT, SELECTED YEARS, 1945–1955
(Billions of dollars)

END OF YEAR	RAILWAY CORPORATIONS			NONRAILWAY CORPORATIONS			TOTAL		
	LONG-TERM	SHORT-TERM	TOTAL	LONG-TERM	SHORT-TERM	TOTAL	LONG-TERM	SHORT-TERM	TOTAL
	Gross corporate debt								
1945	11.9	3.5	15.4	33.4	50.7	84.1	45.3	54.2	99.5
1948	11.1	2.9	14.0	51.7	73.1	124.8	62.8	76.0	138.8
1952	11.5	3.1	14.6	76.5	110.5	187.0	88.0	113.6	201.6
1955	11.5	2.7	14.2	99.6	118.6	218.2	111.1	121.3	232.4
	Net corporate debt								
1945	10.8	3.2	14.0	27.5	43.8	71.3	38.3	47.0	85.3
1948	9.9	2.6	12.5	42.6	62.7	105.3	52.5	65.3	117.8
1952	10.3	2.8	13.1	63.0	94.9	157.9	73.3	97.7	171.0
1955	10.5	2.4	12.9	82.0	101.9	183.9	92.5	104.3	196.8

Source: U. S. Department of Commerce, *Survey of Current Business*, May 1956, p. 13.

The formulation of such objectives must precede interpretation. Thus, suppose the objective is to compare the extent of increase in long-term and in short-term corporate debt between 1945 and 1955, both for gross debt and for net debt. This is easily done by converting each time series into index form with the 1945 figure as 100 per cent. The result, shown below for the net debt of railway and nonrailway corporations separately, now brings out the main trends for net debt at a glance:

	RAILWAY CORPORATIONS		NONRAILWAY CORPORATIONS	
	LONG-TERM	SHORT-TERM	LONG-TERM	SHORT-TERM
1945	100	100	100	100
1948	92	81	155	143
1952	95	88	229	217
1955	97	75	298	233

Alternatively, if the objective is to compare the proportion of total corporate debt that is of the long-term variety as between railway and nonrailway corporations, and the variation in these proportions over time, the total debt of each class of corporation can be represented as 100 per cent. For net corporate debt, this is shown below.

	RAILWAY CORPORATIONS			NONRAILWAY CORPORATIONS		
	LONG-TERM	SHORT-TERM	TOTAL	LONG-TERM	SHORT-TERM	TOTAL
1945	77	23	100%	39	61	100%
1948	79	21	100%	40	60	100%
1952	79	21	100%	40	60	100%
1955	81	19	100%	45	55	100%

Again, the main findings on the question at hand now emerge clearly, the moral of which is that judicious use and transformation of cross-classification tables can yield significant results easily and neatly. This subject will be taken up again in Sec. 11.3.

3.3.   CHI-SQUARE AND MEASURES OF ASSOCIATION

There are two distinct problems in setting up a relationship—establishing its existence, and measuring the extent of relationship once it is established. If sample data are used, establishing the existence of a relationship means determining the extent to which the observed relationship has actually been brought about by sampling variation, and this is where chi-square analysis enters the picture.

3.3.1.   Chi-Square Analysis

Chi square is a statistic that can be applied to a contingency table—a cross-classification table depicting the relationship between two discrete variables—to estimate the probability that the observed relationship is actually the result of sampling variations in the data. Essentially the reasoning is as follows:

1. The *null hypothesis* is advanced that no relationship exists between the particular factors in the population, and that any observed relationship (in the sample data) is due solely to sampling variations.

2. The statistic, chi square (χ^2), is computed as a measure of the extent of agreement between the observed values and the values that *would have been obtained* under the null hypothesis, i.e., on the assumption of absence of any true relationship. This is the reason why the null hypothesis is set up in the first place—to provide the rationale for χ^2 and for the accompanying probability calculation.

3. Given the computed value of χ^2, the probability is ascertained (usually from tables) of a relationship reflected by that particular value being obtained purely as a result of sampling variations.

4. If this probability is low, it seems very unlikely that the observed relationship would have been brought about *entirely* by sampling variation. The likelihood, therefore, appears that the relationship is not due to sampling variation and thus really exists. Hence, the null hypothesis is rejected. On the other hand, if this probability is not low, there is a good presumption that the observed relationship exists only because of the vagaries of sampling variations, and the null hypothesis is accepted—no evidence of a true relationship is uncovered.

In practice, this borderline probability is generally taken as .05, which reflects a compromise between the danger of wrongly concluding that a true relationship does exist (i.e., rejecting the null hypothesis when it is true, which will occur one time out of every twenty at this probability level) and the danger of erroneously concluding that the observed relationship is nothing more than sampling variation (i.e., accepting the null hypothesis when it is false). In statistical parlance, these two pitfalls are known as Type I and Type II errors, respectively.

Chi square is defined as follows:

$$\chi^2 = \sum_{i=1}^{m} \left[\frac{(X_i - \Theta_i)^2}{\Theta_i} \right]$$

where X_i is the observed value for cell i, and
Θ_i is the corresponding expected value under the null hypothesis, there being $i = 1, 2, \ldots, m$ cells in the contingency table.

The manner in which the expected values are obtained and χ^2 computed is best explained with reference to an actual example. For this purpose, we can take the data in Table 3.2, and ask whether the apparent association between income level and stock ownership really exists (in the population) or could have been brought about by sampling variations.

Table 3.4
COMPUTATION OF EXPECTED VALUES UNDER THE NULL HYPOTHESIS

Income level	Owning stock	Not owning stock	Total
Under $3,000	$\frac{275}{3119} \times 988 = 87$	$\frac{2844}{3119} \times 988 = 901$	988
$3,000–4,999	$\frac{275}{3119} \times 923 = 82$	$\frac{2844}{3119} \times 923 = 841$	923
5,000–7,499	$\frac{275}{3119} \times 730 = 64$	$\frac{2844}{3119} \times 730 = 666$	730
7,500–9,999	$\frac{275}{3119} \times 231 = 20$	$\frac{2844}{3119} \times 231 = 211$	231
10,000 and over	$\frac{275}{3119} \times 247 = 22$	$\frac{2844}{3119} \times 247 = 225$	247
TOTAL	275	2,844	3,119

We begin by setting up the null hypothesis that the observed association between these two factors is due solely to sampling variations and not to any systematic cause. If so, then the proportion of spending units owning and not owning stock would be expected to be the same at all income levels, and the best estimate of these two proportions is given by the total number of sample members in each stock-ownership position, i.e., 275/3,119 for stock owners, and 2,844/3,119 for non-stock owners. It then follows that the expected number of sample members in each cell under the null hypothesis would be the appropriate one of these two proportions multiplied by the number in the sample at that income level. Thus, the number earning less than \$3,000 and owning stock that would be expected in a sample of 3,119 under the assumption of the null hypothesis is:

$$\frac{275}{3,119} \times 988 = 87$$

The computation of the expected numbers for each cell in the table is illustrated in Table 3.4. Note that the marginal totals remain the same as in the original table. The expected values obtained in this manner are substituted along with the actual values in the formula for χ^2 as follows:

$$\chi^2 = \frac{(40 - 87)^2}{40} + \frac{(46 - 82)^2}{46} + \frac{(66 - 64)^2}{66} + \frac{(37 - 20)^2}{37} + \frac{(86 - 22)^2}{22}$$
$$+ \frac{(948 - 901)^2}{901} + \frac{(877 - 841)^2}{841} + \frac{(664 - 666)^2}{666} + \frac{(194 - 211)^2}{211}$$
$$+ \frac{(161 - 225)^2}{225} = 301.026$$

The next step is to ascertain the probability of obtaining values of χ^2 exceeding particular figures purely as a result of sampling variations. Such a table is reproduced on p. 551 of the Appendix, showing values of χ^2 corresponding to specified probabilities and particular "degrees of freedom." The latter reflects the number of independent relationships between the cells of a table, and hence influences the values of χ^2 corresponding to particular probabilities. In a 2 × 2 table, the reader can verify that there is only one independent relationship (degree of freedom); for once one of the four cell values is known, the values of the other three cells are automatically fixed given the marginal totals. Similarly, experimentation would indicate that Table 3.4 has four degrees of freedom—if as few as four cell values are known, the values of the other six cells are predetermined.

The degrees of freedom associated with any size contingency table can be ascertained as: $(r - 1)(c - 1)$, where r is the number of rows in the table and c is the number of columns. In the present case, we have $(5 - 1)$ $(2 - 1) = 4$, as before.

Turning to Appendix Table A3, we see that a χ^2 value of 301.026 with four degrees of freedom far exceeds even the .01 probability level. Hence, we conclude that the probability of obtaining the observed relationship between income and stock ownership purely as a result of sampling variations is far below .01, and, because it is so low, the observed relationship undoubtedly actually exists.

All this is predicated on the assumption that the basic theoretical requirements for the applicability of the chi-square test have been met. These include:

1. Independence of the sample observations,
2. Selection of each observation in a random probability manner from the population at large (unrestricted sampling),
3. Data in original units, not percentages,
4. A large sample (50 or more) with a certain minimum number in each cell—usually 5 is sufficient.

In the present example, all requirements but the second are met. Since a stratified sample design was used in selecting the sample members, each of the latter was not selected from the population at large. However, each member was still selected in a probability manner, so the relaxation of this requirement is of minor significance, especially in view of the conclusive nature of the results.

In other instances, relaxation of one or more of the preceding requirements is not so minor. Often, the situation is encountered where the independence or the random nature of the observations is in considerable doubt or may clearly not exist. Yet some indication may be desired of the existence of the observed relationship.

The chi-square test is also applied at times to population data. The justification for the statistical analysis in such a case rests on the assumption that these data represent a selection of observations from an infinitely larger population, and that for generalization it is desirable to ascertain the extent to which the variables are related to each other in this particular population. It is on this basis that chi-square tests are carried out in many business and economic non-survey problems.

Essentially there are two alternatives in such a situation. One is not to apply chi square or any other test if invalid theoretically. This is the more rigorous approach. The other alternative is to apply chi square anyway and present the results with some such qualification as: "If the observations were independent and randomly selected, this is what the chi-square test indicates . . . " Although this approach is frowned upon by theoreticians, from the point of view of practical expediency it can prove useful if properly interpreted.

A second principal use of chi square is in establishing agreement between a sample-based distribution and some hypothetical or population distribution. Thus, the 1955 distribution of income shown in Table 3.2 might be compared with the 1949 Census distribution to ascertain whether any significant changes might have taken place; or an attempt might be made to test whether the distribution in Table 3.2 can be described by a normal curve, etc.

The application of chi square in these cases is the same as outlined before, with two exceptions. First, the hypothetical or population distribution serves as the basis for computing of the expected values of the sample distribution under the null hypothesis. Second, the degrees of freedom associated with the test depend on the nature of the population distribution. If this is either an actual population distribution or a hypothetical distribution not based on a particular mathematical curve or frequency function, the degrees of freedom are one less than the number of class intervals in the distribution. If the sample distribution is being fitted to some mathematical frequency function, such as the normal curve, the degrees of freedom are reduced further by the number of restrictions imposed in the process of fitting the data to the curve. This, of course, requires a knowledge of the frequency function. Thus, the frequently used normal curve imposes three restrictions on any set of data fitted to it, because the distribution of expected values has the same mean, standard deviation, and sample size as the observed sample data.

More detailed material on the application of chi square in these various uses is provided by the references listed at the end of this chapter.

3.3.2. Measures of Association

Measuring the extent of relationship in a contingency table is a difficult task and is, in fact, often best avoided where possible. A principal reason for this is that the degree and nature of association can vary drastically with the system of classification. For example, if we have the following 4 $\times$ 4 table,[8]

	b_1	b_2	b_3	b_4
a_1	0	5	0	0
a_2	5	0	0	0
a_3	0	0	0	5
a_4	0	0	5	0

and combine neighboring classes, the result looks like perfect association:

	b_1, b_2	b_3, b_4
a_1, a_2	10	0
a_3, a_4	0	10

---

[8] Based on L. A. GOODMAN and W. H. KRUSKAL, "Measures of Association for Cross Classifications," *Journal of the American Statistical Association*, December, 1954, p. 737

But if we combine rows 2, 3, and 4 and columns 2, 3 and 4, the result is an entirely different picture:

	b_1	b_2, b_3, b_4
a_1	0	5
a_2, a_3, a_4	5	10

To an extent this ambiguity can be avoided in any particular case by adhering to the system of classification as originally developed for the data at hand. However, this is not always feasible and is likely to break down, in any event, when a measure of association is desired for comparative purposes.

All this does not mean that there are no valid measures of association, but rather that the selection of a measure of association must be considered in the light of the problem at hand and that it must be interpreted with due caution of possible limitations, particularly so when comparison of association in different tables is involved.

The numerous measures of association that are available can be divided into two broad classes—the standard and the probabilistic models. The standard measures are those based largely on x^2 itself and include:

For a 2 × 2 table, there is:

$$Q = \frac{a_{11}a_{22} - a_{12}a_{21}}{a_{11}a_{22} + a_{12}a_{21}}$$

Where the a's are as follows:

a_{11}	a_{12}
a_{21}	a_{22}

For a larger table, the most appropriate measure would seem to be:

$$A = \frac{x^2/N}{(Minimum \ number \ of \ rows \ or \ columns) - 1}$$

This measure has the advantage of ranging between zero and one—zero representing complete independence and one representing total association. For example, the degree of association between income level and stock ownership (Table 3.4) by this measure is:

$$A = \frac{301.026/3119}{2 - 1} = .097$$

Unlike correlation measures, this value does not have any analytical significance in itself. It does not, for example, indicate the "proportion of total variance in one factor explained by the other," as does the coefficient of correlation, nor do similar measures of association.

The more recently developed probabilistic measures of association are much more individualistic in nature in that the formula for the measure itself will vary according to the nature of the problem. Some are based on an attempt to quantify the extent to which one's ability to predict an attribute is improved by knowledge of the other attribute. Thus, suppose a survey on businessmen's expectations yields the following results:

Industry	Optimistic	Pessimistic	Total
Producers' goods	41	62	103
Consumers' goods	84	61	145
Transportation	9	18	27
TOTAL	134	141	275

We may now ask: How much is our ability to predict whether or not a business executive is optimistic increased if we know the industrial classification of his firm than if we did not have this information? The resultant measure of association can be represented as follows:

$$L = \frac{\begin{array}{c}\text{Probability of error if} \\ \text{industry is not known}\end{array} - \begin{array}{c}\text{Probability of error if} \\ \text{industry is known}\end{array}}{\text{Probability of error if industry is not known}}$$

With no knowledge of industry classification the best "guess" of whether or not a particular executive is optimistic would be that he is not, for the preceding tabulation indicates that most sample members were pessimistic. The probability of such a guess being correct is the relative frequency of pessimistic people in the sample, or $^{141}\!/_{275} = .513$. Hence, the probability of error in this first case is $1 - .513$, or $.487$.

If the industry classification of the executives' firm is known, the best guess about his outlook is obviously the response with the highest frequency in each classification, i.e., optimistic for consumers' goods, and pessimistic for the other two industry categories. The probability of being correct is the frequency of occurrence of these answers in the sample, so that the probability of being wrong in this second instance is the complement of the former, i.e.,

$$\begin{array}{c}\text{Probability of error} \\ \text{if industry is known}\end{array} = 1 - (^{62}\!/_{275} + {}^{84}\!/_{275} + {}^{18}\!/_{275}) = 1 - {}^{164}\!/_{275} = .404$$

The value of L is then:

$$L = \frac{.487 - .404}{.487} = .17$$

It is important to note that this measure is applicable only if all industries are not uniformly more optimistic than pessimistic, or vice versa. (Why?) If so, other measures of association have to be sought.

There are a variety of other probabilistic measures of association, the specific formula depending on the conditions of the problem and on what assumptions are used to construct the model. Thus, if the aim is to learn the extent to which outlook indicates industrial classification of the respondent, a different result is obtained, though with much the same formula. If the two factors under consideration are symmetrical in the sense of there being as much interest in ability to "predict" one factor from another as vice versa, a different formula is obtained. If weighting methods are introduced, yet another form is obtained, and similarly if other types of modifications are made. Clearly, therefore, a measure of association has to be hand-tailored to fit the problem.

3.4. ANALYSIS OF VARIANCE

In taking up the analysis of variance, we leave the simplified world of one- and two-way relationships and enter the realm of multivariate analysis—relationships between any number of factors. This is much the more realistic situation, for the explanation of social and business phenomena almost invariably involves more than one other factor.

Variance analysis is essentially a method for ascertaining from sample data whether one factor really influences another factor or whether the observed association was probably the result of sampling fluctuations. The technique has the advantage of allowing for the influence of such other factors for which data may be available, and in fact permits the simultaneous determination of the significance of each factor in turn on the characteristic under study. It possesses the further advantage of yielding estimates of the relative importance of each of the factors that are found to be significant.

Unfortunately, all of these advantages do not come without disadvantages. One disadvantage is that the computations increase sharply in amount and complexity as the number of factors involved increases and with various other considerations. The second main disadvantage is that the method is applicable only if the individual sample observations were randomly and independently selected and if the variance in each cell is approximately the same (homoscedasticity). The latter is not the case, for example, with income data, where the variance within a given income bracket rises steeply with the level of income. In many such instances, however, a mathematical transformation can be made to offset this tendency.

Complex as variance analysis may become at times, the intuitive basis for the technique is not difficult to follow. It rests on the segregation of the total variance in a set of data into a number of component variances, each representing a different factor in the problem. One of these component variances is the estimated sampling variation in the data, while each of the others combines an estimate of the same sampling variance with an estimate of the variance, if any, due to the influence of that particular factor. The significance of each of the factors under consideration is judged by comparing the component variance for that factor with the estimated sampling variance in the data. If the former exceeds the sampling variance by a margin sufficiently large that it could hardly have been brought about by sampling variation alone, that factor is considered to have a significant effect on the characteristic under study.

For example, suppose we want to determine from sample data the separate effects of income, assets, and size of family on the durable goods purchases of families in a given year. Assuming there is more than one observation in each cell, we could determine by variance analysis the significance or non-significance of each of the following factors:

1. Income alone
2. Assets alone
3. Size of family alone
4. Interaction between income and assets—the tendency for particular combinations of income and assets to influence purchases more than other combinations
5. Interaction between income and size of family
6. Interaction between assets and size of family
7. Interaction between income, assets, and size of family

Items 4, 5 and 6 are known as first-order interactions, while item 7 is a second-order interaction.

Thus, to test the effect of income, we would go through the following steps:

1. Set up the null hypothesis that income has no effect on purchases, i.e., that any observed effect of income is actually due to the vagaries of sampling fluctuations. This step is necessary because, as with chi-square analysis, it serves as the basis for estimating the probability that the observed differences could have been caused solely by sampling variations.

2. From the total variance in durable goods purchases, separate that component which reflects the sampling variance and that portion which reflects whatever income effect there may be as well as sampling variance. The so-called F ratio is then computed, as noted previously:

$$F = \frac{sampling\ variance\ +\ variance\ due\ to\ income,\ if\ any}{sampling\ variance}$$

Concomitantly, the number of degrees of freedom is determined for both numerator and denominator, representing in each case the highest number of independent observations permissible, given the sample size and the variance.

3. The validity of the null hypothesis is judged by determining from the appropriate probability distribution table the likelihood that the excess of

the variance containing the income effect over the estimate of just the sampling variance could have been produced purely by sampling variations. The larger this excess for the same combination of degrees of freedom, the less is this likelihood and the greater the possibility that income does influence purchases. (If the numerator were actually less than the denominator, the null hypothesis is immediately accepted, though if it is much lower, the possibility of error arises—either in the computation or in the algebraic segregation of the component variances.) In effect, therefore, if the computed value of F exceeds the value given in the F-distribution table at the significance level adopted in the study (usually .05), the null hypothesis is rejected and income is asserted to influence durable goods purchases. Otherwise, the null hypothesis is accepted.

An illustration of the application of variance analysis to survey data is provided in Supplement A to this chapter. The example also illustrates the complexity of some of the calculations as well as the manner in which estimates of the relative importance of different factors can be obtained by this technique. Although the computations may seem forbidding at first sight, the principle is a simple one, and, once it has been mastered, the computations generally become routine.

3.4.1. Covariance Analysis

Essentially an extension of variance analysis, the analysis of covariance moves one step further and permits the effect of certain interacting forces to be held constant while testing whether or not other variables affect the factor under study. Thus, in the preceding example, there is a strong basis for suspecting that income and family size are interrelated with each other. By covariance analysis, it is possible to adjust the income figures for differences in size of family, test whether income significantly affects durable goods purchases after family size differences have been eliminated in this way and, if so, then compute for each income level numerical estimates of the variation in purchases with changes in income—still holding family size constant. These estimates are obtained through the use of regression analysis, which is covered in the next section.

Thus, covariance analysis is a more powerful tool than variance analysis, though its applicability is subject to much the same conditions as the latter.

3.5. REGRESSION ANALYSIS

While the chi-square test and, primarily, also analysis of variance aim at the testing of hypotheses, the principal objective of regression analysis is measurement. Since a large number of variables can be handled with comparative ease, regression analysis is a very widely used tool of statistical analysis for economic research. During their development, the terms *regression analysis* and *correlation analysis* possessed sharply different meanings, with regression analysis pertaining to the *nature* of the relationship and correlation analysis pertaining to the *extent* of the relationship. However, since most current economic and business studies utilizing this approach are concerned as much with one aspect as with another, the original distinction between the two terms has begun to fade.

3.5.1. Relation Between Two Variables

3.5.1.1. *Graphical approach*. The simplest means of judging the existence and character of a relation between two variables is by plotting the

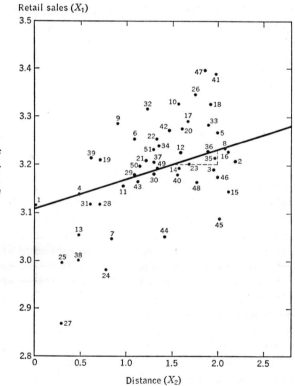
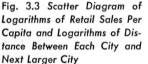

Fig. 3.3 *Scatter Diagram of Logarithms of Retail Sales Per Capita and Logarithms of Distance Between Each City and Next Larger City*

data in the form of a scatter diagram, with each point representing one observation and indicating, preferably, which observation. Thus, Fig. 3.3 presents a scatter diagram of the relationship between the logarithms of retail sales per capita in 1954 in a systematic sample of Illinois cities with 10,000 or more population and the logarithms of the distance between each city and the nearest larger city. Each point represents one city, the number next to the point indicating which city (see Table 3.5); the ordinate represents that city's per capita sales and the abscissa indicates the distance between that city and the larger community. (As a general rule, the "dependent variable" —the one which is presumed to depend, at least in part, on the value of the other, independent variable—is plotted on the vertical scale.)

The clustering of the points in Fig. 3.3 from the lower left to the upper right-hand part of the diagram reveals the existence of some positive correlation between the two variables—as distance between cities rises, sales in the given city increase. The diagram also indicates, by virtue of the spread of the points, that the relationship is not a close one.

If desired, a quick approximation of the nature of this relationship can be obtained by drawing a freehand line through the middle of the clusters of these points, as is shown in Fig. 3.3. A linear (straight) line has been used, as the locus of the points does not appear to warrant anything more sophisticated. Such a line could be drawn simply by inspection, or a more methodical approach can be adopted, such as the following:

1. Divide the diagram into three or four vertical sections, each having about the same width.
2. Mark the vertical center of the points in each section midway in the section, using some distinctive symbol.
3. Draw a straight line passing through these symbols as closely as possible, i.e., with the least vertical deviations.

Rough criteria of the "goodness of fit" of the line can be applied by ascertaining whether there are as many points above the line as below, with each type well distributed over the range of the observations; and whether the deviations of the individual observations from the line are as small as possible, on the average. Often, two or three different lines will be drawn before a satisfactory one is obtained.

The freehand line provides two useful types of information. One is the extent of change in one variable associated with the other. Thus, marking off two well-separated points on the line, forming a right triangle, and computing the ratio of the ordinate to the abscissa,[9] reveals that, on the average, per capita retail sales in a city rose (fell) 2 per cent with each increase (decrease) of 10 per cent in distance between the two cities. Second, the line also indicates the direction and extent of deviation of each city's sales from the sales that would be expected on the basis of the observed relationship. By highlighting these deviations, the determination of other relevant factors is facilitated.

---

[9] This is illustrated in Fig. 3.3 for the abscissa at 1.5 and 2.0.

The main advantages of the graphical approach are speed and the visual aids provided; the main disadvantage is the subjective nature of the regression line thus obtained, in the sense that the lines fitted by two different persons are hardly likely to coincide. Also, this method does not permit statistical significance tests to be applied, which can be a serious handicap if the numerical estimate is a matter of dispute. Whether to use this graphical approach depends largely on the relative importance of these considerations in a given problem. Also important is one's skill in fitting freehand lines, particularly if the relationship is not well defined or is curvilinear. In general, drawing accurate freehand lines becomes more difficult as the dispersion of the observations increases.

3.5.1.2. *Algebraic approach.* The algebraic approach to regression analysis seeks to provide precise estimates of the extent and nature of a relationship. This it does by means of two main tools—the coefficient, or index, of determination as the measure of the extent of the relationship, and the regression equation as the indicator of the nature of the relationship.

The regression equation measures the degree of change in the dependent variable (X_1) associated with, or caused by, changes in the independent variable, X_2. For the time being, we abstract from the case of interdependence (which is taken up in Chapter 4, pp. 166ff.), and assume that changes in one variable can be said to be determined at least in part by the other variable, but not the reverse.

If the regression is linear, the relationship is represented by the equation:

$$X_1 = a + bX_2 \tag{3.4}$$

where a is the intercept of X_1 at the point where X_2 is zero, and b is the slope of the relation—reflecting the change in X_1 that accompanies a unit change in X_2.

For curvilinear relations, additional terms are added to equation (3.4), the general form of the relation being:

$$X_1 = b_1 + b_2X_2 + b_3X_2{}^2 + b_4X_2{}^3 + \cdots + b_nX_2{}^n \tag{3.5}$$

Equation (3.5) is known as an nth degree relation because the highest power of X_2 in (3.5) is n. As a general rule, a second-degree relation provides a good "fit," as defined shortly, if the relationship appears to have one bend in it; a third-degree relation is adequate if there are two bends in the relationship; etc.

Computationally and otherwise, the lower the degree of the equation, the easier it is to manipulate. It is therefore important to note that the simple equation (3.4) can also be used if the relation between the original variables is curvilinear but can be transformed into a linear one. Thus, in many cases a logarithmic transformation of both X_1 and X_2 will result in a straight-line relation, since interactions in economic life are often of geometric rather than of arithmetic form; then X_1 and X_2 in (3.4) would represent the logarithms of the original values. In other cases, such as when one of the variables has an upper or lower limit, the logarithmic transformation of only one variable —the other one—will sometimes produce the desired linearity. Thus, the percentage of family income spent on a certain category of goods and the average price paid can often be approximated by a semi-logarithmic function of family income.

The values of the parameters, b_1, b_2, b_3, etc., in (3.5) are estimated from the original data by the so-called principle of least squares. Application of this principle yields those estimates of the parameters which minimize for that form of regression equation the sum of the squares of the deviations of the observations from the regression line, i.e., from the value that observation would have if it had coincided with the regression line. This sum reflects the variance of the observations about the regression equation, or the variance in the dependent variable that remains unexplained after the effect of the independent variable has been taken into account. Thus, the variance of the dependent variable, X_1, can be segmented as follows:

$$\begin{array}{ccc} \textit{Variance in} & \equiv \textit{Variance in } X_1 \textit{ explained} & + \textit{Variance in } X_1 \textit{ not explained} \\ X_1 & \textit{by } X_2 & \textit{by } X_2 \end{array}$$

(3.6a)

or algebraically:

$$\frac{\Sigma(X_1 - \bar{X}_1)^2}{N} \equiv \frac{\Sigma(X_{1c} - \bar{X}_1)^2}{N} + \frac{\Sigma(X_1 - X_{1c})^2}{N}$$

(3.6b)

where X_{1c} represents the estimates of X_1 yielded by the regression equation. Thus, $(X_{1c} - \bar{X}_1)$ reflects that portion of the original variation, $X_1 - \bar{X}_1$, explained by X_2, leaving $(X_1 - X_{1c})$ as the portion of the original variation not explained by X_2.

Mathematical application of the least-squares principle to (3.5) yields a set of so-called normal equations which provides the basis for the numerical estimates of the parameters. Their general form is:[10]

$$\begin{aligned} \Sigma X_1 &= Nb_1 + b_2\Sigma X_2 + \cdots + b\Sigma X_2{}^n \\ \Sigma X_1 X_2 &= b_1\Sigma X_2 + b_2\Sigma X_2{}^2 + \cdots + b\Sigma X_2{}^{n+1} \\ &\cdots\cdots\cdots\cdots\cdots\cdots\cdots\cdots\cdots\cdots \\ \Sigma X_1 X_2{}^n &= b_1\Sigma X_2{}^n + b_2\Sigma X_2{}^{n+1} + \cdots + b_n\Sigma X_2{}^{2n} \end{aligned}$$

(3.7)

For a linear relation this reduces to:

$$\begin{aligned} \Sigma X_1 &= Na + b\Sigma X_2 \\ \Sigma X_1 X_2 &= a\Sigma X_2 + b\Sigma X_2{}^2 \end{aligned}$$

(3.8)

---

[10] From an operational point of view, they can be obtained first by summing the original function, which then becomes the first normal equation, and then by multiplying this equation by X_2, $X_2{}^2$, etc., in turn, which yields each of the following normal equations.

which can be simplified still further by expressing the variables in terms of deviations from their means, i.e., $X_1 = X_1 - \bar{X}$, $X_2 = X_2 - \bar{X}_2$. This has the effect of reducing the vertical intercept (a) to zero, so that the value of b can be estimated directly from the second equation in (3.8):

$$b = \frac{\Sigma x_1 x_2}{\Sigma x_2{}^2}$$

The value of a is then determined by substituting for b in the first equation in (3.8).

The solution of a linear logarithmic regression equation is illustrated in Table 3.5 using the data which served as the basis for the scatter diagram in Fig. 3.3. The result can be represented either as:

$$log \; (per \; capita \; sales) = 3.05 + .105 \; log \; (distance)$$

or

$$X_1 = 2{,}018 X_2{}^{.105} \tag{3.9}$$

In a linear logarithmic regression the exponent of X_2 has a particular significance, representing the *elasticity* of X_1 with respect to X_2. In other words, equation (3.9) tells us that on the average a 10 per cent increase in distance between communities is accompanied by a 1.05 per cent increase in per capita sales in the given (smaller) city. Thus, a linear logarithmic equation implies constant elasticity—a constant reaction in percentage terms; whereas the use of a linear arithmetic relation implies a constant slope—constant reaction in an absolute sense. These are important factors to consider in deciding which, if either, of these two types of regression lines to use in a particular problem.

The *coefficient of determination* (r^2) measures the extent of association, or goodness of fit, between two variables. Based on the segmentation of variances shown in (3.6a), this measure is simply the proportion of the original variance in the dependent variable explained by the independent variable, i.e.:

$$r^2 = \frac{Variance \; in \; X_1 \; explained \; by \; X_2}{Variance \; in \; X_1} \tag{3.10}$$

r^2 can fluctuate between zero and one, the absence of any correlation being indicated by a value of zero, and perfect positive (negative) correlation being indicated by one (minus one), the minus sign applying to the value of r.

In the past the square root of this measure, the coefficient of correlation, has most often been cited as the measure of correlation. Although r and r^2 are uniquely related, the latter is the more meaningful measure whereas to the uninitiated, r can seem misleadingly high.

Computationally, various forms can be used depending on the particular

Table 3.5

LINEAR REGRESSION OF LOGS OF RETAIL SALES PER CAPITA IN ILLINOIS
CITIES IN 1954 ON DISTANCE TO NEXT LARGER CITY

Obser-vation no.	Log of re-tail sales per capita (X_1)	Log of distance to next larger city (X_2)
1	3.125	0.000
2	3.206	2.193
3	3.185	1.954
4	3.133	0.477
5	3.267	2.000
6	3.254	1.079
7	3.046	0.845
8	3.238	2.090
9	3.286	0.903
10	3.329	1.580
11	3.151	0.954
12	3.222	1.591
13	3.052	0.477
14	3.190	1.580
15	3.145	2.127
16	3.227	2.127
17	3.292	1.681
18	3.334	1.929
19	3.209	0.699
20	3.275	1.623
21	3.209	1.230
22	3.252	1.342
23	3.199	1.707
24	2.980	0.778
25	2.998	0.301
26	3.348	1.756
27	2.869	0.301
28	3.117	0.699
29	3.178	1.079
30	3.177	1.301
31	3.116	0.602
32	3.316	1.230
33	3.284	1.903
34	3.238	1.362
35	3.212	1.978
36	3.227	1.903
37	3.205	1.301
38	3.002	0.477
39	3.212	0.602
40	3.176	1.568

Table 3.5—(Continued)

LINEAR REGRESSION OF LOGS OF RETAIL SALES PER CAPITA IN ILLINOIS CITIES IN 1954 ON DISTANCE TO NEXT LARGER CITY

Obser-vation no.	Log of re-tail sales per capita (X_1)	Log of distance to next larger city (X_2)
41	3.393	1.973
42	3.274	1.477
43	3.161	1.114
44	3.048	1.415
45	3.086	2.021
46	3.167	1.991
47	3.401	1.863
48	3.161	1.771
49	3.191	1.342
50	3.197	1.146
51	3.233	1.301
TOTAL	162.798	68.748

$\Sigma X_1^2 = 520.219802 \qquad \Sigma X_1 X_2 = 221.182170$

$\Sigma X_2^2 = 109.161589$

$\Sigma x_1^2 = 520.219802 - \dfrac{(162.798)^2}{51} = .549651$

$\Sigma x_2^2 = 109.161589 - \dfrac{(68.748)^2}{51} = 16.488077$

$\Sigma x_1 x_2 = 221.182170 - \dfrac{(162.798)(68.748)}{51} = 1.729082$

$b = \dfrac{1.729082}{16.488077} = .10487; \; a = \dfrac{1}{51}[162.798 - (.10487)(68.748)] = 3.0508$

$\sigma_u^2 = \dfrac{.549651 - .10487(1.729082)}{51} = .007222; \; \sigma_u = .085$

$r^2 = \dfrac{(1.729082)^2}{(.549651)(16.488077)} = .329895; \; r = .574$

circumstances. If only knowledge of the extent of linear correlation is wanted, the so-called product-moment formula can be used:

$$r^2 = \frac{(\Sigma X_1 X_2)^2}{\Sigma X_1^2 \Sigma X_2^2} \qquad (3.11)$$

If the regression equation is not linear and/or estimates of the regression parameters have already been obtained, the simplest computational form is likely to be the direct algebraic equivalent of (3.10), i.e. (from 3.6b):

$$r^2 = \frac{\Sigma(X_{1c} - \bar{X}_1)^2}{\Sigma(X_1 - \bar{X}_1)^2}$$

which, by various substitutions becomes:

$$r^2 = \frac{b_2 \Sigma X_1 X_2 + b_3 \Sigma X_1 X_2{}^2 + \cdots + b_n \Sigma X_1 X_2{}^n}{\Sigma X_1{}^2} \tag{3.12}$$

For a linear regression, only the first term in the numerator is present, as shown at the bottom of Table 3.5 where the coefficient of determination is computed for the retail sales data. The additional terms enter into the numerator as the power of the regression equation rises.

The coefficient of determination is an abstract measure of relationship in the sense that, just as elasticities, it is independent of the units of measurement used in the regression. This gives it some value as a comparative measure of relationship between regressions in different units, though it also has some serious limitations in this respect which are often overlooked (see below). In addition to the coefficient of determination, there is the *standard deviation of regression* (also sometimes known as the *standard error of estimate*, which is a misnomer because this statistic is not a measure of sampling variation), which reflects the goodness of fit in original units by measuring the deviation of the observations about the regression line, i.e.:

$$\sigma_u = \sqrt{\frac{\Sigma (X_1 - X_{1c})^2}{N}} \tag{3.13}$$

As seen by (3.13), the standard deviation of regression is simply the square root of the variance in X_1 unexplained by X_2. It corresponds symbolically to the ordinary standard deviation. If the residuals are normally distributed, i.e., u, the differences between X_1 and X_2, two-thirds of the observations will be within one δ_u of the regression line, 95.45 per cent within two δ_u's of the line, etc. Clearly, for the same set of data, the lower the value of σ_u, the higher will be the coefficient of determination. (Why?)

3.5.1.3. Rank correlation. A convenient, and often highly efficient, means of measuring the extent of association between two variables is to rank the observations on each variable and then correlate the ranks. The resulting measure of correlation, the so-called coefficient of rank correlation, is then:

$$Coefficient\ of\ rank\ correlation = 1 - \frac{6\Sigma d^2}{N(N^2 - 1)}$$

where d is the difference between the two rankings of the same observation. (If several observations have the same rank, each is assigned the midpoint of the ranks involved.)

The coefficient of rank correlation has the same properties as the coefficient of simple correlation, from which it is derived. (What are these properties?) The coefficient is particularly useful in measuring association between two attributes where continuous data are not easily obtainable, as in the case of preference tests. It also yields a more typical measure of association in the case of variable data subject to extreme observations. Thus, to measure the extent to which city size is related to income per capita by city for the 100 largest cities in the United States, using the actual data would yield a distorted high value for r because of the tremendous influence on r of such cities as New York, Chicago and Los Angeles. Ranking the data first and then computing the coefficient of rank correlation yields a much more meaningful result. This method is particularly useful where qualitative variables are concerned, such as preferences or attitudes.

On the negative side, the coefficient of rank correlation clearly "wastes" information if continuous data are available. Also, this coefficient can not be used for forecasting purposes: though it measures the extent of association, the nature of the relationship is still unknown.

3.5.2. Multivariate Regression

As noted earlier, most variables in economics and business are influenced by more than one other variable, and the nature and extent of such relationships are ascertained by means of multiple regression analysis. Such relations can be represented in their most general form by the equation:

$$X_1 = f(X_2, X_3, \ldots, X_n) \tag{3.14}$$

which says only that X_1 is influenced by X_2, by X_3, $\ldots$, and by X_n. This equation says nothing about the form of the relation. To specify the form, a more explicit formulation must be provided. For example, if X_1 is believed to be influenced in a linear arithmetic fashion by three other (independent) variables, we would have:

$$X_1 = a_1 + a_2 X_2 + a_3 X_3 + a_4 X_4 \tag{3.15a}$$

Or, if the relationship is second-degree in X_2:

$$X_1 = a_1 + a_2 X_2 + a_2 X_2{}^2 + a_3 X_3 + a_4 X_4 \tag{3.15b}$$

Or, if the relationship is linear in the logarithms:

$$X_1 = a_1 X_2{}^{a_2} X_3{}^{a_3} X_4{}^{a_4} \tag{3.15c}$$

and so on.

For algebraic estimation of the parameters $a_1, a_2, \ldots$, the form of the relationship has to be specified before the computations can be carried out. If graphical analysis is employed, this is not necessary.

3.5.2.1. *Graphical approach.* As an extension of the two-variable case, the graphical approach to multiple regression analysis has all the advantages and disadvantages of the latter with, if anything, greater intensity. For, since the multivariate case involves more variables, additional freehand approximations have to be drawn, which increase the danger of error on the

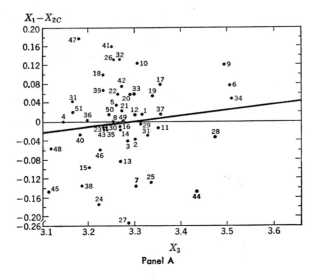

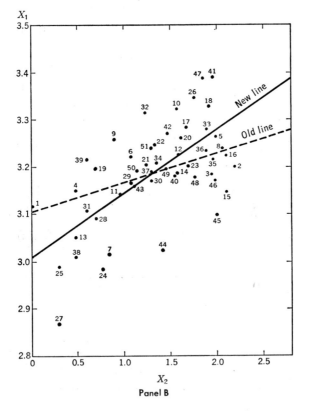

Fig. 3.4. Graphic Regression of Retail Sales Per Capita (X_1) on Distance (X_2) and (opposite) on Income Per Capita (X_3)

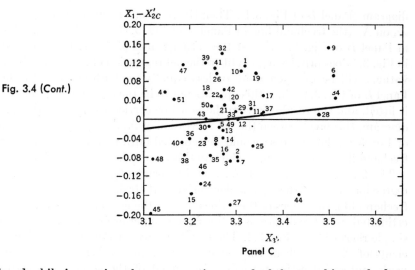

Fig. 3.4 (Cont.)

Panel C

one hand while increasing the comparative speed of the graphic method on the other hand.

The steps involved in the graphical approach are perhaps best described with reference to an actual example. Thus, let us add an income per capita variable to the data in Table 3.5 and seek to determine the regression of retail sales per capita (X_1) on distance (X_2) and on income per capita (X_3), i.e.: $X_1 = f(X_2, X_3)$. Fig. 3.3 represents the first step—a scatter diagram between X_1 and X_2 with a freehand approximation of the regression of X_1 on X_2. The deviations of the observations from this regression line represent, as noted previously, that part of the variation in X_1 not explained by X_2. It therefore behooves us to see to what extent these unexplained deviations can be explained by the other independent variable, X_3.

This is determined by plotting a new scatter diagram, namely, one in which the residuals from the regression line in Fig. 3.3 are plotted against the corresponding values of X_3, as is done in Panel A of Fig. 3.4. The more effective X_3 is in explaining these residuals, the better the relationship between X_3 and the residuals should seem in Fig. 3.4. As is evident from this diagram, some (positive) relationship is apparent but not a very close one. As long as any relationship is apparent, however, a freehand line is drawn to approximate it. Such a freehand line is shown in the diagram; as before it is linear, for there is no presumption otherwise.

It should be noted that the relationship shown in this diagram is a *net* relationship, in the sense that the effect of X_2 has now been presumably eliminated from X_1. We say "presumably" because the foregoing statement rests on the assumption that the freehand line in Fig. 3.3 itself describes the net relationship between X_1 and X_2. To test this assumption, the grid used in Fig. 3.3 and the freehand line obtained there are reproduced on a new diagram (Panel B of Fig. 3.4). Then the residuals from the net regression of X_1 on X_3 (the freehand line in Panel A of Fig. 3.4) are plotted from the line in Panel B of Fig. 3.4 against the actual values of X_2. If the freehand line in Fig. 3.3 does provide a good fit to the net regression of X_1 on X_2, the observations will be grouped more or less equally on both sides of the line in Panel B of Fig. 3.4. Since this appears not to be the case, a new freehand line is fitted, and the residuals from the new line carried over to another scatter diagram, this one between the net regression of X_1 on X_2 and of X_3 (Panel C of Fig. 3.4). The process would be repeated until no further changes in the freehand lines are indicated, which in this case ends with Panel C of Fig. 3.4.

The final scatter diagrams for each independent variable portray the net regression of X_1 on that particular variable. If straight lines were used in the freehand fits, the slopes of these lines (and of the net relationships) are easily estimated from the diagrams in the same manner as described earlier for the simple regression in Fig. 3.3. The results represent the *net* regression coefficients of X_1 on each of the independent variables. With some additional work, numerical estimates can be obtained of the standard deviation of regression and of the coefficient of multiple determination.

It is clear from the above description that the graphical method in the multivariate case requires much more dexterity than when only two variables are involved. Although following various guides does make the process somewhat easier, such as taking up the independent variables in the order of apparent closeness of relationship to the dependent variable, reliable results are likely to be obtained only by those thoroughly experienced in its application. It might be noted, however, that the graphical method can be used prior to using the algebraic approach, in this sense often serving as a basis for specification of the form of the regression function.

3.5.2.2. *Algebraic approach.* The algebraic solution of a multiple regression equation is accomplished in the same manner as before—by setting up and solving a set of normal equations. They are obtained as before (see p. 86), the only difference being that the various powers of X_2 are now replaced by the different independent variables. Thus, the normal equations for (3.15b), after the observations have been expressed as deviations from their respective means, are:

$$
\begin{aligned}
\Sigma x_1 x_2 &= a_2 \Sigma x_2{}^2 + a_2{}' \Sigma x_2{}^3 + a_3 \Sigma x_2 x_3 + a_4 \Sigma x_2 x_4 \\
\Sigma x_1 x_2{}^2 &= a_2 \Sigma x_2{}^3 + a_2{}' \Sigma x_2{}^4 + a_3 \Sigma x_2{}^2 x_3 + a_4 \Sigma x_2{}^2 x_4 \\
\Sigma x_1 x_3 &= a_2 \Sigma x_2 x_3 + a_2{}' \Sigma x_2{}^2 x_3 + a_3 \Sigma x_3{}^2 + a_4 \Sigma x_3 x_4 \\
\Sigma x_1 x_4 &= a_2 \Sigma x_2 x_4 + a_2{}' \Sigma x_2{}^2 x_4 + a_3 \Sigma x_3 x_4 + a_4 \Sigma x_4{}^2
\end{aligned}
\tag{3.16a}
$$

The value of a_1 is obtained from the first normal equation in original units, i.e.:

$$
a_1 = \frac{1}{N} [\Sigma X_1 - a_2 \Sigma X_2 - a_2{}' \Sigma X_2{}^2 - a_3 \Sigma X_3 - a_4 \Sigma X_4]
\tag{3.16b}
$$

A variety of computational techniques exist for solving such equations, the most widely used (and probably the safest as well) being the so-called Doolittle method. The use of this method in deriving estimates of the parameters of an expanded version of the retail sales-distance regression is shown in Supplement B to this chapter. The postulated regression function is:

$$\frac{Per\ capita}{sales} = a_1\ (Distance)^{a_2}\ (Per\ capita\ income)^{a_3}\ \begin{matrix} (Per\ cent\ earning^{a_4} \\ over\ \$7{,}000\ per \\ year) \end{matrix}$$

(3.17a)

or, in corresponding algebraic, logarithmic notation:

$$Log\ X_1 = a_1 + a_2\ log\ X_2 + a_3\ log\ X_3 + a_4\ log\ X_4 \qquad \text{(3.17b)}$$

The numerical solution, obtained in Supplement B, can be represented as:

$$Log\ X_1 = 2.562 + .1203\ log\ X_2 + .1128\ log\ X_3 + .0794\ log\ X_4$$
$$\qquad\quad (.012) \qquad\ (.0023) \qquad\quad (.242) \qquad\quad (.117)$$

(3.18a)

or

$$X_1 = 180.4\ X_2^{.1203}\ X_3^{.1128}\ X_4^{.0794} \qquad \text{(3.18b)}$$

Thus, these results indicate that a 1 per cent increase in retail sales per capita was associated with a 12 per cent increase in distance, an 11 per cent increase in per capita income or an 8 per cent increase in the proportion of the population earning over $7,000 in 1954.

The figures in parentheses underneath the coefficients in (3.18a) are measures of the sampling variation in the estimates. In each case, the figure represents the *standard error* of that particular coefficient; its computation is shown in Supplement B to this chapter. The standard error of a regression coefficient reflects the extent to which sampling variation may have influenced the estimate of that coefficient, and has a meaning for sample data roughly analogous to the standard deviation for population data. In other words, for a population to which the concepts of the normal distribution are applicable,[11] estimates of regression parameters based on randomly selected samples will come within one standard error of the true, unknown figure 68.3 per cent of the time, within two standard errors 95.5 per cent of the time, etc.

This provides a means of testing whether or not the relationship computed from the sample data really exists in the population or could be due solely to sampling variations. This is accomplished by inverting probabilities and using the above standard-error characteristics as a means of estimating the probability that a particular regression coefficient was produced from a

---

[11] This includes almost all univariate populations, for it can be shown in sampling analysis that even if the original population is badly skewed, the distribution of averages (including regression coefficients) based on randomly-selected samples tends toward normality as the sample size increases.

population where the observed relationship is nonexistent. Thus, if a particular regression coefficient is no larger than its standard error, we could reason that such a relationship would be observed in (large) sample data 32 times out of 100 (the complement of 68 per cent) even when the two variables are unrelated in the population. Since this is by no means a low probability, we would be inclined to question the significance of the observed relationship, i.e., doubt that it really exists. And if we are using the 5 per cent significance level as our criterion of significance, we would reject the notion that such a relationship really exists. In fact, for large samples—30 observations or more—the estimate of the regression coefficient would have to be at least 1.96 times its standard error for a coefficient to be adjudged significant (and this critical ratio increases as sample size declines because of the greater spread of distributions based on a relatively few observations).

Even then, we know that we shall be wrong one time out of twenty, on the average, for by definition 5 per cent of the coefficients will exceed their standard errors although based on observations from a population in which the observed relationship is nonexistent. This is a relatively small error, however, which in economic and marketing work can usually be tolerated;[12] in the physical and biological sciences closer tolerances are often required, especially where human lives are at stake. Some of the factors determining the use of standard errors will be discussed in Sec. 8.1.

Turning to the results in equation (3.18a), we see that the coefficient of X_2 is well beyond 1.96 times its standard error while those of X_3 and X_4 are appreciably less. Hence, at the 5 per cent significance level we would infer that per capita retail sales are really influenced by distance and by per capita income, but that there is no evidence of a relationship between sales and the proportion of families earning over $7,000—at least not after the influence of income and distance have been taken into account. If desired, exact significance levels in each case can be estimated from the normal probability distribution table on pp. 549–550; the significance levels of the coefficients of X_2, X_3 and X_4 are .000001, .64 and .50, respectively.

For small samples, the standard error multiples have to be obtained from the so-called t distribution, Table A2 in the Appendix, where u in the stub of the table represents the number of degrees of freedom; this distribution approaches the normal distribution as u increases.

It should be noted that regression analysis is predicated in statistical theory on the assumptions of normality of the underlying distributions, of

---

[12] An additional consideration is the fact that as this type of error—of erroneously rejecting the hypothesis of absence of relationship (the null hypothesis)—is reduced, the probability of mistakenly accepting the null hypothesis is increased. In other words, there is then greater likelihood of inferring from the sample data that the observed relationship is spurious and due solely to sampling variation when in fact such a relationship really exists.

random selection of the observations, and of independence between observations. In many studies, however, the rationale is likely to be somewhat different. Thus, in the present case, the cities were clearly not selected at random. The justification for the statistical analysis, then, is the assumption that the unexplained residuals are the additive result of other causal factors themselves not correlated with the independent variables used, provided also that none of these unidentified factors is considered to be of overwhelming importance.

The extent of association between the dependent variable and the independent variables is measured by the coefficient of multiple determination (R^2) in abstract units and by the standard deviation of regression. Conceptually, R^2 has the same definition as has the coefficient of simple determination in (3.10), i.e.:

$$R^2 = \frac{\textit{Variance in } X_1 \textit{ explained by the independent variables}}{\textit{Variance of } X_1} \tag{3.19a}$$

the computational form becoming, in a manner analogous to (3.12), the following for the example we have used so far:

$$R^2 = \frac{a_2 \Sigma X_1 X_2 + a_3 \Sigma X_1 X_3 + a_4 \Sigma X_1 X_4}{\Sigma X_1{}^2} \tag{3.19b}$$

The standard deviation of regression is, as before, the square root of the variance unexplained in X_1 by the independent variables, or in computational terms in our example:

$$\sigma_u = \sqrt{\frac{\Sigma X_1{}^2 - a_2 \Sigma X_1 X_2 - a_3 \Sigma X_1 X_3 - a_4 \Sigma X_1 X_4}{N}} \tag{3.20}$$

As is shown in Supplement B, the values of R^2 and of σ_u for (3.18) are .377 and .082, respectively. The former indicates that the three independent variables explain 38 per cent of the variation in X_1; the latter, that subject to the validity of the normality assumptions, two-thirds of the observations would be expected to fall within one σ_u of the regression line, 95 per cent within $2\sigma_u$ of the regression line, etc.

It is important to note that the standard deviation of regression applies to the original data, and is not applicable in the case of forecasts or projections. A frequently encountered mistake is to read that "if the values of the independent variables should reach this-and-this level, the predicted value of X_1 is so-and-so, which means that the probability is .68 that the actual value of X_1 under those conditions will lie within one σ_u of the predicted value."

This is not true. The range within which an actual value is likely to deviate from a forecast as a result of sampling variations is not measured by the standard deviation of regression (or the standard error of estimate) but rather by the standard error of the forecast (which is discussed in Chapter 10). This is a more complicated measure than the standard deviation of regression, for it takes into account not only the variability in the original observations but also the extent to which the values of the independent variables exceed the range of the observations (in terms of deviation of these values from their mean) and whether the forecast is for an individual instance or for an average instance at that level. Although this is not the place to delve into the intricacies of this measure (references will be found at the end of the chapter), it is worth noting that this statistic measures only the probability of *random* deviations of the predicted value from the actual value; it can make no allowance for discrepancies brought about by unforeseen events or changes in the basic relationship, which are often far more significant than random deviations.

Both R^2 and σ_u are gross measures in the sense that they describe the association between the dependent variable on the one hand and the independent variables *as a group* on the other hand. There are many situations, however, when it is desired to obtain, in addition, some idea of (a) the extent to which X_1 is related to each of the independent variables, and/or (b) the relative importance of each of the independent variables. To get such information we have to introduce two additional statistical measures: *partial correlation* and the *beta coefficients*.

The coefficient of partial determination measures the extent of association between the dependent variable and any independent variable *after* the effect of one or more other independent variables has been held constant. There are different *orders* of partial determination, depending on how many independent variables are held constant. First-order coefficients are those for which one independent variable is held constant; second-order coefficients indicate two variables held constant, etc.

Conceptually, the coefficient of partial determination is defined as:

$$r_{12.34\ldots n}{}^2 = \frac{\textit{Variance in } X_1 \textit{ explained by } X_2 \textit{ after allowance for } X_3, X_4, \ldots, X_n}{\textit{Variance in } X_1 \textit{ after allowance for the effect of } X_3, X_4, \ldots, X_n} \quad (3.21)$$

where X_1 and X_2 are the variables being correlated, and $X_3, X_4 \ldots X_n$ are those held constant.

From this definition, computational forms are derived, as shown below.

As applied to our example, the computational forms for the first and second order partial-determination coefficients between X_1 and X_2 are:

First-order coefficients:

$$r_{12.3}{}^2 = \frac{(r_{12} - r_{13}r_{23})^2}{(1 - r_{13}{}^2)(1 - r_{23}{}^2)} \qquad r_{12.4}{}^2 = \frac{(r_{12} - r_{14}r_{24})^2}{(1 - r_{14}{}^2)(1 - r_{24}{}^2)} \quad (3.22a)$$
$$= .369 \qquad\qquad\qquad\qquad = .373$$

Second-order coefficient:

$$r_{12.34}{}^2 = \frac{(r_{12.3} - r_{14.3}r_{24.3})^2}{(1 - r_{14.3}{}^2)(1 - r_{24.3}{}^2)} = .505 \tag{3.22b}$$

The direction of the relationship is indicated by the sign of the numerator before it is squared. If the correlation is negative, this can be indicated by a negative sign in parentheses before the actual value of the coefficient, e.g., $r_{13.2}{}^2 = (-).24$, or by showing the square root of the coefficient, $r_{13.2}$, with the appropriate sign. In all of the above instances, the correlation was positive.

As is evident from the above, higher-order coefficients are built up from those of lower order; in a four-variable regression there are no partial correlations above the second order.

It is important to understand the distinction between coefficients such as $r_{13.2}{}^2$ and $r_{13.24}{}^2$. In the former case only X_2 is held constant and no allowance is made for any interaction effects of X_4 on the correlation between X_1 and X_3. With the second-order partial correlation, however, the influence of both X_2 and X_4 is held constant. Hence, the second-order correlation provides a better indication of the *net* relationship between X_1 and X_3; and successively better indications of this relationship are obtained as the order of the partial correlation is raised to hold constant any additional pertinent variables that may exist. Lower-order correlations are nevertheless frequently very useful for indicating the extent to which a relationship is altered as other particular variables are held constant in turn.

An idea of the relative importance of each independent variable in a multiple regression is obtained through the so-called *beta coefficients*. These are simply the ordinary regression coefficients converted into standardized, abstract units, with the result that the relative size of the different beta coefficients indicates the relative contribution made by the corresponding variables to estimating the dependent variable. The beta coefficient, β_{1i}, corresponding to the regression coefficient, a_{1i}, is defined as follows:

$$\beta_{1i} = a_{1i}\frac{\sigma_i}{\sigma_1} \tag{3.23}$$

where σ_i and σ_1 represent the standard deviations of X_i and X_1, respectively.
Applying this conversion to the regression equation in (3.18), we get:

$$log\ X_1 = 3.61\ log\ X_2 + .08\ log\ X_3 + .27\ log\ X_4 \tag{3.24}$$

It is apparent from these results that X_2 has by far the main influence on X_1 of all the independent variables included in this regression. In fact, the influence of X_3 and of X_4 is almost negligible relative to that of X_2.

This is not the only means of evaluating the relative importance of different independent variables. Another approach lies in determining what part of the variance in X_1 is explained by each independent variable, based on a technique for segregating the explained variance into components explained directly and components explained indirectly by each independent variable; references are appended at the end of this chapter.

3.5.3. Adequacy of Regression Functions

Adequacy of a function is basically its ability to satisfy the original objectives for which it was set up. Essentially, there are two such objectives: description of conditions during the period, or space, under observation, and prediction of the level of the dependent variable either in space or time or under specified hypothetical conditions (such as, say, the probable effect on consumption expenditures of a contemplated change in excise taxes). If the objective is description, one or more of four measures of statistical adequacy can be used:

1. The coefficient of determination and the standard deviation of regression as indicators of "goodness of fit" of the function to the data.
2. The ratios of the estimates of the coefficients to their standard errors, as indicators of the significance of each independent variable in influencing the dependent variable. The beta coefficients are also of value here for measuring the relative importance of the different variables.
3. Partial correlations, for measuring not only the extent of the "net" relationships between X_1 and the independent variables but also the extent of intercorrelation among the independent variables. If two independent variables are closely correlated with each other, one is undoubtedly redundant—though which one to eliminate should depend primarily on *a priori* considerations rather than on statistical considerations.
4. In the case of time-series studies, the presence of serial correlation in the residuals of the regression function. Presence of serial correlation indicates that certain regularities are still present in the unexplained variance, and hence that there exists one or more other pertinent variables as yet unidentified. On the other hand, absence of serial correlation in the residuals does not necessarily indicate that everything is fine, for there may still be pertinent missing variables that are not correlated in any systematic fashion with the residuals. The application of regression functions to time series analysis is discussed at further length in Chapter 8.

If prediction is the main objective of a regression function, the above criteria still remain useful but they become subservient to the central issue of *predictive ability*. Unfortunately, this is as yet a characteristic which bears no discernible relation to any of the usual correlation measures. The main criterion of adequacy, therefore, becomes simply the errors of extrapolation. Admittedly, application of this criterion is often difficult because of lack of additional data that can be used to test the predictive ability of the function. In the case of time series, one often simply has to wait until new observations become available. Alternately, in selecting the sample period one can make a more or less arbitrary division of the available data into a period of observation and a period of extrapolation. Furthermore, the fact that a particular function yields highly accurate forecasts at one time does not mean that it will continue to do so, especially if conditions change.

In view of these dilemmas, *a priori* non-statistical considerations of the adequacy of the hypothesis underlying a particular regression function assume dominant importance, and whether one hypothesis yields a better fit to the data than another, therefore, is emphatically not decisive. From a statistical point of view, significance of partial correlations and of regression coefficients becomes more important than their actual magnitude.

In closing this section, it is not inappropriate to repeat the oft-cited warning that correlation measures only association and not causation. Absence of correlation does not even necessarily indicate absence of causation, for an underlying relationship between two variables may be camouflaged by the interactions of other pertinent variables. If correlation is indicated, proof of causation must depend on *a priori* considerations, not on the correlation itself.

3.6. FACTOR ANALYSIS

Developed originally in psychological work, factor analysis is a multivariate technique that aims to identify the underlying factors or forces affecting the relationship between a set of variables. Though used almost entirely in education and psychology, it appears to be a technique that would be worth considering for certain types of business and economic research as well. The approach is predicated on the assumption that the original variables introduced in a multivariate analysis exhibit largely superficial manifestations of the true relationships, and that beneath these superficial relationships are certain factors common to various (linear) combinations of these variables which, when extracted and identified, reveal the true forces giving rise to the observed relationships.

Table 3.6

A FACTOR CORRELATION MATRIX

CORRELATION MATRIX OF PRODUCT-MOMENT r's FOR 20 ADVERTISING VARIABLES[a]

Variable	K	2	3	4	5	8	9	10	11	12	13	14	18	20	21	22	26	29	31
K Readership																			
2 Size of Ad	62																		
3 Number of Colors	37	-07																	
4 Number Illustration	28	35	24																
5 Sq. In. Illustration	67	71	21	25															
8 Number Type Sizes	28	54	21	22	27														
9 Largest Type	49	64	32	21	45	54													
10 Headline Size	43	49	26	23	31	25	55												
11 Largest Prod. Ident.	39	41	28	04	33	41	66	26											
12 Body Type Size	24	19	18	-07	17	25	23	25	25										
13 Pica Width	35	25	28	-11	28	24	24	25	22	49									
14 Number Copy Blocks	30	57	20	54	23	40	29	22	14	-05	-01								
18 Number Words	31	62	11	24	24	43	32	23	24	-03	12	61							
20 Number Prod. Ident.	40	61	18	33	36	-06	37	24	30	05	16	62	62						
21 Number Prod. Facts	19	30	-02	25	26	16	19	-02	08	-03	-17	38	49	35					
22 Number Prod. Benefits	29	51	11	30	22	37	31	16	20	-08	00	59	68	62	54				
26 Pictures of Use	33	29	14	52	32	14	13	-02	08	-04	-13	45	16	29	35	37			
29 Surround	32	49	-11	12	38	20	44	45	15	24	22	-04	00	20	-38	-19	-17		
31 Previous Schedule	47	53	16	20	44	17	27	46	14	02	29	26	39	40	18	34	06	-18	
34 Brad-Vern Schedule	23	22	01	04	21	08	06	15	03	-04	04	09	19	17	02	22	10	-17	50

[a] Decimals omitted.

Source: TWEDT, op. cit., p. 210.

For example, the proportion of readers of a magazine recalling an advertisement may be hypothesized to depend on the following variables:[13]

Size of ad

No. of colors

No. of separate illustrations

Square inches of illustration

No. of type sizes

Point size of largest type

Point size of headlines

Largest type: product identification

Point size of main body copy

Pica width of copy measure

No. of copy blocks

No. of words in advertisement

No. of product identifications

No. of product facts

No. of product benefits

No. of pictures of product in use

Readership of surrounding material

Brad-Vern totals (measures of type)

Previous schedule, 1949

To insert all of these variables in a multiple regression relationship is very awkward, assuming even that sufficient observations are available to yield reliable estimates of the parameters. In addition, the proponents of factor analysis would argue, intercorrelation among the independent variables is likely to be so extensive that such relationships as are derived by multiple regression may not be very meaningful anyway. The sounder approach, according to them, lies in delving beneath these "surface" relationships to find the forces common to all of them, including readership. This is done by analyzing the matrix of simple correlations of all the variables—a tabular representation of the simple correlation of each variable in the study with every other. Such a matrix is reproduced in Table 3.6, pertaining to the magazine readership problem discussed earlier. Only correlations above the diagonal are shown since the table is symmetric, i.e., $r_{ij} = r_{ji}$.

A series of algebraic manipulations is carried out on these data with the objective of extracting and identifying the underlying factors in the study.[14] The result of these manipulations is a set of "factor loadings," which shows the relative weight of each of the extracted factors on each variable included in the factor analysis. As an example, the factor loadings for the advertising problem are shown in Table 3.7. The variables in Table 3.7 have been rearranged from the order used in Table 3.6 to place next to each other all variables having the highest loadings in any one factor. In this particular example, six underlying factors were extracted, so Table 3.7 contains six columns of factor loadings.

These factor loadings can be interpreted in three ways. In one sense, they represent the relative importance of each factor in influencing each observed variable. Thus, given measures, or indices, for the six factors, the best pre-

---

[13] This example is based on D. W. Twedt, "A Multiple Factor Analysis of Advertising Readership," *Journal of Applied Psychology*, Vol. 36, No. 3, June, 1952, pp. 207–215.

[14] Working procedures are described in the references listed at the end of this chapter.

Table 3.7

FACTOR LOADINGS AND COMMUNALITIES OF 20 ADVERTISING VARIABLES[a]

| | CENTROID LOADINGS | | | | | | | ROTATED LOADINGS | | | | | | |
Variable	I	II	III	IV	V	VI	h_c^2	PC (F_1)	S (F_2)	T (F_3)	In (F_4)	F (F_5)	A (F_6)	h_r^2 (R^2)
K Readership	74	−18	−21	−18	08	−12	6773	**64**	35	28	18	16	09	6766
5 Sq. In. Illustration	68	−13	−10	−13	14	−30	6158	**51**	48	25	06	23	04	6111
26 Pictures of Use	38	37	11	−50	05	−10	5559	**51**	23	−18	09	10	−44	5571
3 Number of Colors	33	−25	−17	−31	−15	13	3358	**49**	−07	23	11	−15	01	3326
1 Size of Ad	87	07	18	30	27	−10	9827	18	**69**	26	45	45	04	9827
21 Number Prod. Facts	35	48	15	−17	−21	−07	4533	20	**37**	−24	28	−12	−35	4498
34 Brad-Vern Schedules	26	19	−39	19	02	−27	3652	21	**37**	−25	−01	07	34	3641
9 Largest Type	71	−36	29	18	00	−06	7538	15	45	**62**	36	12	03	7543
11 Largest Prod. Ident.	51	−33	16	08	−14	−09	4287	18	34	**48**	21	−06	04	4277
8 Number Type Sizes	55	−18	46	11	−28	07	6419	01	37	**47**	47	−16	−19	6405
12 Body Type Size	26	−47	−09	−04	−02	04	3002	12	04	**46**	09	00	25	2982
10 Headline Size	55	−27	−10	18	06	04	4230	26	24	**34**	30	14	27	4233
18 Number Words	64	38	15	30	−18	17	7278	05	46	−10	**71**	00	−03	7291
14 Number Copy Blocks	62	43	21	−08	−04	27	6943	25	27	−13	**65**	10	−33	6937
20 Number Prod. Ident.	66	37	−11	14	04	25	6683	31	29	−20	**64**	19	06	6695
22 Number Prod. Benefits	60	59	13	14	−22	04	6965	14	52	−22	**57**	−06	−17	6958
29 Surround	24	−54	18	20	75	16	1.0097	−03	−13	61	10	**76**	17	1.0064
31 Previous Schedule	55	16	−53	25	04	−19	7092	42	46	−21	19	14	**47**	7087
13 Pica Width	34	−44	−33	08	−07	11	4415	35	−01	34	14	05	**43**	4452
4 Number Illust.	46	27	15	−34	18	07	4599	36	17	−05	27	25	**−40**	4564

[a] Decimals omitted. Boldface indicates factor on which each variable has its highest loading.

Source: TWEDT, op. cit., p. 211.

diction of the first variable, readership, would be obtained from the following equation.

Per cent readership $= .64F_1 + .35F_2 + .28F_3 + .18F_4 + .16F_5 + .09F_6$

The coefficients of the factors are obtained, it will be seen, from the values in the "readership" row of Table 3.7. In a similar manner, each of the other 19 variables could be expressed as a linear function of these six factors.

More specifically, the factor loadings represent the *net* correlation coefficient between each factor and each observed variable. Thus, the value of 64 at the head of the F_1 column indicates that $(.64)^2$, or 41 per cent, of the variance in readership is accounted for by factor F_1 after allowance for the other factors; the figure at the head of the F_2 column, 35, indicates that an additional $(.35)^2$ or 12 per cent, of the variance in readership is accounted for by factor F_2; etc.

The cumulated sum of these squares for each variable is shown in the last column of Table 3.7, the one headed "R^2." The first figure in this column means that roughly 68 per cent of the variance in readership is explained by the six common factors extracted in this analysis. The figure is obtained as the sum of the squares of the readership factor loadings, i.e.:

$$(.64)^2 + (.35)^2 + (.28)^2 + (.18)^2 + (.16)^2 + (.09)^2$$

In a similar manner, the second figure in the R^2 column indicates that these six common factors explain 61 per cent of the variance in the square inches of illustration of the advertisements, and so on.

Third, and in some ways most important, the factor loadings serve as the basis for combining the variables into common groups. This is done on the basis of which factor has the highest loading with each particular variable. In Table 3.7, the highest loadings for each variable are shown in boldface type. Thus, the first four variables in Table 3.7 show the highest loadings with F_1; hence, they are considered to form a common group. Similarly, size of ad, number of product facts, and Brad-Vern schedules have their highest loadings in another factor, so they are considered to represent another common force, F_2. Ideally, each variable would have a distinctly high loading in just one factor, so that the grouping operation becomes fairly simple. As is so often the case, however, this does not work out so neatly in actual practice. Thus, the loadings for number of type sizes in Table 3.7 are equal for both F_3 and F_4. Classification of this variable then becomes largely a matter of judgment. The decision often rests on which of the different groups has the closest kinship to the variable in question. On this basis, number of type sizes was classified in F_3 rather than in F_4.

After the variables have been grouped on the basis of their factor loadings, most psychologists (of those who have gotten this far . . .) will attempt to "identify" the various factors by giving each some meaningful interpretation. This is accomplished by examining the variables grouped under each factor and attempting to find a common bond between them. The manner in which this was done in the advertising readership study illustrated here is instructive, and the relevant paragraphs are reproduced below:[15]

Factor PC has high positive loadings on Readership (.64), Square inches of illustration (.51), Number of pictures showing the product in use (.51), Number of colors (.49), and Previous schedule of advertising (.42). The best measures of this factor are those involving *Pictorial* and *Color* aspects of advertisements, hence the factor designation PC.

Factor S had high loadings on Ad size (.69), Number of product benefits (.52), Square inches of illustration (.48), Number of words (.46), Previous schedule of advertising (.46), and Largest type size (.45). Readership loading on factor S is .35, or 12 per cent of the variance in readership scores is attributable to this factor, which seems to involve *Size* of advertisement.

Factor T had high loadings for Largest type size (.62), Readership of surround (.61), Largest type used for product identification (.48), Number of type size (.47), and Point size of main body copy (.46). In general, this factor seems to be associated with *Typographic* size and variety. Its Readership loading is .28, accounting for 8 per cent of readership variance.

Factor In has high loadings for Number of words (.71), Number of copy blocks (.65), Number of product identifications (.64), Number of product benefits (.57), Number of type sizes (.47), and Ad size (.45). This factor appears to be one of *information*, and its loadings on Readership is .18, accounting for only three per cent of readership variance.

Factor F has only two significant loadings: Readership of surround (.76) and Ad size (.45). The factor designation F is for *Field*—the influence of the surrounding field or background against which the advertisement is seen. Another 3 per cent of readership variance is accounted for by this factor, which has a readership loading of .16.

Factor A has significant loadings for Previous schedule (.47), Number of pictures of product in use (−.44), Pica width of copy measure (.43), and Number of illustrations (−.40). This factor is difficult to interpret, but tentatively it is called A, for *Advertising* schedule previously run. It accounts for less than 1 per cent of readership variance; the criterion loading is .09.

3.6.1.   Evaluation

To some exponents of the method, factor analysis is the only truly valid technique of multivariate analysis in that it delves beneath the surface and brings out the "basic" characteristics and associations between observed variables.[16] Most statisticians and researchers, however, will take such allegations with more than just a grain of salt. The fact of the matter is that

---

[15] TWEDT, *op. cit.*, p. 212.
[16] See, for example, R. CATTELL, *Factor Analysis* (Harper & Bros., 1952), Chapter 1.

the interpretation of the extracted factors rests on highly subjective judgment and is at best only as good as the analyst using the technique.

On the other hand, the principles of factor analysis rest by now on a solid mathematical foundation, and methods are available for rigorous extraction of factors (though this is not true of all factor extraction procedures). Utilizing these methods—which unfortunately require a considerable amount of computation, preferably with electronic computers—factor analysis can provide a useful supplement to other multivariate techniques; it is not a replacement for them. Rather, factor analysis is most useful as a preliminary technique for setting up hypotheses, and at times testing them. Thus, if it is not clear which of a large number of variables is most pertinent in a particular problem, distinguishing between them by factor analysis is a much wiser procedure then selecting a few on the basis of an examination of simple correlation coefficients. Thus, if working hypotheses are difficult to develop or a number of alternative possibilities exists, the factorization procedure can often help to make them more precise.[17]

Supplement A *to Chapter 3*	# Illustration of Application of Variance Analysis[18]

Table 3.8 shows the percentage of magazine audiences in each of five economic brackets reached by *Life* Magazine, based on eight surveys taken at different periods of time.

It is desired to know (*1*) whether the relative audience reached by *Life* has really increased over the period of these eight reports or whether the observed percentage increases are due to sampling variation, and (*2*) whether

---

[17] In a slightly facetious vein, factor analysis is a godsend for those with little imagination. Applying the technique to almost any collection of variables will yield factors, which can then be identified in some way or other to provide working, if not final, hypotheses. Indeed, some psychologists counsel that a factor analysis should be undertaken with an "open mind"—with no "preconceived" notions of what the instrumental factors may be.

[18] Reproduced, by permission of the publisher, from FERBER, ROBERT, *Statistical Techniques in Market Research* (New York: McGraw-Hill Book Co., 1949), pp. 286–290.

significant differences exist in *Life's* audience coverage at various economic levels.

Table 3.8
PERCENTAGE OF TOTAL POSSIBLE AUDIENCE REACHED BY LIFE MAGAZINE, BY ECONOMIC CLASS AND AT VARIOUS PERIODS OF TIME

Report	Top 20 per cent	Upper Middle 20 per cent	Middle 20 per cent	Lower Middle 20 per cent	Bottom 20 per cent
1	30	19	16	12	4
2	30	21	17	11	6
3	33	22	19	13	6
4	33	21	19	14	8
5	33	25	19	14	9
6	37	27	20	15	11
7	37	26	18	16	9
8	37	26	20	15	7

Source: *Continuing Study of Magazine Audiences*, Report No. 8, August 15, 1946.

Since the data are in percentage form, the first step in solving this problem is to convert the percentages into a form in which they are independent of the variances. This transformation is effected by applying the conversion formula $X = $ arc sine $\sqrt{\text{percentage}}$. The analysis of variance is then performed on the values of X, disregarding the fact that the X values represent angles. The transformed data are shown in Table 3.9.

Table 3.9
ANGULAR TRANSFORMATION OF LIFE AUDIENCE DATA
(Angle Signs Are Omitted)

Report	Top 20 per cent	Upper middle 20 per cent	Middle 20 per cent	Lower middle 20 per cent	Bottom 20 per cent
1	33.2	25.8	23.6	20.3	11.5
2	33.2	27.3	24.3	19.4	14.2
3	35.1	28.0	25.8	21.1	14.2
4	35.1	27.3	25.8	22.0	16.4
5	35.1	30.0	25.8	22.0	17.5
6	37.5	31.3	26.6	22.8	19.4
7	37.5	30.7	25.1	23.6	17.5
8	37.5	30.7	26.6	22.8	15.3

We now have a two-way classification problem to consider, the data being classified by economic class and by date (number of report). In order to answer the first part of the problem, we have to determine the significance of the differences between the various rows (periods of time); and in order to answer the second part of the problem, the significance of the differences between columns (economic levels) must be determined. Hence, there are two F ratios to be computed, one for rows (F_1) and one for columns (F_2). These ratios are

$$F_1 = \frac{variance\ between\ rows}{sampling\ variance\ of\ the\ data}, \quad F_2 = \frac{variance\ between\ columns}{sampling\ variance\ of\ the\ data}$$

Let us denote X_{ij} as the value in the ith row and jth column, $\bar{X}_i$ as the mean of the ith row, $\bar{X}_j$ as the mean of the jth column, and $\bar{X}$ as the over-all sample mean. Then, as in the previous problem, the variance between columns will be equal to $m \sum_j (\bar{X}_j - \bar{X})^2/(k - 1)$, there being k (5) columns and m (8) observations in each column. In a similar fashion, the variance between rows will equal $k \sum_i (\bar{X}_i - \bar{X})^2/(m - 1)$, since there are m rows and k observations in each row.

Each of these two variances is an estimate of the sampling variance in the data plus the effect, if any, of the particular factor involved (time in the case of rows, and economic level in the case of columns). To determine the presence of such effects, we must have an estimate of the sampling variance alone, the denominator of the F ratio. Now the effect of sampling variations on any particular value X_{ij} is $(X_{ij} - \bar{X}) - (\bar{X}_i - \bar{X}) - (\bar{X}_j - \bar{X})$. The first term measures the deviation of the particular value from the sample mean; this is the usual measure of sampling variation if no influences other than sampling variations are present. If, however, the rows and/or columns do influence the value of X_{ij}, this non-sampling effect is removed by the next two terms. For instance, if the rows have no effect on X_{ij}, i.e., if the value of X_{ij} is independent of the row in which it may be situated, then $\bar{X}_i$ will equal $\bar{X}$ and the second term will vanish. If the row does influence the value of X_{ij}, this effect is obviously the difference between the mean of the row and the over-all mean. The same is true for columns. Consequently, by subtracting these non-sampling effects from the deviation of X_{ij} from the over-all mean, one is left with a pure measure of sampling variation.[19] By eliminating the parentheses, this expression for the sampling variation reduces to $X_{ij} - \bar{X}_i - \bar{X}_j + \bar{X}$. The sampling variance is then the sum of squares of all such residuals divided by their degrees of freedom

$$\frac{\sum_i \sum_j (X_{ij} - \bar{X}_i - \bar{X}_j + \bar{X})^2}{(m - 1)(k - 1)}$$

---

[19] This assumes that there is no interaction effect between rows and columns. In two-way classification problems with one observation in each cell, interaction effects cannot be measured. If the interaction cannot be assumed to be zero on *a priori* grounds in such problems, the analysis-of-variance techniques cannot be applied.

The number of degrees of freedom is $(m-1)(k-1)$ for this variance because in any row (or column) all the values are determined if one less than the total number of values in that row (or column) is fixed. In other words, if as few as $(m-1)(k-1)$ cell values are given, the remaining values may be ascertained from the row and column means.

Table 3.10

VARIANCE-ANALYSIS COMPUTATIONS FOR LIFE AUDIENCE DATA

(1)	(2)	(3)	(4)	(5)	(6)	(7)	(8)	(9)
Report	Top 20 per cent	Upper middle 20 per cent	Middle 20 per cent	Lower middle 20 per cent	Bottom 20 per cent	Total	$\bar{X}_i$	$\bar{X}_i{}^2$
1	8.2	0.8	−1.4	−4.7	−13.5	−10.6	−2.12	4.4944
2	8.2	2.3	−0.7	−5.6	−10.8	− 6.6	−1.32	1.7424
3	10.1	3.0	0.8	−3.9	−10.8	− 0.8	−0.16	0.0256
4	10.1	2.3	0.8	−3.0	− 8.6	1.6	0.32	0.1024
5	10.1	5.0	0.8	−3.0	− 7.5	5.4	1.08	1.1664
6	12.5	6.3	1.6	−2.2	− 5.6	12.6	2.52	6.3504
7	12.5	5.7	0.1	−1.4	− 7.5	9.4	1.88	3.5344
8	12.5	5.7	1.6	−2.2	− 9.7	7.9	1.58	2.4964
TOTAL...	84.2	31.1	3.6	−26.0	−74.0	18.9	.....	19.9124
$\bar{X}_j$........	10.52	3.89	0.45	− 3.25	− 9.25	.....	.....	.....
$\bar{X}_j{}^2$.......	110.6704	15.1321	0.2025	10.5625	85.5625	222.1300	.....	.....

$$\sum_i \sum_j X_{ij}{}^2 = (8.2)^2 + (8.2)^2 + (10.1)^2 + \cdots + (-5.6)^2 + (-7.5)^2 + (-9.7)^2$$
$$= 1,894.39$$

$$\bar{X} = \frac{18.9}{40} = 0.4725$$

Sum of squares between rows = $5[19.9124 - 8(0.4725)^2]$	=	90.63
Sum of squares between columns = $8[222.13 - 5(0.4725)^2]$	=	1,768.08
Total sum of squares = $1,894.39 - (8)(5)(0.4725)^2$	=	1,885.46
Residual sum of squares = $1,885.46 - (1,768.08 + 90.63)$ =		26.75

The F ratios to be computed are now as follows:

$$F_1 = \frac{(m-1)(k-1)}{m-1} \frac{k \sum_i (\bar{X}_i - \bar{X})^2}{\sum_i \sum_j (X_{ij} - \bar{X}_i - \bar{X}_j + \bar{X})^2}$$

$$F_2 = \frac{(m-1)(k-1)}{k-1} \frac{m \sum_j (\bar{X}_j - \bar{X})^2}{\sum_i \sum_j (X_{ij} - \bar{X}_i - \bar{X}_j + \bar{X})^2}$$

As before, computational simplifications are feasible. $k \sum_i (\bar{X}_i - \bar{X})^2$ reduces to $k\left(\sum_i \bar{X}_i^2 - m\bar{X}^2\right)$, and $m \sum_j (\bar{X}_j - \bar{X})^2$ becomes $m\left(\sum_j \bar{X}_j^2 - k\bar{X}^2\right)$. The sum of squares of the residuals is best computed as the difference between the total sum of squares and the sums of squares between rows and between columns

$$\sum_i \sum_j (X_{ij} - \bar{X}_i - \bar{X}_j + \bar{X})^2 = \sum_i \sum_j (X_{ij} - \bar{X})^2$$
$$- k \sum_i (\bar{X}_i - \bar{X})^2 - m \sum_j (\bar{X}_j - \bar{X})^2$$

The total sum of squares is easily computed as $\sum_i \sum_j X_{ij}^2 - mk\bar{X}^2$. And, to further reduce the amount of calculation, 25.0 is subtracted from each observation; as noted previously, this procedure does not alter the values of the F ratios. The calculations are shown in Table 3.10.

The analysis of variance of this problem is presented in Table 3.11.

Table 3.11
ANALYSIS OF VARIANCE OF LIFE AUDIENCE DATA

Variance	Sum of squares	Degrees of freedom	Estimate of sampling variance
Between rows.............	90.63	7	12.95
Between columns..........	1,768.08	4	442.02
Residual................	26.75	28	0.96
TOTAL................	1,885.46	39	

From this table, F_1 is computed to be 12.95/0.96, or 13.49, and F_2 is 442.02/0.96, or 460.44. Both values of F are obviously significant, as may be verified from Appendix Table A4; the critical (0.05) value for F_1, with $n_1 = 7$ and $n_2 = 28$, is 2.36, and the critical (0.05) value for F_2, with $n_1 = 4$ and $n_2 = 28$, is 2.71. These results lead us to conclude that the *Life* magazine audience does vary significantly between economic levels, as would be suspected from examining the data, and that a significant increase in the relative size of *Life's* audience has occurred through time. Judging from the relative size of F_1 and F_2, it also appears that the variation in the audience between economic levels is much more pronounced than the variation through time.

Once again, however, it must be recalled that these results are dependent upon the absence of any interaction between economic level and time.

For an application of variance analysis for purposes of sample design, see Sec. 5.5.

Supplement B *to Chapter 3*	Doolittle Solution of Multiple Regression Equation

Multiple regression equations are being solved with increasing frequency by means of electronic computers. There is no doubt that these computers produce solutions far more quickly and efficiently than a desk calculator, particularly if the solution of a number of different equations is desired. On the other hand, if only one or two multiple regression equation estimates are desired, and if each equation involves fewer than five variables, the use of desk calculators may well be quicker. To be sure, the computation time required by the computer is a small fraction of the time required by the desk calculator, but what is generally overlooked is that, in many situations, days and even weeks of waiting time have to elapse before the problem is put into the computer. Situations have occurred where, by the time a problem does get placed in the computer, the necessary deadline, or the date for action, has long since passed.

Partly for this reason, this Supplement might be useful in showing how a four-variable regression equation can be solved on a desk calculator. As a general rule, this solution will take between two and three hours, after the cross-products have been obtained. The time required for the latter depends on the number of observations and on the number of significant digits used.

The entire solution is presented in Table 3.12 on page 113. The first step is the so-called "forward solution," shown by the 14 numbered lines in the table. The first three lines represent the normal equations corresponding to equation (3.17b) on page 113. The cross-products in deviation units are shown in the first four lettered columns of lines 1–3. The following three columns, those headed by (e), (f), and (g), are inserted to allow the necessary data to be obtained for estimating the standard errors of the coefficients.

Table 3.12

DOOLITTLE SOLUTION FOR FOUR-VARIABLE REGRESSION EQUATION

Line	Direction	(a) X_2	(b) X_3	(c) X_4	(d) X_1	(e) c_2	(f) c_3	(g) c_4	(h) Check
1	Normal equation	16.488077	-.662974	-2.265586	1.729082	1	0	0	15.288599
2	Normal equation	-.662974	.394534	.711766	.021253	0	1	0	.464579
3	Normal equation	-2.265586	.711766	1.880128	-.043014	0	0	1	.283294
4	Line 1	16.488077	-.662974	-2.265586	1.729082	1	0	0	15.288599
5	Line 4 ÷ (X_2, line 4)	1.000000	-.040209298	-.137407534	.104868627	.060649887	0	0	.927251795√
6	Line 2		.394534	.711766	.021253	0	1	0	.464579
7	Line 4 × (X_3, line 5)		-.026657719	-.091097623	.069525173	.040209298	0	0	.614743833
8	Line 6 + Line 7		.367876281	.620668377	.090778173	.040209298	1	0	1.079322833√
9	Line 8 ÷ (X_3, line 8)		1.000000000	1.687166063	.246762779	.109301143	2.718305170	0	2.939928842√
10	Line 3			1.880128	-.043014	0	0	1	.283294
11	Line 4 × (X_4, line 5)			-.311308585	.237588894	.137407534	0	0	2.100768687
12	Line 6 × (X_4, line 9)			-1.047170622	-.153157853	-.067839763	-1.687166063	0	-1.820996851
13	Line 10 + line 11 + line 12			.521648793	.041417041	.069567771	-1.687166063	1	.563065834√
14	Line 13 ÷ (X_4, line 13)			1.000000000	.079396409	.133361319	-3.234294960	1.916998580	1.079396409√

Back solution—a_i's

$a_4 = .079396409$
$a_3 = -.112807852$
$a_2 = .120314217$

$a_4 = (14d);$
$a_3 + a_4(9c) = 9d;$
$a_2 + a_3(5b) + a_4(5c) = 5d;$
Check: $a_2(1a) + a_3(1b) + a_4(1c) = 1d$

Back solution—c_{i2}'s

$c_{42} = .133361319$
$c_{32} = -.115701549$
$c_{22} = .074322459$

$c_{42} = (14e);$
$c_{32} + c_{42}(9c) = (9e);$
$c_{22} + c_{32}(5b) + c_{42}(5c) = (5e);$
Check: $c_{24}(1a) + c_{34}(1b) + c_{44}(1c) = 0$

Back solution—c_{i3}'s

$c_{43} = -3.234294960$
$c_{33} = 8.175097864$
$c_{23} = -.115701549$

$c_{43} = (14f);$
$c_{33} + c_{43}(9c) = (9f);$
$c_{23} + c_{33}(5b) + c_{43}(5c) = (5f);$

Back solution—c_{i4}'s

$c_{44} = 1.916998580$
$c_{34} = -3.234294947$
$c_{24} = .133361319$

$c_{44} = (14g);$
$c_{34} + c_{44}(9c) = (9g);$
$c_{24} + c_{34}(5b) + c_{44}(5c) = (5g);$

$Na_1 = \Sigma X_1 - b_{12}\Sigma X_2 - b_{13}\Sigma X_3 - b_{14}\Sigma X_4$
$51a_1 = 130.688428$
$a_1 = 2.562518$

$R^2 = \dfrac{a_2\Sigma x_1 x_2 + a_3\Sigma x_1 x_3 + a_4\Sigma x_1 x_4}{\Sigma x_1^2} = .376632$

$\sigma_u^2 = \dfrac{\Sigma x_1^2 - (a_2\Sigma x_1 x_2 + a_3\Sigma x_1 x_3 + a_4\Sigma x_1 x_4)}{N-m} = \dfrac{\ \ }{51} = .006718333$

$\sigma_u^{*2} = \sigma_u^2\left(\dfrac{N-1}{N-m}\right) = .007147163$

$\sigma_{a_i} = \sigma_u^* \sqrt{c_{ii}};\quad \sigma_{a_2} = .023048;\quad \sigma_{a_3} = .241720;\quad \sigma_{a_4} = .117052$

$\sigma_{a_1} = \dfrac{\sigma_u}{\sqrt{N-m}};\quad \sigma_{a_1} = .011956$

In effect, four separate sets of equations are being solved in Table 3.12, namely:

Step 1:

$$a_2\Sigma x_2{}^2 + a_3\Sigma x_2 x_3 + a_4\Sigma x_2 x_4 = \Sigma x_1 x_2$$
$$a_2\Sigma x_2 x_3 + a_3\Sigma x_3{}^2 + a_4\Sigma x_3 x_4 = \Sigma x_1 x_3$$
$$a_2\Sigma x_2 x_4 + a_3\Sigma x_3 x_4 + a_4\Sigma x_4{}^2 = \Sigma x_1 x_4$$

Step 2:

$$c_{22}\Sigma x_2{}^2 + c_{23}\Sigma x_2 x_3 + c_{24}\Sigma x_2 x_4 = 1$$
$$c_{22}\Sigma x_2 x_3 + c_{23}\Sigma x_3{}^2 + c_{24}\Sigma x_3 x_4 = 0$$
$$c_{22}\Sigma x_2 x_4 + c_{23}\Sigma x_3 x_4 + c_{24}\Sigma x_4{}^2 = 0$$

Step 3:

$$c_{32}\Sigma x_2{}^2 + c_{33}\Sigma x_2 x_3 + c_{34}\Sigma x_2 x_4 = 0$$
$$c_{32}\Sigma x_2 x_3 + c_{33}\Sigma x_3{}^2 + c_{34}\Sigma x_3 x_4 = 1$$
$$c_{32}\Sigma x_2 x_4 + c_{33}\Sigma x_3 x_4 + c_{24}\Sigma x_4{}^2 = 0$$

Step 4:

$$c_{42}\Sigma x_2{}^2 + c_{43}\Sigma x_2 x_3 + c_{44}\Sigma x_2 x_4 = 0$$
$$c_{42}\Sigma x_2 x_3 + c_{43}\Sigma x_3{}^2 + c_{44}\Sigma x_3 x_4 = 0$$
$$c_{42}\Sigma x_2 x_4 + c_{43}\Sigma x_3 x_4 + c_{44}\Sigma x_4{}^2 = 1$$

The actual solution is illustrated in lines 4–12 of the table. The basis for the solution is the successive elimination of coefficients. Taking the first set as an example, in lines 6–9, a_2 is eliminated from the equations, in accordance with the computational directions shown. In a similar way, a_3 is eliminated in the course of the computations described in lines 10–13. The result, on line 14, is an equation in one unknown, from which estimates are immediately obtained of the last coefficient in this set of equations, namely, a_4.

The estimates of the coefficients of each set of equations are obtained in a series of so-called "back solutions," as shown at the bottom of Table 3.12. The procedure in each case is to solve for the last coefficient in the set, from line 14. The value of this coefficient—a_4 in the first case—is then substituted in the equation implicit in line 9 which, as will be seen, is an equation in two unknowns—a_3 and a_4. With a_4 determined from line 14, the value of a_3 can now be estimated by direct substitution. In a similar manner, these two coefficients are substituted in the equation implicit in line 5 and the value of a_2 is estimated.

The identical procedure is followed in the solution of the c_{ij}'s, with the exception that the X_1 column is replaced by the particular column which is relevant to that set of equations. Thus, for solving for c_{42}, c_{32}, c_{22}, the c_2 column is pertinent.

Notice that various automatic checks are incorporated throughout this solution. Essentially these checks are of two types. One type is designed to make sure that the calculation procedures in the forward solution are carried out properly. It is for this purpose that we have the so-called "check" column at the end. The figures in this column for lines 1–3 are obtained as the sum of all of the other figures in that line. The computations for lines 4–14 are then carried out on the figures in this column in the same manner as on the figures in any other column. As a result, if the computations are correct, the sum of the individual figures shown in lines 5, 8–9, and 13–14 should equal the corresponding figure in the check column. As a rule, there may be a difference in the last two decimal places, but, if the difference goes any further than this, a mistake in computation is likely. (For those who like algebraic manipulation, an interesting exercise is to prove algebraically that these checks are correct.)

The second type of check is incorporated in the back solution. This check is designed to make sure that there is no slipup in the estimation of the regression coefficients in the course of the back solution. It is a simple check, carried out by substituting the estimates of the regression coefficients into any, or all, of the normal equations. As a rule, however, substitution in the first equation is sufficient. In the same way, checks can be made of the estimates of the c_{ij}'s. An additional check in the latter case is possible by virtue of the fact that c_{ij} is equivalent to c_{ji}. In other words, c_{42} should be the same as c_{24}, c_{34} should be the same as c_{43}, etc.

These various checks constitute one of the prime virtues of this method of solution. They are not conclusive, however, since they guard primarily against the danger of isolated computational mistakes. They do not guard against mistakes in the procedure of solution. For example, if a particular line is multiplied by the wrong figure, the result may still check out but the solution will be wrong.

The bottom of the table presents the formulas used to compute the coefficient of multiple correlation, the standard deviation of regression, and the standard errors of the regression coefficients. As is evident, it is in connection with the latter that c_{ij}'s are needed. Actually, only the c_{ii}'s are needed for estimating the standard errors of the regression coefficients. The c_{ij}'s enter in computing the standard error of the *difference* between two net regression coefficients. The formula for this standard error is:

$$\sigma_{a_i - a_j} = \sigma_u{}^* \sqrt{c_{ii} + c_{jj} - 2c_{ij}}$$

PROBLEMS

1. Discuss the advantages and limitations of the Lorenz Curve and of Pareto's alpha as analytical measures of comparative income distribution.

2. *Sales Management's* estimates of "net effective buying income" per household for each of 100 Metropolitan County Areas in 1959 are given on page 116 (*Sales Management Survey of Buying Power*, July 10, 1960, pp. 751–761).

Central city	*Est. buying income per household*	Central city	*Est. buying income per household*
Akron, Ohio	$6,861	Memphis, Tenn	$6,043
Albany, N. Y	6,811	Miami, Fla	6,832
Altoona, Pa	5,600	Minneapolis, Minn	6,782
Atlantic City, N. J	6,272	Montgomery, Ala	5,713
Austin, Tex	5,818	Muskegon, Mich	5,837
Baltimore, Md	6,755	New Castle, Pa	6,515
Beaumont, Tex	5,990	New Haven, Conn	8,198
Binghamton, N. Y	6,872	New York, N. Y	7,809
Boston, Mass	7,698	Newark, N. J	8,294
Brockton, Mass	6,412	Norfolk, Va	6,503
Buffalo, N. Y	6,919	Ogden, Utah	6,062
Canton, Ohio	6,530	Oklahoma City, Okla	5,894
Cedar Rapids, Iowa	6,046	Omaha, Neb	6,372
Charleston, W. Va	6,397	Paterson, N. J	8,172
Chattanooga, Tenn	5,301	Peoria, Ill	7,020
Chicago, Ill	8,022	Phoenix, Ariz	5,929
Cincinnati, Ohio	6,322	Pittsburgh, Pa	6,829
Cleveland, Ohio	7,711	Portland, Maine	6,226
Columbus, Ohio	7,486	Provo, Utah	5,472
Dallas, Tex	6,193	Quincy, Mass	5,634
Davenport, Iowa	6,776	Reading, Pa	6,917
Denver, Colo	6,668	Richmond, Va	6,626
Des Moines, Iowa	6,278	Rochester, N. Y	7,172
Duluth, Minn	5,801	Sacramento, Calif	7,408
El Paso, Tex	6,390	St. Joseph, Mo	5,914
Elkhart, Ind	6,436	St. Louis, Mo	6,653
Erie, Pa	6,770	Salt Lake City, Utah	6,328
Eugene, Ore	5,845	San Bernardino, Calif	5,900
Fall River, Mass	6,181	San Francisco, Calif	7,732
Fort Wayne, Ind	6,745	Santa Rosa, Calif	6,019
Fresno, Calif	6,252	Sarasota, Fla	5,630
Gary, Ind	7,055	Seattle, Wash	6,309
Grand Rapids, Mich	6,558	Sioux City, Iowa	5,931
Hamilton, Ohio	6,899	South Bend, Ind	7,553
Harrisburg, Pa	6,567	Springfield, Ill	6,506
Hartford, Conn	8,711	Springfield, Mo	5,275
Honolulu, Hawaii	7,836	Stockton, Calif	6,630
Huntington, W. Va	5,453	Syracuse, N. Y	6,756
Jackson, Mich	6,334	Tampa, Fla	5,422
Jacksonville, Fla	6,185	Toledo, Ohio	7,638
Johnstown, Pa	5,611	Trenton, N. J	8,315
Kansas City, Mo	6,668	Tulsa, Okla	6,032
Lakeland, Fla	5,276	Utica, N. Y	6,305
Lansing, Mich	6,889	Waco, Tex	5,122
Lincoln, Nebr	6,287	Washington, D. C	8,197
Los Angeles, Calif	6,898	Wheeling, W. Va	5,631
Louisville, Ky	5,797	Wilkes-Barre, Pa	5,741
Macon, Ga	5,560	Winston-Salem, N. C	6,027
Madison, Wis	7,230	York, Pa	6,201
Manchester, N. H	6,525	Youngstown, Ohio	6,993

a) Classify these data in a frequency distribution with class intervals $500 wide, beginning from $3,000.

b) Compute the mean and the standard deviation. Assuming normality, within what income limits would you expect to find 90 per cent of these cities? What proportion of cities would you expect to find having average buying incomes per family between $5,000 and $6,000? Compare your estimates with the true answers as obtained from the above array. What light does this throw on the validity of the normality assumption?

c) Compute whatever other measures you think sufficient to test the normality assumption and then evaluate the reasonableness of the assumption in this problem.

d) Compute the median and the mode. How would you interpret the mean, the median, and the mode in the present case? What does the relationship between these computed measures tell you about the skewness of the distribution? Explain why.

3. The median of a frequency distribution can be estimated graphically as the abscissa of the point of intersection of the ogive of the distribution and the ordinate representing half the observations.

a) Verify this principle by estimating the median of the data in Problem 2 from the ogive and comparing the result with your answer in 2d.

b) How would you estimate the mode of a distribution from an ogive?

4. Devise three situations involving requests for some descriptive measure of central tendency of the buying income distribution in Problem 2 in which you would recommend, alternately, the mean, the median, and the mode as the most appropriate measure.

5. Toss 10 pennies into the air 100 times and record the number of heads on each toss. Prepare the results in the form of a frequency distribution listing the number of tosses having 0 heads, 1 head, 2 heads, etc., and plot the resulting distribution.

Does this look like a reasonably normal distribution? Test your opinion by computing the percentage of observations lying within the mean plus and minus various multiples of the standard deviation and comparing the results with the area under corresponding sections of the normal curve. (As a check on the computations, compute the mean and the standard deviation in two independent ways.)

6. Tests show that the life of brand Y tire is approximately of normal distribution with an average life of 23,000 miles and a standard deviation of 2,500 miles.

a) Out of 400 new tires of this brand put into service by the ABC Delivery Service, what are the replacement needs likely to be after each tire has covered 15,000 miles? 20,000 miles? 25,000 miles?

b) What are the odds that any one tire is likely to last for 30,000 miles?

7. The XYZ Company's radio tube has an average life of 3.5 years, a standard deviation of half a year, and is approximately of normal distribution. The retail sales of this tube in the past five years were as follows:

Period	Number of tubes sold
Last year	110,000
Two years ago	90,000
Three years ago	95,000
Four years ago	75,000
Five years ago	60,000

Assuming that these tubes were put into use at the time of sale, what is the best estimate of the company's potential replacement market during the coming year?

8. A survey provides the following data on sleeve length and collar size of shirts worn by men.

Collar size	SLEEVE LENGTH Under 33″	33″ and over	Total
15 & under	41	52	93
Over 15	24	83	107
TOTAL	65	135	200

a) Test the significance of this relationship.
b) Measure the extent of association in two different ways, one using an "orthodox" statistic and the other a probabilistic model.

9. Apply a probabilistic model to measure the extent to which one's ability to predict stock ownership is increased given income, using the data in Table 3.2. How do you explain the results?

10. The table below gives income-distribution data for a sample of department store A's active credit accounts by local and suburban areas.

Family income	Philadelphia accounts	Non-Philadelphia accounts	Total
Under $2,000	51	22	73
$2,000–$3,500	234	122	356
Over $3,500	182	176	358
TOTAL	467	320	787

(Adapted from D. F. Blankertz, "Shopping Habits and Income," in the January, 1950, issue of the *Journal of Marketing*, page 575.)

Is there a significant difference between the income distributions of the store's credit accounts by locality?

11. The classification of the net buying income per household in 1959 of 20 randomly selected Metropolitan County Areas by four regions is as follows:

East		Midwest	
Hartford, Conn.	$8,711	Akron, Ohio	$6,861
Harrisburg, Pa.	6,567	Fort Wayne, Ind.	6,745
New Haven, Conn.	8,198	Peoria, Ill.	7,020
Trenton, N. J.	8,315	Springfield, Ill.	6,506
Rochester, N. Y.	7,172	Youngstown, Ohio	6,993

South		West	
Austin, Texas	$5,818	Lincoln, Neb	$6,287
Dallas, Texas	6,193	Eugene, Ore	5,845
Jacksonville, Fla	6,185	Santa Rosa, Calif	6,019
Norfolk, Va	6,503	Seattle, Wash	6,309
Winston-Salem, N. C.	6,027	Los Angeles, Calif	6,898

a) Do these figures indicate that significant differences exist among the four regions in the buying income per family in large and medium-sized cities?

b) What additional information would you need to obtain a more reliable answer to the above question?

12. A study is made to estimate the effect on non-response rates in personal interviews of the income level of the area interviewed and of the interviewers used. A test survey yields the following non-response rates for 36 interviewers cross-classified by these two factors.

NON-RESPONSE RATES OF 36 INTERVIEWERS

(All figures are percentages)

INCOME LEVEL OF INTERVIEWERS	INCOME LEVEL OF AREA INTERVIEWED		
	High	*Middle*	*Low*
High	12, 8, 7, 12	16, 9, 12, 11	17, 8, 16, 19
Middle	9, 11, 8, 13	7, 12, 15, 13	13, 14, 11, 14
Low	11, 10, 14, 12	12, 14, 11, 16	11, 9, 13, 14

Determine:

a) whether either of these two factors affects the rate of non-response;

b) the presence of interaction;

c) the relative importance of the two factors, if significant.

13. One of the most useful means of isolating the effect of various factors from each other is the so-called Latin Square, a method used extensively in agriculture but rarely in marketing research. Thus, where four separate factors are involved in an experiment with, say, four observations on each, the following Latin Square arrangement might be used:

Aα	Bβ	Cγ	Dδ
Bγ	Aδ	Dα	Cβ
Cδ	Dγ	Aβ	Bα
Dβ	Cα	Bδ	Aγ

The four factors are represented by the rows, columns, Latin letters, and Greek letters. Each cell represents one observation at a given level of each of the four factors. It will be noted that each Latin and Greek letter appears only once in each row, in each column, and in conjunction with each other. In this way, 16 observations enable the effects of the various factors to be evaluated, whereas a complete experiment with all factors in combination with each other would require 256 observations. (Interactions are assumed to be zero.)

The analysis of variance is carried out in the usual manner, each factor having 3 degrees of freedom. Thus, the variance due to Latin letters would be

$4 \sum_{k} (\bar{X}_k - \bar{X})^2/3$, where $\bar{X}_k$ is the mean of the observations containing the kth Latin letter and $\bar{X}$ is the over-all mean. The random sampling sum of squares of the experiment is best computed as the residual of the four factor variances deducted from the total variance, with 3 degrees of freedom.

Suppose, for example, that a test is made to determine the influence of various factors affecting readership by placing four different ads of the same size in four different magazines, in four different sections of the magazine, and in four positions on the page. By placing a total of 16 ads and then securing readership percentages on each ad, the following Latin Square was obtained. The rows represent position on page; the columns, particular magazines; the Latin letters, week of month; the Greek letters, types of ad.

Magazine

Position on page	1	2	3	4
a	Aα 16%	Bβ 24%	Cγ 19%	Dδ 13%
b	Bγ 15%	Aδ 17%	Dα 16%	Cβ 17%
c	Cδ 17%	Dγ 18%	Aβ 21%	Bα 15%
d	Dβ 21%	Cα 21%	Bδ 22%	Aγ 18%

Carry out the analysis of variance and determine the significance and relative importance of each of the four factors.

14. Disposable national income and U. S. factory sales of passenger cars annually from 1948 to 1960 are shown below.

Year	Passenger car sales (000)	Disposable income ($000,000,000)
1948	3,669	189.3
1949	4,957	189.7
1950	6,504	207.7
1951	5,068	227.5
1952	4,148	238.7
1953	5,926	252.5
1954	5,350	256.9
1955	7,661	274.4
1956	5,610	292.9
1957	5,935	308.8
1958	4,122	317.9
1959	5,469	337.3
1960	6,525	354.2

Source: *Automobile Facts and Figures, 1961*, p. 5; *Handbook of Basic Economic Statistics*, 1961, p. 237.

a) By plotting scatter diagrams of this relationship on arithmetic and log-log paper, what form of function do you think would best fit the data?

b) Test your belief by computing the simple linear regression of scrappage (S) on national income (Y) as an arithmetic function (S = a + bY) and as a logarithmic function (log S = log a' + b' log Y).

c) How do you interpret the corresponding pairs of regression coefficients?

15. A researcher correlates the aggregate sales of washing machines (S) with total disposable income, Y, and comes out with a regression equation, S = a + bY. He then decides that the relationship would be more meaningful if expressed in per capita units, and so he divides both the variables by population, N, and obtains as his final function:

$$\frac{S}{N} = a + b\frac{Y}{N}$$

Comment on the validity of this procedure. If the procedure is not valid, what alternative method would you recommend?

16. Estimates made by the authors of U. S. expenditures for durable goods, personal income, and personal income lagged one quarter, all on a per capita basis and adjusted for price variations, are shown below, by quarters, 1935 to the third quarter of 1941.

Year	Quarter	Lagged income (Y_{-1})	Current income (Y)	Durable consumption expenditures (C)
1935	1	$446	$465	$40.72
	2	465	472	41.01
	3	472	478	42.87
	4	478	488	45.16
1936	1	488	530	46.70
	2	530	531	51.15
	3	531	538	52.17
	4	538	546	54.97
1937	1	546	559	56.46
	2	559	548	55.92
	3	548	519	54.77
	4	519	504	45.50
1938	1	504	498	41.94
	2	498	506	40.28
	3	506	516	41.35
	4	516	531	47.24
1939	1	531	537	48.14
	2	537	539	49.04
	3	539	559	51.07
	4	559	566	53.89
1940	1	566	565	56.15
	2	565	578	57.83
	3	578	606	58.45
	4	606	634	62.80
1941	1	634	658	70.03
	2	658	680	73.62
	3	680	685	70.40

a) Estimate the multiple regression of C on Y and Y_{-1} by means of the graphic method. Find the coefficient of multiple determination by this method.

b) Check the accuracy of your estimates by applying the mathematical method.

c) Which of the two independent variables has the greater relative effect on the dependent variable? By what margin?

d) How is the relationship between C and Y, and C and Y_{-1}, affected when the other independent variable is held constant?

17. In working with two independent variables, one of which is simply a lag of the other, as in $S = f(Y, Y_{-1})$, some people prefer to compute:

$$S = a + bY + cY_{-1}$$

and others prefer

$$S = a' + b'Y + c'(Y - Y_{-1})$$

a) List the differences and similarities in the estimates of the regression and correlation coefficients obtained by working out each of these functions. Where there are differences, show how they can be reconciled, if at all.

b) Is there any advantage of one form over the other? If so, what?

18. Following is the average price and quality ranking of different grades of a canned food product:

Grade (Descending quality)	Average price (Cents)
1	24.2
2	23.7
3	21.2
4	23.7
5	24.1
6	22.6
7	22.8

To what extent is price associated with quality?

SELECTED REFERENCES

Frequency Distributions

Hardly any elementary statistics text would dare to omit a discussion of the description and analysis of frequency distributions, and this subject is generally covered also in many of the intermediate and advanced texts. The following references, therefore, represent only a small portion of the total number of such sources available.

An excellent non-technical introduction to the concepts underlying frequency distributions, and to statistical analysis in general, is provided by the little book by TIPPETT, *Statistics* (New York: Oxford University Press, 1943). The construction of frequency distributions is explained clearly in any of the following texts: F. E. CROXTON and D. J. COWDEN, *Applied General Statistics* (Prentice-Hall, Inc., 1955);

WERNER HIRSCH, *Introduction to Modern Statistics* (New York: Macmillan Co., 1957); D. F. PADEN and E. F. LINDQUIST, *Statistics for Economics and Business* (New York: McGraw-Hill, 1956); F. C. MILLS, *Statistical Methods* (New York: Henry Holt Co., 1955); ERNEST KURNOW, G. J. GLASER and F. R. OTTMAN, *Statistics for Business Decisions* (Homewood, Ill.: Richard D. Irwin, Inc., 1959); W. A. NEISWANGER, *Elementary Statistical Methods* (New York: Macmillan Co., 1956); J. E. FREUND and F. J. WILLIAMS, *Modern Business Statistics* (New York: Prentice-Hall, 1958); A. E. WAUGH, *Elements of Statistical Method* (New York: McGraw-Hill, 1952); and W. A. WALLIS and H. V. ROBERTS, *Statistics* (Glencoe: The Free Press, 1956). All of these books also discuss the measurement of the various attributes of the frequency distribution, perhaps the most elementary discussion being found in the book by PADEN and LINDQUIST and a fairly detailed discussion being found in CROXTON and COWDEN. The book by WAUGH contains a good discussion, in Chapter 8, of the higher moments of a frequency distribution.

Useful monographs on the lognormal distribution are: R. GIBRAT, *Les Inegalités Economiques: La Loi de l'Effet Proportionnel* (Paris: Recueil Sirey, 1931) giving a very simple short-cut for approximating the parameters and illustrating applications to various economic variables; and J. AITCHISON and J. A. C. BROWN, *The Lognormal Distribution* (Cambridge: University Press, 1957).

Chi-Square, Variance and Regression Analysis

A general introduction to the subject of chi-square analysis will be found in the texts by ROBERT FERBER, *Statistical Techniques in Market Research;* R. A. FISHER, *Statistical Methods for Research Workers* (New York: Hafner Publishing Co., 1954); F. C. MILLS, *Statistical Methods;* A. C. ROSANDER, *Elementary Principles of Statistics* (New York: D. Van Nostrand Co., 1951); G. W. SNEDECOR, *Statistical Methods* (Ames, Iowa: Iowa State College Press, 1956); and GUDNY YULE and M. G. KENDALL, *An Introduction to the Theory of Statistics* (New York: Hafner Publishing Co., 1950). The latter text is on a somewhat more advanced level than the others. At the other extreme, a very elementary introduction to the description and analysis of cross-classification data is the subject of the book by HANS ZEISEL, *Say It with Figures* (Harper & Bros., 1950).

All of the same works (excluding ZEISEL) also treat the subject of variance analysis. Particularly thorough treatments of variance analysis and of co-variance analysis are provided in the texts by B. OSTLE, *Statistics in Research* (Ames, Iowa: Iowa State College Press, 1954); ROSANDER, and SNEDECOR. In addition, the article by M. E. BRUNK and W. T. FEDERER, "How Marketing Problems of the Apple Industry were Attacked and the Research Results Applied," (Cornell University, Department of Agricultural Economics Paper #4, January 1953) illustrates how variance analysis and experimental design can be applied to marketing problems; also M. A. MACGREGOR, *Uniformity Trial Experiments in Marketing Research* (Ithaca, N. Y.: Cornell University Department of Agricultural Economics, 1958).

A pragmatic description of the different non-parametric methods of measuring association is SIDNEY SIEGEL's *Nonparametric Statistics for the Behavioral Sciences* (New York: McGraw-Hill, 1956).

An excellent survey article of different concepts of measuring association, with an extensive bibliography, has been published by L. A. GOODMAN and W. H. KRUSKAL, entitled "Measures of Association for Cross-Classification" (*Journal of the American Statistical Association*, December, 1954, pp. 732–765).

The most thorough treatment available of correlation methods and their applications to research is provided by MORDECAI EZEKIEL and K. A. Fox, *Methods of Correlation and Regression Analysis* (New York: John Wiley & Sons, 1959). In addition, good coverage of the concepts underlying regression analysis and of computing methods will be found in the texts by CROXTON and COWDEN, FERBER, FISHER, HIRSCH, MILLS, OSTLE, ROSANDER, SNEDECOR and WAUGH.

Factor Analysis

A very good introduction to this subject is provided by the book by L. L. THURSTONE, *Multiple Factor Analysis* (Chicago: University of Chicago Press, 1950). *Introduction to Factor Analysis* by BENJAMIN FRUCHTER (New York: D. Van Nostrand Co., 1954) also provides a general and fairly easily understood introduction to the subject. The book by R. CATTELL, *Factor Analysis* (Harper & Bros., 1952) is another clearly written introduction to the subject, but is not as unbiased as might be hoped.

One of the best theoretical books on the subject is K. J. HOLZINGER and H. H. HARMAN, *Factor Analysis, A Synthesis of Factorial Methods* (Chicago, University of Chicago Press, 1941). For a variant that was widely used recently, the method of "principal components" (discussed in Sec. 11.4), see M. A. GIRSHICK, "Principal Components" in the *Journal of the American Statistical Association* (1936, pp. 519–528).

4 | Two Basic Approaches

IN PREVIOUS CHAPTERS we have reviewed the design of a research investigation and the more useful techniques that are available for ascertaining quantitative economic relationships. In this chapter we will explore a different and, in a way, broader aspect of the subject, namely, what *are* the relevant relationships in economic and market analysis, and how can various research techniques from economic theory as well as from statistics be of use in detecting such relationships?

4.1. POLICY, STRUCTURE AND PREDICTION[1]

What type of relationships will be relevant in a given case depends on the nature of the problem, as illustrated by Fig. 2.3. From a practical point of view, the problem that leads to the investigation will often be a *policy problem*. Since policy problems may be widely divergent, the number of potentially relevant relations may seem bewildering. All policy problems are, however, formally alike in that the policy maker (whether a private firm or the government, a trade association, or trade union, etc.) aims at realizing whenever possible one or more *targets*. For example, the government's target may be balancing the budget while maintaining employment and preventing inflation, and the firm might want to maximize its profits while maintaining liquidity and increasing the market share.

Various *instruments* are available generally that can be manipulated by the policy maker to attain these targets. These instruments may include such

---

[1] On this subject and on some related topics, see also MARSCHAK'S concise treatment: "Economic Structure, Path, Policy and Prediction," *American Economic Review*, May, 1947, pp. 81–84.

variables as tax rates and the control of credit in the case of a government, or advertising and prices for the individual firm. Other variables, such as population increase and weather conditions in the government's case, or total disposable national income in the case of the firm are clearly not under the policy maker's control, although they affect the target variables. From the point of view of a particular policy maker, these *uncontrollable variables* represent so many data of the problem.

Irrelevant variables are a fourth category. Although neither targets nor instruments nor uncontrollable variables, they are necessary links in solving the problem. Thus, in a profit-maximization problem with unit cost given, the level of total costs may be irrelevant as long as liquidity is guaranteed. Total cost, however, plays a logical rule in the solution, since profits are defined as total revenue less total costs.

Finally, the policy problem, as noted in Sec. 1.4, may be subject to *boundary conditions*. For instance, there may be a requirement that taxes should not surpass a certain level. Or, the projected volume of sales may be stipulated to remain below the existing capacity of the firm. Some of these boundary conditions may refer directly to the range of values that can be taken by the instrument variables. Taxes, for instance, cannot be raised indefinitely, nor can the price of a product.

Seen in this perspective, relevant relationships are therefore:

1. Relationships that govern the dependence of the target variables on the instruments.

2. Relationships that govern the level of the variables subject to boundary conditions.

3. Since no policy decision can be properly evaluated unless its estimated effects are superimposed upon a proper forecast, i.e., a forecast on the assumption that no change in the instruments is contemplated, the relationships of the target variables and of the variables subject to boundary conditions with the uncontrollable variables are equally relevant.

The most effective way to analyze relationships for a given policy problem is to set up a model that describes the interaction among the variables of the three groups mentioned. Model systems of this kind will be discussed in Chapter 9. At this place it is sufficient to note the following three points:[2]

1. The number of instrument variables should at least equal the number of targets. Otherwise the problem is not soluble, a point often overlooked in practical life and one that explains inconsistencies often encountered in political programs.

2. Preferably the number of instruments should exceed the number of targets. In general this will allow for a more flexible policy, and tends to

---

[2] Compare on this subject: J. TINBERGEN, *On the Theory of Economic Policy* (Amsterdam, 1952), and *Economic Policy: Principles and Design* (Amsterdam, 1956). The latter volume contains numerous practical applications to different types of problems.

avoid too drastic a change in the value of a single instrument. In the case of economic policy, this prevents unnecessary hardships through placing the total burden of an adaptation upon specific groups. With marketing policy, the simultaneous change of two or more instruments may avoid customer resistance or retaliation by competitors that otherwise might easily have been provoked.[3]

3. With respect to the model as a whole, a consistent model requires that the number of equations equal the sum of the irrelevant variables and targets. The more complex the problem becomes, the larger, therefore, the number of equations that is required.

4.1.1. Economic Structure

As is clear from the foregoing, in deciding upon a certain course of action the policy maker has to reckon not only with the current values of the uncontrollable variables, but also with a great many economic relationships. The latter are commonly referred to as being part of the *economic structure*, be it the structure of the economy as a whole or that of a certain market. Used in this way, the term "economic structure" refers to the lasting aspects of the economy, or the part of it that is being studied. Hence, it designates the regular, or "normal" characteristics of the economic variables and of the interactions between those variables. Thus, a distinction is made between "normal" values—however defined—of the economic variables and the actual values occurring in a randomly chosen month or year. For example, average yield per acre or average productivity per man-hour are important aspects of economic structure, whereas the yield per acre or productivity in a given year, influenced as they may have been by incidental factors such as prevailing weather conditions or the phase of the business cycle, will not be regarded as such. Period averages or trend values will, therefore, as a rule represent more adequately the prevailing structure of the economy.

The same holds with regard to the relationships that govern the interaction between the current values of the variables. The reaction of total consumption to a change in disposable income, or that of the sales of a product to a change in prices or advertising as observed in a given year, is not decisive since incidental factors may well have intervened. Here again, systematic observation covering a number of such changes is required in order to identify the more permanent aspects of the economy.

Underlying these normal characteristics of the economic variables and of the character and intensity of their interaction are numerous non-economic factors that the economist will usually regard as just so many *data* of the

---

[3] Relevant here is BREMS' analysis of "Implicit and Explicit Bargaining," in *Product Equilibrium under Monopolistic Competition* (Cambridge, Mass., 1951), Part II, particularly p. 165ff.

economic system: their "explanation" does not fall in the realm of economic theory. Demographic, institutional, psychological, sociological and technical factors are perhaps the more important of these variables. The sum total of these factors may be regarded as the basic structure of the economy, and it is this basic structure that is reflected by the normal values and the relationships between economic variables. These normal values and relationships consequently represent the structure of the economy.

The underlying factors of the economy just mentioned alter, as a rule, only gradually or, where major changes are concerned, infrequently. Therefore, one is usually justified in supposing that the resulting economic structure of a country changes but slowly, or at least in a systematic way, provided that no major changes in basic structure do occur.[4]

4.1.2. Quantitative Aspects of Economic Structure

One consequence of the alleged stability of economic structure is the customary procedure of quantifying some of its relevant aspects in terms of relatively simple key figures. Thus, to determine sales quotas, such figures as average consumption per head—or, more refined, average consumption by main income groups—may often prove sufficient. In cases like this, one need not consider the ultimate psychological or sociological aspects of the basic structure that determine consumers' preference scales. For other purposes, however, it is exactly these basic factors that may prove relevant, as when an effective advertising theme has to be developed, or the quality of a product is to be evaluated from the consumer's point of view. The use of such specialized psychological tools as depth questioning and clinical techniques may then become an inevitable part of structural research.

The key figures used to describe quantitative characteristics may be classified into three broad categories:

1. The first category aims at characterizing a certain *variable as such*. Examples are the average, the median and the mode. Useful additional information is provided by the standard deviation (σ_x) and the coefficient of variation, $\sigma_x/\bar{x}$. Other statistics referring to the frequency distribution of the variable studied, such as the semi-interquartile range or the coefficients of an empirically-fitted, theoretical distribution as Pareto's α, serve to complete the picture.

2. The second category describes the existing ratio *between* two variables, such as consumption per family or per head, the rate of turnover of stocks, etc. An alternate means of presentation is to express one variable as a percentage of another. Purchases of a certain group of commodities may be

---

[4] J. TINBERGEN, *Economic Policy: Principles and Design*, Chapter 1, p. 5.

computed as a percentage of total consumer expenditures, in order to assess the relative importance of the group in question. More elaborate variants of this type of key figure are the patterns obtained by cross-classification according to two attributes of the same phenomenon. Cross-classification of total purchases of a product according to households in different income brackets and according to geographical areas is one example. Although cross-classifications of this kind are usually based on survey data and the ensuing patterns consequently refer to one point of time, the percentage distributions thus found can prove to be fairly stable over time. The latter are therefore often regarded as an important indication of the structure of the market. The same holds in the case of the coefficients of input-output tables, to be discussed in Sec. 6.4.

3. The third category of key figures consists of the coefficients of *reaction equations* that explain changes in an economic variable. Demand and supply equations are the principal examples. If we take a simple linear demand equation showing the relationship between demand (v), price (p) and time (t):

$$v_t = \alpha + \beta p_{t-\vartheta} + \gamma t \tag{4.1}$$

there are four types of constants to be reckoned with:

a) The *additive constant, α.* According to Eq. 4.1, α can be written as a linear function of the average values ($\bar{v}$, $\bar{p}$, and $\bar{t}$) of v, p, and t:

$$\alpha = \bar{v} - \beta \bar{p} - \gamma \bar{t} \tag{4.2}$$

The additive constant, α, therefore, belongs essentially among the key figures mentioned in the first category.

b) The *multiplicative parameter, β,* describes the rate of change in demand accompanying a unit change in p. A more convenient key figure is obtained by computing the elasticity:

$$\epsilon_t = \frac{\partial v}{\partial p} \times \frac{p_t}{v_t} = \beta \frac{p_t}{v_t} \tag{4.3}$$

It represents the percentage change of v accompanying a price change of one per cent. It is clear that ϵ is not independent of the numerical values chosen for p and v. When used as a structural key figure, it is therefore customary to compute ϵ as:

$$\bar{\epsilon} = \beta \frac{\bar{p}}{\bar{v}} \tag{4.4}$$

to make it representative of the average elasticity prevailing in the period of observation.

c) The last term, γt, commonly referred to as the *residual trend*, represents the influence of variables that have not been included in the equation, such as changes in consumer preferences, etc. In (4.1), v is expressed as a linear function of time (t). Next to the influence of prices, demand is therefore assumed to increase annually at the same absolute rate, γ.

d) The suffix ($t - \vartheta$) of p, indicates that demand does not react instantaneously to a change in prices, but does so only after ϑ units of time. ϑ therefore indicates the *time lag* that occurs in the demand reaction. Time lags of this kind represent essentially a dynamic element of the economic mechanism, and play an important role in many theoretical business-cycle models.

The dependence of the present values of the variables on the situation in previous periods may manifest itself also in many other forms, as with the accumulation process. In the latter case, the present stock of capital, (k_t), is the sum total of all net investments[5] (i_t) in the past:

$$k_t = \int_0^t i_t \, dt + k_0, \qquad k_0 \text{ representing the initial stock of goods.} \quad (4.5)$$

Another equally important and well-known example of this kind is the manufacturing-progress or learning curve that postulates a relationship between the present level of manpower requirements per unit of product $\left(\dfrac{a}{v}\right)_t$, and total cumulated output of the same product (v_t) in former periods:

$$\log \left(\frac{a}{v}\right)_t = \gamma + \beta \log \int_0^t v_t \, dt, \quad (4.6)$$

where β has a negative sign; for many production processes its value is about $-.3$.[6]

Such long-term relationships serve to relate the past to a nation's present economic structure as well as to its future development possibilities. Equations such as (4.5) and (4.6) are consequently the backbone of many models of economic growth, whereas analogous equations are also used in the theory of advertising.

To summarize: from the economic researcher's and the market investigator's point of view—as distinct from that of their colleagues in other fields as sociology or psychology—the term "economic structure" refers to the regular, or normal, values of the variables; the coefficients describing frequency distributions; such ratios and such patterns resulting from cross-tabulations that can reasonably be assumed to remain fairly stable; and, with regard to interdependence between variables, multiplicative parameters, trend coefficients, and the time-shape of reactions.

It is common usage to call the ratios and coefficients mentioned above

---

[5] Or, more correctly, all gross investments *less* replacements, since the latter do not necessarily equal depreciation changes.

[6] See W. HIRSCH, "Manufacturing Progress Functions," *Review of Economics and Statistics*, May, 1952, pp. 143ff.; FRANK J. ANDRESS, "The Learning Curve as a Production Tool," *Harvard Business Review*, Vol. XXXII, Jan.–Feb., 1954, pp. 37–38.

"structural constants," and the empirical relationships described by such equations as (4.1) and (4.6) as "structural equations."[7]

4.1.3. The Structural Hypothesis

Problem-solving for policy purposes, whether in the field of economics or business, requires that structural constants remain constant in time and space. On the other hand, it is equally clear that no problem can be solved and that policy recommendations are virtually impossible unless a sufficient number of relationships, whether simple ratios or reaction equations, can be assumed to remain reasonably constant. Consequently, the research worker is justified in assuming for purposes of prediction *as a first hypothesis*, that his "structural constants" represent some of the more permanent aspects of the basic structure and, hence, that their numerical values will change but slightly over time and space. Before the actual forecast is made this hypothesis ought, as a matter of course, to be verified by means of a *diagnosis*, as will be discussed in Sec. 10.2.1.

Meanwhile, it is well to remember that these structural parameters may be considered constant only by virtue of this hypothesis. In practice they may fail to remain so when they are re-estimated from a different sample, from data pertaining to another geographic area or to an earlier or later time period.

Apart from sampling errors, there is one major reason for possible discrepancies in our estimates. As noted earlier, the true structure of the economy is governed by numerous factors and interactions, the character of which in many cases is practically unknown, and even if known is often difficult to assess quantitatively. To obtain quantitative estimates, it is therefore necessary to specify beforehand the variables that, according to theoretical or other *a priori* considerations, might conceivably influence the variable studied as well as the mathematical form of this interaction. But the *estimator equation* thus obtained invariably fails to represent adequately all the multivariate aspects of the (unknown) *true structural relationship*. For one thing, not all the relevant variables can be included in the estimator equation, a point to be discussed more fully in Sec. 8.9. As a consequence, there is always a serious risk that a really important variable has been omitted. Then again, the mathematical form of the relationships, as described by the estimator equation, must necessarily remain a rough approximation of the true form. Although the estimator equation may postulate a relationship of a linear or quadratic form, the true form may be much more complicated.

Whether the consequences of errors resulting from erroneous or incom-

---

[7] The term derives from R. FRISCH, "Propagation and Impulse-Problems in Dynamic Economics," *Economic Essays in Honour of Gustav Cassel*, 1933, par. 4.

plete specification prove to be serious depends on the nature of the problem and on the accuracy required. In estimating average consumption per household for different areas as a basis for sales-quota determination, a whole series of successively more refined structural hypotheses is possible, each with a corresponding estimator equation. To start with, we may assume constant per capita or household consumption. Refinements are possible by introducing as explanatory variables in any desired combination, family income, occupational status, family size, education, race, degree of urbanization, etc.

There is no doubt that each of these variables influences the level of consumption, and that in the true structural equation each occupies a well-defined place. The critical question, however, is twofold: whether we will be able to identify the exact influence of these variables from the statistical data, and whether the use to be made of the estimates justifies the required sampling procedures as well as subsequent, possibly elaborate statistical estimates.

Since balance is sought between means and ends, an admittedly over-simplified equation is usually chosen to represent the structure of demand. But whereas this estimator equation might be reasonably representative of most geographic areas, results obtained in some cases will inevitably prove inadequate. This is not to say that the true structural relationships in those cases are necessarily different from that of the others. Rather it means that either the explanatory variables included in the estimator equation are incomplete, or that its mathematical form does not comply with the true structural form.[8]

4.1.4. Structural Change

An important additional reason why a structural hypothesis may prove inadequate is the occurrence of changes in the basic structure of the economy or the market. Well-known are institutional changes, such as revisions in taxation or in import duties, and psychological changes, such as modification of consumers' preference scales due to the introduction of substitute products. In such instances, there is no doubt about the inadequacy of the original structural hypothesis. Other cases, however, may prove more difficult from a methodological point of view, particularly where the study of time series is concerned. Here more often than not, erroneous specification of the estimator equation may be the cause of an alleged change in basic structure.

---

[8] An interesting practical example of this latter type of error in sales-quota estimation is given by D. R. G. COWAN, *Sales Analysis from the Management Standpoint* (Chicago, 1938), p. 60.

For example, an important element of the market structure of a firm is the marginal revenue to be expected from additional advertising. As is shown for the particular product analyzed in Fig. 4.1, the hypothesis of constant marginal returns per family may prove adequate up to a certain number of opportunities for exposure per household. Beyond this limit of, say, 8 opportunities for exposure, marginal revenue tends to decline sharply. Here the hypothesis of a parabolic relation provides a better all-round description of

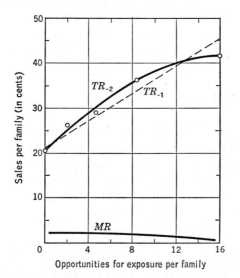

Fig. 4.1. *Systematic Change in Marginal Revenue from Magazine Advertising of a Patent Medicine*

TR_1: *Family total revenue curve, estimated as the partial linear regression of sales per family on "opportunities for exposure per family." The other variables of the estimator equation, kept constant in Fig. 4.1, are: competitive advertising, city size, age, family size, economic class, education, occupation and religion.*
TR_2: *Ditto, fitted as a curvilinear relation to the residuals of TR_1.*
MR: *Marginal revenue curve, derived from TR_2.*

Source: Roberts, H. V., "The Measurements of Advertising Results," *The Journal of Business*, July 1947, pp. 131–155. The points in the figure represent the grouped data for the 1504 families of the sample.

the advertising effect than a simple linear approximation. For this reason, changes over time in the numerical values of the coefficients do not represent necessarily changes in basic structure, since such changes may well be systematic. As will be shown in Sec. 4.3 and Chapter 8, refining the structural equation by a better choice of variables will often suffice, whereas at first sight radical changes in structure may have been expected.

Much of the material discussed in the foregoing, as well as the present subsection, may appear to be just a question of definition. Its importance lies, however, in the fact that forecasts as a basis for policy decisions require constancy of at least some aspects of the economy or the market. From the research worker's point of view, it is wiser to admit the inadequacy of a former structural hypothesis and to look for a better one than to allow himself to be submerged in a sea of ever-continuing structural change. As a matter of fact, assuming that the variability of the structural coefficients is unsystematic *per se* implies renunciation of a scientific approach.[9]

Like other research, a major goal of economic research and market analysis is, therefore, to ascertain what relationships tend to be stable and sufficiently trustworthy to serve as a starting point for further analysis and for prediction.

4.1.5. Two Basic Approaches

As has been suggested by the foregoing, the structure of an economy or market can be approached in two different ways. One possibility is to infer certain properties from a variable observed at a given moment. The second implies the study of the development of a variable over time. The aim of the next two sections is to investigate what relationships of a sufficiently stable nature are to be found with either method.

Elements of observation with the first method are individual, or groups of, units (households, firms, etc.) at a certain *point* of time. With this method, *cross-section analysis*, the relationships to be established refer to systematic differences in the attributes at one point of time between the individual elements of the same universe, such as between different households belonging to a certain group.

With the second method, *time-series analysis*, the comparison covers changes over time in the attributes of the group as a whole. Elements of observation are in this case the successive points of time (or time intervals), such as the individual years in the period, 1929–1959.

It should be noted that, although the relationship derived by either approach may refer to the same attributes, e.g., expenditures on rent as a function of disposable income, the interpretation of these two relations is not necessarily the same. Thus, if cross-section analysis shows that within the same group people with a 10 per cent higher income pay on the average 7 per cent more for rent, it does not follow that, if real national income from one year to the next increases by 10 per cent, deflated average rents paid per household will have to increase by 7 per cent, as in the case of the cross-section. In the time series case, one would assume at least a certain time lag before people adapt to their higher level of income. Apart from this, prefer-

---

[9] See, e.g., J. TINBERGEN, *Econometrics* (London, 1951), p. 205.

ence for more expensive dwellings, as is typical of the higher income brackets, may be due not only to greater purchasing power, but also to certain other factors, such as family size, age, and occupation, that are systematically related to income. But since these factors do not change with income over time in the same systematic fashion, the rent-income relationship as yielded by cross-section analysis can be misleading if applied to changes over time.[10] Consequently, although sub-groups such as different occupations may have the same income elasticity for a certain product, the aggregate elasticity for the group as a whole might be essentially different from the elasticity as derived for either of the two groups separately.

Nevertheless, the cross-section elasticity remains valid, provided its application is restricted to a comparison of the expenditure of members of the same group at a certain point of time. Even without further corrections for difference in sex and other factors, it will prove a useful yardstick in many cases.

For these reasons, which of these two approaches to select in a given situation depends upon the type of relationship desired. However, a complete insight into the structure of the economy or of a particular market requires a knowledge of both types of approaches. Then again, many problems can be solved only by a combination of these two approaches.[11]

The bulk of this chapter is devoted to a discussion of different types of analyses that can be carried out under each approach and to ways and means of facilitating such analyses. The discussion is largely in terms of investigating market structure, which is generally the immediate, if not the principal, objective of such studies. However, much of the material is equally pertinent to problems of diagnosis and prognosis for, as noted in Chapter 1, knowledge of market structure is generally a prerequisite to study of the other two types of problems, and in practice the distinctions between the various stages often become highly tenuous.

Besides these two basic approaches, the subject of "management sciences" is also discussed in this chapter. This subject is essentially a collection of rather specialized problem-solving techniques derived from applied mathematics and from the physical as well as social sciences. Since the observations underlying such studies are derived either from cross-section or time-series data, or perhaps from a combination of both, the results should be interpreted accordingly. For this reason, it would seem appropriate to discuss this subject in this chapter together with the two basic approaches just mentioned.

---

[10] See T. Haavelmo, "Family Expenditures and the Marginal Propensity to Consume," *Econometrica*, Oct. 1947, pp. 335–342, particularly Section 4.

[11] For a good example where both approaches are used simultaneously, see Ruth P. Mack, "Factors Influencing Consumption: An Experimental Analysis of Shoe Buying," New York: National Bureau of Economic Research, Technical Paper No. 10, 1954.

4.2. CROSS-SECTION ANALYSIS

A cross-section analysis studies a particular state of affairs at one moment of time, in order to get a detailed picture of market conditions existing at that moment. The moment of time may be a day, a week, a month, a year or any other convenient interval. The appropriate interval is generally dictated by the nature of the problem, especially when secondary data are used. In some instances, the period may be as short as a quarter or half an hour, like a profile of the TV audience of a particular program, while in other cases the period may be as long as a decade, as in comparing decade averages for capital expenditures with that of total assets of leading corporations. About the only general rule is that the time unit used be suitable for providing the necessary information. A 15-minute profile of the audience of a one-hour program may not provide a representative picture of audience composition. The time interval has to fit the purpose of the study.

Most cross-section studies are carried out with one or more of the following three objectives in mind:

1. To obtain estimates of the size of the market, either in total or by specific components or sectors.
2. To secure information about certain other attributes of the market.
3. To evaluate the degree of competition on company or product sales.

To a large extent this last objective can be considered as a market characteristic, but because of its importance in a free-enterprise economy it is treated here as a separate major objective.

It is important to note that investigation of the other attributes often serves a different purpose than does a study of total market size and of the factors influencing size. Thus, to study what types of people invest in corporate stock is a very different question from the total *amounts* invested by individuals in corporate stock.

Similarly, the subject of so-called "motivation research" (discussed in Sec. 6.5) of determining why people behave as they do, is concerned with market characteristics, not with aggregate amounts.

General methods of approach to each of these three objectives will be discussed in the remainder of this part of the chapter. Though the frame of reference is always in terms of market analysis, the bulk of the material is equally applicable to other types of economic cross-section studies.

4.2.1. Estimating Market Size

An estimate of the total size of the market for a product is generally the starting point of any systematic market study. Such an estimate not only serves as a basis and a check for obtaining breakdowns by different types of markets but also, by relating it to the corresponding industry data, throws light on market share and competitive status.

Estimates of total market size can be obtained in two ways, namely:

1. via supply
2. via demand

Means of obtaining such estimates are discussed in the following pages. Where possible, it is desirable to derive such estimates both ways though rarely is exact correspondence to be expected. This procedure gives some indication of the upper and lower limits of the size of the market as well as of the possible magnitude of errors of estimation. It also highlights weak spots both in the estimation process and in the firm's market position and in this way helps point to areas in which future research might be most usefully directed. The extra work involved is well worth the effort.

4.2.1.1.   *Types of markets.* Before considering means of estimating market size, it deserves to be stressed that markets can be classified in many ways, depending on the criterion of classification. Thus, the market for a good or service can be classified according to the nature of the product, the channels of distribution, the growth trend of sales, degree of competition, the ultimate consumer, etc. Each of these classifications is useful for a particular purpose, and most of them are covered in various parts of this book. In this part on cross-section analysis we shall concentrate on two of them—the nature of the product and the ultimate consumer—for purposes of exposition.

By nature of the product we mean essentially whether a good (or service) is (*a*) a consumer's good, produced primarily for direct sale to families and individuals; (*b*) a producer's good, produced for sale to manufacturers to assist in the production of other goods; or (*c*) a raw material, such as coal, iron ore, etc. Determining the market structure for a consumer's good is generally easier than for the other two categories inasmuch as the demand for the product is synonymous with its ultimate use. The other two types of good involve the problem of *derived demand*, brought about by the fact that the use to which that good is put depends on the demand by families and individuals for the ultimate consumer product which that good helps to manufacture. Thus, the demand for milk-bottle-manufacturing machinery depends on the demand for new milk bottles, which in turn depends on the consumption of milk by consumers.

This example is a relatively simple one. In other cases, the initial user and ultimate consumer may be much further removed, as is true generally for raw materials. In addition, many producers' goods and raw materials are used in the manufacture of more than one consumer good or are used in the manufacture of goods with more than one type of ultimate use. Thus, steel goes into the manufacture of hundreds of different products as well as consumer goods. The same is true of many raw materials. On the other hand, fertilizer is only a single product, though with numerous variations in product composition, that is used in the same form by both producers (farmers) and consumers (home owners). A thorough knowledge of market structure in such cases involves study of the demand and supply picture at each of these various stages of derived demand as well as the ultimate demand for the product(s) in their different uses.

The classification of markets by ultimate consumer is also of major importance in determining market structure for producer's goods and raw materials as well as for consumer goods, as is evident from the preceding paragraphs. It deserves to be stressed that for any particular good there is not one total market but as many "partial markets" or market segments as there are subdivisions imaginable between the users of the product or between certain characteristics of the product itself, such as price level. Particularly with regard to the ultimate consumer, the number of partial markets for a product is practically unlimited. Division of the total market is possible in all sorts of ways—geographic, income, race, sex, family size, occupation, etc.—and for each means of classification there are many different ways of constructing breakdowns. For a more comprehensive discussion, see Sec. 10.3.

When a total market, or population, is subdivided into relevant components, it is said to be *stratified*. Though used mainly in statistical sampling analysis, stratification, defined as a segmentation of the total universe into a number of strata according to varying attributes, applies equally well to economic and marketing analysis. Stratification stems from the inherent heterogeneity of the total market and is a basic consideration in any demand study. The analyst can gain a better understanding of the market structure by breaking up the total into segments, or strata, each of which is relatively homogeneous. Considerations involved in deciding the extent to which stratification should be carried are discussed in Sec. 5.4.

Stratification is also a useful tool of analysis on the supply side, particularly with regard to sources and means of production and, as we shall see shortly, consideration of both demand and supply aspects can check the accuracy of estimates of market structure.

Like so many other aspects of a research study, the market classifications employed will depend on the problem at hand, especially on a determination of which market characteristics discriminate most sharply between sales of the product to different types of users or, in the case of supply, between production of the product among different types of manufacturers or suppliers. The application of this general principle will be discussed in later sections of this and other chapters. (See especially Sec. 11.3.)

4.2.1.2. *Estimating from the supply side.* The starting point for estimating market size from the supply side is production statistics for the product. In many industries such statistics are available from a central trade association office[12] or are published periodically by such government agencies as the U. S. Department of Agriculture, U. S. Department of Commerce or the U. S. Bureau of Mines. If such statistics are not available, fairly accurate estimates can generally be made by deriving relationships between production and employment and labor productivity based on past industry data or on data for one's own company. Labor productivity changes slowly and generally in a uniform manner, while employment figures are almost always available in one way or another.

The next step is to translate the production figures into sales to the ultimate user of the product. For certain types of producers' goods, such as heavy machinery or data-processing machines, this is not too difficult because the manufacturer sells directly to the ultimate user so that production is synonymous with consumption after adjustment for inventory changes of the manufacturers and for foreign purchases or sales of the product, i.e.:

$$Production - change\ in\ inventories\ of\ mfrs + imports - exports$$
$$= Consumption \quad (4.7)$$

Import and export statistics are published monthly by the U. S. Bureau of the Census, though unfortunately not always in the detail required. There is the additional consideration that units of measurement are not always the same in foreign trade and in the domestic market, and particularly that the value of a good locally may well differ from the value placed on it for tariff purposes. Change in inventories is obtainable not directly but as the change in stocks at the beginning and at the end of the given period.

The problem becomes much more complicated when wholesalers and other middlemen enter the picture, as is true of many producers' goods and nearly all consumers' goods. Fig. 4.2 provides a diagrammatic representation of the various stages involved between production and consumption (sales) of a domestic consumer good, assuming only this one channel of distribution. The areas between the rectangles represent the sizes of the various markets at each stage. This diagram assumes no imports of the product, a net increase in manufacturers' and retailers' inventories, and a net decrease in the stocks of wholesalers. In practice, the direction of change at any level could, of course, be either way.

---

[12] A list of such associations is contained in the booklet put out by the U. S. Department of Commerce, *Directory of National Trade Associations*, which is published every few years. The latest edition at this writing is 1956.

Algebraically, the relations needed to equate production with sales to consumers are as follows:

Production − exports − change in inventories of mfrs = Sales to distributors

Sales to wholesalers ≡ Purchases by wholesalers

Purchases by wholesalers − change in wholesaler inventories
                                  = Sales to retailers   (4.8)

Sales to retailers ≡ Purchases by retailers

Purchases by retailers − change in retailer inventories = Sales to consumers

Identity signs are used in the intermediate relations in (4.8) to enable the following relations to appear in clearer fashion. Theoretically, all the relations in (4.8) should have identity symbols, though in practice the different

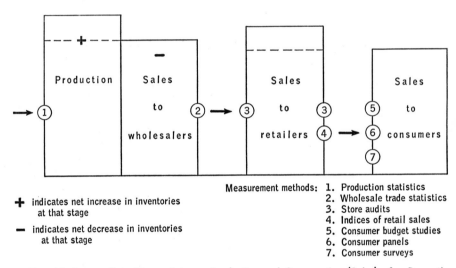

+ indicates net increase in inventories
   at that stage

− indicates net decrease in inventories
   at that stage

Measurement methods: 1. Production statistics
                                    2. Wholesale trade statistics
                                    3. Store audits
                                    4. Indices of retail sales
                                    5. Consumer budget studies
                                    6. Consumer panels
                                    7. Consumer surveys

Fig. 4.2. *Intermediate Stages Between Production and Consumption (Sales) of a Domestic Consumer Good**

data will not always correspond. Not only are there likely to be errors in the individual figures, but allowance has to be made for such factors as breakage and loss in transit at all stages as well as for differences in definition and coverage of the various sources of information.

For direct estimation purposes, (4.8) can be combined into a single equation, i.e.:

---

* Assuming only one channel of distribution.

Production + imports − exports − net change in mfrs' inventories − net change in wholesalers' inventories − net change in retailers' inventories = sales to consumers (4.9)

Data for such estimates would usually be obtained from a variety of sources, the standard ones being government statistics, trade associations (of middlemen as well as of producers), and statistics for one's own firm (particularly if it represents a substantial part of the industry production). At times, considerable ingenuity will be required, particularly in imputing data on part of an industry to the whole. The principal alternative means of estimating the market size at each stage are shown at the bottom of Fig. 4.2.

If several channels of distribution are involved in the sale of a product, relations such as (4.8) and (4.9) have to be derived for each channel. Such would be the case for a product like window glass, which is sold for construction purposes, to home owners direct, and for various miscellaneous purposes such as mirrors. On the other hand, there are products, even consumer goods, with a relatively simple channel of distribution. This is true of automobiles, for example, where the factories sell to dealers who deal direct with the public.

4.2.1.3. *Estimating from the demand side.* The effective demand for a product can be estimated either by attempting to arrive at an aggregate directly or by obtaining components of the aggregate in various ways and building up the aggregate from these components. The principal means of obtaining aggregate demand estimates directly consist of sample surveys of users or potential users of the product, surveys of informed company personnel, including perhaps outside consultants, and study of recent sales and consumption trends. The latter approach relates to time series and is discussed in a later section. The other two are taken up in Chapters 5 and 6 on sampling techniques. The main focus of this section therefore is on the use of components in arriving at an estimate of total effective demand, an approach that has not received too much attention in recent years.

This approach consists of estimating demand as the sum of new demand plus replacement demand. The latter is derived as the product of three factors, namely,

1. The number of demand units
2. Average use per demand unit—the number available (for durable goods) or average consumption per unit of time (for nondurables)
3. Average usable life of the good, the reciprocal of which is used in the product.

To take an example, if the roughly 50,000,000 families in the United States own an average of 1.5 radios each, with the average life of a radio being 10 years, the total replacement demand in an "average" year would be computed as:

$$50,000,000 \times 1.5 \times \frac{1}{10} = 7,500,000$$

Since this is an average figure, it is best treated more as a long-run normal than as a specific forecast for a particular year. The latter, however, can be obtained from this estimate by suitable adjustments for factors considered distinctive to that year—expected rise in incomes, age distribution of existing goods, radically new models, etc. At the same time, this average is highly useful in itself, particularly as a basis for expansion programs and other long-run planning.

In a similar way, new demand is obtained as the product of the probable number of new demand units and ownership-per-demand unit. If there is a tendency for more than one such product to be purchased per customer, overlapping of demand units between new demand and replacement demand must be considered, since a customer may be in the market to replace an old model and at the same time to buy an additional one as well.

One of the main advantages of this approach is the information it provides via the three components on the structure of demand. Thus, it throws light on the extent and concentration of ownership of the product as well as on its usable life (which for manufactured goods especially does not often correspond with physical life). The dispersion of demand units by these various factors is of particular value, and such data are often obtained as a by-product of this approach.

In practice, the derivation of each component is likely to be a problem in itself, and the estimation procedures used for a single product may differ substantially from one component to another. We therefore turn to a consideration of means of estimating each component separately.

NUMBER OF DEMAND UNITS. The determination of a demand unit for a product depends on two main requirements:

1. It must be suitable as a basis for estimating sales, or average use per unit.
2. The total number of demand units should be ascertainable as simply as possible.

Essentially, the principal determinant is the nature of the available data. This is particularly true of many consumer goods for which the demand unit can reasonably be argued to be any of a number of possibilities—the family, the household, the spending unit, or the individual. TV sets are a case in point—some are bought for household use (console models), while others are bought for individual use (portables). In such cases, if data are available for one unit but not for the other, the choice of a demand unit is clear.

Where possible, the nature of the ultimate consumer will dictate the choice —such as individuals in the case of clothes and jewelry, and families in the case of homes and cars. In some instances, where the product is a very large item not many of which are likely to be needed or produced in a year, the demand unit may be taken as the product itself. Such might be the case, for example, with ships. Effective demand would then be determined as the product of the number of ships and their average life. With most other types of goods, however, the demand unit should be chosen to coincide as closely as possible with the ultimate consumer. Thus, the demand unit for men's clothing should be men (not all consumers); the demand unit for home air-conditioning systems should be households; etc. On the other hand, the demand unit for automobile tires might well be the number of automobiles in use, perhaps even car-miles, for consumption of tires depends almost entirely on the number and rate of use of automobiles.

AVERAGE USE PER USER. The usual source of information on the use per demand unit for consumer goods is survey data. Cost-of-living surveys are conducted periodically by the U. S. Bureau of Labor Statistics; farm management studies are made by the U. S. Department of Agriculture and by various state agencies; and in addition there is the host of studies of the consumption of individual products carried out by individual firms, trade associations, and private publications. For certain types of durable goods, such as homes, housing facilities, cars, and some large appliances, ownership data are obtainable from the decennial U. S. Census of Housing. Though these data unfortunately may be somewhat out of date by the time of publication, they may nevertheless prove useful for purposes of weighting and extrapolation.

In some instances, the necessary data will not be available from secondary sources, and a special survey would then have to be undertaken. In such cases, as well as in others, it is important to allow for any dispersion in ownership that may exist among different population groups. If such variation does exist, stratification is indicated among the population groups as well as in the sample design. Ideally, each such population group would constitute a separate market with a separate set of estimates of effective demand derived for each market, the extent of separation dictated by what is needed to render each group homogeneous with only random, or erratic, variations in ownership remaining within the group as well as by the availability of data on the relative sizes of the different strata. In actual practice, however, only a breakdown by the two or three most important criteria is likely to be feasible, for beyond this point the extra costs involved are usually not offset by the gains from further stratification.

With regard to *producers' goods and raw materials*, the estimation of average use is more difficult because:

1. Most such products are used in a variety of final products.
2. In some cases their use is determined by the final product, e.g., textile machinery, and in other cases by the function performed, e.g., coal.

Stratification is particularly important for such goods with regard to both the different uses of the product and the variation in size of the firms utilizing the product in each use. The former stratification is the basis for distinguishing between the different markets for the product, a distinction that can be made according to either the technical uses of a product (such as the different types of machines run by electric motors) or the economic structure of the using industries (for electric motors it might be farm machinery, auto industry, machine tool industry, etc.). Distinction by economic structure is likely to be more amenable to market analysis because of the more data available on this basis. However, a fair amount of data by type of use is currently obtainable in the U. S. Census of Manufactures.

Variation in size of user is generally a major criterion for stratification in conducting a survey to obtain accurate ownership or use data. Where much

Table 4.1

TECHNICAL COEFFICIENTS FOR MATERIALS CONSUMED BY
AUTOMOBILE INDUSTRY, 1958

Materials	Auto consumption (000)	Usage per vehicle (Est. of technical coefficient)[d]
Steel (tons)		
Strip	562	.11
Bar	1,651	.32
Sheet	6,705	1.31
Alloy (other than stainless)	1,043	.20
Stainless	68	.013
All forms	10,125	1.97
Malleable iron (tons)	320	.062
Copper (tons)	96[a]	.023[e]
Lead (short tons)	418[b]	.081
Zinc (tons)	250	.049
Nickel (pounds)	2,609	.51
Rubber (long tons)		
Natural	302[c]	.059
Synthetic	559[c]	.11
Reclaimed	135[c]	.026
Upholstery leather (square feet)	26,700	5.20
Cotton (478 pound bales)	190	.037

[a] New passenger cars.

[b] Includes amount used in tetraethyl lead and in replacement batteries.

[c] Excludes mechanical rubber goods such as rubber weather stripping, grommets, and motor mounts used in automobiles.

[d] Estimated by dividing total consumption by total vehicle production—5,135,000.

[e] Estimated by dividing total consumption by total new passenger car production—4,258,000.

Source: *Automobile Facts and Figures, 1959–60*, p. 60.

variation in size exists, as is invariably the case, such data also serve the highly useful purpose of throwing light on the extent of concentration of ownership or use.

With a raw material, effective demand depends on the demand for the various end uses of that material. There is then a whole series of special markets, one for each end-use, the demand unit in each case being the end-use product. Hence, estimates are required of the amount of that raw material going into each product—the so-called technical coefficients. Such data are generally available for individual products, as shown in Table 4.1 for automobiles, and the problem becomes one of culling these different sources and reconciling them with one another. However, care has to be exercised in equating different units of measurement, especially when foreign trade statistics are used.

The computation of technical coefficients is shown in Table 4.1. The estimates shown in this table are very rough, are applicable to 1958, and make no allowance for differences in the amounts of materials used in different type cars. They do, however, illustrate the general concept, and it is figures such as these that are then applied to estimates of other levels of production. Where data are not available, as is often true for various minor uses of a raw material, estimates can generally be made with regression techniques, such as by relating amounts sold for such uses in past years to amounts sold for all other purposes.

AVERAGE USABLE LIFE. Breakage, deterioration and obsolescence have to be taken into account in estimating the average usable life of a product. Considering the difficulty of making separate allowances for each of these factors, average usable life is invariably estimated in a more direct manner.[13] Perhaps the easiest way of doing so, if the necessary data are available, is to calculate the ratio of items in use to sales. This provides an accurate estimate of average usable life, however, only if there is no trend in sales, for it can easily be shown that the estimate will be biased downward if sales are rising and will be biased upward if sales are declining.

A more reliable as well as more informative approach is the construction of mortality, or survivor, curves on the basis of records of the product, sample surveys, or observation. Table 4.2 presents mortality data for tumblers as compiled from records kept in a drugstore, which provide a basis not only for computing average life of the product but also various other useful data. Thus, column 2 of the table shows how many tumblers may be expected to survive a given number of weeks, column 4 the extent to which one particular cause (breakage) accounts for mortality, and column 5 the average life of tumblers surviving a given time.

---

[13] It is perhaps needless to note that this problem is not pertinent to a product that does not last longer than the time unit under consideration, generally a year, or to a raw material, which is generally physically consumed when used.

Table 4.2

MORTALITY TABLE FOR TUMBLERS

(1) Weeks	(2) Survivors	(3) Breakage	(4) Mortality chance (Breakage in pct. of survivors)	(5) Average life of survivors (In weeks)
1– 2	1,000	112	0.112	8.8
3– 4	888	168	0.189	7.8
5– 6	720	149	0.131	7.4
7– 8	571	137	0.240	7.0
9–10	434	90	0.207	6.9
11–12	344	80	0.233	6.5
13–14	264	58	0.220	6.2
15–16	206	65	0.316	5.6
17–18	141	33	0.234	5.8
19–20	108	37	0.343	5.2
21–25	71	39	0.549	5.4
26–30	32	23	0.719	3.0
31–35	9	9	—	—

Source: Brown and Flood, "Tumbler Mortality," *Journal of the American Statistical Association*, December, 1947, p. 566.

The survivorship data in column 2 provide the basis for estimating average life as well as for plotting a "survivor curve" for the products. Curves for tumblers and for three other products are shown in Fig. 4.3. The steeper the middle sections of these curves, the more concentrated replacement demand will be.

Fig. 4.3. Survivor Curves for Selected Products

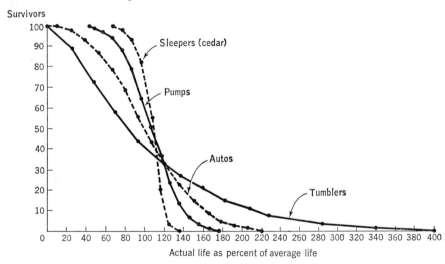

Source: Tumblers: Table 4.2. Others: Kurtz, *Life Expectancy of Physical Property* (N. Y.: McGraw-Hill Book Co., 1930).

Table 4.3

LIFE TABLE FOR CURTAINS AND DRAPERIES IN THE LIVING ROOM

(Based on 197 households in the Wilmington, Del., urbanized area, 1954)

(1) Age in years[a]	(2) Units[b] in inventory	(3) Units[b] removed	(4) Units[b] exposed to risk of removal	(5) Removal rate	(6) Survival rate
0	205	0	205	0	1.0000
1	154	24	178	.1348	.8652
2	102	16	118	.1356	.8644
3	105	20	125	.1600	.8400
4	65	10	75	.1333	.8667
5	21	2	23	.0870	.9130
6	49	10	59	.1695	.8305
7	22	12	34	.3529	.6471
8	12	0	12	0	1.0000
9	10	0	10	0	1.0000
10	4	4	8	.5000	.5000
11	0	0	0	(c)	(c)
12	0	0	0	(c)	(c)
13	2	0	2	0	1.0000
14	1	4	5	.8000	.2000
15	3	0	3	0	1.0000
16	4	0	4	0	1.0000
17	6	0	6	0	1.0000
18	0	0	0	(c)	(c)
19	4	0	4	0	1.0000
20	0	0	0	(c)	(c)
21	0	0	0	(c)	(c)
22	0	0	0	(c)	(c)
23	0	0	0	(c)	(c)
24	4	0	4	0	1.0000
25	0	4	4	1.0000	0
26	0	0	0	0	0

[a] All items assumed to have been acquired on January 1 of the year of acquisition.
[b] Number of curtain and drapery panels in sample households.
[c] When there are no inventory and no removal, the removal rate is indeterminate. For this model a survival rate of 1 was assumed, which yields a maximum figure. If a survival rate of 0 had been assumed, the mean service-life expectancy would have been 6.1 instead of 6.8 years, a decrease of 10 per cent. If the data had been smoothed, the estimate would fall between these extremes.

Source: J. L. PENNOCK and C. M. JAEGER, "Estimating the Service Life of Household Goods by Actuarial Methods," *Journal of the American Statistical Association*, June, 1957, p. 178.

Such actuarial curves are obtainable in two general ways. One approach is through observation of a group of items put into use at the same time, recording the length of life of each item, unless complete records are available, as in the case of railroad cars. This can be highly accurate but is a very slow process. For consumer goods the method is likely to be impractical if the life span is several years because of the difficulty of keeping track of individual items. The second approach is quicker and more economical. It merely involves asking a sample of users of the product the length of time it has been in use and, if discarded, the age of the item at that time. The manner in which these data are used to derive a survival curve is illustrated in Table 4.3. Unfortunately, this approach is also not without disadvantages, the principal ones being systematic changes in quality, bias in the replies of the respondents on the age of particular items, and a tendency to forget altogether about items no longer in use.[14]

It should be emphasized that average life estimates, particularly of durable goods, are applicable in a normative sense only, being subject to sharp cyclical variations. For short-run forecasting, therefore, these estimates would have to be adjusted for cyclical factors, which is possible if time series are available on average life and business activity in the industry.

4.2.2. Market Characteristics and Partial Markets: Income

Qualitative as well as quantitative factors are involved in the determination of market characteristics. Though the concern is no longer with market size as such, quantitative factors enter, nevertheless, the aim now being to ascertain the characteristics and dispersion, or degree of concentration, of the market for a product. At the same time, qualitative considerations become of major importance both in terms of the product as well as the user. In effect, the total market for a product is subdivided into various partial markets, and attempts are made to assess the dispersion of the users in each. The basis for setting up these partial markets is such factors as occupation, sex, family size, region, city size, and social class, not to omit the quality and other distinctive characteristics of the product itself (such as brand, price, year produced, etc.). When dealing with these partial markets, it is sometimes useful to treat such essentially quantitative criteria as age and income in a qualitative fashion by the use of class limits. Although stratification might have been effected by a continuous variable, partial markets can then be considered qualitatively distinct, as in the case of one market for the lower and another for the higher income brackets.

The data for such analyses are generally obtained from sample surveys, either survey data obtained from secondary sources or from surveys carried out specifically to provide the necessary data. Since general survey techniques are the subject of the next chapter, we shall restrict the discussion in this section to a few analytical tools of use in determining market characteristics.

  4.2.2.1. *Gross and net effects.* If 80 per cent of spending units in the Northeastern part of the United States own life insurance as against 71 per

---

[14] For a good discussion of the various problems involved in using this method, see J. L. PENNOCK and C. M. JAEGER, "Estimating the Service Life of Household Goods by Actuarial Methods," *Journal of the American Statistical Association*, June, 1957, pp. 175–185.

cent in the South, does this mean that region accounts for a 9 percentage point differential in life insurance ownership? Probably not, for this differential reflects the *gross* effect of region—the effect before taking into account differences in the characteristics of the spending units living in these regions. Thus, if the distribution of income differs in the two regions, as is true, and if life insurance coverage varies by income level, as is also true, the observed regional difference may be entirely explained by income so that the *net* effect of region on life insurance coverage in this case is zero.

This distinction between net and gross effects is the same as the difference between partial and simple regressions. The net effect, like the partial regression coefficient, is the *ceteris paribus* assumption in economics: it serves to eliminate from the relation under study the interfering effects of other variables included in the analysis.

Table 4.4

INTERACTION EFFECT OF INCOME ON LIFE INSURANCE COVERAGE BY REGION

(1) *Income level*	(2) PER CENT OF SPENDING UNITS IN EACH GROUP *Northeast*	(3) *South*	(4) *Assumed per cent of spending units covered by life insurance in each group*[a]
Under $1,000	6%	24%	46%
$1,000–1,999	15	18	60
2,000–2,999	19	18	76
3,000–3,999	21	15	85
4,000–4,999	17	10	91
5,000–7,499	16	9	93
7,500 or more	6	6	93
TOTAL	100%	100%	

Average coverage in Northeast (Col. 2 × Col. 4) = 80%
Average coverage in South (Col. 3 × Col. 4)   = 71%
[a] Same coverage by income level assumed in each region.
Source: Adapted from *Life Insurance Ownership Among American Families, 1952,* University of Michigan, Survey Research Center, 1953, pp. 8, 11.

Table 4.4 illustrates the manner in which interacting variables can produce an apparent effect when in reality none may exist. In this case, variation in income distribution by region, combined with a relation between income level and life insurance holdings, leads to a 9 per cent differential in overall life insurance coverage by region, shown at the bottom of the table.

This table also suggests one approach to ascertaining the influence of a particular factor, namely:

1. Determine the relationship between the subject under study and other relevant factors (in this case, life insurance coverage to income level).

2. Ascertain if the distribution of the population by these other relevant factors changes as the first factor varies (in this case, how income distribution varies by region).

If no relationship exists in *either* case, the gross effect may then also be the net effect. Thus, if life insurance coverage were independent of income level and other supposed relevant factors, *or*, if the distribution of income and of these other relevant factors were the same in the two regions, the net effect of region would be the same as the gross effect. If relationships hold in both cases, as is true in Table 4.4, part of the apparent effect due to the first factor is only a gross effect. This becomes apparent from cross-tabulations of the relevant factors, as is done in Table 4.4.

The present example is a highly simplified one since all the measured effect is seen to be attributable to a single factor. In most practical problems. several other factors may be involved and the gross effect of one is attributable in part to each of these other factors and in part to a net effect of its own. Again, however, the approach is the same as above, through the use of cross-tabulations. Precise estimates of the net effect due to each of a number of different factors can be obtained through the application of regression methods in conjunction with variance analysis.[15]

4.2.2.2. *The elasticity concept.* The elasticity of demand or supply with respect to various influencing factors is one of the most useful tools of economic analysis both in cross-section and in time-series studies. This is due in part to its abstraction from units of measurement, which renders such measures comparable as between different commodities, and in part to the tendency for economic relationships to be independent of units of measurement and be more valid in terms of percentage changes than in terms of absolute amounts. This is particularly true when changes over time are involved, which may lead to substantial differences in level though to little change in the basic relationship.

The derivation of elasticity estimates from cross-section data will be illustrated with reference to the income elasticity of family recreation expenditures. This elasticity is defined as the percentage difference in expenditures associated with a one per cent difference in income, or in a more operational sense as:[16]

$$\epsilon = \frac{Percentage\ change\ in\ expenditure}{Percentage\ change\ in\ income}$$

---

[15] For one example of the technique, see M. E. KREININ, J. B. LANSING, and J. N. MORGAN, "Analysis of Life Insurance Premiums," *Review of Economics and Statistics,* Vol. 39, No. 1, February, 1957, pp. 46–54.

[16] Properly stated, the denominator should be an infinitesimal, percentage, or change in income, since the elasticity is not necessarily constant over the whole range of the expenditure curve.

This income elasticity can refer to consumption expressed either in volume or in money units. Using cross-section data, estimates of its numerical value are possible in at least two ways. The first involves fitting a regression line between expenditures and income, and then estimating the elasticity from the parameters of this line. As noted in Chapter 3, if the regression is logarithmic, i.e.,

$$C = aY^b \tag{4.10}$$

then the exponent of Y is the income elasticity. The proof follows from the algebraic definition of income elasticity, which is:

$$\epsilon = \frac{\dfrac{dC}{C}}{\dfrac{dY}{Y}} = \frac{dC}{dY} \times \frac{Y}{C} \tag{4.11}$$

Differentiating (4.10) and substituting in (4.11)

$$\epsilon = \frac{abY^{b-1}}{aY^b} \times Y = b \tag{4.12}$$

By the same procedure the income elasticity can be obtained for any regression form, though only for equations of the type as (4.10) will the elasticity be the same for all values of Y. This constancy property is very convenient, but it is not an unmixed blessing if the response of consumption expenditures to a given relative change in income varies with the level of income, as is generally true if a broad range of incomes is considered. A general form for the consumption function or "Engel curve" is suggested by Fig. 4.4. The mathematical function applied there is the so-called sigmoid curve that closely resembles the logistic. This particular curve appears to fit equally well the case of almost saturated demand and the case where less urgent needs are concerned. If this type of curve were to be generally valid, as probably might be true where the money expenditures of homogeneous social groups on large categories of products are studied, the important inference is that the income elasticity is higher for the low income brackets than for the higher ones, and the reverse, that it declines when the level of income increases.[17] When applied to one specific product, many exceptions to this general rule are, however, to be expected. This holds particularly in those cases where consumption is measured in volume terms and where, next to income, other factors such as family size, profession, etc., play a dominant role.[18]

---

[17] J. AITCHISON and J. A. C. BROWN, "A Synthesis of Engel Curve Theory," *The Review of Economic Studies*, 1954–55, pp. 38–39.

[18] See for detailed tabulations of the income elasticities per income class, for instance, *Income and Household Size, Their Effects on Food Consumption*, Market Research Report No. 340, U. S. Department of Agriculture (Washington, D. C.: U. S. Gov. Printing Office, June 1959), pp. 8–16, Tables 2 and 3.

Expenditure per person on individual economy (£)

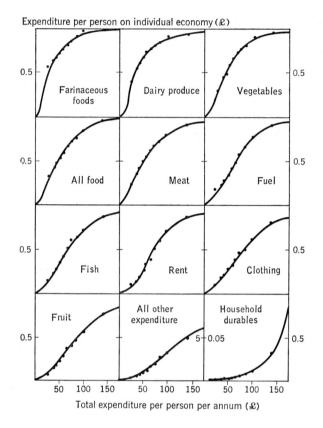

Fig. 4.4. *Relation Between Money Expenditure and Income, for Different Products, United Kingdom, 1937–38* [*]

Source: J. Aitchison and J. A. C. Brown, "A Synthesis of Engel Curve Theory," *Review of Economic Studies*, 1954–55, p. 41.

Total expenditure per person per annum (£)

Alternately, the income elasticity could be estimated directly from the pertinent frequency distributions without recourse to regression techniques. This is easily done through the use of the following approximation of (4.11):

$$\epsilon = \frac{\bar{C}_2 - \bar{C}_1}{(\bar{C}_2 + \bar{C}_1)/2} \Bigg/ \frac{\bar{Y}_2 - \bar{Y}_1}{(\bar{Y}_2 + \bar{Y}_1)/2} \tag{4.13a}$$

where the subscripts 1 and 2 indicate neighboring class intervals and the bars denote averages.

The use of (4.13) to compute the income elasticity of consumer expenditures on recreation is illustrated in Table 4.5. It is seen from column 6 of this table that recreation expenditures in 1950 were most sensitive to a rise in income between the $2,000 and $5,000 income levels. Below the $1,000 level, very little money was available for recreation after living expenses had been paid; in this range a 10 per cent rise in income led to an increase of only 4 per cent in recreation outlays. As soon as income is large enough to take care of bare necessities, a sharp rise in recreation expenditures takes place; here recreation expenditures are "elastic," since a proportionate increase in income produces on the average a more than proportionate rise in these expenditures. Between the $5,000 and $10,000 income levels the relative increase in recreation outlays declines somewhat, though the elasticity turns upward again in the higher income levels. At the same time, it should be noted that income elasticities of such items as tobacco, alcoholic beverages, and recreation tend to be uniformly underestimated in family budget studies. (Why?)

Table 4.5
CALCULATION OF INCOME ELASTICITIES OF FAMILY RECREATION EXPENDITURES IN LARGE CITIES IN THE NORTHERN U. S., 1950

(1)	(2)	(3)	(4)	(5)	(6)
		Average	AVERAGE PER CENT		*Income*
	Average	*income*	INCREASE IN		*elasticity*
Income level	*expenditure*	*after taxes*	*Consumption*	*Income*[a]	*(4)/(5)*
Under $1,000	$ 30	$ 601	35.6%	87.6%	.41
$1,000–1,999	43	1,538	79.7	49.6	1.61
2,000–2,999	100	2,552	47.9	30.6	1.57
3,000–3,999	163	3,475	36.2	25.0	1.45
4,000–4,999	235	4,468	12.0	19.7	.61
5,000–5,999	265	5,447	19.4	19.6	.99
6,000–7,499	322	6,630	8.0	23.0	.35
7,500–9,999	349	8,350	56.2	68.5	.82
10,000 and over	622	17,055	—	—	—

[a] Based on general formula: $\dfrac{x_2 - x_1}{(x_2 + x_1)/2}$

Source: U. S. Bureau of Labor Statistics and Wharton School, University of Pennsylvania, *Study of Consumer Expenditures, Incomes and Savings, Statistical Tables, Urban U. S.—1950*, Vol. IX, p. 10.

Income elasticities are often interpreted as indicating whether a certain product is a luxury or a bare necessity. The reasoning is that if the income elasticity of a product is between zero and one—inelastic—demand changes less than proportionately as income varies, thus indicating that a certain amount is probably needed by the family largely irrespective of income. On the other hand, an elasticity greater than one indicates that demand rises more than proportionately as income increases, and hence the product is a luxury item. A negative elasticity generally denotes an "inferior" good—it is being replaced by other goods as income rises.

The weakness of this generalization is evident; namely, a product can be a luxury item to one family, or group of families, and a necessity to others. Even in the case of such a supposedly clear luxury category as recreation expenditures, sharp differences in elasticity are evident, and this makes no allowance for even sharper differences that may exist between individual families.[19]

From an analytical point of view, a more valid use of income elasticity is as an index of demand, or market, saturation with respect to the commodity under study. Thus, income elasticities might serve as a useful tool in estimating sales potentials of different markets, such as in determining sales quotas for different areas. However, as indicated earlier, cross-section coefficients can not always be used for extrapolation over time. Although they may prove valuable for evaluating the long-term net effect of income changes, they are not always representative of dynamic short-term changes.

Income elasticities refer either to the value or the volume of a commodity bought. The difference between the two can be considerable, due to differences in quality preference between different income brackets. Apart from this, the percentage of effective users may differ with income. The exact relationship between these elasticities can be expressed as follows:

$$\epsilon_{Vy} = \epsilon_{\bar{v}y} + \epsilon_{xy} + \epsilon_{py}$$

and:

$$\epsilon_{vy} = \epsilon_{\bar{v}y} + \epsilon_{xy} \qquad (4.13b)$$

hence:

$$\epsilon_{Vy} = \epsilon_{vy} + \epsilon_{py}$$

where V = total dollar sales per income interval
v = total volume of sales per interval
$\bar{v}$ = average volume sold per effective user
x = percentage of effective users per interval
p = average price paid
y = income

The relationship between these different elasticities may prove useful in directing promotional effort and product policies. Thus, if:

$\epsilon_{\bar{v}y}$ is low, but ϵ_{xy} is high, non-users may probably be more easily persuaded to become users than in other cases.

$\epsilon_{\bar{v}y}$ is high, but ϵ_{xy} is low, emphasis should be laid upon increasing sales per customer.

ϵ_{py} is high, the qualitative features of the higher priced items of the product line should be emphasized, or quality itself might prove an efficient instrument.

To illustrate the latitude for change in emphasis on promotional effort for different products, Table 4.6 presents estimates of the four elasticities for a number of products. In practice, the required data are best obtained by means of a consumer panel.

---

[19] For a more reasonable approach to this problem, based on the theory of opportunity cost, see R H. HOLTON, "The Distinction Between Convenience Goods, Shopping Goods, and Specialty Goods," *Journal of Marketing*, July, 1958, pp. 53–56.

Though not as common, coefficients expressing the influence of many other variates besides income, particularly age and family size, can also be computed.

4.2.2.3. *Marginal distribution analysis.* The elasticity measure is useful as an indicator of individual reactions. However, it provides little idea of aggregate impact on expenditures of changes in, say, income, because no allowance is made for the different number of families nor for the existing expenditure level at each level of income. Hence, from an aggregative point of view an increase in total outlays for a good at a level of income characterized by high income elasticity may be considerably less than the increase in

Table 4.6

INCOME ELASTICITIES OF VARIOUS MARKET CHARACTERISTICS FOR SELECTED PRODUCTS, NETHERLANDS, 1935–36

	ELASTICITIES WITH RESPECT TO INCOME OF			
Product	Average money sales[a]	Average sales per effective user[a,c]	Per cent of effective users[b,c]	Average price paid[b]
Women's dresses	1.75	.47	.51	.78
Men's shirts	1.07	.33	.21	.53
Women's stockings	.67	.36	.05	.27
Marmalade	.56	.36	.09	.10
Potatoes	− .12	− .28	—	.16

[a] Elasticities derived from the formula: $\log V$ (or: $\log \bar{v}$) $= \alpha + \beta \log Y$
[b] Elasticities derived from the formula: x (or p) $= \alpha + \beta \log Y$
[c] "Effective user" is defined as a household buying at least one item during the twelve months covered by the sample period.

expenditures brought about by a rise in incomes at a low income-elasticity level.

A measure of this aggregate impact can be obtained with the aid of so-called marginal distribution coefficients. These can be defined as the relative additional sales which can be expected at each income level if every demand unit increased its expenditures to those of the average demand unit at an income level one per cent higher. In computational terms these coefficients are obtained at each income level as the product of the number of demand units, average expenditures per unit, and income elasticity, the results totaled and converted to a base of 100 per cent.

The procedure is illustrated for recreation expenditures in Table 4.7. This table brings out strikingly the difference between the elasticity concept and marginal distribution analysis. It shows that the income category with the highest elasticity would, if incomes rose uniformly, account for less than 5 per cent of the total increase in expenditures, whereas the even smaller group of households within the $5,000–$5,999 bracket with an elasticity of only .99 would account for almost 15 per cent. From an aggregate point of view, the $3,000–$5,000 bracket would clearly be the most important in the event of a rise in incomes, accounting for more than one-third of the overall rise in recreation expenditures.

The assumption of uniform increase in incomes is at times not too realistic and is a weakness of the approach followed in Table 4.7, particularly if the class intervals are rather broad. However, it is possible to alter this approach to correct for this weakness, simply by postulating different increases in incomes at each level.

Table 4.7

MARGINAL DISTRIBUTION COEFFICIENTS FOR RECREATION EXPENDITURES

(1)	(2)	(3)	(4)	(5)	(6)	(7)
Income level	Est. number of families in population (000)	Ave. exp. per family	Total exp. (000)	Income elasticity	Marginal demand (000)	Marginal dist. coeff.
Under $1,000	500	$ 30	$ 15,000	.41	$ 6,150	.3%
$1,000–1,999	1,200	43	51,600	1.61	83,076	4.7
2,000–2,999	1,900	100	190,000	1.57	298,300	16.9
3,000–3,999	2,500	163	407,500	1.45	590,875	33.5
4,000–4,999	1,800	235	423,000	.61	258,030	14.6
5,000–5,999	1,000	265	265,000	.99	262,350	14.9
6,000–7,499	600	322	193,200	.35	67,620	3.8
7,500–9,999	300	349	104,700	.82	85,854	4.9
10,000 and over	200	622	124,400	.90[a]	111,960	6.4
TOTAL	10,000		$1,774,400		$1,764,215	100.0%

[a] Estimated.

Source: Number of families in population—rough estimates of authors. Other data–Table 4.5.

The last column of Table 4.7 also allows for another interpretation. Since income elasticities are narrowly related to the degree of saturation, income brackets with high elasticities are also income brackets where demand is still relatively unsaturated and where people, as soon as the opportunity presents itself, are willing to expand consumption of the product studied at a greater rate than in the low-elasticity brackets. If the high-elasticity brackets also contain a relatively large number of households, this combination might under certain circumstances serve as a guide for promotional effort and product-line policies.

Another shortcoming of this approach and of income elasticities as here computed is omission of the influence of a multitude of other relevant factors, so that the results obtained are gross effects rather than net effects. Correction for these other factors is possible, but only after extensive analysis based on cross-tabulations.

4.2.3. Prices and Competition

Analysis of competitive position is a continuing source of study in a
dynamic economy, and for good reason. Solely to maintain market position
requires constant study of the effect of changes in prices and in competitive
practices on sales of one's own product, not to mention the possible inroads
that other industries might make. Competition has to be gauged not only in
terms of other companies producing the same or similar products, but also in
terms of competition between industries for the consumer dollar. Thus,
increased purchases of durable goods can mean less sales for non-durable
goods producers, and a rash of technological innovations can lead to increased
total expenditures, with concomitant effects on the banking industry in the
form of a sharp decline in time deposits.

A systematic analysis of competition has to include the effects of three
broad forces with respect to one's own and to competitive products—price
differentials, quality differentials, and differences in promotional techniques.

In effect, such differences as price and quality serve as the basis for distinguishing a whole set of partial markets from the product side. From a
marketing point of view, partial markets set up on this basis of classification
are of major importance because of the strategic role of price and quality as
competitive weapons. Not only is it important to ascertain the relationship
between price and quality—for clearly, to a certain extent, one can substitute
for the other—but it is also important to be able to anticipate the effect on
sales of changes in competitive price as well as of changes in one's own price.
In the latter sense the elasticity concept proves highly useful once again, for
by relating sales or expenditures to price and other relevant variables, the
elasticity of sales with respect to price can be ascertained at different price
levels. Since this is generally done with the aid of observations over time, a
discussion of various forms of price elasticities is postponed to the next section. It is worth noting, however, that cross-section data can also be used to
secure elasticity estimates, at times avoiding the difficulty encountered in
time-series data of very high intercorrelation between fluctuations in price
and fluctuations in income.

In the cross-section approach, one of these variables is held constant while
the other varies. A dummy form for doing so is shown in Table 4.8 holding
price constant. For each level of price, the relationship between sales and
income can be determined graphically or algebraically. Similarly, price-
expenditure data could be collected for observations with much the same
income, and price-elasticity estimates obtained.

With aggregates, however, as for geographic areas, differences in income
distributions among areas may produce faulty estimates. Obtaining the data
may also constitute a major difficulty, requiring not only special surveys but
often manipulation of prices in selected market areas as well.

From a broader social point of view, interest in this area is generally focussed on the degree of competition or monopoly in the economy. This is not the place to undertake a discussion of the pros and cons of this controversial subject,[20] but it is worth noting that a principal measure of concentration is the Lorenz Curve described in the preceding chapter. As noted there, numerical estimates of the degree of concentration can be derived as the ratio of the area under the curve described by the plotted points to the

Table 4.8

FORM FOR ESTIMATING EFFECT OF INCOME ON SALES,
BY PRICE RANKING

Price per unit	Rank number	Average income per capita	Average expenditure per capita
$.18	A1	Y1	C1
	A2	Y2	C2
	A3	Y3	C3
	A4	Y4	C4
.20	B5	Y5	C5
	B6	Y6	C6
	B7	Y7	C7
	B8	Y8	C8
	B9	Y9	C9
	.	.	.
	.	.	.
	.	.	.

area under the diagonal. By far the most difficult analytical problem in such cases is not statistical, but rather defining the scope of competition for a particular product or firm.

4.3.   TIME-SERIES ANALYSIS

This second main approach to economic and marketing analysis complements the first, focusing interest on the derivation of behavior patterns through time. As a general rule, structural research in these areas is concerned with one or more of the following five subjects:

1. Seasonal variations
2. Cyclical effects
3. Price changes
4. Long-term trends
5. Market potentials

---

[20] For such a discussion, see National Industrial Conference Board, *Economic Concentration Measures: Uses and Abuses*. Studies in Business Economics, No. 57, 1957.

Price changes are listed separately because of their central importance as an instrument of policy and hence transcend the usual fourfold time-series breakdown—seasonal, cyclical, secular, and irregular. The same policy point of view holds for market potentials, which in a book of this kind clearly deserve separate treatment. On the other hand, seasonal variations are given short shrift in this section, which is not concerned with statistical techniques for decomposing time series; that is the subject of Chapter 7. Our concern is with the type of problems encountered under each of the other four general headings listed above and the analytical techniques that are available to cope with each. It should be noted that the sharp demarcations drawn here are made primarily to facilitate the exposition; in practice, these various categories are likely to require simultaneous consideration.

4.3.1. Cyclical Effects

The business "cycle" is typified by rhythmical, though not always periodic, fluctuations in production, prices, wages and other economic indicators.[21] These fluctuations can manifest themselves on the following levels:

a) Cyclical movements for the national economy as a whole.
b) Cyclical movements in various sectors, or industries, in the economy.
c) Cyclical movements in individual firms.

The questions facing the analyst are essentially two:

1. How is activity in the particular sector or firm influenced by the cyclical position of the economy as a whole?
2. What is the best economic policy for mitigating any unfavorable effects resulting from such movements?

An answer to the second question rests heavily on the nature of the answer to the first question, which is essentially a problem in market structure. The approach involves, first, measuring cyclical movements, and second, relating those movements to the measure of activity in the relevant sector or firm.

The usual basis for gauging the extent of cyclical movements is income or production, depending on which is most suitable to the problem at hand. The Federal Reserve index of physical production is a very good overall measure of activity in manufacturing and mining industries, and hence is a desirable analytical indicator for evaluating cyclical influences on the sales of many producers' goods or raw materials. On the other hand, in the bank sector,

---

[21] For a good treatise on the theory of business fluctuations, see J. TINBERGEN and J. J. POLAK, *The Dynamics of Business Cycles* (Chicago: University of Chicago Press, 1950).

bank deposits are best related to national income, and, in the consumer sector, expenditures or sales of most consumer goods are best related to disposable personal income (aggregate personal income after deduction of income taxes).

When income figures are used, it is generally desirable to deflate them for changes in prices and in population. This enables the price component to be segregated more easily from the income component and also permits separation of cyclical forces from those caused by secular changes in population.

Once the appropriate cyclical measure has been selected—for the sake of simplicity we shall assume it is income—its relation to the specific measure of activity is usually established by regression analysis and estimates obtained

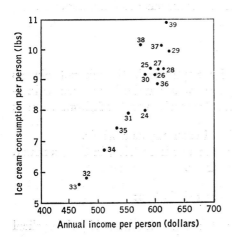

Fig. 4.5. Relation Between Ice Cream Consumption and Income, 1924–39

Source: H. Staehle, "Relative Prices and Postwar Markets for Animal Food Products," *Quarterly Journal of Economics*, February, 1945, p. 272.

of the income component or income elasticity.[22] Such a relation is quickly obtained graphically, especially if only two variables are involved, as is illustrated in Fig. 4.5. By plotting the points on double logarithmic paper, the slope of a freehand-fitted line yields a ready estimate of income elasticity.

Where different markets exist for a product, the above approach has to be carried out separately for each market. This is particularly necessary since changes in income are not likely to be distributed equally among all groups as business activity fluctuates, and the effect of such changes is not likely to be the same for all groups either, because income elasticities may vary from one group to another. In such cases, estimates of the overall effect could be constructed by aggregating these individual effects, as illustrated in Table 4.9 for a hypothetical producer's good. The example in Table 4.9 is a simple

---

[22] An alternative is the reference cycle approach. This involves establishment of peaks and troughs in income, and computation of the extent and direction of change in the specific measure of activity between successive highs and lows. If desired, these changes can then be related to the change in income in each case.

one, but the same general procedure can be used to introduce the effect of other variables as well, e.g., prices.

This general procedure has the advantage not only of highlighting probable strong and weak areas of future sales but also aids in assessing the reliability of the sales estimates by focusing attention on figures for individual markets and on the assumptions underlying the various figures. Thus, since Table 4.9 refers to a producer's good, the expected income-change figures in column 4 will be derived estimates, based on a prior relationship between sales or consumption of the consumer goods produced by these industries

Table 4.9

ESTIMATION OF OVERALL EFFECT OF CHANGE IN INCOME
ON SALES OF A PRODUCER'S GOOD

(1)	(2)	(3)	(4)	(5)	(6)
				ESTIMATED RISE IN SALES	
Industry (user)	*Current annual sales (000)*	*Income elasticity*[a]	*Expected rise in income*[b]	*In per cent* $(3) \times (4)$	*In thousands* $(2) \times (5)$
A	1,500	.4	15%	6%	90
B	2,000	.1	10	1	20
C	1,000	.6	5	3	30
D	2,500	.2	20	4	100
E	3,000	.7	10	7	210
TOTAL	10,000				450

Estimated overall rise in sales $= \dfrac{450}{10,000} = 4.5\%$

[a] Of product concerned.
[b] Of corresponding user industries (consumers).

(assuming they are all consumer goods industries) and personal disposable income. If they are not consumer goods industries, the relationship would have to go further back still. In many cases also, allowance has to be made for inventory changes.

An ideal approach for gauging cyclical effects lies in the establishment of lead-lag relationships, e.g., a measurable lag taking place between the change in overall income or other cyclical indicator and the concomitant change in sales or expenditures. Unfortunately, such relationships are not easily established in cyclical studies, though more easily obtained with respect to price effects and to certain types of short-term forecasting. Thus, construction expenditures can be related to building contract awards at earlier times, and manufacturers' sales depend in large measure on the stream of new orders in preceding periods. Such relationships are highly useful when cyclical analysis is carried out for individual sectors, for estimates of construction expenditures or manufacturers' sales can generally be translated on the one hand into sales of, or expenditures on, specific products utilized in these industries and on the other hand into anticipated changes in income or production of these sectors. In a similar manner, effects other than income can be taken into account.

4.3.2. Price Movements

4.3.2.1. *Price effects*. The apparatus supplied by economic theory for measuring the effect of a change in price on sales or consumption is the traditional negative sloping demand curve, which indicates how large a quantity will be consumed at a given price. The assumption underlying this relationship is that the prices of all other goods remain constant, as do income, tastes of consumers and other relevant factors, i.e., the *ceteris paribus* assumption.

Though the demand curve is not usually linear in an arithmetic sense, the relationship when plotted on double logarithmic paper often turns out to be approximately linear. This is the premise for estimating empirical demand curves by means of the relationship:

$$C = aP^b Z^c \qquad (4.14)$$

where C is consumption expenditures, or sales, of the given product,

P is the price of the product,

Z represents a conglomeration of other relevant factors, each of which would be spelled out separately in practice.

Use of the hyperbolic form, $C = aP^b$, yields the very convenient property of a constant price elasticity (b). This form cannot be used indiscriminately, however, but should be justified on the basis of both *a priori* considerations and by statistical means.

Reflecting as it does the relative change in expenditures brought about by a one per cent change in price, the price elasticity is often the *major aim* of empirical studies of price effects. Estimates of this elasticity can be obtained by compiling price and expenditure data through time and deriving a relationship on the basis of these observations. In either case, it is of the utmost importance to allow for possible interacting effects on the demand curve of other relevant factors, as is done by Z in (4.14). Indeed this step is essential to cope with the problem of *identification*. Thus, the form $C = aP^b$ can as easily represent a supply curve as a demand curve, or some mixture of the two. The way to be sure of deriving a true demand curve is to include relevant variables affecting demand in the right-hand side of (4.14) along with price; this serves to isolate the price-effect on the demand side from that of the other factors.[23] (The same is true with respect to the price effect on the supply side, if the other relevant factors included under Z in (4.14) pertain to supply considerations.)

---

[23] See Sec. 8.1.1.

Income and the prices of all other products are generally the principal additional demand variables included in the *ceteris paribus* assumption. These factors are clearly not independent of each other. Thus, if incomes rise while prices remain unchanged, the rise in consumption expenditures depends on both the price and income elasticities of the product. However, if incomes remain unchanged while the prices of the product and of competing products move differently, the change in consumption will depend not only on the price elasticity of the product but also on the *substitution elasticity*. The latter is defined as the per cent change in the ratio between the consumption of the product studied (C_1) and all other products (C_2) as a consequence of a one per cent change in the corresponding price ratio (P_1/P_2):

$$\frac{d\dfrac{C_1}{C_2}}{\dfrac{C_1}{C_2}} \bigg/ \frac{d\dfrac{P_1}{P_2}}{\dfrac{P_1}{P_2}} \tag{4.15}$$

These various elasticities are related in the following manner:[24]

Price elasticity
$$= -(W)\ (Income\ elasticity) + (1 - W)\ (Substitution\ elasticity) \tag{4.16}$$

where W represents the proportion of income spent on the given product.

This general formula leads to several basic propositions regarding the role of price in influencing market demand, which can be summarized briefly as follows (proofs are left to the reader in the exercises at the end of this chapter):

1. As the proportion of income spent on a product rises, the price effect becomes more closely related to income elasticity of the product and less to the substitution elasticity.
2. A high coefficient of variation in expenditures for a product after allowance for income effects increases the likelihood of a high elasticity of substitution.
3. The higher the relative price level, the greater is the tendency for substitution.
4. Differences in price elasticities for the product among the various partial markets for the product are likely to increase as the spread between the levels of income in these markets widens; this requires some *a priori* reasoning. (See Sec. 4.2.2.2.)
5. As the level of income varies over time, the price elasticity will vary, most likely inversely.

---

[24] J. R. HICKS, *Value and Capital*, 1939, p. 309.

6. Price elasticity increases as the elasticity of substitution increases. In other words, if two producers make and sell an undifferentiated product, any price difference tends to capture the entire market for the producer with the lower price.

A formula analogous to (4.16) may under some specific assumptions be applied to the elasticity of demand for the product of the single firm. If we assume the price elasticity of demand for a certain category of products to be constant and the elasticity of substitution between the product of firm A and all other products to be likewise, constant (as is usually the case over a fairly large interval of the price ratio), the following formula applies, if the existing ratio of A's price to that of competitors differs not too much from unity:[25]

$$\epsilon_{AA} = s_A \epsilon + (1 - s_A)\epsilon_S \qquad (4.16a)$$

where: ϵ_{AA} = price elasticity for A's product
   ϵ = price elasticity for all products of the same category
   ϵ_S = elasticity of substitution between A and all other products (B) of the same category
   s_A = market share of A

This *law of market shares* leads to the following propositions with regard to the price elasticity for a particular firm:

1. Since the numerical value of ϵ_S is usually much larger than that of ϵ, the price elasticity is lower for a competitor with a large share in the market than for one with a small share. Assume, $\epsilon = -.3$ and $\epsilon_S = -2.0$. For a firm holding a share of only 10%, the price elasticity would be -1.83, whereas a firm with a market share of 60% would be faced with the much lower elasticity of $-.98$. This among others explains why a price leader will more readily "lead" in times of rising prices than when prices fall.[26]

2. As product differentiation increases, substitution possibilities decline, with the result that price elasticities will decline also. Equation (4.16a) is a partial elasticity, referring to the consequences of a change in A's price when competing prices remain constant. The reverse effect of a change in competing prices, while A keeps his prices unchanged, is given by:

$$\epsilon_{AB} = (1 - s_A)(\epsilon - \epsilon_S) \qquad (4.16b)$$

Assuming ϵ_S to be again larger than ϵ, product differentiation causes a firm's own sales to be less sensitive to aggressive price policies of competitors.

---

[25] See P. J. Verdoorn, "The Intra-bloc Trade of Benelux," Appendix A; "The Cross-elasticities of Export Demand" in E. A. G. Robinson, (ed.), *The Economic Consequences of the Size of Nations* (London: Macmillan, 1960), pp. 319–321.

[26] See in this context J. Dean, *Managerial Economics* (New York: Prentice-Hall, 1951), p. 435.

3. If product differentiation is pushed so far as to make ϵ_S equal ϵ, price policies of competitors cannot affect the firm's sales any more. This is the case of isolated selling:[27] the producer has virtually become a monopolist.

Where complementarity enters the picture, price elasticity (and substitution elasticity, except for identical products) is likely to decline in importance, and the more so as the relative importance of the product declines. Since the same product may have several different uses, it is important to analyze consumption characteristics of the product in each of its different markets. Thus, plumbing fixtures in the new housing market is a complementary product, constituting only a small part of the total cost of a house. A price decline in this market is therefore likely to have hardly any effect on sales. On the other hand, a price decline in the replacement market can have a substantial effect on sales since no complementarity is involved.

It might be noted that the derivation of substitution elasticities for individual products is often an end in itself, throwing considerable light on the extent that one product is likely to be substituted for another. Such studies are particularly useful in the case of closely competing products, such as meat and cheese, or still more closely, beef and pork, or butter and margarine. In such cases, it becomes necessary to measure the influence on the level of consumption not only of the price of the good itself but also of the price of the competing good. This can be done with regression analysis by including these prices in the regression function as separate variables and fitting the function first with consumption of one commodity as dependent and then with consumption of the other commodity as dependent, e.g.:

$$C_i = aP_i^b P_j^c Z^d$$
$$C_j = aP_i^{b'} P_j^{c'} Z^{d'}$$

(4.17)

where i and j denote the competing products.

The coefficients, c and b' in (4.17) represent the *cross-elasticities* of demand —the effect of a relative change in the price of one product on consumption of the other product. Thus, in a study of beef and pork consumption made some time ago, the regular and cross-elasticities of demand were, as follows:[28]

| | ELASTICITY WITH RESPECT TO PRICE OF | |
	Beef	*Pork*
Beef	−1.5	1.0
Pork	0	−2.1

In other words, a 10 per cent increase in the price of beef led to no change in pork consumption but to a 15 per cent decline in beef consumption; whereas a similar increase in pork prices led to a 10 per cent rise in beef consumption and a 21 per cent decline in pork consumption.

---

[27] See TRIFFIN, *Monopolistic Competitors and General Equilibrium Theory* (Cambridge: Harvard University Press, 1949), p. 104.

[28] J. TINBERGEN, *Econometrics*, p. 103.

4.3.2.2. *Price determination.* In the preceding section we have discussed means of evaluating the effects of price fluctuations. Of equal importance, however, is the problem of determining the factors that influence the course of market prices. Such information is of major importance in a competitive market as a prerequisite to anticipating competitors' reactions under changing conditions as well as to sound determination of one's own market prices. This information serves more generally as a basis for understanding the economic system and predicting the effects of particular changes that may be brought about either by legislation or by the workings of the system.

Price Formation. In a competitive economy, price is the result of the interaction of demand factors with supply factors, so that it is no longer sufficient to consider demand factors alone, as was done in the preceding section. Here, such supply factors as changes in the cost structure and available capacity have to be considered in conjunction with demand elements. Since these factors are generally interdependent, with relations differing according to the nature of the product and the market structure, studies of price determination are not easily fitted into a common mold. As a general rule, however, such studies involve the following procedures:

1. A thorough economic analysis aimed at identifying factors of importance for both the product and its market structure.
2. Compilation of statistical data on these various factors, usually on a time-series basis.
3. A statistical analysis leading to the empirical derivation, usually by regression methods, of the relations between price and the other variables indicated by the prior economic analysis. Such relations may involve variables from both the demand and supply sides and will at times be derived by econometric methods.

To illustrate the derivation of such relations, consider a product the demand for which is influenced solely by its price (p) and by average family income (y), and the supply of which is affected solely by unit costs of production (k) and by average price (p). We can then express these relations in the form of a simple econometric model, as follows:

Demand:	$v = ap + by$	(4.18)
Supply:	$v = cp + dk$	(4.19)

Since p and v are interdependent, i.e., endogenous, and since our primary aim is to obtain the price effect, we can solve these two equations for p and v in terms of the other, presumed exogenous variables, k and y;

$$p = \frac{b}{c - a} y - \frac{d}{c - a} k \qquad (4.20)$$

$$v = \frac{bc}{c - a} y - \frac{ad}{c - a} k \qquad (4.21)$$

Estimates of the parameters of the price relation, (4.20), can then be derived by multiple regression analysis.

In practice many variants of this approach exist. Whatever method is used, two basic precepts of economic theory are worth noting:

1. The more constant is demand and the more variable is supply over time, the more important will be the general level and slope of the demand curve in price determination. In the extreme case, changes through time will trace out the demand curve for the product.
2. If supply is relatively more stable than demand, price changes will be governed mostly by the level and slope of the supply curve and by "shifts" in the demand curve. In the extreme case, price changes conform to the supply curve for the product.

Though there are rarely extreme cases in practice, the first rule does typify most agricultural products while the second corresponds most often to industrial goods. Demand for food is relatively constant from year to year, while substantial shifts can take place in crop production. In industry, on the other hand, demand is much more variable and consequently has a much greater impact on price determination. Apart from these considerations, product differentiation is much more common, introducing elements of monopolistic price formation and, not surprisingly, a much lower degree of price flexibility.

Cost Analysis. Another approach to price determination involves the segmentation of price into its various components, e.g.:

1. Unit costs, excluding depreciation.
2. Markup for depreciation and profit margins (or reduction for losses, as the case may be).

The first category includes the average out-of-pocket expenses of production, which a producer will seek to cover in any case (or else there is no reason to produce, at least as far as profits are concerned). The main components of these expenses are the costs of raw materials and wages, both of which are generally available for current as well as past periods. Given a "materials budget" for a particular product—the amounts of the different materials used to produce the product—the change in unit cost over time is readily computed. The process is illustrated for a fictitious product in Table 4.10. Note that material prices and labor cost, etc., are first converted into index numbers, to make the weights in column 2 correspond with the percentage composition of unit costs in the base year.

If substantial variations in output occur during the period studied, the effect of the level of output on unit costs has to be taken into account. This can be done by revising the weights for the materials (column 2 in Table 4.10) for every time period and computing the cost index with these different weights—a Paasche index series.

Table 4.10

CALCULATION OF AN INDEX OF UNIT COSTS

(Index of unit costs in 1959 relative to 1955)

(1)	(2)	(3)	(4)	(5)
	Weight in	RELATIVE	PRICE	*Unit cost*
Material	*base year*	*1955*	*1959*	*(2)(4)/100*
A	10%	100	130	13.0
B	45	100	115	51.8
Wages	30	100	125	37.8
Miscellaneous	15	100	120	18.0
				120.6

Variations in these unit costs will generally explain a substantial portion of the variation in prices, especially in relatively stable periods when gross profit mark-ups are relatively stable. Where this is not the case, a measure of entrepreneurial behavior has to be sought to explain the difference between

Fig. 4.6. Profits and Output: U. S. Steel Corporation, 1928–38

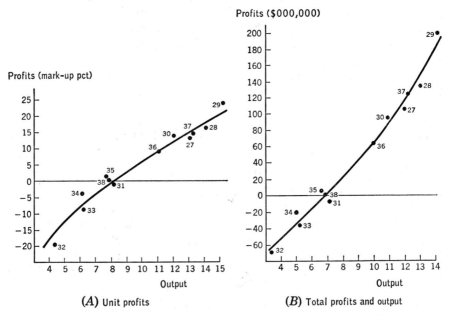

(A) Unit profits

(B) Total profits and output

Source: TNEC Papers, 1940, Vol. I.
  Profit: "Net sale and operating revenues," excluding "intercompany items" (p. 238, Table 6) less "operating costs," excluding "intercompany items," (p. 237, Table 5 in TNEC Papers). Column 2 less column 6, depreciation being included in costs.
  Output: Millions of tons shipped (p. 285, Table 38 in TNEC Papers).

price and unit costs. This leads in most cases to explaining the variations in markups or in profit margins. Here again the causal mechanism differs from one product to another. The principal factors, however, are likely to be the level of sales or degree of capacity utilization, inventories, sales expectations and demand and supply elasticities. The level of activity, as reflected in sales or output, is likely to be most important. An instance of this is shown in Fig. 4.6 for the U. S. Steel Corporation. The relationship is not always this close, and other factors have to be introduced as well.

4.3.3. Long-term Changes

4.3.3.1. *Growth trends.* Despite Lord Keynes' well known dictum, "In the long run we are all dead," concern about long-run changes is a central facet of economic and marketing analysis. The factors entering into growth are many and arise from both the demand and supply sides. Thus, a list of the principal factors making for long-run growth would include the following:

Supply side	*Demand side*
Quality improvement	Changes in consumption habits
Falling prices as a result of:	Population increase
a) increased production	Increased income per capita
b) technological improvements	Price and quality changes in
c) lower profits because of in- creased competition	substitute products
Advertising and promotional efforts	

A similar tabulation can be constructed of forces making for long-run decline. Even in an expanding economy, growth of some industries often leads to the decline of others as an item of conspicuous consumption, e.g., autos vs. silverware. The decline in those cases is often, however, of a relative rather than of an absolute nature.

Statistically, various curves are available for describing and, hopefully, projecting these trends, and some of them are reviewed in Sec. 7.4. Almost all of them are based on the assumption of growth characterized by some form of expanded S-shaped curve reflecting the fourfold phases of growth, as follows (see Fig. 4.7):

1. Experimentation and development (small but increasing sales).
2. Growing popularity (rapidly rising sales; still increasing absolute rate of change).
3. Increasing saturation (leveling sales; decreasing rate of change).
4. Maturity (more or less level sales).

Derivation of some such statistical trend can be useful for descriptive purposes. However, as far as analyzing and explaining the growth trend, it is far more desirable to break down overall sales or consumption into its component causal factors and study the trend in each. Thus, total sales or consumption can be reduced to a per capita basis, so that the effect of population growth can be studied separately. If income and price elasticity estimates can be obtained (including estimates of substitution and cross-elasticities), the effects of higher standards of living and of substitute products can be isolated. Of course, not all such factors can be isolated. However, the trend remaining after these other factors have been removed can then be studied

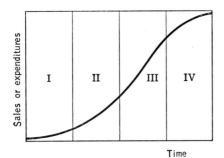

Fig. 4.7. A Hypothetical Growth Curve

separately as indicative of their combined influence, using some type of growth curve, if warranted. (See Sec. 7.4.2.3.)

Such an analytical approach produces a great deal more information than the more or less mechanical application of growth curves to any and all series. It is a much more useful approach to long-run forecasting as well, indicating the relative importance of the different causal factors and permitting account of the trend in each in evaluating the long-run trend for the product.

4.3.3.2.   *Structural change.* An abrupt change in a trend or relationship at a particular point of time is known as a structural change. Such changes generally occur as the result of a change in government policy, e.g., taxes, or of a sudden calamity of widespread proportions, such as a war, whereas the effects of a major depression often may closely resemble those of severe structural changes. An example of the latter, brought about by the 1929–33 depression, is shown in Fig. 4.8. Similar changes occurred among many other products and relationships at that time, probably caused by the sharp changes in income distribution resulting from the very high levels of unemployment. Thus, in Fig. 4.8, the demand for eggs during the 1920's was relatively inelastic (.4), whereas the onset of the depression years brought about a sharply higher elasticity (.9)—people became much more price-conscious.

Whether or not a structural change occurs is often a matter of perspective. The events of World War II sharply altered the nature of many heretofore stable relationships, as shown with regard to disposable income and consumer expenditures in Fig. 4.9. By 1949, there was considerable speculation whether a change in the basic structure of this relationship might have occurred, but the points for later years, plotted in Fig. 4.9, tend to refute this theory. In this particular case, the disturbance in the relationship, though long lasting, seems to have been only temporary.

Detection of a structural change is carried out partly by statistical examination of the relations considered, as in Figs. 4.8 and 4.9, but largely through study of the background situation. Support for a structural change must be

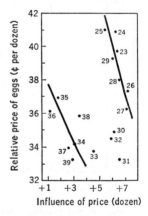

Fig. 4.8. Shift in the Demand for Eggs, 1923–39

Source: H. Staehle, *op. cit.*

found in some aspect of the background situation and then must be confirmed by statistical analysis. What may seem like structural change at times is often remedied by inclusion of an omitted variable. Determination of whether a structural change did occur is therefore largely a matter of definition. At the same time, it is important to note that even well-established structural relations may at one time or another prove to be unreliable for forecasting purposes.

From an analytical point of view, a change in basic structure requires the use of separate trends or other relationships for each period, as in Fig. 4.8. If a change in structure has not taken place, a single trend or relationship can be applied to all the observations. However, if some of the observations are known to be affected by peculiar circumstances, such as is true of the observations for 1941–1947 in Fig. 4.9, they are best omitted from any fitted relationship.

The objective of much empirical work in this area is to derive relationships encompassing all types of business and external conditions, for such relationships are likely to involve the fewest assumptions insofar as forecasting is

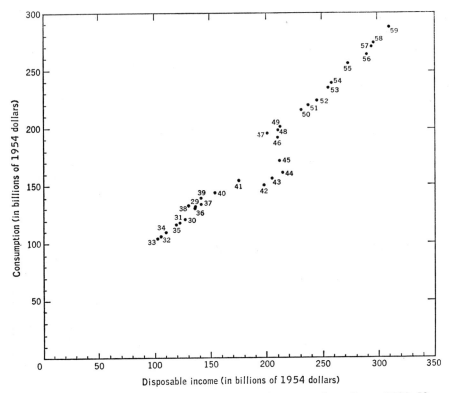

Fig. 4.9. *Relationship Between Disposable Income and Consumer Expenditures, 1929–59*

Source: U. S. Department of Commerce, *Annual Supplement to the Survey of Current Business,* July, 1960, p. 8; *U. S. Income and Output,* pp. 118–119.

concerned. In practice, however, such an ideal is rarely obtainable, especially considering the relatively few decades for which necessary data are available, and the fact that structural breaks in relationships often occur.

4.3.4. Market Potentials

4.3.4.1. *Concepts.* The potential demand for a product includes not only the present level of sales or purchases but also the demand that could still be attracted under various assumptions regarding market conditions and consumer behavior, i.e.:

Potential demand = current demand + potential expansion

Current demand is easily estimated by equating it with current levels of sales or purchases. The extent of potential expansion, however, is a much more difficult problem and has led to much confusion in the past with regard to both the meaning of the term and means of deriving empirically useful estimates. From both points of view, the most important thing to remember is that potential expansion can be defined in many different ways, and the primary task in deriving empirical estimates is to set up a definition that is pertinent to the problem at hand. In many respects this is best accomplished by considering the reverse side of the coin—market saturation. If market saturation is high, potential expansion is likely to be low; and if market saturation is low, potential expansion is clearly high.

Market saturation can be defined in terms of certain successively broader maximal market concepts, particularly:

A. Current demand for one's own product, e.g., brand A automobiles.
B. Total effective demand—the demand for all competing makes of the same product, e.g., total automobile purchases.
C. Short-run economic maximum—the total market that might be secured in the near future through stipulated changes in the price, quality or promotional aspects of the product. The "near future" is restricted to two to three years, so that expansion of productive facilities is of little consequence.
D. Long-run economic maximum—the total market that might be secured in the longer run (the time period suitably specified) allowing for expansion of productive facilities, population increase, higher standards of living, and similar factors. Extended to the extreme this represents the "psycho-sociological maximum size of the market"—the primary restraint on this maximum being psychological or sociological saturation of consumers with the product.

These various levels of market saturation are illustrated in Fig. 4.10. It is perhaps needless to note that except for such essentials of life as bread and salt, the distance between C and D is likely to be very great. In addition, A will correspond with B only in the case of a monopoly for a particular product, as with most utilities when a study is restricted to a particular area. From the short-run point of view, the distance between B and C will indicate in most instances the expansion potential of the market, and hence the severity of competition that can be expected in the near future. As a rule, the closer B approaches to C, the more intense is the competition among producers likely to become.[29]

The above definitions provide the basis for empirical study. For such study, however, definitions C and D have to be projected and qualified

---

[29] The ideas expressed in the foregoing derive from J. GOUDRIAAN, "Enkele opmerkingen over commerciele expansie," in *Van Boekhouden tot Bedrijfsleer* (*Opstellen aangeboden aan Prof. Volmer*), (Netherlands, 1934), pp. 120-1.

against the social and economic structure of the system at the point of time to which the estimates are to refer. This means specifying all relevant variables that might influence demand at a given future time,[30] particularly: population, level and distribution of income, prices (including those of

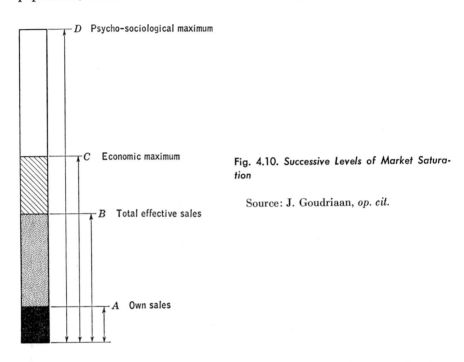

Fig. 4.10. *Successive Levels of Market Saturation*

Source: J. Goudriaan, *op. cit.*

substitutes), costs of production, productive capacity, and scope and nature of promotional efforts. To obtain realistic results on market potential, the specification of the instrument variables is best placed under two conditions:

1. It should be such that in combination with other variables it results in the highest attainable value of the volume of sales.
2. The level of sales should be *economically* attainable, i.e., sales at the margin should at least cover costs of producing and marketing the product.

In some instances, this will be possible only in a limiting sense, for the optimum value of one variable may not be consistent with that of another,

---

[30] In some instances, the "future" time might be specified as the present, or the most recent year. This is done if a check is sought on the effectiveness of current marketing policies.

or certain combinations (such as top quality and a drastic price reduction) may not satisfy the second condition. The optimal combination will then be sought, for which the technique described in the Supplement to Chapter 1 can be extremely helpful.

4.3.4.2. *Empirical approaches.* Irrespective of the method of approach, the relative degree of market saturation, or of market potential, can be computed as follows:

$$\frac{Present\ consumption,\ or\ sales}{Economically\ maximal\ consumption,\ or\ sales,\ by\ appropriate\ concept}$$

Numerous approaches can be taken to the estimation of the economic maximum. Some of the more useful ones are reviewed in the following paragraphs.

Size of population. One of the simplest, and at times the most accurate, approach is to ascertain the maximum number of units of the product that could be used by each demand unit and multiply this figure by the estimated number of demand units at that future time. Thus, only one central air-conditioning system would be used by a private household, so the market potential for such systems in private dwelling units would be the predicted number of such units. A similar approach applied to individual dwellings would be for such appliances as washing machines and (full-size) refrigerators, not more than one of which is likely to be used per dwelling. The same approach can also be applied to the consumption of certain foodstuffs, such as milk or salt where the psychological-sociological maximum is likely to serve as a good approximation to the economic maximum.

The limitation of this approach is that no allowance is made for other limiting factors. Thus, not all families can afford to buy washing machines, so that an estimate based solely on extent of potential use may be unrealistic. Where such other factors are relatively unimportant, however, this is a highly effective approach.

Equating potential with current maxima. In some situations consumption per demand unit of the heaviest-using segment of the market may serve as an indicator of maximum potential use. This is possible only, however, if there is a reasonable basis for doing so, such as may be true of the consumption of soap, personal cosmetics, certain clothing articles, and of plate glass windows in commercial buildings. This approach would not be reasonable where physiological, social or other factors prevent such potential equality. Thus, purchase of technical books is influenced by education and its potential can not be based on maximum usage by the higher-educated groups; the high consumption of potatoes in the lowest-income groups can not be carried over to other income levels because of the high degree of negative income-sensitivity of the product.

This approach is also subject to much the same limitation as the previous one in making no allowance for the possible influence of other factors in causing variations in product consumption in different segments of the market. To some extent this can be done by subjective modifications, e.g., deciding that the maximum consumption of potatoes on the average is represented by that of families earning between $2,000 and $3,000 per year, but firm support must then be obtained for the figure being used.[31]

Equating potential with certain minimum conditions. Essentially, this represents a combination of the first approach with cross-section data on family expenditures. It involves determining a cut-off point in the market structure to eliminate those who could use the product but are not in an economic position to do so. All demand units to one side of the cut-off point are assumed to be potential purchasers of the product, while the others are taken out of the picture. Budget data are used to determine the cut-off point, the exact location being generally the point that segregates at least 90 per cent of the existing market from other consumers.

For example, if the annual income of only 4 per cent of those traveling to Europe is under $5,000, the potential market for European travel might be taken as all families with incomes of $5,000 or more in prices of the given year. The number of families with incomes below $5,000 per year traveling to Europe—retired people, students, etc.—is assumed to be counterbalanced by the number of families with much higher incomes who are unable to go because of illness, family obligations, etc.

In practice, the cut-off point could be refined still further by introducing other relevant bases of classification—family size, age, occupation—and setting up different cut-off points for each individual cross-classification. Thus, the income cut-off point might be $4,500 for single individuals, $5,000 for two person families, $6,000 for married couples with one child, etc. If sharp distinctions in the market structure can be found, this approach can yield much more realistic results than the first.

Extrapolation of growth curve. Since most growth curves by definition possess an upper limit, this upper limit can at times be taken to represent the market potential, usually in the long run. This is a very convenient, though highly mechanical, approach. It is subject to two major limitations. One is that the product should have undergone sufficient development so that its current phase of growth is clearly specified and far enough along to permit statistical description. If this is not true—if, say, the product seems only to be first entering its second stage of growth—the fitted curve may either be of an "exploding" variety, i.e., rising at an increasing rate, or yield a wholly unrealistic maximum.

---

[31] A modification of this approach as applied to income levels involves use of a Pareto Curve to establish the cut-off point by selecting that income level corresponding to the number of people owning that product, moving from the highest incomes downward.

Second, inherent in any mechanical extrapolation is the *ceteris paribus* assumption of no change in underlying conditions. And since these extrapolations apply primarily to the long run, the *ceteris paribus* assumption becomes particularly vulnerable. For this reason, this approach is useful at best for rough approximation purposes only.

Intensive study of budget data. This method applies primarily to goods of which a number or varying amounts may be used by each consumer, such as purchase of life insurance or pairs of nylons used by women. Within each segment of the market, data are obtained on the variability of purchases or consumption. A reasonable economic maximum is established for each segment by adopting some statistical criterion yielding reasonably plausible maxima. Thus, in the tabulations shown in Table 4.11 of tool and hardware purchases by occupation, the value of the fourth quintile might be taken as a reasonable average saturation point for each occupation of possible tool purchases in a year. Total market potential is then obtained as the cumulated products of the various fourth quintiles with the estimated number of people in these occupational categories at the future time.

Table 4.11

ANNUAL FAMILY EXPENDITURES ON TOOLS
AND HARDWARE, BY OCCUPATION
(Data hypothetical)

Occupation	Dollar expenditure per year	Fourth quintile
Professional, managerial	1, 1, 1, 2, 2, 2, 3, 3, 3, 3, 4, 6	3
Clerical, sales	1, 2, 2, 3, 4, 4, 4, 5, 5, 5, 6, 6, 8	5
Craftsmen and skilled laborers	4, 4, 5, 6, 6, 6, 7, 8, 8, 8, 9, 10, 12, 16	$8\frac{1}{2}$
Other laborers, excl. farm	6, 6, 6, 8, 9, 9, 9, 10, 10, 10, 11, 11, 12, 12, 14, 15	$11\frac{1}{2}$
Farm laborers	10, 12, 12, 12, 13, 13, 14, 14, 14, 15, 17, 19, 20, 22	18
Retired	1, 1, 1, 4, 8, 9, 11, 12, 14, 20	$11\frac{1}{2}$
Other	1, 2, 4, 4, 5, 7, 9, 18	$4\frac{1}{2}$

Whether the proper average is to be the fourth quintile or something else must be determined not only from examination of the data but also by field surveys to ascertain the nature and extent of use of tools by different people in each occupational class. This may involve a fair amount of expense, but the result is often a highly realistic set of estimates.

Regression analysis. If sales of the product are closely related to certain indexes of business conditions, regression functions can be derived and potential sales (purchases) at some future time estimated by substituting predicted values of the determining variables in these relationships. Thus, the consumption of aluminum (A) can be shown to be closely related to gross national product (Y), the ratio of aluminum prices to copper prices (M), the ratio of aluminum prices to steel prices (L) and a time trend (T) by the equation:[32]

$$log\ A = -3.439 + 2.917\ log\ Y + .002T - .258\ log\ L + .078\ log\ M$$
$$R^2 = .981$$

(4.22)

Aluminum consumption in 1970 can then presumably be gauged by substituting alternative estimates of the independent variables in (4.22), using the highest reasonable estimates as the basis for gauging market potentials.

This approach represents a variant of the analytical forecast (Sec. 10.1.3). Though using the most favorable of the data alternatives, it still represents only a "normal" level of expected sales. In contrast, the methods hitherto discussed aim at the *maximum* level of sales compatible with given conditions. An element usually associated with determining sales potentials is therefore absent from the analytical forecast, unless instrument variables are specifically taken into account, as is true of price in (4.22).

4.4.   RECENT APPROACHES TO DECISION-MAKING

4.4.1.   Perspective on the Problem

During World War II mathematical techniques were found to be useful for solving problems of military logistics, such as deriving an optimum search pattern for destroyers to follow in hunting enemy submarines. Since business problems resemble military problems in many ways, the same techniques were tried after the war on problem-solving in business and economics, and their success has led to the development of the so-called management science techniques. These techniques are of many different forms and levels of sophistication, the unifying element being that all of them make use of theories or principles from the social sciences as well as from the physical sciences in explaining and predicting business phenomena.

The solution of problems through development of such techniques generally requires the use of knowledge from two or more disciplines. As a result, the interdisciplinary approach has become predominant in this area and, since most people do not know more than one discipline, has led to increasing resort to the "team" approach. Presumably teamwork, like marriage, is here to stay; like its analogue the team offers notable advantages and has achieved much success, while the other side of the picture has yet to be explored. Be that as it may, to understand and use these techniques, a background in several social sciences as well as in mathematics and statistics becomes essential.

---

[32] J. ROSENZWEIG, *The Demand for Aluminum*, Bureau of Economic and Business Research, University of Illinois Bulletin, 1957, p. 27.

The concern of the management sciences is with all aspects of business decision-making. As March and Simon point out, this involves studying three different stages of the decision process:[33]

1. How problems get to be recognized as such and are placed on the agenda for action—attention-directing;
2. Specification of alternative solutions to the problem;
3. Choosing among the alternatives.

Investigation of the first two questions leads to the study of organizations and to how information is funneled from one part of an organization to another. This, in turn, leads to the study of such questions as the effect of particular types of organizations on operating efficiency, the effect of inter-personnel relations on organizational behavior, and the effect of particular types of organizations on the compilation and transmission of relevant information.

Such questions have begun to be studied only recently, comprising the subject matter of the new fields of organization theory and of information theory. These questions are studied in part through theoretical study, in part through observation, and in part by laboratory experiments to measure the effect of particular changes in organization or in information channels on such relevant variables as profits and sales.[34] As yet, the work in these areas is on too abstract a level to permit much practical application. As additional developments are made in these areas, such practical application should be forthcoming.

Despite the growing interest in these broader aspects of decision-making, the main contribution of past work has been in developing more effective techniques for dealing with the third of the three principal stages of the decision process, namely, solving the problem of choice. It is in this area that considerable practical application has been forthcoming. Hence, the main focus of this section is on a review of these principal approaches, with relatively minor attention to the other stages of decision-making. The areas we will cover are game theory, linear programming, other management science techniques, and heuristic programming.[35]

Before considering these techniques individually, it is pertinent to note

---

[33] J. G. MARCH and H. A. SIMON, *Organizations* (New York: Wiley & Sons, 1959), Chapter 3.

[34] See MARCH and SIMON, *Organizations;* J. MARSCHAK, "Elements for a Theory of Teams," *Management Sciences*, 1955, pp. 127–137; S. SIEGEL and L. E. FOURAKER, *Bargaining and Group Decision Making* (New York: McGraw-Hill Book Company, 1959).

[35] Some people classify these areas under the general heading of "operations research," defining this term, in effect, as the application of mathematical, logical and analytical techniques from other disciplines to the solution of business and logistic problems. This is such a broad definition, however, that it includes virtually everything, and would therefore seem to possess little analytical meaning. For the present purposes, no such definition is needed.

two considerations underlying the application of these techniques. One is that irrespective of the nature of the problem, the general approach is to construct a model of the problem containing its essential elements. Such a model is invariably constructed in mathematical or statistical terms, for by so doing numerical solutions are obtainable through manipulation of the model; this is why mathematics and statistics play such important roles in these areas. The basis for the model will be derived at times from economic considerations, at times from marketing considerations, or at times from models used to solve a similar problem in one of the other social or physical sciences. For this reason other disciplines come in handy, since the researcher seeks to reduce the problem at hand to its methodological essentials and then draw on other areas of knowledge for models that have proved successful in coping with this particular type of problem. As a result the model for, and solution of, a problem may come about as much through the application of some engineering principle as through the use of marketing research techniques.

Second, all techniques of the management sciences, as well as other research techniques, can be fitted into a generalized framework according to the extent to which each is designed to cope with risk and uncertainty. Essentially, there are three possibilities. First, no risk or uncertainty may be attached to a particular solution. This is the case with which most linear programming problems are designed to deal: given the data and the alternative choices, an optimum solution will indeed be an optimum. There is presumably no question of the optimum varying according to certain probabilities or of there being no basis on which to derive an optimum. Second, alternative solutions exist, each with a particular probability. In effect, we have risk but not uncertainty, as is the case with the classical theories of statistics and of probability. Monte Carlo techniques are among those used for dealing with this situation.

Third, we may be unable to attach risks to particular eventualities. Not enough is known about the true state of affairs, or the nature of the situation may prevent such assessments from being made, e.g., possible actions of competitors. This is the sort of situation in which the theory of games enters; it is a situation where we are in effect trying to do our best in the face of the unknown, the usual approach being that this unknown (either a competitor or a more generalized actor such as "nature") is doing his best to get the better of us. Clearly, such problems can be highly complex and are the most difficult to solve, which is why the development of practical techniques in this area has been so slow.[36]

---

[36] For further, and more detailed, discussions of the difficulties involved, see R. DORF-MAN, P. SAMUELSON, and R. SOLOW, *Linear Programming and Economic Analysis*, Chapter 15.

4.4.2. Linear Programming

Perhaps the best known and most highly refined of the "new" techniques, linear programming is a mathematical technique for deriving with the aid of economic criteria optimal solutions to linear relations involving many variables. The characteristics of the problem are generally the following:

1. Certain inequalities between variables are postulated, taking the form of inequations between variables and of conditions, or restraints, on the admissible values of the variables.
2. There are generally more variables than equations.
3. The inequalities, or inequations, as well as the objective function, are linear.
4. Something is to be optimized—maximized or minimized.

The last two conditions serve to introduce economic considerations and provide a basis for a solution. The first two conditions are primarily mathematical, the most restrictive of which is the third. Progress is slowly being made in solving problems in nonlinear programming, but the amount of work required is considerably greater. Fortunately, most problems can be stated in linear form.

The second condition is what really causes the problem, for if the number of variables was no more than the number of (independent) relations, the problem could be solved in a straightforward manner; indeed, there is then no problem. The following example serves to illustrate the basic principles involved.

Suppose a tool shop has two machines, A and B. Machine A can be operated 12 hours per day and Machine B, 10 hours. Two products are made by the shop. Product 1 requires 3 hours of Machine A and 5 hours of Machine B, while Product 2 requires 2 hours of Machine A and no time on Machine B. Profit is \$2 on Product 1 and \$1 on Product 2. How should the shop allocate its machine time to maximize profit?

The data can be brought together in the following diagram.

| | Product | | |
Machine time	1	2	Capacity
A	3	2	12
B	5	0	10
Profit	\$2	\$1	—

Algebraically, the problem provides the following inequations (letting X_i be the number of units of product i produced):

$$3X_1 + 2X_2 \leq 12 \qquad (4.23a)$$
$$5X_1 \qquad \leq 10 \qquad (4.23b)$$

and the following optimizing condition, or objective:

$$2X_1 + 1X_2 = maximum \tag{4.24}$$

The problem is also characterized by two further restraints, which in this case are superfluous, namely:

$$X_1 \geq 0 \ and \ X_2 \geq 0 \tag{4.25}$$

Because of the simple nature of this problem, the solution is obvious. (What is it?) Nevertheless, the basic principle used in the solution is the same as in more complicated problems and is easily illustrated. It involves the conversion of inequations (4.23) to equations by introducing so-called "dummy" or "slack" variables, for inequalities cannot be solved mathematically. Hence, we introduce $X_3 \geq 0$ in (4.23a) and $X_4 \geq 0$ in (4.23b) to take up any excess time on the machines not required to produce X_1 or X_2. The inequations are now converted to the following:

$$3X_1 + 2X_2 + X_3 \qquad = 12 \tag{4.26a}$$
$$5X_1 \qquad\qquad + X_4 = 10 \tag{4.26b}$$

To be sure, this leaves us with two equations in four unknowns, but here is where the constraints and the objective function enter the picture. Since the latter tells us that X_1 is much more profitable than X_2, it clearly pays as a first approximation to set X_4 equal to zero (utilizing Machine B to capacity), produce as much X_1 as possible, then also try to produce as much of X_2 as possible with Machine A, i.e., use that machine to capacity.

In this particular case, these results provide the optimal solution, since they also satisfy the constraints. Yet it is worth noting that even this simple problem contains 16 possible integer solutions, a number which multiplies tremendously as the number of variables and relations increases. (Can you list them?) A systematic means of solving such problems is therefore needed. Before considering one such general approach, it would seem helpful to state the linear programming problem in general terms. This can be done by extending the above example to $j = 1, 2, \ldots, n$ products and to $i = 1, 2, \ldots, m$ factors of production, such as raw materials, labor, etc.[37] If we let:

$a_{ij} =$ time (or amount) of process i needed in production of X_j—the technical coefficient

$b_i =$ capacity of process i

$c_j =$ return per unit of X_j produced

---

[37] Alternatively, i could be production processes rather than factors of production. Indeed, the same framework could be used for dealing with problems involving other types of activity—sales, distribution, etc.

The generalized data representation is, then:

PRODUCT

i \ j	1	2		n	Capacity
1	a_{11}	a_{12}	$\cdots$	a_{1n}	b_1
2	a_{21}	a_{22}	$\cdots$	a_{2n}	b_2
.	.	.		.	.
.	.	.		.	.
.	.	.		.	.
m	a_{m1}	a_{m2}		a_{mn}	b_m
Return	c_1	c_2		c_n	

Algebraically, we have the following production inequations, each reflecting the fact that the amounts produced of the n products cannot exceed the capacity of each production process.

$$a_{11}X_1 + a_{12}X_2 + \cdots + a_{1j}X_j + \cdots + a_{1n}X_n \leq b_1$$
$$a_{21}X_1 + a_{22}X_2 + \cdots + a_{2j}X_j + \cdots + a_{2n}X_n \leq b_2$$

$$a_{i1}X_1 + a_{i2}X_2 + \cdots + a_{ij}X_j + \cdots + a_{in}X_n \leq b_i \tag{4.27}$$

$$a_{m1}X_1 + a_{m2}X_2 + \cdots + a_{mj}X_j + \cdots + a_{mn}X_n \leq b_m$$

to be maximized by the following objective function:

$$c_1X_1 + c_2X_2 + \cdots + c_jX_j + \cdots + c_nX_n = maximum \tag{4.28}$$

provided that:

$$X_1, X_2, \ldots, X_j, \ldots, X_n \geq 0 \tag{4.29}$$

More briefly, this problem can be reduced to:

Maximize
$$\sum c_jX_j$$

subject to
$$\sum_{j=1}^{n} a_{ij}X_j \leq b_j \tag{4.30}$$

provided that $X_j \geq 0$ $(i = 1, \ldots, m; j = 1, \ldots, n)$

4.4.2.1.   *The simplex algorithm.* Before any solution can be attempted of a linear programming problem on a systematic basis, the inequations have to be converted to equalities by introducing slack variables (waste processes) to account for possible unused capacity, thereby changing the inequations to:

$$\Sigma a_{ij}X_j + X_{n+i} = b_i \tag{4.31}$$

As a result, the problem contains more variables (in this case, processes) than equations and, unless it happens to be of a very simple nature, requires an iterative approach in obtaining a solution. The simplex algorithm, developed by George Dantzig, provides one systematic approach of this nature; it is not the only approach but is as simple to describe as any of the others and is of general applicability.[38]

The simplex method starts with any one of a number of possible "basic" solutions, i.e., one which satisfies the various equations and restraints and which contains no more variables (including slack variables, or dummy processes) than there are equations. An algorithm, or set of computational rules, is then applied to determine whether the substitution of any of the $(n - m)$ excluded variables for one of the m variables included in the basic solution would produce a larger maximum. If so, a substitution is made, according to another rule, and the process is repeated until the "simplex criterion" indicates that no further substitutions would increase the objective function.

It can be shown that the resulting basic set of variables provides the solution—the maximum possible value of the objective function. It can also be shown that each iteration leads to successively higher values of the objective function so that if an optimal solution does exist, it will be found by this method.[39]

The computational steps are best illustrated by a relatively simple example. Suppose a plant can produce any of three products with the following material requirements and profit possibilities:

| | Product | | | |
Material	1	2	3	Capacity
Machine time (minutes)	10	15	9	445
Input A (units)	3	8	4	300
Input B (units)	12	5	7	200
Unit profit	$3	$4	$2	

How much of each product should be produced to maximize revenue? Indeed, might it pay to produce only two products?

Algebraically, we have three inequations:

$$10X_1 + 15X_2 + 9X_3 \leq 445$$
$$3X_1 + 8X_2 + 4X_3 \leq 300 \qquad (4.32)$$
$$12X_1 + 5X_2 + 7X_3 \leq 200$$

to be maximized by the objective function:

$$3X_1 + 4X_2 + 2X_3 \qquad (4.33)$$

provided that $X_1, X_2, X_3 \geq 0$

---

[38] Other methods are covered in the references at the end of this chapter.

[39] Very clear algebraic proofs of these and other propositions related to this method will be found in DORFMAN, SAMUELSON, and SOLOW, *Linear Programming and Economic Analysis*, Chapter 4.

The procedure of solving this problem is, as follows:[40]

1. The first step is to convert (4.32) into equalities by adding slack variables. For ease of computation, these variables are introduced in all equations which, by adding zero coefficients in appropriate places, does not alter anything:

$$10X_1 + 15X_2 + 9X_3 + \quad X_4 + 0X_5 + 0X_6 = 445 \qquad \text{(4.34a)}$$
$$3X_1 + \quad 8X_2 + 4X_3 + 0X_4 + \quad X_5 + 0X_6 = 300 \qquad \text{(4.34b)}$$
$$12X_1 + \quad 5X_2 + 7X_3 + 0X_4 + 0X_5 + \quad X_6 = 200 \qquad \text{(4.34c)}$$

2. We can start the computations with any one of a number of basic solutions. Since question is raised regarding the possible production of only two products, and since the unit return on X_2 is more than on the other two products, we might select initially a basic solution containing as much of X_2 as possible, namely, 29 units. The latter is the most that can be produced with the given capacity, i.e., it is the minimum of $^{445}\!/_{15}$, $^{300}\!/_8$, and $^{200}\!/_5$, since obviously once any single material is exhausted no more product can be produced.

Furthermore, since $X_2 = 29$ uses up virtually all the machine time, the other variables in this solution must be slack variables, X_5 and X_6. (Recall that a basic solution has no more variables than equations, and that the optimal solution will be a basic solution.)

3. The next step is to determine whether this does indeed constitute an optimal solution.

a) For this purpose, we have to solve that part of Equation (4.34) containing the initial basic solution in terms of the constants and of the coefficients of the excluded variables, i.e.:

$$15X_2 + 0X_5 + 0X_6 = 445, 10, 9, 1$$
$$8X_2 + \quad X_5 + 0X_6 = 300, \ 3, 4, 0 \qquad \text{(4.35)}$$
$$5X_2 + 0X_5 + \quad X_6 = 200, 12, 7, 0$$

In other words, this is similar to the Doolittle solution, except that instead of the coefficients of the c's (Supplement B, Chapter 3), we are substituting as constants the coefficients of each of the excluded variables in turn, and except that there is no symmetry here. There are various ways of solving such equations.[41] One such approach is shown in Table 4.12. (If the equations are more numerous, electronic computers will probably be needed.)

The first three lines of this table reproduce the coefficients of Equations (4.34), similar to the Doolittle Solution in Supplement B of the last chapter. Lines 4 and 5 are intermediate steps required to solve for X_2, X_5, and X_6 by

---

[40] The computational procedure follows closely that outlined in Dorfman, Samuelson, Solow, *op. cit.*

[41] These are explained in P. S. Dwyer, *Linear Computations.*

Table 4.12

LINEAR PROGRAMMING SOLUTION BY SIMPLEX METHOD

Line	Item	X_2	X_5	X_6	Constant	X_1	X_3	X_4	Check
1	Eq. (4.34a)	15	0	0	445	10	9	1	480
2	Eq. (4.34b)	8	1	0	300	3	4	0	316
3	Eq. (4.34c)	5	0	1	200	12	7	0	225
4	(1) × ⅓	5	0	0	148.333	3.333	3	.333	160✓
5	(1) × 8/15	8	0	0	237.333	5.333	4.8	.533	256✓
6	(1)/15	1	0	0	29.667	.667	.6	.067	32✓
7	(2)−(5)	0	1	0	62.667	−2.333	−.8	−.533	60✓
8	(3)−(4)	0	0	1	51.667	8.667	4	−.333	65✓
9	Coefficients of objective function (F): Eq. (4.33)	4	0	0		3	2	0	n.a.
10	Current maximum (F'): F_z alternate solutions				(118.667)	2.667	2.4	.267	n.a.
11	Simplex criterion: (9)−(10)					.037	−.4	−.267	n.a.
	Introduce X_1. Drop X_6	X_1	X_2	X_5	Constant	X_6	X_3	X_4	
12	X_1: (8)/(X_1 value in line 8) (X_1	1	0	0	5.962	.115	.462	−.038	7.5✓
13	X_2: (6)−(entry under same variable in line 12) (X_1 value in line 6)	0	1	0	25.692	−.077	.292	.092	27 ✓
14	X_5: (7)−(entry under same variable in line 12) (X_1 value in line 7)	0	0	1	76.578	.268	.278	−.622	77.5✓
15	F	3	4	0		0	2	0	
16	New maximum: F_z alternate solutions				(120.587)	.037	2.554	.254	n.a.
17	Simplex criterion: (15)−(16)					−.037	−.554	−.254	n.a.

n.a.—not applicable

186

successive elimination of variables, the solution being shown in lines 6–8. These lines indicate this basic solution to be $X_2 = 29.7$, $X_5 = 62.7$, $X_6 = 51.7$. They also provide three alternate solutions, namely, one for each time the column of constants is replaced by the coefficients of one of the (three) excluded variables.

b) These alternate solutions provide the basis for evaluating the optimality of this basic solution. They tell us whether the opportunity cost of excluding a variable exceeds the profit obtained from excluding it; if so, inclusion of this variable, in place of another, will lead to a still higher profit figure. The evaluation is made in lines 9–11. The coefficients of the objective function (F) are reproduced in line 9 under the X columns. In the constant column is shown, in parentheses, the maximum profit yielded by this solution, derived by multiplying the basic solution by the appropriate coefficients of F (assigning zero profit to the slack variables) and summing, in other words:

$$F = 4X_2 + 0X_5 + 0X_6 = 4(29.667) + 0(62.667) + 0(51.667) = 118.667$$

The extent to which profit is increased because of the excluded variables is measured in line 10 as the summed product of the coefficients of F for the included variables and the *alternate* solutions for these included variables. Thus, substituting the X_1 column for the constant column yielded alternate solutions: $X_2 = .667$, $X_5 = -2.333$, $X_6 = 8.667$. Accordingly, the contribution to profit excluding X_1 is obtained by multiplying these values by the appropriate coefficients of F, and summing, i.e.:

$$F = 4(.667) + 0(-2.333) + 0(8.667) = 2.667$$

which is the value in the X_1 column in line 10. The other two coefficients are obtained in a similar manner.

Line 11 presents the "simplex criterion," obtained by subtracting for the excluded variables line 10 from line 9. If any difference is positive, it is a sign that the unit profit provided by that variable (product) exceeds the profit obtained from excluding it, so that substituting it for one of the included variables will increase the value of F.

c) In this example, the X_1 column is positive. Therefore, we have to substitute X_1 for one of the included variables. But which one is to be dropped? It can be shown that the most efficient choice is the variable which has the lowest ratio of its solution using the constant column, to its solution using the column of the variable being added, considering positive ratios only.

The three "drop-out" ratios in this case are:

$$X_2 = 29.667/.667 \qquad X_5 = 62.667/-2.333 \qquad X_6 = 51.667/8.667$$

Excluding X_5 because its ratio is negative, X_6 is seen to have the lowest ratio and is therefore dropped.

4. Now a solution has to be derived for the altered set of equations, with X_1, X_2, and X_5 as the included variables. Such a solution could be obtained by starting from scratch and repeating the process shown in lines 1–8 of Table 4.12. A simpler process exists, however, particularly when there are many more equations and variables, which makes use of the previous solution. Known as the "basis-shifting" technique, the basic formula is:[42]

New column of coefficients = Old column of coefficients
$$- \theta \text{ (old column of coefficients for variable introduced)} \quad \textbf{(4.36)}$$

θ is the new level of the variable introduced, in this case, X_1. It is found by dividing the figures in the X_6 line of the old solution (the variable being dropped) by the value in the X_1 column in that line. In other words, θ in this case is obtained by dividing the values on line 8 by 8.667, the X_1 entry on that line. The result is the new set of solutions for X_1, shown in line 12.

Lines 13 and 14 are now obtained by substituting in Equation (4.36). Thus,

$$\text{New constant column, } X_2 \text{ row} = 29.667 - 5.962(.667) \quad = 25.692$$
$$\text{New constant column, } X_5 \text{ row} = 62.667 - 5.962(-2.333) = 76.578 \quad \textbf{(4.37)}$$
$$\text{New constant column, } X_6 \text{ row} = 51.667 - 5.962(8.667) \quad = 0$$

The values, 25.692, 76.578, 0, correspond to the new constant column for X_2, X_5, X_6, respectively (the variables in the old solution). Since X_6 has been dropped, its new value should be zero, as is the case. The other two values are entered in lines 13 and 14 of the constant column.

In a similar fashion, values for the excluded-variable columns of lines 13 and 14 are obtained, in each case an additional check provided by the fact that the X_6 value in Equation (4.37) must be zero. Thus for the X_6 column:

$$\text{New } X_6 \text{ column, } X_2 \text{ row} = 0 - .115(.667) \quad = -.077$$
$$\text{New } X_6 \text{ column, } X_5 \text{ row} = 0 - .115(-2.333) = .268 \quad \textbf{(4.38)}$$
$$\text{New } X_6 \text{ column, } X_6 \text{ row} = 1 - .115(8.667) \quad = 0$$

The result provides all four solutions for the new set of variables, similar to lines 6–8 in the first part of the table.

Application of the simplex criterion in lines 15–17 indicates this basic solution to be the optimal, the differences for all the excluded variables being negative. Though the values usually have to be rounded downward (why?), in this particular case it is possible to produce 5 units of X_1, 26 units of X_2,

---

[42] Dorfman, Samuelson, Solow, *op. cit.*

and none of X_3, for a maximum return of \$121. This is not much more than the return from the first basic solution, since the latter happened to be close to the optimal solution.

4.4.2.2.   *Degeneracy.* A linear programming problem may well have no solution. There may be no basic solution for the variables that will satisfy the given conditions, or any set of values may provide a solution;[43] or several sets of values may provide an optimal solution. The more obvious cases of no solutions can be detected from examination of the conditions of the problem. Other instances will appear in the course of applying the simplex method. Thus, if there is no basic solution—which means that the constants are not independent of any combination of *m-1* columns of coefficients—the values of one or more variables will become zero, as will the value of θ at the basis-shifting stage.

A zero value for θ alone, however, does not necessarily indicate that work should cease. If at the same time, the variable dropped had a drop-out ratio equal to one or more other variables, each of the others should be dropped in turn. If the problem contains many variables, it is not improbable that after several such stationary cycles, a variable is dropped that brings about a better solution.

4.4.2.3.   *Dualism.* Linear programming is applicable to minimization as well as maximization, the simplex and other methods providing the routine for a solution. In addition, it can be shown that every maximization problem can be rephrased into a dual minimization problem (and vice-versa) such that the solution of one also provides a solution to the other, and the optimal (maximum) of F is also the minimum of the objective function of the dual.

The dual of the general maximum case presented on page 183 is obtained by switching the constraints (b's) and the coefficients of F (the c's), and reversing the inequalities, to reformulate the problem as follows:

Minimize
$$\sum b_j Y_j$$

subject to
$$\sum_1^n a_{ij} Y_j \geq c_j \qquad (4.39)$$

provided that $Y_j \geq 0$ $(i = 1, \ldots, m; j = 1, \ldots, n)$

The dual approach often helps solve a problem not easily solved by the other approach. It also may be of considerable significance. Thus, economy of costs of production, or of resource allocation, is a minimization problem. In fact, with given prices, the former can be represented as the dual of the profit-maximization problem solved in Table 4.12.

---

[43] For example, maximize $F = X_1 + X_2$ subject to $X_1 + X_2 \geq 4; X_1 \geq x_2; X_1, X_2 \geq 0$.

4.4.3. The Transportation Model

Though it is a form of linear programming problem, the transportation model is of sufficient practical importance to warrant separate consideration. The problem is one of minimizing the total costs of shipping different amounts of a commodity from origins to destination points, given the shipping cost from each origin to each destination. The shipping cost on any given route is assumed to be the same for all units of the commodity.

The exact nature of the problem and a method of solution are best illustrated by an example. Suppose a company manufactures a product in 3 plants from which 4 markets are supplied. The market requirements, plant capacities and unit shipping costs from each plant to each market are shown in the following tabulation:

SHIPPING COST TO GIVEN MARKET

Plant	1	2	3	4	Plant capacity (units)
1	$9	$6	$4	$7	35
2	2	4	6	3	20
3	6	1	8	6	45
Requirement (units)	30	40	10	20	

How should the total output of these plants be allocated among these markets to minimize transportation costs?[44]

As before, the solution requires the use of an iterative procedure, or algorithm. Starting from an initial allocation of shipments, a test criterion is provided for determining the optimality of the allocation. If the allocation is not optimal, an altered allocation is prepared through use of the algorithm, and the test criterion is applied again. The procedure is repeated until the optimum is obtained, the algorithm being such that each revision brings the solution closer to the optimum.

The algorithm illustrated here is the so-called "index method."[45] It is not the only one, but is a particularly efficient one. The procedure involves first arranging the data in a matrix form such as that shown in Panel A of Table 4.13. Market requirements are shown at the bottom of the column, plant capacities to the right of the rows, and the unit cost of shipping from the ith

---

[44] In actual practice, total capacity (or production) need not equal total market requirements. By adding dummy variables, provision can be made for excess capacity, or even for use of inventories from previous periods.

[45] A more complete description will be found in A. CHARNES and W. W. COOPER, "Management Models and Industrial Applications of Linear Programming," *Management Science*, October, 1957, pp. 47ff.

Table 4.13

INDEX SOLUTION OF TRANSPORTATION PROBLEM

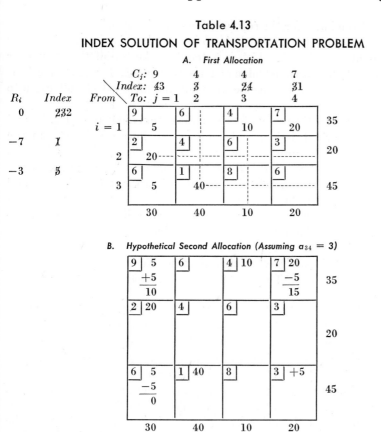

A. First Allocation

B. Hypothetical Second Allocation (Assuming $a_{34} = 3$)

plant to the jth market (a_{ij}) in the upper left-hand corner of cell (i,j). The solution now proceeds as follows:

First Allocation

1. Obtain "index numbers" for each row (R_i) and column (C_j) by computing the difference between the two smallest numbers in the given row or column. The results are recorded on top and to the left of the matrix. For example, $R_1 = 6 - 4 = 2$; $C_1 = 6 - 2 = 4$, etc.

2. Select the row or column with the largest index and allocate as much as possible to the cell with the lowest cost. $R_3 = 5$ has the highest index, and in that row a_{32} $(= 1)$ has the lowest cost. The maximum that can be allocated to this cell, i.e., shipped from Plant 3 to Market 2 is 40 units—the lesser of the capacity of that plant and the requirement of that market. This figure is thereupon entered in that cell, and a line is drawn through the rest of that column to indicate that no more units need be allocated to Market 2.

3. Cross out the index for the row or column used and, using only the cells still available, alter the other index numbers. In this case, the index for R_1 becomes $7 - 4 = 3$, which is entered at the top of that row after crossing out the previous value of 2 for that index. The index for C_2 is also crossed out at this stage because nothing more is to be allocated to that market.

4. Repeat Step 2 for the remaining row and column index numbers. $C_1 = 4$ is now the largest index, and a_{21} has the lowest unit cost in the column. Hence, 20 units are allocated to this cell; this is the minimum of the total for Row 2 and the total for Column 1. Since this exhausts the capacity of Plant 2, a line is drawn through the rest of that row and its index is crossed out.

5. Repeat Step 3 using only the unfilled (zero) cells. All three remaining column index numbers are altered, since now $C_1 = 9 - 6 = 3$, $C_3 = 8 - 4 = 4$, $C_4 = 7 - 6 = 1$.

6. Repeat Step 4. C_3 now has the highest value, the minimum value in that column being $a_{13} = 4$. The most that can be allocated to that cell is 10 (Why?).

7. Repetition of Step 5 for the remaining cells alters the index for R_1 to 2.

8. Repetition of Step 6 indicates the index for C_1 is now highest, with a_{31} in that column lowest. The most that can be allocated to that cell is 5 units. Since this uses up the capacity of Plant 3, cell $(3,4)$ is eliminated.

9. The remaining two cells, $(1,1)$ and $(1,4)$, are obtained by subtracting the cell totals from the marginals. Thus, 5 units can be shipped from Plant 1 to Market 1 because that market has already received 25 of its 30 required units from the other two plants. Similarly, 20 units must be shipped from Plant 1 to Market 4. This completes the initial allocation.

Optimality Check

10. To test the optimality of this solution we compute values for R_i and C_j as follows:

   a) Select an arbitrary value for any one R_i or C_j. Let's say, $R_1 = 0$. This is entered in the R_i column to the left of the matrix.

   b) Compute each of the other C and R values by means of the formula:

$$R_i + C_j = a_{ij}$$

These computations have to be made using *only* stepping-stone cells, i.e., cells with positive shipment allocations. Thus, given $R_1 = 0$, we obtain:

$$0 + C_1 = 9; C_1 = 9$$
$$0 + C_3 = 4; C_3 = 4$$
$$0 + C_4 = 7; C_4 = 7$$

Given these values, we obtain:

$$R_2 + 9 = 2; R_2 = -7$$
$$R_3 + 9 = 6; R_3 = -3$$

and finally:

$$-3 + C_2 = 1; C_2 = 4$$

11. Now comes the acid test. For each zero cell, compute:

$$z_{ij} = R_i + C_j$$

If for any such cell, $z_{ij} > C_{ij}$, rerouting shipments via that route will reduce F. Only if $z_{ij} \leq C_{ij}$ is the present allocation optimal. In the present case we are fortunate, since the optimality condition is seen to be fulfilled for all zero cells. Therefore, no further improvement can be made and the problem is solved.

12. The cost of this allocation is computed as $F = a_{ij}X_{ij}$, where X_{ij} is the number of units shipped from Plant i to Market j.[46] Hence,

$$F = 9(5) + 2(20) + 6(5) + 1(40) + 4(10) + 7(20) = \$335$$

For the sake of exposition, suppose the optimality condition is not fulfilled. Suppose that $a_{34} = 3$, rather than 6, so that $z_{34} > a_{34}$. What then? The following additional steps are involved:

13. Determine what cells will be involved in routing shipments via this route (Plant 3 to Market 4). This is done by means of the "rook's tour" —moving at right angles (after the first move) until one returns to the same row or column. The number of units to be entered in this cell is determined as the minimum value of X_{ij} in each of the other cells toured. (Why?) In this example, the first allocation has been reproduced in Part B of Table 4.13. The rook's tour begins with cell (3,4), where a + sign is inserted to indicate that an addition is to be made. To offset this addition, the tour proceeds up to stepping-stone cell (1,4) where a − sign is inserted.[47] This is offset by a plus move to cell (1,1). From here, a minus move can be made to cell (3,1) which brings us back to the starting point. Since the minimum value of X_{ij} in these stepping-stone cells is 5, this number is added to all the cells with positive signs and subtracted from those with negative signs. The new allocation, shown in the matrix in Part B of the table, assures that the marginal conditions are fulfilled.

14. New values for R_i and C_j are computed by repeating Step 10.

15. The optimality of the solution is computed by repeating Step 11.

---

[46] This sum can also be obtained as $\Sigma R_i a_i + \Sigma C_j a_j$, where $a_i = \Sigma_j a_{ij}$, $a_j = \Sigma_i a_{ij}$.

[47] The tour could just as well have moved sideways to cell (3,1); the result would have been the same. (Why not to cell (3,2)?)

16. The value of F is computed by repeating Step 12. Alternatively, it can be obtained by adding to the old value of F the increments of change in cost resulting from the new routing. Thus, in this case:

$$F' = 335 + 3(5) - 7(5) + 9(5) - 6(5) = 330$$

17. If the optimality condition is not satisfied, Steps 13–16 are repeated as many times as are needed until an optimum is attained.

One convenient property of the transportation problem is that it can often be solved just by pencil and paper, as was the case here. Like the linear programming problem in Section 4.3.2, the transportation problem always has a dual. In any particular case, the problem may require maximization rather than minimization; the procedure, however, is still the same, with the signs reversed in Step 11.

It is also perhaps needless to note that the requirements need not sum to the production capacities. If one sum is more than the other, a row or column of slack variables is introduced, whichever is appropriate. Slack variables are also one means of coping with the problem of degeneracy, if it should occur. Thus, suppose that cell (1,1) in Matrix B of Table 4.13 is empty, so that the rook could not complete its tour. One means of dealing with the problem is to insert for X_{11} a small non-negative number, say α. To offset this addition, α is subtracted from cells (1,4) and (3,1) and the problem-solving process can proceed. In the final solution, α invariably will be zero.

4.4.4. The Monte Carlo Method

Derived originally from gambling considerations, the Monte Carlo Method is a means of solving certain types of problems for which unique solutions cannot be obtained. These problems are too complex to permit derivation and solution of appropriate frequency distributions. The method involves essentially the introduction of random numbers to cope with the situation. As a result, it does not yield a unique answer but serves to indicate the general area within which a solution may lie.

To illustrate the manner in which a problem is handled by the Monte Carlo method, let us consider one way of evaluating the effectiveness of a proposed new inventory policy of a distributor. The measure of effectiveness to be considered is the inverse of the frequency with which inventories are likely to be insufficient to meet customer demand. Clearly, this frequency depends on customer demand, on its level as well as on fluctuations in the level. A general idea of these quantities can be obtained from past experience, but past experience is not likely to be comprehensive enough to yield sufficient data on the full range of plausible alternatives, and on the state of inventories under each alternative. What is needed, therefore, is a realistic model of fluctuations in customer demand based on past experience which can generate the inventory that may be on hand in each case.

Such a model can be set up through the use of the Monte Carlo method. Suppose that the relative frequency of different levels of weekly demand in the past was, as follows:

Units (000)	Average (000)	Relative frequency	Random numbers
1–2.9	2.1	10%	00–09
3–4.9	4.2	25	10–34
5–6.9	6.0	40	35–74
7–8.9	7.9	20	75–94
9 and over	10.4	5	95–99

Assuming that the same general pattern of demand can be expected in the future, this tabulation tells us that in 10 out of 100 weeks customers will need 1,000–2,900 units, or an average of 2,100 units; in 25 weeks out of 100 customers will need 3,000–4,900 units, or an average of 4,200 units weekly, etc. Assuming, further, that the amounts of weekly demand are independent of each other, an artificial demand history can be generated by assigning pairs of random digits to correspond to these relative frequencies—10 random digits to the lowest level of demand, 25 to the next higher level, etc. Then, by selecting pairs of digits in some systematic manner from a table of random sampling numbers, a demand history can be generated for as long as is needed to test the effectiveness of this policy.

Table 4.14

TEST OF INVENTORY POLICY BY MONTE CARLO METHOD

(1)	(2)	(3)	(4)	(5)	(6)
			Random	Depletion of in-	
	Initial	Additions to in-	number	ventory, according	End-of-week
"Week"	inventory	ventory, if any	selected	to random number	inventory
1	10,000		26	4,200	5,800
2	5,800	12,000	87	7,900	9,500
3	9,500		09	2,100	7,400
4	7,400	12,000	53	6,000	13,400
5	13,400		71	6,000	7,400
6	7,400	12,000	38	6,000	13,400
7	13,400		96	10,400	3,000
8	3,000	12,000	12	4,200	10,800
9	10,800		44	6,000	4,800
10	4,800	12,000	65	6,000	10,800

etc.

The procedure is illustrated in Table 4.14. The inventory policy under test is seen to be a beginning stock of 10,000 units supplemented by 12,000 additional units every two weeks. A demand history for the product is generated by random number selection, column 4 of the table, which is translated into inventory depletion in column 5, based on the preceding tabulation. Column 6 of the table shows the end-of-week inventory and serves as a basis for evaluating the cost and effectiveness of this particular policy.

This process could be continued as long as desired, particularly since it can be adopted to electronic machines, thereby producing in an hour or so a demand history covering thousands of weeks. It might be noted that a serial effect can be incorporated in the randomization process to simulate the positive autocorrelation characteristic of most sales data over time.

4.4.5. Game Theory

Theoretical developments in the adaptation of the theory of games to economic behavior have been numerous since the publication of "Theory of Games and Economic Behavior" by John Von Neumann and Oskar Morgenstern in 1947.[48] However, relatively little has been accomplished in adapting this theory to the solution of economic and business problems. To a large extent, this is because even though these problems can be represented as a "game," the rules of the actual game are generally so complicated as to defy the application of theoretical principles of game theory. Then again, since many games can be represented in a linear-programming form (and vice-versa), the approach taken in problems where these techniques might be applicable is to attempt to derive a solution within the framework of linear programming. If a problem can be set up in this framework, the theory of games may not be necessary; and if the problem cannot be set up in a linear programming framework, the theory of games may not be of much help.

For these reasons, a systematic discussion of the theory of games is outside the scope of this volume.[49] Nevertheless, it is pertinent to discuss briefly some of the basic principles and approaches used in the theory of games. The essence of the approach is that any game involves much the same considerations regardless whether it is a parlor game, a military situation, or a problem in business strategy. As an illustration, consider an industry comprised of two duopolists, A and B. Each is faced with making a decision whether to produce during the next year 500,000 units of the product or 1,000,000 units. A figures that its profits under each of these four alternatives will vary between $1,000,000 and $7,000,000 according to the following "pay-off matrix" diagram showing A's expected profits under each alternative.

Production of A	Production of B	
	500,000	1,000,000
500,000	$4m	$1m
1,000,000	7m	3m

---

[48] A review of these developments will be found in the book by DUNCAN LUCE and HOWARD RAIFFA, *Games and Decisions*.

[49] A very clear explanation of the basic principles of the theory of games will be found in DORFMAN, SAMUELSON, and SOLOW, *op. cit.*, Chapter 15.

Thus, if A and B produce the smaller amount, A nets $4,000,000; whereas if B produces 500,000 units and A produces 1,000,000 units A nets $7,000,000. The problem that faces A is that he does not know how much B is planning to produce (and vice-versa). Hence, if A produces 500,000 units, his profit could be as low as $1,000,000 or as high as $4,000,000. If he produces 1,000,000 units, his profits could be $3,000,000 or they could be $7,000,000.

Whereas A wants to maximize his profits, B wants to minimize A's profits. Given this pay-off matrix, B knows that if he produced 500,000 units and if A should happen to produce 1,000,000 units, A would be maximizing his profits—the worst situation for B. On the other hand, if B produces 1,000,000 units, he sees that A might net $3,000,000 if A produced 1,000,000 units, and $1,000,000 if A were to produce only 500,000 units.

What is the solution? Clearly, some criterion is needed to serve as a basis on which A and B can make decisions. Such a criterion is supplied by the theory of games, as proposed by Von Neumann and Morgenstern. The criterion that they proposed, and which has since served as the basis for the development for much of the theory of games, is that each player (in this case, duopolist) acts in a highly rational manner and takes that course of action which will minimize the maximum gain of the other player.

As applied to the present example, this minimax principle means that B will decide to produce 1,000,000 units, because he knows that by so doing A cannot net more than $3,000,000. By similar reasoning, A will also decide to produce 1,000,000 units because his minimum profit under such a course of action will be $3,000,000, which is clearly more than the $1,000,000 that he might have realized had he produced 500,000 units and B produced 1,000,000 units. Since each sees that neither can gain by following a different course, given this pay-off matrix and minimax criterion, both duopolists would end up producing 1,000,000 units.

Even in theory, the situation is not always so simple, and it is not difficult to envisage a situation in which no unique solution exists.[50] It is perhaps needless to note that in practice the situation is far more complicated. For one thing, other factors enter into production decisions in addition to profit possibilities. Second, the range of alternatives is far greater. Third, considerable uncertainty surrounds not only the actions of competitors but also the expected profit levels corresponding to particular levels of output. Fourth, there is no assurance that the same pay-off matrix is being used by all opponents—in fact, in some instances it is not clear that any pay-off matrix at all is being used! Fifth, and by no means last, rational behavior is extremely difficult to define in practice. What may be rational to the executives of one company may not at all be rational to the executives of another company. Aside from economic factors, rational behavior may include such diverse

---

[50] Thus, see Problem 15 at the end of the chapter.

considerations as motivations, aspirations, and personal relationships both within and outside the firm.

For reasons such as these, application of the principles of the theory of games to business problem-solving has been slow. However, attempts have been made. These attempts have extended basically in two different directions.

One approach relates to highly complex problems not previously soluble and consists of an attempt to convert these problems into a type of "game" amenable to a linear programming solution. Such an attempt has been made for the problem of the optimum routing of highways in a city. In standard terms, such a problem is insoluble because of its complexity. The problem involves, in effect, deriving that one of a virtually infinite network of highway systems that will minimize the time spent in transit by the city's population. This could involve a system of as many simultaneous equations as there are automobiles in a city, which is far beyond the capacity of present-day computing facilities.

In dealing with this problem, Cooper and Charnes have transformed it into an n-person non-zero sum game, that is, a game which involves n persons and for which the total winnings are not necessarily offset by the total losses. Instead of dealing with individual cars or trips, they reduce the problem to a manageable form by dividing the city into a relatively small number of points of origin and destination—nodes. At each node, a "player" is stationed who has at his disposal as many cars as there are cars registered in that area. The objective of the player is stipulated to be to send his vehicles to specified destinations in the minimum amount of time. These destinations are determined on the basis of actual traffic surveys, so that the theoretical dispersion of trips approximates the actual state of affairs.

Accordingly, each player is restrained by the fact that his vehicles must go to these different destinations. At the same time, in selecting the minimum transit routes, the player is influenced not only by the current network and condition of existing roads, but also by the amount of traffic on these various roads, all of these factors being specified once again on the basis of traffic surveys. The objective of the problem, which is then put into a linear programming framework for solving, is to obtain a system of assignments of vehicles by the different players which corresponds to an "equalization point"—a position at which alteration of a traffic plan by one player while the traffic plans of other players remain stable will increase the over-all transit time.[51]

In a similar way, it would seem possible to make use of concepts from the theory of games in the solution of other problems. In all such cases the theory

---

[51] Alternatively, if linear programming does not provide a solution, attempts could be made to solve it by simulation methods. This subject is covered in Chapter 9.

of games may provide a facilitating framework, after which one of the mathematical methods is used to obtain a numerical solution.

A second major approach has been to make use of principles derived from the theory of games in the study of business decision-making. A particularly suitable use of these principles has been made in the study of bargaining in a laboratory situation.[52] This study, carried out by Siegel and Fouraker, consisted of testing various principles of the theory of games as applied to bilateral monopoly. It was conducted by bringing two people into a laboratory and designating one as the sole supplier and the other as the sole customer. Each person was given a price list at which he could buy or sell the hypothetical commodity, as the case may be, and was also supplied for each price and quantity a statement of the profit that might be expected. The subjects were then told to bargain with each other, the object being to see if they would maximize their joint returns in different situations. To make the game more realistic, each subject was paid on the basis of his earned profits.

This provides an interesting example of the use of an interdisciplinary approach in dealing with an economic problem, since in the course of these experiments various changes were introduced in the bargaining situation based in part on psychological principles. For example, the level of aspiration was raised by increasing the expected monetary return of each monopolist in turn. Variations were also made in the amount of information available to each of the subjects.

Work of this kind is as yet in a very rudimentary stage. Nevertheless, it would seem to offer considerable promise for throwing light on such highly complicated processes as decision-making, and will therefore be undoubtedly carried out to a much greater extent in the future, not only in the laboratory but in designing projects where decision-making might be observed and even experimented with in actual business situations.

4.4.6. Heuristic Programming

Most of economic theory as well as many of the computational procedures such as linear programming are based on the concept of optimization. Thus, in economic theory the firm attempts to maximize profits, to maximize market share or to minimize cost, subject to various restraints. The techniques of linear programming are based, as we saw, on the same concepts.

Admittedly, these objectives might not always be too realistic. Thus, to what extent do firms consciously attempt to maximize profits or market share? Similarly, is the minimum-cost transportation allocation of a commodity from plant to market actually sought by management?

---

[52] See SIEGEL and FOURAKER, *Group Bargaining and Decision Processes*, McGraw-Hill Book Company, 1960.

Questions of this sort have recently been raised by Herbert Simon in suggesting that the optimizing principle may not necessarily yield an optimum solution. Two principal reasons are advanced for this point of view. One reason is that some problems are so complex that they either exceed the limits of present-day problem-solving procedures or are too costly to solve in this manner. Thus, the game of chess is in theory "a perfect information game," meaning that, with sufficient resources and time, all possible combinations of moves and all possible games could be spelled out, so that to determine the winner of any particular game or the optimum move in a particular position, in theory, is trivial! In actual practice, however, it is clearly an impossible task to carry out this work. The "search costs" of identifying all the possibilities (which number something like 10^{180}) are prohibitive. In such a situation, optimizing is out of the question since it is impossible to reduce the number of alternatives to some manageable form.

For such situations, Simon therefore suggests that we would do better not to seek an optimum solution but rather to seek a "satisficing" solution. By this is meant a solution which is felt to be sufficiently satisfactory for the purposes, considering the conditions of the problem and the objectives involved. Criteria have to be specified beforehand for a satisficing solution to be admitted.

The satisficing criterion is also advocated as a superior approach to the second type of problem where optimization is not feasible. These are problems where well-defined alternatives do not exist, so that one does not know, in effect, what is to be optimized. In such a case, a problem-solving routine is not yet available because one cannot specify an approach which will yield a solution in the absence of a well-defined algorithm. Indeed, the initial objective may be for an algorithm to be derived from the conditions of the problem.

Problems of this sort come very close to the sort of problems that people attempt to solve in everyday life. The application of "heuristic programming" in such a case represents, in effect, an attempt to construct computers that will solve problems by much the same processes that people use in solving their problems. As an illustration, consider a simple problem recently solved by heuristic programming on a computer, namely, the problem of missionaries and cannibals. In the present version, three missionaries are taking three cannibals to church. Until they get to church, the cannibals retain their original gustatory tastes, and will eat the missionaries any time there are more cannibals than missionaries. The party reaches a river and finds on the shore only one boat which cannot carry more than two people at a time. How can the party cross the river without one or more missionaries being eaten?

When first confronted with this problem, a human being is not likely to have any systematic means, or algorithm, for solving it. Essentially, he will approach it by a process of trial and error. It is this same procedure that forms the basis for heuristic programming, and which enabled a computer to solve the problem of missionaries and cannibals. (Can you solve it?)

To be sure, business and economic problems are far more complicated. Yet, the basic problems are essentially the same, particularly where it is not clear what is to be optimized or if anything can be optimized, as is the case with non-numerical problems such as missionaries and cannibals. In such instances, the approach with any particular problem is to attempt to reduce it to its essentials, to specify what would be considered a satisficing solution, and then develop some routine for obtaining a solution that meets this requirement. This solution is then programmed for use by a computer (although a computer is not a prerequisite for heuristic programming).

For example, in the game of chess, a computer is provided with the rules of the game, a programming routine in abstract form, and a satisficing criterion. Thus, the latter might consist of selecting, on the basis of a quick examination, up to seven moves which are both feasible and promising, and then selecting the best move of this group on the basis of complete examination of all possible retaliatory moves two or three moves ahead.

Heuristic programming is as yet in a very rudimentary stage and its success is not yet clear. The approach is undoubtedly more realistic in complex situations than application of the optimizing principle. It has been applied to an assembly-line problem, a situation where the objective was to reduce time spent by a product on an assembly line.[53] The solution obtained was a satisficing solution, since it satisfied the stipulated conditions.

Of course, the initial objective could have been different; it could have been to minimize cost or some other optimal objective. However, in this case the possibilities were too numerous, i.e., the search costs were too high, to enable an optimizing solution to be obtained. For complex problems of this sort—and the assembly-line problem was a simple one—heuristic programming may well provide a means of solving problems not supplied by methods heretofore available.

PROBLEMS

1. How might cross-section data serve as a basis for ascertaining relationships over time? Illustrate.

2. Develop two alternative ways of estimating the size of the market for vacation resorts in the state of Wisconsin. How would you use both approaches to arrive at a single estimate?

3. Illustrate how the diagrammatic representation on pp. 140–141—equations (4.8) and (4.9)—could be modified to serve as a basis for estimating the national market for bituminous coal.

[53] See FRED TONGE, *A Heuristic Program for Assembly Line Balancing* (New York: Prentice-Hall, 1961).

4. Discuss the selection of proper demand units in estimating the demand for coal. Which would you select, and why?

5. A consumer survey is to be made to obtain data for estimating a survivor curve for men's suits. What data should be sought? What conceptual problems would first have to be settled?

6. (For those mathematically inclined) Derive equations (4.13b).

7. Use the following (fictitious) sample data to analyze the demand by income level for pork by applying the elasticity concepts expressed by equations (4.13b).

Income level	Average income	NUMBER OF FAMILIES Total	NUMBER OF FAMILIES Users	PURCHASES PER WEEK PER FAMILY Amount	PURCHASES PER WEEK PER FAMILY Volume (pounds)
Under $1,000	$ 650	50	48	$20.40	3.7
$1–4,999	2,900	75	72	23.00	3.6
5–9,999	7,600	65	60	21.00	3.4
10,000 & over	18,500	55	52	19.20	3.2

8. a) Using the above data, compute the marginal distribution coefficients if the estimated number of families at each income level is, moving up the income scale, as follows (in millions): 13; 17; 12; 9.
   b) What would be the expected increase in the volume of pork sales a decade later when the distribution of families by income level is expected to be, as follows (in millions): 16; 18; 14; 11? What qualifications would you attach to this estimate?

9. a) Using equation (4.16), prove the propositions advanced on p. 163.
   b) (For those mathematically inclined) Derive equation (4.16).

10. Formulate an econometric model for measuring the effect of price fluctuations on sales of home freezers. State the assumptions underlying the model and discuss their validity.

11. Outline successively higher levels of market saturation for residential electric power consumption in the state of Minnesota and discuss how each might be measured.

12. How might management science methods be applied to the preceding problem?

13. How might the inventory policy illustration of the Monte Carlo method (Sec. 4.4.4) be solved mathematically?

14. Devise a model for evaluating the results of the Monte Carlo test of the inventory policy in Table 4.14.

15. Suppose the expected profits in the pay-off matrix on p. 196 if A produces 500,000 units and B produces 1,000,000 units is $5 million rather than $1 million. Show why no solution is then possible using the form of the minimax principle discussed on p. 197.

16. Compare the approach of heuristic programming with that taken in the traffic problem by means of game theory. How do these approaches coincide, and how do they conflict?

17. Construct the dual of the production problem on pages 181–182.

SELECTED REFERENCES

Cross-section Analysis

A broad approach to the use of surveys in marketing and social science research with emphasis on the analytical problems involved is the subject of Part 1 of *Survey Design and Analysis* by HERBERT HYMAN (Glencoe: The Free Press, 1955).

A good discussion of the elasticity concept as applied to cross-section data and the relationships existing among various elasticity measures is "A Complete Scheme for Computing All Direct and Cross Demand Elasticities in a Model with Many Sectors" by RAGNAR FRISCH, *Econometrica* (April, 1959), pp. 177–196.

A rather old but still good monograph on the average life of capital goods is B. E. KURTZ, *Life Expectancy of Physical Property* (1930). Particularly interesting from the theoretical point of view is the article by J. S. CRAMER, "The Depreciation and Mortality of Motor Cars," *Journal of the Royal Statistical Society*, Part I, (1958) pp. 18–59.

Useful examples of the estimation of the service life of consumer goods will be found in the two references mentioned in the text—in the article by J. L. PENNOCK and C. M. JAGER, *Journal of the American Statistical Association* (June, 1957), pp. 175–185, and in the article by G. W. BROWN and M. M. FLOOD, *Journal of the American Statistical Association* (December, 1947), pp. 562–574.

Time Series

A particularly good as well as brief discussion of the theory of time-series analysis will be found in *Econometrics* by VALAVANIS (New York: McGraw-Hill, 1959). Perhaps the most detailed discussion of this subject will be found in *The Analysis of Economic Time Series* by H. T. DAVIS (Bloomington: Principia Press, 1941). Though published in 1941, much of the material in this book is still as up to date as anything else written in this area.

The manner in which time-series analysis is applied to the analysis of business fluctuations is covered in *The Dynamics of Business Cycles* by J. TINBERGEN and J. J. POLAK (Chicago: University of Chicago Press, 1950).

Time-series analysis is also discussed in virtually every business statistics or economics statistics text, references to which will be given in later chapters. However, these discussions are primarily from a point of view of dealing with estimation problems rather than with basic concepts.

Management Sciences

Economic Theory and Operations Analysis by W. J. BAUMOL (Englewood Cliffs, N. J.: Prentice-Hall, 1961) provides excellent material on the application to business and economics of programming methods, game theory and decision theory.

The Cost and Profit Outlook (Philadelphia: Alderson and Sessions, superseded by Alderson Associates) provides in its April, 1957, issue about as good a summary as will be found anywhere on the meaning and application of management sciences. The interrelations between operations research and marketing research are discussed in an article by J. A. HOWARD, "Operations Research and Market Research," *Journal of Marketing* (October 1955).

An easy-to-follow presentation of the meaning of operations research together with examples of applications to business problems is the subject of *Operations Research* (New York: National Industrial Conference Board, 1957). More extensive discussions with means of applying the methods to business problems will be found in *Introduction to Operations Research* by C. W. CHURCHMAN, R. L. ACKOFF and E. L. ARNOFF (New York: Wiley & Sons, 1958).

There are a number of specialized references on linear programming and related techniques. Among the clearer ones are: *Linear Programming and the Theory of the Firm*, by KENNETH BOULDING and W. E. SPIVEY (N. Y.: Macmillan, 1960); *Linear Programming: Fundamentals and Applications*, by R. O. FERGUSON and L. F. SARGENT (N. Y.: McGraw-Hill, 1958); *Scientific Programming in Business and Industry*, by A. VAZSONYI (N. Y.: Wiley & Sons, 1958).

| Part | SURVEY OF RESEARCH |
| Three | METHODS |

THE NEXT FIVE CHAPTERS OF THE BOOK ARE DEVOTED TO AN OVERALL review of the different types of research techniques available for business and economic analysis. Techniques of analyzing cross-section data are the subject of Chapters 5 and 6. Chapter 5 presents a general review of the problems involved in collecting cross-section data, with emphasis on the planning of sample surveys. Chapter 6 then focuses on special applications of the cross-section approach, such as consumer panels, store audits, and end-use analysis. That chapter also contains a discussion of motivation research and of experimentation as a research tool; both of these are subjects that invariably arise in connection with cross-section data.

Techniques used in the second basic approach, time-series analysis, are the subject of Chapter 7, which focuses on the segmentation of time-series data. This material then serves as a springboard for the following two chapters, Chapter 8 dealing with the crucial subject of demand analysis and Chapter 9 with the use of equation systems in research. As will be noted in Part Four, all of this material serves as a basis for the final two chapters, which discuss two of the principal applications of research techniques in business and economic analysis, namely, forecasting and the complete marketing audit.

5 | The Cross-Section Approach

WITH THIS CHAPTER we turn to the practical problems involved in the cross-section approach, particularly to the various means of collecting survey data. A general review of problems in collecting business and economic data that are common to almost all surveys is contained in this chapter, with principal emphasis on data-collection techniques and questionnaire construction. The next chapter focuses on problems encountered in certain special applications of the cross-section approach which are likely to be of increasing value in business and economic research.

We shall begin this chapter with a review of the general nature of a survey operation and what it entails. The discussion proceeds to the relative merits of the different data-collection techniques. Questionnaire construction will be taken up next, followed by a discussion of interview techniques and respondent contact in relation to the foregoing subjects. A brief non-technical review of sampling techniques is provided in the next section, together with a discussion of sampling costs and survey design. The chapter concludes with the problem of verifying survey results.

5.1. THE SURVEY OPERATION

The use of a survey to collect data has many advantages, particularly the up-to-date character of the information obtained and the flexibility it allows of fitting the data directly to the problem at hand. Nevertheless, the cost and time required for most surveys mean that this approach is useful largely for complementary purposes, and most preferably only after other data sources have been exhausted. Prior study of these other sources offers two principal advantages. One is that such a study makes one well acquainted with these

207

data, their merits and limitations. Often sufficient data will be found to render a survey unnecessary. If a survey is to be conducted in any event, this knowledge makes it easier to avoid pitfalls encountered in previous studies. Second, the process of studying these other data tends to produce ideas for new lines of approach that might be incorporated in the planned survey. The frequent tendency to conduct a survey at the slightest provocation is an exceedingly wasteful and inefficient procedure. A good operating rule is to consider a survey akin to surgery—to be used only after other possibilities have been exhausted.

If a survey is to be undertaken, a well-thought-out plan is highly desirable. Such a plan will include:

1. What data are to be obtained—where and when.
2. How they are to be obtained—mail, personal interview, etc.
3. A draft of the questionnaire.
4. Specification of sample size and sample design.
5. Arrangements for field staff, if any.
6. Editing, coding and tabulation specifications.
7. Type of analysis to be carried out.
8. An operating schedule, including time and cost estimates and plans for pretesting, if any.

This plan serves the same purpose for a survey as the outline of a research project does for the project (Chapter 2). The survey plan may be synonomous with the latter, if few other sources of information are available; in that case the first two steps of the general plan outlined in Chapter 2—problem formulation and development of working hypotheses—will be incorporated in the present outline. If the survey represents only part of a larger project, the survey plan will complement the more general outline, and there will be one section in one of the outlines showing how the survey will contribute to solution of the problem.

The complementary character of a well-planned survey operation will generally represent the starting point in a survey plan. This complementary character indicates what data are to be obtained, namely, data that are not available or data to supplement or check material already available that may be obsolete or of doubtful validity. This does not mean that a questionnaire must be restricted to one particular problem, for data can at times be secured efficiently on several matters in the course of a single survey. The overriding necessity in any survey, however, has to be for conciseness and simplicity in the questionnaire, not only to reduce costs but also because the accuracy and completeness of information obtained is generally inversely related to the size of the questionnaire.

Specification of what data are needed leads directly to consideration of how they are to be obtained and of the type of questionnaire to use. Generally, these two decisions have to be made jointly, for the questionnaire form depends in large measure on how the data are to be collected, and, at the same time, specification of a particular question or questionnaire form may predetermine the data-collection method. If a questionnaire contains many open-end questions, for example, collection of the data by mail is not likely to be very successful.

Sample size and sample design are generally the next major decisions to be made, though occasionally they may be predetermined by the nature of the problem. If any personal contact is to be made with sample members, arrangements for hiring, training and supervising field staff will be needed, often one of the sloppiest aspects of a survey. All these decisions together with plans for coding, editing, tabulating and analyzing the data (Chapter 2) lead to the preparation of time and cost schedules for the operation. From a practical point of view, such schedules are perhaps the most important of all, for only in this manner can the feasibility of the survey be assessed. The general tendency is to underestimate both time and cost of a survey, and it is therefore a wise precaution with almost every such schedule to add 10 to 15 per cent to both the time and cost totals before arriving at a judgment of the survey's feasibility. If the resulting totals exceed the limits set for the survey, the entire plan should be re-examined for possible reductions in scope, including the effect of a reduction at one stage on the other aspects of the operation as well as on the nature of the final results.

5.2. DATA-COLLECTION METHODS

A review of the relative merits of the principal methods of data-collection is provided in Table 5.1. No attempt is made here to describe the characteristics of each method, since an extensive literature on this subject is available (references will be found at the end of this chapter), and the reader is presumably acquainted already with the characteristics of each method. Rather, some general pointers are offered here on the conditions under which each data-collection method might be used and on certain characteristics of these methods, based on recent experience.

In general, the conditions under which the data are to be obtained will predetermine the collection method to be used. In this respect, a tabulation such as shown in Table 5.1 can be very handy, for comparison of the relative merits of the different methods with the requirements of the study is likely to make the data-collection method self-evident. Thus, if a relatively few items of data are sought quickly and funds are rather short, resort to the telephone is indicated. If depth interviews and probing techniques are to be employed, personal contact is about the only means of collecting the data.

Each data-collection method has its vociferous proponents who advocate it in preference to others, particularly in the case of personal interviews versus mail questionnaires.[1] However, like the motivation research controversy, the fact of the matter is that each method has its uses and none is superior in all situations. A general guide to the types of circumstances in

Table 5.1
RELATIVE MERITS OF PRINCIPAL METHODS OF DATA-COLLECTION

PERSONAL INTERVIEW	MAIL	TELEPHONE
	Advantages	
Most flexible means of obtaining data	Wider and more representative distribution of sample possible	Representative and wider distribution of sample possible
Identity of respondent known	No field staff	No field staff
Non-response generally very low	Cost per questionnaire relatively low	Cost per response relatively low
Distribution of sample controllable in all respects	People may be more frank on certain issues, e.g., sex	Control over interviewer bias easier; supervisor present essentially at interview
	No interviewer bias; answers in respondent's own words	Quick way of obtaining information
	Respondent can answer at his leisure, has time to "think things over"	Non-response generally very low
	Certain segments of population more easily approachable	Callbacks simple and economical
	Disadvantages	
Likely to be most expensive of all	Bias due to non-response often indeterminate	Interview period not likely to exceed five minutes
Headaches of interviewer supervision and control	Control over questionnaire may be lost	Questions must be short and to the point; probes difficult to handle
Dangers of interviewer bias and cheating	Interpretation of omissions difficult	Certain types of questions can not be used, e.g., thematic apperception
	Cost per return may be high if non-response very large	Non-telephone owners as well as those without listed numbers can not be reached.
	Certain questions, such as extensive probes, can not be asked	
	Only those interested in subject may reply	
	Not always clear who replies	
	Certain segments of population not approachable, e.g., illiterates	
	Likely to be slowest of all	

which different data collection methods are likely to be preferred is provided in Table 5.2. Since the scope of this table is limited to four background variables, even though they are four of the most important ones, it makes no

---

[1] For references pro and con, see H. G. Wales and Robert Ferber, *A Basic Bibliography on Marketing Research*, Sec. 7.3.

allowance for special circumstances arising in almost every survey that may dictate the use of some other method. Limited as it is, however, the table does serve to indicate how preferences for different data-collection methods will vary as the circumstances surrounding the survey change.

Table 5.2 also serves to indicate the value of telephone interviews and the desirability, under certain conditions, of a joint data-collection procedure. The use of telephones is probably the most frequently overlooked data-collection method. This is undoubtedly due to the debacle of the *Literary Digest* presidential poll in 1936, which was widely attributed to selection of the sample from telephone directories, and to the apparent difficulty of holding a person's attention over a telephone for more than two or three minutes. Developments of the past decade, however, appear to have invalidated both of these premises, at least in the United States. The rise in incomes has brought the telephone within the means of the great majority of the population. In quite a few cities, well over 90 per cent of households have telephones, though in some farm areas the proportion of households with telephones was as low as 20 per cent in 1957.[2] With the exception of such areas, studies indicate that the principal deterrent to telephone installation is sociological rather than economic and that, in the latter respect, few significant differences are apparent between telephone homes and non-telephone homes.[3]

At the same time, considerable success has been reported in obtaining information by phone. Interviews of up to twenty minutes duration and encompassing 25 questions and more have been carried out by phone. Interestingly enough, respondents in one such interview test later underestimated the length of the conversation by one-third.[4] Properly conducted, therefore, telephone interviews would seem to possess much greater potentials than has hitherto been believed, though if a fairly extensive questionnaire is to be covered they can not substitute for the other approaches.

The joint use of two data-collection methods is preferred, where possible, mainly for cost considerations. Especially where a wide geographic area is being covered, the use of, say, mail questionnaires supplemented by personal interviews will yield more reliable results per dollar spent than either method alone.[5] Another type of situation in which joint sampling may prove highly efficient is in so-called "double sampling," where the objective is to secure certain basic data from the entire sample supplemented by detailed information secured from a subsample. Thus, estimates may be desired of the socio-

[2] *Farm Telephones*, U. S. Department of Agriculture, Agricultural Marketing Service, Washington, D. C., 1957.

[3] GLENN H. MITCHELL, *Telephone Interviewing*, Ohio Agricultural Experiment Station, Department of Agricultural Economics and Rural Sociology, Department Mimeograph Series No. AE 279, Wooster, Ohio, 1957.

[4] *Ibid.*

[5] For a discussion of sample allocation methods in such cases, see ROBERT FERBER, *Statistical Methods in Market Research*, Chapter IX.

economic characteristics of families purchasing certain major durable goods supplemented by an intensive interview with some of the purchasing families on the factors influencing them to make the purchase. In such a case, mail questionnaires or telephone calls (or both) might be used to obtain the purchase data and personal interviews then conducted with a subsample of the purchasing families.

Though joint approaches can be highly effective, their use presupposes essentially that the respondents' replies will be much the same irrespective of which approach is tried on each respondent. This would appear to be a reasonable assumption in most instances, particularly where factual items are

Table 5.2

A GUIDE TO PREFERRED DATA-COLLECTION METHODS
UNDER ALTERNATIVE SURVEY CONDITIONS

CONDITIONS OF SURVEY				POSSIBLE DATA COLLECTION METHOD(S)[a]			
Funds	*Time*	*Certain precision required*	*Type of data*	*Personal interview*	*Mail*	*Telephone*	*Comments on method*
Restricted	Restricted	Yes or no	Few items			X	Assuming telephone population representative
Restricted	Restricted	Yes or no	Much information	X			If funds permit
Restricted	Ample	Yes	Few items		X	X	Assuming telephone population representative
Restricted	Ample	Yes	Much information	X———X			Non-respondent follow-up needed
Restricted	Ample	No	Few items		X	X	
Restricted	Ample	No	Much information		X		
Ample	Restricted	Yes or no	Few items	X		X	Assuming telephone population representative
Ample	Restricted	Yes or no	Much information	X			
Ample	Ample	Yes	Few items	X		X	Assuming telephone population representative
Ample	Ample	Yes	Much information	X			
Ample	Ample	No	Few items	X	X	X	
Ample	Ample	No	Much information	X———X			Either joint or one method alone.

[a] A line connecting two crosses represents joint use of two data-collection methods. Otherwise, two crosses in the same line indicate that either method could be used.

involved. However, this is less likely to be true for questions on attitudes or motivations where the presence of a personal interviewer may interject a modifying element in the interview situation.[6]

The only data-collection method used with much frequency in business research and not covered in the foregoing is mechanical observation. Its main advantage of yielding highly accurate counts of phenomena—traffic flows, store patronage, etc.—must be balanced against its major disadvantage of providing little or no classifying data for intensive analysis. To offset the latter, this method is often best used in conjunction with another one that

---

[6] Based on unpublished research at the University of Illinois on shopping habits by ROBERT FERBER and MELVIN G. PARSONS. See also MARK BENNEY, DAVID RIESMAN, and S. A. STAR, "Age and Sex in the Interview," *American Journal of Sociology*, Vol. 62 (Sept. 1956), pp. 143–152.

will yield desired supplementary information. Thus, highway traffic analyses are often conducted by counting the traffic passing a specific point during the day and at various intervals during the day, interviewing the driver of every nth car with regard to his origin, destination, purpose of trip, and various personal characteristics. This is, in effect, a double sampling scheme utilizing two data-collection methods.

5.3. THE QUESTIONNAIRE

The questionnaire is in many ways the heart of a survey operation: if it is not properly set up, the survey is doomed to fail. The questions must be clear, simple and to the point. They must be well organized, at least from the point of view of the respondent, and they must be formulated in such a manner as to provide the data insofar as possible in the desired form. This is especially true of a mail questionnaire, which essentially has to speak for itself. If it is not clear, not only may the replies be vague and of little value but many sample members may not bother returning the questionnaire at all.

A questionnaire may be said to possess three main aspects—the general form, question sequence and question wording. In the following pages, attention is given to each of these aspects in turn.

5.3.1. Form

The form of a questionnaire will depend partly on the type of data being sought and partly on the data-collection method to be used. The choice lies between two extremes. On the one hand, there is the highly *structured* questionnaire in which all questions and answers are specified and comments in the respondent's own words are held to a minimum; Panel A of Fig. 5.1 illustrates this type. At the other extreme is the *unstructured* questionnaire, in which the interviewer is provided with a general guide on the sort of information to be obtained, but the exact question formulation is largely his own responsibility, and the replies are to be taken down in the respondent's own words insofar as possible; in some situations tape recorders are used to achieve this goal.

Panel B of Fig. 5.1 presents an unstructured counterpart of the structured questionnaire shown in Panel A. Questionnaires of this type are used largely in carrying out projective tests and in depth interviews, where the aim is to probe for attitudes and reasons for certain actions or feelings. They are also effectively employed in pretest operations where the objective may be to seek more information on a subject as a basis for constructing a structured questionnaire at a later stage. Thus, in a study of family budgeting practices, unstructured pilot interviews may be conducted with a number of families to ascertain the different types of budgeting practices existing in the population. The results may then be used to prepare a structured questionnaire on the subject for use in the main part of the study, or they may be used to prepare a more meaningful unstructured questionnaire.

The main advantages of unstructured questionnaires are the wide range of data obtained and the fact that these data are obtained mostly in the respondent's own words. Such questionnaires are therefore likely to be particularly useful when a problem is first being explored and working hypotheses sought. These advantages also give rise to the main disadvantages of unstructured questionnaires, which are:

1. Different answers to the same question may not be comparable with each other, i.e., they may be in different *dimensions*.
2. Interviewers can easily bias the results, either by interjecting their own interpretation of the respondent's replies or by phrasing the questions in a "loaded" manner.
3. For the above reason, such surveys require highly skilled interviewers.
4. Personal interviews are invariably required.

The first two points are usually most perplexing. Since interviewer bias is discussed in a later section, the focus at this point will be on the dimensionality problem. The problem arises because of the non-directive manner of the question, which allows each respondent to think in a different frame of reference. Thus, in answering a question on policy with regard to changing prices, one businessman may reply in terms of his customers, another in terms of his creditors, and still another in terms of wage rates. The answers are not comparable with each other and the problem becomes one of extracting answer patterns in different dimensions. One manner in which this can be done is, as follows:

Suppose a survey of dealers' attitudes on the relative efficiency of different kinds of promotion results in the following series of answers. This series is exhaustive and ranked by frequency:

Advertising (attractiveness, regularity, etc.)	233
Advertising in local papers	88
Advertising in magazines	42
TV advertising	28
TV program X	20
Spot radio	10
TV program Y	2
	423

In this scheme we find answers with differing degrees of generality. For the sake of mutual comparison, the presentation of results should permit an

INTER-UNIVERSITY COMMITTEE FOR RESEARCH
ON CONSUMER BEHAVIOR

WAVE 2

This is not a questionnaire but rather a statement of what kinds of information are needed for the proposed analysis. You should go into the interview situation with these objectives well in mind and let the respondent structure the interview in so far as he will, but guide him with appropriate probes to get the desired information.

Change

We want to find out what changes have occurred in the family's circumstances since your last visit with them. The reason for asking about change is that non-economic events (such as sickness, accidents, inheritances, change in jobs, births, etc.) which happen to people, frequently influence their financial behavior. Obviously many changes of one kind or another occur in a family's circumstances, but we assume that the respondent will remember those which had the greatest impact on its pattern of living. So note all changes mentioned by the respondent. In the course of talking about change, probe specifically to see if there have been any changes in the composition of the family. If additions have occurred ask about age, sex, relation to MWE, marital status, education and employment status of the new member. If deletions, indicate which member of the family. Using the list of members on the background sheet, review them with the respondent to see that we have all of them.

Record Keeping

We want to find out how people keep track of their finances. In other words, how do they balance their income against their expenditures and savings? Do they keep written records of their income, their expenditures, their savings, or their other financial transactions? If they do, find out as much as you can about these records. How frequently are they brought up to date? What kind of records are they? Some people keep special "books" (balance sheets or income statements) as records, others may only save income-tax records to keep track of these things. What kinds of items are included in these records?

Budgets and Expenditure Plans

People also plan their future finances. We are particularly interested in those who keep written budgets or expenditure plans. If a respondent or a member of his family keeps these, ask for the same information as for records above. In addition, also ask how frequently these budgets or plans are reviewed.

Major Purchases

We want to know about major purchases of goods or services (over $100) made by the respondent or his family since your last visit. What was the price and how was it paid for; e.g., cash installment, borrowing, etc.? Of particular interest are the following: house, car, T.V., refrigerator, freezer, washing machine, dryer, air conditioner, stove or range, additions, repairs, or improvements to a house, a vacation, or own or child's education.

Purchase Plans

We also want to keep track of plans for major purchases of goods or services (over $100). Ask if the respondent or members of his family are planning to spend money on any of the above items. If they do, get a plan-o-meter reading for the item and some indication of its cost and how it will be paid for.

Fig. 5.1. A. *An Unstructured Questionnaire*

St. Louis Study

On this visit we would like to find out what changes have taken place in your personal and financial circumstances and ask your opinion of consumer credit.

1 a. What changes have taken place in your family's circumstances since we spoke with you last? _____

_____

_____

_____

_____

b. Any changes in the composition of your family? ☐ Yes ☐ No
↓

Reductions (identity of member) _____

Additions (age, sex, relation to MWE, marital status, education, employment status)

1. _____
2. _____

c. Let's see, then, your immediate family consists of yourself, ...

_____

The rest of the questions in this form pertain to these members. Please include them in your thinking when answering.

2 a. Do you or any members of your family currently keep any *written* financial records, that is, *written* records of your family's...

	No	Yes	Frequency	What kind of records?	What items are recorded?
Income?	☐	☐ →	_____	_____	_____
Expenditures?	☐	☐ →	_____	_____	_____
Savings?	☐	☐ →	_____	_____	_____
Other?	☐	☐ →	_____	_____	_____
Comments					

b. Do you or any members of your family currently prepare any written budget or expenditure plans of any kind?

☐ Yes ☐ No
↓

Type of (plan) (budget) _____

Items covered.......... _____

Period covered........☐ Yearly ☐ Monthly ☐ Weekly ☐ Other_____

Frequency plan
checked...........☐ Yearly ☐ Monthly ☐ Weekly ☐ Other_____

Frequency plan
revised............. _____

Comments_____

_____

_____

Fig. 5.1. B. Corresponding Structured Questionnaire

3 a. I am going to read you a list of major goods. Have you or any members of your family purchased any of these since our last visit? Do you plan to purchase any of them between now and the end of the year? Let's take the first one...

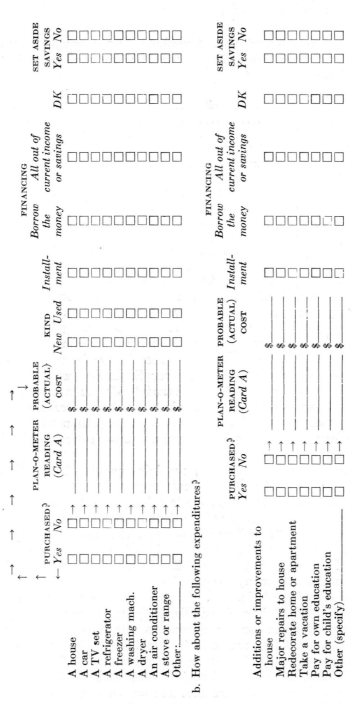

	PURCHASED? Yes No	PLAN-O-METER READING (Card A)	PROBABLE (ACTUAL) COST	KIND New Used	Install-ment	FINANCING Borrow the money	All out of current income or savings	DK	SET ASIDE SAVINGS Yes No
A house			$						
A car			$						
A TV set			$						
A refrigerator			$						
A freezer			$						
A washing mach.			$						
A dryer			$						
An air conditioner			$						
A stove or range			$						
Other:			$						

b. How about the following expenditures?

	PURCHASED? Yes No	PLAN-O-METER READING (Card A)	PROBABLE (ACTUAL) COST	Install-ment	FINANCING Borrow the money	All out of current income or savings	DK	SET ASIDE SAVINGS Yes No
Additions or improvements to house			$					
Major repairs to house			$					
Redecorate home or apartment			$					
Take a vacation			$					
Pay for own education			$					
Pay for child's education			$					
Other (specify)_____								

Fig. 5.1. B. (Concl.)

unambiguous interpretation. Accordingly, main groups comparable by degree of generality are built up from subgroups of an increasingly specific character, as follows:

Advertising specified	190		
Radio		10	
TV Broadcasting		50	
Specified			22
Program X			20
Program Y			2
Not specified			28
Magazines		42	
Newspapers		88	
Advertising not specified	233		
TOTAL	423		

Now, the different dimensions of thinking are revealed and answer patterns are brought out. Thus, TV is seen to be mentioned more frequently than magazine advertising, which was not clear before.

Such a tabulation can serve as the basis for a more highly structured questionnaire seeking more explicit information in each dimension. At the same time, it must be remembered that the feasibility of even such a tabulation depends on the adequacy of the data supplied in the unstructured interview, which in turn depends on the skill of the interviewers in securing all relevant data. If interviewers fail to ascertain that some businessmen speak of the adequacy of profits with reference to their competitors while others do so with reference to industry at large, no amount of rearranging of the data is likely to reveal this difference.

Structured questionnaires, by supplying question formulations in very specific terms as well as the different possible answers, are easier for sample members to answer and also serve to reduce the danger of interviewer bias. They can be used with any of the three main data-collection methods and are practically a "must" on mail surveys. The principal danger is that the process of structuring the answers may bias the results, perhaps by supplying "loaded" answers or by not providing for all possible answers. It is for the latter reason that many structured questions possess a catchall "other" answer (Panel B of Fig. 5.1). "Loaded" answers can best be avoided thorough study of the problem prior to the main survey, supplemented unstructured interviews and discussions with interested parties at n different levels. A further means of control lies in testing alternative form tions of the same questions on mutually comparable pilot samples.

In practice, the final questionnaire in most studies will contain both tured and unstructured questions. The preponderance of structured ques- tions will generally be greater, the lower the degree of skill of the inter wers, and the greater the ease with which the questions can be structured, especially if the data are to be collected by mail. Even in the latter case, however, well-placed open-end questions are feasible and highly useful.

5.3.2. Question Sequence

The position of the respondent is not always a comfortable one. A complete stranger inveigles his, or her, way into the home and starts asking all sorts of questions. The purpose of these questions is often not too clear, and the subject may not be one of any particular interest to the respondent either. It is for these reasons that the introduction to the subject and the sequence of the questions are such major determinants of the quality of the replies received.

    5.3.2.1. *Introduction.* The introduction is best made as simple and as short as possible, especially if a personal interview or telephone approach is used. People are generally interested in the subject of the survey and the time involved but, oddly enough, hardly at all in who is doing it. The introduction can therefore be something like, "How do you do? We are making a study in this area on _____. I would like to ask you a few questions such as . . . " (Question 1 follows.) The interviewer should have some form of identification, however, in case the authenticity of the survey is questioned, and should be prepared, particularly, to assure the respondent that nothing is being sold.

    Introductory letters on mail surveys are also best made very brief. A clever example of such a letter to building contractors, an especially difficult group to contact, is shown in Fig. 5.2. This particular letter "pulled" the unusually high response of 75 per cent.

    5.3.2.2. *Sequence.* The introduction lays the foundation for establishing rapport with the respondent in addition to making the interview possible. Whether or not rapport is maintained depends to a large extent on a clear nd smoothly-moving question sequence. Essentially, this means that the elation of one question to another should be readily apparent to the respondent, with questions that are easiest to answer being placed near the ginning. The first two or three questions are particularly important, for e respondent's attitude toward the entire interview is likely to be influed by them, particularly when the data are being sought by personal tact. These questions are best made straightforward, if possible some t flattering, and should call for simple answers. Asking for one's prefer e often furnishes a good opening of this sort, provided that the answer do ot take too much thought, such as: "Do you prefer office furniture to be o vood or of metal?" A simple factual question also may provide a good open g, such as: "What forms of transportation do you use in going to work

MAGAZINE SERVICE BUREAU

333 North Michigan Avenue Building
Chicago 1, Illinois

July 1951

Attention: Sales Manager

Dear Sir:

Today, one dollar will buy:

> 4 packages of cigarettes, or
> 5 cans of beer, or
> 10 candy bars

Why are we sending you the buck? Frankly to attract your attention.

Sure, we hope you will enjoy the candy bar or the beer, or whatever you spend it for. But we also hope you will take a few moments to help us solve one of our problems.

Your answers to the two questions on the back of this letter will help our client to do a more intelligent job in placing his advertising.

Many thanks for your cooperation. A stamped return envelope is enclosed.

Sincerely,

MAGAZINE SERVICE BUREAU

Director of Research

D. J. Coleman
bet

P. S. Since we are sending this request to only a few representative dealers, your help is doubly important.

DJC

Fig. 5.2. *Covering Letter of a Mail Questionnaire*

Consistent with the objective of establishing rapport, the opening questions will generally seek substantive information of value to the study. The exact questions to be used will therefore depend heavily on the nature of the study. Nevertheless, certain types of questions can be delineated which as a general rule should *not* be asked at the start. These are:

1. Questions that put too great a strain on the memory or the intellect. This introduces the cross-examination and might bring about a tense atmosphere. A question such as: "What can you tell me about our present tariff laws?" should therefore be reserved till later.

2. Questions related to personal wealth: "Have you a savings account?" This question is unpleasant to the man who has none and will seem inquisitive to the man who has one and therefore tends to annoy him.

3. Questions of a personal character: "What is the profession of your husband?" The first impulse of the respondent may be: "What business is that of yours?" If this question is to be asked, it is best placed toward the end—and best reworded to omit "profession" because of the upward bias it may impart.

The value of gaining rapport is of such importance that, if necessary, an opening question may be asked which lies outside the field of the survey. As long as it serves to awaken interest, later questions can be used to steer the discussion in the proper channels. Thus, the question, "Have you been living here long?" is suitable as an opening if the attitude of the housewife toward certain shops is to be investigated. The answer may be of little consequence, but through unconscious remembrance of an earlier environment it helps create the background against which present suppliers can be judged.

Following this opening phase come the questions that are really vital to the interview. Even here, however, questions of only slight interest value are best surrounded by more interesting ones in order not to let attention slip. "Awkward" questions, which create the risk that the respondent may discontinue the interview, are usually relegated toward the end. If the interview is terminated then, considerable information will already have been obtained.

Even after the opening, a connecting thread should run through successive questions. It is not absolutely necessary that each question be logically consistent with the previous one, but if past associations and memories are activated, experiences gained with a product or firm come more clearly into focus. Succeeding questions should make use of these ideas once they have been activated, i.e., they should appeal as much as possible to the frame of reference.

Ideally, the question sequence should conform to the respondent's way of thinking, and this is where unstructured interviews are highly advantageous. Knowing what information is desired, the interviewer can rearrange the order of the questions to fit the discussion in each particular case. With a structured questionnaire the best that can be done is to determine with the aid of pilot interviews the question sequence (and question wording) which is likely to produce good rapport with most people. With skilled interviewers, "free-answer questioning" may be attempted, whereby the interviewer is allowed to follow up the written question with requests for additional information.

Fortunately, it is generally not difficult to obtain information within a frame of reference that is both logical and clear to the respondent. Two such ways worth mentioning are concretizing the general question and interviewing along the time line. In the latter case, the reasons for certain actions are sought by following a "time path," such as:

1. About how long have you had this refrigerator?
2. Can you recall when you bought it?
3. Do you remember where?
4. The circumstances surrounding the purchase?
5. Why did you buy this particular brand and not another one?

By leading the respondent gradually back to the circumstances under which the item was purchased, the reasons for the purchase are more likely to come to the surface.

The concretizing technique involves going from the general to the more specific. The relative merits of life insurance as a form of investment may be sought by asking a series of prior questions on family budgeting and advance planning, allocation of income between saving and expenditures, forms in which saving is put, purposes of each form of saving, and then relative merits of life insurance as well as of other types of saving. Not only does this procedure provide useful background material, but it keeps the main focus away from life insurance as such, thereby countering any bias that may result if the respondent is aware of the specific objective of the interview.

A matter always to be considered in determining the order of questions is the fact that the answer to a given question is a function not only of the question itself but of all previous questions as well. Answers to these previous questions have evoked a certain complex of ideas that are now uppermost in the respondent's mind. These same conscious ideas will enter into the answer formulated to the following question. To the respondent, this is only natural —it enables him to benefit from the economies of thinking: he need not tire his memory and imagination.

If, for example, one question deals with the price usually paid for coffee and the next with the reason for preferring that particular brand, the answer to this latter question may be couched largely in terms of price differences.

In a survey regarding attitudes of women toward advertising in general,[7]

---

[7] A. B. BLANKENSHIP, *Consumer and Opinion Research,* Ch. 6.

a few specific questions were inserted on ladies' dresses. When these preceded those pertaining to advertising in general, the attitude toward advertising proved to be much more favorable than was the case if clothing was dealt with after advertising. The former order apparently made the dress element in advertising dominate to such an extent that advertising as a whole received the benefit of a benevolent attitude toward ladies' fashion advertising.

If this type of bias seems unavoidable, as is the case at times, a split-run technique may be used, in which half the questionnaires use one question sequence and the other half follow an alternate sequence. Differences in replies to the same question on both questionnaires are used as the basis for assessing the presence of bias and for possible corrections for bias.[8]

5.3.3.   Question Formulation

A proper sequence of questions reduces the chances considerably of individual questions being misunderstood. This does not detract from the necessity of making each individual question clear in itself (at least in structured questionnaires), for question misunderstandings can do irreparable harm to a survey, at times without the researcher's knowledge. At the same time, the questions should, in most cases, be impartial in order not to yield a biased picture of the true state of affairs.

The English language being what it is, this is a truly herculean task and is essentially an art rather than a science.[9] Like other fields of art, it is difficult to lay down prescribed rules of procedure, for what is best in one situation will not necessarily be so in another situation. Clearly, there is no "best" way of formulating questions, but at the same time certain guiding principles can be presented, and this is done from four points of view: the requirements of the answers, the requirements of the questions, the different types of question forms, and some comments on question wording.

5.3.3.1.   *Answer requirements.* One means of ensuring that a question meets necessary standards in providing survey information is to consider the requirements that should be met by the answers to that question. Though this is not a sufficient, but only a necessary, condition for question adequacy, this approach also leads one to reflect on what type of information may be expected from that particular question and how useful such information may be relative to the subject of study.

For answers to contribute to solving a problem and be suitable for processing, the following five qualities will be desired: accuracy, unidimensionality, mutual exclusiveness, meaningfulness, and background homogeneity.

---

[8] See ALLAN GREENBERG, "Paired Comparisons in Consumer Product Tests," *Journal of Marketing*, April, 1958, pp. 411–414.

[9] Appropriately enough, the one book devoted exclusively to this subject is entitled, *The Art of Asking Questions* by STANLEY PAYNE (Princeton University Press, 1951).

1. *Accuracy*. Clearly, an answer should be accurate: a fact should be as close as possible to reality, and an opinion should correspond to one's real feelings on the matter.

2. *Unidimensionality*. The answers should be comparable with one another, as discussed in an earlier section. A question such as, "What kind of cigars do you smoke?" flunks this test, for the answer could be in terms of brand, of heaviness, of shape, of price, or in many other dimensions. (In a pilot interview, however, such questions may be used deliberately, to determine how many dimensions may be involved.) Similarly, replies of numerical data to a question should be in the same unit of measurement. "How much milk did your family consume last week?" also flunks, because the answer could be either in money or in physical units.

3. *Mutual exclusiveness*. Answers should not overlap one another, for the problem of interpretation becomes very complicated, if not hopeless. If the reasons for buying a particular model car can include "satisfaction" and "quality" besides "price," "convenience to dealer," "good dealer service," "liked previous model," "good mileage," and "economical," the answers are clearly not mutually exclusive and are not easily interpreted.

4. *Meaningfulness*. Each answer should "make sense" and provide an unequivocal reply to the question. A reply of "pretty fair" or "good" to "How are your sales doing these days?" is not at all clear, for the frame of reference of these adjectives (competitors? own past business? general business? even "doing") is not specified. Perhaps the most frequently encountered non-meaningful answer is "don't know," which can reflect anything from respondent ignorance to refusal to answer the question. An appreciable proportion of "don't know" replies is generally a sign of an inadequate question.

5. *Background Homogeneity*. The frame of reference of the answer should be as similar as possible for different respondents. This means, in effect, that the questions must mean the same to different people and that the perspective from which the question is interpreted should be the same. If both farmers and dealers are asked, "What features would you like to see in a new tractor?" the answers are not easily combined because of the different points of view from which they are given.

5.3.3.2. *Question requirements*. If the question meets the preceding answer requirements, it will very likely be in acceptable shape. At the same time, there are certain standards that nearly all questions should meet as well, namely:

1. *Clarity*. The question should be easily understood. "High-falutin" words should be avoided. The basic criterion is not so much the "King's English" but what will be understood by the least literate, or least intelligent, of those to be interviewed.

2. *Simplicity.* Only one thought should be conveyed at a time. "Do you think the present administration is doing a good job and preventing inflation?" is the sort of question not to ask. It contains two thoughts—doing a good job, and preventing inflation—which are not necessarily coincident. Each of these should be the subject of a separate question.

3. *Concreteness.* The question should conform as much as possible to the respondent's way of thinking. Asking, "How many razor blades do you use a year?" does not correspond to most people's way of thinking. Much more realistic would be to ask, "How many razor blades did you use last week?" Such questions also provide more accurate information, as is true in almost any case where the situation can be focused more sharply. Thus, far superior to, "How often do you buy a suit?" are the dual questions, "When did you last purchase a suit?" and "When did you buy a suit before that?"

In some situations, the reality of the question is vitally important. Thus, to ask a housewife, "Which type of pudding powder do you like best?" is liable to yield replies biased in favor of heavily advertised brands rather than what is actually used. To counteract this danger, the question can be phrased like, "When you want to make a really delightful pudding, which brand do you use?"

It should be noted that these requirements are not always applicable to questions used in unstructured questionnaires. In probing for information on a subject, a question may sometimes deliberately be worded vaguely to see how different people phrase their replies. Indeed, in some projective tests, the aim is to ask very broad questions so that the respondent's mind is left as free as possible.

5.3.3.3. Question form. The two principal question forms are the multiple choice, in which the respondent selects one of the alternative possible answers put to him, and the open-end question, in which the respondent has to supply the answer in his own words. The dichotomous question (two possible answers, usually "yes" or "no") can be represented as a special case of the multiple-choice question. The same is true of categorical questions, such as, "What is your marital status?" in which for all practical purposes the respondent is asked to select one of several alternatives so well known that they may not be read to him.

Multiple-choice questions possess three big advantages: they are easiest for the interviewer to handle (since the exact wording and answer are given), they are simplest for the respondent to answer (the possible answers are presented to him, either orally or in writing), and they are most amenable to statistical analysis (the answers are given and there are no problems of interpretation, presumably). Their main drawback is that of "putting answers in people's mouths"—the answer given may not reflect accurately his real feelings on the subject. For this reason, some multiple-choice questions will be followed by an open-end question, such as, "Would you care to elaborate on your reply?" or, "Do you want to add any further comments to this answer?" or, simply, "Why do you say so?"

The latter are open-end questions and hence give the respondent considerable latitude in phrasing a reply. Getting the replies in the respondent's own words is another major advantage of this type of question. Nevertheless, from an analytical point of view, open-end questions are more difficult to handle, raising problems of interpretation, comparability and interviewer bias, among others.

Occasionally, a modified open-end question will be used, where the respondent is given various alternatives and at the same time left free to suggest other possibilities. Thus, "Do you think the United States should share its atomic secrets with the NATO powers, do so only to a limited extent, or what?" The "what" leaves the respondent free to mention other possibilities. Such a question has to be phrased very carefully, for there is the tendency in such cases to mention listed alternatives and omit others.

A somewhat different approach is exemplified by the "intensity question," in which an attempt is made to find out how strongly a person feels about his answer. Thus, after giving his opinion on United States policy on atomic secrets, the respondent might be asked, "How strongly do you feel about this?" (a) Very strongly, (b) Strongly, (c) Moderately, (d) Not too strongly, (e) Not sure. These answers then serve as a basis for evaluating the stability of opinion on the question, aggregate opinion being presumably less stable, the less strong opinions are reported to be. By asking a number of questions of this type, it is possible by means of "scalogram analysis" to ascertain attitudes on the subject invariant of the wording used in the actual questions.[10] (See Sec. 6.3.5.)

In effect, these various question forms complement each other, and rarely will a questionnaire be encountered that relies on one form alone. Multiple-choice questions constitute the basis of a structured questionnaire, particularly in a mail survey, but, even there, various forms of open-end questions will be inserted to provide a more complete picture of the respondent's feelings and attitudes. In an unstructured questionnaire, open-end questions will predominate, and the exact formulation of the questions will often be left to the judgment of the individual interviewer. In such cases, tape recorders should be used if possible, so that the nature of the reply can be related to the manner in which the question was asked.

5.3.3.4.   *Question wording.* Anybody who has ever taken an oral examination knows that the examiner can put the answers in the examinees' mouth at least nine times out of ten. The same is true in survey operations.

---

[10] Louis Guttman, "A Basis for Scaling Qualitative Data," *American Sociological Review*, April 1944, pp. 139–150. Also, Stouffer *et al*, *Measurement and Prediction* (Princeton University Press, 1950).

The answer is to a large extent a function of the question, and if the question is changed the answer is likely to change too. For example, in one survey, responses to the following two alternate question forms were, as follows:

Question	*Affirmative answers as pct of total answers*
1. Is the service at Johnson's reasonably good?	60%
2. Is the service at Johnson's all you could expect?	25%

In the second question, Johnson's has to meet a higher standard than in the first one. Accordingly, the number of favorable answers to question 2 is smaller by about half.

The suggestive value of question wording can bias the answer in several respects. In this case, both questions leave the standard for good service to the judgment of the person interviewed, though each of them suggests another standard. Therefore, if one wants to ascertain attitudes, the question is best formulated as neutrally as possible (or scalogram analysis might be used). To present a classical example, "Isn't this a nice color?," a person is given the impression that he is expected to like the color. Here, even better than asking, "Do you like *this* color?" (in which the color concerned is also put in a special position) is to show samples and let the respondent choose for himself.

Avoidance of colorful adjectives or undue descriptive phrases is a central tenet of unbiased question wording. Unfortunately, the number of possibilities is legion, and in fact what may be unbiased in one situation will not necessarily always be so.[11]

It is also important to avoid any wording that might suggest to the respondent that he is not meeting certain social or ethical standards unless he gives a particular answer. This kind of "prestige question" often occurs in commercial surveys. Thus, Robinson mentions that in investigating readership of *Gone with the Wind*, answers to the question, "Have you read this book?" received an excessive proportion of affirmative replies. Those people who had not read it apparently were reluctant to say so. This was remedied by rephrasing the question as follows: "Do you intend to read '*Gone with the Wind*'?" This flattered people. Even those who would never read it could pretend that they would do so. But the people who had already read it did not fail to stress this point.[12]

As noted at the beginning of this section, question wording and formulation is more of an art than a science. Where science does enter, however, is in testing the stability and adequacy of replies as a basis for economic and marketing decisions. By changing the wording of questions, their form and even

---

[11] STANLEY PAYNE, *op. cit.*

[12] C. S. ROBINSON, "The New Science of Public Opinion Measurement and Its Implications for Business," *Harvard Business School Alumni Bulletin*, July, 1939.

their sequence, the stability of replies can be examined in relation to numerous other variables. Experimental designs, and particularly split runs, can prove very useful in such work, with the pilot survey providing the basis for determining the extent of experimentation.

5.4. THE INTERVIEWER

In personal interview and telephone surveys a crucial part of the operation rests on the interviewer. A considerable literature has developed on the selection, training and supervision of interviewers (see references at end of chapter), but much remains to be learned about the subject, particularly on interviewer selection and interviewer bias. The variety of purposes of, and conditions under which, surveys are conducted, and the problems of human relationships are such that few hard and fast rules can be formulated for selecting interviewers and avoiding interviewer bias. In this section, we shall review the main problems in dealing with interviewers and various approaches to coping with them.

5.4.1. Selection

The general qualities that an interviewer should possess are easily formulated: extroversion, impartiality to different points of view, friendliness without getting personal, ability to remain calm under many different circumstances, conscientiousness, perseverance, accuracy of reporting, and adaptability. Nevertheless, the selection of successful interviewers remains a most perplexing task. This is partly because it is difficult to judge *a priori* the extent to which an applicant possesses these qualifications, and partly because applicants lacking one or more of these qualifications may become excellent interviewers anyway, while a person having all qualifications may still make a poor interviewer.

Evaluating an applicant's qualifications is done generally by personal interview, by examination of application forms, and by administering tests on various aptitudes, or by some combination of these approaches. A combination approach is generally preferable, particularly one utilizing both application forms and personal interview, since each provides information not easily obtained otherwise. Thus, the application form throws some light on the thoroughness and attention which the applicant gives to details, as well as background information; if he is asked to fill it out in his own handwriting, a revealing impression of his neatness is obtained as well.

On the other hand, the personal interview gives some idea of the tact and poise with which the applicant handles a new situation. Generally, however, the interview helps indicate who will *not* make a good interviewer rather than who will, for the applicant is clearly on his "best behavior" in such a situation.

The value of aptitude tests in interviewer selection is a rather controversial question. For one thing, there is the question of the extent to which such a test measures the desired quality—the validity of the test. Many people who get jitters in any sort of written examination do very well in the field. Then again, there are people who pass such tests with flying colors and are nevertheless unable to handle an actual interview. Under the circumstances, therefore, such tests are best employed as supplementary to the other approaches, and not as absolute criteria. Furthermore, they are likely to be more useful in a negative sense than in a positive sense. In other words, a poor test score is more likely to indicate that the applicant will not make a good interviewer than a good score is likely to indicate that the candidate has the makings of a good interviewer.

A highly effective means of weeding out good interviewers from poor ones lies in the use of the "dummy interview." This technique is applied after interviewers have been selected and have received some training in the type of information to be collected. They are then sent out on "pretest interviews," which are "rigged" in advance, that is, the persons to be interviewed are connected with the sponsor and have been told what to say and how to act to the interviewer when he arrives. The questionnaire turned in by the interviewer can then be matched with the actual information he was given (sometimes by wire recorder) as a basis for assessing the accuracy and completeness with which the data are reported.

Two to three interviews of this type are generally sufficient to yield a very good impression of the capability of a particular interviewer. They can also be used to evaluate an interviewer's ability to cope with difficult situations by arranging for each respondent to act in a different "mood" when the interviewer arrives.

The principal disadvantages of this test are that it can be rather expensive and time-consuming to set up. It is therefore more likely to be preferred if much data are to be obtained in the interview, especially if an unstructured questionnaire is being used, or if the subject of the interview is likely to be somewhat awkward (such as uses of laxatives, savings practices, etc.), or if a series of interviews with each respondent is contemplated, which makes rapport even more important than usual.

It will be noted that no reference has been made so far to experience as a criterion of interviewer competence. In general, experience is not a basic prerequisite for a good interviewer. Experience is helpful, particularly if it is in the same type of survey work for which the applicant is being considered. However, given the other attributes, experience is readily acquired, whereas no amount of experience will compensate for absence of such characteristics as tact or perseverence.

Under certain conditions, experience may actually be detrimental to a good interviewer. Such is the case when an interviewer has had all his experience with one type of questionnaire or survey approach and is faced with using a different approach. What was acceptable previously may be unacceptable now. Thus, an interviewer who has conducted depth interviews may well have trouble using a highly structured questionnaire seeking factual data. Also, an interviewer who has been trained to ask only what is on the questionnaire may find himself lost in a projective test situation where he is supposed to improvise questions that will lead the respondent to talk freely. Such is not always the case, for experience can be a valuable asset in many situations, but the fact remains that its mere presence does not ensure good interviewing, nor does it ensure unbiased interpretation of replies.

5.4.2. Training and Supervision

5.4.2.1. *Training*. Regardless of the amount of experience a staff of interviewers may have had, even if with the same type of operation, training and briefing sessions before a new survey operation are highly desirable for two reasons. One is to acquaint the interviewers with the objectives of the survey, with the type of information they will be seeking and under what circumstances, and to make sure that all instructions are understood. Every survey is new in one sense or another. Avoidance of mistakes and consistency of replies can only be ensured by thorough advance preparations. The second reason for briefing and training sessions is psychological—to give the interviewers "pep talks" and get them interested in the survey more than simply as a means of earning a few extra dollars. Interviewing essentially is a rather lonely job and is much more likely to be done with enthusiasm and conscientiousness if the interviewer feels himself to be part of a team operation with strong support behind him.

If a long or involved interview is required, several sessions may be necessary. In most instances, however, one session will be sufficient (provided the interviewers are already trained), consisting of a description of the survey, means of contacting sample members, method of handling the questionnaire, operating schedules, and various difficulties that might arise and ways of coping with them.[13] Often useful are practice interviews, in which interviewers take turns interviewing each other in the presence of the supervisor. Satisfactory interviews of this type do not, however, guarantee that the interviewer will do all right in the field; they are more in the nature of necessary, rather than sufficient, conditions for good performance.

Written instructions are also of considerable help, preferably used in conjunction with briefing sessions. An effective means of doing so is to have the

---

[13] For a description of how such sessions are run, see MILDRED PARTEN, *Surveys, Polls and Samples* (New York: Harper and Brothers, 1950), Chapter 10.

interviewers study the questionnaire and the written instructions before the meeting, discuss the materials during the meeting, then ask the interviewer to go over the material once again on his own. The latter can be ensured by requiring the interviewer before going into the field to pass an "open book" test at home, consisting of numerous questions on the interview covering all the salient features. By the time the interviewer completes such an examination, he will be thoroughly conversant with the questionnaire, whether he had intended to be or not!

Interviewers with little or no previous experience require advance training before any briefing on the survey at hand. This advance training is carried out with the aid of manuals,[14] meetings and practice interviews. Fully adequate training can be fairly expensive, especially so if turnover is sizeable, since interviewers are paid for the time they spend in this manner. Nevertheless, it is generally an unavoidable cost of a survey operation; it is in fact much less expensive than to have much of the survey itself invalidated because of poor or inconsistent data.

It might be noted that training is as necessary for telephone interviews as for personal interviews, though the emphasis in the former case is heavily on control of respondent interest by oral means alone. Training does not have to be as thorough, however, if telephone interviews are conducted from a central office with a supervisor present to deal immediately with any questions that might arise.

5.4.2.2. Supervision. Too often is interviewer supervision in the field considered unnecessary because training and briefing sessions were held. The result is usually an unhappy one, for these two aspects are complementary rather than substitutes for each other. In any survey, problems are bound to arise which had not been covered or anticipated at the briefing sessions. If the interviewer does not have someone to consult on those problems, he will tend either to ignore them altogether or to decide them on his own, which may or may not be the right decision. Actually, the latter is not too probable because interviewers, being human, are more likely to take the path of least resistance and do what is easiest, which usually means ignoring the problem. Then again, frequent contact with the interviewers during the field operation is beneficial for psychological reasons, in helping maintain morale and interest in the study.

With telephone interviews, supervision is especially easy, and efficient, if the calls are made from a central office. If a problem should arise, the interviewer can consult immediately with the supervisor. When calls are not made

---

[14] An excellent one is *Interviewing With NORC*, University of Chicago, National Opinion Research Center. Also see J. S. ADAMS, *Interviewing Procedures: A Manual for Survey Interviewers*, Chapel Hill, N. C.: University of North Carolina Press, 1958. Various government agencies, such as the Bureau of the Census and the Bureau of Labor Statistics, have their own training manuals.

from a central office, or on personal interviews in a local area, arrangements have to be made for periodic reports by the interviewers to the supervisors. If at all possible, a report should be made at the very start, after the interviewer has completed five to ten calls. By examining the questionnaires and discussing them with the interviewers, potential trouble spots are caught and smoothed out right away. Periodic reports afterward help ensure smooth operations.

In the case of surveys that cover wide geographic areas, the general procedure is much the same, except that each area will probably have a separate field supervisor (who may also do interviewing) with overall coordination effected by a field director traveling from one area to another. The training and preparation of interviewers for the survey may then be carried out in two stages—first by bringing together the area supervisors, and second by having each area supervisor meet with his interviewers, preferably with the field director present at these meetings to ensure uniformity among different areas.

Strictly speaking, supervision ends with the completion of field operations. Actually, however, it is a good idea to keep in touch with the interviewers afterwards as well. Even though this particular survey may have been a one-time proposition, there is no telling when interviewer assistance may be required on another survey. For this reason, many organizations send letters to the interviewers after the field work is in, thanking them for their assistance. At a later date, copies of a final report may be sent as well, if the results are not confidential.

Another desirable practice is to have the interviewers report their impressions of their interviews, of any trouble they might have had, and of possible improvements that might have been made in the questionnaire or in the interviewing procedure. Such a report can be made orally, in group meetings, or on a so-called "interviewer report form," a sample of which is shown in Fig. 5.3. Much useful information is obtained in this manner not only for future reference but also on the sources of error and bias in the present survey, and at the same time the interviewer is more likely to feel that his work is appreciated.

5.4.2.3. *Bias.* By interviewer bias we mean the extent to which an answer is altered in meaning by some action or attitude on the part of the interviewer. The sources of interviewer bias are legion—in fact, the relationship between interviewer bias and overall survey bias appears to be almost in the nature of one order of infinity to another. Despite the numerous forms that have been uncovered already,[15] there is little doubt that many more forms have yet to be detected. If bias can be detected, and there are ways of

---

[15] See references in Hugh G. Wales and Robert Ferber, *A Basic Bibliography on Marketing Research* (Chicago: American Marketing Association, *rev. ed.*, 1962), Sec. 9.2.

INTERVIEWER REPORT FORM

No. _____   Int. _____
1. CONTACT REPORT   Form : _____

			WHERE					RESULTS OF CONTACT					TIME
	WHEN		HOW				Other (ex-	Person(s) talked		R. not	R. too		Other (ex-		SPENT IN
Date	Day	Time	Phone	Pers.	Home	Off.	plain)	to	Int.	home	busy	Ref.	plain)	Con.	Edit.
___	___	___	☐	☐	☐	☐	_____	_____	☐	☐	☐	☐	_____	___	___
___	___	___	☐	☐	☐	☐	_____	_____	☐	☐	☐	☐	_____	___	___
___	___	___	☐	☐	☐	☐	_____	_____	☐	☐	☐	☐	_____	___	___
___	___	___	☐	☐	☐	☐	_____	_____	☐	☐	☐	☐	_____	___	___

IF NOT INTERVIEWED: Please explain circumstances in detail. _____
_____
_____

2. ATTITUDE OF PANEL MEMBER
   a. How would you describe the panel member's attitude in each of the following respects. Please answer both parts of the question in each case.

	IN THIS INTERVIEW					COMPARED TO LAST INTERVIEW		
	Excel-lent	Good	Fair	Poor	Very poor	Better	No change	Worse
Cooperativeness......................	☐	☐	☐	☐	☐	☐	☐	☐
Accuracy of information given...........	☐	☐	☐	☐	☐	☐	☐	☐
(Exact figures for items requested)								
Completeness of information............	☐	☐	☐	☐	☐	☐	☐	☐
(All assets and liabilities)								

3. INTERIM REPORT NO. 1
   Did panel member mention receiving "Interim Report No. 1"?
   No ☐   Yes ☐
                   ↓
   (Exact words of panel member) _____
   _____
   _____

4. INVENTORY OF PERSONAL ATTITUDES
   a. What was panel member's attitude while taking IPA?
   Fully sincere ☐   Partly sincere ☐   Not sincere ☐
                                     ↓   ↓
   Explain: _____
   _____
   _____

   b. Any problems involved in giving the IPA?
      No ☐   Yes ☐
                   ↓
   Explain: _____
   _____
   _____

5. SUMMARY COMMENTS
   Please summarize briefly the overall reaction of the respondent to this interview. Include any information or observations which might be of interest in the analysis of this panel member.
   _____
   _____
   _____
   _____

Fig. 5.3

doing so,[16] adjustments are generally possible. In view of the subtle ways it can occur, prevention through adequate interviewer training and supervision is by far the superior approach. However, since bias may occur under almost any conditions, a general knowledge of the manner in which it takes place is

---

[16] *Ibid.*

indispensable in survey work. In this section, a generalized framework is presented which encompasses the various forms of this bias.

OUTLINE. A general outline of this framework is as follows:

    A. Non-response bias—interviewer-induced
    B. Response bias
        1. Deliberate misrepresentation—cheating
        2. Inadvertent misrepresentation
            a) Interviewer misunderstanding of response
            b) Response understood but interpreted incorrectly
        3. Preconditioning of respondent
            a) Identification bias
            b) Sponsor bias
            c) Other

As indicated by this outline, interviewer bias in the first instance is brought about either by influencing or distorting the answer or by not receiving an answer at all. The latter, the problem of non-response, is broader than the interviewer alone. Conceptually, however, it is a form of interviewer bias as well, to the extent that the non-response is influenced by some action or attitude of the interviewer. In practice, the reasons for non-response, whether to a single question or to the entire interview, are very difficult to allocate by specific factors, but the fact remains that in particular situations non-response is known to be caused by the interviewer "rubbing the sample member the wrong way."

Bias in the answers reported by the interviewer undoubtedly represent the principal sources of trouble and, as noted in the preceding outline, these sources are many. A few comments on each are made in the following paragraphs.

CHEATING. To sit home and fill out questionnaires while sitting by one's fireside can be an almost irresistible urge—especially if it is a cold rainy night, the interviewer knows that he is on his own, and it is a one-time proposition in which checking back seems hardly likely. Though there is nothing a researcher can do about the weather, at least so far, enough can be done in these other respects to reduce the problem to negligible importance.

Proper interviewer selection and training is the first requisite. If an interviewer is conscientious and feels confident that he has been given all the instructions needed to do the job, there is much less incentive for him to do any cheating.

Adequate supervision in the field is another requisite. If a supervisor is in frequent touch with the interviewers, not only is there less opportunity for them to cheat but there will be less inclination as well, since their morale is higher and the "team spirit" will be more in evidence. If no supervisors are present, as in the case of widely dispersed geographic surveys in which interviewers receive instructions by mail, the cheating problem is potentially much more serious.

Realistic schedules are another deterrent to cheating. If an interviewer is given an assignment which he knows cannot possibly be carried out within the stipulated time, the impulse to cheat may be overwhelming, especially if he is anxious to earn the money and fears that slowness on his part may lead to his not receiving further assignments.

Perhaps the strongest deterrent to cheating is use of a system of spot checks. Such a system is useful for gaining information on the impressions made by different interviewers as well as for checking purposes. In a local area, this can be carried out by phone, if the respondent's name and address are given. Otherwise, it is easily done by means of a double-folded postcard sent to every *n*th respondent. Interviewer awareness of the use of spot checking, including precautionary mention that no compensation will be made if cheating is discovered,[17] would serve virtually to eliminate this practice. Unfortunately, many surveys fail to take such simple measures.

INADVERTENT MISREPRESENTATION. The danger of this bias is greatest with open-end questions and depth or projective interviews and is least with multiple-choice questions in which the interviewer simply checks the appropriate category of response. In the former case, the most frequent source of bias is the interviewer's tendency to shorten the respondent's reply and put it in his own words. Misinterpretation easily occurs. If the respondent describes his firm's current sales as "good under the circumstances" and the interviewer writes this down as "good," an important qualification is lost.

In other instances, an interviewer may misunderstand a reply, either without realizing it or by not understanding some term used by the respondent and hesitating to ask for a clarification. The resulting answer can impart a radically different interpretation to the respondent's reply. Thus, a reply to a question on attitude toward federal control of prices in natural gas fields may be "depends on which side you're looking at," which is not the same as "not sure." Here, additional probing would serve to indicate the side taken by *that* respondent and, hence, a definite opinion.

Adequate training is the principal means of counteracting these forms of bias, particularly impressing interviewers with the necessity to use a respondent's own words and to transcribe the *entire* reply. In long, unstructured interviews, this is not easy to do, however, and in such instances a tape recorder may be the only effective means of securing all the information.

Bias of this type is particularly likely to occur in attitude surveys on subjects of wide current interest. In such a case, detection and correction are often possible by subjecting the interviewers to the same questionnaire in

---

[17] This has been upheld by the courts. L. ANDREWS, "Court Decree on the 'Cheater,'" *Journal of Marketing*, October, 1953, pp. 167–169.

advance of the field operations. The relationship between their attitudes and those they report for the respondents can then be studied and appropriate adjustments made if necessary.[18]

PRECONDITIONING. Question sequence and wording are probably the principal culprits in preconditioning respondent answers, but interviewer actions and attitudes may well be a close second. The very presence of an interviewer will tend to make the respondent more careful and cautious in his replies, especially if the questions relate to a matter of personal concern. Thus, employees' attitudes toward their supervisors were found to be much less critical when the information was sought by personal interview than when a mail questionnaire was employed, even though the data collection was carried out by an impartial organization, and no personal identification was requested in either case.[19] Assurances notwithstanding, the respondent is likely to retain some fear that the interviewer might later identify him in one way or another.

In almost any type of interview, the interaction between interviewer and respondent tends to influence the latter's replies.[20] Some forms of preconditioning are overt, others are not. Following are some of the principal forms encountered in economic and business surveys:

Identification bias. Fear of one's responses being identified will lead to modification of replies, as noted in the preceding example. Sometimes this may lead to deliberate misrepresentation, by the respondent's giving the "popular" answer rather than reveal his true feelings.

Sponsor bias. Knowledge of the sponsor of a survey tends to influence the respondent against making critical remarks if the questions relate to that sponsor's products. Even on more general issues, the respondent will tend to give answers in line with the imagined attitude or policy of the sponsor. Thus, an interviewer for a labor union is not likely to get many critical remarks on the labor movement, even from management respondents. For these reasons, use of a "dummy" sponsor, if the survey work is not subcontracted, is often a necessary device for securing accurate data.

Expectation bias. Explaining the objectives of a survey may often influence replies. If the respondent is told that the purpose of a survey is to explore the need for suburban shopping centers, his answers are likely to be in the direction of helping to establish such a need. The purposes of a survey are therefore deliberately left vague, sometimes with the interviewers as well.

---

[18] For one means of making such adjustments, see ROBERT FERBER and H. G. WALES, "Detection and Correction of Interviewer Bias," *Public Opinion Quarterly*, Spring 1952, pp. 107–127. Also J. S. STOCK and J. R. HOCHSTIM, "A Method of Measuring Interviewer Variability," *Public Opinion Quarterly*, Summer 1951, pp. 322–334.

[19] R. L. KAHN, "A Comparison of Two Methods of Collecting Data for Social Research," paper presented at 1952 Annual Meetings of the *American Statistical Association.*

[20] DAVID RIESMAN and MARK BENNEY, "The Sociology of the Interview," *The Midwest Sociologist*, 1955.

Inflection bias. Inflection in the manner of asking a question can influence replies with comparative ease. "Do you favor higher taxes at *this* time?" will yield many more negative replies than "Do you favor higher *taxes* at this time?" As a general rule, the less inflection, the better.

Appearance bias. A white-collar interviewer may secure different information than would a less well-dressed one.[21] Anything unusual about the interviewer in the eyes of the respondent may influence the replies.

Here again, training and supervision are the best preventives for preconditioning. Detection of the numerous forms of this bias is very difficult in any given situation, involving usually some form of experimental design incorporated in the survey operation.[22]

5.5. SAMPLING TECHNIQUES

It is in the nature of a survey operation that only a small number of members of the population are covered. The results obtained are, therefore, hardly ever likely to be perfectly accurate estimates for the population as a whole because of variations brought about by the sampling process.

Perfect accuracy is not necessary anyway;[23] all that is needed are results with a sufficiently high degree of accuracy to be of practical value. In effect, surveys yield information on the probable limits within which the true, unknown values for the population lie. The specification of these limits is a practical problem, depending on the judgment of those who are going to use the results. The sampling problem is to determine what sample size and sample design will yield results within these limits as economically as possible.

Alternately, the sample size and design may be specified by other considerations, such as a desire to maintain comparability with previous studies, and the problem may be simply to measure the accuracy of the results. In either case, the answer is usually not difficult to obtain through the application of probability theory. Much more difficult is the situation where probability methods are not applicable. The various alternatives are discussed in the following sections.

---

[21] D. KATZ, "Do Interviewers Bias Poll Results?" *Public Opinion Quarterly*, Vol. 6 (Summer 1942), pp. 248–268.

[22] For the most comprehensive study of the many forms of interviewer bias, see H. HYMAN, *Interviewing in Social Research* (Chicago: University of Chicago Press, 1954). See also R. L. KAHN and C. F. CANNELL, *The Dynamics of Interviewing: Theory, Techniques and Cases* (N. Y.: Wiley & Sons, 1957).

[23] Perfect accuracy in all respects is impossible, which is clear when we consider the many other sources of error besides sampling variations—coding and editing errors, sample selection errors, interviewer bias, etc. In fact, it can be argued that a sample is more effective than even a census in minimizing *total* errors, because of the greater attention that can then be given to these other sources of error, which often outweigh considerably sampling errors alone.

5.5.1. Probability Selection

Numerical estimates of sample size and sample precision are valid only
when a so-called probability, or random, method of sample member selection
is employed. All this means is that each member of the population has an
equal chance of being selected in the sample. For example, if a sample of 400
is to be chosen from a list of 100,000 people, equal probability means that
each of these 100,000 people must have 4 chances in 1,000 of being picked.
In practice, there are two principal ways of accomplishing this:

1. *Systematic selection.* If a sample of N units is desired from a population
of P units, select every P/Nth name, beginning with a random number
between *1* and N, inclusive. Thus, if we pick every 250th name from the list
of 100,000 people, beginning with a randomly selected number between 1 and
250, we end up with a sample of 400. The important thing is to select the
first number in as random a manner as possible. A random-sampling number
table, as described later, is an easy way of doing so.

Systematic selection is feasible if no list is available, but the population
can be counted. For example, a probability, or randomly-selected, sample
of 300 dwelling units in a city containing about 6,000 units is possible by
instructing interviewers to select every 20th dwelling unit, counting in some
systematic fashion, e.g., numbering all blocks from southwest to northeast
and counting clockwise around each block beginning at the southwest corner.
Actually, the directions would have to be far more explicit and the interviewers would have to be trained to avoid skipping units, but the general
approach is feasible and has been used frequently in population sampling.
It is important also to guard against periodicity in the sampling process.
Thus, if there are 10 homes to every block, a 10 per cent systematic sample
of households to ascertain willingness to pay for paved streets is likely to
yield biased results.

2. *Random-sampling numbers.* Tables of numbers are available which,
according to the best statistical tests that can be devised, are dispersed entirely at random.[24] Part of a table of random numbers is shown in the Appendix (pp. 558–559). The procedure involves numbering all the members of the
population, selecting digits from the table in any *systematic* manner (horizontally, vertically, diagonally, etc.), and including in the sample the units
whose numbers are selected.

In some instances, numbering of all population units is not necessary.
For example, if a sample is to be picked from a city directory containing
624 pages, two columns to a page and 34 names in a column, a six-digit number is needed to identify each sample member. The first three digits would
represent the page number if under 625 (numbers over 624 and 000 would
not be used: why?); the fourth digit, the column number—odd, the left-hand

---

[24] The most complete such set is Rand Corporation, *A Million Random Digits* (Glencoe,
Ill.: The Free Press, 1954). Various smaller sets are available as well.

column, even (including zero), the right-hand column; and the last two digits, the line number. In the latter case, 00 could be omitted and digits up to 68 used (how?). Thus, counts would be needed only in pages and columns selected by the random numbers, and even this can be avoided by using an appropriately marked paper strip.

The precise method of application of random digits depends on the particular problem, but the general approach is always the same: identify each member of the population with a distinctive set of digits and select the sample members on the basis of digit sequences chosen from the random number table.

Random selection of sample members is almost always possible, though a fair amount of ingenuity may be required in some instances, such as in selecting a sample of farmers in Greece. In all cases, the approach involves setting up a list or "frame" to serve as the basis for selecting the sample. Once the frame is set up, the rest is routine.

5.5.2. Unrestricted Sampling

With unrestricted sampling as discussed in the last section, *each* sample member is selected from the population at large. No attempt is made to ensure the representation of particular groups, the theory being that this is taken care of by the process of random selection.[25] Thus, if 40 per cent of a population own their homes, 40 per cent of an unrestricted sample would also be expected to own their homes.

The sampling variance in estimates of averages based on unrestricted samples is proportional to the variance of that characteristic in the population and inversely proportional to the sample size, i.e.:

$$Sampling\ variance = \frac{Variance\ of\ characteristic\ in\ population}{Size\ of\ sample} \quad (5.1)$$

The square root of the sampling variance, the "standard error" is the usual measure of sampling error, and is analogous in sampling analysis to the standard deviation in analysis of populations (Chapter 3). Thus, with a large sample (N about 30 or more), there are 95 chances in 100 that the sample estimate is not more than about two (1.96) standard errors away from the true value and 68 chances in 100 that it is within the one standard error range. For smaller size samples, the probabilities are somewhat lower, and decrease with sample size, as may be deduced from Appendix Table A2 on page 551.

---

[25] This technique is also sometimes called "random sampling." The latter is an unfortunate term, however, for it tends to confuse a sampling *technique* with a method of sample member *selection*. The latter may serve to modify sampling variance formulas, as with systematic selection, but in practice its effect in this respect is usually negligible.

Computationally, (5.1) is easy to apply. The variance of a continuous variable, such as age or income, is $\sigma^2 = \Sigma(X - \bar{X})^2/N$ (Chapter 3), so that the standard error of the mean of such a variable is:

$$\sigma_{\hat{x}} = \frac{\sigma}{\sqrt{N}} \qquad (5.2a)$$

and of a total

$$\sigma_x = \frac{P^2\sigma^2}{N} \qquad (5.2b)$$

P is the size of the population.

The variance of a percentage (p) is pq, where $q = 1 - p$, so that its standard error is:

$$\sigma_p = \sqrt{\frac{pq}{N}} \qquad (5.3)$$

For example, if 30 per cent of 280 men interviewed bought a topcoat within the past year, the chances are 19 out of 20 that the interval $30 \pm 2(2.7)$ per cent contains the true percentage. On the other hand, if an upper limit estimate is desired, we can say that the chances are 19 out of 20 that the true percentage of men who bought a topcoat recently is below $30 + 1.645(2.7)$, or 35 per cent. The multiplier is 1.645 because five per cent of the area under the normal curve is bounded by 1.645σ and the limit of the curve.

If the sample size is less than 30, $N - 1$ is substituted for N in (5.2) and (5.3) and the t-distribution (Appendix Table A2) is used instead of the normal distribution for estimating the probabilities of error. If, in addition, the sample constitutes an appreciable portion of the population, say 4 per cent or more, the expression is modified by $(1 - N/P)$. Thus, (5.3) then becomes:

$$\sigma_p = \sqrt{\frac{pq}{N}\left(1 - \frac{N}{P}\right)} \qquad (5.4)$$

The inversion of (5.1) serves as the basis for estimating sample size, i.e.:

$$N = \frac{\textit{Variance of characteristic in population}}{\textit{Sampling variance}} \qquad (5.5)$$

and correspondingly for (5.2)–(5.4). In other words, having an estimate of the variance in the population and given the allowable margin of error in the survey, the required sample size can be calculated in advance, the accuracy of the estimate depending on the accuracy of the estimated population variance, or on the desired *precision* of the estimate.

Since it is wiser to be safe than sorry, any doubt about the true population variance is best resolved on the conservative side, i.e., toward the higher figure. With percentages, this means selecting the percentage closest to .5 (why?), whereas with a continuous variable it involves selecting the higher of two alternative probable values of the population variance.

For example, suppose an estimate is to be sought by unrestricted sampling of the proportion of households owning two or more television sets. The researcher wants to have 95 chances out of 100 that the sample estimate will be within 5 percentage points of the true figure, and feels that the latter may be anywhere between 25 and 40 per cent.

For estimating the required sample size, the safest estimate of p is .4. By the conditions for accuracy, we have:

$$1.96\sigma_p = .05$$

or

$$\sigma_p = .0255$$

Hence, from (5.3):

$$N = \frac{pq}{\sigma_p{}^2} = \frac{(.4)(.6)}{(.0255)^2} = 369 \qquad (5.6)$$

If N is less than 30 or is appreciable in relation to the size of the population, a new computation should be made taking these factors into account (5.4).

The estimate of the population variance is based generally either on the results of a pilot survey or on past experience. For percentages, there is likely to be little trouble even in complete absence of information because of the limiting value of pq. If no information is available in the case of a variable, a pilot survey is indicated, and yields a good estimate of the variance with only a few observations. This is made possible by the existence of a relationship between the range and the standard deviation of randomly-selected observations, as follows:

$$estimate \; of \; \sigma = (a_n)(range) \qquad (5.7)$$

where a_n is a multiplier that varies with sample size. Its values, and related multipliers for assessing the reliability of the estimate, are given in Appendix Table A6 on p. 557. This table permits estimates of the population variance to be made with as few as two observations, though as a rule it is desirable to have at least four to five observations.

5.5.3. Replicated Sampling

5.5.3.1. *Single drawing per zone.* Instead of selecting one large sample from the population, the sample may be divided into a number of equal subsamples and each subsample selected at random from the population in the same way as every other subsample. The overall sample then consists of a number of *replicating* subsamples, each providing presumably a miniature of the population.

For example, in ordinary unrestricted sampling a shopping survey of N households may be carried out by selecting from the street section of a city directory every (P/N)th address, beginning with a random number between 1 and P/N, P being the number of listed households. (In practice, the city directory would probably have to be supplemented by outside data, e.g., new housing developments, but this does not affect this example.) In other words, if 250 households were to be contacted in a city containing 10,000 households, the household corresponding to a random number between 1 and 40 would be selected as would every 40th household thereafter.

In replicated sampling the procedure is somewhat different. A decision is made on how many replicated subsamples are desirable. The number ordinarily varies anywhere from 2 to 10 or more, with 10 a fairly frequent figure.[26] If we choose 10 as the number of replications, the sample of 250 households is broken up into 10 replicated samples, each containing 25 households. Each subsample is selected separately. One way of doing so is to divide the directory list into 25 equal zones, each containing approximately 400 names. Ten (non-duplicating) random numbers between 1 and 400 are selected. Each of these numbers represents the start of one of the 10 subsamples, the remaining 24 members being selected as every 400th household thereafter. The result is 10 replicating, or *interpenetrating*, samples of 25 each, or an aggregate sample size of 250.

Replicated sampling offers two principal advantages over unrestricted sampling. One is that the replicative design can serve as a basis for detecting various forms of bias in certain instances or for testing the influence of different factors or survey approaches on the subject under study. Since the subsamples are presumably identical with each other except for random sampling fluctuations, the influence of different factors can be gauged experimentally by imposing them on some subsamples but not on others and then noting the significance of any resulting differences. For example, in a survey on advertising recall, different measures of recall could be used with each subsample to ascertain the effect of each on the type of results obtained.

The second principal advantage of replicated sampling is the ease with which sampling errors can be computed in many instances. Thus, in the shopping survey example just mentioned, the standard error of, say, the per cent (p) shopping mostly in neighborhood stores would be:[27]

---

[26] This matter is discussed in Chapter 21 of W. E. DEMING, *Sample Design in Business Research*, New York: John Wiley & Sons, 1960.

[27] If the overall sample constituted an appreciable part of the population, the finite multiplier would have to be attached, and (5.8) becomes:

$$\sigma_p = \frac{r}{k} \sqrt{1 - k/Z}, \text{ } Z \text{ being the size of a zone.} \qquad (5.8a)$$

If, in addition, there are few replications, say less than 8, (5.8a) should be multiplied by $\sqrt{k/(k-1)}$, where k is the number of replications.

$$\sigma_p = \frac{R}{k} \quad for \ 2 \leq k \leq 10 \tag{5.8}$$

where R is the range of p for the k (= 10) subsamples.

In other words, suppose the per cent shopping in neighborhood stores ranges from 18.4% to 29.2% for the 10 subsamples, with the overall percentage being 23.6%. The standard error of this overall percentage is estimated from (5.8) to be:

$$\sigma_p = \frac{29.2 - 18.4}{10} = 1.08\%$$

Equation (5.8) supplies a reliable estimate of the standard error for up to ten subsamples. For larger numbers the range becomes unstable, and the variance of the percentage has to be used, so that (5.8) becomes:

$$\sigma_p = \frac{\Sigma(p_i - p)^2}{k} \tag{5.9}$$

More generally, (5.9) can be represented as the standard error of any ratio, percentage, or mean value by rewriting it as:

$$\sigma_p = \frac{1}{Y} \sqrt{\Sigma(X_i - pY_i)^2} \tag{5.10}$$

where X_i is the value of the numerator from subsample i
      Y_i is the value of the denominator from subsample i
      p is the overall percentage, or ratio, i.e., $(\Sigma X_i)/(\Sigma Y_i)$
      Y is ΣY_i

For example, if we are estimating the average income of those interviewed on the shopping survey, X_i would represent the total income of the respondents in subsample i, and Y_i would represent the number of respondents in that subsample. Similarly, in estimating the proportion having a particular attribute, X_i would represent the number in subsample i having that attribute and Y_i the total number interviewed in that subsample.[28]

5.5.3.2. *Multiple drawings per zone.* The preceding section covered the case where only one observation from each zone was selected for each subsample. More generally, however, it may be considered desirable to make more than one drawing per zone for each subsample. This may be useful for

---

[28] Corresponding standard error formulas for estimates of a total, and of coefficients of variation of a ratio are:

$$\text{For a total: } \sigma_X = \frac{1}{k} Z \sqrt{\Sigma(X_i - pY_i)^2} \tag{5.11a}$$

$$\text{For the coefficient of variation of a ratio: } \sigma_{V_p} = \frac{1}{X} \sqrt{\Sigma(X_i - pY_i)^2} \tag{5.11b}$$

computational convenience, for administrative reasons, or because of the requirements of the sample design.

In any event, the procedure is essentially an extension of the simpler case. If systematic selection is used, the sampling interval is reduced to fit the new requirements, or the zones could be redefined. For example, in the shopping survey mentioned previously, two drawings per zone (per subsample) could be obtained by combining pairs of adjoining zones into new "thick zones" (though some further adjustment of the zones would be needed in this case because the number of original "thin" zones is odd). Alternately, the sampling interval could be reduced from 400 to 200 and the number of subsamples halved.

Similarly, the standard error formulas for this more general case are extensions of those presented in the preceding section. If we let:

X_{ij} be the sample value of Z for the ith zone in the jth subsample; $i = 1, \ldots, m; j = 1, \ldots, k$

Y_{ij} be the sample value of Y for the ith zone in the jth subsample

$\bar{X}_i$ and $\bar{Y}_i$ be the X and Y sample means, respectively, for the ith zone

p_i be the sample proportion in the ith zone having a given attribute, which also may be defined as: $\bar{X}_i / \bar{Y}_i$

R_i be the average of the absolute ranges of the variable $= (\Sigma R_i)/m$

Z be the size of each zone in the population (number of sampling units per zone)

and the other symbols the same as before,

the standard error of the sample percentage, p, becomes:

$$\sigma_p = \frac{R_i}{k \sqrt{m}} \tag{5.12}$$

The more general form, corresponding to (5.9) and (5.10), is:

$$\sigma_p^2 = \frac{1}{k^2} \sum_i \sum_j \{(X_{ij} - \bar{X}_i) - p(Y_{ij} - \bar{Y}_i)\}^2 \tag{5.13}$$

Similarly, the square of the standard error of a total is:

$$\sigma_X^2 = \frac{Z}{k} \sum_i \sum_j (X_{ij} - \bar{X}_i)^2 \tag{5.14}$$

And the square of the standard error of the coefficient of variation of a ratio is·

$$\sigma_{V_p}^2 = \frac{1}{X} \sum_i \sum_j \{(X_{ij} - \bar{X}_i) - p(Y_{ij} - \bar{Y}_i)\}^2 \tag{5.15}$$

As before, the finite multiplier, $1 - (k/Z)$, should be used if the sample constitutes an appreciable part of the population, and the multiplier $k/(k-1)$ should be appended if k is less than about 8.

5.5.4. Stratification

When an unrestricted sample is selected, there is always some danger that it will not provide a representative miniature of the population. Since it is selected by probability methods, there remains the *possibility* that 300 people, all millionnaires, may be selected at random from a city of 100,000, though the probability of this event may be very low. More realistically, certain relevant segments of a population can easily be underrepresented when an unrestricted sample is chosen. Hence, when considerable heterogeneity is present in the population with regard to the subject under study, it is often a good idea to divide the population into segments, or strata, and select a certain number of sample members from each stratum, thus ensuring representation from all relevant segments. Thus, in a survey on consumer credit, the population might be divided into strata by income level and a certain number selected in a true random manner from each income level.

The number of sample members selected from each stratum is set usually in proportion to the size of that stratum in the population (proportional sampling) or allowing in addition for differing degrees of heterogeneity among the strata (disproportionate sampling). In the former case, the size of each stratum is:

$$N_i = \frac{P_i}{P} N = W_i N \tag{5.16}$$

where P_i is the size of the ith stratum in the population.

In disproportionate sampling, the optimum allocation is

$$N_i = \frac{W_i \sigma_i}{\Sigma(W_i \sigma_i)} N \tag{5.17}$$

or

$$N_i = \frac{W_i \sigma_i / \sqrt{C_i}}{\Sigma(W_i \sigma_i / \sqrt{C_i})} N \tag{5.18}$$

if cost data are available, σ_i being the population variance in stratum i and C_i the cost of interviewing a sample member in stratum i.

Illustrations of the allocation of a sample by these different methods are provided in Table 5.3. In this example, marked heterogeneity is present among the income strata, and as a result the disproportionate allocation differs sharply from the proportional allocation, placing more emphasis on representation from the higher income strata. This is highly desirable, for the more variability in a stratum, the larger the sampling variances for the same sample size.

Table 5.3

ALTERNATIVE ALLOCATION SCHEMES OF STRATIFIED SAMPLE OF 400 FOR ESTIMATING OUTSTANDING DEBT PER FAMILY

(1)	(2)	(3)	(4)	(5)	(6)	(7)	(8)	(9)	(10)	(11)	(12)
		BASIC DATA			PROPORTIONAL ALLOCATION	DISPROPORTIONATE (OPTIMAL) ALLOCATION, COSTS EXCLUDED			DISPROPORTIONATE (OPTIMAL) ALLOCATION, COSTS INCLUDED		
Income stratum	W_i	σ_i	C_i	$\sqrt{C_i}$	$(2)(N)$	$W_i\sigma_i$	$\dfrac{W_i\sigma_i}{\Sigma(W_i\sigma_i)}$	$(8)(N)$	$W_i\sigma_i/\sqrt{C_i}$	$\dfrac{W_i\sigma_i/\sqrt{C_i}}{\Sigma(W_i\sigma_i/\sqrt{C_i})}$	$(11)(N)$
Under $2,000	18%	$100	$2.50	1.6	72	1,800	4.1%	16	1,125	3.8%	15
$2,000– 3,999	31	250	2.00	1.4	124	7,750	17.5	70	5,536	18.9	76
4,000– 5,999	24	400	2.00	1.4	96	9,600	21.6	86	6,857	23.4	94
6,000– 7,999	14	700	2.00	1.4	56	9,800	22.1	89	7,000	23.8	95
8,000– 9,999	7	1,000	2.50	1.6	28	7,000	15.8	63	4,375	14.9	60
10,000–14,999	4	1,200	3.20	1.8	16	4,800	10.8	43	2,667	9.1	36
15,000 and over	2	1,800	4.00	2.0	8	3,600	8.1	33	1,800	6.1	24
	100%				400	44,350	100.0%	400	29,360	100.0%	400

Differences in allocation with interview costs taken into account (these would include the unit costs of contacting sample members and carrying out the interview) are seen to be relatively small. Except where interview conditions are radically different, such as with a sample containing both urban and rural families, this is the usual experience, though it is generally a wise precaution, nevertheless, to carry out the calculations both ways.

From the point of view of securing maximum efficiency, i.e., lowest sampling error, disproportionate allocation is highly desirable with stratified samples since most variables in economic and marketing analysis are heterogeneous in nature. Income, expenditure, savings, whether in dollars or in physical quantities vary substantially by all sorts of socio-economic characteristics as do many other variables as well.

The standard error of a stratified sample is simply the square root of the weighted average of the sampling variances of the individual strata, the weights being the squares of the relative sizes of the strata, W_i. For the mean, the latter is σ_i^2/N_i, so that for the entire sample:

$$\sigma_{\bar{X}_i} = \sqrt{\Sigma W_i^2 \frac{\sigma_i^2}{N_i}} \tag{5.19a}$$

For the sum, it is:

$$\sigma_{\Sigma X} = \sqrt{\Sigma N_i \sigma_i^2} \tag{5.19b}$$

which, for optimum allocation, (5.17) or (5.18), reduces to:

$$\sigma_{\bar{X}_i} = \frac{\Sigma W_i \sigma_i}{\sqrt{N}} \tag{5.20a}$$

and

$$\sigma_{\Sigma X} = \sqrt{N} \, \Sigma W_i \sigma_i \tag{5.20b}$$

As before, σ_i would be modified by $(1 - N_i/P_i)$ and N_i replaced by $N_i - 1$ if the strata sample sizes are appreciable in relation to the population sizes and if they are less than 30, respectively.

The same expressions hold for percentages, with $p_i q_i$ representing σ_i^2.

Equation (5.19) serves as the basis for estimating sample size in stratified sampling in the same manner as (5.1) for unrestricted sampling. Now, however, estimates are required of the population variances as well as of W_i for each stratum. Given these estimates and the maximum allowable tolerance, (5.19) can be used to arrive at an estimated total size for the stratified sample. The allocation of N among the various strata is carried out by applying (5.17) or (5.18), as illustrated in Table 5.3.

If the accuracy of the overall sample estimate is the only point at issue, this solves the problem of sample size. If, at the same time, particular levels of accuracy are desired for individual strata, as is often the case, a separate estimation of sample size would have to be made for each stratum based on

(5.1). The final sample size for a particular stratum would then be the larger of the two estimates for that stratum.

Effect of insufficient knowledge. A problem that frequently arises in the application of stratified sampling is that accurate knowledge of the sizes of the various strata is not available, or, if it is available, that lists of the population are not available by individual strata. In the former case, sampling variances such as (5.19) and (5.20) have to be increased by a term to allow for possible errors in the estimation of the W_i, so that (5.19a) becomes:

$$\sigma_{\bar{X}_i} = \sqrt{\Sigma W_i^2 \frac{\sigma_i^2}{N_i} + \Sigma[(\bar{X}_i - \bar{X})^2 \sigma_{W_i}^2]} \tag{5.21}$$

where $\sigma_{W_i}^2$ is the variance of W_i.[29]

The second term is extremely important, for it may at times be large enough to counteract the inherent superior efficiency of stratification, in the sense that the addition it contributes may raise the sampling variance of the stratified sample to that of an unrestricted sample of the same total size. This may not rule out the desirability of stratification (why?), but it could alter substantially the required sample sizes.

The problem raised by non-availability of a separate population list, or frame, for each stratum can be overcome in the following manner.[30] As an illustration, let us take the problem of obtaining a quota sample by income level, assuming that we know the city's families to be distributed in the proportion, 10:30:40:20 in four income levels, A, B, C, D, respectively. If a proportional sample of 400 families is desired, we would want 40 families in income level A, 120 in income level B, 160 in C, and 80 in D.

Sampling is carried out by applying random selection to the city *as a whole*, not to each income level individually, as was formerly done. Each member of the sample is classified in one of the four income levels. As soon as the quota for one income level is filled, all succeeding selected families that happen to be in that income level are discarded. But sampling continues from the city as a whole until all income quotas are filled. For example, if the quota for income level D is filled after sampling only 300 families, sampling continues just as before except that all D families sampled after the 300th family would either be discarded or weighted appropriately in obtaining overall estimates.

In the same manner, a disproportionate sample can be obtained as well, though oversampling of individual strata is much more likely.

---

[29] This variance can often be estimated in terms of the coefficient of variation (V). Since $V = \sigma_{W_i}/W_i$, then $\sigma_{W_i} = VW_i$, with V being an estimate of the probable percentage standard error in the estimate of the weights.

[30] This and succeeding passages are based on ROBERT FERBER, "The Common Sense of Sampling," *Current Economic Comment*, Vol. 11 (August, 1949), pp. 48–56.

This procedure fulfills the requirements of random selection because every member of any particular income level has an equal chance of being included in the sample. Of course, the probability of members of one income level being chosen relative to the probability of selection of members of any other income level is proportional to the relative numbers at the two income levels, but this does not affect the validity of the procedure.[31]

5.5.5. Area and Cluster Sampling

Area sampling is pretty much what the name implies. The population is broken up initially into areas, and a number of these areas are selected either at random or in some stratified manner for inclusion in the sample. The sample members are then selected from these sample areas only, usually with the aid of maps of some kind, e.g., maps of dwelling units. Besides ensuring random selection of the sample members, this procedure reduces interviewing costs as a result of the concentration of interviewers within specific areas. Thus, it is much cheaper to interview 20 farmers in one county than one farmer in each of 20 different counties. Consequently, where the cost of additional materials, e.g., maps, does not nullify this reduced interviewing cost, an area sample may prove more economical than even an unrestricted sample.[32]

A variation of area sampling which reduces interviewer travel and time costs to a minimum is *cluster sampling*. In this type of sample, the sample members are selected in groups instead of individually. For instance, instead of selecting one family from each of 1,000 blocks, a cluster sample could be constructed by selecting ten adjoining families from each of 100 blocks. In some instances, a cluster sample is likely to be more accurate than the corresponding area sample of the same size.

Still another variation is *chunk sampling*, which refers to the selection of sample members in groups from lists of a population. It is particularly useful in sampling internal records because of the ease with which the procedure can be explained to, and carried out by, clerical personnel. For

---

[31] This procedure does affect the standard errors of the resulting estimates. See DEMING, *op. cit.*, Chapter 15.

[32] Note that this method is not the same as the selection method outlined just previously when strata frames are not available. The basic difference is that in area sampling the sample members are chosen from certain predesignated or randomly-selected areas within the population, whereas the sample members in this scheme are drawn from the population at large. Therefore, this is not an area-sampling procedure, and does not require the detailed maps on the basis of which area samples are generally drawn. It might also be noted that greater accuracy can be obtained by retaining sample members in excess of their quota instead of discarding them, and merely weighting the average or aggregate figures for the different strata by the relative sizes of these strata in the population. The sampling error of such an estimate will be less than if excess sample members had been discarded (assuming that every stratum has, at least, its full quota). See Deming, *ibid.*

example, a sample of 500 credit customers of a department store is selected more simply and quickly by taking 50 (probability) chunks of 10 customers apiece rather than by selecting 500 customers individually.

It might be noted that area samples may be either unrestricted or stratified. A sample of blocks selected at random from New York City as a whole would be an unrestricted area sample, but if the blocks were selected separately from each of the five boroughs, a stratified sample would result.

The sampling variance of an area sample depends on the number of stages of randomization involved in the selection of the sample members. As a rule, an area sample will involve two or more stages of randomization. Thus, an area sample in a city may be chosen by first taking an unrestricted sample of districts or census tracts, then an unrestricted sample of blocks within sample districts, and then a random selection of households in each sample block—three stages of randomization. The sampling variance is then, symbolically:

$$\begin{matrix} Sampling \\ variance \end{matrix} = \begin{bmatrix} Sampling\ variance\ in\ the \\ random\ selection\ of\ districts \end{bmatrix} + \begin{bmatrix} Sampling\ variance\ in\ the \\ random\ selection\ of\ blocks \\ within\ districts \end{bmatrix}$$
$$+ \begin{bmatrix} Sampling\ variance\ in\ the\ random\ selection\ of \\ households\ within\ blocks \end{bmatrix} \quad (5.22)$$

Often, the primary sampling units (the districts in the preceding example) will be stratified, in which case one source of randomization will be removed and the sampling variance formula takes the general form of (5.19) with σ_i^2 being replaced by a bracketed expression summing as many different sources of sampling variance as there are stages of random selection.

The sampling variance of a cluster sample follows much the same principles, with an additional term to measure the effect of clustering. For example, the sampling variance of the percentage of an unrestricted sample whose members are selected in clusters is:

$$\sigma_{\bar{X}_i}^2 = \frac{pq}{N}[1 + r(N_s - 1)] \quad (5.23)$$

where N_s is the size of each cluster and r is the intercorrelation between sample members in the same cluster, averaged over all clusters.[33]

If r is zero, (5.23) reduces to the unrestricted sampling variance, as is also true in the trivial case when N_s is one. If the members of a cluster are negatively intercorrelated, (5.23) will yield a lower sampling variance than an

---

[33] For the percentage,

$$r = \frac{[\Sigma(p_i - p)^2/P_c] - [\Sigma p_i q_i/P_c(N_s - 1)]}{pq}$$

where P_c is the number of clusters, and p_i the value of p in the ith cluster.

unrestricted sample of the same size, and the more so the larger is N_s. Unfortunately, in economic and marketing surveys, r is generally positive, and at best zero. Thus, people of the same type generally live next to each other, so that if, say, one household owns a high-priced car, the neighboring household is more likely than otherwise also to own a high-priced car, etc., so that positive intercorrelation results.

The advantage of cluster sampling, and of area sampling, is therefore not likely to be more precision *per se*, but rather greater economy of operation, so that the precision obtained *per dollar spent* is much higher. The absolute precision yielded by these samples is generally about the same as that obtained from an unrestricted sample of the same size. For this reason, a rough but quick estimate of the sample size required in such operations can be obtained by applying (5.5), based on a simple unrestricted sample. However, if clustering is to be used, it would be safer to use (5.23), estimating r from a pilot survey. The subdivision of the sample size by stages of randomization is a more complicated procedure, which seeks essentially to equalize the contribution of each stage to the overall sampling variance.[34]

5.5.6. Sequential Analysis

At present, sequential analysis is applicable primarily to problems in which a decision is to be made as to one of two mutually exclusive alternatives on the basis of sample data. An example of the problem is a manufacturer trying to determine which one of two types of instant coffee is the more popular. By the conventional method, the sample size is set in advance (usually as the minimum sample size that would achieve a desired precision), a sample of the stipulated size is taken, and the data are analyzed after sampling is completed. In sequential analysis, the sample size is not set in advance. Instead, the data are analyzed while sampling is going on. By means of such a running analysis, any clear trend in favor of one alternative is immediately detected. Once the desired precision is obtained, as determined by appropriate formulas, sampling stops. The result is just as reliable as that obtained by the usual procedure, although the sample size may be reduced by more than half.

Though the mechanics of sequential analysis are somewhat complicated,[35] the reason for the method's great advantage is a matter of common sense, and may be illustrated by the following example. Suppose a cereal concern conducts a test to determine whether its recently introduced *Tootsies* cereal is proving more popular than its established *Crackles* cereal. Actually, a

---

[34] See M. H. HANSEN, W. N. HURWITZ, and W. G. MADOW, *Sample Survey Methods and Theory*, Vol. I (New York: John Wiley and Sons), Chapters 8, 9.

[35] For a simplified exposition, see ROBERT FERBER, *Statistical Techniques in Market Research*, Chapter 7.

heavy majority of the people, say 95 per cent, prefer *Crackles*. By the conventional method, the popularity of *Crackles* would not be apparent to the researcher until after a (predetermined) sample of several hundred people had been interviewed and analyzed. But by the sequential method, the running analysis of the cumulative results would bring to light the greater popularity of *Crackles* very early in the sampling process—perhaps after only as few as 10 observations—and with the same reliability as if several hundred interviews were treated by the usual method.

The margin of superiority is not frequently this large, but is generally substantial.

Sequential analysis is only applicable with probability sampling. For this reason, it cannot be applied on a mail survey but only when contact is made by phone or personal interview, and even in the latter cases non-responses cannot be set aside and left till later, as is often done. It is for these reasons that sequential analysis has not yet gained wide use in commercial sampling.

5.5.7. Non-probability Selection

To select sample members from the population in an arbitrary or haphazard manner is usually much the easiest way of doing so. In such a case, the sampling error is not measurable (though sampling error formulas are often used all the same), and the probabilities of sample bias tend to increase sharply because the representativeness of the sample members is in doubt. To some extent the bias can be counteracted by using so-called quota samples, in which stratification is incorporated in the sample design and quotas set for each stratum. The interviewers are then told to select people at their discretion until the quotas are filled. This can give rise to some rather ludicrous results, such as an interviewer having to round out his various quotas by finding a woman, retired, aged 26–35. More important, however, there is no assurance of the representativeness of the sample members *within* each stratum, since interviewers in such a case will naturally tend to select the people most convenient to them.

Nevertheless, non-probability samples are useful in certain situations. This is particularly true where representativeness may be of little importance, as in certain taste-testing experiments. Pilot surveys or exploratory situations are other examples, for the primary aim is to probe for possible hypotheses and different explanations. Quota samples with arbitrary sample member selection are also alleged to be useful in attitude and other studies, on the ground that the main determinant of the attitude is already incorporated in the stratification scheme, so that variations within strata are of little consequence, i.e., the strata are highly homogeneous within and heterogeneous as between each other. However, this is a moot point.

5.5.8. Selecting a Sample Design

With the exception of the possibilities cited in the previous paragraph, a probability method of sample member selection will invariably be preferred. A straight unrestricted sample will be favored if the population is believed to be fairly homogeneous with regard to the subject under study or if stratification is not feasible because of cost or time limitations.

In most economic and marketing studies, stratification is usually highly desirable. The technique of stratification, however, can be a problem at times. Theoretically, the objective is clear: to set up strata with as little variance as possible *within* each stratum and the largest possible variance *between* strata. In this way, the overall sampling error would be reduced to a minimum, for, in a stratified sample, the only contribution to the sampling variance is the variability within strata (and possibly the variance due to uncertainty in the true values of the W_i); the variance between strata is eliminated by the process of stratification. Thus, if all the families in each of the seven income strata listed in Table 5.3 owed the same amount of money, i.e., if σ_i were zero for all i, the sampling variance of the average debt per family would vanish for that sample. (What would be the optimum allocation in such a case?)

The application of this principle in practice can be as much of an art as a science. On the one hand, elimination of the within-strata variance is always possible—by setting up as many different strata as there are differences in the population with regard to the characteristic being measured! If 9,473 families out of a population of 10,000 have different amounts of debt outstanding, 9,473 strata would ensure zero sampling error. (What the cost of such an operation would be is another question!) On the other hand, the number of strata should be manageable from an operational sense and the individual strata should generally be meaningful relative to the problem at hand. In effect, therefore, the solution is likely to be a compromise between these two considerations.

The solution will contain two elements—the *basis* of stratification (income, area, age, etc.) and the *number* of strata to be used. The basis of stratification will generally be that variable, or combination of variables, which is felt to influence most the subject of the study. In a consumer credit study, this might be income and, perhaps, ownership of a business. If there are several possibilities, variance analysis will often prove useful in making the selection, provided the necessary data are available. Thus, if in a consumer credit study, it is not clear whether seven income strata or nine occupation strata serve as the most effective basis of stratification, an analysis of variance might be carried out of the effect of income and of occupation on debt. Suppose the results are, as follows:

	Sum of squares	Degrees of freedom	Est. of sampling variance
Variance due to income	100.62	6	16.77
Variance due to occupation	122.48	8	15.31
Residual variance	542.88	174	3.12

From these data, the variance due to the effect of the seven income strata can be estimated as:

$$\frac{16.77 - 3.12}{7} = 1.95$$

and the variance due to the effect of the nine occupation strata as:

$$\frac{15.31 - 3.12}{9} = 1.35$$

which indicates that income is a more effective basis of stratification. Alternatively, the effect of occupation might be increased further by using more strata. This possibility, too, could be tested by variance analysis. The final determination, however, will have to rest on non-sampling as well as sampling considerations.

Whether an unrestricted or a stratified design is adopted, the question invariably arises of the advisability of superimposing an area and/or cluster design. In a personal interview survey, cluster sampling offers considerable savings in field costs, particularly if a large area is being covered. Against these advantages have to be weighed the effect of clustering on sampling error, i.e., the direction and size of intercorrelation, and the advisability of clustering on substantive grounds. In a "knowledge-testing" survey, for example, failure to contact all the neighbors at the same time may bias the results because of "leaks." Whenever contact between sample members might be detrimental to the study, clustering is clearly ruled out. In the other instances, it becomes a matter of balancing possibly positive intercorrelations against potential cost savings. Means of deriving optimum sampling conditions in such instances are readily available.[36]

Area sampling is invariably preferable when personal contact is to be used and areas of any substantial size are involved. This holds for large cities as well as broader areas. The selection of the type and number of stages in an area design, particularly the primary sampling units, depends to a large extent on the type of units for which data are available. The boundaries of these primary units should be clearly defined and sufficient information available to serve as a basis for further subdivision. These primary sampling units should be as heterogeneous *within* as possible, i.e., they should be as similar as possible to each other, though this may not be too feasible when stratification of the population is being used as well.

---

[36] HANSEN, HURWITZ, MADOW, *op. cit.*, Chapters 6, 7.

The number of primary units depends on the area being covered, the conditions of the problem, and resources available. As with stratification, to reduce sampling variance, the more such units, the better, but, as the number increases, area sampling begins to lose its advantages. The result is, therefore, again a compromise; as a rule 25 to 50 is a minimum number.

The determination of other stages of area sampling is governed by much the same factors, and again much the same compromise has to be made.[37]

In considering two or more alternative sample designs, a standard of comparison is often needed. Such a standard is readily obtained by computing the *efficiency* of one sample design relative to that of the corresponding unrestricted sample. This measure, E, can be computed in either of two ways.

If the question is what sample size is needed to yield a particular accuracy, we have:

$$E = \frac{\text{Sample size required by unrestricted sample}}{\text{Sample size required by alternative sample}} - 1 \qquad (5.24)$$

If the question is what accuracy will be obtained with a *given* sample size, we have:

$$E = \frac{\text{Sampling variance of unrestricted sample}}{\text{Sampling variance of alternative sample}} - 1 \qquad (5.25)$$

In either case, the higher the value of E, the more efficient is the alternative sample design. If E is negative, unrestricted sampling is clearly more efficient.

5.5.9. Estimating Sampling Costs

Sampling costs are of two broad types—*overhead costs*, which are relatively fixed for any particular sampling operation (e.g., interviewer selection and training, preparation of questionnaire forms, selection of sample members, etc.), and *variable costs*, which depend on the scope of the operation and include primarily interviewing costs. For any survey design, a cost function can be constructed combining both types of costs in a form such as:

$$C = a + bN \qquad (5.26)$$

where a is the approximate overhead cost, b is the cost per interview and N is the sample size. The values of a and b are based partly on past experience and partly on the results of the pilot survey, if one is made.

Cost functions, whether of the form of (5.26) or of a more involved form, serve two purposes. First, they provide an indication of the probable cost of the survey, which is indispensable for planning purposes. Second, they serve as a basis for optimum allocation of sample members among strata and sam-

---

[37] For means of computing optimum combinations, see HANSEN, HURWITZ and MADOW, *ibid.*

pling stages to yield either the highest accuracy per dollar for a given total sample size or the lowest cost for achieving a given accuracy. Thus, given a cost function such as (5.26) and a formula for the sampling variance, a knowledge of differential calculus is generally sufficient to compute the optimum allocation of sample members among strata or sampling units (by substituting for N from (5.26) into the sampling variance, differentiating with respect to the size of one stage, and setting the result equal to zero). It is on this basis that the optimal allocation for stratified sampling (5.18) was derived.[38]

In a similar fashion, it is possible to incorporate economic considerations in a sample design. As an example, let us consider a production program being scheduled for men's suits based on a survey of the market potential, say using buying plans data as the basis for the prediction. Such a survey can be wrong in either of two ways:

1. The survey-based estimates may prove too high, in which case less is sold than expected and losses are created because of excess production.

2. The survey-based estimates are too low, so that losses are created in the form of unrealized profits.

Let us assume, for simplicity, that the unit loss in each case is constant within the range of expectations, and that the unit loss is s dollars in the first case and r dollars in the second.

Now we seek an expression for the total dollar risk resulting from possible inaccuracies of the survey, i.e., the mathematical expectation of the loss. This is obtained as follows: We know that many sample estimates taken from the same population in the same way are normally distributed, so that the probability of a particular result falling within the inteval z to $z + dz$ is:

$$P = \frac{1}{\sigma_n \sqrt{2\pi}} e^{\frac{-z^2}{2\sigma_n{}^2}} dz \tag{5.27}$$

where $\qquad \sigma_n = \sigma/\sqrt{N}$

If the sample, N, is selected from a population of size P, the total expected loss in the first case (S) resulting from over-production is the aggregation of the individual losses (s) multiplied by the probability of each occurrence of s (5.27):

$$
\begin{aligned}
S &= P \int_0^\infty \frac{1}{\sigma_n \sqrt{2\pi}} e^{\frac{-z^2}{2\sigma_n{}^2}} sz\, dz \\
&= \int_0^\infty \frac{sP\sigma_n}{\sqrt{2\pi}} e^{\frac{-z^2}{2\sigma_n{}^2}} d\left(\frac{z^2}{2\sigma_n{}^2}\right) \\
&= \frac{sP\sigma_n}{\sqrt{2\pi}}, \text{ since } \int_0^\infty e^{-t}\, dt = 1
\end{aligned}
\tag{5.28}
$$

---

[38] For illustrations of the application of this procedure, see HANSEN, HURWITZ and MADOW, *op. cit.*, Vol. II, Chapter 11.

In a similar manner, the total expected loss with under-production (R) can be shown to be:

$$R = \frac{rP\sigma_n}{\sqrt{2\pi}} \tag{5.29}$$

so that the total expected overall loss is:

$$L = \frac{(r + s)P\sigma_n}{\sqrt{2\pi}} = \frac{(r + s)P\sigma}{\sqrt{2\pi N}} \tag{5.30}$$

Thus, if the standard error of the estimate of total production ($P\sigma_n$) is 2,000 units, the unit loss due to over-capacity (s) is \$3.00, and the unit loss due to under-production is \$1.00, the total expected loss is:

$$L = \frac{(1 + 3)2,000}{\sqrt{2\pi}} = \$3,556 \tag{5.31}$$

To compute optimal sample size, we assume that unit sampling costs are constant, say, b dollars per interview, with overhead costs of a. The cost function is then (5.27) and our aim is to compute that sample size that will minimize total costs for the given tolerance, which are:

$$L + C = \frac{(r + s)P\sigma}{\sqrt{2\pi N}} + a + bN \tag{5.32}$$

which, when differentiated with respect to N, set equal to zero, and solved for N, yields:

$$N = \left[\frac{(r + s)P\sigma}{2b \sqrt{2\pi}} \right]^{2/3} \tag{5.33}$$

Thus, (5.33) indicates the value of N that would balance the costs of the survey against the risk resulting from possible errors in the survey results. This particular formula applies only to the conditions under which it was derived, some of which may well be oversimplified. The general approach to this type of problem, however, is essentially the same.

5.6.   VERIFICATION OF RESULTS

The results obtained from a survey can be checked in two ways:
1. Investigation of possible sources of error, or bias, in the survey.
2. Evaluation of acceptability of results both on theoretical and empirical grounds.

From a logical point of view, these two approaches are related: unacceptability of results should be accountable in terms of one or more sources of error while, on the other hand, detection of major sources of error should lead to explanation of differences between the present results and those of other studies on the same subject. Then again, if the present results differ from previous studies but no sources of error can be found, a change in underlying circumstances, i.e., in basic structure, may be indicated, in which case additional evidence on this point should be sought. Conceivably, also, the present survey may be accurate and the previous ones not, but this inviting path too often leads into a fool's paradise.

5.6.1.   Sources of Error

A checklist on sources of errors in surveys is provided in Table 5.4. Such a checklist is indispensable to the beginning researcher as a basis for a sys-

Table 5.4

CHECKLIST ON ERRORS IN SURVEYS

1. Variability in response
2. Differences between different kinds and degrees of canvass
   a) Mail, telephone, telegraph, direct interview
   b) Intensive vs. extensive interviews
   c) Long vs. short schedules
   d) Check block plan vs. response
   e) Correspondence panel and key reporters
3. Bias and variation arising from the interviewer
4. Bias of auspices
5. Imperfections in the design of the questionnaire and tabulation plans
   a) Lack of clarity in definitions; ambiguity; varying meanings of same word to different groups of people; eliciting an answer liable to misinterpretation
   b) Omitting questions that would be illuminating to the interpretation of other questions
   c) Emotionally toned words; leading questions, limiting response to a pattern
   d) Failing to perceive what tabulations would be most significant
   e) Encouraging non-response through formidable appearance
6. Changes that take place in the universe before tabulations are available
7. Bias arising from non-response (including omissions)
8. Bias arising from late reports
9. Bias arising from an unrepresentative selection of data for the survey, or of the period covered
10. Bias arising from an unrepresentative selection of respondents
11. Sampling errors and biases
12. Processing errors (coding, editing, calculating, tabulating, tallying, posting and consolidating)
13. Errors in interpretation
    a) Bias arising from bad curve fitting; wrong weighting; incorrect adjusting
    b) Misunderstanding the questionnaire; failure to take account of the respondents' difficulties (often through inadequate presentation of data); misunderstanding the method of collection and the nature of the data
    c) Personal bias in interpretation

Source: Based on W. EDWARDS DEMING, "On Errors in Surveys," *American Sociological Review*, Vol. 9 (August 1944), pp. 359–369.

tematic review of the possible weaknesses and shortcomings in the study. It also serves to highlight the very limited information provided by sampling error formulas on overall reliability: as a rule, other sources of error will far outweigh possible sampling variations, *provided* that proper sample design has been employed.

The imposing list in Table 5.4 also serves to reinforce the fact that almost every survey is characterized by errors of one type or another. In most instances these errors are relatively small, and their number need not deter anyone from carrying out a survey. At the same time, however, it is only by systematic review that sizeable errors will be detected when they exist.

Though Table 5.4 is largely self-explanatory, a few points could use amplification.

Variability of response (1). The same respondent can give differing answers to the same question if it is repeated (change of opinion, inaccuracy, bad memory, etc.). In the same way, different members of the family will not always give the same answer at all times even with regard to concretely given facts. The wife sometimes gives the profession of the man differently from his statement, the spouses hold diverging opinions regarding income and rent, and may also disagree on each other's age and the year of their marriage.[39] It is only a statistic such as the number of children which is likely to be given with relatively great accuracy.

Interviewer bias (3). As noted earlier,

a) the respondent may be influenced by the intonation, the choice of words or the appearance of the interviewer;
b) his answer may be misinterpreted by the interviewer;
c) a deviation from interviewer instructions may bias the result.

Verification is often possible in such cases by comparing the results of different interviewers.[40]

Bias of auspices (4). Mention is also needed of the respondent as an independent source of distortion. It is true that in principle each bias in the answer can ultimately be led back to the interviewer, the questions or the way of putting the questions. In a concrete case, it may be at least as fruitful to ask: What reasons can the respondent have had to answer beside the truth, or to exaggerate in a certain direction? The risk always exists that the interviewee's interests originate from another frame of reference than had been expected when drafting the questionnaire. Faulty conclusions from a given answer can often be traced back to this source.

---

[39] See ROBERT FERBER, "On the Reliability of Responses Secured in Sample Surveys," *Journal of the American Statistical Association*, September, 1955, pp. 788–810.
[40] ROBERT FERBER and H. G. WALES, *op. cit.*

Selection bias (9). Thus, interviewing housewives on weekday mornings supplies a larger percentage of response from those who are not employed; the others are not home. A survey on travelling on the day before Christmas may not be representative unless we are investigating peak loads. Surveys during sales or advertising campaigns also create distortions. Questions about seasonal articles asked outside the season meet with slight interest and the answers are accordingly fickle, etc.

Misinterpretation (13b). The investigator who interprets and summarizes the results should either be professionally acquainted with the subject or have himself taken part in the survey. As a rule, he should at least take part in the pilot survey. If he does not know from his own experience the practical difficulties encountered by the interviewee and interviewer in using the questionnaire, his interpretation of the differences in answering will be, to put it mildly, hazardous.

5.6.2.   Evaluating Acceptability of Results

At least three phases are involved at this stage. They may be independent in an operational sense but their results, nevertheless, tend to reinforce one another. They are: plausibility, empirical verification, and theoretical verification.

Plausibility. Do the results make sense? In other words, how do the results compare with generally accepted beliefs on the subject? The latter may not be on too firm a basis, but deserve consideration nevertheless, especially if the report is to secure acceptance by outsiders. Deviations from accepted belief have to be detected and then explained. The search for such an explanation leads into the other two phases of acceptability.

Empirical verification. Known also as "validation," the aim of this part of the work is to compare the results of the study with whatever external data may be available on the subject—other surveys, general statistics, information gleaned from company records, etc. Such comparisons are needed not only for the entire sample but also for the various strata or segments of the market covered in the study.

Any differences that may be uncovered by such comparisons have to be explained in one way or another. The fault may not necessarily lie with the survey, but, if not, the source has to be identified. If the fault lies with the survey, it is better for the investigator to bring this out himself than to have someone else discover it at some later time.

Theoretical verification. Do the results agree with such theory as may exist on the subject? To what extent do they conform with *a priori* reasoning? For example, is it reasonable for a survey to show that at the same income level bachelors spend as much money for food as a couple with two children?

Offhand, this may seem rather far-fetched, and indicate that something may have gone wrong in the survey. However, further investigation may reveal that those who live alone, particularly men, eat outside the home more often than those who are married. The cost of such outside meals is found to be substantially higher than the cost of the same meals at home. In other words, for bachelors part of the price of their freedom is the purchase of calories at a much higher cost than married people. The final phase of this verification analysis would be to show, if possible, that once these differential price effects are eliminated, the quantity of food consumed by a couple with two children exceeds substantially the quantity in the bachelor's diet.

At the same time, theory is not infallible, and observed discrepancies will not always be the fault of the survey. Much of theory is little more than stylized reality, and reality is itself a transitory and variable phenomenon. New theories and revision of existing theory are generally based, in economic and marketing work, on empirical results. It is perhaps needless to note, however, that if survey findings contradict current theory, the findings have to rest on a firm foundation to secure acceptance.

PROBLEMS

1. Prepare a survey plan for ascertaining by personal interview the extent to which farmers in Illinois, Indiana and Michigan are in debt, including:

   > how a probability sample of 600 farmers might be selected,
   > the type of information sought,
   > arrangements for contacting farmers,
   > arrangement for editing, coding and tabulation,
   > how the data are to be analyzed,
   > cost and time schedules.

2. In the preceding example, how might mail and telephone be used to increase the efficiency of such a survey? What disadvantages might be expected from using each of these alternative data collection methods in this problem?

3. Dangers of biased question-wording are emphasized in the text. Can you think of circumstances that would *favor* biased question wording? Give examples.

4. *a*) Draft a structured personal questionnaire form to investigate New Yorkers' knowledge and opinions of Japanese 35 mm cameras.
   b) What respondent classifications and supplementary data might be pertinent?
   c) Modify the questionnaire to make it suitable for a mail survey.

5. List the different types of biases that are likely to be encountered in the survey of New Yorkers' attitudes toward Japanese cameras. What precautions might be taken against each?

6. A survey is to be made by interviewing a sample of purchasers of room air conditioners in the past six months. How might a probability sample of such people be selected with reasonable efficiency?

7. An aluminum manufacturer plans a survey to investigate the market potential for aluminum among residential builders. How might stratification be of value? What strata might be used?

8. a) A local newspaper wants to ascertain the extent to which inclusion of a daily stock market page might increase circulation. How might a survey provide such information? Prepare a draft of the questionnaire.
   b) Discuss the pros and cons of alternative data-collection methods and recommend one approach.
   c) Write out instructions for selection of a probability sample.

9. Discuss the pros and cons of non-probability sampling in conducting taste tests.

10. The following table presents data on the extent of awareness of the current minimum wage based on a sample:

Education	Pop. size	Sample size	Number aware of true minimum wage
Grade school	24,500	120	24
High school	26,500	140	35
College or over	12,000	60	45

   a) What is the estimated proportion in the area aware of the true minimum wage? What is the 95 per cent confidence interval for this estimate?
   b) What is the relative efficiency of the stratified sample in this case?
   c) By hindsight, was the particular sample allocation optimal? If not, what should it have been? In the latter case, how much would the efficiency of the estimate have been increased?

11. a) A household survey is planned to estimate the extent to which cars are used for business purposes. Discuss the data-collection method and the survey design.
   b) How might sequential analysis be applied? What are some possible pitfalls of this technique that might be encountered in this case?
   c) The estimate of the per cent of car-owning families using cars for business is desired within plus and minus 5 per cent with a 95 per cent confidence interval. The overhead costs of the study are estimated at $1,000 and field costs at $1.50 per completed interview. If $1,500 is allocated for the survey, is this amount sufficient? Under what assumptions?

12. Discuss means that might be used by a department store in evaluating the results of a consumer survey in its market area of soft goods purchased in the last six months by type of outlet.

13. A television survey conducted by interviewing one household in each of eight zones using six replicated samples yields the following data on TV ownership this year and last year. The first answer in each cell indicates current ownership; the second, ownership last year.

Zone	SUBSAMPLE 1	2	3	4	5	6
1	Yes	Yes	Yes	Yes	Yes	Yes
	No	Yes	Yes	Yes	No	Yes
2	No	Yes	Yes	Yes	Yes	Yes
	No	No	Yes	No	Yes	Yes
3	Yes	Yes	No	Yes	Yes	Yes
	Yes	Yes	No	Yes	Yes	No
4	Yes	Yes	Yes	Yes	No	Yes
	No	No	Yes	No	No	Yes
5	Yes	No	Yes	Yes	Yes	No
	No	No	No	Yes	No	No
6	Yes	Yes	Yes	No	Yes	Yes
	Yes	Yes	No	No	Yes	No
7	Yes	Yes	No	Yes	No	Yes
	No	Yes	No	No	No	Yes
8	Yes	No	Yes	No	No	No
	Yes	No	Yes	No	No	No

If each zone contains 200 households, estimate and compute the 95 % confidence interval for:

a) the total number of TV sets owned currently in the area.
b) the per cent of households owning TV sets currently.
c) the per cent change in the per cent of households owning TV since last year.

14. In the previous example, assume that the first four zones constitute one "thick" zone, and the next four zones a second one, so that each subsample has then four observations in each thick zone.

a) Redo the preceding estimates on this new basis.
b) Which estimates change and which do not? Why?
c) Discuss the pros and cons of this design versus that used in the preceding example.

SELECTED REFERENCES

Literally hundreds of references are available on the methodological aspects of cross-section analysis and particularly on the pros and cons of different survey techniques. A small selection of these references are listed here. A much more complete selection will be found in *A Basic Bibliography of Marketing Research* by H. G. WALES and ROBERT FERBER (American Marketing Association, 1962).

In addition to references on individual methods, there are several texts which provide good coverage of the entire subject. In particular, *Surveys, Polls, and Samples* by M. B. PARTEN (New York: Harper & Bros., 1950) presents a very clear discussion in Chapters 11–12 of the practical aspects and pitfalls of collecting data by mail or by personal interview, while Chapter 6 discusses questionnaire construction.

Chapters 8 and 9 of *Statistical Techniques in Market Research* by ROBERT FERBER

(McGraw-Hill, 1949) discuss the general design of survey operations. Chapters 3–6 of this book outline sampling principles in some detail and present applications, while Chapter 7 covers the application of sequential analysis to business problems.

Two comprehensive texts on the subject of sampling, with particular emphasis on the design of sample surveys and the measurement of sampling errors, are W. E. DEMING, *Some Theory of Sampling* (New York: Wiley and Sons, 1950) and the two volumes by M. H. HANSEN, W. N. HURWITZ, and W. G. MADOW, *Sample Survey Methods and Theory* (New York: Wiley and Sons, 1953). Volume 1 covers the applications of sampling methods and presents numerous illustrative examples; Volume 2 is more technical. A less comprehensive, but easily understood, book on sampling methods is DEMING's *Sample Design for Business Research* (New York: Wiley and Sons, 1960).

Data-Collection Methods

"Problems of Response in Enumerative Surveys" by W. P. MAULDIN and E. S. MARKS (*American Sociological Review*, October, 1950, pages 649–657) contains an interesting discussion of the problem of obtaining accurate responses to both quantitative and qualitative data. A comparative evaluation of two methods of data-collection will be found in "A Limited Comparison of Two Methods of Data Collection: The Fixed Alternative Questionnaire and the Open-Interview" by H. METZNER and F. MANN (*American Sociological Review*, August, 1952, pages 486–549).

A concise but clear explanation of the meaning of depth interviewing is "What is Depth Interviewing?" (*Printer's Ink*, February 15, 1946, pages 36ff). The same publication contains in its issues of May 30, 1952, and June 6, 1952, two well-written, useful articles by R. A. ROBINSON on the practical considerations involved in conducting a mail survey, with particular emphasis on techniques for increasing response.

The use of tape recorders as a means of data collection is discussed in "Interviewing with Tape Recorders" by J. C. BEVIS (*Public Opinion Quarterly*, Winter 1949, pages 629–634). A related article by A. E. MILLER, "Consumer Interviews by Mechanical Recording" (*Printer's Ink*, October 5, 1945, pages 122ff) discusses the use of the wire recorder to cope with interviewer misrepresentation. For a more recent study on tape recorders, see J. F. Engel, "Tape Recorders in Consumer Research" (*Journal of Marketing*, to be published).

The Questionnaire

The Art of Asking Questions by S. L. PAYNE (Princeton: Princeton University Press, 1951) is "must" reading for those working on questionnaire preparation, and covers numerous ways in which questions can be biased by poor wording. Questionnaire construction and depth interviewing is discussed in "Depth Questioning" by L. M. PARADISE and A. B. BLANKENSHIP (*Journal of Marketing*, January, 1951, pages 274–288); this article covers both structured and unstructured questionnaires. An interesting case for the use of biased questions under certain circumstances is presented by ALFRED POLITZ in "Questionnaire Validity Through the Open-Ended Question" (*Journal of Psychology*, July, 1953, pages 11–16). Sources of bias in question construction are discussed in the following two articles in respects which are self-evident from the titles: P. B. SHEATSLEY, "Closed Questions Sometimes Are More

Valid Than Open" (*Public Opinion Quarterly*, Spring 1948, page 127); H. S
and H. HYMAN, "How Interviewer Effects Operate Through Question
(*International Journal of Opinion and Attitude Research*, Winter 1949–50, pages
493–512).

Of particular pertinence to attitude surveys is "A Problem of Interpretation of
Survey Results" by A. WESTEFELD (*Journal of Marketing*, January, 1953, pages
295–297), which points out that "hark-back" questions tend to be favorable to the
present situation.

The Interviewer

An excellent general discussion of the subject is provided by "Selection, Training,
and Supervision of Field Interviewers in Marketing Research" by V. D. REED and
others (*Journal of Marketing*, January, 1948, pages 365–378). The book by HERBERT
HYMAN, *Interviewing in Social Research* (Chicago: University of Chicago Press, 1954)
is virtually a treatise on interviewing techniques. The volume presents the results of
a six-year study by the National Opinion Research Center of interviewer effects on
survey results.

A very useful manual on interviewing procedures, with emphasis on the psychological aspects of interviewing, is *The Dynamics of Interviewing* by R. L. KAHN and
C. F. CANNELL (New York: John Wiley and Sons, 1957). This book explores the
relationship of questionnaire design and question formulation to the interviewing
situation and contains a number of very useful case studies.

One of the best reviews of interviewer influence is the article by H. W. BOYD, Jr.
and RALPH WESTFALL, "Interviewers As a Source of Error in Surveys" (*Journal of
Marketing*, April, 1955, pages 311–324). Two interesting methodological studies on
interviewer bias are: "Differences in Response Rates of Experienced and Inexperi-
enced Interviewers" by J. DURBIN and A. STUART (*Journal of the Royal Statistical
Society*, Part 2, 1951, pages 163–195); and "Detection and Correction of Interviewer
Bias" by ROBERT FERBER and H. G. WALES (*Public Opinion Quarterly*, Spring 1952,
pages 107–127). "A Method of Measuring Interview Variability" by J. A. STOCK and
J. R. HOCHSTIM (*Public Opinion Quarterly*, Summer 1951, pages 322–334) presents a
novel approach to the measurement of non-sampling errors contributed by interviewer variability.

Sampling Techniques and Design

One of the best books presenting a comprehensive survey of sampling and alternative sampling designs is *Sampling Techniques* by W. G. COCHRAN (New York: Wiley
and Sons, 1953). Although somewhat mathematical and largely theoretical, this
book is very well written and is a first-class reference work. Another excellent book
on the subject is *Sampling Methods for Censuses and Surveys* by F. YATES (New York:
Hafner Publishing Company, 1953).

Application of Probability Sampling to Farm Surveys by E. E. HOUSEMAN (Washington, D. C.: U. S. Department of Agriculture, 1954) is a good illustration of how
this sampling technique is applied in rural areas. Discussion of various sampling
methods and their practical applications will be found in "Selecting Sampling

Methods in Commercial Research" by P. G. Peterson and W. F. O'Dell (*Journal of Marketing*, October, 1950, pages 182–189).

Replicated sampling is discussed in great detail, and with excellent illustrations in W. E. Deming, *Sample Design in Business Research* (New York: John Wiley & Sons, 1960). This is easily the best source on the subject.

Two articles that discuss the application of probability sampling to problems somewhat out of the ordinary are: H. L. Jenkins, "An Application of Probability Sampling to Retail Store Consumer Analysis," (*Journal of Marketing*, April, 1954, pages 399–401); H. L. Jones, "Sampling Plans for Verifying Clerical Work" (*Industrial Quality Control*, January, 1947, pages 5–11).

The theory of sequential analysis is the subject of *Sequential Analysis by* Abraham Wald (New York: Wiley and Sons, 1948). A comprehensive working manual on this technique together with numerous formulas, tables, and computational aids is *Sequential Analysis of Statistical Data: Applications* by the Columbia University Statistical Research Group (New York: Columbia University Press, 1945). Despite its age, this book still contains many of the most recent developments in this area.

Incorporation of economic considerations in sample design is discussed at some length in Robert Schlaifer, *Probability and Statistics for Business Decisions* (New York: McGraw-Hill Book Co., 1959), Part Four. This book also presents, and clearly illustrates, techniques for deciding when sampling is likely to be economical.

The *Table of 105,000 Random Decimal Digits* (Washington, D. C.: U. S. Bureau of Transport Economics and Statistics, 1949) contains enough random decimals for most practical purposes. For those who want the best, they are referred to *A Million Random Decimals* (Glencoe: The Free Press, 1955).

Verification of Results

A discussion of the various factors that affect the usefulness of surveys is the subject of "On Errors in Surveys" by W. E. Deming (*American Sociological Review*, August, 1944, pages 359–369). Another article by Deming, "Some Criteria for Changing the Quality of Surveys" (*Journal of Marketing*, October, 1947, pages 145–157) presents a very clear discussion of validity, reliability, bias, and sampling reliability as related to various sampling methods.

An interesting relationship between the stability of answers and the percentage of "Don't Knows" is discussed in S. C. Dodd and K. Svalastoga, "On Estimating Latent from Manifest Undecidedness" (*Educational and Psychological Measurement*, Autumn 1952, pp. 467–471).

"Sampling in Marketing Research" by T. T. Semon *et al* (*Journal of Marketing*, January, 1959, pp. 263–273) presents a very useful discussion of this general area.

"The Accuracy of Census Measures" by M. H. Hansen, W. N. Hurwitz, and Leon Pritzker (*American Sociological Review*, August, 1953, pages 416–423) discusses the use of post-enumeration surveys as a means of checking the quality of data collected in the various censuses of 1950. The use of self-enumeration forms in improving census data is discussed in "Response Errors in Census Research" by E. S. Marks and W. P. Mauldin (*Journal of the American Statistical Association*, September, 1950, pages 424–438).

6 | Special Applications of the Cross-Section Approach

A NUMBER of special applications of the cross-section approach are considered in this chapter—the consumer panel, store audits, scaling and attitude surveys, end-use analysis, motivation research, and experimentation. The growing importance of these applications is sufficient to warrant separate treatment of each, particularly in view of the sparse and widely scattered nature of the current literature on each of these techniques.

The discussion of each of these techniques provided in this chapter will focus, first, on the uses and limitations of the technique, and second, on the distinctive problems encountered in operation. For this reason, the present discussion supplements that of the previous chapter; the omission in this chapter of the general problems of applying the cross-section approach does not mean that they can be ignored in applying the special techniques considered here.

6.1. THE CONSUMER PANEL

6.1.1. What It Is

A consumer panel is essentially a sample of people who are interviewed repeatedly over a period of time. Strictly speaking, a sample becomes a (continuing) panel operation if its members are interviewed in at least two different points in time on the same general subject. If only two or three "waves" of interviews are involved, however, there is some tendency to use the term "reinterview sample" rather than "panel." Then again, if the same people are interviewed several times on different aspects of the same subject, neither "panel" nor "reinterview sample" may be used to describe the oper-

267

ation. Thus, in the *Life* Study of Consumer Expenditures for 1956 interviews were sought with each sample member four different times during 1956–57 partly because the information desired was too detailed to obtain in one, two or three sessions, and partly because different methods were used to secure particular types of data.[1] In one sense, this was a panel operation, since four waves of interviews were sought, but in another sense this was not, since all the interviews pertained to the same point in time, the year 1956.

In what follows, the discussion will focus on panel operations as first defined in the preceding paragraph. At the same time, much of the material will also be found applicable to the type of operation conducted by *Life Magazine* in its consumer expenditure study.

6.1.2. Uses of Panels

Most consumer panels are of two types. On the one hand is the highly transitory panel set up to measure the effect, or influence, of a particular phenomenon. Usually, such a panel is conducted on a "before and after" basis. Initial interviews are conducted before the phenomenon takes place to record respondent actions or attitudes at that moment. A second set of interviews is carried out after the phenomenon has taken place to ascertain what changes may have occurred in respondent attitudes or actions as a result.

This is a favorite tool of advertising and of social research. Thus, a number of people may be brought together in an auditorium and asked to record their brand preference for a certain product. After exposure to different commercials, the same questions are repeated, the shifts in brand preference being used to ascertain the relative effectiveness of the commercials.[2] Or, antisemitic tendencies in an area may be probed just prior to publication of a series of articles on the subject and reinterviews conducted afterward with the same people to gauge the effect of the articles.[3]

Product-testing and evaluating the probable effect of consumer innovations are other uses to which such panels have been put.[4] In all such cases, care has to be taken to ensure that the observed effects are really attributable to the phenomenon being tested and not to some external factor. Thus, if between the two waves of interviews on antisemitism several significant

---

[1] *Life Study of Consumer Expenditures*, Time, Inc., 1957, Vol. IV.

[2] H. C. Schwerin, "Why Television Commercials Succeed," pp. 321–333 in Robert Ferber and H. G. Wales (ed.), *Motivation and Market Behavior* (Homewood, Ill.: Richard D. Irwin, Inc., 1958). This article was originally presented as a talk at the Marketing Research Conference, University of Michigan, 1955.

[3] C. Y. Glock, "Some Applications of the Panel Method to the Study of Change," pp. 242–250 in P. F. Lazarsfeld and Morris Rosenberg (ed.), *The Language of Social Research* (Glencoe, Ill.: The Free Press, 1955).

[4] For selected references, see H. G. Wales and Robert Ferber, *A Basic Bibliography on Marketing Research*, Sec. 10.7.

scientific advances by Jews are announced, the effect of the newspaper articles on antisemitism may be confounded with that of the news items. The ideal means of handling such a situation is through experimental control, whereby a random subsample is not exposed to the phenomenon while the other subsample is exposed, but in business and the social sciences this is not always feasible.

The second broad category of consumer panels is the continuing kind. Panels of this type are set up often for an indefinite period. The purpose of such a panel may be to serve as a "sounding board" for researchers on a variety of subjects—the so-called "general purpose panel"—or the purpose may be to collect continuing data on a particular aspect of consumer behavior over time, generally at periodic intervals. In practice, the distinction between these two kinds of continuing panels is not too sharp, since a continuing data panel may also be used to secure "general purpose" information.

Continuing data panels have been used in the area of consumer expenditures, consumer saving, public opinion, and radio and TV listenership, among others. Most of these panels operate by mail. Thus, the Market Research Corporation of America (MRCA), has maintained a national monthly consumer panel of several thousand families since 1944 (10,000 in 1962), the members of which report by means of weekly diaries detailed expenditures and amounts purchased of foods, drugs and magazines as well as of various sundry items. A page from such a diary is shown in Fig. 6.1.

From these data, reports are prepared for clients (generally manufacturers or advertising agencies) on monthly or weekly consumer purchases of a particular product by brand, by area, and by any of a number of classifying family characteristics. The reports are used to obtain a profile of the market structure for the product as well as for each competing brand. In this way, strong as well as weak areas in one's sales can be pinpointed, and remedial attempts made where deemed necessary. Given continuing data on the same families, changes in market structure can be observed and, presumably, the effects of particular marketing strategies evaluated, both one's own and those of competitors.

Such data are also useful for a variety of other purposes. For one thing, changes in sales trends can be ascertained more quickly than through the usual order channels, and production and marketing plans revised accordingly. In the same vein, the data can serve as a basis for sales forecasting, especially in the short run. They can also be used to ascertain the effect on product sales of changes in income and other family circumstances, of changes in product characteristics, notably price and packaging, and of particular types of promotional effort. Brand loyalty is another key subject of analysis; a brand that retains much the same customers is in a different marketing situation from another brand that has much the same share of the market but keeps losing old, and gaining new, users all the time.

Food Products
FROZEN

DAY OF
WEEK
AND
DATE
OF
MONTH

WRITE THE BRAND NAME EXACTLY AS IT APPEARS
ON THE PACKAGE

None

FROZEN VEGETABLES

DESCRIBE
(Where Requested)

BEANS (Brand)	Green French Style Green Cut or Wax Style	
BEANS, LIMA (Brand)	Small or Fordhook	
BROCCOLI (Brand)	Whole or Chopped	
CAULIFLOWER (Brand)		
CORN (Brand)	Whole Kernel or on Cob	
MIXED VEGETABLES (Brand)		
PEAS (Brand)		
PEAS & CARROTS (Brand)		
SPINACH (Brand)	Leaf or Chopped	
OTHER VEGETABLES (Brand)		WRITE KIND

None

FROZEN FRENCH FRIED POTATOES & OTHER

| FROZEN FRENCH FRIED POTATOES (Brand) | |
| OTHER FROZEN POTATOES (Brand) | WRITE KIND |

None

FROZEN FRUIT (BERRIES & FRUIT)

WRITE KIND

| (Brand) | |

None

FROZEN FRUIT & DESSERT PIES
(BERRIES, FRUIT, CUSTARDS, ETC.)

WRITE KIND
(Apple, Cherry, Chocolate Cream, Mince, Pumpkin, Etc.)

| (Brand) | |

Fig. 6.1. A Page from a National Consumer Panel Diary

Source: Reproduced with permission of Market Research Corp. of America .

Section
FOODS

QUANTITY	WEIGHT	PRICE		WHERE PURCHASED					
				Check Where Purchased					
		HOW MUCH YOU PAID (Don't include Taxes) (Explain if it was a sample, or purchased with a coupon or as a 1c sale, etc.)		GROCERY STORE					BE SURE TO WRITE FULL NAME OF STORE
HOW MANY PKGS. OR ITEMS OF EACH KIND	AS SHOWN ON LABEL			Independent or Private	Chain	Department or General Store	Frozen Food Plan Service	Other Place	
	(Lbs., Ozs.)	For each	Total if more than one	(5)		(3)		(0)	

FROZEN POTATOES

Fig. 6.1. (Cont.)

Some panels operate through the joint use of mail and personal interview. This is the case with a study launched in 1957 on means of securing accurate, current and continuous data on short-run changes in consumers' financial position. This study, sponsored by the Inter-University Committee for Research on Consumer Behavior and financed by the Ford Foundation, sought to get, among other things, periodic "balance sheet" statements from the same consumers over several years. In most instances, these data were obtained by personal interview. However, a small per cent of the panel members in one area expressed a strong preference for supplying these data by mail, and some refused to supply the data any other way. In such a case, optimum results are likely to be obtained through a flexible approach using both mail and personal interviews.

Saving data obtained frequently from consumer panels can be of great value to both business and government. The amount and composition of consumer savings, in relation to income and other financial magnitudes, are a crucial factor in determining the course of the economy. Since saving propensities are subject to sharp and rapid fluctuation, current data on changes in saving and in these propensities are essential for an intelligent appraisal of the economic outlook as well as of the desirability and effects of particular government policies. Such data are of equally tremendous value in various areas of business, such as sales forecasting, market potentials, and determining investment plans.

Panel techniques to measure radio and TV listenership have been conducted both by mail and by means of mechanical recorders attached to the set.[5] In the former case, families are asked to keep diaries or "logs" of their listening time, which are mailed to a central office every week. In the latter case, a device attached to the radio or TV set records automatically when the set is on and the station to which it is attuned. Tapes are collected periodically and new ones inserted. Mechanical recording of this type has the advantage of eliminating recall or recording errors, but raises the problem of translating the unit of observation from the individual *set* to the individual person or family. There is also the matter of identifying who, if anyone, is actually listening at a particular time when the set is on.

Aside from these problems, radio and TV panel data are useful in much the same manner as expenditure data. Though hated thoroughly by the entertainment industry (a low program rating can mean cancellation of a contract), advertisers rely heavily on them for an analysis of the size and

---

[5] CHARLES H. SANDAGE, *Qualitative Analysis of Radio Listening in Two Central Illinois Counties*, Bureau of Economic and Business Research, University of Illinois, 1949. A. C. NIELSEN, "Two Years of Commercial Operation of the Audimeter and the Nielsen Radio Index," *Journal of Marketing*, January, 1945, pp. 239–255. More recent material will be found in the report of the American Statistical Association Technical Committee on Broadcast Ratings, *Evaluation of Statistical Methods Used in Obtaining Broadcast Ratings*. Washington, D.C.: American Statistical Association, 1961.

composition of program audiences and of changes in these characteristics over time. In a broader sense, such data are useful for evaluating the economic and social impact of radio and TV on the economy. Thus, the extent to which TV serves as a substitute for other leisure time activities, or the extent to which it may serve as an educational medium, can be traced over time with panel data.

6.1.3. Problems of Panel Operation[6]

The repetitive interviewing of the same people, intensified at times by requests for the very same information period after period, gives rise to two problems of major significance to any panel operation: the representativeness of the panel relative to the population, and the effect of panel membership on the information obtained.

6.1.3.1. *Representativeness.* A panel may provide a near-perfect miniature of the population at the start of the operation. However, it is not likely to remain so, for two reasons. One is that the panel, being selected from the population at a particular point in time, reflects only to a limited extent changes in the characteristics of the population over time. Migration, for example, is clearly neglected. The same is true of new family formation and of changes due to unusual circumstances affecting one area or population group but not another. Theoretically, these factors can be, and sometimes are, offset by periodic additions of new, suitably selected families to the panel. Also, in practice this factor is not particularly important in the short run, since changes of significant magnitude generally require many years.

Much more important in distorting panel representativeness is the second factor, non-response. Because of the continuous nature of a panel operation, the non-response rate is inevitably greater than that of a single-interview sample, and the more so, the longer the period of the operation. Non-response can occur for a number of reasons. The respondent may not be in a cooperative mood; he may not be at home; he may be antagonized by the interviewer; he may not like the questions asked; and so on. From an analytical point of view, these various reasons can be combined into two categories: people who could not be contacted, and people who were contacted but refused at some stage or other.

Theoretically, the number of non-contacts could be reduced to zero, given sufficient resources. In practice, this is rarely, if ever, the case. Inability to locate addresses, moving, departures for vacation, and illness are among the principal factors that contribute to non-contacts. On the other hand, the

---

[6] This section is based in large part on ROBERT FERBER, "Observations on a Consumer Panel Operation," *Journal of Marketing*, January, 1953, pp. 246–259. See also G. G. Quackenbush and J. D. SHAFFER, *Collecting Food Purchase Data by Consumer Panel*. East Lansing, Mich.: Michigan State University, 1960.

refusals constitute the hard core of non-response in a survey operation. Despite thorough training of interviewers and careful advance preparations, a certain proportion of those contacted will refuse to cooperate for one reason or another. The refusal rate, the proportion of those contacted who refuse to be interviewed, on the initial wave of a personal interview panel is generally about 15 per cent, the same as on a one-interview survey—provided the respondent is not told of the panel aspect of the operation until the end of

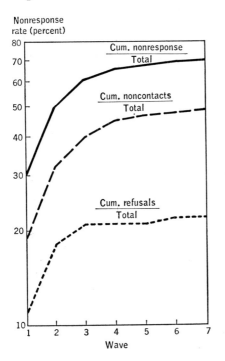

Fig. 6.2. *Nonresponse Rate, by Type of Nonresponse*

Source: Robert Ferber, *op. cit.*

the interview. Additional refusals can be expected on succeeding waves, as boredom and respondent fatigue begin to appear.

Fig. 6.2 shows how non-response can cumulate during a personal interview panel operation. The three lines on the chart portray the cumulative non-response rates over seven waves of interviews for (a) total non-respondents, (b) non-contacts, and (c) refusals.

The general trend of each of these non-response rates is essentially the same, and in accordance with past experience with such operations. Non-response increases most, both absolutely and relatively, in the initial waves and then rapidly declines. The cumulative non-response rates therefore rise rapidly at first and then slowly level off. As is shown by the chart, the refusal rate leveled off fairly early—the cumulative refusal rate by the third interview differed only negligibly from that on the seventh interview—whereas non-contacts continued to mount throughout the operation, though at an apparently decreasing rate. The non-response pattern on a mail panel operation is generally much the same, except that the levels of non-response are likely to be much higher.

In this particular study, non-contacts were relatively high, reflecting limitation of resources, which served to restrict the interview period and the number of call-backs that could be afforded. Given sufficient resources, the refusal rate in Fig. 6.2 would represent, in effect, the theoretical minimum non-response rate that might have been obtained on this study.

Compensation for non-response is made in most panel operations by the recruitment of additional people; in some instances attempts are made to replace non-respondents with people having much the same characteristics. In any event, the non-response problem is a factor to be considered, particularly the extent to which the results are biased by non-response. The evidence on this subject is conflicting. In some cases, non-response tends to be concentrated in particular population groups, which can lead to bias to the extent that the replies of these groups differ from those of groups that have higher response rates.[7] In other cases, bias due to this factor is not apparent.[8] It is clear, however, that tests for the possible presence of this bias are desirable in any event, notably by comparing the distributions of the respondents and non-respondents by all available characteristics felt to influence the subject under study, using chi-square and variance analysis.

6.1.3.2. *Effect of panel membership.* Apart from the factor of non-response is the question of the effect of panel membership as such on the sample results.[9] Presumably, panel members tend to become more self-conscious over time both of their membership in the panel and of their replies. One result of this increased self-consciousness is a possible tendency on their part to modify their replies to questions on personal habits or on matters of social import to bring them more into line with social acceptability. Another, more favorable, result is improvement in the memory of the respondent, which leads to more accurate data where records of past actions (purchases, attitudes, etc.) are requested. Still another possible effect is a tendency to lose interest in the study and to provide less accurate or less comprehensive information. Thus, in a diary-keeping operation, some people will tend to

---

[7] L. O. Brown, *Marketing and Distribution Research;* M. Parten, *Surveys, Polls and Samples*, Chapter 3; S. G. Barton, "Consumer Panels" in Churchman, Ackoff and Wax (editors), *Measurement of Consumer Interest.*

[8] Robert Ferber, *op. cit.* Also, M. G. Sobel, "Panel Mortality and Panel Bias," *Journal of the American Statistical Association*, March, 1959, pp. 52–68.

[9] A summary of early studies on the effect of repeated interviews on sample results will be found in F. L. Ruch, "Effects of Repeated Interviewing on the Respondent's Answers," *Journal of Consulting Psychology*, July–August, 1941, pp. 179–182. None of these early studies, however, was concerned with bias in the measurement of purchase plans or of purchases made.

record their grocery purchases at less frequent intervals as time goes on, thereby increasing the likelihood of omitting purchases.

In any of these instances, however, some form of bias is involved, bias in the sense that the replies obtained by interviewing the panel members are not the same as those that would have been obtained had those people not been interviewed previously.

As with panel mortality, continual checks for bias due to panel membership are needed. In this case, the checks are more difficult because of the numerous ways in which panel membership can produce bias. The approach depends to a large extent on the nature of the particular panel operation. Generally, however, it involves consideration of the various channels through which panel membership may influence the results—loss of interest, irritation, etc.—and the manner in which each of these factors may manifest itself in the data. In the latter respect, the following three effects are likely to be exhaustive: because of panel membership, the data may be affected in terms of:

  a) accuracy of information given
  b) comprehensiveness
  c) cognition.

The first two categories are self-evident, the direction of bias generally being toward less accurate and less comprehensive data. This is not always the case, however, as shown by the following report.[10]

In the present study, which sought to determine, in part, the degree of realization of consumer purchase plans, a very real effect due to the use of the continuous panel technique was detected. The average number of actual purchases reported per family increased consistently with length of panel membership. On the other hand, the average number of purchase plans reported per family actually declined during the first few interviews and, though it increased with additional interviews, never quite reached the level of the initial interview. This leads to the inference, therefore, that the degree of realization of purchase plans is to some extent a positive function of length of panel membership, so that the use of the panel operation tended to increase the fulfillment of purchase plans over time.

Cognition refers to understanding of what is wanted. Often panel members will fail to include pertinent items or will include extraneous data because of misunderstanding of instructions. Though such errors are generally sought and detected on an individual panel member basis, aggregative checks can also be useful in this regard.

Whether or not bias due to panel membership is apparent, most continuing panel operations provide for rotation of panel members, with a restriction

---

[10] ROBERT FERBER, *op. cit.*, p. 258.

on the maximum length of participation of any one family. This not only helps counteract effects of panel membership but also serves to maintain the representativeness of the operation, as noted earlier.

6.2. STORE AND PANTRY AUDITS

6.2.1. Nature and Uses

The essential difference between a store, or pantry, audit and a consumer panel is that in the former case the principal data are obtained not by questioning but by observation. Thus, in the case of a grocery store audit, a sample of stores is visited periodically and data are recorded on inventories on hand, either by observation or copying from store records. Shipments of merchandise received since the last visit will also be recorded, usually from purchase invoices. The combined data are then used for deriving sales estimates by period and by type of store—size of store, location, chain or independent, etc.

Additional data may be sought at times from the store manager or owner for use in conjunction with these sales estimates. Thus, figures may be recorded on the amount of display space accorded different brands of a certain product. The figures will then be used afterward in an attempt to derive a relation between sales and display space. Alternatively, store-audit reports may be tied to external data, such as changes in sales in different areas as related to the extent of local unemployment.

The general principles of store auditing are illustrated in Figure 6.3, which shows the type of data transcribed from store shelves and records, by the A. C. Nielsen Company, the largest firm in this field. Each one of these cards contains an estimate of the sales of an individual product, and brand, as well as other information pertinent to an evaluation of the sales of that item.

A pantry audit differs from a store audit primarily because the data are recorded from examination of the consumer's pantry, rather than from examining store shelves. As a result, sales estimates are not generally practicable. Rather, the usual objective in a pantry audit is to find out what types of consumers buy certain products and certain brands, the assumption being that the contents of the pantry accurately portray the consumer's preferences.

Pantry audits generally are supplemented by direct questioning of the family shopper. These questions will seek reasons and circumstances under which particular products were purchased, in an attempt to relate these factors to purchasing habits. Other subjects may be covered as well, depending on the objectives of the particular survey. In any case, questions will be asked about products obtained without charge and about any unusual contents of the pantry, e.g., a 50-pound bag of sugar in the pantry of a single person living alone.

Store audits invariably are panel operations, for the derivation of sales estimates and compilation of sales trends by store are their principal *raison d'être*. A pantry audit may or may not be set up as a panel operation, since a single visit is often considered sufficient to yield an accurate picture of consumer preferences. Because sales data can hardly be obtained in this

---

PRINCIPLES OF NIELSEN INDEX AUDITING
"BLANK" BRAND TOOTH PASTE (50¢ SIZE)
IN JOHN DOE'S DRUG STORE

FOR JAN—FEB

PURCHASES:

	NO. OF ORDERS	PKGS	VALUE
From manufacturer	1	24	$7.00
From wholesalers	10	62	19.10
Total	86		$26.10

INVENTORY:

January 1	114 pkgs.	
March 1	93 "	
Change		21

CONSUMER SALES

Package	107
Price, per pkg.	$ .41
Dollars, total	$43.87

STORE PROMOTION

	YES	NO
Window displays	☒	☐
Inside advertising displays	☐	☒
Inside goods display	☒	☐
Local advertising, by store	☒	☐
Special price sale	☒	☐
At what price?	$ .39	

Fig. 6.3. A Store Audit Record

Source: A. C. Nielsen, "Evolution of Factual Techniques in Marketing Research," in *Marketing Research and Business Management*, Nugent Wedding, Editor, University of Illinois, Bureau of Economic and Business Research, p. 25.

---

manner anyway—except through the awkward and highly expensive procedure of combining the audit with some sort of diary method—panel methods are rare in the case of pantry audits.

Groceries are not the only products for which store and pantry audits are carried out. The pantry-audit approach is used for products ranging from foods to houses and by organizations varying from advertising agencies to the U. S. Bureau of the Census. The Census Bureau has utilized this approach in its periodic "National Inventory of Housing" in which investigators visit households to ascertain the type of construction, plumbing, heating, and various other features of the house.[11] Private research agencies sometimes use this approach to determine the distribution of durable goods having cer-

---

[11] See U. S. Bureau of the Census, *National Inventory of Housing*, 1956.

tain characteristics by type of consumer. Many of these characteristics, such as the model year or type of motor in a washing machine, are not easily secured by direct questioning, so that accurate data are best obtained through a "pantry audit" approach.

A group of products for which store audits have been used for many years is drugs, both ethical and proprietary. With ethical drugs in particular— those which can be bought only with a doctor's prescription—the average consumer is in no position to supply accurate information: often he does not know what he is purchasing. In addition, the purchasers of particular drugs are likely to be so widely scattered that a sample of prohibitive size would be required to obtain this information with much reliability. As a result, drug store audits, conducted along the same general lines as illustrated in Figure 6.3, were the only means for a long time of obtaining current sales estimates at the consumer level.[12]

6.2.2. Pros and Cons

Accuracy of data is perhaps the principal advantage of the audit method. No question of recall is involved, or of extent of consumer cooperation in maintaining diary records. Admittedly, question remains of the accuracy with which the transcribing is done from store or pantry shelves, but since this is done by a paid employee of the research organization, control of such errors is a relatively simple matter.

In a store audit, the conscientiousness of store managers or owners in keeping past invoices could be a trouble spot, except for the fact that in most instances such records are kept for internal purposes anyway. Since stores are generally reimbursed for their cooperation, an additional incentive is provided for maintaining accurate invoice files.

Another advantage of the store audit method is that it offers the most practicable means of evaluating the effect on sales of variations in display space and location, window displays, and other means of in-store promotion. The method is particularly amenable to use with experimental designs, and a growing trend has been evident in more recent years toward the use of store audits in conjunction with variance or covariance analysis to measure the effectiveness of various promotional devices.[13]

---

[12] More recently, attempts have been made to obtain the same information from samples of physicians.

[13] As examples, see M. E. BRUNK and W. T. FEDERER, "Experimental Designs and Probability Sampling in Marketing Research," *Journal of the American Statistical Association*, September, 1953, pp. 440–452; W. APPLEBAUM and R. F. SPEARS, "Controlled Experimentation in Market Research," *Journal of Marketing*, January, 1950, pp. 505–17; R. J. JESSEN, "A Switch-Over Experimental Design to Measure Advertising Effect," *Journal of Advertising Research*, March, 1961, pp. 15–22.

Furthermore, in some instances, as noted earlier, the audit approach may be alleged to be the only reliable means of getting current sales estimates at the consumer level. This is likely to be particularly true of household audits relating to product characteristics with which consumers are not generally familiar.

On the other hand, the audit approach is not without its drawbacks. A serious practical difficulty has arisen from the refusal of some of the largest food chains in the country to permit audits in their stores. As a result, not only are major gaps left in the sales estimates derived for products and brands of the major food manufacturers, but virtually no information is obtained on sales of the private store brands, some of which constitute substantial portions of the total market. Attempts are made to fill these gaps by means of a variety of indirect methods, such as client manufacturer reports of shipments to these excluded stores and the use of correlation methods to estimate sales based on data from stores in the sample most closely comparable to those excluded. However, such estimates are makeshift procedures at best and little is known of their reliability.[14]

Another difficulty, one that has grown more serious with the spread of supermarket merchandising methods over the years, is the tendency for particular goods to be sold by an increasing variety of stores. In the past, a sample of grocery stores and supermarkets would have been sufficient to cover virtually all sales of packaged foods. To do the same in the 1960's requires not only grocery stores and supermarkets but also variety stores, department stores, drug stores and even discount houses. From a conceptual point of view, the design of such a sample is not difficult. However, from a practical point of view, various difficulties arise, not the least of which is to secure the cooperation of new types of stores, many of which are large chains not particularly interested in allowing such data to be compiled for the benefit of manufacturers.

In addition, it has to be recognized that, at best, store audits measure product sales from retail outlets. Sales not made through the retail channels covered by the store sample are necessarily excluded. With some products, such as food and drugs, these sales are generally insignificant and can safely be disregarded. However, with such products as appliances, TV and radio sets, appreciable "leakage" can occur through wholesalers and other non-retail outlets. Reconciliation of audit-based estimates with manufacturer data on production and shipments can then pose perplexing questions.

A conceptual drawback of the pantry-audit approach is that consumer preferences and the factors underlying them are not at times identifiable from the audit data alone. Thus, if increased display space produces a significant rise in sales, it is often desirable to pursue the matter further and deter-

---

[14] The reluctance of store audit organizations in making data available for impartial tests does not add to general confidence in these procedures.

mine if possible what particular characteristics of the product—the price, the package, the appeal, etc.—led the consumer to buy it.

In the case of a pantry audit, question can be raised further on the extent to which items in the pantry really represent consumer preference. This is particularly true of goods acquired some time ago, or of goods purchased for the first time, where experience with the product may have given rise to new preferences. Essentially, however, these criticisms are not serious, for they are easily remedied with the aid of supplemental personal interviews. Such interviews, which can be conducted in the store or in the home, often can provide sufficient information to overcome this drawback, though they do not usually provide the great amount of detail on consumer behavior derived from a direct interview approach.

All things considered, it is clear that the audit approach and the consumer panel each are able to supply information partly competitive with the other and partly supplementary. Largely because of the evolution and prevailing structure of the marketing research industry, the past emphasis has been on the competitive aspects of these two approaches. However, from an analytical point of view these two approaches are potentially useful supplementary devices, each compensating to a large extent for inherent deficiencies in the other approach.

6.3. SCALING AND ATTITUDE SURVEYS

Although the analysis of attitudes logically lies within the province of Chapter 3, it is best understood after techniques of securing cross-section data have been discussed and has therefore been postponed to this chapter.

The problem of measuring attitudes is encountered in many of the other social sciences besides business and economics. Attitude measurement in business and economics has been a relatively recent development, partly because of the large amount of factual data that has been available in these fields and partly because for a long time little emphasis was placed in the theoretical literature on the possible relevance of attitudes and expectations to business and economic behavior. In the field of economics particularly, it was not until the appearance in the 1940's of considerable literature devoted to the probable influence of attitudes and expectations on business fluctuations that much attention was given to the measurement of these variables.

Currently, attitude measurement serves a wide variety of objectives. In business, attitude measurement is used among other things to:

a) evaluate employee satisfaction with working conditions,
b) gauge community and public sentiment toward a plant or company,
c) select the best personnel for particular types of work,

d) measure user satisfaction with company products,
e) keep track of business confidence,
f) predict the effect of certain changes in company policy, e.g., a new system of salesmen compensation, on employee relations.

In economic analysis, the measurement of attitudes has gained vogue as a possible indicator of business trends. Some have alleged that attitudes may be a tool of major importance for prediction purposes and that the primary issue is how best to measure attitudes rather than whether or not to employ attitudinal variables.[15] Experimentation has already been carried out with regard to both the phrasing of attitudinal questions and the quantification of replies.[16] The former has already been discussed in Chapter 5 and therefore need not be reviewed here. Instead, we will focus on the problem of quantification, which in many ways has been the real stumbling block to the use of attitudinal information in business and economics.

6.3.1. Approaches to Quantification

Numerous approaches to quantification of attitudes have been developed over the years, primarily in sociology and psychology. None is fully satisfactory, the ones that are most reliable and valid from a technical viewpoint generally being the most difficult, and expensive, to apply. The selection of the "best" technique in a particular situation is still a highly controversial question. Hence, a number of the principal techniques are presented on the following pages with a review of the advantages and limitations of each. First, however, it will be useful to differentiate between "reliability" and "validity" as applied to the measurement of attitudes.

By *reliability* is meant the ability of a technique to yield the same results if repeated under invariant conditions. Thus, a series of attitudinal questions on the desirability of resale price maintenance would be adjudged reliable to the extent that repetition of the test under the same conditions produces the same attitude. In some instances, this test can be made by reinterviewing the same people with the identical questions. However, this is not always the best approach partly because of the danger of memory bias and partly because the passage of time may have brought about a true change in the people's attitudes on the subject. Hence, an alternate approach frequently used to test for reliability is to interview samples from different groups of the population and in this way test not only for invariance but also for the extent

---

[15] GEORGE KATONA, *Psychological Analysis of Economic Behavior;* also by KATONA, *The Powerful Consumer.* For a contrary view, see JAMES TOBIN, "On the Predictive Value of Consumer Intentions and Attitudes," *Review of Economics and Statistics,* February, 1959, pp. 1–12.

[16] References will be found in H. G. WALES and ROBERT FERBER, *A Basic Bibliography of Marketing Research,* Sec. 3.2, 12.

to which reliability is affected by variations in socio-economic characteristics —and perhaps by the interviewing situation as well.

By *validity* is meant the ability of an attitudinal technique to measure what one thinks is being measured. Thus, does a series of attitudinal questions on hostility toward labor unions really measure that characteristic or something else? One of the questions proposed may be, "Do you think Walter Reuther is a great American?" Answers to such a question may reflect primarily opinion of Walter Reuther as a person and may have little to do with attitudes toward unions. If so, this question, though perfectly straightforward for some purposes, would be "invalid" for the purpose at hand.

Establishing validity is not generally an easy task, the English language being what it is. Various procedures have been developed for doing so, each best suited for a particular situation. Thus, one approach is to administer the test to groups known to have extreme attitudes on the subject at hand; in the above example the test might be tried out on a group of labor leaders and on a group of known anti-union industry executives. If opposite ratings are obtained from the two groups in accordance with expectations, the test may be considered to possess validity.

Another approach involves obtaining independent opinions from experts in that field of the ability of the test, and of individual questions, to measure the attitude under study. The extent to which these opinions agree is taken as a measure of validity. Yet another approach is to compare results obtained from applying the attitudinal questions on a pretest to such independent criteria as may exist. Thus, results of a scale designed to measure customer satisfaction may be compared with the extent to which the given product is actually used (or bought).

Unfortunately, none of these criteria is foolproof. Each involves at the least the assumption that the criterion selected is an adequate measure of the attribute being tested, a question which itself may have to be validated. In many instances, therefore, validation reduces to a matter of judgment, based on the use of as many different approaches as feasible. In some instances, however, the method of attitude measurement itself will assist in evaluating validity. This will be discussed in connection with scalogram analysis.

6.3.2. Ranking

One of the earliest approaches to attitude measurement, ranking has been used extensively in psychology and sociology. It is most useful where a scale of measurement is not easily constructed but where some ordering of the population on the given attribute (attitude) is desired. Such may be the case, for example, in evaluating salesmen's attitudes toward alternative compensation plans.

To arrive at an attitudinal scale, the *method of paired comparisons* can be used. This method involves showing the respondent all possible pairs of alternatives and having him indicate a preference between each pair. Thus, if four sales compensation plans are being compared—A, B, C, and D, each interviewee would be asked to express a preference between A and B, between A and C, A and D, B and C, B and D, and between C and D, six pairs in all.

In the simplest case, the compensation plans are ranked on the basis of the number of preferences stated for each, the plan with the highest score presumably being the most popular.[17] In the same manner, the consistency—and hence, the reliability—of the answers can be evaluated, based on the property of transitivity.

At best, the result of this procedure is a ranking of alternatives, which may or may not be all that is desired. In addition, the test becomes progressively awkward to administer as the number of items increases. Since n items constitute $n(n-1)/2$ possible pairs, the test tends to become unwieldy altogether if there are more than six items.

6.3.3. Rating

One of the simplest types of numerical scales is the scale of agreement, or of gradational adjectives, assigning integers in sequence to each point or answer. The question can be designed for a graphic answer, as follows:

Please indicate on the scale below your degree of optimism or pessimism regarding the general business outlook for the next year

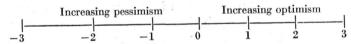

Or, the question can be put more straightforwardly:

Are you optimistic or pessimistic regarding the general business outlook for the next year? Check one.

Very optimistic.............................. □ 2
Optimistic..................................... □ 1
Not sure....................................... □ 0
Pessimistic................................... □ -1
Very pessimistic.............................. □ -2

In either case, the simplest form of rating a person as optimistic or pessimistic would be on the basis of his answer to a single question of this type.

---

[17] For a more rigorous method of ranking the alternatives, see J. P. GUILFORD, *Psychometric Methods* (New York: McGraw-Hill Book Company, 1954), Chapter 8.

However, since question formulation is still more of an art than a science, more valid results are obtainable by basing such a rating on more than one question. Usually, a series of such questions is presented to each person interviewed, all with essentially the same answer categories and all relating to the same general subject, in this case, optimism or pessimism. The numbers opposite the answer categories serve as a basis for scoring, the score for each individual being the sum, or average, of the numbers (ratings) opposite the answers checked. Sums are generally adequate if only relative ordering of individuals on this attribute is desired. (What is the exception?) If, however, the individuals are to be classified as "optimistic" or "pessimistic," averages of the ratings serve as the basis of classification. Thus, by the above classification, all individuals having a positive average rating would be classified as "optimistic" and all those with negative average ratings as "pessimistic."

In a similar manner, the same technique can be used to rank different sectors or industries by degree of optimism. Separate questions of the type just illustrated would be asked for each sector, and the summation would be by sectors over all individuals. The higher the total, or average, rating accorded a sector, the more optimistic presumably is the sample regarding its outlook.

The assignment of numerical ratings is clearly arbitrary, both for values and distance between values. Yet, the technique stands up remarkably well compared to more sophisticated approaches; indeed it yields virtually identical results.[18] Furthermore, these results are practically invariant to the numerical values assigned to different answers as long as these values are assigned by a "reasonable" method—meaning essentially that the sequence of values is changing monotonically.[19]

Scales of this type are also not without limitations. For one thing, much depends on the wording of the questions and on the gradational answer scale that is used. In particular, the "zero point"—the boundary between optimism and pessimism, in the previous example—is not invariant to these variables, which means that the proportion ascribed a given attitude may vary with the nature of the question.

Furthermore, the method gives equal weight to all answers. Thus, the fact that a person may feel very strong about, or very sure of, one answer but not at all of another is disregarded. In addition, establishing the validity and reliability of a test of this type is not always too easy, particularly the unidimensionality of the test. A common method of testing for reliability is to correlate scores of individual questions with the score for the test as a whole,

[18] GARDNER MURPHY and RENSIS LIKERT, *Public Opinion and the Individual* (New York: Harper Bros., 1938); also E. A. RUNDQUIST and RAYMOND SLETTO, *Personality in the Depression* (Minneapolis: University of Minnesota Press, 1936).

[19] ROBERT FERBER, "Gradational Adjectives in Market Surveys," *Journal of Applied Psychology*, 1955, pp. 173–177.

eliminating questions that correlate negatively or not at all with the test average. This is a useful method but by no means foolproof. (Why not?)

Despite these limitations, rating scales have proven very useful in business and economic studies. They are easy to administer, simple to score, and with proper precautions can give valid results.

6.3.4. Equivalent Intervals

Developed by L. L. Thurstone[20] and used primarily in psychology, this technique has received virtually no attention in business or economics. No doubt this is due to the greater simplicity with which rating scales can be administered, and prepared, as well as to the recent development of the scalogram method, to be discussed in the next section. Nevertheless, under certain conditions this approach may be useful and is worth knowing.

As originally evolved, the method consists of submitting to experts on the particular subject a large number (over 100) of attitudinal statements each on a separate card. Each expert, or "judge," is asked to sort the cards into 11 piles on the basis of instructions of the following sort, as given by Thurstone in applying the method to preparing a scale on attitudes toward the church:[21]

1. The 130 slips contain statements regarding the value of the church. These have been made by various persons, students, and others.

2. As a first step in the making of a scale that may be used in a test of opinions relating to the church and religion we want a number of persons to sort these 130 slips into eleven piles.

3. You are given eleven slips with letters on them, A, B, C, D, E, F, G, H, I, J, K. Please arrange these before you in regular order. On slip A put those statements which you believe express the highest *appreciation* of the value of the church. On slip F put those expressing a neutral position. On slip K put those slips which express the strongest *depreciation* of the church. On the rest of the slips arrange statements in accordance with the degree of appreciation or depreciation expressed in them.

4. This means that when you are through sorting you will have eleven piles arranged in order of value-estimate from A, the highest, to K, the lowest.

5. Do not try to get the same number in each pile. They are not evenly distributed.

6. The numbers on the slips are code numbers and have nothing to do with the arrangement in piles.

7. You will find it easier to sort them if you look over a number of the slips, chosen at random, before you begin to sort.

On this basis, each judge comes up with 11 piles of cards, each pile presumably equidistant from its neighboring piles in terms of attitude. The letters A, B, . . . , K are then replaced by the integers 1, 2, . . . , 11, and an

---

[20] L. L. THURSTONE and E. J. CHAVE, *The Measurement of Attitude* (Chicago: University of Chicago Press, 1929).
[21] *Ibid.*, p. 31.

ogive is prepared of the relative frequency with which each statement is placed in a particular pile, one ogive for each statement. The rating corresponding to the median frequency (how is this obtained from the ogive?) is the scale value assigned to each statement. The inter-quartile range of the ratings of that statement is taken as a measure of reliability, or ambiguity, of that statement; the smaller the range, presumably the more reliable is the statement.

These measures—the median and the inter-quartile range—are computed for all the statements, in the preceding example, 130 of them. A small number of the statements, between 12 and 18, are then selected for the final scale on the basis primarily of two criteria: representation from the entire range of attitudes, and high reliability. The statements so selected constitute the scale which is then administered for measuring attitudes on the given subject. Each sample member is presented with all the statements in the scale and is asked to indicate which he would endorse. His score, or scale, on the attitude is computed as the mean of the scale values of the statements he has endorsed.

Clearly, much depends on the acumen of the judges in sorting the statements. Judges not only have to be selected with great care, but there has to be a substantial number of them to offset whatever individual prejudices may exist. Selecting the judges, administering the test to them, and then choosing statements for the final scale are all formidable tasks, particularly since in some subject areas the requisite number of judges may not be available.

It should also be noted that the specification of 11 piles is arbitrary. An odd number is desirable in attitude measurement (why?), but the specification of a particular number in advance is open to question. In addition, like rating scales, the specification of the zero position, the point of neutrality, remains a matter of judgment. Finally, no allowance is contained in this method for differing degrees or intensities of opinion which, perhaps more than any other factor, contributed to the later development of rating methods and of scalogram analysis. Despite these limitations, however, careful application of this method does yield valid results.

6.3.5. Scalogram Analysis

Developed by Louis Guttman just prior to World War II, scalogram analysis is a very elegant technique of measuring attitudes. It copes with two of the principal limitations of virtually all previous techniques: establishing unidimensionality and location of the neutral attitude position irrespective of question wording. The operational procedure can be described as follows:[22]

---

[22] E. A. SUCHMAN and LOUIS GUTTMAN, "A Solution to the Problem of Question 'Bias,'" *Public Opinion Quarterly*, Fall, 1947, pp. 445–455. Also see the chapters on this method in S. A. STOUFFER *et al.*, *Measurement and Prediction.*

" (1) asking a series of opinion questions on the same topic (this series need not be long—in very few cases are more than a dozen questions required in the pretest; for the final study, successful results have been obtained with only four or five questions selected on the basis of the pretest),

" (2) testing these questions to determine whether they all ask the respondent about the same single dimension of opinion,

" (3) asking "How strongly do you feel about this?" after each opinion question in order to determine intensity of feeling,

" (4) obtaining for each respondent an opinion or content score which is the number of the opinion questions to which he gives the *more favorable* answer, and

" (5) plotting content scores by intensity scores to obtain a U- or J-shaped curve, the lowest point of which serves to divide the population into the desired *objective* and *invariant* favorable and unfavorable groups."

The analysis can be carried out in several ways, all relating to the same basic principle and hence yielding essentially the same results. This principle is that if a series of questions are unidimensional and comprise a scale, they can be ordered in such a way that a person's answer to all succeeding questions can be inferred given an affirmative answer to one of them. Thus, consider the following four statements:

1. Total profits next year will be substantially higher than this year.
2. Profits next year will be higher than this year.
3. Business will improve next year.
4. Business next year will be the same or better than this year.

If a person agrees with one of these statements, we can safely assume that he also agrees with all succeeding ones. In this sense, the statements are said to be scalable. For if one person is known to agree with statement 2 and another only with statement 4, we can safely say that the first individual has a higher value on the scale of business optimism than the second.

In practice, the respondent is presented with a series of attitudinal statements on a subject and asked to indicate his extent of agreement with each. A questionnaire of this nature is illustrated in Figure 6.4. As noted in this illustration, the intensities are assigned weights, the selection of the actual numbers being arbitrary and governed only by the requirement of "reasonableness," as defined earlier. On the basis of these weights, each respondent is assigned a score, the possible values in this example varying from 0 to 28. On the basis of these scores, the questionnaires are arranged in descending order in a table which also reproduces the pattern of each respondent's answers. Such a table is portrayed in Figure 6.5 for the 50 subjects answering the questionnaire on "A Nation of Nations."

This table serves as the basis for ascertaining scalability. If the answers are scalable, the pattern for responses should be a simple one, running for each question from the upper left-hand corner to the lower right-hand corner.[23]

---

[23] *Ibid.*, p. 256.

"Let us consider the first question in the table. If response 4 is higher than response 3, and if 3 is higher than 2, and if 2 is higher than 1 (response 0 happens to have no frequency in this case), then the nine people in category 4 should be the top nine people. Actually, six of them are the top six and the other three scatter farther down the column. Similarly, the twenty-seven people in category 3 should be below the first nine people and should go down to the thirty-sixth person $(36 = 9 + 27)$. Again, this is not perfectly true for our data. A similar examination for the other items shows that there is a substantial error of reproducibility in their present form."

A NATION OF NATIONS

QUESTIONS

1. *A Nation of Nations* does a good job of analyzing the ethnic groups in this country.
   ____Strongly agree$_4$ ____Agree$_3$ ____Undecided$_2$
   ____Disagree$_1$ ____Strongly disagree$_0$

2. On the whole, *A Nation of Nations* is not as good as most college textbooks.
   ____Strongly agree$_0$ ____Agree$_1$ ____Undecided$_2$
   ____Disagree$_3$ ____Strongly disagree$_4$

3. Adamic organizes and presents his material very well.
   ____Strongly agree$_4$ ____Agree$_3$ ____Undecided$_2$
   ____Disagree$_1$ ____Strongly disagree$_0$

4. As a sociological treatise, Adamic's book does not rate very high.
   ____Strongly agree$_0$ ____Agree$_1$ ____Undecided$_2$
   ____Disagree$_3$ ____Strongly disagree$_4$

5. Adamic does not discuss any one group in sufficient detail so that a student can obtain a real insight into problems of ethnic group relations in this country.
   ____Strongly agree$_0$ ____Agree$_1$ ____Undecided$_2$
   ____Disagree$_3$ ____Strongly disagree$_4$

6. By providing a panorama of various groups, *A Nation of Nations* lets the student get a good perspective on ethnic group relations in this country.
   ____Strongly agree$_4$ ____Agree$_3$ ____Undecided$_2$
   ____Disagree$_1$ ____Strongly disagree$_0$

7. *A Nation of Nations* is good enough to be kept as a textbook for this course.
   ____Strongly agree$_4$ ____Agree$_3$ ____Undecided$_2$
   ____Disagree$_1$ ____Strongly disagree$_0$

Fig. 6.4. Questionnaire for Scalogram Analysts

Source: LOUIS GUTTMAN, "The Cornell Technique for Scale and Intensity Analysis," *Educational and Psychological Measurement*, 1947, pp. 250–251.

If the initial answer categories are not scalable (reproducible), as is usually the case, attempts are made to combine answer categories for each question until a sufficient degree of reproducibility is achieved. The extent to which combination is carried out depends on whether the given questions do indeed form a scale and on the number of distinct scale types desired. If not many scale types are desired, a much higher degree of reproducibility can generally

Score	1					2					3					4					5					6					7				
	4	3	2	1	0	4	3	2	1	0	4	3	2	1	0	4	3	2	1	0	4	3	2	1	0	4	3	2	1	0	4	3	2	1	0
28	x					x					x					x					x					x					x				
25	x					x						x				x						x					x				x				
25	x					x					x						x				x					x					x				
24	x						x				x						x				x					x					x				
23	x					x					x					x						x						x			x				
23	x					x					x						x				x					x					x				
23		x				x						x					x				x						x					x			
22	x					x					x						x				x						x				x				
21		x				x						x				x					x						x					x			
21		x				x						x				x					x						x					x			
21	x					x						x				x						x					x					x			
21		x				x						x					x				x						x					x			
21		x				x					x						x						x			x					x				
20		x				x					x						x				x						x						x		
20			x			x						x					x				x					x					x				
20	x					x						x				x						x				x					x				
20	x					x					x					x							x				x					x			
19	x					x						x					x				x						x					x			
19	x							x				x				x					x							x			x				
18	x					x					x					x							x			x					x				
18	x					x					x					x								x		x					x				
18	x					x							x			x							x			x					x				
18	x					x						x					x				x					x					x				
17	x					x					x						x					x				x					x				
17	x						x				x						x					x					x				x				
16	x					x					x						x					x				x					x				
16	x							x			x						x				x					x					x				
16	x							x			x					x								x		x					x				
16	x					x					x						x						x				x								x
15	x					x					x						x						x						x						x
15		x					x				x						x						x			x						x			
15	x					x					x						x						x				x					x			
14			x			x							x			x						x					x					x			
14	x					x						x						x				x					x					x			
13			x						x		x							x				x				x						x			
13	x								x		x					x						x					x								x
12			x			x								x		x						x					x								x
12	x					x								x		x						x					x								x
11	x							x				x							x			x					x								x
11		x						x				x						x					x				x								x
10			x					x			x							x				x				x									x
9	x									x	x							x				x					x								x
8			x					x			x							x				x						x							x
7	x									x		x						x				x				x									x
7				x				x			x							x					x				x						x		
7				x				x					x				x					x					x						x		
6				x				x					x					x					x				x						x		
5				x				x					x				x						x				x								x
5				x				x							x	x						x					x						x		
4				x						x	x									x			x				x								x
Freq.	9	27	2	12	0	8	24	0	13	5	10	25	8	7	0	3	7	16	14	10	3	14	5	21	7	9	21	7	12	1	11	19	25	11	4

Fig. 6.5. Pattern of Responses to "A Nation of Nations" Questionnaire

Source: Same as Fig. 6.4.

be achieved than otherwise. Combination of answer categories is accompanied by reshuffling of weights, which leads to a new score for each questionnaire. The new scores serve as the basis for rearranging the questionnaires and preparing a new table similar to that shown in Figure 6.5, from which reproducibility is assessed anew.

This iterative procedure is repeated until a satisfactory degree of reproducibility[24] is attained or until lack of reproducibility is established. Two or three iterations are generally sufficient to complete the analysis. In the process, questions with considerable errors of reproducibility can be pinpointed and eliminated; these questions presumably are not unidimensional with the others.

In actual practice, a so-called "scalogram board" has been devised to facilitate this work. If extensive use is made of this method, such a board can prove a major economy.[25]

The position of neutrality of attitude on the particular subject is obtained by computing for each respondent an "intensity score" reflecting the extent to which he expressed a strong feeling in one direction *or* the other. Medians of these scores are computed for different percentiles of the previously-computed "content" scores. These scores are obtained by asking, after an answer has been given to an attitudinal question, the additional question, "How strongly do you feel about this?" Plotting these "intensity" medians against the corresponding percentiles of the content scores yields a U- or J-shaped curve. The low point of this curve indicates the true division of opinion on the subject among the sample members, a division which can be shown to be invariant to question wording.[26]

> "Intensity of feeling decreases as one moves toward the middle from either end until one reaches a point of least intensity. This point serves to divide the population into positive and negative. *It will stay fixed regardless of the particular opinion questions used or of the way they are worded.* No matter how badly "biased" the questions are, provided only that they deal with the same opinion dimension, the distribution of the population into pro and con will be the same."

As is evident from the foregoing description, construction of a scale by this method entails a fair amount of work, both in the field and afterward. Establishing the validity of a scale by means of scalogram analysis has been

---

[24] One measure of this characteristic is the following coefficient:

$$1 - \frac{Number\ of\ errors\ in\ reproducibility}{Number\ of\ questions \times Number\ of\ respondents}$$

This is not a sufficient measure, however, since the frequencies of particular responses also have to be taken into account. As Guttman notes, reproducibility can be artificially high if one particular response contains almost all the answers.

[25] For directions on preparing such a board, see S. A. STOUFFER, *et. al., Measurement and Prediction*, Chapter 4.

[26] SUCHMAN and GUTTMAN, *op. cit.*

another deterrent to its use, since in some subjects it is feared either that scalability is not likely to exist or that it is unstable from one group to another. Whether or not this is true can only be established by empirical test.

The fact remains that, conceptually, scalogram analysis is perhaps the most elegant of the scaling techniques yet devised. Its administration in the field is no more difficult than numerous types of rating scales, particularly since, once a scale is shown to exist, a subset of the original set of questions is equally valid for further operations.[27] Where rating scales offer a distinct advantage over scalogram analysis and over the method of equivalent intervals is in the ease with which they can be set up and with which the results can be analyzed. However, too often these advantages serve as pitfalls for overlooking lack of reliability or validity.

6.3.6. The Semantic Differential

The semantic differential is a relatively new method of attitude measurement designed to evaluate the different components of attitude. For example, it is all very well to know that a particular respondent thinks that prices are going higher, or prefers one type of beer to another. For operational purposes, it is also necessary to know the reasons for this opinion. These reasons can, of course, be sought by asking "why" questions. In many situations, however, such questions may not be too desirable, either because of their direct nature or because they do not permit more gradation of opinion. The semantic differential is meant to serve as a more objective method in such situations.

The basis of the technique is the use of pairs of polar adjectives on a marked continuum containing generally seven divisions, as follows:

High :   :   :   :   :   :   :   : Low

Thus, in the present case, the respondent would be asked to rate the subject under discussion on the above scale. He might be told that the seven divisions represent, moving from left to right, something like: "very high," "fairly high," "somewhat high," "neither high nor low," "somewhat low," "fairly low," and "very low."

In practice, the respondents are presented with a number of these scales, as illustrated in Fig. 6.6, and are asked to mark these scales at a rapid rate and not think over at any great length the meaning of the particular concepts.[28]

---

[27] STOUFFER, et. al., op. cit.

[28] The technique is described in detail in C. E. OSGOOD, G. J. SUCI, and P. H. TANNENBAUM, *The Measurement of Meaning.* Urbana, Illinois: University of Illinois Press, 1957.

For scoring purposes, this continuum is assigned numbers, such as, 3, 2, 1, 0, −1, −2, −3. Ratings of different respondents on the same scale can then be combined and averages formed to yield an average profile for that subject in the particular dimension.

The example in Fig. 6.6 shows average ratings of the image obtained of three different breweries on nine different dimensions.[29] These profiles were obtained by having respondents rate each company in turn on each of the separate dimensions. The result then shows the extent to which the different companies compare with each other on these different characteristics as well

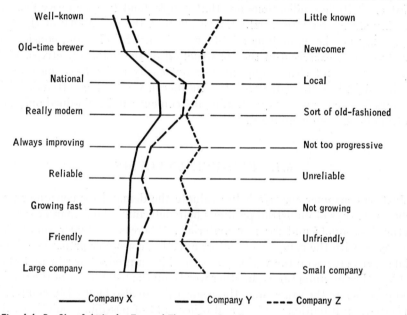

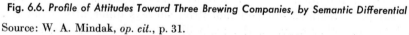

Fig. 6.6. *Profile of Attitudes Toward Three Brewing Companies, by Semantic Differential*

Source: W. A. Mindak, *op. cit.*, p. 31.

as providing some indication of the absolute picture of these companies in people's minds.

To be sure, the same general information could be obtained by a Guttman scale or by a Thurstone scale. The advantage of the semantic differential lies in its much greater simplicity and the ease with which it can be applied. Thus, each reply on any scale yields at the same time an indication of both the *direction* of a person's attitude and of the *intensity* of feeling. At the same time, the semantic differential possesses some of the same advantages of the more intricate scaling techniques, such as helping to segregate components

---

[29] Based on W. A. MINDAK, "Fitting the Semantic Differential to the Marketing Problem," *Journal of Marketing*, Volume 25 (April 1961), p. 31.

of an attitude, making comparison between different components, and helping to avoid stereotyped responses and ambiguous phrases. Furthermore, the many tests that have been made with this technique tend to support both its reliability and its validity. Thus, in one test of attitude toward teaching by TV, a single-item semantic differential seven-point scale using the polar adjectives, "good . . . bad," correlated closely with results obtained from a 21-item Thurstone equal-appearing interval scale.[30]

Unfortunately, unlike the Guttman scale, it has yet to be shown that the neutral point of a semantic differential scale does indeed represent a neutral point of attitude. Indications are that people tend to veer away from expressing strong reactions, with the result that the sensitivity of the technique may not be as high as might be desired.[31] In addition, considerable care has to be exercised in the construction of the polar adjectives. If the adjectives are not clearly opposites or not easily understood, meaningless results might be obtained. This is yet another instance where often definitive answers on adequacy of a questioning instrument can be obtained only after pretests have been conducted.

6.4.   END-USE ANALYSIS

Just as consumer surveys help evaluate the demand for consumer products, so surveys of industrial products help determine the demand for manufactured products and for raw materials. Whereas consumer surveys are concerned with the complex of factors affecting consumer preference, industrial surveys focus on the various uses to which a product or raw material is put by other manufacturers, in other words, on the technology of the production process. At the same time, these surveys can also be used to compile information on intentions to buy and other data of possible predictive value. The sampling methods used in industrial surveys differ little from those employed on other surveys, the main differences being greater stress on stratification by product use and on coverage of major customers for each product use. Where industrial surveys do differ is in the manner in which the data are used to estimate demand—end-use analysis. This approach is important not only for demand analysis but also for survey design, and attention is therefore given to it in this section.

Two approaches to end-use analysis are presented: a micro-economic individual product approach, and the macro-economic input-output method. As we shall see, the two approaches are essentially complementary.

[30] Reported by P. J. DEUTSCHMANN, "The Semantic Differential and Public Opinion Research," paper given at the 1959 meeting of the American Association for Public Opinion Research. Many more instances are reported in OSGOOD et al., op. cit.

[31] Methods of coping with this problem are discussed in W. A. MINDAK, op. cit.

6.4.1. Individual Products

A raw material or a producers' manufactured product is generally used in the manufacture of numerous finished products. Hence, an essential prerequisite to evaluating demand for this good is to ascertain the nature and extent of its various end-uses. In effect, what has to be determined is:

1. The quantity sold of each type of finished product using this good.
2. The number of units of this good used in the manufacture of each of these finished products.

The latter represents the "technical coefficients" of the good in each of its end-uses. Barring any changes in production processes, it is the multiplier that reflects the extent to which a unit of finished product draws upon the good under study.

Table 6.1

CONSUMPTION OF FRICTION BEARINGS AND EQUIVALENT STEEL IN VARIOUS USES, GERMANY

(1)	(2)	(3)	(4)	(5)	(6)
Use	Friction bearings per demand unit	Average weight of bearing (kilograms)	Total weight per demand unit	Crude steel equivalent per kg.	Equivalent consumption of crude steel per demand unit
Passenger cars	28	.31	8.68	3.5	30.4
Trucks (six wheelers)	47	1.62	76.14	3.5	266.5
Tractors (less than 30 HP)	34	.62	21.08	3.5	73.9
Tractors (100 HP)	35	1.55	54.25	3.5	189.9

Source: U. S. Strategic Bombing Survey, *The German Anti-Friction Bearings Industry*, January, 1947, pp. 7ff.

Table 6.1 illustrates how such data can be used to estimate demand for a semi-manufactured product, friction bearings, by various final users, and also how these estimates can be translated into demand for the corresponding raw material, in this case crude steel. Columns 2 and 3 of this table present technical coefficients, estimating the extent to which friction bearings enter into the production of each of the four final product categories listed, first in terms of number and then in terms of weight. Column 5 presents another technical coefficient, the amount of steel used to manufacture each type of friction bearing, which happens to be the same in all four instances. This coefficient serves as the basis for estimating, in Column 6, the amount of steel required to supply friction bearings for each of the final demand units.

Aggregate estimates of the demand for friction bearings, whether in number, weight, or steel equivalent, would be obtained by multiplying the appropriate set of technical coefficients by estimates of total production of each of these final demand units and then summing over all uses.

A table of this form not only serves as an aid in demand estimation. It also pinpoints the principal markets for the product, the amount of raw material required for each use and, from a survey methodological point of view, the types of data required for cost and demand analysis. It might be noted that often such data can be obtained without a formal survey, as a by-product of other activities. Thus, data on extent of use of a product such as friction

Table 6.2
ESTIMATED MARKET POTENTIAL FOR SOYBEAN OIL IN NEW YORK, OHIO AND CALIFORNIA, 1948

Item	United States Total	New York	Ohio	California
Thousand employees, food and kindred products[1]	1353	138	61	97
Per cent of total	100	10	4	7
Soybean oil potential in edible products other than oleomargarine—millions of lbs.	865	87	35	61
Production of margarine—millions of pounds[2]	642	0	86	89
Per cent of total	100	0	13	14
Soybean oil potential in margarine, million lbs.	228	0	30	32
Cost of materials, etc.,[3] of paint & varnish industry—millions of dollars	771	91	78	72
Per cent of total	100	12	10	9
Soybean oil potential in paint & varnish industry—millions of pounds	89	11	9	8
Thousand employees, chemicals and allied products[1]	674	84	40	34
Per cent of total	100	12	6	5
Soybean oil potential, other uses than above	112	13	7	6

[1] Employment mid-March, 1947, "Business Establishments, Employment & Taxable Pay Rolls under Old-Age & Survivors Insurance Program, Part I" (U. S. Department of Commerce, December, 1948).

[2] Bureau of Internal Revenue, Year ending June 30, 1947.

[3] Census of Manufactures, 1947 (U. S. Department of Commerce, 1949).

Source: ARIES and COPULSKY, *op. cit.*, p. 732.

bearings can often be secured by having the salesmen code on their order forms the final demand unit for which the products are being ordered.

In a manner similar to that illustrated by Table 6.1, a demand analysis can be carried out on a geographic basis. To take another example, end use of refined soybean oil in 1948 was found to be 18 per cent in oleomargarine, 66 per cent in other edible products (mainly shortening), 7 per cent in paint and varnish, and 9 per cent in chemicals and allied products.[32] Yardsticks of

---

[32] This example is based on R. S. ARIES and WILLIAM COPULSKY, "Determination of Area Market Potentials for Chemical Process Raw Materials," *Journal of Marketing*, April, 1950, pp. 730–732.

44 EATING & DRINKING PLACES	45 NEW CONSTRUCTION & MAINTENANCE	46 INVENTORY CHANGE (additions)	47 FOREIGN COUNTRIES (exports to)	48 GOVERNMENT	49 GROSS PRIVATE CAPITAL FORMATION	50 HOUSEHOLDS						TOTAL GROSS OUTPUT
—	116	—	—	250	865	92	1,008	1,276	569	21	9,785	44,263
2	251	*	9	134	3,469	2	608	1,528	728	—	22,141	37,636
—	—	*	7	45	—	—	77	217	3	—	1,485	2,663
29	4	—	15	580	—	47	61	919	101	21	1,469	9,838
20	16	*	12	150	21	1	214	301	193	1	9,987	13,321
*	1	—	17	444	5	2,330	174	170	14	36	67	6,002
—	4	—	—	199	—	198	78	35	52	569	1,459	2,892
62	26	—	145	836	57	170	44	154	59	—	344	7,899
27	173	13	321	585	30	—	*	72	156	89	1,491	6,447
198	222	2	30	1,181	42	635	305	812	186	—	1,964	14,050
57	56	1	8	357	15	617	56	680	177	*	2,437	13,670
71	4	—	5	468	4	56	94	168	21	8	709	2,825
34	6	—	14	283	—	1	108	84	30	17	2,065	3,810
25	6	—	3	363	59	1,741	99	205	17	15	341	4,844
—	—	—	130	719	—	876	57	605	13	—	—	12,338
—	*	—	21	524	2	315	98	167	5	—	19	6,387
—	—	—	7	106	—	878	64	42	7	60	397	1,745
—	—	—	9	248	—	1,564	15	67	4	145	13	2,316
32	6	—	46	1,138	24	652	127	280	38	74	537	6,445
57	*	—	11	261	—	116	105	566	82	1,640	66	3,292
—	—	—	6	264	—	—	17	205	11	734	31	1,833
146	1	—	53	1,717	—	338	288	990	84	3,450	1,080	10,312
3	—	—	10	257	—	3	33	85	11	128	—	1,095
23	—	—	2	74	—	—	56	113	83	296	639	1,692
62	4	—	25	608	—	716	161	244	76	1,331	673	5,723
,054	*	—	70	671	1	36	401	1,020	151	2,982	3,128	14,265
2	—	—	14	456	—	1	18	324	1,245	1,203	171	4,001
52	176	—	6	229	—	22	32	184	79	260	630	2,119
164	46	53	112	638	21	32	43	187	85	511	1,934	4,756
307	163	54	—	23	219	30	27	355	195	—	133	9,205
29	52	2	10	798	253	706	74	590	332	266	2,061	9,952
—	—	—	5	2	—	—	—	1,340	126	—	102	2,292
14	190	2	6	1,102	97	572	38	314	186	103	3,860	9,855
386	292	7	80	808	1,061	2,506	149	987	45	2,336	27,107	41,657
123	66	11	—	83	11	44	—	38	148	—	1,269	3,173
118	93	26	—	—	72	400	—	135	32	—	6,993	12,814
710	402	180	—	—	386	84	—	—	223	804	20,289	28,855
121	17	95	—	421	55	134	—	3	38	—	179	5,097
559	76	22	30	2,294	228	819	—	—	83	271	7,333	14,301
—	85	—	—	350	—	—	—	—	5,078	—	7,856	13,385
—	7	392	—	14	—	—	—	128	—	—	2,403	2,944
1	1	13	—	12	—	1	—	30	1	—	—	2,233
,303	960	269	—	—	536	—	—	—	—	—	—	24,711
—	152	—	—	1,030	—	—	—	—	—	—	12,075	13,270
56	342	25	—	—	73	7	—	—	5,464	5,709	154	28,704
—	—	—	851	—	—	—	—	22	—	—	—	4,887
—	—	3	69	12	—	—	—	—	1,313	—	1,325	9,275
503	170	318	74	2,176	1,410	470	73	831	3,458	216	31,308	63,685
—	—	—	—	—	—	—	—	—	—	—	—	—
,951	9,199	1,456	—	1,801	4,254	11,492	—	847	30,058	218	2,116	220,474
—	—	—	—	—	—	—	—	—	—	—	—	—
4,301	13,385	2,944	2,233	24,711	13,270	28,704	4,802	17,320	51,060	33,514	191,625	769,248

area production or activity were sought for each of these end-uses, to serve as a basis for allocating soybean oil consumption by area. Since yardsticks of area activity in manufacturing are generally closely related,[33] the same yardstick was not required for each end use. This is fortunate, for not only may the same area data not be available for different industries but the most appropriate indicator may not be the same for all industries.

Table 6.2 shows the indicators selected to measure soybean potential in 1948 in three principal states—New York, Ohio and California. In each case, soybean oil market potential has been allocated as proportional to the yardstick employed for that end use. The soybean oil potential figures derived in this manner can then be combined to derive aggregate market estimates for the product in each of the three states, and by extension to other areas as well.

As is evident from this example, there is considerable room for ingenuity in end-use analysis. At times, a formal survey may be unnecessary. The best way to ascertain the need for a survey is to set up such an analysis, if only in skeleton form, and see if the analysis can be carried out on the basis of available data. If not, a survey may well be necessary.

6.4.2. Input-Output Approach

6.4.2.1. *Meaning*. Developed by W. W. Leontieff,[34] input-output analysis represents essentially an extension of the end-use approach to consideration of the interrelations between a number of industries, or sectors, of the economy. The idea for such a table has its origins in the "Tableau Economique" developed by Quesney in the mid-Eighteenth Century to represent the interdependence of productive activities. The result of such an analysis is an input-output table, showing the transactions between different sectors during a given period of time. The rows of the table portray shipments, or sales, of each sector from all other sectors, including itself, while the columns of the table represent the purchases of all sectors, in turn, from a given sector. Since the classifications of supplier and purchasing industries are generally identical, an input-output table tends to be square, or a "square matrix," though this need not necessarily be the case.

An input-output table for 1947 is presented in Table 6.3. Based originally on the division of the American economy into 500 sectors, this table shows in summary form the distribution of output in 1947 between 50 combined sectors at producers' prices. This is a square matrix, the same sectors constituting both the rows and columns. The rows represent production, or sales, while the columns represent purchases. Thus, the first row indicates that

---

[33] *Ibid.*, p. 731.
[34] W. W. Leontieff, *The Structure of the American Economy, 1919–29* (New York, Oxford University Press, 1941).

the gross output of the agriculture and fisheries industry in 1947 amounted to $44.3 billion, at producers' prices. Of this total, $10.9 billion represented intrasector transactions—products consumed for its own purposes, such as corn used for feeder cattle. An additional $15.1 billion was sold to the food and kindred products industry, $783 million to tobacco firms, etc. At the same time, columns 46–50 indicate how much of each sector's product went into final demand—inventories, exports, government, private capital formation, and consumers. Thus, consumers are seen to have received $9.8 billion of the products of agriculture and fisheries.

In a similar manner, each column of the table portrays the amount purchased by each sector from all other sectors. For example, agriculture and fisheries purchased $10.9 billion from itself, $2.4 billion from food and kindred products, $64 million from apparel, etc. It also depleted inventories of $2.7 billion, imported $690 million, purchased $813 million from government and $19.2 billion from households (the latter primarily in the form of labor). The column total is equivalent to the row total for each industry, since total purchases are the same as total sales, everything valued at factor prices.

In effect, the columns represent inputs, for the sector *qua* purchaser, and the rows represent outputs, for the sector *qua* producer, from which the name "input-output table" is derived.

6.4.2.2.   *Applications.* The uses of input-output analysis stem from the premise that,[35]

"while the pattern of shipments from one sector to others may change quite significantly from year to year as the requirements placed on the economic system by end-product consumers vary, the pattern of inputs into any given sector tends to be more stable and more predictable. A going establishment in a given industry normally represents a collection of machinery and equipment adapted to processing certain materials, and a collection of persons (both in labor and management) skilled in handling, using, and transforming these same materials. Hence abrupt and capricious changes in input patterns are unusual, even where the firm's customers change, and where they result from technological innovations or for other causes, one is likely to know of them and hence be able to take account of their probable effects. Input-output analysis thus attempts to take advantage of the typical stability of input patterns in order to obtain reasonable answers to many complex and difficult problems of economic analysis."

One of the chief advantages of this method is that it can answer questions on the nature and disposition of the product of each industry.

First, the data can be used to compute for each industry, or sector, its direct purchases from every other industry per dollar of output. This is done

---

[35] W. D. EVANS, "Marketing Uses of Input-Output Data," *Journal of Marketing*, Vol. 17, July, 1952, p. 12.

by adjusting the total purchases of each purchasing industry for inventory change, to relate total purchases (output) to the current year. Then each figure in the column is divided by the adjusted total. As applied to iron and steel in Table 6.3, for example, we find that for each dollar's output, there was required 32.3 cents of internal transfers (bars, ingots, etc.), 11.1 cents of materials of other fabricated metal products industry, and so on. Hence, we see where the supplies come from.

Second, we can determine how much of each industry's product goes to every other. In part, this is indicated by the rows of Table 6.3. In addition, however, a determination can be made of the importance of iron and steel in the output of every other industry. For iron and steel, this is obtained for each industry by dividing its purchases of iron and steel by its total current output. The result is shown in Column 2 of Table 6.4.

Third, since the results obtained so far apply only to direct purchase of a product, we may extend them to include indirect purchases as well. Thus, from Table 6.3 it is apparent that the motor vehicle sector purchased substantially from fabricated metals, which in turn was a major user of iron and steel. Such indirect purchases are incorporated in the figures shown in Columns 3 and 4 of Table 6.4. As is evident from these columns, sectors which made no direct purchases of iron and steel nevertheless become important once these indirect purchases are taken into account. Column 3 of the table expresses direct and indirect requirements in relation to the gross output of each industry, and Column 4 presents the same estimates in terms of the iron and steel requirements for \$100 of that sector's output delivered to end-product consumers.

Fourth, it is possible to estimate from Table 6.3 the disposition of each sector's output to final demand categories, the categories shown in Columns 46–50 of Table 6.3. Thus, we may estimate the extent to which iron and steel is used for new construction in the furniture sector, or for exports in motors and generators, or for gross private investment in metalworking machinery, etc. As a result, a picture is obtained not only of the extent to which other sectors are customers for a given product but also of the type of uses into which the product enters.

6.4.2.3. *Mathematical formulation.* The derivation of the data for the third and fourth applications listed above involves multivariate analysis. The method is conceptually a simple one, and since it also serves to indicate how this general approach can be translated into mathematical terms, it is useful to outline the principal steps.[36]

Let us denote by X_{ij} the shipments of sector i to sector j. Then the output of any sector, i.e., the figures in any row of Table 6.3, can be represented by the following expression:

---

[36] Based on U. S. Department of Labor, *The 1947 Interindustry Relations Study*, BLS Report No. 33, pp. 18–24.

Table 6.4

COMPARATIVE DISTRIBUTION OF GROSS IRON AND STEEL OUTPUT, 1947

(1)	(2) Direct purchases per $100 production	(3) TOTAL DIRECT AND INDIRECT REQUIREMENTS PER $100 OF Gross production	(4) TOTAL DIRECT AND INDIRECT REQUIREMENTS PER $100 OF End-product deliveries
Purchasing Sector			
1 Agriculture and fisheries	$ 0.01	$ 0.60	$ 0.84
2 Food and kindred products	0.01	1.79	2.16
3 Tobacco manufactures	—	1.30	1.88
4 Textile mill products	—	1.26	1.47
5 Apparel	0.01	1.88	2.22
6 Lumber and wood products	0.16	2.45	3.01
7 Furniture and fixtures	3.37	9.11	9.15
8 Paper and allied products	—	1.47	2.24
9 Printing and publishing	—	1.76	2.03
10 Chemicals	0.04	2.56	3.26
11 Products of petroleum and coal	0.05	1.24	1.94
12 Rubber products	0.48	3.33	3.40
13 Leather and leather products	0.02	1.81	2.51
14 Stone, clay and glass products	0.48	2.69	2.97
15 Iron and steel	32.28	100.00	150.76
16 Nonferrous metals	0.53	2.83	4.87
17 Plumbing and heating supplies	9.87	20.88	21.41
18 Fabricated structural metal products	23.87	39.72	40.55
19 Other fabricated metal products	21.33	34.48	36.34
20 Agric'l, mining, and constr. machinery	16.16	29.75	30.96
21 Metalworking machinery	7.82	16.47	17.07
22 Other machinery (except electric)	9.02	18.02	19.49
23 Motors and generators	10.77	19.66	20.05
24 Radios	0.78	6.00	7.03
25 Other electrical machinery	3.42	9.82	10.61
26 Motor vehicles	7.73	16.13	23.51
27 Other transportation equipment	9.25	17.83	19.32
28 Professional and scientific equipment	0.76	4.77	5.22
29 Miscellaneous manufacturing	0.76	4.68	4.90
30 Coal, gas, and electric power	0.48	1.55	1.82
31 Railroad transportation	1.54	2.97	3.12
32 Ocean transportation	—	2.00	2.22
33 Other transportation	0.06	1.28	1.32
34 Trade	—	1.28	1.30
35 Communications	0.02	0.74	0.76
36 Finance and insurance	—	0.91	1.06
37 Rental	—	0.63	0.64
38 Business services	—	2.58	2.66
39 Personal and repair services	—	3.52	3.72
40 Medical, educ., and nonprofit org's	—	1.24	1.25
41 Amusements	—	1.44	1.67
42 Scrap and miscellaneous industries	9.40	19.67	20.19
43 Undistributed	2.91	10.25	11.52
44 Eating and drinking places	—	1.51	1.51

Source: Reproduced from EVANS, *ibid*, Table 2.

$$X_{i.} = X_{ia} + X_{i1} + X_{i2} + \cdots + X_{ii} + \cdots + X_{in} \qquad (6.1)$$

where $X_{i.}$ is the total output of sector i, there being $n + 1$ sectors. X_{ii} is the amount of intra-sector transactions, and X_{ia} represents shipments to autonomous, or final demand, sectors. The other $n - 1$ sector demands interrelate with demand for the product of sector i.

In a similar fashion, the total purchases of a particular sector, the figures in any row of Table 6.3, can be expressed as follows:

$$X_{.j} = X_{1j} + X_{2j} + \cdots + X_{jj} + \cdots + X_{nj} + X_{aj} \qquad (6.2)$$

with $X_{.j}$ representing the total purchases (output) of sector j.

Now, the total requirements (direct and indirect) for products of interconnected sector i by sector j will clearly depend on the level of activity of sector j. Thus, the amount of iron and steel needed by motor vehicle manufacturers will depend on the number of motor vehicles to be produced. In effect, then, we have:

$$X_{ij} = F_{jj}(X_j) \qquad (6.3)$$

so that the function (6.1) becomes:

$$X_{i.} = X_{ia} + F_{i1}(X_1) + F_{i2}(X_2) + \cdots + F_{in}(X_n) \qquad (6.4)$$

(Why is there no F_{ia}?)

The F_{ij} will vary with the values of i and j, and in theory could assume innumerable forms. Partly for simplicity and partly because it seems reasonable, let us assume that the demand by sector j for the product of sector i is always proportional to the output of sector j. In other words, F_{ij} becomes a_{ij}, a constant, and (6.3) becomes:

$$X_{ij} = a_{ij}X_j \qquad (6.5)$$

a_{ij} is the technical coefficient, representing the amount of the product of sector i required to produce one unit of the product of sector j. This coefficient multiplied by the output of sector j, X_j, as in (6.5), indicates the amount of i's product needed by sector j during the given period.

The relation (6.4) can now be represented as:

$$X_{i.} = X_{ia} + a_{i1}X_1 + a_{i2}X_2 + \cdots + a_{ii}X_i + \cdots + a_{in}X_n \quad (6.6)$$

or (letting X_i be equivalent to $X_{i.}$ for simplicity):

$$X_{ia} = -a_{i1}X_1 - a_{i2}X_2 - \cdots + (1 - a_{ii})X_i - \cdots - a_{in}X_n \quad (6.7)$$

The system of interindustry relations can therefore be represented by the following set of simultaneous equations:

$$X_{1a} = (1 - a_{11})X_1 - a_{12}X_2 - \cdots - a_{1n}X_n$$
$$X_{2a} = -a_{21}X_1 + (1 - a_{22})X_2 - \cdots - a_{1n}X_n \qquad (6.8)$$
$$\cdots \cdots \cdots \cdots \cdots \cdots \cdots \cdots \cdots$$
$$X_{na} = -a_{n1}X_1 - a_{n2}X_2 - \cdots + (1 - a_{nn})X_n$$

The parameters, a_{ij}, are presumably known from external sources, and the autonomous or end-product demands, X_{ia}, are given. Hence, (6.8) can be solved for the values of X_i—the required production levels of the different sectors to achieve the predesignated levels of final deliveries. The data in Columns 3 and 4 of Table 6.4 were obtained in this manner.

The solutions are usually not easy to obtain and require the use of high-speed computers. Such solutions can be of great value, however, since with their aid predictions can be made of changes in outputs of different sectors as final demand is varied. Thus, among other things, the results can be used to study:

> a) possible increases in industry production associated with alternative increases in production of other goods,
> b) adequacy of manufacturing facilities for different levels of final demand,
> c) how soon expansion of existing capacity may be needed,
> d) industries that may become bottlenecks in war production,
> e) effect on other sectors of depressed activity in one particular sector.

Input-output data can also be used in conjunction with other methods to arrive at an overall prediction of levels of activity in a future period. Thus, these other methods may be used to predict gross national product in a future period and, subsequently, the levels of the different final demand sectors. The structure of the system in the future period is derived through the use of the interindustry relations derived from the input-output data.

6.4.2.4. Limitations. Input-output analysis contains, unfortunately, some formidable limitations. For one thing, the number of sectors into which the economy can be divided is limited by available data as well as by computer and other resource capacities. The largest division attempted so far—500 sectors in 1947—is almost negligibly small relative to the thousands and thousands of products turned out by the economy. As a result, each sector tends to represent a heterogeneous conglomeration of goods and services, and it is not clear how representative overall sector figures are for individual products (and companies). Ideally, what would be required for product analysis is a separate extended input-output table for each sector contained in the larger analysis.

Second, the linearity and constancy of the technical coefficients, a_{ij}, is a matter of dispute. These are very convenient assumptions from a computational point of view, but it is not clear how realistic these assumptions may be. The question is especially difficult to answer because in many instances the estimation of a_{ij} has to be based on inadequate data.

Third is the question of the stability of the technical coefficients and of the interindustry relations over time. If input-output analysis is to be used for prediction of future activity, or even for conditional forecasts, stability of these relations is an essential prerequisite. This is a question which arises with almost any forecasting tool and the present case is no exception. An input-output table is a major undertaking, the results of which are generally not obtained until two or three years after the end of the period under study. Stability of the relations over time is therefore especially important. As yet, relatively little work has been done on this problem.

Fourth is the time and resource factor. Because of the nature of the method, substantial computer facilities and data sources are required. The method is therefore not likely to be developed by individual companies, except as an extension of a larger input-output table developed by government or by a group of firms or industries. In practice, input-output tables have been developed either by governments or by research agencies, notably by the project headed by Professor Leontieff at Harvard University. At the same time, increasing attention has been given to the uses of the method for regional analysis, where in many ways it may prove more practicable than on a national level.[37] The method is as yet relatively new and its full potentials do not seem to have been developed.

6.5. THE PLACE OF MOTIVATION RESEARCH

6.5.1. What It Is

The meaning and usefulness of so-called motivation research has been one of the most hotly debated issues in business research circles in the postwar years. The meanings range from its very narrow interpretation as the application of projective techniques to the determination of the motivations underlying consumer (market) behavior all the way to the very broad definition as the search for the "why" of consumer behavior irrespective of what techniques are employed in the process.[38]

Here, as with operations research, question has been raised regarding the "newness" of the subject, not so much on the application of psychological techniques to business research problems—which is a fairly recent development—but rather on the emphasis on "why" questions. As many researchers have pointed out,[39] reasons for consumer actions possess numerous dimensions and can be derived in a variety of ways—by psychological projective techniques, by scaling techniques, by depth interviews, by statistical analysis

---

[37] For an example, see WERNER HIRSCH, "An Application of Area Input-Output Analysis," paper delivered at annual meetings of Regional Science Association, December 28, 1958.

[38] For a variety of different interpretations and a somewhat different perspective on the subject, see ROBERT FERBER and H. G. WALES, ed., *Motivation and Market Behavior* (Richard D. Irwin, Inc., 1958).

[39] *Ibid.*

of survey data, even by time-series analysis. Insofar as economic and marketing research is concerned, the important question is not to uncover the inner motivations for particular actions but rather to identify motivations on a level where remedial steps can be carried out. Thus, the fact that a certain proportion of consumers may harbor inner resentment against a ball-point pen because its round tip recalls unpleasant childhood experiences may be very interesting, but this is not something marketing policy can alter. However, something certainly can be done if it is found that consumers have the erroneous impression that this particular pen, like cheaper ball-point pens, is subject to excessive skipping.

Because market motivations can be sought in so many different ways, many of them competitive with each other, albeit from different disciplines, it seems generally preferable to approach this problem with a broad perspective. Such an approach permits the researcher to select for any given problem whichever technique appears best suited to the conditions at hand. Such an approach also tends to place in the background the basically fruitless controversy over the meaning of "motivation research" and helps the researcher concentrate on the broader question of "consumer market motivation" or, more simply, on the reasons for consumer behavior.

6.5.2. Some Projective Techniques

The approach advocated above requires some working knowledge of many different techniques. Since economic and business researchers are likely to be weakest on the psychological side, it would seem useful to present here brief explanations of techniques from the area that have proven of value in studying market motivations. All of these techniques are of the "projective" variety—where the respondent in supplying information tends unconsciously to project his own attitudes or feelings on the subject under study.

It should be stressed that the following presentation is meant solely to introduce the reader to the different techniques and is not a substitute for careful study of them. Pertinent sources will be found in the references listed at the end of the chapter. The techniques discussed in this section also by no means exhaust the possibilities; only the more important ones are mentioned.

6.5.2.1. *Word association.* The respondent is asked to mention the first word that comes to mind, ostensibly without thinking, as the interviewer reads each word on a list. If the interviewer says "hot," the respondent may say "cold"; if the word is "government," the response may be "taxes"; etc. The general technique is to use a list of as many as 50 to 100 words, reading them rather rapidly to the respondent and securing a matching word after each word on the list is read. The first few words are generally "softeners," meant to get the respondent used to the idea, with the "key words" contained near the middle of the list.

The objective of the test is to find out what connotations are applied to these key words. These key words may be a proposed new trademark, the name of an existing product, a generic name, or even just a word that is being considered for heavy promotional use. Analysis of the matching words supplied by the respondents presumably indicates whether the given word should be used for the contemplated purpose.

This technique is a quick, easy one to apply, but what it shows is a moot point. Answers are likely to be given in a number of different dimensions that can not be reconciled with each other on the basis of such brief replies. Thus, the word "government" may lead some people to think of a type of political system, others of a level of government (local, state, federal), and still others of specific governmental functions. Hence, the analytical problem can at times become unmanageable. Then too, in the case of unfamiliar words, the reliability of a person's reply is highly doubtful: the history of fashion and of advertising is replete with instances of slogans or styles that were highly unpopular at first but then became symbols of the times.

Though used frequently in advertising research, considerable work has to be done on establishing the reliability of this technique—indeed, of all projective techniques. Preliminary indications are that it does yield reliable results when applied to words or names that are widely known and which possess "unidimensionality"—essentially one type of meaning.

6.5.2.2. *Sentence completions.* Here, the interviewer reads the first part of a sentence, such as, "I think trading stamps . . . ," and the respondent provides the last part, again as quickly as possible. Several sentences of this type might be put to the respondent on the same subject. Analysis of the replies for the same respondent presumably reveals his attitude toward that subject, and the combination of these attitudes of all the sample members is then taken to reflect the views of the population.

This technique is of broader applicability than word associations, for it permits not only the testing of words but of ideas as well, and can often serve as a useful basis for developing hypotheses and making up questionnaires. Thus, if the question is whether rising prices at a particular time are good or bad for consumer purchases, people may be asked to complete the sentence: "As a result of the recent rise in prices, my personal financial position. . . . " The replies can then serve as a basis for more intensive analysis of the question with other techniques.

Like word associations, this technique is quick and easy to use but often leads to difficult analytical problems, particularly with regard to multidimensionality of response. This can be taken care of to some extent by making the phrase that is read to the respondent very specific. To what extent this then remains a "projective psychological" technique, however, becomes a moot point. Indeed, it can be argued that direct questioning (e.g., "What effect do you think the recent rise in prices will have on your personal financial position?") is always possible in such cases and will produce at least as reliable replies.[40]

6.5.2.3. *Picture frustration*. In this more esoteric test, the respondent is shown a cartoon of some situation with two or more people in the scene. Facial and other identifying characteristics of these people are blurred, usually with the exception of sex, and in general an effort is made to represent the scene as neutrally as possible. One of the people says something, contained in a balloon at the top, which invites an answer from the other person. The balloon for the latter, however, is left blank, and the respondent is asked to fill it in.

The picture is "frustrating" in the sense that the respondent is asked to interpret a scene that is not clear to him. Hence, he is impelled to "project" his own feelings into such interpretations as he may supply. If the scenes touch upon the subject under study, the respondent presumably reveals his feelings on this subject without realizing it. Thus, in a study of brand loyalty a picture may be used in which one woman is saying to another, "I like to change brands of flour every few months just for variety." By replying to this comment, the respondent reveals her feelings on the subject.

Although the reliability of this technique has yet to be established, evidences are that it does produce useful results when skillfully applied.[41] Analysis of the data in particular is a difficult task involving once more the problem of multidimensionality. In addition, there is always the danger that some aspect of the scene may bias the replies.

6.5.2.4. *Thematic Apperception Test (TAT)*. Essentially similar to the preceding approach, the TAT is also based on use of scenes but without any dialogue. Instead, the respondent is asked to make up a story about, or description of, the scene—how it happened to take place, what is going on in the scene, a description of the people in it, and what is likely to take place later on. Here again, the respondent is supposed to project his own attitudes in the narration.[42]

The TAT is much more vague, and hence more troublesome analytically, than the Picture Frustration Test. Although it has been used with some success in commercial research, its validity is not yet well established for this purpose or even in clinical psychology, where it was first developed.[43]

---

[40] R. L. WESTFALL, H. W. BOYD, and D. T. CAMPBELL, "The Use of Structured Techniques in Motivation Research," *Journal of Marketing*, October, 1957, pp. 134–139.

[41] For example, E. M. ROGERS and G. H. BEAL, "Projective Techniques: Potential Tools for Agricultural Economists," *Journal of Farm Economics*, August, 1959, pp. 644–648.

[42] For some commercial research applications of this and the preceding test, see MARTIN ZOBER, "Some Projective Techniques Applied to Marketing Research," *Journal of Marketing*, January, 1956, pp. 262–268.

[43] GARDNER LINDZEY, "Thematic Apperception Test: Interpretive Assumptions and Related Empirical Evidence," *Psychological Bulletin*, January, 1952, pp. 1–25.

6.5.2.5. *Rohrschach Test.* This most widely-known of the psychological projective tests also seems to be the most dubious. Not unrelated is the vague nature of the test: the respondent is asked to interpret the form of ink blots and explain what each means to him. In doing so, his inner feelings are presumably brought out. In actual practice, however, considerable doubt surrounds the value of the test even in clinical psychology when administered by highly skilled personnel.[44] Despite all the publicity it has received, the value of this test to commercial research remains an open question, to say the least.

6.5.2.6. *Error-choice technique.* Unlike the Rohrschach Test, this approach has received little attention though it seems rather promising.[45] It involves asking the respondent a number of multiple-choice questions with all the answer-choices presented being either wrong or with the truth indeterminate. By putting the answers at opposite extremes it is reasoned that the respondent's bias, if any, is indicated by the answer selected. Thus, one question may relate to the current federal minimum hourly wage, the choices being $1.35, $1.25, $.85, $.75 (the true figure at this writing is $1.15). The direction of the answer selected from the true figure presumably provides an indication of any labor-management bias he may have.

The results obtained from this test do not appear to be invariant of the conditions under which it is administered or of the characteristics of the respondent.[46] However, it does present interesting possibilities in economic and marketing surveys, particularly in the use of questions with indeterminate answers for bias detection.

6.5.2.7. *Depth interviews.* Whether long, probing interviews are projective or not is a matter of opinion. Essentially, it would seem to depend on the manner in which the interview is carried out. With sufficient time and interviewer skill, depth interviews can be projective in nature.

What is the difference between a projective depth interview and a non-projective depth interview? Essentially, it lies in the nature of the questions asked—indirect questions often on seemingly irrelevant subjects provide information that can be related to the respondent's behavior or attitude toward the product or subject under study. Thus, the respondent may be questioned first on his frequency of air travel, and, at a later stage, he might be asked his opinion of the feelings of relatives toward a third person who gets killed in an airplane accident. Reluctance to fly can then be related to responses to questions of the latter nature.

---

[44] D. B. LUCAS, "Can the Clinical Techniques be Validated?" in *Consumer Behavior and Motivation,* Bureau of Economic and Business Research, University of Illinois, 1956.
[45] K. R. HAMMOND, "Measuring Attitudes by Error-Choice: An Indirect Method," *Journal of Abnormal and Social Psychology,* 1948, pp. 38–48.
[46] *Ibid.*

Third-person personification of this type is used heavily in projective depth interviews. One of the first, and most successful, of all asked housewives what kind of housewife they thought was represented by a particular shopping list. Two lists were used, each on matched samples, with one list containing (among other items) a brand of instant coffee and the other list containing the same items but with regular coffee of the same brand rather than instant coffee. From respondents who did not use instant coffee, a very clear impression emerged that the housewife who purchased instant coffee was lazy and inefficient, whereas in direct questioning these respondents only complained of the inferior taste of this product.[47]

Depth interviews do not have to be projective to be useful, however, and much useful information can be obtained by direct "why" questions. This is particularly true in product tests where a fairly comprehensive set of opinions on the product under study can be obtained in this manner.

6.5.3.   A Note on Sample Size

An advantage often cited for projective methods, generally by psychologically-oriented researchers, is that, because of the nature of these methods, sample sizes can be fairly small, often less than 50, and also need not be selected in any particular representative manner. The rationale for this is asserted to be that psychologically people are basically alike, so if the feelings and attitudes of even a few are known, the results can be imputed to the population at large.

If this rationale were true, research would be greatly simplified. Then, as one author notes,[48] sampling would be no problem at all: one could simply interview friends and relatives. Unfortunately, however, all indications are that this rationale is fallacious. People are clearly not alike insofar as motivations or psychological attributes are concerned, and variability in this respect seems to be no less than for socio-economic characteristics. This is borne out by the many different types and dimensions of abnormal psychology. Hence, sampling considerations can not be ignored in studies utilizing projective techniques. It is fully as important in this type of study as in any other to follow proper sampling methods and use sampling error measures where applicable. There is also no question about the feasibility of probability sampling in such cases.[49]

---

[47] MASON HAIRE, "An Application of Projective Techniques in Marketing Research," *Journal of Marketing*, April, 1950, pp. 649–56.

[48] WILLIAMS, R. J., "Is It True What They Say About Motivation Research?" *Journal of Marketing*, October, 1957, pp. 125–133.

[49] ZOBER, *op. cit.*; HAIRE, *op. cit.*; and various other studies.

6.5.4. Selection of Method[50]

Motivating influences in market behavior can be studied in numerous ways; the most desirable approach depends on the nature of the particular problem and on the time and resources (money and personnel) available. In many instances, two very different approaches can be applied to the same problem and, if both approaches are valid, with essentially the same results. Thus, a nonprojective questionnaire using direct questions yielded much the same results on attitudes toward purchases of instant coffee as did the projective approach described earlier.[51]

In selecting a particular technique, especially in deciding whether or not to use a projective technique, the following classification of respondent awareness of motivation is useful:

First, the reason may be obtainable from the respondent, he knows the reason, and will tell it if asked.

Here, direct questioning is all that would be needed, if a survey were made on the subject. If consumers don't like the taste of a particular pudding, the reason why is readily ascertainable by direct questioning.

Second, the reason may be obtainable from the respondent, he knows the reason, but does not want to admit it.

Such situations are likely to arise when the reason involves or implies social disapproval, ridicule, or may place the respondent in an unfavorable light. That many people may refuse to fly because they are afraid of heights; that some may refuse to consider buying a small car, such as the Ford Falcon, because of the sense of inferiority it gives them on the road, that some stout girls don't diet because they think they will never be asked out anyway are not reasons likely to be derived from answers to direct questions. Where reasons of such a nature are suspected, projective techniques are eminently suitable. They allow the respondent to express his feelings without embarrassing him and without direct questioning.

Third, the reason may be obtainable from the respondent, it relates to some underlying social or psychological attitude, but he is not aware of it.

Projective techniques are well suited in such a problem, as illustrated by the example of why people did not buy instant coffee, namely, because of apparent identification of purchases of this "substitute" product with inferior housekeeping.

---

[50] This section is based on ROBERT FERBER, "Projective Techniques from an Analytical Point of View," in *Consumer Behavior and Motivation*, pp. 106–107.

[51] Westfall, *op. cit.*

Fourth, the reason may be obtainable from the respondent, it relates to some behavior, socio-economic or environmental characteristic, but he is not aware of it.

Thus, Alfred Politz relates that quick pick-up in a car was found to be related to the softness of the accelerator pedal in the respondent's car, leading to the inference that the way to "increase" pick-up, at least in the minds of consumers, was to soften the spring on the accelerator pedal rather than to increase horsepower. In such problems, projective techniques are likely to be of little value because the consumer could not provide the necessary information, consciously or otherwise.

Fifth, the reason is one which is not obtainable from the respondent by a survey technique.

Thus, sales of a cereal may be low because the amount of display space allotted to it in stores may have been reduced. The income elasticity of housing expenditures by farm families has been higher than that of urban families in the past largely because the farmer did not have as many varied outlets for spending money on other things as did urban families. Here, the study of aggregates or the compilation and analysis of non-consumer data are likely to be most fruitful.

Thus, by this classification, projective techniques are of principal value in detecting two of five possible sets of "why" categories. This is no measure of their importance in relation to other techniques but is rather an indication of the type of situations to which they are most suitable. From a problem-solving point of view, the value of such a classification may be questioned, because a given problem is not likely to fall automatically into one of the above five categories, and thus this classification resembles to some extent a Bayes Theorem type of solution (given the probability attached to each event, the overall probability is easily computed). But even such solutions can be of value. Basically, the selection of a proper technique is up to the insight and ingenuity of the researcher in formulating the problem, in recognizing alternative hypotheses, and in devising suitable test procedures. At the same time, however, *a priori* reasoning supplemented by suitable pretests and examination of preliminary data will often lead in a given problem to elimination of anywhere between one and four of the above five possibilities. At the least, it should serve to crystallize one's thoughts on the nature of the reasons for the observed actions and thereby aid in the selection of an optimal research technique.

In considering alternative approaches to a "why" problem, it is important to remember projective techniques are as yet in an early stage of development, with the validity of many of them remaining an open question. Under the circumstances, there would seem to be some reason for placing most reliance on the more straightforward statistical methods in any given problem with only supplementary use of projective techniques. Nevertheless, in pretesting and in searching for hypotheses they can be highly valuable. Confirmation can then be sought by more established methods.

[6.6.   CONTROLLED EXPERIMENTATION[52]

Most research in business and economics is based on operating data or on actual, observed behavior. This is counter to the practice in the physical sciences, where research is based heavily on controlled experiments. Other things equal, the latter approach is generally preferable, for it enables the effects of particular factors to be isolated and measured. In practice, however, other things are not equal, for strict control of conditions when dealing with markets and people is a very different matter from dealing with plants or animals in a laboratory.

Nevertheless, the use of controlled experiments is possible in many economic and marketing problems, undoubtedly on a much wider scale than they have actually been used. Although the extent of control may not be as rigorous in some instances as might be possible in the physical sciences, useful results can still be obtained. It is an approach that will gain increasing recognition in the social sciences and that can be used with either cross-section or time-series data.

6.6.1.   Characteristics of the Method

An experiment might be defined as an investigation in which a factor, or variable, under test is isolated and its effect(s) measured. That is, conditions are set up under which it can be determined precisely what happens when a hypothesized solution (the variable under test) is put into effect.[53] The requirements of an experiment are highly exacting. They include the ability to measure effects and that of isolating the tested factors from the possibly confounding influence of other factors.

In its simplest form, the experiment might be conceived as measured in terms of the *difference* between the phenomenon under observation *after* the changing factor is injected into the situation and the phenomenon's value

---

[52] Much of this section is based on or abstracted from ROBERT FERBER, SIDNEY COHEN and DAVID LUCK, *The Design of Research Investigations*, American Marketing Association, 1958.

[53] The older idea that only one variable may be tested at a time is no longer true. With multivariate analysis, the simultaneous effect of several variables may be measured and correctly attributed to the causal factors.

before the injection.[54] If p and p' represent the before and after values, respectively, we may represent the measurement as:

$$p' - p = d \qquad (6.9)$$

In most real life conditions, things are more or less in flux, so some change might have taken place even if the experimental controls had not been altered. To take this into account we establish a "control" group within the framework of a particular type of design that is comparable with the "test" group but does not have the change injected—therefore showing presumably what would have happened without that change. Thus, if we label values of the control group with the subscript c, while designating values of the test group with the subscript t, our formula becomes:

$$p_t' - p_t = d_t \qquad (6.10)$$
$$p_c' - p_c = d_c$$

so that:

$$d_t - d_c = experimental\ results \qquad (6.11)$$

The all-important advantage of the experiment is that it demonstrates empirically the effect of the factor under test. Therefore it has the advantages of being predictive and of being directly relevant to the proposed solution. It is the most exacting of designs, however, for two large "if's" must be satisfied: (1) *if* the experiment is carried on under conditions adequately representative of those in which the tested solution will subsequently be applied, and (2) *if* the demonstration is so conducted that no extraneous factors happen to be present and bias the results. The latter may be particularly troublesome in a time-series experiment.

6.6.2. Types of Control

The essence of experimentation is having control over the factors that would affect the results. Control is impossible unless one can (1) determine the factors or variables that would influence a study's results, and (2) measure accurately the extent to which the test factor is introduced and its results. One is on safer ground if, in addition, (3) he also can measure the effects of the other influencing variables.

Control may take any of the following four forms: (1) to direct the changes in the variables, (2) to measure the effects of changing variables by using matched groups, (3) to cancel out their effects, or (4) rotation of factors. The

---

[54] For an excellent article on the nature of an experiment, see S. A. STOUFFER, "Some Observations on Study Designs," *American Journal of Sociology*, January, 1950, pp. 355–61. Also, in more detail on retail store experimentation, see W. APPLEBAUM and R. F. SPEARS, "Controlled Experimentation in Marketing Research," *Journal of Marketing*, January, 1950, pp. 505–517.

traditional notion of control was the first, that of *manipulating* the phenomena at will. The laboratory scientist can manipulate temperature, diet and air pressure, for example, and one can think of a number of forces that might be varied at will in most investigations. A situation in which *all* important variables can be manipulated is indeed an enviable one from the research standpoint. Situations amenable to this sort of control are rare in the social sciences. A more likely situation is one for which groups of variables can be held constant. For example, a silviculturist cannot manipulate the size of trees at will and cannot even grow them to exact sizes, but he can select matched groups of identical trees with respect to the aspects under study. If all the factors are thus held constant by selection, the effects of one variable factor could be measured.

This type of *matching* control is employed in marketing studies. Radio and television studies of selling effects have attained simultaneous matching of the subjects in many aspects.[55] If data are available on all vital aspects of the subjects or phenomena observed, and the sample is large enough to allow matching groups to be formed, true experimentation is often possible.

Permitting a number of factors to vary but *compensating* for their effects is a third type of control. If the precise effects of humidity on the test is known, the test can be conducted regardless of humidity and the results adjusted therefore. If Magazine R has 200,000 circulation and Magazine W has 350,000, we can compensate for W's larger circulation in certain situations by a $\frac{4}{7}$ reduction in appropriate magnitudes relating to that magazine.

Rotation is the fourth type of control. The characteristics of the various subjects in the research (e.g., different cities, stores, persons) do not need to be measured, but the factor under test is rotated successively between them so that different characteristics are offset. A series of studies conducted by Cornell University of apple marketing in retail stores illustrates the method.[56] To test the effects of bruised apples on sales, 12 stores were selected and combined into four groups of three stores each. Lots with certain degrees of bruising were placed on sale for equal periods in each group of stores and the lots rotated so that every store carried at one time or other all the different types of lots. Thus the varying characteristics of these stores and their clienteles were offset since apples of differing bruising qualities had equal sales exposure in each store.

Rotation experiments are capable of many adaptations. The Cornell apple research tried a number of time periods, such as twice-daily, daily and weekly rotations. Size of packaged unit, prepackaging versus bulk, price changes

---

[55] Detailed explanation of a matching procedure is given in "NBC Study of Radio's Effective Sales Power," National Broadcasting Company, September, 1952, pp. 23–32.

[56] MAX BRUNK and W. T. FEDERER, *Methods of Research in Marketing*, Paper No. 4, Department of Agricultural Economics, Cornell University Agricultural Experiment Station, January, 1953.

and types of display similarly have been tested in such designs for fruit marketing.

6.6.3. Two Examples

1. Experimental control provides a means of selecting the more effective of alternate methods. It may be particularly useful in a pretest to a larger study or to a series of studies. Thus, to ascertain the effect of trading stamps on probable response to a series of mail questionnaires, a two-page questionnaire with 50 trading stamps was mailed to 235 households in a middle-income area in Boston. An additional 221 households in the same area were sent the same questionnaire without trading stamps, and 213 more households were sent the same questionnaire with an accompanying letter offering them 100 trading stamps or 25 cents in coin on return of the questionnaire.[57] Random selection was used in choosing the sample households.

Returns were obtained from 29 per cent of the households sent trading stamps, from 27 per cent of those offered 100 stamps or 25 cents, and from 22 per cent of the households not receiving stamps. The response rate from households sent or offered stamps or coin is significantly higher than that from households receiving no extra inducement. The difference between the 29 per cent return and the 27 per cent return is not significant.

Hence, the trading stamp or coin inducement appears to have raised the rate of return by 25 to 30 per cent. This would not be the end of the matter in practice, however, for the decision on whether or not to use one of these incentives depends on cost considerations as well as on an evaluation of the applicability of the results to other areas to be sampled. The experiment serves to provide the necessary data.

2. Experimental control may also be necessary at times to detect and avert biased results, as illustrated by the second example.[58] A product use test of two types of hosiery was carried out on 516 female employees of three factories of the company involved. Half were given a fitted pair of "A" stockings and half a fitted pair of "B" stockings, by systematic random selection. Each employee was requested to record daily the number of hours the stockings were worn. When torn, the employee was asked to rate the product by a number of characteristics, and was then given a pair of the other stockings to wear and the same procedure was repeated.

That the results of such a test not using this design would have been biased is evident from Table 6.5.[59] The brand worn first was rated generally more

---

[57] Adapted from R. D. BRENNAN, "Trading Stamps As An Incentive in Mail Surveys," *Journal of Marketing*, January, 1958, pp. 306–7.

[58] Based on ALLAN GREENBERG, "Paired Comparisons in Consumer-Product Tests," *Journal of Marketing*, Vol. 22, April, 1958, pp. 411–414.

[59] *Ibid.*, p. 413.

favorably than the brand worn second. Furthermore, the same was found true of the presumedly objective data on hours each brand was worn before tearing, as shown below:[60]

	A	B
a) Average number of hours when worn first	130.3	116.3
b) Average number of hours when worn second	115.9	100.3
Ratio, a/b	1.12	1.16

If experimental control had not been maintained, the brand worn first would clearly have been adjudged superior, and a possibly expensive error

Table 6.5
RATINGS OF STOCKINGS WHEN WORN FIRST VERSUS SECOND

Attribute	Rating of A When "A" Stocking Worn First	Rating of A When "A" Stocking Worn Second	Rating of B When "B" Stocking Worn First	Rating of B When "B" Stocking Worn Second
Resiliency	More favorably	Less favorably	More favorably	Less favorably
Seams straight	More favorably	Less favorably	More favorably	Less favorably
Durability	More favorably	Less favorably	More favorably	Less favorably
Snagging	More favorably	Less favorably	Less favorably	More favorably
Feeling	More favorably	Less favorably	More favorably	Less favorably
Luster	Less favorably	More favorably	Less favorably	More favorably
Softness	More favorably	Less favorably	More favorably	Less favorably
Bagging	Less favorably	More favorably	More favorably	Less favorably

Source: Greenberg, *ibid.*, Table 1, p. 413.

in production and marketing might have been committed. In fact, virtually no difference is evident between the two brands so that a decision on which one to produce can rest primarily on production and related considerations.

6.6.4. A Note of Caution

Because experiments are carried out under controlled conditions, considerable care has to be exercised in interpreting and generalizing the results. In the many cases where variables cannot be identified or adequately controlled, to set up a pseudo-experimental design can be misleading.

An interesting example along this line is cited by Brunk.[61] Suppose milk bottled in glass and in paper is sold side by side, using a "matching" experimental design, and the paper container substantially outsells the glass. To interpret this as meaning that if a store carried milk in paper cartons only, it would sell more than in glass would be imputing something beyond the design of the experiment—for it shows only what happens when *both* are displayed. Thus, people who select paper over glass may have only a slight

---

[60] *Ibid.*, p. 413.
[61] Max Brunk, "How Marketing Research Has Helped the Apple Industry," *Journal of Farm Economics*, December, 1953, pp. 961–23.

preference for paper, whereas the minority choosing glass might have deep-seated preferences. If this were true, the latter group might refuse to buy milk if it were offered only in paper cartons, whereas the others would be willing to buy it in glass when offered no choice.

Design of an experiment in any event demands careful thinking and anticipation. Correct appreciation of the potentialities and obstacles in the project's situation is essential, and recognition must be given to both the desirability of minimizing the span of inference and the avoidance of an impracticable approach. All of the variables affecting the results materially should have been identified and reckoned with. And after the data have been brought together and analyzed, the limitations inherent in the research approach and character of the data should be strictly observed.

PROBLEMS

1. *a*) Given the soybean oil production figures for the U. S. for 1948 in Table 6.2, compute the aggregate market potential for this product in each of the three states shown.
   b) Derive technical coefficients for soybean oil in each of its uses.

2. *a*) Derive estimates of the ultimate disposition of gross output of chemicals among the first five industries listed in Table 6.4 using the data in Column 4 of that table and the data in Table 6.3.
   b) Set up an algebraic relation for deriving such estimates for any number of purchasing sectors.

3. *a*) What considerations should be taken into account in evaluating the applicability of the results of the trading stamp experiment (p. 314) to other areas?
   b) Suppose that the costs per returned questionnaire are as follows:

50 trading stamps with questionnaire	$1.18
100 stamps or 25 cents on return:	
100 stamps requested	1.12
25 cents requested	1.26
No inducement	1.06

   Which method would you suggest be used in the future? Why?

4. What adjustments would you make in the design of the camera survey discussed in Problem 4(*a*) of Chapter 5 if an additional objective of that survey were to pinpoint personality characteristics accounting for differences in interviewer performance?

5. *a*) What changes would you make in the plan for the farm survey mentioned in Problem 1 of Chapter 5 if it were to be undertaken as a panel operation, with the sample members being interviewed every three months for two years?

b) Given the focus of the operation on farm debt, what sort of data might be collected in the course of the panel that would otherwise not be obtainable?

6. A survey is being planned in a metropolitan area to measure the effect on consumer durable goods purchases of the consumer-goods rating publications, *Consumer Reports* and *Consumer Research*. Discuss the problem of experimental design and suggest one design that may be expected to yield the necessary information.

7. There are several sections of an economics course, one taught by one instructor over open-circuit TV and the others taught by other instructors by the usual classroom lecture method. At the end of the semester, it is proposed to evaluate the effectiveness of the TV approach by comparing grades of the TV class with those of the other classes and by having all the students fill out questionnaires on their satisfaction with the course. Comment on the adequacy of this approach.

8. *a*) A savings institution wants to investigate the influence of the interest rate it pays on time deposits on, (*a*) its own depositors, (*b*) non-depositors. Discuss the problem of sample design, indicate the type of data that should be sought, and prepare a questionnaire for the survey.
   b) Suppose the institution is secretly planning to raise its interest rate in the next few months and is willing to finance a before-and-after survey. How might the preceding plans be improved?

9. *a*) Discuss the pros and cons of a telephone panel of 100 nationally-known economists and business leaders who are surveyed on the business outlook every three months.
   b) How would this compare with a similar survey every three months, but speaking with 100 different people each time?

10. A consumer panel operation is being planned on durable goods ownership and use. Under what conditions would you recommend mail questionnaires and under what conditions would you recommend personal interviews?

11. Design a store audit experiment for determining whether apples wrapped in a cellophane bag sell any more than unwrapped apples if:
    a) the selling price is to be the same in both cases,
    b) unwrapped apples are to be sold for one cent a pound less than the wrapped apples.

12. How might the reliability and the validity of the responses in the study on the effect of interest rates be evaluated if:
    a) the survey is to be based on one interview only,
    b) the survey is to be a panel operation.

13. Describe how the method of equivalent intervals might be used in assessing consumer attitudes toward socialized medicine, including preparation of sample questions and derivation of attitude rankings for the different questions.

14. Prepare a Guttman-type questionnaire for the preceding problem, and discuss its practical application. Which of the two approaches (scalogram or equivalent intervals) would you choose, and why?

15. To elicit support for the hiring of members of a minority group as sales clerks, a community organization asked all those who had indicated their previous support of this policy to shop for one specific week at a grocery chain that had hired several sales clerks belonging to this minority group. The experiment was designed to test whether employment of these people would decrease sales (as employers feared) or increase sales.

Results were obtained by telephone interview of a subsample of those contacted. After study of the data, it was reported that "over 58% of all those solicited responded by purchasing during the designated week and spent over $6,500. All but a very small fraction of these had changed their shopping habits in order to underline their support of fair employment."

"The experiment was a test of the customer's religious and ethical desire to reward fair employment. The results show the affirmative response in dollars and cents that merchants can expect if and when they change their policies."

Comment on a) the research design and on, b) the interpretation. Can you think of a better approach?

SELECTED REFERENCES

Consumer Panels

A general discussion of the use of panel methods in commercial research is contained in *Samples, Polls and Surveys* by M. B. Parten, Chapter 3. A description of the types of problems encountered in a panel operation is discussed in *Collecting Financial Data by Consumer Panel Techniques: A Case Study* by Robert Ferber (University of Illinois Bureau of Economic and Business Research, 1959). Methods of keeping track of response rates and measuring bias in a personal interview consumer goods panel operation are the subject of "Observations on a Consumer Panel Operation" by Robert Ferber (*Journal of Marketing*, January, 1953, pages 246–259). Much the same subject is covered, with reference to a weekly mail consumer panel, in *Problems of Establishing a Consumer Panel in the New York Metropolitan Area* (Washington, D. C.: U. S. Department of Agriculture, Bureau of Agricultural Economics, May, 1952); also M. G. Sobel, "Panel Mortality and Panel Bias" (*Journal of the American Statistical Association*, March, 1959, pp. 52–68). "The Use of Panels in Social Research" by P. F. Lazarsfeld (*Proceedings of the American Philosophical Society*, November, 1948, pages 405–410) describes one of the pioneer applications of the panel technique to measuring social attitudes. For another application, see G. G. Quackenbush and J. D. Shaffer, *Collecting Food Purchase Data by Consumer Panel* (East Lansing, Mich.: Michigan State University, 1960).

Measuring Inventories

The National Inventory of Housing (Washington, D. C.: U. S. Bureau of the Census, 1956) illustrates the application of the method in the field of housing research. The use of the store audit method in marketing research is discussed in "Evolution of Factual Techniques in Marketing Research" by A. C. NIELSEN (in *Marketing Research and Business Management*, Champaign, Ill.: University of Illinois, Bureau of Economic and Business Research, 1952); also "Observation and Audit Techniques for Measuring Retail Sales," by E. E. HOUSEMAN and B. LIPSTEIN (*Agricultural Economics Research*, July, 1960, pp. 61–70).

Scaling Methods

Perhaps the best general reference work on different types of scaling methods is *Psychometric Methods* by J. P. GUILFORD (New York: McGraw-Hill, 1954). This book covers ranking methods, rating methods, equivalent intervals and scalogram analysis. A more theoretical discussion of various approaches to scaling is *Theory and Methods of Scaling* by W. S. TORGERSON (New York: Wiley and Sons, 1958).

The pioneer reference on the use of numerical ratings in attitude measurement and still well worth reading is *Public Opinion and the Individual* by GARDNER MURPHY and RENSIS LIKERT (New York: Harper & Bros., 1938).

The method of equivalent intervals appeared originally in *The Measurement of Attitude* by L. L. THURSTONE and E. J. CHAVE (Chicago: University of Chicago Press, 1929).

An excellent review of the place of scalogram analysis as well as of the theory of latent structure in attitude measurement is provided by S. A. STOUFFER in Chapter 1 of *Measurement and Prediction* by STOUFFER et al. (Princeton: Princeton University Press, 1950). This book is probably the best single source on scalogram analysis, being devoted mostly to this subject and written partly by LOUIS GUTTMAN. Another excellent reference on the subject, explaining the theoretical role of scaling analysis, is "The Principal Components of Scalable Attitudes" by LOUIS GUTTMAN in *Mathematical Thinking in the Social Sciences*, edited by P. F. LAZARSFELD (Glencoe: The Free Press, 1954), pages 216–257.

Numerous articles on the pros and cons of the methods and on various refinements have appeared in the periodical literature, particularly in the *Public Opinion Quarterly*. A number of these references will be found in *A Basic Bibliography on Marketing Research* by H. G. WALES and ROBERT FERBER.

The basic, and original, reference on the semantic differential is *The Measurement of Meaning* by C. E. OSGOOD, G. J. SUCI, and P. H. TANNENBAUM (Urbana, Ill.: University of Illinois Press, 1957). Related material of interest from the viewpoint of applications are: W. A. MINDAK, "Fitting the Semantic Differential to the Marketing Problem" (*Journal of Marketing*, April, 1961, pp. 28–33); W. T. NORMAN, "Stability-Characteristics of the Semantic Differential" (*American Journal of Psychology*, December, 1959, pp. 581–584; R. MEHLING, "A Single Test for Measuring the Intensity of Attitudes" (*Public Opinion Quarterly*, Winter, 1959–60, pp. 576–578).

End-Use Analysis

The input-output approach is discussed in great detail in *The Structure of the American Economy* by W. W. LEONTIEFF (New York: Oxford University Press, second edition, 1951). Applications to general economic analysis are discussed in "The Interindustry Relations Study for 1947" by W. D. EVANS and M. HOFFENBURG (*Review of Economics and Statistics*, November, 1959, pages 360–369). The use of other techniques applicable to end-use analysis is illustrated in an article by R. S. AIRES and WILLIAM COPULSKY, "Determination of Area Marketing Potentials for Chemical Process Raw Materials" (*Journal of Marketing*, April, 1950, pages 730–732).

Motivation Research

A broad review of the different approaches to motivation research is provided in *Motivation and Market Behavior* edited by ROBERT FERBER and H. G. WALES (Homewood, Ill.: Richard D. Irwin, Inc., 1959). The psychological approach to motivation research is emphasized in the book by D. L. LEONHARD, *Consumer Research with Projective Techniques* (Shenandoah, Iowa: Ajax Corp., 1955). Another book devoted to this subject, focusing on the benefits of motivation research and discussing some of the administrative aspects is *Motivation Research and Marketing Management* by J. W. NEWMAN (Boston: Harvard University Graduate School of Business, 1957).

Experimentation

The Design of Research Investigations by ROBERT FERBER, SIDNEY COHEN, and DAVID LUCK (American Marketing Association, 1958) provides a simple explanation of the meaning and use of controlled experimentation in marketing research. The article by S. A. STOUFFER, "Some Observations on Study Designs" (*American Journal of Sociology*, January, 1950, pp. 355–361) is well worth reading for the material in it on concepts of experimentation in the social sciences.

Various means of using controlled experiments as a tool of survey research are discussed in Chapter 6 of *Survey Design and Analysis* by HERBERT HYMAN (Glencoe, the Free Press, 1955). Illustrations of how experimentation has been used in the field of retailing will be found in the article by WILLIAM APPLEBAUM and R. F. SPEARS, "Controlled Experimentation in Marketing Research" (*Journal of Marketing*, January, 1950, pp. 505–517). More detailed description of the use of experimentation in particular situations will be found in "NBC Study of Radio's Sales Power" (National Broadcasting Company, September, 1952) and in the various studies on apple marketing by MAX BRUNK and W. T. FEDERER (a very informative one is "Methods of Research in Marketing" Paper No. 4, Department of Agricultural Economics, Cornell University Agricultural Experimental Station, January, 1953).

7 | Time-Series Analysis

W E NOW TURN from techniques of analyzing cross-section data to techniques of analyzing time-series data. The general economic relations sought in the study of time series have been covered, it will be recalled, in the second part of Chapter 4. This chapter and the following three supplement that discussion by presenting, and evaluating the adequacy of, specific statistical techniques applicable to time-series analysis. The present chapter deals with the decomposition of time series while the following ones take up special applications of time-series analysis to demand analysis, model systems, and forecasting.

No attempt is made in any of these chapters to present statistical techniques in detail except for those few techniques that are not already covered adequately in numerous statistical texts. Rather it would seem much more useful to concentrate on an evaluation of the relative adequacy of the various techniques for providing valid results under practical operating conditions; details of the statistical procedures are provided in the references at the end of this chapter.

The analysis of time series is used to investigate both the current state of affairs and economic structure—seasonal patterns, lags, etc. (compare Sec. 4.1). Generally, the same techniques may at times serve as a basis for structural research as well as for diagnosis and prognosis. For this reason, the order of presentation in this chapter will be governed by the individual research techniques rather than by research observations.

7.1. THE SEGMENTATION PRINCIPLE

Segmentation has long been, and continues to be, the basis for much of time-series analysis. In accordance with this principle, a time series can be

321

decomposed into four basic parts—trend (T), cyclical (C), seasonal (S), and erratic movements (E). The series, say Y, can then be represented either in a multiplicative sense or in an additive sense. In the former case, which tends to characterize better most economic events, we have:

$$Y = T \times C \times S \times E$$

Methods are sought to measure one or two of these components at a time. As estimates of the different components are obtained, that particular factor can, if desired, be eliminated by dividing these estimates into the original data. Thus, if trend estimates are derived, dividing these figures into Y yields the trend-adjusted series, i.e.:

$$\frac{Y}{T} = C \times S \times E$$

This adjusted series can then be segmented in a similar fashion between the three remaining factors. Of course, if the unit of observation is a year or some multiple, seasonal effects are not pertinent. One of the factors can be obtained as a residual, which simplifies the analysis but which can also introduce substantial bias to the extent that the estimation of the other factors remains more or less arbitrary.

Actually, this analytical framework can greatly oversimplify the true state of affairs, particularly through the implication it provides that there is "one trend" and "one cyclical" to estimates. There may be not one but several trends and cyclical patterns superimposed on one another, and the problem may be to segregate them from each other.[1] This restriction as well as the danger of compounding errors in residual estimates should be kept in mind in all time-series analyses based on this general approach.

7.2.   ERRATIC INFLUENCES

Interest in time-series data is not so much in the actual level of particular figures as in the general pattern or movement of the series. Differences in a single month or week may, therefore, be of incidental importance, particularly since the figure at any single time will be affected in part by numerous erratic and temporary factors—a labor stoppage, tie-up of shipments, bad weather, etc. Hence, means are sought of eliminating these so-called erratic influences[2] and bringing the general pattern of movement more sharply into

---

[1] For examples, see E. FRICKEY, *Economic Fluctuations in the United States* (Cambridge: Harvard University Press, 1942).

[2] The alternate term "random influences" is not used here because of the danger of identifying such influences as being of a statistically random nature. Such an identification can be highly misleading.

focus. Two general approaches are available for this purpose: moving averages, and what may be called "point correction."

7.2.1. Moving Averages

It can be shown that the average period of a series which consists of purely random digits is three time units. Hence, the ups and downs of a series brought about by purely incidental forces acting on the data can be attenuated by means of a three-period moving average.

Such an average may be unweighted or weighted. Thus, the unweighted three-month moving average would be:

$$February = \frac{January + February + March}{3}$$
$$March = \frac{February + March + April}{3}$$
$$etc.$$

With monthly data such an average has the advantage of adjusting the data not only for erratic influences but also, to a large extent, for differences in the number of working days or calendar weeks in each month.

A corresponding weighted three-month moving average would be:

$$February = \frac{January + 2(February) + March}{4}$$
$$March = \frac{February + 2(March) + April}{4}$$
$$etc.$$

Such a weighted moving average provides progressively less smoothing than the unweighted form as greater influence is assigned to the middle month. It is used at times to eliminate disturbances of a less pervasive nature from a series of data, such as the shift in the date of Easter between March and April from one year to another.

Five-period and seven-period moving averages may also be used to eliminate erratic fluctuations. In particular, a five-period average with weights 1, 2, 3, 2, 1 has been found useful on long time series on monthly data.[3] Much more complex methods can be and are used as well, particularly when electronic computers are available.[4]

---

[3] JULIUS SHISKIN and HARRY EISENPRESS, *Seasonal Adjustments by Electronic Computer Methods* (New York: National Bureau of Economic Research, Technical Paper 12, 1958).

[4] *Ibid.* Also F. R. MACAULEY, *The Smoothing of Time Series* (New York: National Bureau of Economic Research, 1931).

Perhaps most widely used is the twelve-month moving average, e.g.:

$$July = \frac{January + 2(February) + \cdots + 2(December) + January, \text{ } next \text{ } year}{24}$$

or:

$$July \text{ } 1 = \frac{January + February + \cdots + November + December}{12}$$

$$August \text{ } 1 = \frac{February + March + \cdots + December + January}{12}$$

$$July = \frac{July \text{ } 1 + August \text{ } 1}{2}$$

This moving average not only greatly reduces the effect of erratic influences but it also eliminates the seasonal fluctuations. Hence, this single step serves to bring into sharp focus the trend-cyclical pattern of the series. For relatively short time series, however, this procedure has the disadvantage of lagging six months behind the actual data. (Why?) In addition, this procedure is likely to be more appropriate for eliminating seasonal variation than for correcting for erratic variation, as noted below.

7.2.2.   Point Correction

Smoothing procedures such as moving averages have the serious disadvantage of ironing out characteristic points of a time series. As a result, turning points of cycles can be camouflaged, and it becomes difficult to judge when certain events begin to be manifested in the data. To some extent, this shortcoming is mitigated by the use of weighted moving averages which, by assigning the largest weight to the current month, help preserve its individuality. This raises something of a paradox, however, for, to the extent that individuality is preserved, smoothing is not achieved. Since the contour of these patterns differs so drastically in practice from one period to another, a weighting system that works in one instance may fail in another.

The problem is a perplexing one, for which no fully satisfactory solution exists as yet. It serves to emphasize the desirability of "point correction" whenever possible: correcting the data in advance on the basis of exact knowledge of the nature of the disturbance rather than relying on purely mechanistic adjustment procedures. Perhaps the simplest such correction is to express sales or production on a working-day basis to eliminate variations in the number of working days from week to week or from month to month. The correction may not be as simple in the case of a labor stoppage, but even in such a situation some form of point correction would seem more desirable than automatic use of a moving average. As a general rule, point correction would seem to be the first step in adjusting a time series for erratic variations, with some type of moving average introduced, if necessary, after these corrections have been made.

7.3. SEASONAL FLUCTUATIONS

The measurement of the nature and scope of periodic fluctuations in a time series within a year has one or both of two objectives: to find out what they are like, and to get rid of them. Knowledge of seasonal patterns is essential to understanding how the economy and firms operate and is a prerequisite for market diagnosis and forecasting within the period of a year. At the same time, such knowledge is needed for proper evaluation of short-run business and economic trends, for ascertaining the extent to which certain movements reflect seasonal changes rather than the working of more underlying forces.

The two objectives generally go hand-in-hand, for before seasonal variation can be eliminated, it must first be measured. Various means are available for doing this, all but one being covered very adequately in the statistical texts. Hence, we shall confine ourselves in this section to a review of the principal such methods, going into detail only for the method not generally available in English, a method developed by Abraham Wald.

7.3.1. Monthly Averages

Perhaps the simplest means of deriving a seasonal monthly index is to average all the figures for January, all the figures for February, etc., and then divide each of these averages into the overall monthly average. In this way, an estimate is obtained of the extent to which each month on the average deviates from the average level. This deviation is taken to represent the seasonal effect attributable to that particular month. Alternately, differences could be obtained instead of quotients, which is even quicker but presupposes no substantial changes in scale over the period studied.

The same procedure is applicable to weekly data, quarterly data, and to data on any similar basis.

The method is a very simple one and quick to apply. However, it is basically a first approximation method because it fails to allow for any trend in the data or for the possibility that the series may end at a different cyclical level than the point at which it starts. If the latter is true or a pronounced trend in the data does exist, the use of such a seasonal index to eliminate seasonal effects is likely to produce a "saw-tooth" pattern in the adjusted series. (Why?) Although rough corrections can be devised for such influences, none is particularly adequate, and for more precise work other methods are used.

7.3.2. Link Relatives

Each month is linked to the one immediately preceding, usually by dividing the latter into the former. Differences may also be used, though usually the amplitudes involved are large enough that ratios are to be preferred, as in the case of the number of unemployed which may vary substantially from one month to another; normally, seasonals are proportional rather than additive. Averages of these ratios are obtained for the different months and a seasonal index is derived by cumulatively adjusting for trend.

Like the method of monthly averages, this method is a simple one and quick to compute. The seasonal index derived in this manner is a more sophisticated one than that obtained by monthly averages and likely to be more reliable. However, use of this index to eliminate seasonal effects from the original data is subject to the same possible shortcomings noted earlier. The seasonal index is a rigid one—the same percentage correction for a particular month regardless of changes in economic structure.

Furthermore, the trend correction is for linear effects only, so that a non-linear trend or sharp cyclical fluctuations would be reflected in part in the seasonal index. In addition, each abnormally high or low figure brought about by erratic forces serves to distort two ratios and the corresponding monthly averages as well. For this reason, point correction is particularly desirable before working with link relatives. An additional precaution is to select as the "average" ratio for the month either the median of the individual ratios for the month or the arithmetic mean of the ratios after excluding the highest and the lowest for each month.

7.3.3. Ratio-to-Moving-Average

With monthly data, a 12-month total, or average, encompasses the entire range of seasonal variation within a year and hence effectively eliminates seasonal influences. Such an average, which therefore reflects almost entirely trend and cyclical forces and contains virtually no seasonal effect, can serve as a basis for isolating the seasonal influences by dividing the average into the actual figure for the given month. By this reasoning, the resulting quotients reflect only seasonal and erratic effects, i.e.:

$$\frac{T \times C \times S \times E}{T \times C} = S \times E$$

The erratic effects are eliminated by some averaging process, as before. In the simplest case, this would involve computing the mean, median, or an adjusted mean for all the quotients for each month. The result, however, again is a rigid index. A more flexible procedure is to prepare a separate time-series chart for the ratios for each month and then fit a trend to the data if it seems warranted, doing so either freehand or by algebraic means. This makes it possible to allow for changes in the seasonal pattern over time and also permits further adjustment of the data for erratic fluctuations. If such trend lines are fitted, separate seasonal indices are obtained for each year, the appropriate seasonal index being read off or computed from the trend lines. Dividing the original data by these seasonal indices provides the seasonally-adjusted series.

The method is a very flexible one, and therein lies what is perhaps its main shortcoming. Selection of trend lines for the monthly ratios is essentially an arbitrary procedure. This is particularly true of fitting freehand lines, and considerable controversy still exists over the wisdom of "following the curves" as against keeping curvature to an absolute minimum. A compromise procedure sometimes used, if enough data and computing facilities are available, is to fit a moving average to the ratios for each month and then decide if a trend line should be fitted, and what form of a line.

The ratio-to-moving-average method also entails a lot of computations besides lagging about six months behind the current month. Nevertheless, its aforementioned advantages are such that it is undoubtedly the most widely used technique in technical time-series studies, particularly when a long series of data is available and the principal objective is to eliminate seasonal effects from the data. The method also forms the basis for the electronic-computer approach to seasonal adjustment.[5]

7.3.4. Fixed Regression Coefficients

Multiple regression methods can also be used to derive seasonal indices. The method is suitable only if extensive computing facilities are available and is not particularly flexible but does offer the convenience of incorporating in a single equation both seasonal and nonseasonal effects. It also enables tests to be made on the results for the statistical significance of different seasonal effects.

The method is based on the use of dummy variables, as follows (Sec. 8.7):

Suppose quarterly corporate profits (P) are to be estimated on the basis of a regression on quarterly corporate sales (S), both seasonally unadjusted. The following regression equation is set up:

$$P = a + bS + c_1Q_1 + c_2Q_2 + c_3Q_3 \tag{7.1}$$

The Q's are dummy variables, one for each quarter except Q_i takes the value 1 if that particular quarter is involved; otherwise it takes the value, 0. Thus, for data for all the first quarters, Q_1 is 1 and Q_2 and Q_3 are zero; for all second quarters, Q_2 is 1 and Q_1 and Q_3 are zero; etc.

---

[5] JULIUS SHISKIN and HARRY EISENPRESS, *op. cit.*

Estimates of the parameters, a, b, c_1, c_2, c_3, are obtained by the usual methods, and the estimates of the c's represent the seasonal influences attributable to the specified quarters. These seasonals are measured with respect to the fourth quarter instead of with respect to a "normal" or average level. However, seasonals in the ordinary sense are easily derived from the c's (How?), bearing in mind that the four seasonals must total zero.

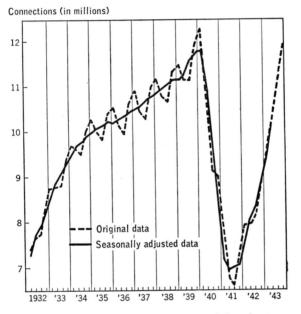

Connections (in millions)

Original data
Seasonally adjusted data

1932 '33 '34 '35 '36 '37 '38 '39 '40 '41 '42 '43

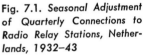

Fig. 7.1. *Seasonal Adjustment of Quarterly Connections to Radio Relay Stations, Netherlands, 1932–43*

In (7.1) linear effects are assumed for the seasonal factors, but non-linear effects can also be incorporated by using logarithms. Furthermore, the form of the seasonal can be determined partly by inspection; it need not be the same for all quarters.

7.3.5. Moving Regression Coefficients

This highly flexible method was developed by Abraham Wald in the mid-1930's. However, partly perhaps because of the computational work involved and partly perhaps because the original publication was not in English,[6] it has never received much attention in the United States. Nevertheless, the method possesses unusual features which clearly merit it further attention. Thus, by means of this method automatic allowance is made for changes in the amplitude of seasonal patterns even in the face of sharply moving and changing trends, as shown in Fig. 7.1.

---

[6] ABRAHAM WALD, *Berechnung und Ausschaltung von Saisonschwankungen* (Beitrage zur Konjunkturforschung, No. 9), Vienna, JULIUS SPRINGER, 1936.

The basic principle is rather simple: deviations from a 4-quarter (or 12-month) moving average serve as the basis for computing regression coefficients measuring the amplitude of the seasonal for the given quarter (month) relative to that of the period as a whole. These regression coefficients are then used to correct the deviations for shifts in amplitude, which in turn serve as the basis for the (moving) seasonal index and for seasonal adjustment of the original data.

Application of the method is illustrated by the data in Table 7.1. Essentially the following steps are involved, and are illustrated by Table 7.1 (capital letters refer to the correspondingly labeled sections of the table).

Step 1. Weighted 4-quarter moving averages are computed from the original data. The results are shown in Section B.

Step 2. Deviations are obtained by subtracting the moving averages from the actual figures for the corresponding quarters. This is shown in Section C.

Step 3. The constant, k, is computed as a basis for deriving seasonal regression coefficients. This constant is computed by summing the deviations for each quarter, obtaining quarterly averages, adjusting these averages to add up to zero, and dividing each of the four resulting averages by the sum of the squares of all four averages. The calculations are illustrated at the bottom of Table 7.1.

Step 4. The result of the last step is four estimates of k, one for each quarter. These estimates are transferred to the top of Section D in Table 7.1, and are multiplied by the corresponding deviations from Section C.

Step 5. Seasonal "regression coefficients" are estimated by computing weighted 4-quarter moving totals of the data in Section D. The results are shown in Section E. These regression coefficients make allowances for the moving seasonal amplitude in the data.

Step 6. The actual seasonal effect in each quarter is now estimated by multiplying these seasonal regression coefficients by the "rigid averages," i.e., the values of a. The results are shown in Section F.

Step 7. The original data in Section A are now corrected for the seasonal effect by subtracting from them the estimate of the seasonal influence for the appropriate quarters obtained in Section F. The results are shown in Section G.

All in all, the method offers the advantages of high flexibility with precise methods of estimation. On the other side of the ledger, the results lag about one year behind current figures and require for diagnostic purposes extrapolation of the seasonal regression coefficients.

Table

ELIMINATING SEASONAL INFLUENCES

Year	Actual figures (× 1000)				Weighted four quarter moving average[a]				Deviations from the average[b]			
	A				B				C			
	I	II	III	IV	I	II	III	IV	I	II	III	IV
1930	348.3	399.8	442.7	504.6	......	......	450.3	500.6	....	....	− 7.6	4.0
1931	559.9	590.9	627.1	685.0	547.6	593.2	638.3	682.9	12.3	− 2.3	−11.2	2.1
1932	740.8	766.6	773.7	826.5	723.2	759.2	793.6	824.1	17.6	(7.4)	−19.9	2.4
1933	874.4	877.1	881.8	934.3	851.4	878.4	903.8	926.3	23.0	− 1.3	−22.0	8.0
1934	970.0	961.3	950.6	1006.3	945.4	963.0	979.5	991.5	24.6	− 1.7	−28.9	14.8
1935	1029.8	997.7	982.0	1040.2	1000.0	1008.2	1015.8	1021.5	29.8	−10.5	−33.8	18.7
1936	1056.9	1016.3	997.1	1066.7	1025.7	1030.9	1039.1	1047.7	31.2	−14.6	−42.0	19.0
1937	1095.6	1046.8	1033.0	1100.2	1056.0	1064.7	1073.0	1082.0	39.6	−17.9	−40.0	18.2
1938	1128.6	1085.3	1073.8	1138.2	1091.9	1101.7	1110.0	1118.1	36.7	−16.4	−36.2	20.1
1939	1156.5	1122.3	1121.3	1203.5	1128.6	1142.7	1161.3	1168.0	27.9	−20.4	−40.0	(28.5)
1940	1239.4	1093.3	923.5	904.1	1139.6	1077.5	981.7	872.1	(50.0)	(−17.0)	(−58.2)	(32.0)
1941	772.7	682.9	664.4	730.3	788.4	734.3	715.9	734.6	(43.0)	(−22.0)	(−46.0)	(15.0)
1942	799.4	805.5	824.7	893.4	769.9	810.4	850.7	897.9	(29.5)	(− 4.9)	(−26.0)	(−4.5)
1943	958.9	1023.9	1118.5	1204.8	962.0	1037.6	1114.4	1187.3	(−3.1)	(−13.7)	(4.1)	(17.5)
1944	1261.5	1304.8	......	......	......	......	......	......	....	....	....	....

7.4. TREND ANALYSIS

The objectives of trend determination are similar to those of measuring seasonal fluctuation. On the one hand, trend determination indicates long-term movements, thereby providing a basis for planning long-run market expansion, investment planning, etc. On the other hand, for studying short-run influences, particularly cyclical variations, it is highly desirable, if not essential, to eliminate trend effects from the data. Doing so, however, requires the use of a method either to measure trend or to eliminate trend more or less implicitly, and it is to a review of the principal such methods that we now turn.

7.4.1. Moving Averages

What a time-series analyst would do without the ubiquitous moving average is hard to say. As in the measurement of seasonal variation, moving averages are frequently used for trend analysis. Only the objective now is not to eliminate trend but to isolate it.

For this purpose, the data are generally combined into annual (non-overlapping) totals or averages, so that seasonal variation is no longer a factor. A

7.1

BY WALD METHOD

Year	D COLUMN (C) × k				E Seasonal regression coefficients (weighted moving four quarter totals of column (D))				F Seasonal influence column (E) × rigid average 26.9 −10.6 −28.2 11.9				G Original figures, corrected for seasonal influences (column A−column F)			
	0.0152	−0.0060	−0.0159	0.067												
	I	II	III	IV	I	II	III	IV	I	II	III	IV	I	II	III	IV
1930	....	......	0.121	0.028	....	....	....	....	....	....	....	....	....	....	....	....
1931	0.187	0.014	0.178	0.014	0.379	0.400	0.434	0.445	10.2	− 4.2	−12.2	5.3	549.7	595.1	639.3	679.7
1932	0.268	−0.044	0.316	0.016	0.485	0.555	0.597	0.644	13.0	− 5.9	−16.8	7.9	727.8	772.5	790.5	818.7
1933	0.350	0.008	0.350	0.054	0.707	0.743	0.774	0.787	19.0	− 7.9	−21.8	9.4	855.4	885.0	903.6	924.9
1934	0.374	0.010	0.460	0.099	0.843	0.921	0.983	1.049	22.7	− 9.8	−27.7	12.5	947.3	971.1	978.3	993.8
1935	0.453	0.063	0.537	0.125	1.114	1.165	1.189	1.212	30.0	−12.3	−33.5	14.4	999.8	1010.0	1015.5	1025.8
1936	0.474	0.088	0.668	0.127	1.290	1.365	1.421	1.495	34.7	−14.4	−40.1	17.8	1022.2	1030.7	1037.2	1048.9
1937	0.602	0.107	0.636	0.122	1.488	1.470	1.445	1.419	40.0	−15.6	−40.7	16.9	1055.6	1062.4	1073.7	1083.3
1938	0.558	0.098	0.576	0.135	1.384	1.361	1.300	1.245	37.2	−14.4	−36.7	14.8	1091.4	1099.7	1110.5	1123.4
1939	0.424	0.122	0.636	0.191	1.287	1.345	1.541	1.699	34.6	−14.3	−43.5	20.2	1121.9	1136.6	1164.8	1183.3
1940	0.760	0.102	0.925	0.214	1.834	1.990	1.948	1.910	49.3	−21.1	−54.9	22.7	1190.1	1114.4	978.4	881.4
1941	0.654	0.132	0.731	0.101	1.828	1.675	1.515	1.361	49.2	−17.8	−42.7	16.2	723.5	700.7	707.1	714.1
1942	0.448	0.029	0.413	−0.030	1.150	0.926	0.613	0.392	30.9	− 9.8	−17.3	4.7	768.5	815.3	842.0	888.7
1943	0.047	0.082	−0.065	0.117	0.179	0.014	....	....	4.8	− 0.1	− 0.3	0.1	954.1	1024.0	....	....
1944	....	....	....	....	....	....	....	....	....	....	....	....	....	....	....	....

Calculation of the rigid averages and k, based on the totals of columns C–I to IV inclusive.

Total........................	242.7	−85.1	−281.6	107.3
Average.....................	27.0	−10.6	− 28.2	11.9 Σ = 0.1
Correction.................	−0.1			
Rigid average (=a).........	26.9	−10.6	− 28.2	11.9
a^2.......................	723.6	112.4	795.2	141.6 Σ = 1772.8

Season multiplicator

$$k = \frac{a}{\Sigma a^2} \quad\quad 0.0152 \quad\quad -0.0060 \quad\quad -0.0159 \quad\quad 0.0670$$

[a] For the third quarter we get, e.g.: $\mathrm{III} = \dfrac{\mathrm{I + II + III + IV + I}}{8}$

[b] Deleted figures have been put into brackets. Italics represent corrected deviations pertaining to lags or leads of the moving average with respect to actual development. Generally as few observations as possible are scrapped when using WALD's method. In this example, however, in order to calculate the rigid normal (a), only the figures up to the third quarter of 1939 inclusive were used, because the years of occupation would prove useless for the calculation of the "normal" seasonal. For the computation of the seasonal regression they had, of course, to be used (columns D-E) in order to eliminate the remaining systematical pattern.

moving average is then selected of a length equal to the average period of the cycle in the series—the average distance from trough-to-trough or from peak-to-peak. To the extent that this can be done—means of determining periodicity are discussed later in this chapter—application of the appropriate moving average will smooth out the ups and downs in the data as well as a preponderant part of such erratic effects as may be present, and leave a series of data which changes gradually over time.

The optimum moving average can vary considerably with the particular data. For rayon production in the United States, an average of as few as two years may be adequate because of the tendency for each year to represent either a temporary peak or trough. Overall industrial production in the United States generally goes through a cycle of three to four years, whereas business activity in many European countries may go through a cycle of as much as nine years before a new peak, or trough, is reached. In the construction industry, on the other hand, cycles of 18–20 years are not uncommon.

The moving-average method of determining trend has the big advantages of flexibility and of presenting perhaps a more realistic picture of long-run movements. This is because the data are not forced into any particular form, as is true when mathematical functions are used. At the same time, the method does possess some severe limitations. One drawback derives from the purely descriptive nature of the moving average: it does not indicate much about the nature of the trend development and is therefore of little value for the interpretation and understanding of trend movements. Hence, moving averages are better suited for studying deviations from trend rather than the trend itself.

Then too, moving averages assume that the time series is subject to a definite and relatively stable periodicity. This is not necessarily true, however, especially if a series spans a period characterized by major erratic disturbances—war, revolution, etc. To the extent that this is the case, no single moving average can eliminate entirely these cyclical-erratic fluctuations.

Finally, the moving averages necessarily miss as many observations as the length of the average, half at the beginning and half at the end (actually half plus one if the moving average is an even number). To avoid this loss of data, one of the other approaches to trend analysis has to be used.

7.4.2. Mathematical Trends

This is perhaps the most common means of determining trend. By means of a prior hypothesis or by visual examination of the data, a particular function form is selected and fitted to the data either freehand or by algebraic means, usually the latter by least-squares techniques. Different procedures are possible, however, depending on the form of the function selected. The function forms available are virtually innumerable, varying from the very simple to the highly complicated. The three main categories are first degree polynomials—corresponding with the hypothesis of constant growth, polynomials of higher degree, and the so-called growth curves.

7.4.2.1. *Constant growth.* This hypothesis is perhaps the most frequent in practice. A certain flexibility is possible since constant growth can be defined as referring either to a constant absolute change per unit of time or to a constant percentage rate of change. In either case, the mathematical form of the trend is a polynomial of the first degree, *viz.*:

$$Y_t = a + bt \tag{7.2a}$$

or

$$log \ Y_t = a + b \ log \ t \tag{7.2b}$$

where Y_t is the estimate for the observation in the given year and t is time. (Subscripts seem unnecessary here and will therefore be omitted in what follows.)

The assumption underlying (7.2b) is often preferable since economic and business time series are more likely to vary by a constant rate than by a constant amount. This can be tested quickly in a particular case by plotting the observations on arithmetic and on semi-logarithmic paper and determining which plot, if any, exhibits essentially a straight line.

The logarithmic trend is a transformation of the exponential function:

$$Y = A(1 + m)^t \tag{7.2c}$$

where m represents the fixed percentage rate of change. Another way of writing (7.2c), often used to represent a residual trend in demand analysis or to characterize the trend-component of a variable in models of economic growth, is the form:

$$Y = Ae^{rt} \tag{7.2d}$$

The constant e denotes the base of the natural logarithms ($e = 2.718$ . . .) whereas for small values of r, the latter approaches m.[7] If r is small, (7.2b) is used as estimator equation with logs to the base 10 (as normally will be the case). The value of r is found by multiplying b by 2.303.

In arithmetic units or in logs, the method of fitting linear trends is quick to apply. This is particularly true if the number of years is odd, in which case shifting the origin to the middle year causes $\Sigma t/n$ to be zero.

7.4.2.2. *Polynomials of higher degree.* Linear trends, whether logarithmic or not, are highly inflexible. Their use can often be defended, however, since many series can be approximated very well by a linear trend over considerable periods of time. On the other hand, if a curvilinear trend appears more suitable, polynomials of higher degree can be introduced into (7.2). Thus, if the trend evidences a bend, a parabolic function can be used, i.e.:

$$Y = a + b_1 T + b_2 T^2 \tag{7.3}$$

If two bends are apparent, a third degree polynomial can be used, i.e., adding the term, $b_3 T^3$, to (7.3), and so on.

The number of bends in a series can generally be determined by plotting the data, preferably on both arithmetic and semi-log chart paper. Often an upward bend in a series when plotted on arithmetic paper may vanish when

---

[7] This is easily seen since:

$$r = log_e (1 + m) = m - \tfrac{1}{2}m^2 + \tfrac{1}{3}m^3 \pm \cdots \quad (1 \geq m > -1)$$

plotted on semi-log paper, so that conversion to logarithms conserves one degree of freedom.

Another criterion for selecting a polynomial trend of appropriate degree is to examine the differences in the original series. This criterion is based on the fact that with a trend of the . . .

first order, the differences are constant from year to year,
second order, the second differences—the differences of the differences—
  are constant from year to year,
third order, the third differences are constant,
nth order, the nth differences are constant.

Often, however, the situation is not clear-cut. Selection of a function can then be made on *a priori* grounds or by the purely statistical expedient of selecting the higher-degree polynomial and measuring the degree of significance of the coefficient of the highest-order term.[8]

An alternate approach, if tentative trends are to be computed for many series, lies in the use of the so-called "orthogonal polynomials."[9] This method permits successively higher degree terms to be added to a given polynomial without the necessity of recomputing all the lower order coefficients.

7.4.2.3.   *Growth curves*. From a theoretical point of view, the so-called "logistic curve" is perhaps the most appropriate: it is about the only mathematical trend derived in an attempt to approximate "growth" as such.[10]

The underlying assumptions are that the annual absolute rate of increase varies:

1. proportionately to the level in the given year; the rate of increase therefore rises as the value of the series rises.
2. proportionately to the difference between the variable itself in the given year and its maximum value, i.e., saturation level. Hence, the rate of increase declines as this difference decreases.

Both of these assumptions have been verified for various biological as well as economic phenomena.[11]

Its equation is:

$$Y = \frac{k}{1 + ce^{bt}} \tag{7.4}$$

where b, c, and k are parameters, k representing the maximum value of Y, i.e., the saturation level.

  e is the base for Neperian logarithms, 2.718 . . .

---

[8] Such a test can be carried out by variance analysis. See ROBERT FERBER, *Statistical Techniques in Market Research*, pp. 396–399.

[9] R. A. FISHER, *Statistical Methods for Research Workers*, 12th edition, Chapter 5.

[10] J. TINBERGEN, *Econometrics*, pp. 57–60.

[11] RAYMOND PEARL, *Biology of Population Growth*. Also SIMON KUZNETS, *Secular Movements in Production and Prices*.

The curve describes an expanded, but still perfectly symmetrical, S sweep. The derivation of estimates of its parameters, however, is a laborious procedure, and is best done only if there are strong *a priori* grounds to expect the trend to follow this pattern.[12] For this reason, the *Gompertz Curve* is eminently more suitable. It has a very similar form to the logistic, its equation being:

$$Y = ka^{b^t} \tag{7.5a}$$

with k again as the saturation level. This value will be higher than the corresponding value of k for the logistic to the extent that the observations are clustered below the point of inflection of the curve. In both instances, however, the reliability of k is highly questionable.[13]

For just describing the sweep of a series of data, the Gompertz Curve is preferable to the logistic. However, an important improvement is possible with the logistic curve, since its use enables one to take into account the effect on growth of the business cycle. Thus, (7.4) can be written as:

$$Y = \frac{\dfrac{b'}{a'}}{1 + \dfrac{c'}{a'}\, e^{-b't}} \tag{7.5b}$$

The parameters, a' and b', can be estimated as the parameters of the regression equation:

$$\frac{\Delta Y}{Y} = b' - a'Y \tag{7.6}$$

At the same time, this may serve as a simple test for the presence of a logistic trend. Before doing so, an additional term can be introduced into (7.6) to represent cyclical fluctuations in the economy, e.g.:

$$\frac{\Delta Y}{Y} = b' - a'Y + d\frac{\Delta X}{X} \tag{7.7}$$

where X represents, say, an index of industrial production. In this way, estimates of the parameters, a' and b', are obtained largely independent of cyclical influences.[14]

The integration constant, c', in (7.5b) can be estimated in various ways. A quick, approximate method is to determine c' from (7.5b) for a "normal"

---

[12] Criteria for selecting the logistic curve, as well as computational procedures, will be found in CROXTON and COWDEN, *Applied General Statistics*, 2d edition, Chapter 13.

[13] H. T. DAVIS, *The Analysis of Economic Time Series*, p. 527.

[14] For an example of this method as applied to measuring automobile demand, see CHARLES ROOS and VICTOR VON SZELISKI, *Dynamics of Automobile Demand*, 1939.

year. The saturation level thus obtained is that to be expected in "normal" cyclical conditions.[15]

A further refinement is to estimate the saturation level using per capita data. In this way, the influence of population growth is kept separate, and the absolute saturation level can be varied with the expected size of the population.

7.4.3. Eliminating Trend

If the objective of the analysis is to study patterns or to derive relationships after trend effects are eliminated, the statistical description of trend becomes of incidental importance. If a trend equation has been derived anyway, the equation can serve as the vehicle for trend adjustment, usually by taking as the new observations the deviations of the original values from the corresponding estimate computed from the trend equation. However, prior derivation of a trend equation is not the only means of adjusting data for trend. In particular, two alternate means are worth mentioning.

One such approach lies in incorporating trend variables in a *multiple regression,* if multiple regressions are to be used. If the period is relatively short, the use of a straight-line trend is usually justified, and may be so in other instances as well. If the assumption of linearity proves unwarranted, this fact would show up in an analysis of the residuals, to the extent that the residuals are subject to autocorrelation.[16] In that case, some form of non-linear trend can be considered. It should be emphasized, however, that statistical results cannot be decisive in making such a decision; heavy emphasis must be placed on *a priori* hypotheses and such economic factors as may be known.

With a linear trend, the rationale of this approach is that the trend variable(s) will eliminate the trend element from the dependent and explanatory variables, thereby revealing the net, trend-adjusted relationship between the dependent variable and the other variables in the equation. To the extent that the trend is actually linear, this can be an effective approach, and is usually called *"time-regression."*

An alternate approach is to convert the data into *first differences;* ratios could be used also, but differences are generally easier to work with. Thus, suppose we want to derive the cyclical relationship, if any, between investment expenditures (I) and level of production (P) in relation to capacity (C). If we were to follow the previous approach and include a trend variable, the basic equation form might be:

---

[15] A simple and less arbitrary method is given in H. T. DAVIS, *The Theory of Econometrics,* 1941, pp. 222–224.

[16] For the appropriate statistical tests, see GERHARD TINTNER, *Econometrics,* Chapter 11; also ROBERT FERBER, *op. cit.,* Chapter 13.

$$I_t = a + b\left(\frac{P}{C}\right)_t + cT_t \tag{7.8}$$

The alternate approach is to convert the data into first differences, thereby using the following transformation:

$$I_t - I_{t-1} = a' + b'\left[\left(\frac{P}{C}\right)_t - \left(\frac{P}{C}\right)_{t-1}\right] \tag{7.9a}$$

or:

$$\Delta I_t = a' + b' \Delta \left(\frac{P}{C}\right)_t \tag{7.9b}$$

where under certain conditions, $a' = c$ (Sec. 8.9.3, footnote 53).

This procedure has the advantage of reducing the number of variables while at the same time the trend effect is virtually eliminated. Aside from the trend-adjustment procedure, the method also has certain other advantages. Thus, it may provide a means of avoiding autocorrelation and multicollinearity effects, the presence of which indicates omission of certain systematic factors from the relationship (though their absence does not of itself validate a derived relationship). Then too, first differences prove useful where it is believed that changes in particular variables are more decisive than actual levels. For example, the well-known, and highly controversial, acceleration principle in business cycles is based on such an hypothesis—that investment (net change in capital stock) is a function of the change in the level of production.

First differences have disadvantages too, not the least of which is the exaggeration of erratic influences. Also, the method may not at times fully eliminate trend and multicollinearity effects. If such effects are not fully eliminated, it is often possible to find another transformation of the original data that will do the job.[17]

7.5. CYCLICAL FACTORS

If the segmentation principle is followed, the cyclical effect is obtained as a residual, the result of smoothing the original data and dividing them by estimates of the trend and seasonal factors. As noted earlier, this procedure has the advantage of simplicity but raises the danger of substantial uncertainty due to the residual nature of the estimates.

Alternately, estimates of the cyclical effect can be sought directly, which is generally done by setting up criteria for turning points and then seeking

---

[17] See D. COCHRANE and G. H. ORCUTT, "Application of Least Squares Regression to Relationships Containing Auto-Correlated Error Terms," *Journal of the American Statistical Association*, Vol. 44 (1949), pp. 32–61.

to identify them from an examination of a time-series graph of the data. In actual practice, the data are likely to be adjusted first for erratic and seasonal variations, the latter if the unit of observation is less than a year, and even for trend too if the series covers several decades or more. The result is therefore a combination approach, involving initially application of the segmentation principle followed by identification and delineation of individual cycles largely by visual examination and case study, bringing in whatever additional pertinent information may be available.[18] In this way, the cyclical characteristics of a series can be determined, particularly the average duration and amplitude of a cycle.

Mathematical means of cyclical description can also be employed, if desired, primarily through fitting the cyclical data to a trigonometric function. To the extent that the data conform to a particular function form, a very useful descriptive picture of cyclical variations can be obtained in this manner.[19] This functional approach is especially useful for decomposing a series of data into cycles of different length.

7.6.   LAGS AND PERIODICITY

Apart from their relevance to time-series analysis, ability to determine lags between series and the average period of a series is important for regression analysis and for market diagnosis and prognosis. In the case of lags, for example, an important question that frequently arises is the extent to which activity in a particular industry or sector leads or follows general business developments. Though this magnitude will not be the same for all cycles, its variability is generally sufficiently small so that an average can have much significance for interpreting and understanding market forces.

7.6.1.   The Average Period

Perhaps the simplest way to estimate the average period of a series—the average distance between successive peaks or successive troughs—is to eliminate trend (and seasonal factors, if pertinent) and then divide the average of the number of peaks and troughs into the total number of observations. Alternately, if the series is plotted as deviations from trend, the average period can be obtained as the quotient of half the number of times the series intersects the horizontal (zero) axis and the total number of observations.

---

[18] See A. F. BURNS and W. C. MITCHELL, *Measuring Business Cycles* (New York: National Bureau of Economic Research, 1946). For a critical discussion of this general approach, see the August, 1947, and May, 1949, issues of the *Review of Economics and Statistics*.

[19] For details, see H. T. DAVIS, *Analysis of Economic Time Series*, Chapter VII.

More rigorous methods are available, but they are rather complicated and laborious.[20] A potentially very useful approach is the "periodograph method" of Armstrong, which provides a profile of the cycle as well as an estimate of the average period.

The simplest of the algebraic methods, and one that at the same time provides a fairly precise estimate, is to use the serial correlation coefficient, ρ (defined by equations 7.17 or 7.18 below), as the basis for calculating the average period. The estimating equation for the average period (T) is then:

$$\cos \frac{2\pi}{T} = \rho \qquad (7.10)$$

where π is the usual trigonometric symbol for 180 degrees. Thus, if ρ is .13, we have:

$$\cos \frac{360°}{T} = .130, \text{ or } T = \frac{360°}{82°30'} = 4.35$$

Some estimates of the average period (T), obtained by means of (7.10), are given in Table 7.2 for different countries and periods.

Table 7.2
ESTIMATES OF AVERAGE PERIOD, T

Country	Branch of industry[a]	Period	Estimate of T in years
Germany	Pig iron	1882–1895	5.7
Germany	Pig iron	1896–1909	4.7
United States	Total industrial production	1901–1914	4.0
United States	Iron and steel	1901–1914	3.6
United States	Total industrial production	1921–1937	6.2
United Kingdom	Total industrial production	1924–1936	5.9
Belgium	Pig iron	1920–1938	8.4
Netherlands	Total industrial production	1923–1936	10.4

[a] The series refer to volume of output of the branches concerned.

Source: P. J. VERDOORN, *De Verstarring der Productiekosten*, Haarlem, 1943, Table 40, p. 156.

This method provides useful results when, for example, for purposes of trend elimination the length of a moving average has to be determined. Also, as will be shown below, whether or not ρ is interpreted as an indicator of the average period, its computation is necessary in order to evaluate properly the long-term influence of lagged variables.

From the point of view of assessing as correctly as possible the average period, the approach has the disadvantage that only one rough "overall"

---

[20] DAVIS and NELSON, *Elements of Statistics*, 1937, pp. 137–140; C. E. ARMSTRONG, "The Short-Term Business Cycle," *Review of Economic Statistics*, May, 1936.

average is obtained. If, for instance, several cyclical movements are super-imposed in the same series, a single value of T is not very meaningful. Another disadvantage is that the estimate of T fails to provide any indications either of the variability in the average or of the profile of the cycle. For this purpose, periodogram, or periodograph, analysis is required. This is particularly important if periodicity is to be used as a basis for prediction. Extrapolating cyclical patterns on the basis of the average period, as is occasionally suggested, can be highly misleading because of the generally high variability in the average. Unlike long-term trend projections, average periods provide no basis whatsoever for indicating basic directions of movement even one to two years hence.

7.6.2. The Single Lag

In measuring lagged reactions it is customary to distinguish between discrete lags and distributed lags.

With *discrete lags*, the underlying assumptions are that the reaction of y on x starts only after ϑ units of time and that the full adaptation of y is then completed at that very same moment. A discrete lag, therefore, presupposes a structural equation of the form:

$$y_t = \gamma + A x_{t-\vartheta} \qquad (7.11)$$

where ϑ, measured in the same units as t, indicates the length of the lag.

Distributed lags, on the contrary, allow for the possibility that the adaptation process, once started, may take some time. A distributed lag, consequently, can be represented by:

$$y_t = \gamma + \alpha_1 x_t + \alpha_2 x_{t-1} + \alpha_3 x_{t-2} + \cdots \qquad (7.12)$$

In practice, distributed lags are often treated as discrete lags if the full adaptation takes less than one time unit, say less than one year. In this case, ϑ is considered to represent the average length of a distributed lag that expires within one unit of time following the change of x. Equation (7.11) is then said to represent a *single lag*, in distinction to the *distributed lag*, spread over a number of time units, as implied by (7.12). With a single lag, ϑ is therefore always less than unity.

This average length, ϑ, of the single lag between two time series may usually be estimated by any of the following three approaches:

Visually. Each series is plotted on a sheet of transparent graph paper with the same time (horizontal) scale. The units of this scale should be sufficiently small to allow for an appropriate estimate of ϑ, e.g., monthly intervals if t is being measured in years. The sheets are placed on top of each other, held against a light, and shifted back and forth horizontally until the peaks and troughs of the two series seem to cover each other most completely. The difference between the dates on the two charts at any point is then the estimate of the average lag.

Simple correlation. Instead of attempting to obtain an estimate by visual examination, simple correlation coefficients can be computed between the two series, first lagging one series by one unit, second using a two-unit lag, and so on. The lag corresponding to the highest correlation coefficient thereby obtained is then taken as the best estimate of the average lag.

Formula estimation. A less familiar method rests on a multiple regression between the one variable and the other variable both at the current value and at a lagged value clearly preceding the likely average lag. For example, suppose the average lag of the series, x_t, is sought relative to the series, y_t, ϑ being expressed in annual units. The lag is known to be less than one year. The following multiple regression is set up:

$$y_t = \gamma + \alpha x_t + \beta x_{t-1} \tag{7.13}$$

The conventional estimate of the average lag, ϑ, is then:[21]

$$\vartheta = \frac{\beta}{\alpha + \beta} \tag{7.14}$$

Thus, if α were .4 and β were .2, the weighted average lag is estimated as one-third of a year, or four months.

It should be noted that the influence of the lagged series, $x_{t-\vartheta}$, on y will almost always be less than suggested by the sum of the regression coefficients, $\alpha + \beta$, as one might expect from writing (7.13) as:

$$y_t = \gamma + (\alpha + \beta)\{(1 - \vartheta)x_t + \vartheta x_{t-1}\} \tag{7.15}$$

This difference between A in (7.11) and $(\alpha + \beta)$ in (7.15) is due to the fact that since the autocorrelation of the series for x_t is in practice always less than unity, the variance of the weighted sum of x_t and x_{t-1} is necessarily smaller than that of $x_{t-\vartheta}$. The sum $(\alpha + \beta)$ as estimated from (7.15) is accordingly higher than the estimate of A from (7.11), where $x_{t-\vartheta}$ ought to have a variance equal to that of x_t or x_{t-1}. This situation is illustrated by Fig. 7.2, referring to the output of the iron and steel industry in the period 1901–1913. The variables are measured in first differences of logarithms and, assuming $\vartheta = .37$, $\Delta \log x^*$ is defined as:

$$\Delta \log x^* = .63\Delta \log x_t + .37\Delta \log x_{t-1}$$

As a consequence of the weighting procedure, the standard deviation of $\Delta \log x^*$ is in this case only .058 as against .098 for $\Delta \log x_t$ and .099 for $\Delta \log x_{t-1}$.

To estimate A from (7.15), it clearly is necessary to correct $(\alpha + \beta)$

---

[21] J. TINBERGEN, *Statistical Testing of Business Cycle Theories*, Vol. II: *Business Cycles in the United States of America*, Geneva, 1939, p. 46.

for the difference in variance between x_t and $(1 - \vartheta)x_t + \vartheta x_{t-1}$. The appropriate correction is:[22]

$$A = (\alpha + \beta) \sqrt{1 - 2\vartheta(1 - \vartheta)(1 - \rho_{x_t x_{t-1}})} \qquad (7.16)$$

As is easily seen, the correction term under the square-root sign depends

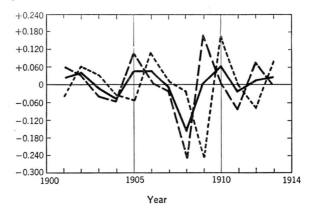

Year

Fig. 7.2. Damped Variance Due to Weighting Subsequent Pairs of Annual Data

− − − Volume of production in the current year (x_t).
------ Ditto, in the preceding year (x_{t-1}).
——— Lagged volume of production $(x^*_{t-\vartheta})$
$(x^*_{t-\vartheta} = .63x_t + .37x_{t-1})$.

All variables are measured as first differences of logarithms.

Source: DOUGLAS, PAUL H.: The Theory of Wages, Chicago, 1934. Statistical Appendix, Table I.

on the size of the lag as well as on the value of ρ, and hence on the average periodicity of the explanatory series, x_t.

The coefficient of autocorrelation, ρ, is calculated as:

$$\rho_{x_t x_{t-1}} = \frac{\Sigma x_t x_{t-1}}{\Sigma x_t^2} \qquad (7.17)$$

---

[22] In order for the variance of the right-hand side of (7.11) to equal that of (7.15), we have, if the variance of x_t is σ_t^2:

$$A^2 \sigma_{t-\vartheta}^2 = (\alpha + \beta)^2 \{(1 - \vartheta)^2 \sigma_t^2 + \vartheta^2 \sigma_{t-1}^2 + 2\rho \vartheta(1 - \vartheta)\sigma_t \sigma_{t-1}\}$$

Assuming further:

$$\sigma_{t-\vartheta} \sim \sigma_t \sim \sigma_{t-1}, \text{ it follows that:}$$

$$A = (\alpha + \beta) \sqrt{(1 - \vartheta)^2 + \vartheta^2 + 2\vartheta(1 - \vartheta)\rho}$$

which leads to (7.16). The same result is obtained by assuming the series for x_t to follow a sinusoidal pattern. See, P. J. VERDOORN, De Verstarring der Productiekosten, Haarlem, 1943, App. B. The more general approach presented here has been suggested by A. P. BARTEN.

If in addition to x_t and x_{t-1} a linear trend term is included in the estimator equation (7.15), the required formula can be shown to be as follows:

$$\rho_{x_t x_{t-1}} = \frac{\Sigma x_t x_{t-1} \Sigma t^2 - \Sigma x_t t \Sigma x_{t-1} t}{\Sigma x^2 \Sigma t^2 - (\Sigma x_t t)^2} \tag{7.18}$$

When ρ is needed for estimating the length of a moving average, (7.18) has to be used if the time series is subject to a trend and (7.17) if it is not.

Table 7.3

CORRECTION FACTOR, $\sqrt{1 - 2\vartheta(1 - \vartheta)(1 - \rho)}$, FOR ESTIMATING THE TOTAL EFFECT OF AN EXPLANATORY VARIABLE WITH A SINGLE LAG

ρ	*Corresponding average period, T*	LAG, ϑ, AS A DECIMAL FRACTION OF THE TIME UNIT				
		0.1 or 0.9	*0.2 or 0.8*	*0.3 or 0.7*	*0.4 or 0.6*	*0.5*
−1.000	2	0.800	0.600	0.400	0.200	0.000
−0.809	2.5	0.821	0.649	0.490	0.363	0.309
−0.500	3	0.854	0.721	0.608	0.529	0.500
−0.222	3.5	0.883	0.780	0.698	0.643	0.624
0	4	0.906	0.825	0.762	0.721	0.707
0.174	4.5	0.923	0.858	0.808	0.777	0.766
0.309	5	0.936	0.882	0.842	0.817	0.809
0.500	6	0.954	0.917	0.889	0.872	0.866
0.623	7	0.966	0.938	0.917	0.905	0.901
0.707	8	0.973	0.952	0.936	0.927	0.924
0.766	9	0.980	0.963	0.952	0.945	0.942
0.809	10	0.983	0.969	0.959	0.953	0.951

Table 7.3 gives values of the reduction factor, $\sqrt{1 - 2\vartheta(1 - \vartheta)(1 - \rho)}$, for alternative combinations of ϑ and of ρ, together with the average period corresponding to ρ as calculated from (7.10).

7.6.3. Distributed Lags

Estimating the effect of a distributed lag can be rather complicated because both the time-path of the reaction and the number of time units involved may still be unknown. As Nerlove aptly puts it:[23]

"Distributed lags arise in theory when any economic cause (for example, a price change or an income change) produces its effect (for example, on the quantity demanded) only after some lag in time; so that this effect is not felt all at once, at a single point of time, but *distributed* over a period of time. Thus, when we say that the quantity of cigarettes demanded is a function of the price of cigarettes taken with a distributed lag, we mean, essentially, that the full effect of a change in the price of cigarettes is not felt immediately, and that only after some passage of time does the quantity of cigarettes demanded show the full effect of the change in the price of cigarettes."

---

[23] MARC NERLOVE, *Distributed Lags and Demand Analysis*, U. S. Department of Agriculture, Agriculture Handbook 141, 1958, p. 4.

To paraphrase an example given by Nerlove, suppose the demand for margarine in a given year (Q_t) is a linear function of the average price of margarine (P) in the current year and of the average price in past years as well, i.e.:

$$Q_t = a + b_0 P_t + b_1 P_{t-1} + b_2 P_{t-2} + \cdots + b_n P_{t-n}$$
$$= a + \sum_0^n b_i P_{t-i} \tag{7.19}$$

Suppose a tax is levied in year t which raises the average price of margarine by, say, dP. The demand function in year, $t + 1$, then becomes:

$$Q_{t+1} = a' + b'_0(P_{t+1} + dP) + b'_1 P_t + b'_2 P_{t-1} + \cdots + b'_n P_{t-n} \tag{7.20a}$$

and in year, $t + 2$:

$$Q_{t+2} = a'' + b''_0(P_{t+2} + dP) + b''_1(P_{t+1} + dP) + \cdots + b''_n P_{t-n}$$
$$\text{etc.} \tag{7.20b}$$

Thus, the effect of the price change is distributed over time, in this case the more so as time moves on.

In a more general sense, product demand could be conjectured to depend on current and past prices (relative perhaps rather than absolute) as well as on current and past incomes (Y) and on other variables (Z), i.e.:

$$Q_t = f(P_t, P_{t-1}, \ldots, Y_t, Y_{t-1}, \ldots, Z_1, Z_2, \ldots) \tag{7.21}$$

In any given case, the problem is to identify the variables that enter into (7.21), specify the form of the relationship, and then estimate the parameters. As applied to the lag terms, this means determining how far back the effect of the lag may have been manifested. Assuming these lags exert causal effects on the dependent variable, this could be interpreted from a statistical point of view as including as many lagged variables as are necessary to maximize the correlation between these variables and the dependent variable.[24] Actually, however, this is a highly empirical point of view, the validity of which would seem to depend on the approach taken to the solution of this problem. (Why?) Essentially, there are three such approaches, to which we now turn.

7.6.3.1. The purely empirical approach. This approach seeks to select the most appropriate distributed lag based solely on empirical tests. Thus, if the function form being used is (7.19), the approach involves successive computation of the regression of quantity on price, adding each time another earlier lagged variable. The procedure stops when the coefficients of the lagged variables begin to show erratic or non-meaningful variations.

---

[24] IRVING FISHER, "Note on a Short-Cut Method for Calculating Distributed Lags," *Buletin de l'Institut International de Statistique*, 1937, pp. 323–328.

This procedure was applied by Alt[25] to measuring the relation between quarterly fuel oil consumption and new orders for 1930–39. Four regressions were computed, the results of which were as follows:

$$Y_t = 8.37 + 0.171X_t \qquad (7.22a)$$
$$Y_t = 8.27 + 0.111X_t + 0.064X_{t-1} \qquad (7.22b)$$
$$Y_t = 8.27 + 0.109X_t + 0.071X_{t-1} - 0.005X_{t-2} \qquad (7.22c)$$
$$Y_t = 8.32 + 0.108X_t + 0.063X_{t-1} + 0.022X_{t-2} - 0.020X_{t-3} \quad (7.22d)$$

Equation (7.22b) was chosen as "best" because the coefficients of X_{t-2} and of X_{t-3} in the two later equations showed symptoms of erratic variation, especially by virtue of the alternating signs of the coefficient of X_{t-2}.

Statistically, this approach tends to yield the "best" results, at least in terms of goodness of fit. The method is also relatively easy to apply, especially if a high-speed computer is available. However, the interpretation of the results is open to question in the sense that no theoretical foundation is advanced to justify the selection of a particular distributed lag. Then, too, use of regression results to specify the period of a distributed lag can be misleading if the lagged variables are highly intercorrelated.

7.6.3.2.   *Specifying the form of the distribution.* By the previous approach, the distribution of the lag over time is determined empirically, as

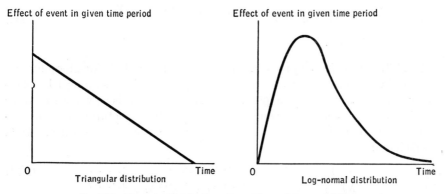

Fig. 7.3. Alternate Distributions Over Time of Lagged Effects

the estimates of the coefficients of the lag terms. An alternate approach is to specify the form of this distribution on the basis of *a priori* reasoning and develop the distributed lag function on the basis of this specification. Thus, a very simple, and often justifiable, assumption is that the effect of a given event over time is approximated by the "triangular distribution." In other words, the effect exerts its maximum influence in the time period in which it

---

[25] Quoted in NERLOVE, *op. cit.* See F. F. ALT, "Distributed Lags," *Econometrica,* Vol. 10 (1942), pp. 113–128.

occurs, and then tapers off in intensity by equal decrements, reaching zero at some future period.[26] The distribution curve is shown in Fig. 7.3.

Logarithmic normal and other exponential curves have also been proposed as possible distributions for lag effects.[27] The former distribution is appropriate if an event exerts relatively small effect at first, rises quickly to a maximum and then gradually tapers off, as shown in Fig. 7.3. (Why not the arithmetic normal curve?) In the latter case, the main influence is assumed to take place in the initial time period, with subsidiary effects following an elongated, inverted-S shape: this may be generally more realistic than the triangular distribution but is achieved only at the expense of a considerable increase in computational effort.

In all of these instances, once the form of the lag function is derived, the trial-and-error regression approach is used, as before, to select the final empirical function. Thus, with the triangular distribution the following successive regressions would be run and the regression with the highest correlation would be selected as "best":

$$Y_t = a + b \frac{2X_t + X_{t-1}}{3} \tag{7.23a}$$

$$Y_t = a + b \frac{3X_t + 2X_{t-1} + X_{t-2}}{6} \tag{7.23b}$$

$$Y_t = a + b \frac{4X_t + 3X_{t-1} + 2X_{t-2} + X_{t-3}}{10} \tag{7.23c}$$

etc.

7.6.3.3.   *Koyck's approach.* An ingenious method of side-stepping this trial-and-error process has been devised by Koyck.[28] Assuming the coefficients for the influence of the previous year to decrease as a geometric rather than as a linear function of time, the corresponding structural equation permits the derivation of a simple estimator equation that is linear in its coefficients:

$$Y_t = \gamma + \beta X_t + \beta\lambda X_{t-1} + \beta\lambda^2 X_{t-2} + \cdots \tag{7.24}$$
$$\lambda Y_{t-1} = \lambda\gamma \qquad + \beta\lambda X_{t-1} + \beta\lambda^2 X_{t-2} + \cdots$$

$$\overline{}$$

$$Y_t = \gamma(1 - \lambda) + \beta X_t + \lambda Y_{t-1} \tag{7.25}$$

Alternatively, instead of (7.25) the form:

$$\Delta Y_t = \gamma(1 - \lambda) + \beta X_t - (1 - \lambda) Y_{t-1} \tag{7.25a}$$

---

[26] FISHER, *op. cit.*

[27] *Ibid.;* also ALT, *op. cit.*

[28] L. R. KOYCK, *Distributed Lags and Investment Analysis*, Amsterdam, 1954, Ch. II. See also L. M. KLEIN, "The Estimation of Distributed Lags," *Econometrica*, October, 1958, pp. 553–566.

can be used as an estimator equation if, for instance, new investment (ΔY_t) is explained as a function of current output (X_t), and total capital stock at the end of the preceding year (Y_{t-1}). If there is no *a priori* preference for a linear as against a geometric formulation of the time shape of the reaction, as is usually the case, (7.25) or (7.25a) recommend themselves strongly from a practical point of view. Practical applications as well as some implications of this approach will be discussed in the next section as well as in Sec. 8.8. Here it may suffice to note that the total influence on Y of a sustained change of X is given in the first instance as the sum of an infinitely decreasing geometric series:

$$A = \frac{\beta}{1 - \lambda}$$

Taking into account the necessity for a reduction as in the case of the single lag (7.16), the total influence of a change in X is estimated from (7.25) or (7.25a) as:

$$A = \frac{\beta}{\sqrt{1 + \lambda^2 - 2\lambda\rho_{y_t y_{t-1}}}} \tag{7.25b}$$

which is discussed in Sec. 8.8.1. (Compare line 8.34 in Table 8.2, p. 374.)

A distributed lag of the form (7.24) implies rapidly decreasing weights for the earlier years. Consequently, beyond a certain point of time, the addition of earlier observations with their corresponding weights has but a very slight effect on Y. A yardstick to evaluate the time required for the effectuation of the first half of the total effect of a sustained change in X is found in the *median time lag*, Θ. A formula for Θ is easily derived as follows. The sum of the first Θ terms of the series β, $\beta\lambda$, $\beta\lambda^2$, . . . , is given by:

$$B_\Theta = \beta \frac{1 - \lambda^\Theta}{1 - \lambda} \tag{7.25c}$$

Since $B_\Theta = \frac{1}{2} A$, it follows from (7.25b) that:

$$1 - \lambda^\Theta = \tfrac{1}{2}$$

and

$$\lambda^\Theta = \tfrac{1}{2}$$

Hence:

$$\Theta = - \frac{log\ 2}{log\ \lambda}$$

If λ, for instance, is found to equal .7, $\Theta = - \dfrac{.301}{-.155}$, or about 2. Half of the total effect of a given change in X will therefore manifest itself within the first two years.

7.6.3.4. *A priori models.* The first approach was almost purely statistical. The preceding approach was part theory (specification of the distribution of the lag) and part statistical (selection of the "best" function). The third approach to be discussed here is accordingly almost purely based on theory. It involves derivation not only of the lag distribution but also of the specific function to be used on the basis of *a priori* reasoning. Statistical analysis is applied only afterward, to test the adequacy of the derived function for explaining the phenomenon under study.

In effect, this approach involves setting up a model to explain the given phenomenon and to yield an equation for empirical testing. As an example of such a model, let us attempt to explain variations in the demand for new cars.[29] This demand can be said to depend on the services desired from automobiles, which is presumably why automobiles are purchased. The flow of services obtained from automobiles can be assumed approximately proportional to their stock, the number of different makes and models in the hands of consumers. The marginal rate of substitution between cars of different ages is assumed to be reflected in the annual rate of depreciation, d, a rate presumed constant for all models and over time. If we add one more assumption, namely, that new car purchases in period t are adjusted for make and model, and can hence be represented by a single variable, X_t, then the stock of automobiles during period t, S_t, is equivalent to:

$$S_t = X_t + (1 - d)X_{t-1} + (1 - d)^2 X_{t-2} + \cdots \qquad (7.26)$$

Since equation (7.26) is a distributed lag function of the same form as equation (7.24), we can perform the same manipulation on it as we did in the former case to obtain:

$$S_t = X_t + (1 - d)S_{t-1} \qquad (7.27)$$

Now we need a demand function. This we obtain by postulating that the demand for the services of automobiles, as manifested by the demand for a certain stock, is dependent upon the price of automobiles (P), real disposable income (Y), and a number of other factors—population, highways, suburbanization—which for simplicity we represent by the single variable, Z. The demand function is, then (assuming a linear homogeneous arithmetic relation):

$$S_t = aP_t + bY_t + cZ_t \qquad (7.28)$$

Substituting (7.28) and (7.28) lagged one time unit in (7.27), we can eliminate S_t and S_{t-1} from (7.27) to obtain:

$$aP_t + bY_t + cZ_t = X_t + (1 - d)(aP_{t-1} + bY_{t-1} + cZ_{t-1})$$

or

$$X_t = aP_t + bY_t + cZ_t - (1 - d)(aP_{t-1} + bY_{t-1} + cZ_{t-1}) \qquad (7.29)$$

[29] Adapted from MARC NERLOVE, *op. cit.*, pp. 89–91.

Under suitable conditions, the parameters of (7.29) would be estimated by least squares of the form:

$$X_t = a'P_t + b'Y_t + c'Z_t + d'P_{t-1} + e'Y_{t-1} + f'Z_{t-1} \qquad (7.30)$$

Given estimates of the parameters of (7.30), the four parameters of (7.29) can be estimated by equating corresponding terms, i.e.:

$$
\begin{aligned}
a &= a' \\
b &= b' \\
c &= c' \\
d &= \frac{d' - a}{a} \quad \text{or} \quad \frac{e' - b}{b} \quad \text{or} \quad \frac{f' - c}{c}
\end{aligned}
\qquad (7.31)
$$

To avoid the awkward situation created by the use of the six equations in (7.31) to estimate the four unknowns in equation (7.29), two additional restraints can be imposed on the coefficients.

By setting up such a model, the question of the nature and form of distributed lag is allowed for. This does not mean that the problem is eliminated, for the lag terms, if any, have to be specified in the model in one way or another. The restraints suggested by Nerlove are:

$$\frac{a}{d'} = \frac{b}{e'} = \frac{c}{f'}$$

Nevertheless, from an analytical point of view, this approach is worth using if for no other reason than that it tends to produce more thorough consideration of the various facets of the problem.

PROBLEMS

1. Listed below are quarterly U. S. consumer durable goods expenditures for 1951–58, in billions of dollars. Derive a seasonal index by:

   a) Link relatives
   b) Ratio-to-moving averages
   c) Moving regression coefficients

Year	I	II	III	IV
1951	7.3	7.2	6.9	8.0
1952	6.1	7.4	6.6	9.0
1953	7.4	8.6	8.2	8.8
1954	7.1	8.2	7.6	9.5
1955	8.7	10.0	9.8	11.1
1956	8.8	9.6	8.9	11.2
1957	9.2	10.1	9.7	11.3
1958	8.3	9.1	8.8	11.4

Source: U. S. Department of Commerce, *U. S. Income and Output*, pp. 154–155; U. S. Department of Commerce, *Survey of Current Business*, July, 1959, p. 18.

2. Discuss the relative merits of fitting a growth curve to the above data

    a) for trend elimination
    b) for trend projection

3. Using the durable goods expenditure data in Problem 1, select a method for segregating cyclical fluctuations and apply it to identifying turning points.

4. What is the average period of the durable goods expenditure series, to judge by the turning point data? Compare this result with that obtained by using the serial correlation coefficient to estimate periodicity.

5. *a*) Write out a complete set of instructions to a research assistant for determining empirically any distributed lags in the relationship between monthly per capita income and monthly per capita retail sales. Assume that a retail price index is the only other variable in the relationship.

    b) Develop an *a priori* model for deriving the distributed lag in income.

6. Income elasticities obtained in time-series consumption studies generally differ systematically from those obtained from comparable cross-section data. Figure out possible reasons for these differences and the probable directions of their effects.

7. Review the pros and cons of distributed lags for analyzing the effect of U. S. Government budget appropriations on business cycles. What alternatives can you suggest as related to different objectives?

8. *a*) Derive an index of cyclical variation for the data shown below on annual ordinary life insurance purchases in U. S. companies (in billions of dollars) by fitting a trend line to the data and computing residuals from the trend. Justify your selection of the trend equation used.

    b) Contrast the above result with that obtained by using first differences of the original data.

    c) Before using these data for extrapolation purposes, what adjustments might be considered?

1921	$ 6.2	1940	$ 7.0
1922	6.7	1941	7.9
1923	8.3	1942	7.0
1924	8.7	1943	8.0
1925	10.1	1944	9.2
1926	10.5	1945	10.6
1927	10.8	1946	16.2
1928	11.7	1947	16.1
1929	12.3	1948	15.8
1930	11.9	1949	15.9
1931	10.2	1950	18.3
1932	7.9	1951	19.0
1933	6.8	1952	21.6
1934	7.4	1953	24.9
1935	7.6	1954	26.8
1936	7.3	1955	32.2
1937	7.6	1956	38.9
1938	6.7	1957	48.9
1939	6.9	1958	50.8

Source: *Life Insurance Fact Book*, 1959, p. 23.

9. Discuss the practical advantages and disadvantages of the segmentation approach to time-series analysis. Illustrate with reference to the analysis of fluctuations in unemployment. Can you suggest any alternative approaches?

10. Using the data in Table 7.1, obtain seasonal adjustment factors by the method of link relatives. Compare the results of this method with those of Wald's method.

11. How might the concept of distributed lags be applied to the measurement of seasonal influences? Illustrate by setting up a model for isolating seasonal factors in monthly retail sales.

12. Indicate what changes would have had to be made in the calculation of seasonal effects by Wald's method (Table 7.1) if ratios-to-moving-average were used rather than deviations from the moving average.

SELECTED REFERENCES

Segmentation and Related Techniques

Most of the texts listed in the references under "Frequency Distributions" in Chapter 3 cover the statistical analysis of time series. About as complete a presentation as is available of the various methods for isolating seasonal, cyclical, and trend elements in time series is available in the text by CROXTON and COWDEN. Other fairly complete discussions of time series analysis will be found in the texts by MILLS, WAUGH, WALLIS and ROBERTS.

A more advanced treatment of time-series analysis will be found in the econometrics texts of TINTNER and TINBERGEN. The latter has a particularly good discussion of trend analysis and growth curves. TINTNER presents various approaches to trend analysis including the use of orthogonal polynomials and the transformation of series into differences to eliminate trend. This book also has a very good presentation of the more sophisticated means of isolating cycles, such as periodogram analysis and correlogram analysis.

Perhaps the most detailed analysis of time series, presented from a mathematical point of view, is *The Analysis of Economic Time Series* by H. T. DAVIS (Bloomington: The Principia Press, 1941). This book contains considerable material with examples of the fitting of different types of trends to economic data.

An earlier reference on the segmentation principle with applications to business cycle analysis, and still very much current, is *Economic Fluctuations in the United States* by E. FRICKEY (Cambridge: Harvard University Press, 1942). A fairly thorough discussion of the application of moving averages to time-series data will be found in an even earlier reference, *The Smoothing of Time Series* by F. R. MACAULEY (New York: National Bureau of Economic Research, 1931). The application of electronic computers to the measurement of seasonal variation is discussed in considerable detail in *Seasonal Adjustments by Electronic Computer Methods* by JULIUS SHISKIN and H. EISENPRESS (New York: National Bureau of Economic Research, 1958). This publication also illustrates how fixed regression coefficients may be applied to the measurement of seasonal variation.

The reference cycle approach to cyclical variation is described clearly in *Measuring Business Cycles* by A. F. BURNS and W. C. MITCHELL (New York: National Bureau of Economic Research, 1946). For a discussion of the pros and cons of the approach, see the August, 1947, and May, 1949, issues of the *Review of Economics and Statistics*.

The problems introduced by serial correlation in economic time series are discussed in the texts by EZIEKIEL and FOX, and FERBER.

The use of variance analysis as a means of trend determination is covered in the texts by R. A. FISHER and FERBER.

Lags

A well-written general introduction to the measurement and use of lags in monthly data will be found in Chapter 22 of the text by CROXTON and COWDEN. A rigorous approach to the measurement of the average period is presented in *Elements of Statistics* by H. T. DAVIS and W. F. C. NELSON (Bloomington: Principia Press, 1937, pages 137–140). The estimation of the average profile of a business cycle index is illustrated by "The Short-term Business Cycle" by C. E. ARMSTRONG (*Review of Economic Statistics*, May, 1936, pages 62–66).

A very clear summary of the various means of measuring distributed lags will be found in *Distributed Lags and Demand Analysis* by MARC NERLOVE (U. S. Department of Agriculture, 1958). Individual approaches to the measurement of distributed lags will be found in the article by IRVING FISHER, "A Note on a Short-Cut Method for Calculating Distributed Lags," (*Buletin de L'Institut International de Statistique*, 1937, pages 323–328) and in the article by F. F. ALT, "Distributed Lags" (*Econometrica*, 1942, pages 113–128). The monograph by L. N. KOYCK, *Distributed Lags and Investment Analysis* (Amsterdam: North Holland Publishing Company, 1954) presents a summary of these methods as well as a detailed presentation of the ingenious technique devised by the author to circumvent the problem of infinite lags. An alternative method has been developed in a forthcoming book by FRANKLIN FISHER, *A Priori Information and Time Series* (Amsterdam: North-Holland Publishing Co).

8 | Special Applications of Time-Series Analysis: Demand Analysis

THE USE of time-series analysis for the purpose of measuring and establishing systematic relationships is manifold and widespread. In the case of individual products, the derivation of demand and price equations are well-known examples, while, in the case of such aggregates as national income, the construction of forecasting and policy models has been attempted with varying degrees of success.

In estimating the coefficients of a particular relationship, either complete model systems or a single-equation approach can be used. In the first case, the coefficients of all equations constituting the model are estimated simultaneously. In the second, estimates are restricted to coefficients entering that particular equation. As will be shown, simultaneous estimation with equation systems has certain theoretical advantages over the single-equation approach. This is true even in instances such as estimating the demand equation for a single product. Nevertheless, practical, useful estimates of model systems for individual products are as yet scarce, partly because of lack of data. Especially in the area of demand analysis, however, such applications are likely to be much more numerous in the future.

Since price analysis has been discussed already in Sec. 4.3, the present chapter deals with demand analysis, concentrating on the single-equation approach. Modifications required in the case of complete model systems are discussed as part of the following chapter.

8.1. SPECIFICATION OF VARIABLES

The aim of empirical demand functions is to explain as fully as possible the changes in demand over time. For this purpose it is necessary to specify

353

in advance the variables that affect demand for the product under consideration. Here either theoretical or practical considerations may serve to detect the variables that are to be included in the demand function.

From a theoretical and policy-making point of view, the hero (or culprit) of many demand investigations is *price*. As noted in Chapter 4, however, one cannot hope to find a meaningful price-quantity relationship by comparing time series for these two variables alone. All that results in such a case is a

Log of volume

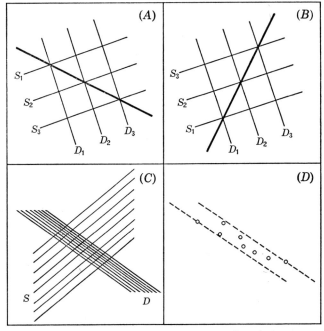

Fig. 8.1. *Effect of Shifting Demand and Supply Curves on Estimation of Demand Relationships*
S: supply curves; D: demand curves.
Subscripts denote points of time.

picture of the general direction of the "historical path" of the points of intersection of a shifting demand curve with a supply curve that, likewise, is subject to shifts. If an increase in demand due to non-price factors coincides with contracting supply, this path may be inclined negatively, as shown by Fig. 8.1A. If, on the other hand, the same favorable shift in demand is accompanied by expanding supply, the inclination may just as well be positive (Fig. 8.1B) although the elasticities of demand and supply are the same in either situation.

Only where the amplitude of the shifts in one of the two curves is small relative to that of the other can meaningful results be anticipated. This applies, for example, to some agricultural products where changes in crop size surpass considerably demand fluctuations resulting from cyclical change. This situation is depicted by Figs. 8.1C and 8.1D. But even in a case like this the statistical series for volume and price require careful processing in order to isolate the effect of price on demand from those of other, intervening factors. Thus, effective demand generally has to be calculated in per capita terms whereas prices ought to be deflated by dividing by a cost-of-living index. In order to eliminate long-term tendencies on the demand and supply side, the use of either trend elimination or first differences may be desirable.[1] (These two devices will be discussed later in this section.)

With due exception for certain agricultural and related products, this approach, as a rule, tends to produce inadequate results. From a theoretical point of view, the obvious approach to demand analysis as well as to price analysis would be recourse to simultaneous estimation and, more specifically, the *reduced-form approach* as illustrated by equations (4.20) and (4.21) in Section 4.3. In the simple case presented there, it is possible to derive the four coefficients of the original demand and supply equations (i.e., the "structural equations" 4.18 and 4.19) from the estimates of the four coefficients of the reduced-form equations (4.20) and (4.21). As is often the fate of theoretically elegant solutions, however, this particular approach has seldom met with success in deriving demand equations for individual products. The noteworthy exception to this rule is Tintner's analysis of processed meat. His indirect estimates of the coefficients of the demand and supply equations as derived from the reduced-form coefficients are:[2]

| | ELASTICITIES WITH REGARD TO | | |
	Price	*Income*	*Cost of processing*
Demand equation	− .79	+ .56	
Supply equation	+ .35		− .22

A practical obstacle in applying this method is that it often proves impossible to compute the structural coefficients of the demand equation from those of the price and volume equations of the reduced form. Apart from this, the standard errors of the coefficients of the structural equation tend to be fairly large, whereas errors in the specification of variables included in the structural equations may influence the results unduly as compared with a direct estimate of the demand equation itself.

Presumably because of these difficulties, direct estimates of the demand equation are as yet predominant. In order to avoid meaningless results it is

---

[1] The best known work along these lines is that of HENRY SCHULTZ, *The Theory and Measurement of Demand*, Chicago, 1938. His results refer to the price elasticity of demand with regard to wholesale prices of a diversity of such agricultural products as barley, wheat, sugar, cotton, buckwheat, and hay.

[2] G. TINTNER, *Econometrics*, pp. 170–172.

accordingly imperative that in addition to prices other relevant factors governing demand are introduced into the demand equation. Even though we may be interested only in the price elasticity of demand as such, the inclusion of the other relevant factors remains a *sine qua non*, as long as least-squares estimates are applied to the demand equation.

Focusing our attention on consumer goods, one of the more important of these other factors is the general level of *consumption prices* measured at the retail level. As a rule, a cost-of-living index is used for this purpose. A second important factor is real disposable personal income, i.e., aggregate private income less corporate savings and net of direct taxes, corrected for changes in the cost of living. Disregarding other more specific factors as well as trend, one form of the demand equation is:

$$v = \gamma y^\beta p^\epsilon q^\eta \tag{8.1}$$

where:

   v = demand, measured in physical units (or alternatively, deflated demand, such as value of total sales divided by a retail price index),
   y = real disposable income,
   p = unit price of v (alternatively, a retail-price index of v),
   q = cost of living index.

As shown in Sec. 4.3, the exponents β, ϵ and η are computed as the coefficients of the multiple linear regression of log v upon log y, log p and log q. They represent the elasticities of v with regard to y, p and q. The use of the exponential relationship yields constant elasticities, whereas using a linear equation:

$$v = \beta^* y + \epsilon^* p + \eta^* q + \gamma^* \tag{8.2}$$

constant regression coefficients result. Thus, with the linear expression (8.2) we obtain a constant marginal propensity to consume, $\beta^* = \dfrac{\partial v}{\partial y}$, whereas in equation (8.1) the income elasticity is assumed to be constant: $\beta = \dfrac{\partial v}{\partial y}\dfrac{y}{v}$. In the case of time series, as pointed out by Schultz, both approaches tend to give approximately the same results, if the elasticity in the linear case is computed for the average values $(\bar{v}, \bar{y},)$ of v and y. The reason is, that "*within the neighborhood of the representative point* on the demand curve there is no very significant difference between the fits of several types of curves."[3]

In equation (8.1) the exponent β of y therefore clearly represents the average value of the income elasticity if y can be taken to represent per capita or per family income. Less clear, however, is the interpretation of ϵ and η. Economic theory assumes a relationship between demand, the price of the product concerned, and all other prices. According to Sec. 4.3, the formula

---

[3] H. Schultz, *op. cit.*, p. 557.

for the price elasticity of demand as derived by Allen and Hicks, is:

$$\epsilon_{vp} = -w\beta + (1 - w)\epsilon_{vr} \tag{8.3}$$

where ϵ_{vp} and ϵ_{vr} are respectively the price elasticity of demand and the price elasticity of substitution with regard to the price (r) of all other products, w denoting the share of the consumer's total expenditure on v. This raises the question how the price elasticities, ϵ and η, of equation (8.1) can be interpreted in terms of the parameters of the Allen and Hicks equation (8.3).

If we suppose that the demand equation had been of the form:

$$v = \gamma y^\beta p^{\epsilon'} r^{\eta'} \tag{8.4}$$

so as to relate v to r instead of to q, a relation with (8.3) is easily established by introducing money income ($Y = yq$) instead of real income (y) as an explanatory variable. Let us assume, for argument's sake, that the deflator, q, of money income is measured as the weighted geometric index of all prices:

$$q = p^w r^{1-w} \tag{8.5}$$

This makes it possible to write equation (8.4) as:

$$v = \gamma Y^\beta p^{\epsilon'-w\beta} r^{\eta'-(1-w)\beta} \tag{8.6}$$

In this equation the exponent of p represents the price elasticity of demand. It therefore equals the right-hand side of (8.3):

$$\epsilon' - w\beta = -w\beta + (1 - w)\epsilon_{vr} \tag{8.7}$$

and consequently:[4]

$$\epsilon' = \epsilon_{vr}(1 - w) \tag{8.8}$$

With regard to η', it should be borne in mind that the Allen and Hicks formula presupposes the consumer to be fully aware of price changes and, moreover, to react rationally. As long as his total purchasing power (y) remains the same, a one per cent increase in r must then have the same effect as a one per cent decrease in q. This condition will be referred to as the *proportionality condition*. It implies that the coefficients of p and r have the same numerical value but the opposite sign:

$$\eta' = -\epsilon' \tag{8.9}$$

Taking into account (8.8) and (8.9), the price elasticities of (8.4) can now be expressed in the parameters of the Allen and Hicks formula:

$$v = \gamma y^\beta p^{\epsilon_{vr}(1-w)} r^{-\epsilon_{vr}(1-w)} \tag{8.10}$$

According to (8.5), $r = q^{\frac{1}{1-w}} p^{\frac{w}{1-w}}$. Hence, r in (8.10) can be replaced by a function of q and p:

$$v = \gamma y^\beta p^{\epsilon_{vr}} q^{-\epsilon_{vr}} \tag{8.11}$$

[4] See R. STONE, "The Analysis of Market Demand," *Journal of the Royal Statistical Society*, Vol. CVIII, Parts 3 and 4, Sec. 2.3.2.1.

Comparison of the coefficients of (8.11) with those of (8.1) shows that:

$$\epsilon = -\eta = \epsilon_{vr} \qquad (8.12)$$

The important conclusion therefore is that, regardless of the share of the product studied in the consumer's total outlay, ϵ equals the price elasticity of substitution and η must have the very same absolute value but the opposite sign. This conclusion, however, is subject to two restrictions. First, that the assumption of rational behavior and price awareness is justified for the product under consideration; second, that the cost-of-living index can reasonably be approximated by the geometric average of all retail prices.

Taking these requirements for granted, the obvious thing to do, therefore, would seem to be to replace (8.1) by the simpler form:

$$v = \gamma y^\beta (p/q)^\epsilon \qquad (8.13)$$

However, the cost-of-living index, q, is not normally a weighted geometric average, but some other type of index number. More important is the fact that the proportionality conditions, although acceptable from the static-equilibrium point of view, do not necessarily apply to those cases either where the process of adaptation to a new equilibrium level takes time or where the condition of perfect price awareness is not actually fulfilled. With regard to the latter, one could imagine, for example, consumers to be less price conscious in the case of habitually bought items that imply only a small outlay at the time. Conversely, they might be much more price conscious in the case of durables bought at rare intervals. If consumers do react in this way we would expect $-\epsilon < \eta$ in the first case and $-\epsilon > \eta$ in the latter.[5] For this reason one is, as a rule, not justified in forcing $-\epsilon$ and η into equality, and independent estimates of both ϵ and η are to be preferred wherever possible.

Apart from the three variables just discussed, a *trend* usually has to be added as a fourth. Including the latter, the demand equation becomes:

$$v = \gamma y^\beta p^\epsilon q^\eta e^{\rho t} \qquad (8.14)$$

where e denotes the base of the natural logs, viz., 2.718 . . . , and ρ the approximate annual rate of growth, measured as a decimal fraction (see Sec. 7.4). It should be remembered that if v is measured in logarithms to the base 10 (as is usually the case) and not in natural logs, the regression coefficient is: $\dfrac{\partial \log_{10} v}{\partial t}$. To find the value of ρ, the latter magnitude has to be multiplied by $\dfrac{1}{\log_{10} e}$ or 2.303, as noted in Sec. 7.4.2.1.

When included with other variables in a regression equation, it is customary to call $e^{\rho t}$ a "residual trend" and the estimating procedure with the help

---

[5] See, for example, R. STONE, *op. cit.*, Sec. 2.3.3.3 and 5.1.8.

of the latter "time-regression." The trend serves as a "catch-all" to represent the aggregate effect of the trend components of all factors affecting demand not included explicitly in the equation, such as population growth, technical and institutional developments with concomitant changes in consumers' preference scales, etc.

Since the exact nature of the component parts of the residual trend is not known, it is often desirable to insert those components that are known as so many variables in the equation, in order to reduce the degree of uncertainty with regard to extrapolation. The easiest factor to deal with is population growth, by dividing both v and y by total population or, depending upon the character of the product,[6] by the number of households. Denoting total population (or households) by P, (8.14) becomes:

$$\frac{v}{P} = \gamma \left(\frac{y}{P}\right)^{\beta} p^{\epsilon} q^{\eta} e^{\rho t} \tag{8.15}$$

Equations (8.14) and (8.15) can be considered as the *general form of the demand function*. Depending on the specific requirements of the product studied, other factors have to be added, of course. Some of these specific factors will be discussed summarily below.

Of the two general forms just given, (8.15) at first sight may seem the more correct since the income elasticity refers to income per head or per household rather than to total income. An increase of average income by, say x per cent, that is not accompanied by a change in population increases demand by βx per cent. But the same increase of total income due to an x per cent expansion of population, average income remaining the same, augments demand not by βx per cent but by the same x per cent. If, however, total population expands gradually, the trend term in (8.14) guarantees that this equation yields essentially the same numerical value for β as (8.15). The principal merit of (8.15), consequently, is a reduction of the algebraic value of the trend coefficient, ρ, and hence a better demarcation of the no man's land represented by the latter. But if no trend term is included, the computation of v and y on a per capita or per household basis becomes essential for a correct interpretation of β.

8.2. DISTRIBUTION OF INCOME

The use of either (8.14) or (8.15) assumes that demand is influenced by changes in average income. In addition, shifts in income distribution also will affect the pattern of demand to a certain extent. One reason for this is that the Engel curves describing the relation between consumption and income

---

[6] See Sec. 4.2.1.

tend to be curvilinear, as shown by Fig. 4.4 (Sec. 4.2). Although these curves can, as a rule, be approximated by a double-log function over a large range, changes in distribution of income, especially in the highest and lowest brackets, can alter demand even if average income remains unaffected.

A second reason is that the demand reactions of different groups of income-earners are not necessarily the same even within the same income brackets. Thus the consumption habits of farmers are not the same as those of city workers. Apart from this, consumption habits based on non-wage income may be more "sticky" than those of manual workers and employees, at least downward.

Since changes in distribution of income often closely parallel those in average income, or take place but gradually, their influence will be represented partly by β and partly by ρ in many cases. In other instances, however, it may be desirable to include shifts in income distribution as a special factor in the demand equation. One way to do this is to use a series representing a parameter of a theoretical function describing the frequency distribution of income. This method relies, therefore, upon the *interpersonal* distribution of income. Although the Pareto curve admittedly does not represent very well the slope of the cumulative distribution at its lowest and highest levels, its coefficient, α, might in some cases serve well as a general indication, particularly of changes in distribution within the intermediate brackets.[7]

Nevertheless, Pareto's α will prove inadequate if income elasticities for the extreme brackets differ considerably from those in the intermediate ranges. With regard to the highest brackets, the suggestion therefore has been advanced to insert in the demand equation in addition to average total income $\left(\dfrac{y}{P}\right)$ also the share received by, say, the upper 5% of all income-earners, thereby leading to the following demand function:[8]

$$v = \gamma \left(\frac{y}{P}\right)^{\beta_1} \left(\frac{y_1}{y}\right)^{\beta_2} \tag{8.16}$$

Here y_1 denotes the income of the upper 5 per cent of all taxpayers.[9] If we write demand as an explicit function of the average incomes $(\bar{y}_1, \bar{y}_2)$ of respectively the upper μ per cent and of the lower $(1 - \mu)$ per cent of all income-receivers, we have:

$$v = \gamma y_1^\kappa y_2^\lambda \tag{8.17}$$

---

[7] See Sec. 3.1 and Fig. 3.2.

[8] R. FERBER, "A Statistical Study of Factors Influencing Temporal Variations in Aggregate Service Expenditures," in Lincoln H. Clark, ed., *Consumer Behavior: Research in Consumer Reactions* (New York: Harper & Bros., 1958), pp. 394–419.

[9] Data on the percentage distribution of income at the higher income levels are given by S. KUZNETS, *Shares of Upper Income Groups in Income and Savings* (New York: National Bureau of Economic Research, 1953).

It is easy to show[10] that:

$$\beta_1 \sim \kappa + \lambda \tag{8.18a}$$

and
$$\beta_2 \sim \kappa - \frac{\lambda\mu}{1 - \mu} \tag{8.18b}$$

For this reason β_2 in equation (8.16) tends to become a small negative figure if the marginal propensity to consume in the upper brackets, and consequently also κ, approaches zero. The term with y_1, therefore, serves essentially as a cleaning variable.

Apart from the poor fit of the Pareto curve, an additional difficulty arises with the lowest income brackets. Frequency distributions of personal income are often based on income-tax returns. The latter, however, do not take into account incomes and people below the tax exemption limit. Due to strong curvilinearity of the Engel curves when income becomes very low, Pareto's α tells only part of the story in periods of severe changes in unemployment.[11] In such times, the number of unemployed as a percentage of the gainfully occupied or total dependent working population might therefore serve as a correction-factor for average income.

Another approach, often applied successfully in the construction of business-cycle models and in market research, makes use of the *functional* distribution of income, i.e., of a partitioning as to sources of income.[12] The two main categories generally distinguished are wage income (L) and non-wage income (Z), the latter comprising such items as paid-out profits and dividends, interest and rent. By this formulation, (8.14) becomes:

$$v = \gamma \left(\frac{L}{q}\right)^{\beta_1} \left(\frac{Z}{q}\right)^{\beta_2} p^\epsilon q^\eta e^{\rho t} \tag{8.19}$$

One advantage of this distinction is that major differences in income elasticity are taken into account. A second advantage is that it becomes easier to allow for the stickiness of non-labor expenditure by using a time lag. Also, for those products where expenditures out of farm income play a considerable role, it may be desirable to separate farm income from non-farm income, introducing a special variable for the former. In that case L and Z in (8.19) would refer to the non-farm share of disposable income. Difficulties to be expected with the practical application of (8.19) as a result of multicollinearity will be discussed below.

---

[10] On the condition that $\frac{y}{P} \sim \zeta \bar{y}_1^\mu \bar{y}_2^{1-\mu}$, where ζ, here assumed constant, represents a multiplicative correction for the difference between the geometric and arithmetic mean.

[11] See Sec. 4.2, particularly Fig. 4.4.

[12] See KLEIN and GOLDBERGER, *An Econometric Model of the United States, 1929–52*, p. 51.

8.3.   CLOSELY COMPETING PRODUCTS

The elasticity of substitution, $\epsilon = \epsilon_{vr}$ in (8.12), refers to all other items of the consumer's budget. Hence, it can be considered as a weighted average of all the elasticities of substitution with regard to these other products. The numerical values of these elasticities can be either high or low, according to the existing possibilities of direct substitution. Since there is nothing to guarantee perfectly parallel movement of the prices of closely competing products with the cost-of-living index, there is a strong argument for introducing into the demand equation prices of competing products wherever the latter are of sufficient importance. The relative importance of the price-volume substitution to be expected from a one per cent change in the price of a competing product—say the jth product—is not only determined by the elasticity of substitution between the product studied (v_1) and the jth product, but also by the share of the latter in total consumer outlays. Denoting this share by w_j, the cross-elasticity concerned can be written as: $\epsilon_j = w_j \epsilon_{vp_j}$.

Taking into account the prices of the competing products, 2, 3, . . . , etc., the demand equation, at least as far as prices are concerned, takes the form:

$$v_1 = \gamma p_1{}^{\epsilon_1} p_2{}^{\epsilon_2} p_3{}^{\epsilon_3} \ldots q^{\eta} \tag{8.20}$$

where p_1 and ϵ_1 represent the price and the price elasticity of substitution of v_1 with regard to all other products, $p_2, p_3, \ldots$, and $\epsilon_2, \epsilon_3, \ldots$, the prices and cross-elasticities of the separately specified competing products, and q and η, the cost-of-living index and the price-substitution elasticity of v_1 with regard to all other products, except the specified ones.

Presupposing again perfect price awareness and rational behavior throughout, the proportionality condition would require in the present case:

$$-\epsilon_1 = \epsilon_2 + \epsilon_3 + \cdots + \eta \tag{8.21}$$

Starting from (8.21), as we are often obliged to do as a consequence of intercorrelation, (8.20) can be written alternatively as:[13]

$$v_1 = \gamma \left(\frac{p_1}{q}\right)^{\epsilon_1} \left(\frac{p_2}{q}\right)^{\epsilon_2} \left(\frac{p_3}{q}\right)^{\epsilon_3} \cdots \tag{8.22}$$

The necessity of introducing prices of competing goods depends upon the characteristics of the product studied. In the case of major aggregates, such as total expenditures on clothing, possibilities of direct substitution are less than for individual products. Particularly with individual foods, price substitution plays an important role, and is often found where it would not have

---

[13] See R. STONE, *The Measurement of Consumers' Expenditure and Behaviour in the United Kingdom, 1920–1938*, Cambridge, 1954, Vol. I, pp. 262, 277–278, 321.

Table 8.1

PRICE-VOLUME SUBSTITUTION FOR CONDENSED MILK, UNITED KINGDOM, 1928–38[a]

SUBSTITUTION ELASTICITY WITH REGARD TO

Equation number[b]	Income elasticity[c]	Own price	Fresh milk price	Tea price	Margarine price	Cheese price	All other products	Residual trend coefficient	R^2[d]
(1)	(2)	(3)	(4)	(5)	(6)	(7)	(8)	(9)	(10)
52	−.53 (.18)	−.60 (.55)	—	—	—	—	.60 (.55)	−.011 (.032)	.07
53	−.53 (.18)	−.78 (.55)	1.40 (.95)	—	—	—	−.62 (.99)	−.029 (.031)	.19
58	−.53 (.18)	−1.27 (.55)	1.87 (.91)	1.09 (.55)	—	—	−1.69 (1.04)	−.063 (.028)	.37
63	−.53 (.18)	−1.31 (.37)	2.14 (.61)	1.34 (.38)	1.03 (.24)	—	−3.20 (.78)	−.056 (.019)	.74
67	−.53 (.18)	−1.23 (.32)	2.25 (.53)	1.06 (.35)	.80 (.23)	.43 (.19)	−3.32 (.68)	−.047 (.016)	.82

[a] The analysis is based upon the first differences of the logarithms. The standard errors of the elasticities are given between parentheses.
[b] Stone, *op. cit.*, Table 106.
[c] *A priori* coefficient based upon family-expenditure statistics.
[d] Since an *a priori* coefficient has been used to represent the influence of income, R^2 in this case shows the proportion of the variance of the first differences of demand adjusted for the influence of income, which is accounted for by the price variables.

Source: R. STONE, *The Measurement of Consumers' Expenditure and Behaviour in the United Kingdom, 1920–1938*, Cambridge, 1954, Vol. 1, Table 106, pp. 323–324.

been expected on *a priori* grounds. The substitution between such products as cheese and meat, investigated by Staehle,[14] serves as an example. For this reason, a detailed study of consumption habits is a prerequisite to adequate specification of a demand function.

The dependence of demand for one product on prices of competing products is illustrated by an analysis by Stone of the demand for condensed milk in the United Kingdom. As shown by Table 8.1, relative price alone, $\left(\dfrac{p}{q}\right)$, contributes virtually nothing to the explanation of fluctuations in demand.

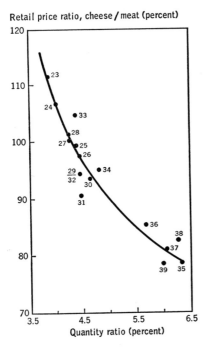

Fig. 8.2. *Substitution Between Cheese and Meat*

Source: H. Staehle, *loc. cit.*

It is only after the introduction of the prices of fresh milk and tea as directly competing products that the value found for ϵ approaches significance at the .05 level. A satisfactory overall explanation is possible if margarine and cheese prices are taken into account.

The income elasticity, β, as shown by Column 2 is not estimated from time series but has been derived from family-expenditure statistics, a device that will be explained below. Its negative value ($-.53$) suggests that condensed milk in the country and period studied must have been considered

[14] H. STAEHLE, "Relative Prices and Postwar Markets for Animal Food Products," *Quarterly Journal of Economics*, February, 1945, p. 263.

as an inferior product. The elasticity with regard to "all other products," η, (Column 8) has been estimated on the assumption of proportionality. It therefore equals the sum, with attached negative sign, of the other price-elasticities. The value of η, however, need not necessarily be positive. Prices of competing products remaining the same, an increase in the cost of living will lower the relative price of the latter and hence promote substitution.

A preliminary method often used to investigate the existence of price-volume substitution between two products is to plot the volume ratios (v_1/v_j) of the products concerned against their price ratios (p_1/p_j), as illustrated in Fig. 8.2. The appearance of a well-defined negative slope can be taken as an indication that the products are mutually competing. It therefore points to the desirability of including p_j as a separate variable in the demand equation of v_1. On the other hand, this preliminary test cannot establish the reverse. If, for example, the income elasticities or trend coefficients show markedly different values for the two products concerned, this fact alone may well overshadow the price-volume substitution.

Nevertheless, this method has sometimes been used successfully in the case of international trade to study the price-substitution relationship between the exports of the same product from two countries to a third one, or that between imports and home production in the home market.[15] Another field where this device might be employed is price competition between two firms on the same product. Recorded, successful attempts are, unfortunately, very few as a consequence of changes in quality and promotional effort that are difficult to measure. One example, however, will be given later on.

8.4. COMPLEMENTARY PRODUCTS

With products and services like telephones and telephone-calls, or cameras and films, the possession or use of some other product or service (v_2) can be a prerequisite for the use of the product under analysis (v_1). In such a case, an adequate explanation of v_1 may require the introduction in the demand equation of a new variable representing the critical influence of v_2. What variable to select for this purpose is more often than not a matter of judicious choice. Thus, the best explanation of the demand for car tires is no doubt found by including total vehicle miles as an explaining variable. Apart from a slight influence of income due to the flexibility of average miles per tire, the relationship found will then be largely a technological one. Though the latter may yield a technical coefficient of great importance, the main economic problem still remains unsolved until a satisfactory explanation for total vehicle-mileage has been found. In cases like this an explanation in two stages

---

[15] See, J. Tinbergen, *Econometrics*, pp. 133–137.

might therefore prove the best approach toward a *complete* explanation of the demand for v_1.

In seemingly less complicated cases, the choice of the variable representing complementarity is not always self-evident. Trial-and-error may then be the best approach. In explaining the aggregate category of services labelled as "user-operated transportation" (comprising such items as automobile servicing, parking, rental and insurance), the number of automobiles in use, total vehicle miles per year, and the age distribution of cars may all seem equally suitable. However, after experimentation with each of these variables, the proportion of passenger vehicles more than three years old turned out to be the only variable next to disposable income to have a significant influence upon demand.[16]

8.5.   QUALITY CHANGES

Homogeneity of the product and constancy of quality during the period of observation are usually two tacit assumptions underlying demand analysis. Actually, even with single products changes in quality either of the product itself or those of close competitors are apt to occur quite frequently. In either case, "shifts" of the demand function are the inevitable result as quality alterations affect the consumer's preference schedules and consequently the level of demand at given incomes and prices. In addition, apart from the level of demand as represented by γ in (8.14), such changes may also affect the income and price elasticities. Since quality characteristics are seldom measurable, one is lucky if a suitable index for an important aspect of the product's quality can be found. Stone, working on the hypothesis that " . . . more beer will be drunk if stronger, and to that extent better, beer is obtainable at a given price," used annual average gravity as a quality indicator representing "strength." The subsequent analysis showed a significant partial correlation of consumption in bulk barrels on average gravity, thus confirming his *a priori* expectations.[17]

Another example illustrating the influence of quality upon a firm's competitive position is given by Brems. Analyzing new car registrations, the ratio between Ford and Chevrolet registrations (v_F/v_C) are explained not only by the ratio between the corresponding prices (p_F/p_C), but also by that of the maximum brake horsepower (h_F/h_C), the latter serving as an index of quality:[18]

---

[16] R. FERBER, "A Statistical Study of Factors Influencing Temporal Variations in Aggregate Service Expenditures," *op. cit.*, pp. 400 and 407, Table 2.

[17] R. STONE, *The Measurement of Consumers' Expenditure and Behaviour in the United Kingdom*, 1954, Vol. I, pp. 180, 388, and Table 110, p. 390.

[18] H. BREMS, *Product Equilibrium Under Monopolistic Competition*, Cambridge, Mass., 1951, pp. 36–46.

$$\frac{v_F}{v_C} = .782 \left(\frac{p_F}{p_C}\right)^{-1.79} \left(\frac{h_F}{h_C}\right)^{1.51} \qquad (8.23)$$

The equation suggests that in the period concerned (1932–50) a 1 per cent reduction of Ford's prices relative to that of Chevrolet was accompanied by an improvement in Ford's competitive position of 1.79 per cent. A one per cent increase in Ford's relative quality as measured by the horsepower ratio tended to result in a 1.51 per cent increase in the relative position of Ford.

In the majority of cases, however, simple indicators like those just mentioned are not available. We can only hope then that quality has changed but gradually and thus is taken care of in a satisfactory way by ρ, the coefficient of the residual trend.

If the analysis deals with an aggregate of heterogeneous products, difficulties may arise over the interpretation of the income and price elasticities. With heterogeneous categories of products, it is usual to estimate the volume series by dividing either an unweighted unit-price or a weighted price index into the total value of sales. If the latter procedure is followed, the volume series represents not only changes in the number of items sold but also changes in quality, since demand is measured not in physical units but in equivalent sales per deflated dollar. The number of units sold per equivalent dollar varies inversely with changes in the quality that the consumer happens to prefer. To a large extent these changes are induced either by shifts in income per capita or by shifts in the level of relative prices. In the latter case, we have the phenomenon of price-quality substitution: if the weighted average price of a certain category of products rises faster than that of other categories, consumers may shift to lower-priced items within the same category.

As for the income effect, it was noted already (Sec. 4.2.2.2) that the average price paid can often be approximated as a semi-logarithmic function of income. The interpretation of the elasticities β and ϵ is moreover complicated by the fact that their numerical value depends not only upon the deflator of money sales but also upon the price series used for estimating ϵ.

The type of analysis required for the interpretation of the coefficients in a given case can be illustrated as follows. Let the effect on volume of, say, purchases of women's dresses, regardless of the price brackets in which they are sold, be governed by the structural equation:

$$v = \gamma' y^{\beta'} \left(\frac{\bar{p}}{q}\right)^{\epsilon'} \qquad (8.24)$$

where v represents demand in physical units,

$\bar{p}$ is a fixed-weight price index of all women's dresses,

y represents real income per head,

q is the cost-of-living index.

If $\tilde{p}$ is not known, we can choose as an estimating equation:

$$v = \gamma y^\beta \left(\frac{p}{q}\right)^\epsilon \tag{8.25}$$

where v is again the number of dresses, and p the average unit price obtained by dividing y into total sales value. Now, we may assume that average unit prices are governed by a structural relation of the form:

$$p \sim \pi \tilde{p} y^\zeta \left(\frac{\tilde{p}}{q}\right)^\xi \tag{8.26}$$

where ξ represents the elasticity of price-quality substitution. Its algebraic value is therefore negative. The second exponent, ζ, can be approximated by the average value of the price-income elasticity measured over the relevant interval of the semi-logarithmic price-income function. Starting from (8.26) we can write p as an explicit function of $\tilde{p}$, y and q, and substitute this function in the right-hand side of (8.24). Rearrangement of the exponents results in:

$$v = \gamma \pi^{-\frac{\epsilon'}{1+\xi}} y^{\beta' - \frac{\epsilon'\zeta}{1+\xi}} \left(\frac{p}{q}\right)^{\frac{\epsilon'}{1+\xi}} \tag{8.27}$$

Comparing (8.27) with the estimator equation (8.25), the coefficients of the latter can be expressed in terms of the coefficients ϵ' and β' of the structural equation (8.24):

$$\beta = \beta' - \frac{\epsilon'\zeta}{1+\xi} \tag{8.28}$$

$$\epsilon = \frac{\epsilon'}{1+\xi} \tag{8.29}$$

In this case, β will be larger than might have been expected on the basis of pure volume data obtained from, say, budget statistics. It will therefore represent neither the increase of volume-sales to be expected with a one per cent increase of real income per head, nor need it equal exactly the (deflated) value increase, unless $-\dfrac{\epsilon'}{1+\xi}$ happens to equal unity, which will not generally be the case. The numerical value of ϵ will also surpass that of the structural elasticity of substitution, ϵ', since $\xi < 0$. A reliable prediction of the effect of income and price changes upon the value and volume of demand requires therefore that their effects upon average unit prices, as represented by (8.26), are also reckoned with.

Other specifications of the estimator equation can be dealt with in an analogous manner.

8.6. OTHER SPECIFIC VARIABLES

The particular nature of a product may sometimes require the use of other kinds of explanatory variables than those already mentioned. Well-known examples in the case of durables (automobiles, furniture, etc.) are such variables as liquid assets held by households, or per capita (or per household) stock of the product concerned. More involved reasoning in terms of these variables has led to different kinds of theoretical models of the demand for durables, that allow the age structure and average life of the existing stock also to be taken into account. Demand equations based upon these models are not only more satisfactory from a theoretical point of view but have been shown applicable in practical research.[19]

A more trivial example of the need for a specific "character" variable is the influence of average winter temperatures upon the demand for coal. Other examples could easily be cited. Although their contribution to the explained variance as measured by the β coefficients[20] may often be marginal in the sense of not being too important from the statistical point of view, their inclusion may nevertheless lead to more precise estimates of the coefficients of the other variables. Their role tends, besides, to become more important in the case of market diagnosis where recent developments are evaluated against the background of a demand equation derived from a previous period. Anything that contributes to the explanation of the actual situation carries more weight, since an exhaustive explanation is usually considered as the ultimate goal.

8.7. DUMMY VARIABLES

Dummy variables provide a valuable supplement in demand analysis and in other areas where regression methods are used. Essentially, they can serve two purposes: they provide a means of quantifying qualitative variables and they can be of assistance in deriving unbiased estimates where quantitative variables are involved. This they do by providing a basis for

---

[19] For examples see M. J. Farrel, "The Demand for Motorcars in the United States," *Journal of the Royal Statistical Society*, Series A, Vol. 117, Part 2, 1954, p. 171; G. C. Chow, *The Demand for Automobiles in the United States, A Study in Consumer Durables*, Amsterdam, 1957; R. Stone and D. A. Rowe, "The Durability of Consumers' Goods," *Econometrica*, April, 1960, pp. 407–416; J. S. Cramer, "The Depreciation and Mortality of Motor-Cars," *Journal of the Royal Statistical Society*, Series A, 1958, pp. 18–59; *Idem*, "A Dynamic Approach to the Theory of Consumer Demand," *Review of Economic Studies*, 1957, pp. 73–86.

[20] See Sec. 3.5.

replacing the original variable by a "proxy" variable possessing more desirable properties.

The procedure followed in replacing a qualitative variable is to assign numbers to each attribute. This is particularly simple in the dichotomous case, where the presence of the attribute can be assigned the value *1* and its absence the value *0*.[21] For example, in a regression analysis of the factors influencing the price of a car, one variable might be presence or absence of automatic shift. For cars that have automatic shifts, this variable, say x_4, would be given the value 1; for cars that do not have automatic shift x_4 would be given the value 0.

Dummy variables provide a flexible method of handling explanatory factors that exert nonlinear effects on the dependent variable. In that case, the particular independent variable can be subdivided into a number of dummy variables, thereby retaining the linear form but at the same time preserving the true relationships between the variables. For example, medical expenditures tend to vary in a curvilinear fashion with age, first being relatively high, then declining, and finally moving up again. If age is an independent variable in such a regression study, it could be subdivided into a number of dummy variables, each representing a particular age bracket, and each taking the value 1 if the observation (respondent) is in that age bracket, and taking the value 0 otherwise. Thus, instead of forcing age into a parabola or other mathematical form, we might represent "age" by, say, five different variables:

$$x_1 = \text{under 10 years of age}$$
$$x_2 = \text{10–19 years of age}$$
$$x_3 = \text{20–39 years of age}$$
$$x_4 = \text{40–59 years of age}$$
$$x_5 = \text{60 years of age and over}$$

If a particular respondent happens to be 42 years of age, for that observation x_4 would take the value 1 and all the other age variables would take the value 0.

The form of the function, assuming for simplicity that age is the only independent variable, might be as follows:

$$x_0 = \alpha + \beta_1 x_1 + \beta_2 x_2 + \beta_3 x_3 + \beta_4 x_4 \tag{8.30}$$

Note that one age variable is omitted. The reason for this is that if this equation included all the dummy variables for this classification (age), the estimates of the regression coefficients would be indeterminate. Intuitively, this is evident from the fact that in its present form, equation (8.30) allows

---

[21] If logarithms to the base 10 are used, 1 and 2 might be substituted for 0 and 1.

for all possible age values. If all five age dummy variables were included in this form together with the constant term, the equation becomes over-identified and estimates of the regression coefficients are indeterminate.[22]

The best known application of dummy variables is the determination of seasonal influences in demand. Every month, or quarter, except one is represented by a separate dummy variable, as noted in Section 7.3.4. If logarithms are used, all months, or quarters, show a constant percentage shift with respect to the nth month or quarter.

An alternate approach is to have one age variable, with different values for each age bracket. Thus, if this variable is, say, x_1, it might be given the value 1 for those under 10, 2 for those 10–19, 3 for 20–39, etc. This method saves degrees of freedom but does not allow for a specific form of nonlinear relationship. If the size of the class intervals varies substantially, the values can be made more realistic by assigning them in rough proportion to these class intervals. Thus, using the upper limit points of the age intervals, the possible values for x_1 would be 1, 2, 4, 6, 8 (assuming 80 as the upper limit of the last class interval). This was the approach used by Stone in allowing for quality variations in beer (Sec. 8.5).

In using dummy variables of this type, indeterminate estimates can be eliminated by omitting one dummy variable from each system of classification (age, education, etc.) or by removing the constant term. In the latter case, equation (8.30) becomes:

$$x_0 = \beta_1 x_1 + \beta_2 x_2 + \beta_3 x_3 + \beta_4 x_4 + \beta_5 x_5 \tag{8.31}$$

With equation (8.31) the coefficients and standard errors may be estimated in the usual way except that the product moments are computed about zero rather than about the mean values.

Dummy variables may be used only with each other or with other types of variables. In either case, in estimating regression coefficients and evaluating their reliability, dummy variables are treated just like any other variable in a regression function. In other words, the usual formulas apply both for estimating the coefficients and for computing standard errors. Indeed, the computations are likely to be considerably easier to the extent that more observations have zero or unit values.[23]

In the case of ordinal variables, as illustrated by gradational adjectives, each possible answer is assigned a numerical value on some continuum to correspond with the actual answers. For example, suppose that a person is presented with the following multiple choice questions:

---

[22] See D. B. SUITS, "Use of Dummy Variables in Regression Equations," *Journal of the American Statistical Association*, December, 1957, pp. 548–551.

[23] For a practical, clearly-illustrated example, see J. B. LANSING and D. M. BLOOD, "A Cross-Section Analysis of Non-Business Air Travel," *Journal of the American Statistical Association*, December, 1958, pp. 928–947.

How do you think that business next year will be compared to what it was this year?

_____Much better
_____Somewhat better
_____About the same
_____Somewhat worse
_____Much worse

For analytical purposes, these adjectives could be assigned the values, -2, -1, 0, 1, 2, respectively, in the order of listing. Alternately, they could be assigned the values 1, 2, 3, 4, 5, if it is desirable for some reason to get away from negative values.

Admittedly, the numerical values assigned are largely arbitrary. Despite this fact, such work as has been done in this area indicates that the results obtained by such a procedure tend to be invariant, for all practical purposes, to any reasonable method of assigning these numbers. By "reasonable method" is meant that the numbers assigned correspond to some underlying continuum in the qualitative variables which effectively exists in the respondents' minds in answering this question.[24]

8.8.   DYNAMIC ELEMENTS

One aspect of specification sometimes overlooked is the *time shape* of demand reactions. Demand may adjust itself instantaneously to a change in income or prices. Alternatively, the adjustment may extend over a period of time, in which case *a priori* information about the time path followed in the process of adaptation to the new equilibrium level is generally scarce. Since divergent forms of the time shape are possible, it is often necessary to test empirically the main possibilities, each as a different hypothesis. Two major categories of the time shape of reactions are considered here—lagged reactions and the quasi-accelerator.

8.8.1.   Lagged Reactions

The simplest case of a lagged reaction is the *single lag,* corresponding to a structural equation of the form:

$$y_t = \gamma + A x_{t-\vartheta} \tag{8.32}$$

where ϑ indicates the length of the lag as a decimal fraction of the time unit and is less than unity. Three different methods of specifying this lag relationship are to be found in the literature:

---

[24] ROBERT FERBER, "Gradational Adjectives in Market Surveys," *Journal of Applied Psychology*, June, 1955, pp. 173–177.

1. First, there is the straight-forward method discussed in Sec. 7.6.2:

$$y_t = \gamma + \alpha x_t + \beta x_{t-1} \tag{8.33}$$

2. More involved is the use of the preceding value of the dependent variable instead of x_{t-1},[25]

$$y_t = \gamma + \alpha x_t + \lambda y_{t-1} \tag{8.34}$$

3. Alternatively, instead of lagging the dependent variable, we may give it a lead of one unit.[26]

$$y_t = \gamma + \alpha x_t + \mu y_{t+1} \tag{8.35}$$

where the algebraic value of μ ought to be negative.

Equations such as (8.34) and (8.35) are often used if the dependent variable is supposed to react with a lag of the same length upon *all* the explanatory variables of the estimator equation. Apart from this, (8.34) recommends itself as a particularly flexible estimator equation. As things are, it can represent a structural equation with a single lag (as 8.32)[27] just as well as one with a distributed lag of the Koyck type that is represented by (7.25).

At the same time, this very flexibility may prove a serious handicap. Without further knowledge about the nature of the time shape of the reactions studied, an empirical equation of the form (8.34) generally does not permit identification of the underlying structural equation, making it impossible to judge whether a distributed lag or a single one is implied. This uncertainty is a major limitation of this approach, especially since many practical purposes require at least an approximate knowledge of the time shape itself. A second disadvantage is that only a small fraction of the change in the dependent variable is really "explained" if λ approaches unity, as may be the case with rapidly expanding demand.

Just as in the case of the "straightforward" equation (8.33) the total or long-run influence (A) of x_t as well as the length of the lag (ϑ) can be determined from the coefficients of (8.34) and (8.35). The formulas are given in Table 8.2. For purposes of illustration, Table 8.3 presents the results of a practical application of the three estimator equations to labor demand in

---

[25] As an example, see the consumption function of KLEIN and GOLDBERGER, *loc. cit.*, pp. 51 and 63.

[26] TINBERGEN'S wage equation may serve as an example: See *Statistical Testing of Business-Cycle Theories*, Vol. II: *Business Cycles in the United States of America*, Geneva, 1939, Sec. 3.1.

[27] That this actually is the case may readily be seen if (8.32) is written as:

$$x_t = \frac{1}{A} y_{t+\vartheta} = \frac{1}{\delta A} (1 - \vartheta) y_t + \vartheta y_{t+1} \tag{8.36}$$

where δ is a correction factor to maintain equality between the variance of $y_{t+\vartheta}$ and that of the weighted sum of y_{t-1} and y_t (see Sec. 7.6). This expression is the basis for (8.35). Lagging all its variables with one unit, an explicit function of x_{t-1} in y_t and y_{t-1} is obtained. Substitution of this function for x_{t-1} in (8.33) leads directly to (8.34` the iron and steel industry as explained by volume of output during the period, 1901–1913. (See also Sec. 7.6, Fig. 7.2.)

Table 8.2

FORMULAS FOR ESTIMATING TOTAL EFFECT (A)
AND TIME LAG (ϑ) FOR A SINGLE LAG

No.	Estimator equation[a]	ϑ	A
8.33	$y_t = \alpha x_t + \beta x_{t-1}$	$\dfrac{\beta}{\alpha + \beta}$	$(\alpha + \beta)\sqrt{1 - 2\vartheta(1 - \vartheta)(1 - \rho_{x_t x_{t-1}})}$
8.34	$y_t = \alpha x_t + \lambda y_{t-1}$	$\dfrac{\lambda}{1 + \lambda - 2\lambda\rho_{y_t y_{t-1}}}$	$\dfrac{\alpha}{\sqrt{1 + \lambda^2 - 2\lambda\rho_{y_t y_{t-1}}}}$
8.35	$y_t = \alpha x_t + \mu y_{t+1}$	$\dfrac{-\mu}{1 - \mu}$	$\dfrac{\alpha}{\sqrt{1 + \mu^2 - 2\mu\rho_{y_t y_{t+1}}}}$

[a] Additive constants are omitted.

Table 8.3

EXPLANATION OF LABOR DEMAND (y) AS A
FUNCTION OF TOTAL OUTPUT (x)

(Iron and Steel Industry, United States, 1901–1913)

No.	Estimator equation[a]	ESTIMATES OF R	ESTIMATES OF ϑ	ESTIMATES OF A[b]	Estimates of A, uncorrected for reduction of variance[c]
	$y_t = \underset{(.162)}{.641 x_t}$	.781	—	.641	—
8.33	$y_t = \underset{(.076)}{.835 x_t} + \underset{(.047)}{.497 x_{t-1}}$	.962	.373	.789	1.332
8.34	$y_t = \underset{(.128)}{1.038 x_t} + \underset{(.156)}{.702 y_{t-1}}$	.933	.363	.791	3.483
8.35	$y_t = \underset{(.142)}{.701 x_t} - \underset{(.164)}{.320 y_{t+1}}$	.847	.242	.699	.531

[a] The variables are measured as first differences of the logarithms of the index numbers (1899 = 100). Additive constants are omitted. Standard errors are given between parentheses.
[b] $\rho_{x_t x_{t-1}} = -.387$; $\rho_{y_t y_{t-1}} = -.164$; $\rho_{y_t y_{t+1}} = -.150$.
[c] Calculated by assuming: $\rho_{x_t x_{t-1}} = \rho_{y_t y_{t-1}} = \rho_{y_t y_{t+1}} = 1$, i.e., by assuming perfect linear correlation.
Source for original data: PAUL H. DOUGLAS, The Theory of Wages, New York, 1934, Statistical Appendix, Tables I and V.

Table 8.3 leads to the following conclusions:

1. Comparison of the results of the first and the second estimator equations show that the total correlation and the efficiency of the estimates of the coefficients can be improved considerably by allowing for a single lag.

2. As might have been expected, the results for ϑ and A obtained with the three estimator equations are not identical, although the correspondence between the estimates from (8.33) and those from (8.34) is certainly satisfactory. A value of .80 for the total elasticity of labor demand in the iron and steel industry is plausible, indicating that a short-run adaptation of a higher

volume of output tends to be accompanied by slightly increasing returns. A value of this order of magnitude is, moreover, confirmed by data covering the inter-war period.[28]

3. The interpretation of (8.34) serves as a good example of an equation of this type representing a single lag. First, the only case where the single-lag hypothesis would lead to inconsistent estimates of the lag itself—the case where the value of ϑ (computed as: $\lambda/(1 + \lambda - 2\lambda\rho)$) surpasses unity—does not exist here, since ρ is negative ($-.164$). Second, a straightforward test of the single-lag hypothesis is found in (8.33). Since the estimate of the total effect (A) obtained with this equation is the same as that shown by (8.34), and the estimate of (8.33) is, moreover, the more reliable of the two, there is no statistical reason to decide in favor of a distributed lag. Third, a slowly decreasing series of weights (.7, .49, .34, .25, .18, etc.) for the influence of output changes in all previous years seems hardly applicable to labor demand in the iron and steel industry.

4. The last column of Table 8.3 emphasizes the need to take into account the coefficient of autocorrelation in estimating the total effect of a sustained change of the independent variable. The suggestion sometimes made of calculating A under the assumption of perfect linear development,[29] i.e., $\rho = 1$, may easily lead to incorrect conclusions and even nonsensical results, particularly where the actual values of ρ are low.

In demand analysis single lags may or may not prevail, depending on the psychological and institutional conditions in the country studied as well as on the nature of the product itself. Often, however, single lags may be expected with regard to income. Assuming the straightforward-estimator equation is used, the influence of income may be represented as:

$$v_t = \gamma y_t^{\beta_1} y_{z_{t-1}}^{\beta_2} \tag{8.37}$$

Due to the stickiness of consumption out of non-labor income (Z), the lagged term may play even a more important role if the functional distribution of income is taken into account, as in the following relation:

$$v_t = \gamma \left(\frac{L}{q}\right)_t^{\beta_1} \left(\frac{Z}{q}\right)_t^{\beta_2} \left(\frac{Z}{q}\right)_{t-1}^{\beta_3} \tag{8.38}$$

A single lag may also prevail with regard to price reactions. This might be the case where a continually bought product involves only a small outlay at a time. Other examples of single lags sometimes encountered are the influence

---

[28] An analysis of the corresponding series for the U. S. Steel Corporation for the period 1929–1938 (T.N.E.C. Papers, Vol. I, 1940, Pamphlet 6, p. 223ff.) points to an elasticity of .84 (P. J. VERDOORN, *op. cit.*, p. 108, Table 29).

[29] KLEIN and GOLDBERGER, *op. cit.*, p. 63.

of liquid assets held by households, the stock of durables already available, etc.

As soon as the process of adaptation takes more than one time unit—in the case of annual data more than one year—a single lag is insufficient for measuring demand reactions. One of the methods mentioned in Sec. 7.6 for approximating a distributed lag will then be necessary. The method to choose may sometimes follow logically from *a priori* reasoning as in the example of the demand for new cars discussed there. The same is true of those cases where the income reactions of the consumer are supposedly governed by their expectations regarding "permanent" income rather than by current income. As argued by Friedman, this "expected income" can be approximated as the weighted average of actual income in the present and all previous years, if the weights are chosen as the successive terms of a declining geometric series with, consequently, rapidly diminishing values for the earlier years. A correction to this weighting scheme is, however, necessary to allow for the normal rate of increase of real income per head. Disregarding this correction, expected income (y^e) represents basically a distributed lag of the form (7.19):

$$y_t^e = (1 - \lambda)(y_t + \lambda y_{t-1} + \lambda^2 y_{t-2} + \lambda^3 y_{t-3} + \cdots) \qquad (8.39)$$

The multiplier, $(1 - \lambda)$, is the reciprocal of the sum of the convergent series $1, \lambda, \lambda^2, \lambda^3, \ldots$ etc., and makes the sum of the weights equal to unity. In order to verify his "permanent income" hypothesis, Friedman used an analogous series of geometrically declining weights, $e^{\beta(t-T)}$ instead of λ^{t-T} as used in (8.39), T denoting the rank number for each of the preceding years. Selecting a value of .4 for β (corresponding with $\lambda = .67$), a satisfactory explanation of total deflated consumption by means of expected income could be obtained in this way.[30] The same device was successfully exploited by Chow in explaining changes in the stock of automobiles, also using an *a priori* estimate of .4 for β.[31]

As shown in Sec. 7.6, independent estimates of λ are easily obtained by the use of Koyck's approach. This method may also be used if the declining series of weights sets in *after* the second preceding year.[32] Using again the derivation (7.20), we have:

$$
\begin{aligned}
v_t &= \alpha y_t + \beta y_{t-1} & + \beta\lambda y_{t-2} + \beta\lambda^2 y_{t-3} \cdots \\
\lambda v_{t-1} &= \qquad\quad \alpha\lambda y_{t-1} & + \beta\lambda y_{t-2} + \beta\lambda^2 y_{t-3} \cdots \\
\hline
v_t &= \alpha y_t + (\beta - \alpha\lambda)y_{t-1} & + \qquad\qquad \lambda v_{t-1}
\end{aligned}
\qquad (8.40)
$$

---

[30] M. Friedman, *A Theory of the Consumption Function*, National Bureau of Economic Research, No. 63, Princeton, 1957, pp. 142–148.

[31] G. Chow, *Demand for Automobiles in the United States*, Amsterdam, 1957, Ch. IV.

[32] L. M. Koyck, *Distributed Lags and Investment Analysis*, Amsterdam, 1954, p. 39 and the applications in Ch. IV.

Since (8.40) can be applied to the original data as well as to their logarithms, this particular specification provides a flexible tool for investigating the time shape of demand reactions, if the interpretation of a distributed lag is not open to question. Apart from difficulties of interpretation, difficulties of estimation also may arise if a distributed lag is assumed with regard to one variable, e.g., income, whereas other variables, say, price, are supposed to act instantaneously. In cases like this, the structural equation may take the form:

$$v_t = \epsilon p_t + \eta y_t + \eta \lambda y_{t-1} + \eta \lambda^2 y_{t-2} + \cdots \tag{8.41}$$

The corresponding estimator equation:

$$v_t = \epsilon(p_t - \lambda p_{t-1}) + \eta y_t + \lambda v_{t-1} \tag{8.42}$$

is no longer linear in the coefficients. Independent estimates of λ, ϵ and η are, therefore, impossible. A way out is provided by conditional regression, i.e., by assuming a set of reasonable values for λ and selecting the value that maximizes the coefficient of multiple correlation, R.

For this purpose the transformed variables:

$$p_t' = p_t - \lambda p_{t-1}$$

and

$$v_t' = v_t - \lambda v_{t-1}$$

are computed for alternative values of λ, where λ as a matter of course is assigned values between zero and unity. Estimates of α and β and the corresponding values of R are calculated for each separate value of λ from the new estimator equation:

$$v_t' = \alpha p_t' + \beta y_t \tag{8.43}$$

The value of λ, corresponding with the highest R is retained as the best estimate, provided the estimates for α and β are acceptable.

Table 8.4 serves the double purpose of illustrating first the procedure just mentioned, in the first part of the table, and second, the case where an estimator equation as (8.34) or (8.42) is compatible with a distributed lag, as shown in the last three columns. In both cases the results refer to the explanation of deflated automobile prices (p) as a function of automobile stock per capita (x) and of expected income per capita (y).[33]

The results obtained by conditional regression applied to Koyck's approach suggest that the residual variance as indicated by $(1 - R^2)$ in Column 3 tends to a minimum in the neighborhood of $\lambda = .50$ ($\beta = .7$).

---

[33] In both approaches the income data are those of the Department of Commerce (CHOW's I_d, Table 1, Column 4), excluding the World War II period. Results for $\lambda = 0$ for the first approach and $\lambda = .667$ for the second are therefore not strictly comparable with his equations (1d) and (1e), *op. cit.*, pp. 32, 34 and 35.

Compared with using only the current value of income ($\lambda = 0$, $\beta = \infty$), the residual variance has been reduced by about 40%. An exact estimate of the value of λ for which the variance is a minimum could be obtained by interpolation, but the present procedure does not justify such a degree of precision.

Table 8.4

ESTIMATES OF THE DISTRIBUTED LAG BY CONDITIONAL REGRESSION

(Automobile prices, 1921–1953, U. S. A.)

(1) Selected a Priori Values for	(2)	(3) I: ESTIMATOR EQUATION $\log p - \lambda \log p_{-1} = \epsilon(\log x - \lambda \log x_{t-1}) + \eta \log y$	(4) ELASTICITIES WITH REGARD TO[a,b] Stock of Cars	(5) Expected Income	(6) II: ESTIMATOR EQUATION $\log p = \epsilon \log x + \eta \Sigma e^{\beta(t-T)}(1 - e^{-\beta}) \log y$	(7) ELASTICITIES WITH REGARD TO[a,b] Stock of Cars	(8) Expected Income
β	λ	$1 - R^2$	(ϵ)	$\left(\dfrac{\eta}{1-\lambda}\right)^{c,d}$	$1 - R^2$	(ϵ)	(η)
.2	.819	.071	−1.01 (.15)	2.38 (.27)	.056	−1.05 (.06)	2.36 (.06)
.3	.741	.064	−1.02 (.14)	2.14 (.20)	.049	−1.02 (.06)	2.14 (.05)
.4	.667	.059	−1.03 (.13)	2.03 (.16)	—	—	—
.5	.607	.057	−1.03 (.12)	1.96 (.14)	.055	−1.01 (.06)	1.97 (.05)
.6	.549	.055	−1.03 (.11)	1.93 (.12)	—	—	—
.7	.497	.055	−1.03 (.11)	1.87 (.11)	.060	−1.01 (.07)	1.90 (.06)
.8	.449	.055	−1.03 (.10)	1.85 (.10)	—	—	—
.9	.407	.056	−1.03 (.10)	1.83 (.10)	.066	−1.02 (.07)	1.85 (.06)
1.0	.368	.057	−1.03 (.10)	1.81 (.09)	.	.	.
∞	0	.093	−1.01 (.09)	1.73 (.08)	.	.	.

a Standard errors, measured as a decimal fraction of the elasticities, are given in parentheses.
b Since the value of λ is unknown, the standard errors should essentially be considered as minimum values.
c Standard errors refer to η, not to $\eta/(1 - \lambda)$.
d Elasticities are uncorrected for differences in variance.
Source for original data: See G. CHOW, *op. cit.*, Table 1, p. 32.

The results of Friedman's approach, correlating price directly with the weighted sum of the present and all previous values of y, are given in Columns 6 and 8.[34] The minimum variance in this case is obtained in the neighborhood of $\lambda = .67$ ($\beta = .4$), thus confirming Friedman's original findings. Good correspondence of the estimates is apparent between Friedman's method and that of Koyck with regard to ϵ and η. It is less satisfactory in the case of λ. The comparison given in Table 8.4 suggests that:

1. The discriminatory power to establish an optimal value of λ is considerably greater with the approach of Friedman than with that of Koyck.

---

[34] In order to maintain comparability with KOYCK's approach, the weighted sum of the logs of y_t has been used as an explanatory variable.

2. The optimal values of λ found with the latter approach do not necessarily correspond with those of the former.

The reason for these different results is the same: that for a given value of λ, the residuals of the two estimator equations are not identical, unless the residuals of Friedman's equations happen to be uncorrelated. Koyck's approach, therefore, should essentially be considered as a second-best approximation of λ. However, since in many cases the statistical data for the required number of previous years are not available, a second-best approximation is often better than none at all.

A different kind of lagged reaction is the *ratchet* or *Modigliani effect*, as studied in theoretical economics. It has been applied with varying success in the analysis of aggregate consumption.[35] According to this effect, consumer behavior depends not only on present income but on highest previous income (y_m) as well:

$$v_t = \gamma y_t^{\beta_1} y_m^{\beta_2} \ldots \tag{8.44}$$

Since y_m is the highest observed value of y for the years preceding t, its value can only rise; it can never fall. It might therefore represent the lasting effects on consumption habits of a higher income earned in earlier years. A more refined hypothesis, that aims at the same ultimate effect, assumes a one-sided stickiness of the demand equation. It is conceivable that the income elasticity of a product might be higher when income rises than in periods when income drops correspondingly; and again, that the absolute value of the price elasticity with falling prices may surpass the same value found in the case of an increasing price.[36]

8.8.2. Quasi-Accelerator

The second category of dynamic elements refers to the *quasi-accelerator*. In a demand function of the form:

$$v_t = \gamma' + \beta_1' y_t + \beta_2' \Delta y_t + \cdots \tag{8.45a}$$

or its exponential equivalent:

$$v_t = \gamma y_t^{\beta_1} \left(\frac{y_t}{y_{t-1}}\right)^{\beta_2} \cdots \tag{8.45b}$$

demand is assumed to depend upon the rate of increase and not exclusively

---

[35] F. MODIGLIANI, "Fluctuations in the Saving-Income Ratio: A Problem in Economic Forecasting," *Studies in Income and Wealth*, Vol. XI (New York, National Bureau of Economic Research, 1949). J. DUESENBERRY, *Income, Saving and the Theory of Consumption Behavior*, 1949, Ch. VII.

[36] For applications, see M. J. FARREL, "Irreversible Demand Functions," *Econometrica*, April, 1952, pp. 171–186.

upon the prevailing level of income, y_t.[37] Thus, a consumer may well use a temporary increase in income to purchase durable equipment. Apart from this, it is important to remember that average service life of durables is often extremely flexible. The average age of household goods tends therefore to increase in times of falling income. Due to the consequent postponement of normal replacement in the downswing of the cycle, replacement purchases tend to be concentrated in recovery.

An analogous effect is sometimes encountered with regard to prices. Writing p' for p/q:

$$v_t = \gamma p_t'^{\epsilon_1} \left(\frac{p_t'}{p_{t-1}'} \right)^{\epsilon_2} \cdots \tag{8.46}$$

Here, the last term may represent the effect of speculative motives. In other instances, consumption plans made some time earlier may prove to be inflexible in terms of volume, rather than of value. In both cases we may expect ϵ_2 to have a *positive* value. Equation (8.46) therefore represents only another way of writing a single lag as long as $\epsilon_1 < -\epsilon_2$, since:

$$p_t'^{\epsilon_1} \left(\frac{p_t'}{p_{t-1}'} \right)^{\epsilon_2} = p_t'^{\epsilon_1 + \epsilon_2} p_{t-1}'^{-\epsilon_2} \tag{8.47}$$

Equations of the type of (8.45a) or (8.45b) may serve as a general approach for investigating the existence of a single lag or quasi-accelerator. A significant value for β_2 with the same sign as β_1 points to a quasi-accelator; a significant value with the opposite sign to a single, or perhaps a distributed, lag. The main advantage of a function of the form (8.45a) as compared with (8.33) is that the correlation between y_t and Δy_t is usually smaller than that between y_t and y_{t-1}.

8.9.   THE EFFICIENCY OF THE ESTIMATES

It follows from the foregoing that the number of separate variables that might possibly affect demand is impressively large. To be sure, a large number of variables conveys, no doubt, a touch of realism. But if valid conclusions are to be drawn at all, the specification of the demand equation must be such that the sampling variations of the coefficients remain acceptable

---

[37] Reactions of this type have been investigated by RUTH P. MACK in survey data ("The Direction of Change in Income and the Consumption Function," *Review of Economics and Statistics*, Nov., 1948, pp. 239–259) and in time series, *Factors Influencing Consumption: An Experimental Analysis of Shoe Buying*, National Bureau of Economic Research, Technical Paper 10, 1954, pp. 20–21, 45 *et seq.* Also, R. STONE and D. A. ROWE, "Some Studies of the Market Demand for Durable Goods," (Paper read for the 17th European Meeting of the Econometric Society, Kiel, 1955); M. J. FARREL, "The New Theories of the Consumption Function," *Economic Journal*, Dec., 1959, pp. 694–695.

from the statistical point of view. The formula for the standard error, as mentioned in Sec. 3.5, is:

$$\sigma_{b1.234\ldots n} = \frac{\sigma_1}{\sigma_2} \sqrt{\frac{1 - R^2_{1.2\ldots n}}{(1 - R^2_{2.3\ldots n})(N - n - 1)}} \tag{8.48}$$

where

σ_1 and σ_2 denote the standard deviations of the explained variable, x_1, and that of the explanatory variable, x_2, for which σ_b is being computed respectively,

N is the number of observations in the sample period,

n is the number of explanatory variables.

The standard error therefore will increase for sheer lack of degrees of freedom if n becomes unduly large relative to N. Moreover, the greater the number of explanatory variables, the greater becomes the risk of multicollinearity between the latter ($R_{2.3\ldots n}$), since all economic phenomena are necessarily interdependent. Finally, there must exist a reasonable ratio between the residual variance of x_1 as shown by the numerator under the square-root sign and that of x_2, if explained by the other variables, in the denominator $(1 - R^2_{2.3\ldots n})$. The acceptance of x_2 as an explanatory variable therefore clearly requires a further and tangible contribution to the reduction of the residual variance of x_1 beyond that already provided by the other variables of the set 3, 4, . . . , n.

These two requirements—economic realism of the explanation as represented by the inclusion of *all* the theoretically relevant variables, and the efficiency of the estimates—do not necessarily go together. An optimal position between the two must therefore be found. The practical solution is to include in the demand equation only those variables the contribution of which was comparatively important during the sample period, whereas variables with only minor contributions are discarded, however relevant from a theoretical point of view.[38]

This procedure inevitably leads to a second-best, or even third-best, specification from a theoretical point of view. In addition, omitting relevant variables may lead to overstating or understating the influence of some of the retained variables. But to use Frisch's analogy: "In target shooting the result depends not only on the correct aiming but just as much on the steadiness with which one pulls the trigger. If for some particular reason it is impossible to pull the trigger steadily when one aims *exactly* at the target,

---

[38] It is important to note that a theoretically relevant variable may have exercised no influence at all if its standard deviation during the period of observation was relatively small, as is brought out by the definition of the β-coefficient (Eq. 3.23). Regression analysis in such cases does not therefore refute the alleged relevance of the variable concerned, but simply shows that its influence there and then, as compared with that of other variables, was negligible.

it is quite conceivably better to aim deliberately a little on the side of the target. And so in statistical analysis it may be found safer deliberately to leave some bias in the regression coefficients by not including a certain variable in the analysis.[39]

Since the marginal contribution of a certain variable is generally not known beforehand, the usual procedure is to test successively alternative sets of mutually consistent hypotheses including the probably relevant variables. The procedure is illustrated in Tables 8.1 (condensed milk) on page 363, and 8.5 (clothing), on page 396.[40]

An indication whether a certain variable may be pertinent can be obtained by computing the matrix of first-order correlation coefficients among all the variables considered relevant on grounds of *a priori* reasoning. The joint contribution of any two variables (x_2, x_3) to the variance of x_1 is then computed as:

$$R^2_{1.23} = \frac{r^2_{12} + r^2_{13} - 2r_{12}r_{13}r_{23}}{1 - r^2_{23}} \tag{8.49}$$

A second means of increasing the efficiency of the estimates is to use as many observations as are available, since σ_b varies inversely with the square root of the degrees of freedom. However, nothing is gained by adding observations that are statistically less reliable. It should also be noted that using quarterly or monthly data instead of annual data does not necessarily increase the amount of independent information in the ratio of $4:1$ or of $12:1$, unless one happens to be especially interested in the mechanism of short-term reactions.

One possibility sometimes overlooked is to combine postwar observations with those of the interwar period. This not only has the advantage of increasing N, but in some cases also that of reducing multicollinearity, since empirical patterns of cyclical development show considerable differences, and the trends of such variables as prices and income are often divergent for the two periods considered. To be sure, the pattern of demand for some products may have also changed. But closer analysis of such differences and their causes may well add valuable information to knowledge of basic structure.

---

[39] R. FRISCH, *Statistical Confluence Analysis by Means of Complete Regression Systems*, Oslo, Universitetets Økonomiske Institutt, 1934, p. 85.

[40] In testing the different hypotheses it is important to use a sufficient number of digits with the solution of the normal equations when explanatory variables are numerous or highly intercorrelated. (Sec. 3.5) This applies not to the original data where sometimes even the second digit is hardly significant, but to the processing of the moments. Omission of digits in the latter case may lead to indeterminacy of results and, consequently, to nonsense parameters, e.g., numerical values of, say, -210.36 and 211.36 for the elasticities of an intercorrelated pair of variables as p and q. With more careful processing the really irrelevant variables—those not providing any independent contribution—tend to show negligible absolute values even if intercorrelation is considerable.

Apart from judiciously decreasing n and increasing N, there are various other possibilities of improving the efficiency of estimates. The first refers to suitable specification of the form of the relation between demand and a given set of explanatory variables. One point to decide upon is whether a linear or logarithmic relation will be used. Reasons for generally preferring the latter have been discussed in Sec. 3.5. An example of its advantages with the analysis of time series is the case of rapidly increasing demand, as shown by the number of telephone calls in the beginning of this century. Here we cannot expect the same absolute change in real national income, say of one billion dollars in 1962 prices, to have the same effect upon the number of calls in 1962 as in 1890. In cases like this, the relation is rather between the relative changes of the variables. The income elasticity may, admittedly, also not have been constant, but it is no doubt the more stable of the two coefficients considered.

Another question in deciding upon the functional form of the demand equation is how to deal with the trend component of the variables. The usually applied method is that of "time-regression"—a regression including trend as a separate variable (8.14). Other methods aim either at directly eliminating the trend component from each of the series concerned, or at differencing the latter over time.

Both methods require transformation of the different variables $(x_1, x_2, \ldots)$ or their logarithms into new ones $(x_1', x_2', \ldots)$, the coefficients of regression being computed from the transformed equation:

$$x_1' = \alpha + \beta x_2' + \gamma x_3' + \delta x_4' \qquad (8.50)$$

In either case there are different ways of defining the relationship between x' and x, the principal such ways being discussed below.

8.9.1. Direct Elimination

The following are some of the transformations that have been applied in the direct elimination of trend:

$(A\text{-}1)$[41]	$x_t' = x_t - \tilde{x}_t$	*(Absolute deviations)*
$(A\text{-}2)$	$x_t' = \log x_t - [\log x]_t$	*(Logarithmic deviations)*
$(A\text{-}3)$	$x_t' = \dfrac{x_t}{\tilde{x}_t}$	*(Trend ratios)*
$(A\text{-}4)$[42]	$x_t' = 100 \left(\dfrac{x_t}{\tilde{x}_t} - 1 \right)$	*(Percentage deviations)*

---

[41] For practical examples, see H. Schultz, *The Theory and Measurement of Demand*, 1938, p. 527.

[42] See J. Tinbergen, *Business Cycles in the United Kingdom, 1890–1914*, Amsterdam, 1951.

Here, $\tilde{x}_t$ represents the trend values, however defined, of x_t, and $[log\ x]_t$ those of $log\ x_t$. The regression coefficients $\beta,\ \gamma,\ \ldots$ etc., obtained from the transformations $(A\text{-}1)$ and $(A\text{-}2)$ will not usually be the same as those obtained with the time regression. However, identical coefficients are obtained if x_t or $[log\ x]_t$ have been fitted as linear trends to x_t and $log\ x_t$, respectively.[43]

$(A\text{-}3)$ leads to the same results as $(A\text{-}4)$. At any point of time the elasticity of x_1 with respect to x_2 is given as:[44]

$(A\text{-}3\text{-}1)$
$$\epsilon_{12} = \frac{\partial x_1}{\partial x_2}\frac{x_2}{x_1} = \beta\,\frac{x_2'}{x_1'}$$

in the case of the $(A\text{-}3)$ transformation.

For that of the $(A\text{-}4)$ transformation, we have:

$(A\text{-}4\text{-}1)$
$$\epsilon_{12} = \frac{\partial x_1}{\partial x_2}\frac{x_2}{x_1} = \beta\,\frac{x_2' + 1}{x_1' + 1}$$

The last two transformations, therefore, assume not constant elasticities for the actual values of x_1 and x_2 but for their trend values. Hence, changes in the value of ϵ_{12} occur only as a consequence of deviations of x_1 and x_2 from their trend values and not as a result of changes in the latter.

8.9.2. Differencing Over Time

The following transformations are most common in this category:

$(B\text{-}1)$ $x_t' = \Delta x_t$ (*Absolute first differences*)

$(B\text{-}2)$[45] $x_t' = \Delta\ log\ x_t$ (*First differences of logs*)

$(B\text{-}3)$[46] $x_t' = 100\,\dfrac{\Delta x}{x_t}$ (*Percentage first differences*)

$(B\text{-}4)$[44] $x_t' = \dfrac{x_t}{x_{t-1}}$ (*Link relatives*)

where:

$$\Delta x_t = x_t - x_{t-1}$$
$$\Delta\ log\ x_t = log\ x_t - log\ x_{t-1}$$

Here, the transformations $(B\text{-}2)$ and $(B\text{-}3)$ yield constant elasticities for the actual values, whereas in the case of $(B\text{-}4)$ equation $(A\text{-}3\text{-}1)$ applies

---

[43] R. FRISCH and F. V. WAUGH, "Partial Time Regressions as Compared with Individual Trends," *Econometrica*, 1933, p. 387.

[44] SCHULTZ, *op. cit.*, p. 528.

[45] Used by STONE throughout his *Measurement of Consumers' Expenditures and Behaviour in the United Kingdom*. As an example, see Table 8.1.

[46] Used in the Dutch forecasting model, *Central Economic Plan, 1961*. The Hague: Central Planning Bureau, 1961, pp. 113–127.

again. Just as in the case of direct trend elimination, the coefficients found with (B-1) by differencing the original series will not normally equal exactly those obtained with time regression.

As is easily seen, the difference transformation results in a particular form of trend elimination since the mean of the transformed series equals the difference between the last and the first observation of the original data divided by the number of observations of the latter less one.

Unfortunately, it is difficult to say beforehand whether trend elimination or differencing will lead to more efficient estimates. Since many variables are dominated by a trend component, it would seem only reasonable to expect a reduction of multicollinearity, particularly if the period studied covers many years. This, however, does not imply that standard errors should decrease accordingly. Precisely because of the elimination of that part of the variance of the dependent variable that is most easily "explained" by time regression, viz., its trend component, the total correlation for the transformed series is always lower than that for the original ones. This factor in many cases may offset the decrease in multicollinearity.

Direct trend elimination of types (A-1) or (A-2) may indicate the effect of this general approach, if at least linear, or logarithmic linear, trends are used. As noted previously, coefficients of regression in this case are the same as those obtained from time regression. Moreover, this particular transformation leaves the residual variance unaffected.[47] As a consequence, the computed standard errors are the same, apart from the gain of one degree of freedom due to the reduction in the number of explanatory variables by one (see equation 8.46).

As a rule, direct trend elimination is mainly used if it is desirable to highlight such short-term movements as the Kitchin or the Juglar cycles in business-cycle research. As a means of increasing the efficiency of the estimates, trend elimination may also be useful for the study of longer periods, where secular movements can be eliminated by using a moving average of the original data as trend (Sec. 7.4).

Compared with trend elimination, the first difference transformation offers two additional advantages. First, the occurrence of significant autocorrelation of the residuals renders unreliable the usual formula (8.48) for the standard error of the coefficients, and the efficiency of the estimates will be overestimated.[48] If the residuals obtained by applying regression analysis to the original series show significant positive autocorrelation, as often happens to be the case, more satisfactory results may be obtained by using first

---

[47] FRISCH and WAUGH, *loc. cit.*

[48] H. WOLD, *Demand Analysis*, New York, 1952, p. 44. See also Sec. 13.4 and 15.2, where a method for correction is suggested.

differences instead of the original series.[49] Although not always necessary, this device presents a means of improving the efficiency of the estimates.

The existing degree of autocorrelation of the residuals can be estimated with the aid of the Von Neumann Ratio of the mean-square successive difference to the variance of the residuals:[50]

$$\frac{N}{N-1}\frac{\Sigma(\Delta u_t)^2}{\Sigma u_t^2} \tag{8.51}$$

where N represents the number of observations, u_t the residuals, and Δu_t their first differences, Σu_t being assumed to equal zero.

The value of this ratio is $2N/(N-1)$, if the successive values of u_t form a purely random series, i.e., if they are normally distributed and independent. The upper and lower values of the ratio at a given significance level depend on N. These limits are shown for selected values of N in Appendix Table A5. Positive autocorrelation is assumed present at the .05 or .01 level if the ratio, for given N, falls below the lower limit, and negative autocorrelation if the ratio exceeds the upper limit. (Why?)

A second advantage of the first-difference transformation is that the differences between the time shapes of the explanatory variables tend to become more pronounced than with straightforward trend elimination. Intercorrelation therefore may be reduced considerably. If the accompanying decrease in total correlation is not too large, first differences here again may provide a method of reducing the standard errors. This is particularly likely when the hypothesis to be tested implies a large number of explanatory variables, as where the existence of time lags for two or more variables is being tested simultaneously.

First differences, finally, may prove a useful device for linking data for the interwar period to those for the postwar years. Time regression, as well as trend elimination, suffers from the difficulty that the hypothesis of a sustained constant rate of change as implied by the residual trend cannot readily be applied to the period covered by World War II and the immediately following years. First differences may therefore provide a better method of dealing with structural change where the latter has not affected basically the parameters being investigated.

8.9.3. Conditional Regression

A more direct attack on multicollinearity is to impose side conditions on the parameters. Thus we may use *a priori* information on some relation that

[49] D. COCHRANE and G. H. ORCUTT, *op. cit.*, pp. 32–61 and 356–372. For a more refined approach to this problem, see C. HILDRETH and J. Y. LU, *Demand Relations With Autocorrelated Disturbances*. East Lansing, Mich.: Department of Agricultural Economics, Michigan State University, Technical Bulletin 246, November, 1960.

[50] See, for example, G. TINTNER, *Econometrics,* New York, 1952, pp. 252–255.

the parameters must satisfy in order to secure more efficient estimates. This procedure is analogous to that of stratified and ratio sampling where *a priori* information is heavily exploited as a means of reducing sampling errors. (How?) Just as with the sampling methods mentioned, however, the reliability of regression analysis depends on whether the conditions imposed are justified when applied to the population being studied. For this reason, the devices summarily discussed below are commonly referred to as *conditional regression*.[51]

From a technical point of view, three separate categories of conditional regression may be distinguished. The first category contains *relationships* that are supposed to exist *between parameters*. Thus, one such relationship with regard to price elasticities, viz., the proportionality condition, assumes either $-\epsilon = \eta$ as in (8.12), or $-\epsilon_1 = \epsilon_2 + \epsilon_3 + \cdots + \eta$ as in (8.21). The proportionality condition does not necessarily apply to continuous adaptation of consumer expenditure patterns, as reflected by time-series data covering a relative by short interval of time. But the error thereby introduced need not be large. For example, testing this condition on many different foods, Stone found significant differences in only two out of 37 cases.[52] For other products, however, the difference may well be larger.

An estimator equation sometimes encountered in the earlier studies of demand is:

$$V = \alpha Y^\beta p^\epsilon \qquad (8.52)$$

where $V = vp$ and $Y = yq$. Although this form may seem attractive in some cases, it tacitly assumes equality between β and η, an assumption that is difficult to defend. Consequently, (8.52) is less sound basically than (8.12) and (8.21).

A well-known application of conditional regression to another field is the Cobb-Douglas function:

$$v = \gamma a^\lambda c^\mu \qquad (8.53)$$

v denoting volume of output, a labor and c capital. Presupposing $\mu = 1 - \lambda$, (8.53) can be written:

$$\frac{v}{a} = \gamma \left(\frac{c}{a}\right)^{1-\lambda} \qquad (8.54)$$

This form permits λ to be estimated by simple regression. The reliability of an estimate of λ obtained in this way clearly depends upon the validity of the hypothesis: $\mu = 1 - \lambda$. As is evident from (8.53), this form of conditional regression does not allow for returns to scale.[53] Wherever the role

---

[51] H. WOLD, *Demand Analysis*, Sec. 2.6.

[52] *The Measurement of Consumers' Expenditure*, . . . , *op. cit.*, p. 328 and Table 107.

[53] See J. TINBERGEN, "Professor Douglas' Production Function," *Revue de l'Institut International de Statistique*, 1943, pp. 37–48.

played by the latter happens to be important, it might therefore easily lead to unrealistic results.

In the cases discussed, the *sum* of two or more parameters has been subjected to a side condition. In other situations the *ratios* of the two may be fixed in advance, as when a linear demand equation includes an allowance for the functional distribution of income, e.g., equation (8.19) where the exponential form is used. In this case separate estimates of the marginal propensities to consume (β_1, β_2, β_3) may be derived from sample survey data for each of the three main categories of disposable income: wage income (L), non-wage income (Z) and farm income (F). Defining:

$$\tilde{\beta}_2 = \frac{\beta_2}{\beta_1} \quad and \quad \tilde{\beta}_3 = \frac{\beta_3}{\beta_1} \tag{8.55}$$

the three variables are combined into one, and a new estimate of β_1 is obtained by applying time series data to the following form:

$$v = \beta_1 \left(\frac{L}{q} + \tilde{\beta}_2 \frac{Z}{q} + \tilde{\beta}_3 \frac{F}{q} \right) \tag{8.56}$$

In this way the usually high intercorrelation between different types of income can be avoided whereas the main differences in the propensity to consume are included automatically.[54]

The second category imposes an even more drastic condition by directly "pegging" the numerical value of one of the parameters. Using a chosen value as an *a priori* coefficient, the estimates for the other parameters are then subject to the side condition implied by the specific value chosen for the pegged coefficient. If, say, β in (8.50) is used as an aprioristic coefficient, the estimator equation for the coefficient of x_3', x_4', etc., becomes:

$$x_1' - \beta x_2' = \alpha + \gamma x_3' + \delta x_4' + \cdots \tag{8.57}$$

with the new series ($x_1' - \beta x_2'$) as dependent variable. Sometimes this procedure may be inevitable if multicollinearity between the explanatory variables is such as to make some of the coefficients unidentifiable.

Another case in point is the use of the functional approach in measuring the influence of income (8.19). Income earned from different sources tends to be highly correlated, and sample survey data on consumption habits of non-wage and farm income separately are not always available. Direct estimates from time series as well as *a priori* fixing of the ratios among the consumption parameters (8.55 and 8.56) are then impossible. If, however, data regarding consumption of wage earners are available, the functional approach still can be applied by using an *a priori* coefficient to indicate the

---

[54] See L. R. KLEIN and A. S. GOLDBERGER, *An Econometric Model of the United States*, pp. 57–62.

probable effect of changes in L, and estimating the coefficients of Z and F, or that of the combined series representing $(Z + F)$, by means of (8.57).

If either multicollinearity between Z and prices is feared, or a less elaborate approach is thought desirable (because of limited computational capacity, lack of time, etc.), the still simpler device of choosing an aprioristic coefficient for total disposable income, y, may be preferable.[55]

Simplified approximations of the demand equation can be obtained by combining two or more of the devices hitherto discussed. Noteworthy is Stone's approach, which implies the following:

1. Logarithmic first difference transformation.
2. *A priori* coefficients for the income elasticities as obtained from family-expenditure statistics.
3. Use of the proportionality condition.

In the absence of closely competing products, the resulting estimator equation is of the form:[56]

$$\Delta \, log \, v - \tilde{\beta} \, \Delta \, log \, (y/q) = \alpha + \epsilon \, log \, (p/q) \tag{8.58}$$

where the *a priori* coefficient is represented by $\tilde{\beta}$.

In this way, a full-fledged structural equation containing four parameters of the following form,

$$v = \gamma y^{\beta} \left(\frac{p}{q}\right)^{\epsilon} e^{\rho t} \tag{8.59}$$

is approximated by estimating only two coefficients with the use of time-series data.

The trend term $e^{\rho t}$ is readily obtained from (8.58):[57]

$$\rho = 2.303\alpha \tag{8.60}$$

However elegant from the statistical point of view, functional forms such as (8.58) aim, before anything else, at securing efficient estimates for the different price parameters, as shown by Table 8.1. But this is not to say that they also represent an ideal analytical approach where changes in non-price variables are concerned. As has been demonstrated by one of the authors, the influence of variations in income and/or relative prices may be over-shadowed more often than not by that of specific factors.[58] This is particu-

---

[55] As an example, see H. STAEHLE, "Relative Prices and Postwar Markets for Animal Food Products," *Quarterly Journal of Economics*, February, 1945; in particular, p. 252ff. and Figs. II and III.

[56] R. STONE, *Measurement of Consumers' Expenditures*, . . . , *op. cit.*, Ch. XX, Sec. 4.

[57] Assuming serial independence of the residuals of the transformed series. STONE, *loc. cit.*, Ch. XIX, Sec. 9.

[58] R. FERBER, "A Statistical Study of Factors Influencing Temporal Variations in Aggregate Service Expenditures," in *Consumer Behavior: Research in Consumer Reactions*, L. H. Clark, ed., New York, 1958, especially p. 405ff.

larly so if the series studied deal with single products or services rather than broad aggregates. Terms representing those specific factors or dynamic elements as discussed in the foregoing can, however, be added wherever necessary. Thus, the addition of $\Delta^2 \log y$ in (8.58) or of $\Delta \log y$ in the untransformed equation might be used to allow for the existence of a single lag or quasi-accelerator.

Apart from this, information extracted from sample survey data requires careful handling when used in the analysis of time series. First, family budgets are not equally reliable for all products. Thus, a reputed downward bias is found where expenditures on alcohol and tobacco are concerned. This led Stone to estimate income elasticities for these products directly from time series.

Second, and more important, is the question whether a cross-section analysis is representative of developments over time.[59] Provided that the survey data are sufficiently detailed, such sources of error as are due to the systematic association of family size, occupation and age with income, can be eliminated by suitable specification of the estimator equation for β. As an example, consider the following relation that is comparatively easy to handle:

$$\log v = \alpha + \beta \log y + \lambda n + \zeta k \qquad (8.61)$$

v and y denote total consumption per family (either in money or volume units) and total disposable family income, respectively,

n is the number of persons (or, preferably, adult equivalents) per family,

k is a dummy variable equalling 1 in the case of clerical employees' families, and 0 for those of manual laborers.

As is evident from (8.61), one additional unit of family size is supposed to change consumption by $100(10^\lambda - 1)$ per cent. This method of allowing for family size, though admittedly rough, makes it possible to avoid constructing complicated consumer-unit scales for the purpose of "deflating" v and y, while taking care of systematic variance in consumption due to differences in family size.

Similarly, $100(10^\zeta - 1)$ indicates the percentage difference in consumption between clerical and manual labor, income and family size being the same. This variable illustrates the importance of taking into account other relevant factors in estimating income elasticities. Thus, suppose the true elasticities, β_1 and β_2, for clerical and manual workers were equal. Even in this case, the income elasticity for the sample as a whole, if computed regardless of social class, does not necessarily take the same absolute value as β_1 and β_2, as shown by Fig. 8.3.

But although the sources of error due to the association of other factors

---

[59] See T. HAAVELMO, "Family Expenditure and the Marginal Propensity to Consume," *Econometrica*, October, 1947, pp. 335–342, especially Sec. 4.

with income may have been successfully removed[60] we cannot be sure that the net-elasticity upon income does represent consumer behavior over time. *A priori* estimates for β remain therefore a second-best solution, according to the theoretical economist. But then, a second-best solution may be preferable to an impeccable, theoretical approach that is unable to produce numerical estimates with a reasonable degree of precision.

The third form of conditional regression is of a more experimental nature. It is also less ambitious. Instead of accepting in advance one of the side conditions as the correct one, the procedure consists in the repeated substitution of different values for the pegged parameter. For each value of the latter,

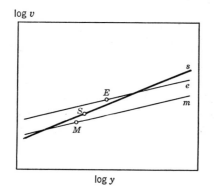

Fig. 8.3. Regression of Consumption on Incomes

M and m: point of gravity and regression line for manual labour, respectively.
E and e: ditto, for clinical employees.
S and s: ditto, for total sample, regression not corrected for differences in social classes.

corresponding values of the other parameters are estimated by regression analysis.

If, for instance, we are not sure of the correct value of β in (8.57), but .5 and 1.0 are judged reasonable lower and upper limits, β can be fixed successively at .5, .6, etc., up to 1.0. This procedure results in a possible range of estimates for γ and δ. In some cases these ranges may be narrowed if for certain values of β the corresponding values of γ and δ are not acceptable on the basis of *a priori* expectations of their sign and size, or by standard errors and total correlation. Alternatively, this method can be applied with other side

---

[60] For some excellent studies in this field, see H. S. Houthakker, "The Econometrics of Family Budgets," *Journal of the Royal Statistical Society,* Part 1, 1952, pp. 1–20; and L. R. Klein, "Statistical Estimation of Economic Relations from Survey Data" in *Contributions of Survey Methods to Economics* (New York: Columbia University Press, 1954). For a related method of applying information from survey data to time-series analysis, see V. G. Lippitt, *Determinants of Consumer Demand for Housefurnishings and Equipment* (Cambridge, Mass.: Harvard University Press, 1959).

conditions where the sum of the parameters or their ratios are fixed in advance.

One advantage of this method is that, in case of uncertainty with regard to the fixed parameter, at least some information about the other parameters, such as possible minimum and maximum values, can be obtained. Another advantage is that the influence of changes in the fixed parameter upon the other coefficients are shown unambiguously.[61]

This method takes on an altogether different twist if used to ascertain the "best" value for the *a priori* coefficient itself, or that for the ratio among a pair of parameters. An innocent application is the determination of the average lag between two variables by assuming different values for this lag and selecting the value that yields the highest coefficient of simple correlation (Sec. 7.6). More complicated, however, are the consequences if Koyck's distributed lag has to be estimated from (8.43). Since the "best" value is not based on *a priori* information, sampling errors obtained for the corresponding values of the other parameters are invalidated to some unknown extent. Although this kind of application is sometimes unavoidable, it is well to remember that inferences obtained thereby are less reliable than those inferred from straightforward regression analysis. Statements in terms of possible ranges are therefore to be preferred.

8.10.   EVALUATION OF RESULTS

An adequate evaluation of final results of a demand analysis has to reckon with five different points of view. *First*, the degree of confidence placed in the coefficients of an empirical demand function depends chiefly upon the reliability of the time series used. A fact sometimes overlooked is that careful selection and adequate processing of data is more important than acrobatics with an elaborate specification.

Second, it is well to remember that demand analysis has to serve a specific purpose, either a practical or a scientific one. The specification must be compatible with this purpose and fit in logically with the "data" and "unknowns" of the problem at hand. (See Fig. 2.3.) Thus, a first-difference transformation might be well suited to bring out short-term reaction patterns, but is less appropriate if a study of long-term shifts in demand is contemplated.

Third, statistics such as the coefficient of correlation may provide a general indication whether the overall explanation of demand during the period studied has been reasonably successful. However, as noted in Sec. 3.5, R tells nothing whatsoever about the accuracy of the parameter estimates, or about

---

[61] A number of interesting applications is given in H. Wold and L. Jureen, *Demand Analysis*, Secs. 15.1 and 17.2.

their ability to forecast future developments.[62] For the first purpose standard errors are the more suitable yardstick, whereas the coefficients of partial correlation (Sec. 3.5) may give a more refined indication, particularly if a choice is to be made between two alternative hypotheses. Finally, a check on the influence on the standard errors of serial correlation between the residuals is provided by the *Von-Neumann ratio.* Correlation coefficients, standard errors and the Von-Neumann ratio, therefore, are generally considered indispensable criteria for an evaluation of a demand function from an empirical point of view.

Fourth, just as important as the latter is validation of the results against theoretical and practical *a priori* considerations.[63] Although furnishing some indications of possible signs of parameters, economic theory, unfortunately, seldom provides indications of their size, unless the famous tripartite classification of inferior goods, necessities and luxuries with their ensuing requirements as to sign and size is regarded as such. Here it is empirical research that has to classify a given product rather than economic theory. In some cases, however, economic reasoning can establish *a priori* conditions for the ratio expected among a pair of coefficients.[64] Practical evaluation, on the contrary, is based either upon the commonsense plausibility of the numerical values obtained, or upon the results of analogous investigations of the same or related products. Criteria thus obtained need not be decisive for the acceptance or rejection of a coefficient, but wherever differences are sizeable, an explanation is required. The latter is indispensable if the results are to be made plausible to colleagues in the same field.

Fifth, although not generally thought necessary, a complete evaluation requires study of the residuals of successive years of the period studied. The reason for this is twofold. First, even a satisfactory Von-Neumann ratio may conceal systematic discrepancies, such as the fact that every turning point has been missed. A specification suffering in this respect is less suitable as an estimator equation for short-term forecasts. Consequently, the standard errors and other statistics just mentioned tell only part of the story, and visual inspection either by partial scatter diagrams or by graphs showing the time series of the computed and actual values with the contributions of each of the explanatory variables is required to complete the picture, as illustrated by Fig. 8.4.

The other reason is that a closer analysis of the time shape of the residuals may indicate that a specific variable has been omitted from the specification. The failure of a theoretically important variable to appear with a coefficient

---

[62] The problem of evaluating forecasting ability is discussed in Chapter 10.

[63] See Sec. 2.5.

[64] Examples are the *Hotelling-Jureen* condition and the *Törnqvist* theorem regarding the ratio between two cross-elasticities and that among the income and price-elasticity. See WOLD, *op. cit.*, Secs 6.3, 6.5 and 15.1.

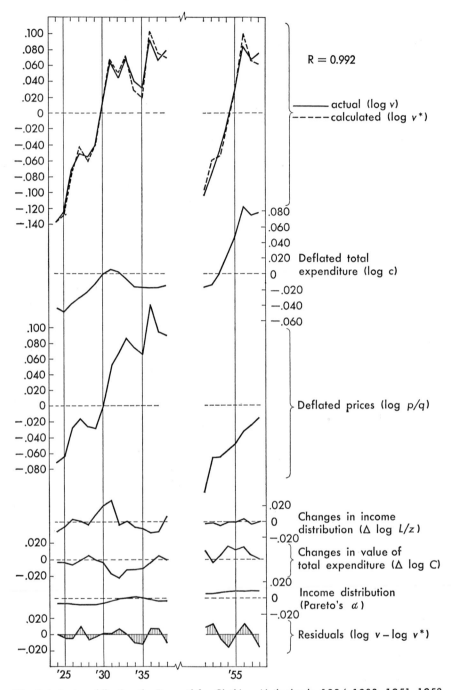

Fig. 8.4. *Factors Affecting the Demand for Clothing, Netherlands, 1924–1938, 1951–1958*

Reproduced by courtesy of the Central Planning Bureau, The Hague.

of the expected sign and size can sometimes be attributed to incidental factors known to have been present in certain years. Deviant case analysis applied to the study of time series may also be fruitful from the heuristic point of view.[65] As noted in Sec. 3.5, this procedure is, however, by no means ideal from the statistician's point of view. The difficulty is that clues based on the sample period cannot reasonably serve as a basis for formulating new hypotheses if the new ones are to be tested with the same sample observations.[66] But this is not to say that one ought to accept estimates of parameters of the theoretically best specification as valid, although the residuals point to the latter as being glaringly incomplete.[67] Testing a hypothesis is one thing; evaluating its completeness another.

It should be stressed that each of these five aspects should be considered in reporting the results of a demand study. They may serve as so many checks on overstating the merits of a certain specification or on otherwise sweeping conclusions. To be sure, inferences from, say, 15 sample years, each covering the reactions of some millions of consumers, may seem more trustworthy than inferences made from a regression analysis based upon a sample survey with fifteen individuals as respondents. But it is clear from the foregoing that the number of factors affecting shifts in demand over time is considerable, and only a few can be represented in the demand equation. For this reason the small number of time-series observations only permits conclusions of very approximate validity.

| *Supplement to Chapter 8* | Demand Analysis of Clothing |

Following is a case study of a time series analysis of the demand for clothing.

This case study is of particular interest since it illustrates most of the concepts discussed in the present chapter, such as conditional regression,

---

[65] For an application, see RUTH P. MACK's analysis of shoe buying, *op. cit.*, p. 45ff.

[66] For a discussion of this point, see T. J. KOOPMANS, "Methodological Issues in Quantitative Economics," *Review of Economics and Statistics*, May, 1949, p. 90.

[67] Actually, the parameters of an incomplete specification can be accepted as valid if the explanatory variables concerned are perfectly uncorrelated with the one that has been omitted. Unfortunately, this hardly ever occurs in practice.

the proportionality conditions, the quasi-accelerator, measuring the influence of income distribution, the use of the Von Neuman ratio and beta coefficients as additional criteria, as well as evaluation of the results against previous cross-section analyses.

Table 8.5

TIME-SERIES ANALYSIS OF THE DEMAND FOR CLOTHING[a,b]

(Netherlands, 1924–1938 and 1951–1958)

(1)	(2)	(3)	(4)	(5)	(6)	(7)	(8)
	ELASTICITIES WITH REGARD TO		INFLUENCE OF				
Equation number	Deflated total expenditure (log c)	Deflated prices (log (p/q))	Changes in functional distribution of income (Δ log (L/Z))	Changes in total expenditure (Δ log C)	Pareto's α	R²	N.R. (von Neumann Ratio)
1	1.28 (.06)	−.70 (.05)	—	—	—	.968	1.27
2	1.24 (.06)	−.70 (.05)	.20 (.49)	—	—	.974	1.22
3	1.27 (.10)	−.70 (.05)	—	—	.001 (21.58)	.968	1.27
4	1.14 (.06)	−.76 (.04)	.26 (.31)	.47 (.32)	—	.982	1.65
5	.98 (.11)	−.77 (.04)	.33 (.27)	.49 (.30)	.041 (.61)	.984	1.94

a General form of the demand equation:

$$log\ v = \beta_1 + \beta_2\ log\ c + \beta_3\ log\ (p/q) + \beta_4\ \Delta\ log\ (L/Z) + \beta_5\ \Delta\ log\ C + \beta_6\alpha$$

where the series for v, c and C are on a per capita basis. For the evaluation of β_6 it should be borne in mind that the unit chosen for log v and α is .001.
b Standard errors measured as a decimal fraction of the coefficients are given in parentheses.

The analysis refers to the demand for clothing in the Netherlands for the combined periods, 1924–1938 and 1951–1958. The marginal contribution of each of the independent variables to the explained variance of demand can be evaluated from .the coefficients of determination presented in Table 8.5. Reliable data on disposable income of households not being available for the interwar period, per capita demand has been related to total deflated consumption per head. The coefficient represents, therefore, the expenditure elasticity rather than income elasticity, the former being necessarily larger than the latter. Since it appeared to be impossible to identify the influence of prices separately for both p and q, conditional regression had to be applied by imposing the proportionality conditions. The long-term influence of the distribution of income is represented by Pareto's α.

Short-term dynamic influences appear to affect demand where changes in the value of total consumption are concerned ($\Delta\ log\ C$) as well as in the case of changes in the distribution of income as represented by $\Delta\ log\ (L/Z)$, where L is the total wage bill and Z aggregate non-labor income.

The coefficients of the expenditure- and price-elasticities are reasonably stable for all the equations investigated. As judged by the correlation coefficients and the von Neumann Ratios, of the five equations shown in Table 8.5, the fourth and fifth are to be preferred. The contributions of each of the explanatory variables to the explanation of the standard deviation of demand as measured by the beta-coefficients, are:

	log c	$log \dfrac{p}{q}$	$\Delta \, log \dfrac{L}{Z}$	$\Delta \, log \, C$	α
Eq. 4	*.60*	*−.90*	*.10*	*.13*	—
Eq. 5	*.52*	*−.91*	*.13*	*.14*	*.09*

A check on the estimates of the expenditure elasticities is possible, the values obtained from Equations 4 and 5, i.e., 1.14 and .98, corresponding well with those found from two available family-expenditure surveys:

	ϵ_{vc}
1935/36	1.07
	(.06)
1951	1.02
	(.06)

A value fairly close to unity may therefore be considered representative of the long-term influence of real expenditure per head.

In Equation 5 the relative standard error of the coefficient for Pareto's α is .61. Although the coefficient is not significant at the 5 per cent level, this may be no reason to reject the equation since the introduction of α leads to a sizeable improvement in the von Neumann Ratio and brings the long-term influence of real expenditure still more in line with the values obtained from the family-expenditure studies.

The residual variance of Equation 5, as represented by the standard error of regression, is .0095, or $2\frac{1}{4}$ per cent, showing that even for the period of observation high coefficients of correlation are not necessarily associated with great accuracy of the estimates.

PROBLEMS

1. Set up a time-series model to estimate consumer demand for nylon auto tires for replacement purposes, taking into account competitive forces as well as overall economic conditions.

2. How might income elasticities computed from consumer panel data, for the same families over time, compare with the usual cross-section and time-series elasticities, say for clothing?

3. Discuss the pros and cons of a logarithmic vs. arithmetic form of demand relation in analyzing:
   a) per capita consumption of bread
   b) per capita consumption of aluminum.

4. (For those mathematically inclined) Derive the relations (8.28) and (8.29).

5. To what extent, if any, would you expect the equality between the various elasticities, equation (8.12), to be altered in each of the following studies, and in what direction. Explain why.
   a) the demand for aluminum siding over time
   b) the demand for margarine over time
   c) the demand for Brand X cigarettes on a cross-section basis.

6. Set up a time-series demand relation for Brand Y washing machines, a dominant producer in the industry. Give definitions of the various elasticities, and state with reasons what sort of relations, if any, might be expected between them. Illustrate with reference to the demand for food.

7. Discuss how quality considerations might be taken into account in each of the following studies:
   a) time-series demand for room air conditioners
   b) cross-section demand for wool dresses
   c) time-series demand for auto tires
   d) time-series demand for TV sets
   e) cross-section demand for readership of weekly "picture" magazines.

8. Comment on the following relation suggested in a time-series study of the demand for life insurance in the U. S. How might this relation be improved?

Sales $= \alpha + \beta$ *(Real national income)* $+ \gamma$ *(Pareto's alpha)*
$+ \delta$ *(Wholesale price index)* $+ \epsilon$ *(Sales, lagged one year)*

9. Devise a lagged relation for estimating the influence of advertising on sales of grocery store merchandise.

10. (For those mathematically inclined) Derive the time lag and total effect of single lags for equations 8.33–8.35 (Table 8.2).

11. Discuss the desirability of using lagged variables in each of the following demand studies. If lagged variables are desirable, explain what types of lags you would recommend and for which variables.
    a) demand for men's dress suits
    b) demand for liquid assets
    c) demand for vacation travel
    d) demand for own home.

12. *a*) Derive the estimator equation (8.42) given the structural equation (8.41).
    b) Under what conditions might the structural equation in this case also serve as the estimator equation?

13. Evaluate the pros and cons of deflating for price and population changes a relation estimating the demand for medical care. What alternatives might be preferable? Under what conditions?

14. Write down the computational forms for estimating equation (8.61).

15. The amount a car-owning family spends on car repairs annually is hypothesized to depend on number of cars owned, plans to buy a new car within the next year, age of present cars, condition of present cars, whether the car is a compact, foreign or regular size, income level, and presence of teen-agers. Write a regression function incorporating these ideas and prepare instructions for estimating the parameters and their standard errors.

SELECTED REFERENCES

Specification

The specification of single-equation demand relationships is illustrated with reference to numerous agricultural commodities in *The Theory and Measurement of Demand,* by HENRY SCHULTZ (Chicago: University of Chicago Press, 1938). This work is replete with discussions of the specification of variables and the elimination of trend. A more general approach to demand analysis, with emphasis on the use of simultaneous equations, will be found in *Econometrics* by GERHARD TINTNER (New York: Wiley & Sons, 1952) as well as in the econometrics text of L. R. KLEIN. Particularly important from a theoretical as well as practical point of view is H. WOLD and L. JUREEN's, *Demand Analysis* (New York: John Wiley & Sons, 1952).

The literature is full of all sorts of demand studies for different commodities and using different approaches. The ones mentioned below represent only a small sample of this total with emphasis on those which possess either special methodological value or particular substantive interest. Perhaps the most comprehensive set of demand studies for individual non-durables is contained in *The Measurement of Consumers' Expenditure and Behaviour in the United Kingdom, 1920–1938,* by RICHARD STONE (Cambridge: Cambridge University Press, 1954). This book presents demand studies for a number of individual consumer goods and also contains an excellent description, in the first part, of the theoretical assumptions and measurement techniques used in obtaining the demand relations.

A number of interesting demand studies have been undertaken of consumer durable goods. Among these are: M. J. FARREL, "The Demand for Motor Cars in the United States" (*Journal of the Royal Statistical Society,* 1954); G. C. CHOW, *The Demand for Automobiles in the United States* (Amsterdam: North Holland Publishing Company, 1957); RICHARD STONE and D. A. ROWE, "The Durability of Consumers' Goods" (*Econometrica,* April, 1960, pp. 407–416); V. G. LIPPITT, *Determinants of Consumer Demand for House Furnishings and Equipment* (Cambridge: Harvard University Press, 1959).

The work by LIPPITT is particularly interesting since it presents a novel approach for combining both cross-section data and time-series data in a demand study. Another approach of this sort is discussed in a demand study for food by JAMES TOBIN, "A Statistical Demand Function for the U. S. A." (*Journal of the Royal Statistical Society,* 1950, pp. 113–149).

Methods of increasing the available information by using time series for the separate states instead of national aggregates are skillfully discussed and illustrated in the forthcoming book of C. Kaysen and F. Fisher, *The Demand for Electricity in the United States* (Amsterdam: North-Holland Publishing Co.).

A number of demand relations for consumer services will be found in "A Statistical Study of Factors Influencing Temporal Variations in Aggregate Service Expenditures" by Robert Ferber (in L. H. Clark, editor, *Consumer Behavior: Research in Consumer Reactions*, New York: Harper & Bros., 1958, pp. 394–419). Discussion of the specification of demand relations on an aggregate basis will be found in *An Econometric Model of the United States, 1929–1952* by L. R. Klein and A. S. Goldberger.

For a fairly comprehensive bibliography of post-war demand studies and demand projections, see *Bibliography on Demand Analysis and Projections* (Rome: Food and Agricultural Organization of the United Nations, 1959, Supplement, 1960; a revised tri-lingual edition is intended for 1961). A much less complete survey, but covering also pre-war studies, is given by Robert Badouin, *L'Elasticite de la Demande de Biens de Consommation* (Paris: Armand Colin, 1953).

Lags

References covering different approaches to the measurement of lags have already been presented in the bibliography to Chapter 7. In addition, the ratchet effect is discussed in *Fluctuations in the Savings-Ratio: A Problem in Economic Forecasting*, by Franco Modigliani (New York: National Bureau of Economic Research, Studies in Income and Wealth, Vol. XI, 1949). The rationale for this effect is discussed from a broad sociological and psychological point of view in *Income, Saving and the Theory of Consumption Behavior*, by James Duesenberry (Cambridge: Harvard University Press, 1949). The application of this effect to individual demand studies is discussed in "Irreversible Demand Functions" by M. J. Farrel (*Econometrica*, April, 1952, pp. 171–186). The use of the quasi-accelerator is illustrated in "The Direction of Change in Income and the Consumption Function," by R. P. Mack (*Review of Economics and Statistics*, November, 1948, pp. 239–259). The concept of lags is also discussed and made use of in the automobile demand study of Chow.

Trend Elimination and Serial Correlation

A basic article on the elimination of trends is "Partial Time Regression as Compared with Individual Trends," by Ragnar Frisch and F. V. Waugh (*Econometrica*, 1933).

The nature of the bias in parameter estimates introduced in serial correlation as well as various transformations for eliminating this correlation are discussed in two articles by David Cochrane and G. H. Orcutt in the 1949 issues of the *Journal of the American Statistical Association* (pages 32–61 and 356–72). The econometrics text by Tintner also discusses this question in some detail and presents a number of examples of how such transformations might be made. A refined method applying conditional linear regression has been suggested by Hildreth and Lu, *Demand Relations With Autocorrelated Disturbances* (East Lansing, Michigan: Department of

Agricultural Economics, Michigan State University, Technical Bulletin 246, 1960).

Statistical Confluence Analysis by Means of Complete Regression Systems by RAGNER FRISCH (Oslo: Universitets Okonomiske Institutt, 1934) is a basic work on the use of this schematic though laborious analysis of the influence of multicollinearity on the parameters obtained from different specifications of the demand equation.

Problems introduced by serial correlation in demand functions as well as the subject of conditional regression are discussed in *Demand Analysis* by H. WOLD (New York: Wiley & Sons, 1952). Other good treatments of the latter subject will be found in the study by LIPPITT mentioned previously.

For the derivation of income elasticities from family-budget data, see "The Econometrics of Family Budgets," by H. S. HOUTHAKKER (*Journal of the Royal Statistical Society*, 1952, pp. 1–20) as well as "Statistical Estimation of Economic Relations from Survey Data," by L. R. KLEIN (*Contributions of Survey Methods to Economics*, New York: Columbia University Press, 1954).

9 | Special Applications of Time Series: Economic Models

THE USE of equation systems in estimating economic relationships from time series is the focal point of this chapter. Though the construction and analysis of equation systems are, in principle, equally applicable to cross-section data, in practice their main use is with time series. Therefore, this discussion would seem most appropriate in this chapter.[1] At the same time, this enables us to lead into recent developments relating to the simulation of economic and market behavior, a topic closely connected with both equation systems and time-series data.

Following these sections, we are then in a good position to discuss the forecasting problem, with particular reference to the adequacy of equation systems for prognosticative purposes.

9.1. EQUATION SYSTEMS

9.1.1. The Concept of a Model

The aim of all economic and market analysis is to describe the operations of the real world in one or more of its aspects, preferably with sufficient generality and precision to enable useful predictions to be made about future developments. The movement of business or economic activity is, however, determined partly by the non-economic conditions under which firms and consumers operate and partly by the manner in which these economic units

---

[1] For an interesting application to cross-section analysis, see I. HOCH, "Simultaneous Equation Bias in the Context of the Cobb-Douglas Production Function," *Econometrica*, Vol. 26, October, 1958, pp. 566–579.

react to actions of other economic units and to changes in this environment. The specification of these inter-relations within a certain scope of activity is the purpose of a "model." Though not necessary, such specification is generally sought in equation form, for this is the most precise means of specifying economic relations, of testing their adequacy, and of subjecting them to further analysis.

The equations represent a "model" in the sense that their objective is to portray developments in the real world in simplified yet useful form. The model is derived by attempting to approximate and simplify actual conditions by means of certain basic assumptions, or propositions, which then serve as the basis for the construction of the equations. The model can be a very complicated one, involving numerous inter-related equations, or it can consist of perhaps a single linear equation in two variables.

For example, an explanation of variation in unit sales of a product (S_i) may be advanced in terms of the price of the product relative to other prices (P_i/P) and of gross national product (Y). It may further be hypothesized that the relationship is arithmetic linear. This "model" leads, then, to the following equation:

$$S_i = \alpha + \epsilon(P_i/\bar{P}) + \beta Y + u \qquad (9.1)$$

The parameters to be estimated from available data are α, β, and ϵ. In addition, the variable, u, is added as a "stochastic" term to indicate that in practice the relationship (9.1) will not be exact, but rather that the estimate of S_i derived from (9.1) can be expected to deviate from the corresponding actual value because of the effect of other, presumably erratic, influences affecting S_i, and of errors of measurement. These influences are generally assumed to be random in nature and normally distributed, so that u will average out to zero. If this assumption can be made, the estimation problem becomes less difficult, as discussed later. Once the parameters have been estimated, various tests can be applied to evaluate the adequacy of the equation in approximating actual product sales, as well as the adequacy of the assumptions used in estimating the parameters.

Although this example provides a highly simplified representation of a model, it nevertheless serves to illustrate what goes into the construction of an economic model. Essentially, the process can be said to involve four more or less distinct steps, as follows:

1. Specification of a set of hypotheses purporting to explain the (one or more) phenomena being studied. These hypotheses may be based on past studies, empirical findings and/or *a priori* reasoning.
2. Translation of these hypotheses into a form amenable for testing, usually into mathematical equations, and for identification of the individual relations.

3. Estimation of the parameters of the model. This step necessitates generally prior assumptions of various mathematical characteristics of the variables so that a proper estimation procedure can be specified, as will be discussed shortly.
4. Evaluation of the adequacy of the model and of the underlying assumptions and hypotheses, generally by empirical tests.

This is not the place to discuss the first step, which permeates all analytical work and is as much an art as a science. In the following sections, therefore, we shall focus on the last three steps, which are most distinctive to model construction. First, however, it would seem desirable to secure an idea of the various components of a model and of how models can vary.

9.1.2.　Ingredients of a Model

A complete model generally consists of a system of one or more mathematical equations explaining how different variables are related to each other. In the formulation of the model, decisions are required on a number of different characteristics or ingredients, the most important of which are reviewed in this section.

9.1.2.1.　Stochastic properties. An equation system such as (4.18) and (4.19), or like (7.21), is *non-stochastic* because it contains no allowance for possible deviations of empirically-estimated values of the variables from the actual values or of errors in our measurements of the data. From the point of view of pure theory, this is not a serious limitation, for many useful and provocative results can be obtained without regard to empirical data: the acceleration principle is one such example.

For evaluating the adequacy of a particular model, however, or for any empirical applications, such an assumption is clearly most unrealistic. Aside from the fact that virtually all empirical data in economics and business are subject to errors of measurement, the estimated value of a variable from a functional relation will deviate from the true value for a number of reasons. Thus, the functional relation will rarely be complete (unless it is a definitional equation), because it is out of the question to include the myriad of variables that influence economic events. Rather the objective is to include the principal variables, which may be difficult enough as it is and which, when accomplished, means that at any given time a certain margin for error has to exist because of the pertinent variables that have been omitted. Then, too, the estimates of the parameters are subject to error, a factor which will also serve to bring about individual errors in the estimates of the dependent variable.

These various sources of error can hardly be specified individually. The expedient invariably selected, therefore, is to represent these sources of error by a single random, or stochastic, variable which is appended to each of the functional relations of the model. With equation (9.1), this is the variable u. Its presence tells us that for any observation period, t, the estimate of S_i obtained from (9.1) will differ from the corresponding actual value by a margin, u_t. Hence, u serves as the gauge of error. Clearly, the smaller is u, the more accurate is the functional relation. In this way, u also serves as a basis for selecting an estimation procedure in a particular case, namely, to select that estimation procedure which will minimize some mathematical combination of the u's. Specification of the properties of the u's—their relation to each other and to the observed variables—is an essential prerequisite to selection of an efficient estimation procedure. We will discuss this matter at further length in the section on estimation. Suffice it to say that although for theoretical analysis a stochastic variable can often be discarded, for any empirical work such a variable, and specification of its properties, is essential. However, it should be noted that, though the stochastic variable ought to allow for errors of measurement, the different estimation procedures discussed in this chapter all disregard errors of observation.

9.1.2.2. *Types of equations.* A model may consist of many different equations, all serving to indicate the inter-relations among the variables in the system. The equations that enter into a model may be said to consist of three general types: definitions, technical relations and behavior relations. Following is a model containing all three of these types of equations. It seeks to explain the formation of national income (Y) in terms of expenditures of the private sector of the economy (X^p), of the government sector (X^g), and of the amount of tax receipts (T). The equations are:[2]

$$Y = X^p + X^g \tag{9.2a}$$
$$X^p = X_o + \alpha(Y - T) + u \tag{9.2b}$$
$$T = T_o + tY + v \tag{9.2c}$$

where X_o and T_o are constants, and u and v are unobservable random variables

Equation (9.2a) is a *definition:* it says that national income is equivalent to total private expenditures plus total government expenditures.

Equation (9.2b) is a *behavior relation:* it says that total private expenditures are related to national income less tax receipts.

Equation (9.2c) is a *technical relation:* it shows how tax receipts vary with national income.

Note that definitional equations do not have any stochastic property. Equation (9.2a) is an identity, and therefore errors of estimation are irrelevant. On the other hand, behavior relations are stochastic, for the purpose of

---

[2] Adapted from J. Tinbergen, *Economic Policy: Principles and Design* (North Holland Pub. Co., 1956), p. 233.

equations such as (9.2b) is to relate the behavior of one sector or variable to that of other sectors; hence the stochastic variable, u.

Technical relations may or may not be stochastic. Thus, the tax rate in the hypothetical country depicted by equations (9.2) may be such that (9.2c) is the exact formulation. If, say, the tax is \$1 million plus 10 per cent of national income, then T_o and t are specified and there is no source of error (at least theoretically). It may be, however, that T stands for a multitude of individual taxes, and that equation (9.2c) is a simplified approximation to total tax determination. In that case, the equation for empirical purposes would have to include a stochastic variable, as it does—the variable, v.

Technical relations may arise out of the legal-institutional framework of an economic system, as is the case with equation (9.2c), or they may arise out of engineering or physical production processes. Illustrative of the latter is equation (6.5), which relates the amount of the product of industry j required by industry i in its production processes by means of the technical coefficient, a_{ij}. This is a stochastic relation. (Why?)

Any particular model need not contain all three types of equations. The basis of most models, however, is the behavioral relations, as determined by the hypotheses advanced to explain the phenomena under study. These equations are supplemented by technical relations and definitional equations as needed.

9.1.2.3.   *Types of variables.* The variables of a model can be classified in various ways. Three means of classification are especially important from the point of view of estimation of parameters as well as for assessing the predictive and general diagnostic value of a model. These are the distinction between *exogenous* and *endogenous* variables, the distinction between *lagged* and *current* variables, and the distinction between *instantaneous interacting* and other variables.

The last two distinctions have already been encountered in earlier parts of this book. If X is not only influenced by Y but also affects the value of Y in the same time period, the two variables are said to be in instantaneous interaction with each other, or *interdependent.* Thus, price and quantity are interdependent in the demand-supply model represented by equations (4.18) and (4.19). Quantity is not only affected by the price of the product but, in the *same* time period, price is in turn influenced by quantity: the two variables interact with each other. On the other hand, the assumption underlying the model represented by equation (9.1) is that gross national product and relative price affect the sales of the product but not vice-versa.

This distinction is particularly important from the point of view of statistical estimation, for a basic assumption underlying least-squares estimation is that the variable whose fluctuations are to be explained—the "dependent" variable—is affected by the explanatory, or "independent," variables but that the latter are not in turn affected by the dependent variable in the same time period. If this assumption does not hold, as in the case of equations

(4.18) and (4.19), least-squares estimation is subject to a certain bias, the degree of which is difficult to evaluate.

Note that for two variables to be interdependent, the interaction must be instantaneous. If all relations between two variables are one-way directed, or unilateral, the two variables are said to be *recursive*, a phenomenon which offers various computational advantages, as will be shown later.

The distinction between lagged and current variables permeated the closing sections of the preceding chapter, and therefore needs no further elaboration.

Endogenous variables are those that affect one or more other variables of the system and are in turn influenced by one or more of the latter; while *exogenous variables* affect the variables of the system without being influenced by them. In effect, the endogenous variables are the variables whose fluctuations the model seeks to explain. On the other hand, exogenous variables are those outside the scope of the system, which can be taken as given: their fluctuations do not have to be explained within the scope of the given model because they are known in advance. This knowledge may come from engineering considerations, from the institutional framework of the system, or from any external sources.

The classification of variables as exogenous or endogenous depends as much on the nature and objectives of the model as on the variables themselves. The same variable that is classified as exogenous in one model may be classified as endogenous in another. Various criteria can be used in making this classification, but perhaps the most precise is the so-called "causal principle," which "regards as exogenous those variables which influence the remaining (endogenous) variables but are not influenced thereby."[3]

Thus, in the equation model (9.2), government expenditure would be regarded as exogenous, since it is not affected by the other variables: its value at any time is presumably known on the basis of government policy. However, the other three variables in the model are endogenous within the framework of the model. Tax receipts depend on Y, which depends on private (as well as government) expenditures, which in turn depend on Y and on tax receipts. Hence, these three variables interact with each other.

If, however, equations (9.2b) and (9.2c) were to be considered as two separate models (Why not 9.2a too?), then Y might be treated as exogenous in (9.2c) and Y and T as exogenous in (9.2b). The basis for doing so in each case would be on the assumption that, in (9.2c), T is not sufficiently important to exert much effect on Y and that, in (9.2b), total private expenditures do not exert much effect on either Y or T. In a capitalistic system, the latter assumption is clearly most dubious, though perhaps not the former.

This use of the so-called "modified causal principle" is widespread, for in its absence the application of least-squares techniques to a single-equation

[3] T. C. Koopmans, ed., *Statistical Inference in Dynamic Economic Models*, p. 394.

model such as equation (9.1) or (9.2b) cannot be justified. In the case of equation (9.1), the principle may well be applicable if the product is of small importance relative to the total economy, or relatively stable. This would be true of something like purchases of men's topcoats in the former instance and perhaps of total food expenditures in the latter. However, to the extent that the assumption is used where it is not true, biased estimates of the parameters are obtained.

This three-way classification of variables can be merged into a single classification, *jointly dependent* vs. *predetermined* variables, as is depicted in Fig. 9.1. Predetermined variables are those that are given from external sources, i.e., outside the scope of the current model. They may possess this

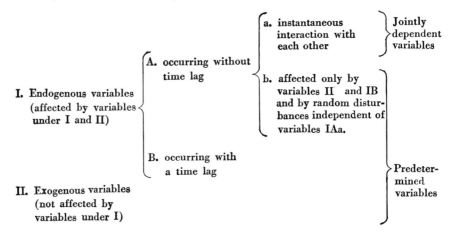

Fig. 9.1 *Classification of Variables*

Source: Koopmans, *op. cit.*, Table 7.1, p. 406.

characteristic either because of their exogenous nature, or because they are lagged endogenous variables. The jointly dependent variables are those whose fluctuations the model seeks to explain: they are instantaneously interacting variables occurring without time lag.

If there is only one such variable in the model, we have a straightforward least-squares estimation problem.

From the point of view of diagnosis or prediction, it is clearly desirable to relate endogenous variables insofar as possible to exogenous or lagged endogenous variables. (Why?) Given the complexity of the economic system and the interdependence of business and economic events, however, this ideal is not easily achieved. See, however, Sec. 10.1.3.1.

9.1.2.4.   *Static vs. dynamic.*   In model construction the use of the term "dynamic" is restricted to those models in which lagged values occur for one or more endogenous variables. Consequently, equation systems containing only current values of the endogenous variables are considered as static. Interpreted in this way, a dynamic model has the property that a change in one of the exogenous variables at time $t = 0$ may lead to a more or less sustained movement of the system at $t = 1$, $t = 2$, $t = 3$, etc., even if all exogenous variables remain unchanged after the initial "impulse" at $t = 0$. This is usually referred to as the endogenous development pattern of the system: it depends not only on the parameters of the system and on the type of impulse but also on the initial values of all the variables at $t = 0$.

With a static model, equilibrium is reached again within the same period. Consequently, it cannot show a purely endogenous development. An example of such a static model is 9.3.a − 9.3.c, where the adaptation of demand and prices to a change in income or wage rates is instantaneous. The same system would have been a dynamic one if demand in 9.3.a had reacted upon the lagged instead of upon the current values of prices, i.e., on $P_{t-\vartheta}$ instead of upon P_t. Other examples of structural equations that may give rise to dynamic systems are 4.5 and 4.6 as well as the several forms discussed in Sec. 8.7. Clearly, dynamic models are essential where the endogenous movements of a system through time are to be considered. They tend therefore to be more realistic, particularly where annual or quarterly models are concerned. Nevertheless, dynamic equations representing an accumulation process, such as 4.5, form an integral part of long-term models. Static models too may be useful, as for those policy problems where the final equilibrium reached after a sustained change of an instrument is the main point of interest rather than the time shape of the reaction.

9.1.2.5. *Instruments of policy.* From an analytical point of view, especially with regard to policy formation, it is useful to identify the *instrument* variables in a model. These are the variables subject to control by the policy makers. Thus, in the model represented by equations (9.2), T could be replaced by, say, rY, where r is a variable representing the tax rate, or tax structure. Such a variable is essentially an *instrument* of economic policy, for it can be varied within a wide range at the will of the policy makers. It is an exogenous variable, as is true of many instrument variables, though the reverse is not true: exogenous variables are not necessarily instrument variables, as in the case of climate. (See Sec. 4.1.)

Being at the control of the policy makers, whether they be business leaders or government officials, the values of these instrument variables can be altered systematically or experimentally to ascertain the effect of changes in policy on other variables in the system. Thus, in equations (9.2), by varying r, the effect of contemplated changes in the tax rate structure on income formation can be evaluated and, presumably, an optimum policy selected. Similarly, in equation (9.1) product price, P_i, could be treated for some producers as an instrument variable. In that case, an analysis can be carried out of the effect of variations in price (relative to the general price level) on product sales, an evaluation that can aid considerably in establishing the most desirable price under given conditions—values of P and Y—for attaining a desired level of sales. Indeed, the objective in constructing many models is to determine the effect of alternative changes in policy, as manifested through the instrument variables in the system, on industry or overall national activity.

9.1.3.   Specification

Before a model can be subjected to empirical test, its *structure* has to be specified.[4] By "structure" is meant all the properties of the equations of the model, including those needed for estimation purposes. This includes:

> the equations of the model and the functional form assumed for each,
> the exact definition of the variables entering into each equation and the classification of each as exogenous or endogenous, or as predetermined or jointly dependent,
> the parameters to be estimated,
> the nature of the stochastic variables, and what relationships, if any, exist among these variables as well as between each of them and the other variables in the model.

As an example, consider the following, highly simplified model:

1. Demand for a commodity (X_d) depends on its price (P) and national income (Y), in a linear logarithmic relation.
2. Supply (X_s) depends on price and the wage rate (W), also in linear logarithmic form.
3. Demand equals supply.
4. Wages and national income are exogenous; the other variables are not.
5. The residual of the demand equation (u) is normally distributed, averages out to zero, and is not correlated with any of the other variables.
6. The same is true of the residual of the supply equation.

Given this information, our model becomes:

$$X_d = aP^b Y^c u \tag{9.3a}$$
$$X_s = dP^e W^f v \tag{9.3b}$$
$$X_d = X_s \tag{9.3c}$$

---

[4] Based on J. MARSCHAK, "Statistical Inference in Economics," in T. J. KOOPMANS, *op. cit.*, pp. 8, 14.

By taking logarithms, these equations can be converted into the usual, more manageable arithmetic form. Thus, equation (9.3a) becomes:

$$X'_d = a' + bP' + cY' + u'$$

where

$$X'_d = log\ X,\ P' = log\ P,\ Y' = log\ Y$$

Specification of a model is not only necessary from a statistical point of view but is also useful in a more general sense as a result of having to state explicitly the nature of the underlying relationships in the model. This serves to sharpen the model and also helps to focus attention on any questionable assumptions about the model that may not yet have come to light.

9.1.4. Identification

Another essential prerequisite to statistical estimation of parameters is verifying that each equation in the model is unique in the sense that it cannot be confused with any other equation, or combination of equations, in the model. For example, suppose that the model represented by equations (4.18) and (4.19) is instead the following:

$$\text{Demand:} \quad X = aP + u \qquad (9.4a)$$
$$\text{Supply:} \quad X = cP + v \qquad (9.4b)$$

Statistically, neither equation is identifiable since one cannot be distinguished from the other: both involve a relation between the same two variables and nothing else. Hence, although according to the usual economic theory, a should be negative and c positive, empirical measurement can only result in the same sign for both parameters.

Similarly, there is no basis for distinguishing between either of the preceding two equations and a combination of them. Thus, suppose we multiply equation (9.4a) by a constant, k, and equation (9.4b) by a constant, n, and add the two. We obtain:

$$X(k + n) = P(ak + cn) + uk + vn \qquad (9.4c)$$

which is again an equation in the same two variables as before.

Lack of identification in a model does not necessarily mean that the model should be rejected. Rather it is a sign that additional specification is needed before statistically meaningful results can be obtained.

In the preceding illustration, the trouble can be remedied by introducing additional variables, as in equations (4.18) and (4.19), so that the two equations become clearly distinct. In some instances, identification can be obtained solely by imposing additional restrictions on the stochastic variables. Thus, if the demand curve is perfectly stable while the supply curve fluctuates sharply, we can impose the condition: $\sigma_u^2 = 0$. The equations are then "strongly identified," and an estimate of the coefficient of P is clearly an estimate of the slope of the demand curve. (Why?)

Such strong identification is unfortunately not too frequent, and as an alternative partial or "weak" identification may be the best that can be obtained. Thus, it is not likely that a demand curve remains perfectly stable, but it is likely for many products that demand will fluctuate less than supply. We then have the "weak" restraint: $(\sigma_u^2/\sigma_v^2) < k$, with k a constant less than unity and preferably as close to zero as possible. However, unless k is close to zero, stronger identification by insertion of additional variables is to be desired.

The preceding model notwithstanding, identification is not generally achieved by a quick glance. In a model containing several equations, it is not easy to determine whether a linear combination of two or three equations yields a relation in the same variables and of the same form as another equation. Thus, consider the following model:[5]

$$C = aY + u \qquad (9.5a)$$
$$I = bP + cP_{-1} + dK_{-1} + v \qquad (9.5b)$$
$$W = eY + w \qquad (9.5c)$$
$$C + I = Y \qquad (9.5d)$$
$$P + W = Y \qquad (9.5e)$$
$$K - K_{-1} = I \qquad (9.5f)$$

The model seems well specified, but a little algebraic manipulation soon indicates that a relation statistically identical to equation (9.5b) can be derived by various combinations of these equations, the proof of which is left as an exercise for the reader.

Fortunately, a quick rule is available that provides a necessary, and often a sufficient, condition for establishing identification of individual relations. Let:

H be the total number of variables in the system (excluding stochastic terms),
H^* be the number of variables in the particular equation,
K be the number of equations in the model.

Then: the equation is just-identified if: $H - H^* = K - 1$
the equation is over-identified if: $H - H^* > K - 1$
the equation is under-identified if: $H - H^* < K - 1$

If an equation is just-identified or over-identified, estimates of its parameters can be derived by multivariate methods, as we shall soon see. If an equation is under-identified, meaningful estimates of its parameters cannot

---

[5] Adapted from L. R. KLEIN, A Textbook of Econometrics, p. 95.

be derived, and further consideration has to be given to the specification of that equation, and perhaps of the model as a whole.

The degree of identification is not necessarily the same for all equations in a model. This characteristic is best determined for each (behavioral) equation separately, unless the model contains only one equation in which case the above rule is redundant. (Why?) Thus, applying the rule to equation (9.5b), we obtain: $H - H^*$ equal to 4 while $K - 1$ is 5; hence the equation is under-identified, as noted earlier. On the other hand, for equation (9.5a) we have $H - H^*$ equal to 6 and $K - 1$ is still 5, so this equation is over-identified. Similarly, it can be established that both equations (9.4a) and (9.4b) are under-identified, in the absence of any further restraints on the stochastic variables, while both equations (4.18) and (4.19) are just-identified.

9.1.5. Estimation

If a model consists of a single equation with all variables but one predetermined, and with the stochastic elements averaging out to zero and independent of the predetermined variables and of each other, the parameters can be estimated by straightforward application of the least-squares technique. For example, the parameters of equation (9.1) could be estimated in this fashion if we can assume that:

1) $P_i/\bar{P}$ and Y are predetermined
2) $\Sigma u_i = 0$
3) $\Sigma u_{it} u_{i,t-j} = 0$ **(9.6)**
4) u_i is not related to $P_i/\bar{P}$ or to Y

Though not explicitly stated (and perhaps, at times, not realized!), these assumptions underlie every application of the least-squares technique in estimating the parameters of a single equation. Least squares is invariably used for single-equation estimates because of the convenient properties of the resulting estimates.[6] (What are these properties?)

The principal difficulty in applying least-squares techniques arises when a particular equation has more than one dependent variable. If this occurs within the context of a single-equation estimate—as if equation (9.4a) were considered by itself—least squares is not applicable. This does not mean that the least-squares technique could not be applied anyway—it often is—

---

[6] The fact that alternative criteria can be used for estimating parameters of single equations is hardly ever considered. For some such alternatives, see A. WALD, "The Fitting of Straight Lines if Both Variables Are Subject to Error," *Annals of Mathematical Statistics*, Vol. 11, 1940, pp. 284–300 (also in HANS THEIL, *Linear Aggregation of Economic Relations*, pp. 116–119); T. T. SEMON, "An Alternative Statistical 'Line of Best Fit,'" *Journal of Marketing*, January, 1960, pp. 73–74.

but rather that the estimates obtained of the parameters are biased in the sense that if successive estimates were to be obtained from different samples, the average of the estimates will not usually equal the true mean in the population. Thus, misleading estimates are possible of such possibly crucial parameters as demand elasticities or marginal propensities.[7]

If interdependence is present, an estimation technique is sought that will allow for this factor and still yield unbiased estimates of the parameters. At the same time, it is desirable that these estimates have the following properties, particularly the first one listed below:

Minimum variance—for that form of function the unbiased estimates result in the lowest possible error variance for the parameters.

Consistency—as the sample size increases toward infinity, the estimate approaches the true value asymptotically, i.e., the estimate converges stochastically to the true value.

Efficiency—as the sample size increases toward infinity, the distribution of the estimates of the parameter approaches a normal distribution with the true value as the mean and the variance less than any other estimate asymptotically and normally distributed about the same mean.

These properties as well as lack of bias are satisfied by the least-squares technique when the necessary conditions (9.6) are fulfilled. Insofar as possible, estimation techniques with similar properties are sought in the case of interdependence, though this is not always possible. The principal techniques available for this purpose are summarized in this section.

9.1.5.1. Recursive method. If the interdependence between endogenous variables in the equation of a model is not simultaneous, the least-squares technique may still be applicable. For example, consider a simplified model of the well-known Cobweb Theorem:

Demand:	$P_t = aX_t^d$	**(9.7a)**
Supply:	$X_t^s = bP_{t-1}$	**(9.7b)**
Equilibrium:	$X^d = X^s$	**(9.7c)**

In effect, this is a system of two (behavioral) equations in three variables—X, P, and P_{t-1}—for by virtue of the identity (9.7c), X^d and X^s become one variable. In equation (9.7b), X is determined by the price in the previous period, which is a lagged endogenous, and hence predetermined, variable. Equation (9.7a), considered by itself, contains two interdependent, variables. However, because it is part of the system containing equation (9.7b), the value of X_t is obtained for any given time from the supply equation. For this reason, P_t and X_t in the demand equation are no longer interdependent in an

---

[7] For a rough idea of the magnitude of such biases, see T. HAAVELMO, "Methods of Measuring the Marginal Propensity to Consume," *Journal of the American Statistical Association*, March, 1947, pp. 105–122.

instantaneous sense. Rather the model is recursive in that each of the equations now describes a cause-and-effect relation. Furthermore, the endogenous variables form a *recursive causal chain*, meaning that in each equation there is one endogenous variable which is dependent on predetermined variables and/or other endogenous variables which have already been estimated from previous equations.[8]

More generally, a recursive system can be represented as follows:

$$Y_1 = f_1(Z_1, Z_2, \ldots, Z_n)$$
$$Y_2 = f_2(Y_1, Z_1, Z_2, \ldots, Z_n)$$
$$Y_3 = f_3(Y_1, Y_2, Z_1, Z_2, \ldots, Z_n) \qquad (9.8)$$
$$\cdots\cdots\cdots\cdots\cdots\cdots$$
$$Y_n = f_n(Y_1, Y_2, \ldots, Y_{n-1}, Z_1, Z_2, \ldots, Z_n)$$

The first relation contains one endogenous variable, Y_1, which is dependent only on exogenous variables, the Z's. The second equation contains two endogenous variables but one of them, Y_2, is dependent on the Z's and on Y_1, which is already given by the first equation. Similarly, Y_3 is estimated by the third relation in terms of predetermined and already-estimated endogenous variables. Thus, we have a recursive causal chain, with every endogenous variable but the first acting initially as an effect and then as a cause.

It is important to note that a system need not contain only behavioral equations to be recursive. Thus, consider the relations among saving (S), consumption (C), income (Y), and investment (I) as assumed by the following model:

$$Y = f(I) \qquad (9.9a)$$
$$C = g(Y) \qquad (9.9b)$$
$$S = Y - C \qquad (9.9c)$$

This model is recursive if the assumption that investment is exogenous can be justified. If so, equation (9.9a) yields an estimate of income, which then serves to determine consumption in equation (9.9b). Y and C together yield S in equation (9.9c).

When a system is recursive in this manner, the least-squares technique is valid for each equation in turn. In practice, the parameters of equation (9.9a) would be estimated first. These estimates would then be used to estimate the value of Y for each observation on I. The estimated values of Y are then inserted in equation (9.9b) and least squares used to estimate the parameters of that equation.

Determination of whether a model is indeed recursive is a matter outside the scope of the particular model. By minor changes in one or more equa-

---

[8] H. Wold and L. Jureen, *Demand Analysis*. Particularly see H. A. Simon, "Causal Ordering and Indentifiability," in Hood and Koopmans, *Studies in Econometric Method* (N. Y.: John Wiley & Sons, 1953), Chapter 3.

tions, a model sometimes can be manipulated so that it becomes recursive though originally without this property.

9.1.5.2. *Instrumental variables.* This is essentially a makeshift approach designed to yield justifiable and relatively quick estimates of parameters of a single equation. The basic approach is to add as many predetermined variables to the particular equation as are necessary for the total of such variables to equal the number of parameters in the equation to be estimated. The rationale for selecting additional variables is that the equation is presumably part of a larger system in which these variables would be present. The predetermined variables selected are presumably those that would influence most strongly the endogenous variables in the equation at hand and also that are not highly intercorrelated with each other or with any predetermined variables in the equation. The original equation is then multiplied by each predetermined variable in turn (the old as well as the new), thereby yielding as many equations as there are parameters to be estimated. Substituting computed product sums for the variables in the equations and solving the resulting system of equations yields the desired estimates.

As an example, suppose that steel output (X) is said to depend on price (P), available capacity (C), and profits (Q). We assume that all the variables but C are interdependent, and that the form of the relation is, as follows (the constant term is dropped for convenience):

$$X = a_1 P + a_2 Q + b_1 C + u \qquad (9.10)$$

We wish to obtain rough estimates of the parameters, even though a complete model is not available, and least squares is not applicable to this equation. (Why?)

Applying the method of instrumental variables, we see that there are three parameters to be estimated but only one predetermined variable in the equation. Hence, two more predetermined variables are needed. Where do they come from?

We reason that if equation (9.10) were part of a larger system, output would surely be affected by the level of inventories at the beginning of the period, say H, and by the demand for new cars, say D (since the automobile industry is one of the biggest customers of the steel industry). We assume that both H and D are predetermined.

Our next step is to multiply equation (9.10) in turn by each of the three predetermined variables available and sum over all the observations, i.e.:

$$\Sigma CX = a_1 \Sigma CP + a_2 \Sigma CQ + b_1 \Sigma C^2 \qquad (9.11a)$$
$$\Sigma DX = a_1 \Sigma DP + a_2 \Sigma DQ + b_1 \Sigma DC \qquad (9.11b)$$
$$\Sigma HX = a_1 \Sigma HP + a_2 \Sigma HQ + b_1 \Sigma HC \qquad (9.11c)$$

We now have a set of three equations in three unknowns, so that solution of these equations yields estimates for a_1, a_2 and b_1.

9.1.5.3. *Two-stage least squares.* Notwithstanding their elegance and the ease of estimation, instrumental variables have the serious drawback of the results being too much dependent on the particular choice of the variables used as multiplicands for the normal equations (9.11a–9.11c). As is aptly pointed out by Stone:[9]

"As a general rule this method has not been used because experience at an early stage of the inquiry suggested that alternative estimates with different instrumental variables were highly erratic."

A very useful method, remotely resembling instrumental variables, but one much less dependent on the selection of variables, is provided by two-stage least squares. The crucial point of this method is the replacement of the jointly dependent explanatory variables by the systematic part of their regression on the predetermined ones. The purpose of the first stage, therefore, is to estimate this systematic part. Referring again to the steel example in equation (9.10), prices (P) and profits (Q) are estimated as a linear function of *all* predetermined variables:

$$P = b_{11}C + b_{12}H + b_{13}D + u_1 \qquad (9.11\text{d})$$
$$Q = b_{21}C + b_{22}H + b_{23}D + u_2 \qquad (9.11\text{e})$$

In the second stage, the output equation (9.10) is successively multiplied by:

1. Each of the predetermined variables appearing in this equation (here, therefore, only by C).

2. The part of the dependent explanatory variables that is systematically related to all predetermined variables, in the present case, therefore, by $P - u_1$ and by $Q - u_2$.

Summation over all observations of the values thus obtained results in three equations:

$$\Sigma CX = a_1 \Sigma CP + a_2 \Sigma CQ + b_1 \Sigma C^2 \qquad (9.11\text{f})$$
$$\Sigma (P - u_1)X = a_1 \Sigma (P - u_1)P + a_2 \Sigma (P - u_1)Q + b_1 \Sigma (P - u_1)C \qquad (9.11\text{g})$$
$$\Sigma (Q - u_2)X = a_1 \Sigma (Q - u_2)P + a_2 \Sigma (Q - u_2)Q + b_1 \Sigma (Q - u_2)C \qquad (9.11\text{h})$$

By solving this system for a_1, a_2 and b_1, asymptotically unbiased estimates for these coefficients are obtained.[10] For purposes of practical computations,

---

[9] R. STONE, *The Measurement of Consumers' Expenditure and Behaviour in the United Kingdom, 1920–1938*, Vol. I, p. 298.

[10] See H. THEIL, *Economic Forecasts and Policy* (Amsterdam: North-Holland Publishing Co., 1958), Ch. 6; also, H. THEIL and T. KLOEK, "The Statistics of Systems of Simultaneous Economic Relationships," *Statistica Nederlandica*, 1959, pp. 65–89; T. KLOECK and L. B. M. MENNES, "Simultaneous Equations Estimation Based on Principal Components of Predetermined Variables," *Econometrica*, 1960, pp. 45–61.

the first stage is usually integrated with the second. As compared with straightforward least squares, the computations required may become considerable. Compared with other methods for estimating simultaneous relationships, however, this burden remains modest.

9.1.5.4. Reduced forms. If a system of equations is just-identified, the easiest method of estimation is to solve each endogenous variable algebraically in terms of only predetermined variables. Such is the case for the model represented by equations (4.18) and (4.19). The solution of the endogenous variables, x and p, in terms of the predetermined variables, y and k, is shown on p. 166. Each equation of this solution can now be fitted by least-squares techniques. Estimates of the four parameters of the original equations can be obtained by a suitable transformation. Thus, if the coefficients of the reduced equations (4.20) and (4.21) are represented as:

$$A = \frac{b}{c - a}, \quad B = \frac{d}{c - a}, \quad C = \frac{bc}{c - a}, \quad D = \frac{ad}{c - a} \quad (9.12a)$$

we have:

$$a = \frac{D}{B}, \quad c = \frac{C}{A}, \quad b = A(c - a), \quad d = B(c - a) \quad (9.12b)$$

The method of reduced forms can also be applied to a particular equation in a model even if the other equations are not just-identified, provided that this equation does have this property. In other words, if equation (4.18) were just-identified but equation (4.19) were not, least-squares estimation would still be applied to the reduced forms of the equations. This is a very convenient property since often the focus in a model is on a particular equation, such as a demand function, and estimation of the parameters of the other equations is of relatively little interest. If the demand function contains interdependent variables but happens to be just-identified, estimates of its parameters can still be obtained by reduced forms with relative ease.[11]

9.1.5.5. Limited information. This method is roughly analogous to the method of instrumental variables in that it is applicable to a single equation. It serves to remedy the arbitrary characteristic of the latter method by yielding estimates of the parameters of the particular equation on the basis of information concerning the other variables that appear in the model. For this purpose, complete specification of the other equations is not required, as long as they are linear in the variables. It is sufficient to know which exogenous variables are not contained in the equation studied. The estimates obtained by this method are considerably more reliable than by instrumental variables, but the amount of computation is considerably greater too.

The basic approach lies in the conversion of the model into reduced forms. Since the model is assumed to have as many equations as there are interdependent variables, it is possible to express each of these variables in terms

---

[11] See GERHARD TINTNER, *Econometrics*, pp. 166–172.

of only predetermined variables, though a fair amount of algebra may sometimes be involved in the process.

If the particular equation happens to be just-identified, the parameters are estimated by the least-squares method outlined in the preceding section. More often than not, however, the equation may be over-identified; there is essentially more information than is necessary to estimate the parameters. In that case, the least-squares technique does not apply, and the so-called *maximum likelihood* method has to be used. Maximum likelihood represents a broad approach to the problem of point estimation. The method is based on the formulation of a joint distribution function of the sample observations in terms of the parameters to be estimated; this function is known as a *likelihood function*. By applying calculus, the function is used to derive those estimates of the parameters which, if they were the true values, would maximize the probability of obtaining the given sample of observations.

Thus, if we have a set of independent sample observations, X_1, X_2, . . . , X_n, drawn presumably from a normally-distributed population, the distribution function is the normal curve:

$$\frac{1}{\sigma\sqrt{2\pi}} e^{-\frac{(X-\mu)^2}{2\sigma^2}} \tag{9.13a}$$

where μ is the true mean and σ^2 is the population variance.

The likelihood function L is derived by applying this function to the joint distribution of the sample observations, $p(X_1, X_2, . . . , X_n | \sigma, \mu)$ to obtain:

$$L = \left(\frac{1}{\sigma\sqrt{2\pi}}\right)^n e^{-\frac{1}{2\sigma^2}\sum_1^n (X_i-\mu)^2} \tag{9.13b}$$

We then seek those estimates of the parameters, μ and σ, which maximize L. This is done by first converting L into logarithms, to make it more amenable for maximization, then differentiating L in turn with respect to each of the parameters, setting the resulting equations equal to zero, and solving for μ and σ. With the equation by equation approach of the limited information method, the estimates are:

$$est \ of \ \mu = \Sigma X_i/n$$
$$est \ of \ \sigma^2 = \Sigma(X_i - \mu)^2/n \tag{9.13c}$$

which are the usual least-squares estimates.

The results, nevertheless, can be quite complicated. Their derivation necessitates the use of matrix algebra and is outside the scope of this book. Suffice it to say that the numerical solutions can be fairly lengthy, though considerably facilitated by electronic computers.[12] In over-identification, there is no simpler means of obtaining estimates of the parameters that is

---

[12] For detailed examples of the technique together with numerical illustrations, see L. R. KLEIN, *op. cit.*, pp. 125–133, 169–183; G. TINTNER, *op. cit.*, pp. 172–189.

statistically justifiable. In addition, the estimates obtained in this manner are consistent but not efficient, in accordance with the definitions given earlier.

9.1.5.6. *Full information*. The limited-information method is applicable to the estimation of parameters either of a single equation or of a complete system. However, it fails to exploit all available information. For this purpose, all equations of the system must be specified, and the method of full information enters into the picture.

This method involves the application of maximum likelihood techniques as well as the simultaneous estimation of *all* the parameters in the system. The approach is to form a joint distribution of the stochastic variables in the system, usually with the assumptions of joint normal distribution (similar to equation 9.13b), zero means, constant variances, and no intercorrelation between the stochastic variables. A likelihood function is then set up and a transformation is made for the stochastic variables in terms of the relations between these variables and the other variables (interdependent and predetermined) in the system. This likelihood function is maximized, as before, by partial differentiation with respect to each parameter in turn and setting each of these partial derivatives equal to zero. The result is a set of as many simultaneous equations as there are parameters to be estimated, so that parameter estimates can be obtained by the usual algebraic methods.

From a computational point of view, a considerable amount of work is involved for two or more endogenous variables. This is especially so because, even if the original model was linear, nonlinearities in the parameters tend to enter in the process of transforming the joint distribution of the stochastic variables into a joint distribution of the interdependent variables. Unfortunately, there is no other means currently available for getting estimates of parameters of a model that seeks to take into account all available information.[13] In many instances, the full-information approach can be avoided, particularly if interest lies only in estimating the parameters of one equation, in which case the limited-information method can be used—or least squares if the equation is just-identified. Alternatively, if the system can be set up so that it is recursive, or if all the equations happen to be just-identified, the computational task is lightened considerably.

9.1.6. Evaluation

The adequacy of a model is evaluated in essentially the same way as is any hypothesis, though the process may be more intricate because of the size and scope of some models. Before empirical estimates of the model parameters

---

[13] For a detailed treatment of the application of this method, see L. R. KLEIN, *ibid*, pp. 50–62, 100–121, 160–168, 211ff.

have been derived, the adequacy of the theoretical model has presumably already been established to the satisfaction of the researcher. After the parameters have been estimated, further tests of the adequacy of the model are indicated, these tests focused primarily on the empirical results. These tests may be classified into two general groups, those relating to the purely statistical properties of the model and those tests dealing with substantive implications.

9.1.6.1. *Statistical properties: serial correlation.* Once estimates of the parameters have been obtained, tests can be carried out on the validity of the assumptions underlying the estimation procedure employed. Thus, the stochastic variables are assumed to be each independent over time—no autocorrelation. Previously their values were unknown. However, given estimates of the parameters, the values of these stochastic variables can now be estimated as the residuals of the estimates of the (endogenous) variable estimated from each equation. These residuals can then be subjected to the usual tests for autocorrelation. (See Sec. 8.9.2.)

In addition, assumptions can be tested regarding intercorrelation between stochastic variables, as well as between the stochastic variables and the predetermined variables. These variables are invariably assumed to be mutually independent, and, if this assumption is not true, biased estimates of the parameters will result.

The residuals are also useful for examining the appropriateness of the form of the relationship. If they show a particular pattern over time, or in relation to the endogenous variables, another specification may be more suitable.

If the residuals are correlated significantly with each other, then presumably one seeks to discover what variables have been omitted from the model that might account for the systematic pattern in the residuals and incorporate them in the model, thereby eliminating the serial correlation and improving the efficiency of the estimates.

Often, however, this procedure is not feasible. The missing variables may not be known, or if known may not be quantifiable, or so many variables may be involved that it is hardly practicable to include them all. Whatever the reason, the question often arises of how to adjust for serial correlation when no other variables can be incorporated in the model.

Two courses of action are possible. By one approach, an attempt is made to anticipate the presence and nature of serial correlation and modify the form of the model by means of an appropriate transformation. Thus, an estimating equation for aggregate consumption expenditures in the U. S. is fairly likely, on the basis of past experience, to exhibit serial correlation in the residuals. If there is no good reason to believe that the function under consideration may be different from the others in this respect, consideration might well be given to attempting to anticipate this effect.

A simple transformation that is often effective involves the use of first differences rather than actual magnitudes. Thus, if serial correlation is expected in a regression of sales of a product (S) on price (P) and on gross national product (Y), a regression equation of the following form might be used instead of the form depicted by equation (9.1):

$$S_t - S_{t-1} = b(P_t - P_{t-1}) + c(Y_t - Y_{t-1}) \tag{9.14}$$

The hypothesis underlying the use of this equation is that the residual of the original form, u_t, is perfectly correlated with its preceding value with a correlation coefficient of unity. If so, then:

$$u_t = u_{t-1} = S_{t-1} - a - bP_{t-1} - cY_{t-1} \tag{9.15a}$$

so that:

$$S_t = a + bP_t + cY_t + S_{t-1} - a - bP_{t-1} - cY_{t-1} \tag{9.15b}$$

which becomes equation (9.14). In practice, a constant term must be included anyway in the first-difference form to comply with the requirement that the sum of the residuals in the estimator equation equals zero. A constant is also desirable here to allow for a trend (Sec. 7.4.3), perhaps, on the basis of *a priori* reasoning.

Perhaps a more realistic assumption than equation (9.15a) is that the residuals are correlated, but not with unit correlation, i.e.:

$$u_t = \rho u_{t-1} \tag{9.16a}$$

This assumption leads to a somewhat more complicated equation, one of the form:

$$S_t = a' + bP_t + b'P_{t-1} + cY_t + c'Y_{t-1} + dS_{t-1} \tag{9.16b}$$

In many instances, however, the assumption underlying equation (9.14), though not strictly fulfilled, is sufficient to correct for the serial correlation effect. Particularly if degrees of freedom are not too plentiful, that equation is to be preferred, if possible, over equation (9.16b). This is especially true in the case of equation systems where serial correlation in the residuals of the reduced-form equations is relevant rather than that of the original equations.

There is of course no assurance that the transformation selected will indeed correct for serial correlation effects.[14] Hence, the use of a transformation does not obviate the need for testing the residuals of the transformed equation for serial correlation. If serial correlation is detected then, the task of devising further transformations may become rather complicated, especially from a conceptual point of view. Hence, such advance transformations are made generally only when there is reasonable assurance of their effectiveness or if first differences are preferred anyway for other reasons.

---

[14] There is also some danger that the transformation will yield biased results. See HILDRETH and LU, *op. cit.*, where a practical method is presented for estimating ρ.

The second approach involves empirical determination of the pattern of the serial correlation and then devising an appropriate adjustment to correct for it. Thus, an estimating equation may be set up of the form:

$$u_t = a_0 + a_1 u_{t-1} + a_2 u_{t-2} + \cdots \tag{9.17}$$

The parameters of this equation are estimated by the least-squares technique and as many parameters used as are statistically significant; usually two or three will be sufficient. The result can then be used to transform the original equation and arrive at an adjusted form (See Sec. 10.2.1). Alternatively and more simply, the original equation can be transformed and estimates made by applying to each variable the same pattern of serial correlation as was detected in the residuals. For example, if only a_1 and a_2 are significant in equation (9.17), the transformation of the original equation becomes:

$$S_t - a_1 S_{t-1} - a_2 S_{t-2} = b(P_t - a_1 P_{t-1} - a_2 P_{t-2}) \\ + c(Y_t - a_1 Y_{t-1} - a_2 Y_{t-2}) \tag{9.18}$$

Estimates are derived using this equation.

This procedure may at times be more involved than that outlined above since the form of the serial correlation may not be as simple as that exemplified by equation (9.17). Yet the nature of the relationship is generally discernible. Unfortunately, the procedure becomes involved in the case of equation systems where specification of the estimating equation (9.17) requires an attempt to detect patterns in residuals of the reduced form equations. (Why?)

9.1.6.2. *Other statistical properties.* Supplementing study of the validity of the underlying statistical assumptions are tests designed to determine the reliability of the parameter estimates. Primarily this entails ascertaining the significance of the various coefficients, both singly and in combination with each other, by computing first standard errors and then ratios of the coefficients to the standard errors. The tests of significance are essentially the same as before, though the computation of standard errors of coefficients estimated by the limited or full information methods can be rather involved; computational procedures are given in the various econometrics books listed at the end of this chapter.

In addition to these tests of significance, standard errors of the coefficients will be desired for establishing confidence intervals for the estimates of the various parameters as well as for the estimates of the interdependent variables. In conjunction with an evaluation of the substantive value of these intervals, these tests constitute a principal basis for judging the adequacy of a model.

Note that the usual goodness of fit criterion applied to the simultaneous estimate of a structural equation is even less satisfactory than it is for a single equation fitted by least squares. The reason is that the maximum likelihood approach does not yield minimum variance estimates for single equations as does the straightforward least-squares approach. In other words, the variance of estimates obtained from an equation fitted by maximum likelihood as part of a larger model will be at best equal to—though usually more than—the variance of estimates obtained from the same equation fitted alone by the least-squares technique. Hence, the coefficient of determination in the former case cannot be any larger than for the least-squares case, and is invariably less.

9.1.6.3. Substantive implications. Questions on the substantive implications of a model tend to fall under five general headings. Since each is covered at varying lengths in other parts of the book, they will be reviewed rather briefly at this point.

1. The extent of agreement of the estimates with *a priori* notions of the values of the parameters has to be examined, excluding those used as restrictions in the estimation process. Thus, if one *a priori* restriction on the estimation of steel output (equation 9.10) is that the relation be homogeneous, the results can not constitute a test of this property. Alternatively, however, a constant term could have been added to equation (9.10) with the intent of testing the homogeneity of the relation.

In general, such *a priori* notions are best expressed in the form of hypotheses, if for no other reason than because they are less likely to be overlooked in this way. Often contradiction of an *a priori* notion can lead to major revisions and improvements of a model. Thus, if a price elasticity of demand comes out positive when there are strong reasons for believing it to be negative, the model might well need reworking.

2. The implications of the results have to be assessed, particularly in the light of such other information about the signs and magnitudes of the parameters as may be available. If, for example, a model yields a propensity to consume exceeding unity, a second look at the composition of the model is clearly indicated. When a number of different variables and relationships are involved in the same system, unexpected interaction effects are not unlikely to appear in the final results. For this reason, a satisfactory multi-equation model is generally achieved only after a number of tests with alternative equation forms and model formulations.[15]

Apart from the validity of equation specifications, attention must be given to the possibility that the basic data used in the estimation may turn out to be incompatible with some of the substantive requirements of the model.

---

[15] For examples of the application of this trial-and-error approach to model construction for public policy formulation, see P. J. Verdoorn and C. J. van Eyck, *Experimental Short-Term Forecasting Models* (The Hague: Central Planning Bureau, July, 1958).

3. The extent to which the results correspond with previous studies on the same subject warrants examination. If the present results conflict with the other studies, explanations have to be sought, a process that will generally point either to noncomparabilities, to inadequacies of one or the other study, or to changes in basic structure. In the latter case, the question may well be asked whether such a change can be incorporated into the model, something which, if successful, would impart to the model much greater generality.

4. The ability of the model to explain fluctuations in the endogenous (interdependent) variables during the period of observation needs study. Such an analysis is not carried out in terms of the goodness of fit, though coefficients of determination can still serve as useful descriptive measures. Rather the focus of such a study is on the detection of systematic patterns in the residuals or of any unusual disturbances in the estimates that may be linked to factors or events not incorporated in the model. As noted previously, presence of systematic patterns, even if not statistically significant, may be indicative of missing variables. With unusual disturbances, if the cause can be identified, it may be possible to allow for such disturbances through the use of dummy variables. Thus, if the savings-income ratio is found to be unusually high during periods of rationing, even after allowing for other factors, a "rationing variable" may be introduced, taking the value unity in periods when rationing exists and being zero otherwise.

5. The acid test of a model is its predictive ability. The fact that a model survives all other tests with flying colors does not mean it will yield reliable predictions, as has been noted in Chapter 3. The only way to find out is to subject the model to the test and see how well the equations work beyond the period of observation. Some yardsticks for evaluating the forecasting performance of a model will be discussed in Sec. 10.4.

As can be seen from the preceding material, evaluation of the adequacy of a model brings to bear as much pertinent external data as is available—and which has not already been used in the model—and involves examination of the results from many different perspectives. Ideally, for a model to be acceptable, it should:

a) satisfy all the statistical prerequisites—justify the assumptions underlying the estimation procedures, have statistically significant coefficients, explain variations in the endogenous variables within the range of tolerable error and without systematic or highly unusual disturbances,

b) make "sense" from a substantive point of view—the estimates should reconcile with such other information as is available and with *a priori* expectations,

c) survive the acid test of predictive accuracy.

The extent to which a model is adequate in the absence of one or more of these conditions depends on the circumstances and objectives of the particular study.

9.2. SIMULATION OF MARKET BEHAVIOR

The objective of most models is to describe or predict aggregate market behavior. The econometric approach outlined in the preceding section attempts to attain this objective through the formulation of relations representing aggregate behavior. Presumably, these relations are derived from functions describing micro-economic behavior, since markets are composed after all of individuals—consumers, firms, institutions, etc. Actually, however, this is generally not the case, primarily because of the difficulty of deriving aggregate relations from individual relations. To do so brings in the so-called aggregation problem, i.e., cumulating relations for economic units to obtain a single aggregate relation. The process takes in all sorts of mathematical difficulties and necessitates the use of various approximation procedures in order to obtain an aggregate relation.[16] As a result, hypotheses are generally either framed in terms of aggregate behavior to begin with, or it is assumed that the aggregate and the individual relations correspond, which is true only for certain linear relationships.

An alternative approach to the analysis of aggregate behavior is to simulate individual behavior by setting up functions specifically designed to explain or estimate the action of individuals, apply these relations in experimental or artificial situations and aggregate the results. In other words, instead of estimating aggregative behavior by deriving functional relations between aggregates, the simulation approach uses functional relations for *individuals* to estimate behavior for *individuals* and then derives aggregates by summing the (numerical) results for all individuals studied.

This general approach has a wide variety of applications, all relatively recent. In the field of business and military testing, it has gained widespread recognition under the name of the *Monte Carlo* method as a relatively inexpensive means of evaluating the effects of particular policies or programs.[17] Not only is the simulation approach economical, but it permits policies to be evaluated which could not be tried out in practice under actual operating conditions. Thus, the extent of damage and losses incurred by alternative dispersals of a given military force would hardly be estimated by actual test. However, with the aid of mathematics and of high speed computers, each

---

[16] For a discussion of these problems, see HANS THEIL, *Linear Aggregation of Economic Relations* (Amsterdam: North-Holland Publishing Company, 1954).

[17] For a simple description of the method, see ROBERT SCHLAIFER, *Probability and Statistics for Business Decisions*, pp. 320–328.

dispersal situation could be *simulated*, stochastic variables introduced to allow for unforeseen contingencies, and estimates obtained of the probable effects of each dispersal situation.[18]

In a similar fashion, simulation can be used to assess the relative economies that might be achieved from alternative locations of warehouses, or from alternative promotional plans, or from alternative transportation arrangements. In each case, a model is constructed to describe individual behavior, the nature of the "individual" varying with the problem at hand. Stochastic elements are introduced, and the model is subjected to a sequence and variety of actual conditions. An estimate of behavior is derived under each set of conditions for each individual, and these estimates are aggregated to obtain totals.[19]

To cite another example, simulation could be used to evaluate the extent to which traffic jams are likely to result under different road systems. Each car-owner would have a certain "travel function," an equation or series of equations indicating his likelihood of travel and his travel route as a function of such factors as relation of location of home to place of work if employed, work schedules, shopping habits, availability and condition of particular roads, etc., as well as of a stochastic element to represent unexpected trips. To derive the traffic pattern at any particular time, these travel functions would be fed into a high-speed computer together with the given travel conditions, the exogenous variables. The computer could then determine for each car whether it would be on the road during that period and, if so, what route would be followed. Aggregating these individual results yields traffic densities at different points in the road network for various times of the day. By varying the condition and network of available roads, optimum traffic patterns can be determined and road construction planned accordingly.

Theoretically, the same results might be obtained solely by mathematical analysis. In practice, however, the derivation of the requisite mathematical functions becomes so complex that simulation turns out to be the only feasible approach.

The full uses and ramifications of simulation methods as applied to business and economics have yet to be developed. Illustrative of the breadth of its application is an attempt by Guy Orcutt and his associates to simulate the workings of the U. S. economy.[20] Because of the basic implications of this study for economic and marketing analysis and because it serves to highlight the concepts used in putting simulation techniques into practice, the bulk of this section is devoted to a description of this particular study.

---

[18] For examples, see "Economics and Operation Research: A Symposium," in *The Review of Economics and Statistics*, August, 1958; also the article in the same issue by STEPHEN ENKE, "An Economist Looks at Air Force Logistics."

[19] For some business applications, see the references at the end of this chapter.

[20] GUY ORCUTT, *et al.*, *Microanalysis of Socioeconomic Systems: A Simulation Study*. Harper & Bros., 1961.

9.2.1. The Orcutt Model

9.2.1.1. *Objective.* In its broadest formulation, this model seeks to describe the behavior of the economy through simulating the interaction between and within households, firms, financial institutions, and other decision-making units. To date, however, the focus of activity has been on the household sector, and a description of this component of the model is sufficient to indicate how it works. The principal objective of the model of the household sector described here is to simulate the demographic and economic changes in this sector—change in population, income, consumption, debts, etc., as well as in the distributional characteristics of these aggregates.

9.2.1.2. *Components of the model.* Four components may be said to enter into the composition of the model: units, inputs, outputs, and operating characteristics.

Units. The unit of observation is the decision-making unit. In the case of households, two types of decision-making units are involved, individuals and households. In some instances, the decision or event pertains to the individual, e.g., marriage, illness and related expenditures, whereas in other instances it is the household or family that is the decision unit, as with purchase of a home, entrance of wife into the labor force, etc. Hence, the model incorporates two distinct units of observation and has to simulate the behavior of each but with provision for the fact that one unit is at times part of the other.

Inputs. Before the model can generate a decision for any individual or household, certain information must be available about that unit, i.e., whatever information would be required in order for a decision to be made. Thus, a "decision" whether an individual goes on living from one time period to another may depend on the individual's age, sex, occupation, physical condition, etc. This information represents the inputs needed by the model before a determination can be made whether that individual dies in the current period or lives beyond this period. Similarly, a decision to buy a house by a given household may depend on its financial position, current living conditions, household composition and income level. These factors would be the inputs for this decision.

In effect, the inputs correspond to the predetermined variables of the model systems discussed previously; they are variables required to be known for a given period in order for particular decisions to be made.

Outputs. The outputs are the decisions or the outcomes accompanying the inputs fed into the model. The continued life or death of an individual is an output, as is a decision by a household whether or not to purchase a home in a particular period. A variable that is an output for one type of decision may serve as an input for another type of decision. Thus, if a decision is made for a certain household to buy a house, a decision is next needed on the manner in which the house is to be financed.

Operating characteristics. An output is derived by means of a functional relationship linking that output to a given set of inputs. The functional relation is stochastic, to reflect the uncertainties of economic life. Furthermore, it yields not the output itself but the probability that a particular output will result. These probability distributions linking outputs to inputs are known as "operating characteristics" of the system.

For example, the probability that an unmarried person will marry may be assumed to depend on sex, age, month, and state of business conditions. A function or table is then constructed to enable this probability to be determined (an output) given the values of these determining factors (inputs); this is then an operating characteristic of unmarried individuals.

Each decision made by a unit or each event occurring to it requires a separate operating characteristic function. In the course of a month or even a week, a household or individual may make literally hundreds of decisions of an economic nature, particularly since decisions not to act have to be made as well as decisions to take certain actions. Hence, a complete model of individual market behavior requires an enormous number of operating-characteristic functions and involves numerous problems of estimation and of data collection. It is only because of the advent of electronic computers that such an approach can even be considered.

Operating characteristics are essentially behavior equations and the objective in each case is to formulate as realistic a relationship as possible. Following are some examples of operating characteristics that have been formulated to derive various outputs. In each case, P represents the probability of a given event and E represents the expected amount accompanying certain decisions:[21]

Death (of an individual):

$$P = F_1 \ (Age, \ race, \ sex, \ month) \tag{9.19}$$

Divorce (of a married couple):

$$P = F_2 \ (Duration \ of \ marriage, \ month, \ aggregate \ income \ change) \tag{9.20}$$

Birth (of an individual):

$$P = F_3 \ (Age \ and \ parity \ of \ woman, \ aggregate \ income \ change, \ time) \tag{9.21}$$

Sex of new-born children:

$$P \ (child \ will \ be \ male) \ = \ .514 \tag{9.22}$$

---

[21] Adapted from G. H. Orcutt, *Some Operating Characteristics of Household Units.* Mimeographed memorandum.

Marriage:

P (*of a male getting married*) $= F_4$ (*Sex, age, marital status, month, change in aggregate income*)   (**9.23a**)

P (*male i, if he is getting married, chooses female of age k*)[22] $= F_5$ (*Sex, age and marital status of i and of k*)   (**9.23b**)

Ownership of liquid assets:

P (*household has liquid assets*) $= F_6$ (*marital status, age, education, and race of head, interval since marriage if any, mortgage debt of household, personal debt of household*)   (**9.24a**)

E (*assets if owned*) $= F_7$ (*same variables as in preceding function*)   (**9.24b**)

Purchases of durable goods:

P (*household purchases any durables*) $= F_8$ (*same variables as in preceding function, and liquid assets*)   (**9.25a**)

E (*durable goods purchased*) $= F_9$ (*same variables as in preceding function*)   (**9.25b**)

The ten functional relations listed here clearly represent only a fraction of the economic (including demographic) outputs of a decision unit during a given period of time. Yet, for each such output, a different functional relation, or operating characteristic, is required.

In each case, the form of the functional relation is specified either from past knowledge or on the basis of *a priori* reasoning. The parameters of the relations are estimated by least-squares techniques, except for a case like equation (9.22) where the best estimate is a single value. The data requirements for such a task are, accordingly, far beyond what has ever been collected in the past on any systematic basis. Yet, for the model to present a realistic picture of consumer behavior, reliable operating-characteristic functions is a basic prerequisite.

9.2.1.3.   *How the model works.* A population of several thousand individuals is specified as of a certain date, say t. Presumably, this population represents a miniature in certain essential respects of the actual population studied, in this case of the U. S. population. The size of the population depends partly on the requirements of precision of estimation and partly, as a limiting factor, on the capacity of the available computers for storing and processing the data. In the case of the present model, the population contains 5,000 individuals.

For each individual, all necessary summary information is specified— identification number, age, sex, education, membership in household, marital

---

[22] The assumption is that the male takes the initiative—clearly a most artificial one!

status (including identity of spouse if married), employment status, occupation if any, etc. Corresponding information is stored for each of the different households in this population—data on the household composition, home residence status, ownership of mortgages and other debts, ownerships of goods, ownership of other assets, etc.

All of this information together with such general economic and other data needed as inputs is stored in a data processing machine, as illustrated by the "Summary information storage" box in Fig. 9.2. In addition, there are stored in the machine the previously derived operating characteristics, estimates of the parameters of the relations or precomputed tables of various probabilities, e.g., the probability of a male getting married. Finally, the machine stores a set of random numbers, a routine for applying them and routines for feeding inputs into the operating characteristics to obtain desired outputs for each individual and household, as shown in Fig. 9.2.

Given this information, the objective is to ascertain how the characteristics of the population and its aggregate welfare change over time. We start at time, t, and feed each decision unit in turn into the computer. As the decision unit enters the computer, the various operating characteristics are brought into play, together with the associated inputs and operating routines. Thus, the first "decision" made by, or imposed upon, unit i is death: its characteristics (inputs) are fed into operating characteristic F_1 (equation 9.19), and a decision is made with the aid of the random number routine if the unit survives.[23] If the unit survives, it is then fed successively into operating characteristics F_2, F_3, F_4, etc., and the entire series of outputs is obtained for that unit—divorce if any, birth (to a married couple), marriage (if unit is single), employment, purchasing behavior, assets, debts, etc.

The procedure is diagrammed in Fig. 9.2. The result of the process is a revised set of characteristics of the decision unit as of time, $t + 1$, one month later. In a similar fashion, all other decision units are advanced in time, the entire population thereby moving into time, $t + 1$. The model is assumed to be recursive, so that there is no simultaneous reaction between decision units. This does not rule out the possibility, however, that the action of one decision unit is influenced by the (prior) action of another, i.e., that the output of unit i serves as an input for unit j.

By the same general procedure, the process can be continued indefinitely, the outputs of one period serving as the inputs for the next period. At the same time, exogenous elements, such as changes in fiscal policy, war, and unusual weather conditions, can be introduced as desired; they would constitute additional inputs at the particular times.

---

[23] For example, suppose that the probability of an individual of that age, race, and sex, surviving that month is .991. A three-digit random number is selected by the machine. If the digit is 991 or less (treating 000 as a higher digit), the individual "survives"; if not, he dies and is eliminated from the population.

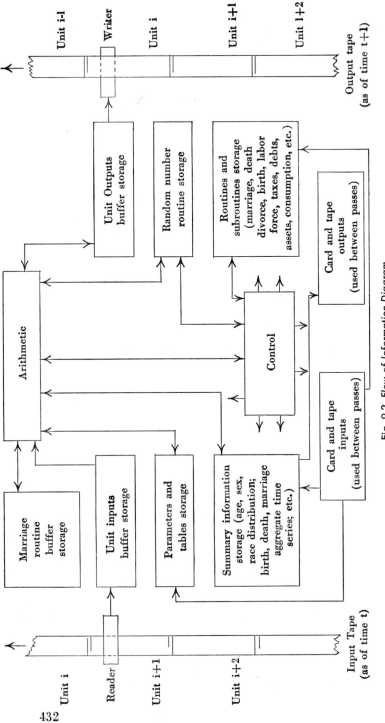

Fig. 9.2. Flow of Information Diagram

Source: G. H. Orcutt, *Some Operating Characteristics of Household Units.* Mimeographed.

Given the outputs for the individual decision units, a picture of aggregate behavior in each period is readily obtained by aggregating the individual outputs. Thus, the total births in the population at time, $t + 1$, is the sum of the outputs of applying operating characteristic, F_3, to each decision unit in the population at time, t. This is a matter of simple arithmetic and hence is immeasurably simpler than trying to derive the aggregate counterpart of F_3, especially if the latter should be nonlinear. The addition process is handled by machine, which can also be set to produce desired distributions and aggregates.

In practice, some adjustments may have to be introduced into the simulation process to maintain comparability of the model with reality. For example, the preset probability of a child being born male is .514. However, by the very nature of the stochastic process certain deviations from this probability are bound to occur. If there are 1,000 births in period, $t + 1$, the random number routine is not likely to yield exactly 514 males; the figure may be 510, or 525, or even further from 514. Because of the small size of the simulated population relative to the real population, such differences from the predetermined probability can be substantial, especially after several periods of time have elapsed.

To bring the simulated probabilities back into line with the "true" figure, correction factors have to be introduced in future periods. Thus, if the proportion of males after some periods starts to move well above .514, the simulated probability might be lowered in future periods to make the average move closer to .514. Conceivably, however, such differences may be indicative of a shift in basic structure, i.e., a change in this probability of .514 to some other value. If such a change does appear to have occurred—the decision would have to be based largely on such external evidence as is available—no correction factors may be needed.

9.2.1.4. *Evaluation.* The advantage of a model of this sort derives from two basic characteristics: the analysis of units of observation at the micro level, and the introduction of a probabilistic element in these micro-reactions. Because of the focus on the individual household, or the individual firm, it may be possible to describe more realistically the behavior of a specified endogenous variable in terms of the exogenous variables, if for no other reason than because it becomes possible to observe individual units and think in terms of their behavior, something which is very difficult to do when working with aggregates.

The probabilistic element provides for the element of uncertainty which affects every aspect of human behavior, and by doing so on numerous individual units makes it possible to introduce erratic influences in individual behavior in a more realistic manner than is possible with stochastic error terms in macro-economic models.

At the same time, the degree to which a model of this type can simulate actual economic activity is yet to be determined. For one thing, much more efficient data-processing systems than are now available will be needed to process the huge number of units, inputs, operating characteristics and program routines required to yield the necessary flow of outputs. This may be only a matter of time.

Second, is the problem of deriving operating characteristics, the difficulty of which is greatly intensified by the paucity of available data. In numerous instances, completely new theories are required to explain various economic or demographic phenomena and derive realistic operating characteristics. Thus, how can changes in birth rates be predicted, considering the unforeseen shifts that have taken place in such rates over the past decades? Or purchases of houses, automobiles, washing machines? Or deposits to savings accounts? Answers to each of such questions necessitate long, extensive studies in their own right.

Estimation is a third problem, question arising regarding the validity of the assumption of independence of output both among decision units and among operating characteristics. Detecting changes in operating characteristics is another knotty problem on which further research is required.

Overcoming these obstacles is in many ways a tremendous task. Yet, even if the attempts are not fully successful, simulation models should be of real use in guiding economic and business policy.

9.3.   FORECASTING WITH MODEL SYSTEMS

In considering the application of model systems to prediction problems, it is useful to distinguish between three forms of forecasts.

1. A model may be used to derive an *unconditional forecast*, one which seeks to predict what will happen to the dependent variables in some future period. This is the most difficult and hazardous forecast to make. In order for it to be accurate, not only must the functional relations remain valid in the period of extrapolation, but accurate predictions are required of the predetermined variables in the model. In some instances, the latter may not be difficult, such as government expenditures or births in the next year. In other instances, however, such forecasts may constitute the biggest stumbling block of all. This is particularly true of short-run forecasts with models in which some of the predetermined variables are lagged endogenous variables. The values of such variables may not themselves be known at the time the forecast is made.

2. Instead of sticking one's neck out altogether, a *conditional forecast* may be made, a forecast which is assumed valid only if the predetermined variables take on certain stipulated values. In other words, the forecast is condi-

tional on the validity of the assumed levels of the predetermined variables. At the same time, the value of the forecast does not necessarily depend on the predetermined variables actually taking the assumed values. As a basis for planning, it is clearly useful to know what levels the endogenous variables might reach *if* the predetermined variables were to be at certain levels. Indeed, from a policy point of view, a number of such conditional forecasts may be prepared, corresponding to alternative, plausible combinations of values for the predetermined variables. Since the latter are generally not accurately known, such forecasts can provide the most useful indication of the probable range within which the endogenous variables may fall and of their sensitivity to possible fluctuations in the predetermined variables at their forecasted levels. In this way, steps can be taken to prepare for a wide range of eventualities.

3. A model may be used to draft a *plan* or *target* for future operations. Desired levels are selected for the endogenous variables on the basis of external considerations, and the problem becomes one of ascertaining what (feasible) combinations of the predetermined variables will bring about the desired result. This is an area in which linear programming techniques can be used jointly with econometric analysis. For example, suppose the government decides that it should take such steps as are possible to assure a national income the following year of at least Y_1, in deflated prices. If the model represented by equations (9.2) were a valid base for such plans, the question becomes: What (feasible) combinations of the predetermined variables will bring about a national income of at least Y_1? Also, if there are several such alternatives, which combination should form the basis for government policy? By linear programming techniques, these combinations can be ascertained, as well as some idea of the stability of these different possibilities. Judgments would then be required on the feasibility of the various combinations, and policy is then influenced accordingly.[24]

The same approach applies at the level of the individual firm. Thus, the various instruments appraised by the marketing audit—price, promotion, product line, etc.—can be combined into a set of equations relating these instruments to sales and profits instead of representing them in graphs, as was done in the Supplement to Chapter 1. In either case, a plan or target is set in terms of the *endogenous* variables, sales and profits, and feasible combinations of the other variables are sought which will assure realization of the plan.

This type of forecast is essentially an inversion of the other two forms.

---

[24] For an illustration of the application of this technique, see H. B. CHENERY and K. S. KRETSCHMER, "Resource Allocation for Economic Development," *Econometrica*, October, 1956, pp. 365–399. For a general discussion of the use of model systems in economic planning, see J. TINBERGEN, *Economic Policy: Principles and Design*.

Nevertheless, the validity of the model system in the projected area remains crucial to the success of this approach.

Various technical considerations enter into these different types of forecasts. These considerations are best discussed in connection with the next chapter on alternative approaches to forecasting. (See Sec. 10.1.3.) Some of the more important of these technical considerations are discussed in this next chapter.

PROBLEMS

1. Given the system (4.18)–(4.19) in the following dynamic form:

$$\text{Demand:} \quad v_t = 6p_t + 2y_t$$
$$\text{Supply:} \quad v_t = 4p_{t-1} + 3k_t$$

a) Obtain an equation showing:

    i) how price varies over time

    ii) how quantity varies over time

b) Compute the values of each of these two variables for years 1 to 5 given the following information:

Year	p_t	y_t	k_t
0	4		
1		3	3
2		4	3
3		5	4
4		3	4
5		4	5

2. In Chapter 7 it was stated (p. 349) that "under suitable conditions" the parameters of equation (7.29) could be estimated by the least-squares technique. Enumerate these conditions.

3. Given the following demand-supply model, with Y representing income:

$$\text{Demand:} \quad X = aP + bY + u$$
$$\text{Supply:} \quad X = cP + v$$

Which equation is identified, and which is not? Why?

4. Prove algebraically that equation (9.5b) in the model on p. 412 is not identified.

5. Instead of estimating the parameters of equation (9.11) by instrumental variables, as shown in the text, why not simply add H and D to the equation with their own parameters and solve the whole thing by least squares?

6. Prove that if the under-identified demand function, $X = aP + u$, is solved by adding an instrumental variable, Y, the estimate of a is $\Sigma XY/\Sigma PY$.

SELECTED REFERENCES

Models

Economic Models by E. F. BEACH (New York: Wiley & Sons, 1957) contains a simple and clear discussion of the concepts of econometric models and of the problems of specification and identification. At a somewhat higher level but also easy to understand is *An Introduction to Econometrics* by VALAVANIS (New York: McGraw-Hill, 1959). More detailed coverage of these questions will be found in *A Textbook of Econometrics* by L. R. KLEIN (Evanston: Row Peterson and Company, 1953), Chapter 3, and in *Econometrics* by GERHARD TINTNER (New York: Wiley and Sons, 1952), Chapter 7. Part I of the latter book contains a number of practical illustrations of the applications of econometric models. Basic concepts are discussed in a fairly rigorous manner in the article by JACOB MARSCHAK which is included in *Statistical Inferences in Dynamic Econometric Models* edited by T. KOOPMANS (New York: Wiley and Sons, 1950).

Economic Policy: Principles and Design (Amsterdam: North-Holland Publishing Co., 1956) by J. TINBERGEN, dealing with 21 different kinds of models in relation to several categories of problems, may be cited as giving the best examples of how a model should be constructed to suit the requirements of a given policy problem.

The various forms of estimating parameters of equation systems are covered in detail in the textbook by KLEIN. They are also presented in the book by VALAVANIS, which has a particularly clear section on the use of instrumental variables. The method of "two-stage least squares" is set forth in H. THEIL, *Economic Forecasts and Policy*, Chapter 6 (Amsterdam: North-Holland Publishing Co., 1958). *Demand Analysis* by H. WOLD (New York: Wiley & Sons, 1953) has perhaps the most complete exposition of the application of recursive methods.

An example of the use of first differences for business cycle research and of various approaches to evaluating equation systems is provided in the monograph on *Experimental Short-term Forecasting Models* by P. J. VERDOORN and C. J. VAN EYK (The Hague: Central Planning Bureau, 1958; available on request). An empirical business-cycle model for the United States is presented by KLEIN and GOLDBERGER in *An Econometric Model of the United States, 1929-1952* (Amsterdam: North-Holland Publishing Company, 1955).

Simulation

The simulation model of the United States economy described briefly in this chapter is covered in full detail in G. H. ORCUTT *et al.*, *Microanalysis of Socioeconomic Systems: A Simulation Study* (New York: Harper & Brothers, 1961). The uses of simulation methods in managerial training is described in an article by O. B. SCHENK, "Mathematical Models of Market Simulation" (*Journal of Marketing*, April, 1960, pages 69–74). An interesting example of the use of simulation in studying business fluctuations is described in *Computer Models of the Shoe, Leather, Hide Sequence* by K. J. COHEN (New York: Prentice-Hall, Ford Foundation Doctoral Dissertation Series, 1960). A very good example of the potential applications of simulation is provided in *Simulation of Trust Investment* by J. B. CLARKSON (New York: Prentice-Hall, Ford Foundation Doctoral Dissertation Series, 1962). For another good example, see "Simulation in Organizational Research" by E. W. MARTIN, JR. (*Business Horizons*, Fall, 1959, pp. 68–77).

Additional references on simulation will be found in "Bibliography on the Use of Simulation in Management Analysis" by D. G. MALCOLM (*Operations Research*, March–April, 1960).

PRACTICAL
APPLICATIONS

PART THREE OF THE BOOK HAS AIMED TO PROVIDE A SURVEY OF INDI-
VIDUAL research techniques, their peculiarities, advantages and disadvantages. Having made this survey, we are now ready in this part to
consider the application of these techniques to some of the principal
research situations encountered in practice. To this end, two such
general problem situations are considered. First, in Chapter 10, the
application of alternative research techniques to perhaps the most
basic problem situation of all is considered, namely, forecasting. Here
the focus is on evaluation of the advantages and disadvantages of
different techniques for solving this problem.

A very different problem situation is considered in Chapter 11—
the coordination of a variety of research techniques to bear on a single
cluster of interrelated problems. The type of problem selected for this
purpose is a very general one, namely, the complete marketing audit.
As will be seen, however, this generality is of real value for this purpose since it enables many different problem situations to be considered and accordingly brings up the selection of research techniques
for numerous purposes.

439

10 | Forecasting

No problem is of more basic interest to economists and businessmen than trying to predict the future. The challenging nature of the problem as well as its importance have given rise to numerous methods and procedures for obtaining accurate predictions, many accompanied by considerable controversy over their reliability. It would therefore seem most appropriate in a book of this type to devote one of the last chapters to a review of these different approaches to forecasting. This helps to demonstrate how a wide variety of different methods are brought to bear on the same problem, and also how the application and evaluation of these methods is interrelated with policy decisions.

This chapter is divided into four main sections. A review of the principal forecasting methods is provided in the first section, followed by a section on the relation between diagnosis of current conditions and selection of a forecasting method. The knotty question of fitting the forecasting procedure to the needs of the policy makers is considered in the third section while different means of evaluating forecasts and forecasting methods is the subject of the concluding section.

10.1. ALTERNATIVE APPROACHES

Different forecasting methods are not necessarily competitive with one another. In some instances, one method serves to supplement another. Some methods are applicable primarily to the very near future—a month, a quarter, at most a year—while others are best used for longer-term forecasting. What is being forecasted may also serve to narrow the range of choice. The fact remains, however, that an appropriate forecasting method can best be

441

chosen when the various possible approaches are known, including the peculiarities of each. To this end, it seems useful to classify forecasting methods under four general headings:

Mechanical extrapolation
Surveys of anticipations or of expectations
Analytical forecasts
Judgment forecasts

The different individual methods are discussed in connection with each of these general approaches.

10.1.1. Mechanical Extrapolation

The rationale underlying extrapolation procedures is that some past tendency or trend in the variable being forecasted reflects what is going to happen. Accordingly, an attempt is made to quantify this tendency or trend and to derive a forecast by extrapolating the relation into the future. No consideration is given to possible determinants of past or future fluctuations in the variable except for the use of time as an explanatory factor. Thus, by this approach, sales of the food industry would be forecasted by using past sales of the same entity, with perhaps explicit inclusion of a time trend. Factors other than time that affect food sales are not included explicitly, presumably because of the regularity of past trends.

Mechanical extrapolation methods range in sophistication from simple naive models to complex trend functions. Since these methods have already been covered in past chapters, they will be treated only briefly at this point, with primary reference to their forecasting potential.

10.1.1.1.   *Mathematical trends.* This general class of methods includes those in which a mathematical relation is derived between time and the variable to be predicted. Linear trends, polynomials and growth curves were discussed in Sec. 7.4. In each case, the variable being predicted is treated as the dependent variable and time is the independent variable. As in the case of growth curves, the form of the relationship may be rather complex. In addition, periodic variations in the level of the dependent variable may be incorporated in a trend function.[1]

Whatever the trend equation used, the reliability of the forecast obtained rests on the validity of projecting the particular trend relation into the future. In general, such a projection is likely to be most valid relative to other methods for long-term estimation, particularly in the case of a rapidly growing product whose specific demand determinants are not easily pinpointed. Thus, in the 1920's and early 1930's the manifold uses for electricity

---

[1] See H. T. DAVIS, *The Analysis of Economic Time Series*, especially Chapters 2, 7.

could hardly have been predicted although the eventual development of such uses seemed hardly in doubt. Extrapolation of a fitted growth curve to predict future per capita consumption of electricity in the United States would have been at that time about as good a method as any.

For short-run projection, mathematical trends are not likely to be as effective as other mechanical projection methods. This is partly because a sizeable series of data is used in fitting a trend or growth curve and partly because a smoothed, long-run curve is sought. As a result, short-run fluctuations tend to be treated as erratic in nature and are largely ignored.

10.1.1.2. *Moving averages.* The method of moving averages, with perhaps seasonal adjustments superimposed, is likely to be a more efficient mechanical projection method for predicting short-run movements than mathematical trend relations. It is a more flexible approach, easy to apply, and allows for short-run variations in the given series.

As noted in Sec. 7.4, a disadvantage of the method is that the moving average necessarily lags the current period by half the length of the average. Thus, the most recent figure for a five-month moving average is two months back of the current date. To predict next month's figure, therefore, is equivalent essentially to forecasting the level of the moving average as of *last* month. To the extent that the moving average follows a regular pattern, this procedure can facilitate the prediction problem. On the other hand, this procedure is likely to become less reliable as more forward predictions are attempted, in which instance regularity of the moving-average pattern tends to become more questionable and the occurrence of unforeseen factors more likely.

10.1.1.3. *Naive models.* The simplest of the mechanical, or any other, forecasting methods, naive models are intrinsically appealing, particularly to people in a hurry or to those who do not want to fool around with statistics. The naiveté of the method derives from its inherent rationale: what has happened in the past will continue to happen in the future.

Various types of naive models are available, some more sophisticated than others. To cite a few examples:

1. The simplest is the no-change model, that is, the anticipated level of the variable in the next period (X_{t+1}^*) is equal to its current actual level (X_t).

2. A slightly more refined model is that based on equal change, i.e., the change from the current period to the next period $(\Delta X_{t+1}^* = X_{t+1}^* - X_t)$ will be equal to the change that has taken place between the last period and the current period $(\Delta X_t = X_t - X_{t-1})$.

3. More refined still is to postulate that the expected change is a certain proportion of the past change, e.g.:

$$\Delta X_{t+1}^* = \rho \, \Delta X_t$$

with ρ estimated by observation or, if one wants to become really refined, by averaging or regression techniques. In the latter case, one is using the autocorrelation in the data. From a statistical point of view, this is no longer a particularly naive model but is nevertheless likely to be classed in this category from a substantive point of view. (Why?)

4. Still more refined naive models can be constructed by including adjustment terms for seasonal variations, for erratic movements in the data and for other factors.

It may seem somewhat paradoxical to note that when a naive model is used in business forecasting it is generally one of the first two types. The reason appears to be that the first two types are particularly simple to apply, require a minimum amount of data or computation, and therefore appeal to the large number of statistical laymen confronted with the unpleasant task of making a forecast. In such an instance, one or the other of the first two models is an easily rationalized "out." In fact, a recent study has shown that some forecasters in this category use these models without being aware of it![2]

At the same time, those acquainted with statistical methods tend either not to use a naive model at all or select one of the first two models if faced with a situation where a naive model seems the best solution. Naive models of types 3 and 4 find their most frequent use as yardsticks for the evaluation of the adequacy of more elaborate forecasting methods, which is discussed in a later section of this chapter.

Despite their analytical shortcomings, naive models do have a place in the forecaster's repertoire, particularly for forecasting a month or a quarter in advance. Thus, Chicago area employers who used naive models to predict changes in employment two months ahead between 1952 and 1959 were found to be fully as accurate as employers in the same industry using other methods.[3] In addition, a more sophisticated naive model approach was found to be more accurate in predicting railroad carloadings one quarter ahead over a 25-year period than an elaborate system of traffic manager reports.[4]

A simple naive model is likely to be most successful if conditions are fairly stable or are changing in a uniform and monotonic manner. This is particularly true of the type 2 naive model, which tends to be superior to the type 1 model in all instances but relative stability. The latter situation though not common is, however, not to be ignored. Thus, in the Chicago area employers' manpower predictions, many firms were apparently faced with a situation where steadily rising needs for manpower occasioned by higher levels of activity were being offset by mechanization and increased productivity. In

---

[2] ROBERT FERBER, N. R. CHEN, and FADIL ZUWAYLIF, "Chicago Area Employers Labor Force Anticipations: An Interview Study," *Journal of Business*, July, 1961.

[3] *Ibid.*

[4] ROBERT FERBER, *The Railroad Shippers' Forecasts*, Chapter 3.

many of these situations, the type 1 model proved highly efficient for short-term forecasting.

10.1.2. Survey Data

The survey approach is based on the premise that, if you want to know what is going to happen in a particular sector, go out and ask those who will be making things happen! However, this is not as simple or as rational as it sounds. For one thing, surveys are very expensive, probably the most expensive of any forecasting method, apart from the fact that, as noted in earlier chapters, designing meaningful questions and obtaining reliable answers is not an easy task. Then too, there is always the possibility, if not likelihood, that those responsible for future actions may not have a clear idea themselves of their future actions because of uncertainty or other factors. (What others?) Nevertheless, the approach is an intriguing one and has gained widespread use and some spectacular successes. Some of its principal applications are reviewed in this section.

10.1.2.1. *Consumer purchases.*[5] Essentially, there are two basic approaches to forecasting by sample surveys—the direct and the indirect. By the direct approach is meant securing information on people's attitudes, plans, and purchase intentions with regard to the items under study and preparing forecasts directly from that material. In the indirect approach, the researcher uses the survey method to predict one or more variables closely related to the items under study and then prepares forecasts of those items by means of some previously derived relationship between them and the other variables.

The approach to employ depends on the item being forecasted.[6] If it is a distinctive one not purchased frequently (this could include anything from a stapler to a house), the direct approach will probably be preferred. In this case, a series of questions might be devised that would yield information required for forecasting the probable sales of the item. The information required and how it is to be used would have to be determined in advance, presumably by experimental study.

If, on the other hand, the item is one purchased more or less daily (such as bread) with little advance planning, the best method may be to use the sample to predict variables to which the item is closely related and then use the relationship between the item and those variables to forecast sales. Thus, if

---

[5] Part of this section is reproduced from the article by Robert Ferber, "Sales Forecasting by Sample Surveys," *Journal of Marketing*, Vol. 19, July, 1955, pp. 1–13.

[6] In some instances, it may be feasible (and this is certainly desirable) to utilize both approaches and thereby check the forecast derived by one approach against the forecast derived by the other—though the forecasts cannot be considered fully independent of each other.

the number of loaves of bread sold is found to be closely related to average family income and to the number of family units, the primary function of sampling in such a case would be to assist in predicting income and family formation rather than to predict bread sales directly. This does not mean that the sample could not throw light on such factors as people's attitudes toward bread in relation to competing products—for example, prebaked rolls—thereby also indicating to some extent the adjustment that might be needed to correct the forecast obtained from the income-family-formation relationship for such additional considerations. Thus, this indirect method basically involves joint use of sampling with regression or some arbitrary factors method.

Note that the durability of a good is not a major determinant of the feasibility of forecasting its sales through sampling. Durability does, however, influence the approach to be followed, for, if the good is perishable (and hence likely to be purchased on short notice), the chances are that the indirect method will be indicated. This would seem to be true of large items—night club expenditures and tickets to sports events—as well as of such small items as certain foods and haircuts. Some items in this category, like vacation tours, would, however, require considerable advance planning, and for these the direct approach, or some combination of the two, would be preferred.

Similarly, frequency and size of purchase indicate the feasibility of the sampling method only insofar as they reflect the extent of advance planning and thinking involved in the purchase. By this standard, the frequency of purchase is probably of greater relevance than the size because of the close association between frequency and extent of planning of a given purchase.

Does this mean, then, that the sales of any product can be forecast by sampling? Not necessarily. But a sample survey may succeed in forecasting sales of items in the following categories:

1. A good purchased after advance planning and thought, thus permitting prediction of sales from knowledge of the distribution of those plans by time and by other pertinent characteristics.
2. A good purchased frequently and with relatively little thought, sales of which are known to be closely related to certain general characteristics, for example, income and number of families.

Forecasting sales of durable goods by following the first approach has received increasing attention in recent years, particularly the possibility of using data on expectations (of either future personal or general events), attitudes on the current situation (e.g., whether the present is a "good time to buy"), or intentions to purchase. The degree of success is still a controversial question and will probably remain so for many years. The evidence so far indicates that data on intentions to purchase may contribute substantially to increasing the accuracy of forecasts. However, this is less likely for anticipations of future conditions and for attitudes regarding the present situation, although this is evidence that they too influence purchases.[7] People in an optimistic frame of mind—whether because of higher anticipated income or because of prospective disposal of a mother-in-law—are more likely to make purchases than those who are pessimistic.

Nevertheless, anticipations data do not seem to add much to forecasting accuracy. For one thing, anticipations appear to be much more subject to instability than purchase plans. For another thing, anticipations are not the sole determinant of purchases. (What other factors are involved?) The studies made so far indicate that after other factors have been taken into account, such as income and purchase plans, anticipations data provide no net increment to forecasting accuracy.[8] At the same time, other studies have shown that data on purchase intentions, when properly obtained, provide valuable clues to future purchases.[9] Although the record is somewhat spotty, a much higher proportion of those who report purchase plans make a purchase than those who report no purchase plan. This is particularly true for large durable goods such as houses and cars, due no doubt to the fact that the more expensive an item is, the more likely its purchase is to be planned for some time in advance.

The result is that buying plans studies appear to be growing in popularity. Annual studies of buying plans were carried out on a national scale between 1944 and 1959 for the Federal Reserve Board by the Survey Research Center of the University of Michigan. Beginning with 1960, these studies have been conducted on a quarterly basis by the U. S. Bureau of the Census. At about the same time, the National Industrial Conference Board launched a bi-monthly series of such studies using telephone interviews. The telephone approach has considerable cost advantages, but poses other problems that can only be overcome by personal interview. (What problems?)

In the field of marketing, a large number of such studies have been undertaken by business firms, though for obvious reasons they are not usually published. Indications are, however, that purchase plans and preference surveys are of value not only for predicting purchases of particular items but

---

[7] George Katona, *Psychological Analysis of Economic Behavior* (New York: McGraw-Hill Book Company, Inc., 1951), Chapter 8. Also by Katona, *The Powerful Consumer* (New York: McGraw-Hill, 1960).

[8] James Tobin, "On the Predictive Value of Consumer Intentions and Attitudes," *Review of Economics and Statistics*, February, 1959, pp. 1–11.

[9] Robert Ferber, *Factors Influencing Durable Goods Purchases*, Bureau of Economic and Business Research, University of Illinois, Bulletin #79, 1955. Also F. Thomas Juster, *Consumer Expectations, Plans and Purchases: A Progress Report*, National Bureau of Economic Research, Inc. Occasional Paper #70, 1959.

also for predicting the brands that people will select when they decide to make the purchase.[10]

Surveys for predicting consumer purchases are not without disadvantages, some of them serious. For one thing, they are very expensive. Second, a period of experimentation may be needed before tangible results are obtained. Third, a major development occurring between the time that the survey is made and the time the purchases are scheduled to take place may upset completely the forecast. As with other forecasting methods, the shorter the interval before the forecast is desired, the more accurate is the prediction based on the survey likely to be.

10.1.2.2. *Business expenditures.* Perhaps the most notable success achieved by surveys is in the prediction of capital expenditures, a key factor in business fluctuations and long one of the principal stumbling blocks to successful economic forecasting. The initiation of quarterly surveys of anticipated capital expenditures after World War II appears, as of the early 1960's, to have provided a solution to the problem. The merits and shortcomings of this approach can be evaluated by reviewing the principal such surveys in the United States.

Surveys are being used to collect two types of forward data on capital spending in the United States. One type of data is anticipated capital expenditures, collected quarterly by the U. S. Department of Commerce Office of Business Economics (OBE) and the Securities and Exchange Commission (SEC), and annually, in the late fall, by McGraw-Hill and its periodical, *Business Week*. The OBE-SEC survey, the more extensive of the two, relates to private nonfarm businesses, both corporate and noncorporate. Reports are filed quarterly by corporations registered with the SEC, by companies filing reports with the Interstate Commerce Commission, and by a sample of unregistered companies reporting to OBE. During the first two months of a given quarter, the respondent reports actual capital outlays in the preceding quarter and anticipated outlays in the current quarter and the next quarter. In January-February, firms also report anticipated outlays for the entire current year as well as actual outlays in the past year. The sample covers primarily the largest firms. Hence, although the sample size is only about 9,000 of roughly 4,000,000 businesses in the country, coverage in terms of assets averaged 57% in 1958 and was over 80% for 9 of 18 major industrial groups.

As Fig. 10.1 shows, the annual predictions have generally been correct in the direction of movement and often close to the actual change. The principal exception was 1950 when the Korean War jolted economic activity. Other-

---

[10] SEYMOUR BANKS, "The Prediction of Dress Purchases for a Mail Order House," *Journal of Business*, University of Chicago, January, 1950, pp. 48–58. Also, SEYMOUR BANKS, "The Relationships Between Preference and Purchase of Brands," *Journal of Marketing*, October, 1950, pp. 145–157.

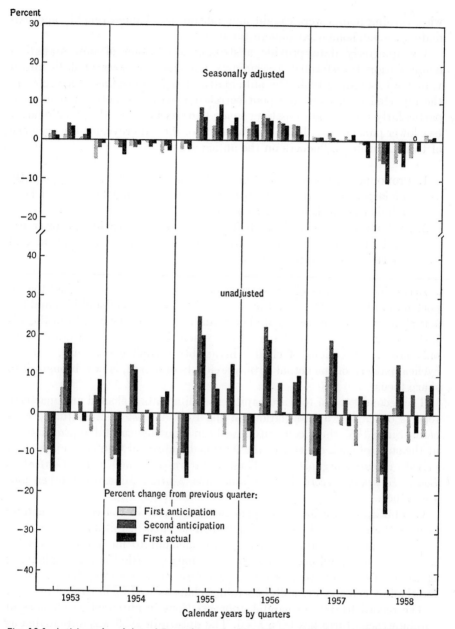

Fig. 10.1. *Anticipated and Actual Expenditures for New Plant and Equipment, United States, 1953–58*

Source: U. S. Bureau of the Budget, *An Appraisal of OBE-SEC Estimates of Plant and Equipment Expenditures, 1947–1958*, p. 39.

wise, turning points were caught and substantial changes roughly approximated, though somewhat underestimated.

The quarterly data provide a striking illustration of how statistical manipulation transformed a seemingly questionable body of data into a valuable forecasting tool. The anticipated changes in outlays derived from the reported data exhibited poor correlation with the actual movements, particularly the first anticipations made two weeks before the given quarter (see lower panel of Fig. 10.1). Examination of the data revealed the presence of two disturbing influences on the anticipations:

1. Pronounced seasonal variations in the anticipations, often apparently of larger scope than actual change after seasonal factors had been eliminated, as is evident from Fig. 10.1.
2. Systematic biases relative to the actual values, serving to lower the first and third quarter anticipations and to raise the second and fourth quarter anticipations.

Accordingly, a series of transformations was undertaken to adjust the reported data for these factors, the anticipations for seasonal and bias and the actual magnitudes for seasonal. The resulting changes derived from the adjusted data exhibit remarkable improvement (top panel, Fig. 10.1). Not only are the directions of change invariably predicted correctly, but the cyclical pattern of the actual data, previously obscured, is now brought into sharp focus.

The second type of forward capital spending data collected are quarterly reports on capital appropriations of the 1,000 largest manufacturing concerns. Since 1955 these concerns have been reporting capital appropriations at the start of each quarter to the National Industrial Conference Board, a private research organization. These data are published in the *Conference Board Business Record* in the issues for March, June, September and December.

Capital appropriations may play an earlier role in the capital spending process than do anticipated expenditures. In effect, capital appropriations constitute authority undertaken by management to incur obligations for new plants and equipment, a step which may precede the actual planning of the expenditures. In this sense, therefore, capital appropriations could foreshadow changes in capital spending plans as well as in capital outlays.

The record to date of capital appropriations in anticipating changes in capital expenditures has been good. The upturn in 1958 was anticipated as was the earlier downturn in 1956.[11] Nevertheless, the experience with these data is as yet too limited to warrant any conclusive judgment of their value.

---

[11] *Business Record*, December, 1959, p. 529ff.

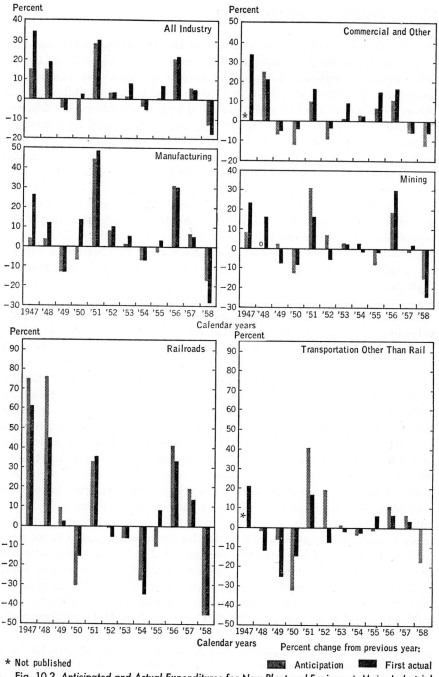

Fig. 10.2. *Anticipated and Actual Expenditures for New Plant and Equipment, Major Industrial Divisions, United States, 1947–58*

* Not published

Source: U. S. Bureau of the Budget, *An Appraisal of OBE-SEC Estimates of Plant and Equipment Expenditures, 1947–58*, pp. 52–53.

In particular, it is not clear to what extent the capital appropriations data add to what is already obtained from the surveys of anticipated outlays. In this sense, it is pertinent to note that capital appropriations possess two limitations distinctive to that type of data. One is that capital appropriations are inherently linked with the capital budgeting process. If a firm has no capital budget, as is true for the majority of small and medium-sized firms, capital appropriations possess little meaning in themselves. For this reason, the coverage of the capital appropriations survey has to be limited for the time being primarily to the largest firms in the country.

The second limitation derives from the greater separation that exists between capital appropriations and actual spending. A capital appropriation represents an intention to spend, but it says nothing about the timing of the expenditure or possible conditions that might cause the expenditure to be postponed or canceled altogether. To some extent, this limitation can be taken into account by refining the survey procedure, but the fact remains that, particularly with capital appropriations data, relatively small changes, say 10% or less, may not have much significance.

From an overall point of view, it is clear that surveys are of considerable value in predicting capital expenditures. At the same time, it is evident that the surveys are by no means infallible, and that instances can happen, as occurred in 1950, when events occurring after the anticipations or the appropriations had been reported brought about substantial, unexpected changes in actual expenditures. In addition, it is apparent that something akin to the law of large numbers serves to make the predictions for industry or sector totals more accurate than would be the case for individual firms. To what extent this averaging process may be expected to continue in the face of a major letdown in economic activity is a question that has not yet been answered.

10.1.2.3. Business operations. Surveys of business firms have been used at various times and in different countries to predict such operating variables as sales, prices, profits and inventories. Surveys of this type are made periodically in the United States by Fortune Magazine of its subscribers, by Dun and Bradstreet in the process of collecting credit information, by the National Industrial Conference Board of its industry members, by the U. S. Department of Labor in collaboration with the individual states on manpower requirements, and by a number of trade associations and publications.[12] In addition, the OBE-SEC and McGraw-Hill capital expendi-

---

[12] They have also become a popular social pastime at meetings of various business and professional groups. Those attending the meeting are asked to record their predictions of particular business and economic variables, these predictions then serving as the basis for subsequent discussion. Presumably, everyone benefits from hearing everybody else talk. . . . In the more affluent groups, the person whose prediction by retrospect proves most accurate may win a prize, such as a free dinner.

ture surveys also ask for anticipations regarding sales and, at times, selected other variables.

Similar surveys are conducted in Canada, England, Netherlands, West Germany, South Africa and other countries, often with official or quasi-official sponsorship.

From a methodological point of view, it is instructive to divide these various surveys into two groups, according to whether quantitative information on expected change or only directions of movement are sought. The quantitative surveys are those that request of the respondent a prediction of the level or per cent change in the set of variables being studied. Thus, the OBE-SEC and Canadian government surveys ask for the anticipated level of next year's sales; Fortune has asked for the expected percentage change in sales or profits, etc. The period being forecasted is generally the next year, though the horizon may be as little as two months ahead (such as with U. S. manpower requirements).

Whether it is because of the longer horizon or other factors, the record of these quantitative surveys has been rather spotty. As noted earlier, quarterly forecasts of U. S. railroad carloadings by shippers have been no superior to what could have been obtained from a naive model formulation. The OBE-SEC data appear to have presaged shifts in annual sales somewhat better but do not appear to exhibit the high degree of accuracy characteristic of the capital outlay plans. The state manpower requirements data do a good job of approximating actual trends, better so than various naive models, but major contributing factors are no doubt the brief horizon (two months) and the relative stability of employment during the periods studied.[13]

Overall, two inferences seem to be warranted on the value of these quantitative surveys for predicting business behavior:

1. Forecasting errors are likely to increase as the amplitude of the variable being predicted rises or as the variable is more amenable to short-run manipulation as a policy instrument. Thus, employment fluctuations as measured by the coefficient of variation are smaller than those of sales. As might be expected, relative errors in employment forecasts tend to be also smaller than those of sales.

2. Businessmen are likely to forecast more accurately changes in conditions affecting their own firm or industry than changes on the national business scene. This was demonstrated conclusively by various studies (unpublished) of the Fortune surveys undertaken by Franco Modigliani in the early 1950's.

[13] ROBERT FERBER, "The Railroad Shippers' Forecasts and the Illinois Employers' Labor Force Anticipations: A Study in Comparative Experience," in *The Quality and Economic Significance of Anticipations Data* (Princeton: Princeton University Press, 1960), pp. 181–199.

A possible third inference is that accuracy of prediction increases as the forecasting horizon declines. Such an inference seems logical on an *a priori* basis, but the available data do not bear out this point as conclusively as might be desired.

The second form of these surveys seeks a judgment of the direction of movement of a particular variable. The nature of such a survey can best be illustrated by describing what is perhaps the best known of this type, the Munich Business Test (MBT). Since the early part of 1950, the IFO—Institut für Wirtschaftsforschung—has been sending monthly questionnaires to firms in Western Germany asking for information on the past direction of change in particular variables, and on the expected direction of change. The variables covered relate to the firm's operations, and include sales, new orders, production, inventories, and buying and selling prices. For most of these variables the respondent is asked to indicate whether the level in the current month relative to the preceding month is up, down, or about the same. At the same time, the respondent is asked to predict whether the level of the same variable next month will be higher, lower, or about the same as it is this month. In some cases, such as capital expenditures, the question is framed with reference to the level of expenditure in the corresponding month of the preceding year.[14]

Altogether, the survey covered, as of the early 1960's, more than 150 commodities at the manufacturing level, about 90 in wholesale trade and about 50 in retail trade. The data are published in the form of weighted percentages two or three weeks after the questionnaires have been sent out, the weight being the size of the respondent firm. Three percentages are presented for each variable and each month, namely, the proportion of firms reporting an increase, the proportion reporting no change, and the proportion reporting a decrease; the sum of these proportions is 100%. In contrast to the quantitative surveys, no information is requested on numerical magnitudes of the variables involved.

The analyses that have been made of the MBT indicate that the predictions are considerably more successful than chance in anticipating turning points, in many ways the acid test of a set of forecasts.[15] Furthermore, it appears that the firms are better able to predict turning points concerning quantity and value variables, such as sales and production, than they are able to predict changes in prices. This finding is basically consistent with the inferences noted previously relating to quantitative surveys. In most instances, a firm has relatively little control over its selling or buying price, especially in the short run, compared to the control that it can exert on such more instrumental variables as sales and production.

Another finding of the MBT is that the firms in consumer goods industries

---

[14] HANS THEIL, *Economic Forecasts and Policy*, Netherlands, North-Holland Publishing Company, 1958, Chapter 4.
[15] *Ibid.*

tend to predict a given variable more accurately than do firms in the producer goods industries or even firms in the same industry that are further removed from the consumer. For example, the forecasts of shoe retailers have generally been more accurate than the forecasts of shoe wholesalers, and in turn have usually been more accurate than the forecasts of shoe manufacturers, which in their turn have generally been more accurate than the forecasts of leather traders, tanneries, and traders of hides. Again, this is not inconsistent with the findings of various other surveys, and may well be explained by the fact that the amplitude of business activity tends to be smaller for the consumer goods industries than for the producer goods industries. The severity of business fluctuations tends to increase as the stage of operations moves further away from the consumer level.

The survey of businessmen's expectations conducted by Dun and Bradstreet in the United States seeks essentially the same information, though on a quarterly basis. The results obtained have been quite similar to those of the MBT, showing that businessmen appear to be better able to predict directions of movement in the short run than the amount of change.[16] It is interesting to note that the accuracy of the Dun and Bradstreet predictions do not seem to be as uniformly high as those of the respondents to the MBT, which may be explained in large measure by the longer horizon with which the Dun and Bradstreet respondents are confronted.

All in all, it would appear that for short-run forecasting, particularly of variables relating to a firm's own operations, this approach might be preferable to that of seeking more detail by asking for numerical values. At the same time, it also seems clear that even this type of survey is not likely to be too reliable if the forecasting horizon extends beyond two or three months.

It is important to note, however, that prediction need not be the only function of such surveys. In particular, some survey of this general nature seems indispensable if a study is being made of end-product uses of a particular product over a long period of time and of the technical changes that may influence the demand for the product in its different uses. In such a case, a less reliable survey producing numerical data may yet be preferable to a more reliable survey producing qualitative judgments of the anticipated directions of change. Indeed, if a quantitative survey is properly constructed, the qualitative data can always be obtained as a special case.

10.1.3. Analytical Forecasts

In this type of approach, which essentially combines diagnosis with prediction, explanations are sought of the factors influencing the variable to be predicted and a mathematical relationship is derived between these factors

---

[16] MILLARD HASTAY, "The Dun and Bradstreet Surveys of Businessmen's Expectations," *Proceedings of the Business and Economics Section, American Statistical Association,* September, 1954, pp. 93–123.

and the given variable. The forecast is made by substituting anticipated values for the determining factors in the equation. Alternatively, the forecast may be predicated on the use of certain other variables or indexes as advance indicators of future changes, which may or may not be formulated as an explicit mathematical relationship.

10.1.3.1. *Single equation approach.* An analytical forecast may be formulated in terms of a single equation or as part of a complete model system. Since the mechanics of both approaches have already been discussed in the preceding chapters, this discussion will focus on forecasting considerations.

The ideal single forecast equation is one that provides a close relationship between the variable being forecasted as dependent and a number of other variables, all of which are lagged. In that case, given the parameters of the equation and confirmation of its validity, the prediction problem is essentially solved, since the values of the independent variables required for the forecast are presumably known at the time the forecast is prepared. It is for this reason that so much time is devoted to the search for lead indicators and that the diffusion index approach has gained prominence.

The logic underlying the *diffusion index* approach is that a change in the direction of business conditions becomes more likely as this change is experienced by an increasing proportion of firms in the given industry or sector, i.e., as the movement becomes more diffuse. Hence, cyclical changes may be anticipated by keeping track of the proportion of firms undergoing movements counter to the prevailing trend. Unfortunately, in practice, problems seem to arise which may negate the value of this approach. In particular, there is the difficulty of securing the necessary data quickly enough to anticipate an actual turn as well as that of differentiating between a false alarm and the real thing.[17]

Whatever the merits of the case, the fact remains that a pure lag-lead relationship between the explanatory and the dependent variables remains more the exception than the rule. Except for such clear-cut situations as construction contracts preceding construction expenditures, at least one independent variable is generally in current time units. In such instances, the best that can be expected is to have all the explanatory variables as exogenous. Even then, however, a valid equation for the period of observation does not solve the forecasting problem but rather breaks it down into two separate problems: evaluating the applicability of the equation to conditions in the new period or sector, and forecasting the values of the explanatory variables. The former problem has already been discussed. The latter problem often tends to be overlooked in considering the analytical approach to a forecasting problem, and is equally important.

In effect, using current exogenous variables shifts the forecasting problem

---

[17] For the pros and cons of the approach, see the articles by Geoffrey Moore and by Stephen Valavanis in the *American Statistician*, October, 1957.

from the dependent variable to the explanatory variables. Hence, the question must be asked: is this shift desirable? The problem is of sufficient importance to justify a closer analysis. The forecasting error, in the case of a linear regression equation with one explanatory variable only, is given by:

$$u_a = y - \alpha - \beta(x + u_x) \quad \left\{ \begin{array}{l} \textit{Total} \\ \textit{ex-ante} \\ \textit{error} \end{array} \right. \qquad (10.1)$$

where y is the dependent variable, x the explanatory variable, and u_x the forecasting error of the latter, as a consequence of the fact that the current values of x for the next year are still unknown at the time of the forecast. u_a, however, depends not exclusively on u_x, but also on the systematic error, u_s, that still would have been obtained if x were exactly known, i.e., in the case of an "*ex post*" forecast:

$$u_s = y - \alpha - \beta x \quad \left\{ \begin{array}{l} \textit{Systematic} \\ \textit{ex-post} \\ \textit{error} \end{array} \right. \qquad (10.2)$$

It follows from (10.1) and (10.2) that there exists a simple relation between the three types of error:

$$u_a = u_s - \beta u_x \qquad (10.3)$$

Studying the results of a number of forecasts, regression forecasts are to be preferred if the sum of the squares of the *ex ante* errors is smaller than that of the errors obtained from direct forecasts of the dependent variable itself. Denoting the last mentioned errors by u_d, this condition is represented by the inequality:

$$\Sigma u_a^2 < \Sigma u_d^2 \qquad (10.4)$$

Substitution of the right-hand side of (10.3) in (10.4) gives:

$$\Sigma u_s^2 - 2\beta \Sigma u_s u_x + \beta^2 \Sigma u_x^2 < \Sigma u_d^2 \qquad (10.5)$$

Assuming that u_s and u_x are uncorrelated, the second term in the inequality vanishes. After replacement of β by:

$$\beta = \epsilon \frac{\bar{y}}{\bar{x}} \qquad (10.6)$$

where ϵ is the average elasticity, and $\bar{y}$ and $\bar{x}$ represent the average of y and x over the period studied, the condition (10.4) takes the form:

$$\sum \left(\frac{u_x}{\bar{x}} \right)^2 < \frac{1}{\epsilon^2} \left\{ \sum \left(\frac{u_d}{\bar{y}} \right)^2 - \sum \left(\frac{u_s}{\bar{x}} \right)^2 \right\} \qquad (10.7)$$

As is evident from (10.7), whether or not a regression estimate should be preferred over a direct one depends not only on the ratios involving u_d, u_s and u_x, but also on the elasticity implied by the estimator equation. If this elasticity shows, for example, a value of only .5, relative errors of .10 and .05 for u_d and u_s, respectively, set an upper limit as high as .17 for the forecasting error of x. With an elasticity of 2.0, however, the much higher precision of .043 would be required.

As is clear from (10.3), the two component parts of the final error may cancel out to some extent. Where many predetermined variables are involved, this chance increases,[18] although according to all rules of probability cumulative effects are likewise apt to occur.

The validity of a single equation as providing a more or less *complete structural relation* is another question that arises in economic and business forecasting. As noted in previous chapters, interdependence of variables is perhaps more the rule than the exception in many fields. Unless the "independent" variables are truly independent of the "dependent" variable, the equation has to be incorporated in a complete model as predictions from a single structural equation are inevitably subject to bias, the extent of which is usually unknown. Unbiased single equation estimates, however, remain sometimes possible if solution of the system results in a just-identified reduced-form equation from which the dependent variable can be predicted, as illustrated in Sec. 9.1.5.

These various reservations notwithstanding, the fact remains that in certain situations the single-equation approach may turn out to be most effective for forecasting. This is particularly true in demand analysis if the product or brand exerts relatively little influence on variables that might affect it, as might be the case for anything from shoelaces to washing machines. In such a situation, if a reasonable demand equation has been derived relating quantity to price and, say, disposable income, it may be possible to estimate the total demand for the product concerned under the assumption that relative prices will remain unchanged. This assumes, of course, that estimates of disposable income are available from some external sources.

Such a procedure offers an important frame of reference for decisions to be taken in the next period and also a basis for considering additional refinements. These refinements might consist of estimating the expected average relative price for the market as a whole and the influence of contemplated changes in the firm's marketing mix on shifts in its market share. Also, depending on the capability of the firm, its product line, and similar factors, some allowance could be incorporated for an autonomous rate of growth.

Essentially, this approach is much the same as that used in most judgment forecasts. The big difference, however, is the explicit quantification of the effect of each determining factor separately, and the basis thereby provided for constructive evaluation of the forecasting technique.

---

[18] In one case of model systems, differences between conditional and unconditional forecast errors were found to be relatively small. See P. J. VERDOORN and C. J. VAN EYK, *op. cit.*, p. 92.

10.1.3.2. *Complete model systems.* The technical considerations entering into the use of a model system for prediction are in many ways similar to those entering into the use of single equations, but with varying degrees of emphasis in each case. Some of the more important of these technical considerations are discussed below.

PREDICTING PREDETERMINED VARIABLES. Prediction of particular variables with a model system requires, first, the derivation of the reduced-form equation corresponding to each of these variables. As a result, the number of supposedly predetermined, or exogenous, variables in one of these equations may turn out to be much larger than the number of variables originally thought to influence the variable being forecasted. The statement made in the preceding section on the shift of the problem from prediction of the independent variable to the prediction of a set of "predetermined" variables applies equally to model systems. Although there is perhaps more opportunity for cancellation of prediction errors in predetermined variables, the main difficulty remains. This is especially true when the model is to be used for short-run unconditional prediction: in such cases the predetermined variables may have to be predicted with the aid of supplementary models, the models being related to each other in much the same way as estimates of the various interdependent variables are derived in a recursive system.

SERIAL CORRELATION IN RESIDUALS. It is by now standard practice to test the residuals of the time-series estimates of a dependent variable for the presence of serial correlation. Methods for doing so were discussed in Sec. 8.9.2, and possible means of adjusting equations for serial-correlation effects were covered in the previous chapter. It should simply be noted here that the use of first differences is a very simple device that may lead to more accurate forecasts, somewhat apart from its general effectiveness in minimizing serial-correlation effects, in much the same manner as a ratio estimate is at times a more efficient sample statistic than the mean value. By using a model to forecast absolute (or percentage) changes from the preceding period's level, forecasting bias in levels is largely eliminated.

It should be emphasized that the validity of any adjustment approach selected depends, as in so many other instances, on the applicability, for extrapolation purposes, of estimates of the parameters of the adjustment relation, e.g., equation (9.17), for the period of observation. As was noted in Sec. 3.5.3, the statistical effectiveness of a purely empirical approach in the period of observation may affect the generality of the results for extrapolation purposes. If at all possible, the results for the period of observation should be evaluated in the light of other than statistical grounds.

ERRORS IN FORECASTS. Since the probability of accuracy of a point estimate is zero, forecasts should preferably be presented in terms of ranges. For a single-equation prediction, the so-called standard error of the forecast is available for allowing for the probable effect on the forecast of sampling errors in the data.[19] The same concept is valid for model systems, though the computational process is so complicated as to be prohibitive in the case of model systems with interdependent variables.[20]

These procedures do not allow for possible errors in estimating the predetermined variables or for changes in structure. The latter is especially difficult to allow for, but errors in estimating predetermined variables can be allowed for in the forecasts to some extent by hypothesizing ranges within which these variables may lie. Forecasts are then prepared for alternative values within these ranges, usually three—high, middle and low values of the predetermined variables.

STABILITY OF STRUCTURE. A model is valid for predictive purposes only if the structure of the system—the estimates of the parameters—can be assumed to be unchanged in the future period. If this is not so, the model is less suitable for prediction unless the required changes can be made in the estimates of the parameters. This may be possible in some instances, as in the case of a shift in the tax structure, and depends in part on the nature and extent of the shift. If the shift is of such a nature that all previous relations are invalidated, estimation of the new structure may be a very difficult task. If only one or two equations are involved, the task is likely to be much easier.

How does one detect a change in structure? This is a very difficult question to answer. It involves generally critical evaluation of the effect of possible events that may have brought about a change in structure combined with empirical study of the accuracy of such forecasts as have been made with the model. As noted earlier, estimation of tolerance intervals for reduced form forecasts is not usually feasible. Nevertheless, standard errors can be computed for forecasts made directly from structural equations, as is shown in Sec. 10.2.1.1.

If, in such a case, the forecasts fall outside preset acceptable limits, reasons for the discrepancies must be investigated. Possibly the hypothesis had not been sufficiently refined, or perhaps the estimates of the predetermined variables were in substantial error, in which case corrected values should be substituted and the distribution of the revised forecast errors compared with the tolerance range.[21] (Why?) If forecast errors deviate more than would be expected by chance, a change in structure is not unlikely.

The final decision on a possible change in structure has to rest on economic and institutional considerations. Statistical tests can highlight the possibility

---

[19] M. EZEKIEL and K. FOX, *Methods of Correlation and Regression Analysis*, Chapter 19; also ROBERT FERBER, *Statistical Techniques in Market Research*, Chapter 13.

[20] T. M. BROWN, "Standard Errors of Forecast of a Complete Econometric Model," *Econometrica*, April, 1954, pp. 178–193.

[21] A means of carrying out this test is illustrated in CARL CHRIST, "A Test of An Econometric Model for the United States, 1921–1947," in *Conference on Business Cycles*. New York: National Bureau of Economic Research, 1951. See also L. R. KLEIN, *op. cit.*, pp. 272–275.

of such a change but are not likely to provide explanations for unusual discrepancies.

KEEPING MODELS CURRENT. As a model is used to provide continuous predictions over time, the period of observation tends to depart increasingly further from the period of extrapolation. This serves to reduce the reliability of the forecasts and makes it more difficult to detect any structural changes that may occur. (Why?) To remedy this situation, it is a good idea to recompute the estimates of the parameters as new data become available. However, unless the sample period is very short, it is important to leave some years between the sample period and the forecasting period to test the model. For, if adding new observations alters appreciably the estimates of the parameters, the new reduced form should be tested before being used for forecasting and policy decisions.

10.1.4. Judgment Forecasts

This "seat-of-the-pants" approach is probably still the most popular in general business operations, though it is declining in importance with the expansion of organized research activities. The approach is in some ways similar to the preceding one in that an attempt is generally made to understand the forces affecting the variable in question and to predict on the basis of anticipated changes in these forces and their effects. It involves a considerable amount of intuition and foresight. Thus, the reasoning underlying a forecast of gross national product for the next year might run something as follows, in abridged form:

"Expenditures of federal, state and local governments next year are likely to rise about $2 billion because of increased interest charges on the debt, more road-building and school and institutional building (about $3 billion more) offset only in part by a possible $1 billion reduction in defense costs. Private capital outlays are likely to rise by $2.5 billion, to judge by the business climate and recent anticipations surveys.

"Inventories generally are already high in relation to sales, so the past high rate of inventory accumulation is hardly likely to continue; the prospects are for inventory liquidation of roughly $2 billion.

"Consumer incomes are likely to move up further, accompanied by a possible rise of $1 billion in durable goods purchases, $1.5 billion in service expenditures, and a $0.5 billion drop in nondurable goods purchases, a net increase of $2 billion. Foreign balances are likely to average out to zero, with a slight trade deficit offset by repayment on debt and net capital inflows. All things considered, therefore, next year's gross national product will probably rise by $4.5 billion at current prices."

In some instances, an alternate forecast may be derived for the same item by a different variant of this approach, such as predicting gross national product by considering the factors of production—changes in wage and salary incomes, in corporate incomes, in rents, etc. The two forecasts are then compared for possible discrepancies, not only in the totals but also for internal consistency. Thus, does the ratio of consumer expenditures to disposable income "make sense" as obtained from the two sets of forecasts? Is the anticipated change in transfer payments consistent with what is expected for unemployment, social security eligibility, etc.? To the extent that discrepancies are found, adjustments are made in the various forecasts until everything appears consistent.

In a similar fashion, predictions can be made of such microvariables as product sales or prices. Thus, anticipated sales of urethane rubber may be derived by summing the anticipated changes in demand for the product by furniture manufacturers, auto plants, and other users of the product. The price of crude oil may be predicted on the basis of an evaluation of the domestic demand relative to supply and the probable exports and imports of crude oil, and so on.

Clearly, the approach is a highly flexible one and permits a multitude of factors to be taken into account. All sorts of data can be brought to bear on the forecast too—national trends, sales reports, and, perhaps, salesmen's anticipations (tempered for their usual inveterate optimism), dealer reports, the political situation, etc. The method is also very quick and painless to apply—no digging around for weeks for all sorts of figures, no computers to bother with, no statistical tests to run, no large staffs, not even any blond assistants to distract one's attention!

This type of forecast is especially advantageous when there are a large number of variables for which relatively little data are available or when erratic or intangible factors are expected to play a major role. For example, fluctuations in sales of an aircraft manufacturer will depend to a large extent on the vagaries of military policy as well as on the size of the government's military budget. In such a case, a judgment forecast may well be the only means of arriving at any sort of prediction.

There is little doubt that the ease and speed with which judgment forecasts can be made assure their continued popularity for years, if not decades, to come. Nevertheless, their shortcomings are such that their successful use will continue to be limited to persons with unusually keen intuitive judgment; little progress in forecasting techniques can be expected from this area. The lack of a rigorous structure for the forecast means that no estimates are available of the precise effect of particular determining variables on the variable being predicted. Pinpointing errors and using this knowledge to improve future predictions becomes therefore a highly arbitrary affair. For example, the degree to which a prediction is in error because of faulty evaluation of the effects of individual determining factors and because of mistaken forecasts of the extent of change of these factors can hardly be determined, and in many instances is ignored. By its very nature, the method abets a less-than-rigorous attitude toward profiting from decomposition of past errors of prediction.

By the same token, it becomes extremely difficult to pinpoint the role of judgment and the nature of all underlying assumptions in such predictions. Indeed, a primary advantage of the analytical approach is the obligation placed on the forecaster to specify the basic assumptions on which the various relationships are based and to examine their internal consistency in a rigorous fashion, e.g., the problem of identification. Identification of relations in a judgment forecast is hardly possible. In fact, much of the flexibility of the method is due to the ease with which certain equations that are usually thought relevant can be changed or suppressed. Full evaluation of a judgment forecast therefore requires reconstruction of the underlying model and testing its internal consistency as well as the plausibility of any coefficients accepted implicitly by the forecaster. In this sense, the example cited previously, forecasting gross national product, is somewhat atypical because the "model" underlying it is a definitional equation. Evaluating a judgment forecast of crude oil prices may be more typical, for this would very likely involve specifying the underlying demand and supply relationships, testing their consistency, and examining the basis for values assigned to the parameters, in some instances implicitly.

Although the judgment approach does have a place in the kit of the "compleat forecaster," as noted above, all things considered the more rigorous analytical approach would seem preferable where choice is possible. If the judgment method is used, specifying the assumptions underlying the predictions and examining their validity at a later time on an *ex post* basis are to be highly recommended.

10.2. DIAGNOSIS AND FORECASTING

Given a general knowledge of the availability and suitability of different forecasting methods, one is then in a position to evaluate the general conditions under which a forecast is to be made and the procedures indicated under these conditions. In this section, we shall consider the role that diagnosis plays in the forecasting procedure as well as the various steps to take in arriving at a forecast and evaluating its adequacy. The next section then turns to some basic questions of forecasting strategy in relation to policy decisions.

10.2.1. Diagnosis

After the discussion of the general aspects of the diagnosis in Sec. 1.1.1 and 1.2.2 it should be clear that no reliable prediction is possible without a thorough diagnosis of recent developments. The main objects of study in macro-analysis are dynamic factors, as outlined in Sec. 9.1.2.4, and the behavior in the base period of such exogenous factors as the level of government expenditure and export demand. For the individual firm, apart from present cyclical conditions and their ramifications, recent shifts in instrument variables, competitive conditions and autonomous demand comprise the main topics of interest. Some of the techniques used for this purpose will be discussed in Sec. 11.5 and 11.6.

Within the framework of the forecast the role of diagnosis can best be illustrated with reference to the analytical method. Using additive relationships, the most general way of writing a prediction of x_t for the period T is given by:

$$x_T^* = x_0 + \Phi_{T-0}^* + w_T^* \qquad (10.8a)$$

where x_T^* is the expected value of x_t at $t = T$,

x_0 is its actual value in the base period,

Φ_{T-0}^* is the expected combined systematic effect in the time-interval, $0 \rightarrow T$, of all factors entering the forecasting equation or model,

w_T^* is the expected value of the residual of the ex post forecast, w_T being defined as:

$$w_T = x_T - x_0 - \Phi_{T-0} \qquad (10.8b)$$

If the forecasting equation refers to the original observations of x_t and not to a first-difference transformation, w_T can be written as the difference between the systematic ex-post errors, as shown by (10.2), at $t = T$ and $t = 0$:

$$w_T = u_T - u_0 \qquad (10.8c)$$

Determining the structure of the forecasting equation or model is clearly a main objective of structure research. In forecasting, the remaining task for the diagnosis is therefore twofold:

1. To explain as exhaustively as possible, by means of the forecasting equation or model, and with the help of any other available information, the actual level of x_t in the base year, x_0.
2. To decide whether or not w_T^* in (10.8a) ought to be given a non-zero value. For this there may be three sets of reasons:
   i) Analysis of x_0 has shown $t = 0$ without further corrections to be inadequate as a base year, as, for instance, if short-run factors not specified in the equation are prevalent.
   ii) Even in the absence of such factors, the performance of the forecasting equation needs correction.
   iii) New factors not already present at $t = 0$ are expected to be operative at $t = T$.

This investigation may also point to the desirability of revising the coefficients of the existing equation or to the need for a new specification.

10.2.1.1. *Applicability to future period.* Whether or not changes in the equation or model are required depends essentially on the answer to the following questions:

Has a change in structure taken place? This is particularly likely if "something new" has been added to the economic scene—war, rationing, tax legislation, etc. In such instances, the relations used in the past may no longer be valid or new variables may have to be added. A change in structure does not only take place when some new development occurs. A continuation and intensification of a current development may have much the same effect, as might have been the effect of the deepening of the depression in 1932 on the income-consumption relationships (Fig. 4.9). It is especially desirable to look for changes in structure when the forecast or the values of the determining variables appear likely to fall outside the current range of observation. (Why?) Particularly pertinent in this respect is the next question.

Are boundary conditions likely to become operative? If the forecast relation indicate probable sales to be 140 million tons of ingot steel next year but capacity production is only 130 million tons, clearly the latter figure is the more realistic expectation. Alternatively, the forecast relations may indicate that consumer credit outstanding by next December 31 could reach $50 billion under present conditions. However, long before that figure is reached it seems probable that the government will take steps to reduce the volume of borrowing. The final forecast has to take this eventuality into account. To cite another example, in forecasting price trends allowance has to be made for the tendency of prices to remain relatively stable within wide ranges of demand and supply; but, if demand is likely to approach capacity, the short-run reaction may be a sharp jump in prices.

Might the form of the relations have changed? This is a question that should be raised instinctively whenever forecasting moves beyond the range of the past observations. The question is particularly pertinent with mathematical trends, where a simple function may provide a good approximation to the period of observation but may prove entirely inadequate for prediction purposes. In fact, diagnosis may indicate that a relation highly effective for describing current trends is of little value for prediction purposes. Thus, beyond a certain point a parabolic trend becomes ridiculous (Why?), and even a linear trend is hardly likely to go on indefinitely.

The same question is pertinent to analytical relationships. In the early 1950's, many predictions were made that U. S. aluminum production would continue to expand into the 1960's at a rate roughly 50 per cent in excess of the growth of gross national product, as was true of past decades.[22] That

---

[22] J. E. ROSENZWEIG, *The Demand for Aluminum: A Case Study in Long Range Forecasting* (Champaign, Illinois: Bureau of Economic and Business Research, University of Illinois, 1957), Chapter 4.

available markets might not be large enough to absorb the output in view of declining military aircraft production and increasing competition from other metals was generally overlooked.

The rationale behind a statistical relationship has to be reassessed continually and appropriate adjustments made in the form of the relationship as needed. The next question is particularly useful for this purpose.

How accurate is the function in extrapolation on an ex post basis? Some indication of the predictive reliability of a function can often be obtained by fitting the function to only part of the period of observation and using the remainder of the period as the part to be predicted. Thus, if the period of observation for a mathematical trend describing production of natural gas is 1947–1960, for testing purposes the relation might be fitted to 1947–56 and the result used to predict production in 1957. The period of observation might then be extended to include 1957, and the resulting relation used to predict 1958 production, and similarly for 1959 and 1960. As one measure of the validity of the function, the average absolute error of prediction can be compared with the average error of estimate in the period of observation. The trend of these predictive errors can also be examined for any systematic or explosive tendencies. More rigorously, tolerance intervals can be computed to see if the predictions lie within them; if not, investigation of a change in structure or in the form of the relation may be indicated.

The application of these procedures to the natural gas problem mentioned above is shown in Table 10.1. The functional relation used, a semi-log linear trend between energy and time, is not especially sophisticated and might be difficult to justify on *a priori* grounds. (Why?) Nevertheless, it does serve to illustrate the procedure, which is a fairly general one.

Table 10.1

EVALUATION OF PREDICTIVE ABILITY OF TREND IN PRODUCTION OF NATURAL GAS[a] BY *Ex Post* EXTRAPOLATION

Period of observation	FORECAST[b] Period	*Estimate*	*Actual*	AVERAGE ABSOLUTE ERROR IN Pd. of obs.	Pd. of forecast	*Two-sigma tolerance interval*[c]
1947–56	1957	12.8	11.7	0.2	1.1	11.5–13.6
1947–57	1958	13.3	12.1	0.3	1.2	12.5–14.1
1947–58	1959	14.0	13.0	0.3	1.0	12.5–15.7
1947–59	1960	14.8		0.4		13.9–15.7
Average		13.7		0.3		

[a] In thousands of trillions of British thermal units.
[b] Based on functional relation: 1947–56: $log\ Y_c = 2.892459 + .018579t$
1947–57: $log\ Y_c = 2.908293 + .035785t$
1947–58: $log\ Y_c = 2.922897 + .017134t$
1947–59: $log\ Y_c = 2.937592 + .033223t$

[c] Based on standard error of forecast, as discussed in Sec. 10.2.2.5.
Source for original data: *Statistical Abstract of the U. S., 1960*, p. 526.

As is evident from this table, the predictive equation appears to be consistently overshooting the mark; the natural gas production for 1957–60 is just barely, and for 1958 not at all, contained within the lower bounds of the 95 per cent tolerance interval. In addition, the error of the forecasts is seen to average considerably higher than the error of the function estimates in each period of observation. The evidence seems clear, therefore, that the present trend function is not likely to prove reliable for predictive purposes.

The same general procedure can be applied to other means of mechanical extrapolation and to relations derived by the analytical approach. In the latter case, however, it should be noted that tolerance intervals are applicable only to estimates of structural equations; they are not obtainable for reduced-form relations.[23]

10.2.1.2. *Incidental factors.* A major function of diagnosis in a forecast situation is to determine to what extent the forecast derived from the functional relation may have to be modified because of the possible influence of special factors in the period ahead. Thus, if inventories of room air conditioners are unusually high at the start of the season, a sales forecast for such air conditioners, accurate as it may be, cannot serve as the basis directly for a production schedule. Similarly, anticipated sales of wine in Italy may have to be raised well above the figure derived from the functional relation in a year when Rome is the site of the World Olympic Games and of a number of other special events.

To be sure, if such phenomena occur with some regularity, adjustment factors can at times be incorporated into the functional relations. Thus, if the effect of presidential nominating conventions on TV summer audience ratings could be isolated, a dummy variable reflecting this could be added to the relation and assigned the value 1 in a presidential year and 0 otherwise (assuming the effect to be additive). However, numerous events that may influence the forecast substantially occur either uniquely or with very low frequencies, and for these an *a priori* adjustment seems preferable.

Such considerations are particularly applicable to forecasts of operational variables pertaining to the individual firm—sales, production, etc. Being on a lower level of aggregation, incidental factors are likely to be of greater importance to the individual firm than to the industry or to the economy as a whole. This is especially so for a firm that serves primarily a particular region or consumer group. For example, in 1959 a general increase in the price of bread took place in the United States, an increase large enough to enable Canadian bread bakers to export bread profitably to the large border cities of the United States, but not much farther. As a result, a 1960 sales

---

[23] For a discussion of the interpretation of tolerance intervals, see W. A. WALLIS, "Tolerance Intervals for Linear Regressions," in *Proceedings of the Second Berkeley Symposium on Mathematical Statistics and Probability* (Berkeley: University of California Press, 1951), pp. 43–51.

forecast made at that time for an American baking firm selling heavily in the Buffalo or Detroit area required modification of the functional relation estimate to allow for this intensified, though presumably temporary, competition.

To take another example, if a firm in a highly competitive field receives unfavorable publicity in a given year, some adjustment may be indicated in a near-term sales forecast derived from an analytical relationship. This was the situation faced by Revlon, the cosmetics producer, in late 1959 as a result of the Congressional hearings on TV quiz shows, which had been sponsored by Revlon among other firms, and which turned out to have been rigged, apparently without the knowledge of top management.

Forecasts for an individual firm may also be influenced by changes in instrument variables. Thus, if the firm assigns its account to a new advertising agency that is about to try a radically different form of promotion than that used previously, the possibility of pronounced effects on future operations may have to be introduced. Continuing surveys of such factors as brand awareness and product acceptance are particularly useful for detecting the impact of changes of this nature.[24] If the shift should appear to be permanent, an appropriate revision may be needed in the forecast relation.

10.2.2. Forecast Stages

The process of arriving at a particular forecast, after the diagnosis has been completed, may be divided into five stages or steps, as discussed below.

10.2.2.1. *Selection of a forecasting method.* Selecting a forecasting method involves bringing together the various considerations covered in Sections 10.1 and 10.2.1 as well as such related matters as available data and time and resources. It is perhaps needless to note that at this stage the form of the relationship must be specified as well as the variables that enter into it.

10.2.2.2. *Collection and estimation of required data.* Not only do data have to be collected for the different variables included in the forecast relation, but the predetermined variables generally have to be estimated for the current period. Such basic indicators as gross national product, consumer expenditures, corporate profits, and capital expenditures are hardly ever available for a given year before the end of the first quarter of the following year. However, since forecasts for, say, 1963 are usually prepared about the end of 1962, this means that the values of any such predetermined variables included on a current basis in the forecast relation have to be estimated for 1962. This is not a task to be tossed off lightly because some of these estimates are subject to considerable margins of error, for example retail sales, a large part of which take place just before Christmas.

---

[24] For one account of such surveys, see *Advertising Agency*, November, 1949, pp. 50ff.

Related to the collection of data in the case of long-term structural estimates is the proper choice of a base period. For example, if investment outlays are to be predicted on the basis of, among other variables, the ratio of an index of capital stock to an index of capacity operations, the nature of the relationship obtained may depend in large measure on the base period selected. Selection of a base period when capital stock was unusually low relative to productive capacity may yield a very different forecast than would use of a "more normal" base period. Considerable diagnosis and experimentation may be required before an informed decision can be made.

10.2.2.3. *Adjusting the forecast relation.* Estimation of the parameters of the relation by suitable means is only a preliminary step at this stage. The characteristics of the estimates derived from the relation have to be studied and appropriate corrections applied as needed. Perhaps the most frequent of these corrections relates to removal of serial correlation effects. This may involve consideration of additional variables that may have previously been thought not relevant to testing different transformations of the original data, as described in Section 9.1.6.1.

In the case of model forecasts, a change of coefficients or even suppression of an entire equation may be indicated at times. To paraphrase an example given by Klein,[25] an equation explaining fluctuations in consumer credit may have to be drastically altered or removed altogether if the government were to impose a ceiling on the amount of credit outstanding. In such an instance, the effect of the shift cannot be ascertained simply by adjusting the reduced form equation for the direct effect on the variable being forecasted. The effect may be indirect as well and is therefore ascertained by combining this new equation with the other structural relations in the system, then deriving new reduced form relations.

10.2.2.4. *Consideration of alternative forecast conditions.* Invariably the values of the exogenous variables in the forecast period—and at times even in the current period—are subject to considerable uncertainty. To cope with this problem, alternative reasonable levels for these variables may be assumed and forecasts derived for each of these alternatives. If the expected amount of competitor advertising next year is between $14 million and $17 million, sales forecasts might be derived for each of these two advertising figures in turn, thereby providing some indication of the effect on sales of these alternative events.

If the values of several exogenous variables are subject to uncertainty, the usual practice is to combine in one alternative mutually consistent values of these variables leading to a relatively high prediction, in another alternative consistent values leading to a relatively low prediction, and perhaps in a third alternative those values that appear to be most "reasonable" or most

---

[25] *A Textbook of Econometrics*, p. 254.

likely. This form of prediction has the advantage of indicating the probable range of variation in the predetermined (exogenous and instrumental) variables as well as the extent to which variations in these variables may produce different conditions.[26] Alternative hypotheses relating to variables beyond the policy maker's control are customarily referred to as *data alternatives;* hypotheses relating to instrument variables are referred to as *policy alternatives.*

10.2.2.5.   *Appraisal of forecast.* After a forecast figure has been derived, some *a priori* evaluation is needed of its reliability. Such an evaluation can be carried out in part by statistical means and in part by what we may term plausibility checks.

STATISTICAL EVALUATION. If the forecast is derived from a mathematical trend or from an analytical equation, its reliability can generally be evaluated by computing the standard error of the forecast and an estimate thereby obtained of the range of sampling error to which the forecast may be subject. To illustrate, consider the linear trend equation for natural gas production for the period, 1947–57, which is, from Table 10.1:

$$log \ Y = 2.908293 + .035785t \qquad (t_{1952} = 0) \qquad (10.9)$$

The variance formula for a forecast based on this relation is:[27]

$$\sigma_f^2 = \frac{m\sigma_u^2}{N-2} \left\{ 1 + \frac{12}{N^2 - m^2} t^2 \right\} \qquad (10.10)$$

where σ_u is the standard deviation of regression,

m is the forecast range form $t = 0$,

N is the length of the period of observation

This expression is applied in a manner analogous to that of other standard error expressions. Thus, the 95 per cent tolerance interval for the 1958 forecast of natural gas production would be obtained as:

$$2.908293 + .035785(6) \pm 2.62 \sqrt{\left[\frac{6(.003388)}{9} \left\{ 1 + \frac{12}{121 - 36} 36 \right\} \right]} \qquad (10.11)$$

or between 12.5 and 14.1 thousand trillion thermal units.

The standard error of the forecast reflects the dispersion of the data in the period of observation, and hence sampling errors in the estimates of the parameters of (10.11), as well as the increased variation to be expected as the extrapolation departs farther and farther from the center of the period of observation. This declining reliability is illustrated in Fig. 10.3, which contains estimates of Y for 1947–57 and forecasts for 1958–60 as well as the corresponding tolerance interval.

[26] For an example, see P. J. VERDOORN, "Complementarity and Long-Range Projections," *Econometrica*, October, 1956, p. 449.

[27] H. T. DAVIS. *Analysis of Economic Time Series*, p. 518.

Formulas are available for a host of other mathematical trends. Study[28] of these formulas before selecting a trend equation can be highly instructive regarding probable reliability of a forecast. Thus, one finds that a forecast based on a polynomial trend is subject to considerable instability because the tolerance interval depends, among other things, on the time interval raised to twice the power of the highest degree polynomial. In other words, if (10.9) were parabolic, the standard error, σ_f, would contain a term, t^4.

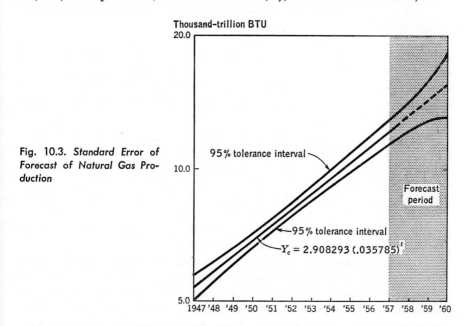

Fig. 10.3. *Standard Error of Forecast of Natural Gas Production*

The general formula for the standard error of an analytical forecast based on a linear estimator equation with only one explanatory variable, e.g., $Y = a + bX$, is:[29]

$$\sigma_f^2 = \sigma_y^2 + \sigma_u^2 + (\sigma_b x)^2 \tag{10.12}$$

where σ_y is the standard error of the mean of the dependent variable, y,
   σ_u is the standard deviation of the residuals in the period of observation,
   σ_b is the standard error of the regression coefficient,
   x is $X - \bar{X}$
This relation, like equation (10.10), is useful not only for evaluating a

---

[28] *Ibid.* Chapter 11.
[29] For the multivariate case, see M. EZEKIEL and K. Fox, *Methods of Correlation and Regression Analysis*, p. 320; R. FERBER, *Statistical Techniques in Market Research*, pp. 393–395.

forecast but also for providing general pointers on means of decreasing forecast errors. Three such means are indicated from these relations:

1. Use more observations in deriving the forecast relation.
2. Work as closely as possible to the mean of the independent variable. (Why?)
3. Seek better estimators, to reduce $\sigma_u{}^2$. As noted in an earlier chapter, however, goodness of fit itself is not always a reliable criterion of predictive ability.

The last of these means serves to emphasize that the standard error of forecast is not an all-inclusive measure of predictive reliability. It makes no allowance for such non-sampling and, often much more important, considerations as structural shifts, faulty selection of function form, or omission of relevant variables.

Standard errors of forecasts based on equation systems can also be computed though the computations tend to be rather involved.[30] In the case of reduced form equations derived from models containing many equations, the necessary computations, though theoretically possible, may become too complex for actual use.[31] As an alternative, comparisons can be made of the normality of the distribution of the ratios of the forecast residuals to the standard deviations of regression of the different equations, a procedure discussed at greater length in Section 10.4.

PLAUSIBILITY CHECKS. The plausibility of a forecast can be tested in a number of ways, depending on the context within which the forecast is made and on the ingenuity of the forecaster. Essentially, the aim is to bring to bear on the derived prediction whatever other data, procedures or reasoning may be available to assess its adequacy. Three such approaches of fairly wide applicability are mentioned below.

1. *Derivation of alternative forecasts.* If there is much uncertainty regarding the validity of the method used, forecasts may be derived by alternative methods and the results compared. In a similar way, stability of the forecast can be tested against alternative hypotheses by adding or deleting appropriate variables or by varying the form of the relation. Thus, an equation model forecast of investment expenditures may be compared with the results of a small-scale survey of investment plans, if such a survey is feasible. Or, if it is not clear whether change in income distribution should be included in a relation seeking to explain fluctuations in home freezer purchases, forecasts could be derived alternately including and excluding this variable, and the results compared.

---

[30] KLEIN, *op. cit.*, Chapter 6. T. M. BROWN, "Standard Errors of Forecast of a Complete Econometric Model," *Econometrica*, April, 1954, pp. 178–192.

[31] P. J. VERDOORN and C. J. VAN EYCK, *Experimental Short-Term Forecasting Models* (The Hague: Central Planning Bureau, July, 1958), pp. 84ff.

To the extent that alternative estimates are close to each other, the resulting forecast is presumably more reliable. This is not always true, however, for the possibility that the same biases underlie both forecasts always exists. Thus, a prediction of aluminum production based on a regression on national product and time may be virtually the same whether a linear or a curvilinear relation is assumed. Both may contain large errors, nevertheless, if another highly relevant variable, such as the ratio of aluminum prices to that of other metals, were omitted from the relation.

2. *Comparison with the past.* How consistent do the implications of the forecast appear to be with changes that have taken place during analogous periods in the past? If, for example, a 15 per cent rise in production is predicted for the year following a recession period, how does this compare with the revival in similar periods in the past, such as 1958–59? Can the differences be accounted for in terms of the different situations prevailing in these other years? If not, might the forecast be unrealistic? Questions of this type may provide either further support for the forecast or a basis for re-examining some of the basic underlying assumptions.

3. *Common sense evaluation.* Does the forecast seem reasonable from a common sense point of view? Thus, if the results of an econometric model point to a decline of 20 per cent in the number of telegrams sent as a result of a 10 per cent rise in prices, does this make sense with what is known about the composition of the market? Cross-section data on the extent to which business, government, consumers, etc., send telegrams can be very helpful in such a case, indicating, on the one hand, the reasonableness of the forecast in terms of market composition and, on the other hand, what sort of promotional measures might be considered in an attempt to avert part of this loss, i.e., to shift the demand curve to the right.

10.3. FORECASTS AND POLICY DECISIONS

10.3.1. Policy Alternatives

Forecasts are an instrument of policy. Hence, if the results obtained from a forecasting procedure are not compatible with the targets of the policy maker, the values of the instruments that are at the control of the policy maker may have to be changed. If so, policy alternatives are developed.

As a rule, the aim of these policy alternatives is twofold:

1. Quantification of the issues involved in the current policy discussion. Such quantification, combined with appropriate use of data alternatives, can add considerably to the meaningfulness of the policy discussion, whether it be in business or in government.
2. Seeking an optimum solution to the policy maker's problem.

In the latter case, linear programming can help in formalizing the procedure, as noted previously. Unfortunately, the methods developed to date are not often powerful enough to discriminate between meaningful and non-meaningful alternatives, and therefore still need to be handled very carefully.[32] Theoretically, mathematical decision functions would provide an objective answer to this problem, but the construction of such functions in practice is as yet an unsolved problem.[33]

Attaining an optimum solution, therefore, is essentially a subjective matter, requiring consideration of data alternatives, policy alternatives, reasonableness of particular forecasts, and risks involved in particular courses of action. It may be argued that selection of a particular forecast, and policy, is something for the policy maker to do, not the researcher. It is nevertheless the task of the researcher to indicate different policy alternatives, the forecasts that are obtained under these various conditions, and the reliability of these forecasts. In particular, it is the task of the researcher to define what is meant by an optimal solution and to bring out the components of this solution.

For example, an optimal solution may be defined as one that, to paraphrase Theil, will "maximize welfare subject to the actual (and generally unknown) constraints."[34] It is up to the policy maker to indicate the framework within which welfare is to be maximized—whether it is to be in terms of employment, stable prices, market share (for the business firm), or something else—as well as the nature of the constraints to be imposed on the solution. Thus, the objective of a national policy may be stipulated to be the growth of real national product by at least 4 per cent annually subject to the constraints of: (a) consumer prices stable within 3 per cent of their current level, (b) unemployment less than 5 per cent of the labor force, (c) a balanced budget, and (d) a favorable balance of trade.

The forecaster then seeks to ascertain, on the basis presumably of a comprehensive model of the economic system, whether these targets are likely to be realized next year. The likelihood of attaining the objective will undoubtedly vary with the manner in which various instruments of economic policy are used—tax rates, monetary policy, fiscal policy, etc. Ideally, "optimal reaction functions" would be developed relating the policy maker's optimum values—in this case economic growth, consumer prices, unemployment, etc.—to the effectiveness of the instruments in bringing about changes in the uncontrolled variables. Once obtained, such functions, accompanied by an evaluation of their reliability, bring out clearly the probable effect on the desired objectives of particular manipulations of instruments. They

---

[32] C. J. VAN EIJK and J. SANDEE, "Quantitative Determination of an Optimum Economic Policy," *Econometrica*, January, 1959, pp. 1–13.

[33] For an outline of one theoretical procedure, see KLEIN, *op. cit.*, pp. 261–264.

[34] HANS THEIL, *Economic Forecasts and Policy*, p. 431.

are also a basis for determining what combinations of policy instruments are most likely to yield the desired objectives.[35]

10.3.2. Strategic Forecasts

The strategic forecast is a variant of the policy alternatives. Its objective is not to arrive at the most probable values of the dependent variables but rather at some point of minimum risk. Thus, in defending the U. S. Government's forecast of national income for 1946, Arthur Smithies said:[36]

"If policies are based on, say, an assumed national income, it is not a matter of indifference whether the estimate turns out to be too high or too low. It is much better to have a program of unemployment relief and not use it than to need it and not have it. But if national income is assumed at a low level, there is danger that policies may be adopted which will be inflationary if national income, for other reasons, turns out to be high. The risk of inflation must be weighed against the risk of failure to provide for unemployment. The strategic assumption should be selected so as to minimize the risks of being wrong.

"It is frequently much easier to change policy in one direction than in another. It is easy to reduce taxes but hard to increase them. On the other hand, it is risky to keep taxes too high or to retain controls too long. But the strategic assumption should be based in part on the ease or difficulty with which policies based on it can be changed.

"Economists delude themselves and the country when they assert that policy should be flexible enough to provide for a wide range of contingencies. The machinery of government of the United States is so complex that there are severe limits to flexibility. I do not see how we can hope to devise methods to guard against inflation and deflation at the same time. Even though both may be equally probable, the strategic assumption should give greater weight to the alternative that is considered to be the more dangerous."

In this sense, Smithies notes that the forecasts at that time, though much too low, nevertheless appear in a more favorable light. Had transitional unemployment been high and acute shortages taken place, a possibility in those circumstances, the government was well prepared to cope with the situation.

The danger with such a strategic forecast is that one is likely, as Smithies remarks, to be hoisted with one's own petard. Others may interpret the forecast as representing the most probable value and act accordingly aggrieved when the forecasts differ substantially from actual values.

Strategic forecasts may also give rise to conflicting considerations. Thus, in estimating the effect of a price cut on revenues of an electric utility, there

---

[35] A more comprehensive and rigorous treatment of this problem will be found in THEIL, *op. cit.*, Chapters 7–9.

[36] Comment in *American Economic Review*, May, 1947, p. 85.

is the risk on the one hand of increasing demand above current capacity and, on the other hand, of financial losses of revenue, part of which might be devoted to increasing capacity. In the first instance, the strategic forecast would imply a relatively high load estimate whereas in the other instance a conservative prediction would be indicated.

10.4. EVALUATING FORECASTING METHODS

The *ex post* evaluation of forecasting methods is generally the most neglected aspect of forecasting, even though in many ways it is potentially the most useful. Systematic recording and study of past forecasts are by far the best means of pinpointing biases and increasing predictive accuracy. It is unfortunate that these forecasts tend to be forgotten after the period in question has past, unless, of course, the forecast turned out to be unusually accurate! It is the inaccurate forecasts that often provide valuable lessons for the future.

Principal means of evaluating forecasting methods are discussed in this section. Note that the perspective taken here is very different from that taken in Section 10.2.2.5. In the latter case, the *a priori* evaluation of a *particular* forecast was considered; here it is the *ex post* evaluation of the *method itself*.

10.4.1. Absolute Accuracy

Forecast errors can be recorded and evaluated in two principal ways, each complementary to the other: ascertaining the absolute accuracy of the forecasts and ascertaining their comparative accuracy. In the former case, the objective is to determine:

1. the extent to which the forecasts deviate from the actual values, and
2. whether the errors are consistent in any particular direction, namely, the biases in the forecasts.

The results then provide a basis for investigating the reasons for the discrepancies and what can be done to reduce them.

The deviation of the forecasts from the actual values may be gauged by the following measure of percentage error:

$$\sum \left| \frac{Actual\text{-}Forecast}{Actual} \right| \Big/ \begin{array}{l} Number\ of \\ forecasts \end{array} \tag{10.13}$$

Note that, in averaging, absolute values of the deviations are used. (Why?)

Examination of the individual deviations with regard to sign can also serve to detect bias in the forecasts, namely, to the extent that patterns appear to be present in the deviations. Another approach may be useful in this case, however, one that yields a more general, graphic picture of the situation. This involves plotting the percentage error of the forecast against the actual percentage change in the variables, as illustrated by Fig. 10.4. Since the same percentage grid is used on both axes, any drift of the forecasts from the 45-degree line is indicative of bias—underestimates if the points fall below the line and overestimates if they lie above the line. Thus, Fig. 10.4 shows at a glance that the forecasts of prices and, to some extent, of the exogenous variables were systematically too low. The diagram also provides an indication of the absolute and comparative percentage errors of the forecasts, highlighting the unbiased forecasts of value compared with the wide deviations in forecasts of various exogenous variables.

An alternative measure of predictive accuracy can be obtained by dividing the root-mean-squares of the residuals by the same statistic for the annual changes of the estimand during the period of observation. Note that the units of measurement ought to be the same and that the root mean square deviations are taken from zero, not from the mean.[37] Thus, if $A_{i,t}$ is the actual level of the ith variable in period t, if $E_{i,t}$ is the corresponding predicted variable, and if s_{A_i} is the root mean square of the period-to-period changes in the estimand over the period of observation, we have:

$$u_{i,t} = A_{i,t} - E_{i,t}$$

and the measure of predictive accuracy is:

$$u'_{i,t} = \frac{u_{i,t}}{s_{A_i}} \tag{10.14}$$

For the forecasts for a number of variables $i = 1, 2, \ldots, n$, at t, we have the *standardized root mean square residual* as the root mean square of the values obtained from (10.14) for each of the n variables:

$$u'_t = \sqrt{\frac{1}{n} \Sigma u'_{i,t}} \tag{10.15}$$

In a similar way, a predictive measure can be derived for the forecasts of the same variable over a number of periods.

This measure is generally obtainable directly from data already calculated and in some ways is more manageable algebraically than (10.13). It also yields a measure of forecast accuracy independent of the levels of the actual variables, which is not true of the previous measure. Like (10.13), it can be

---

[37] P. J. VERDOORN and C. J. VAN EYCK, *op. cit.*, pp. 58ff.

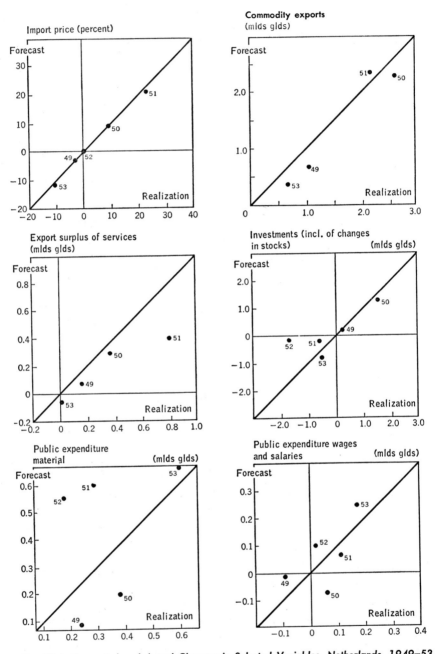

Fig. 10.4. *Forecasted and Actual Changes in Selected Variables, Netherlands, 1949–53*

Source: Central Planning Bureau, *Scope and Methods of the Central Planning Bureau.*
The Hague, 1956, p. 58.

used to compare forecasts of different variables or trends in accuracy of forecast of a single variable. Thus, whether a model is able to yield forecasts as
accurate as the estimates obtained in the period of observation can be tested
by determining whether the frequency distribution of (10.14) corresponds
to a normal distribution.[38] If the mean of the distribution is significantly
different from zero, bias is indicated; and if the variance significantly exceeds
unity, growing dispersion of the forecasts may be indicated.

Another measure of predictive accuracy with similar virtues to that of
(10.15) is the following one proposed by Theil, *viz.*, the *coefficient of inequality*:[39]

$$U = \frac{\sqrt{\Sigma u_{it}^2}}{\sqrt{\Sigma A_{it}^2} + \sqrt{\Sigma E_{it}^2}} \tag{10.16}$$

This measure has the convenient property of varying between zero and
unity; the lower the forecast errors, the closer is U to zero. The measure is
not independent of additive transformations. Thus, if each value in the following pair of series,

$$
\begin{array}{lrrrr}
\text{E:} & -3 & 5 & 10 & -4 \\
\text{A:} & -1 & 7 & 7 & -1 \\
\end{array}
$$

is increased by 100, i.e.:

$$
\begin{array}{lrrrr}
\text{E:} & 97 & 105 & 110 & 96 \\
\text{A:} & 99 & 107 & 107 & 99 \\
\end{array}
$$

U declines from .23 to .01 although the correlation is .95 in both instances.[40]

10.4.2. Comparative Accuracy

Apart from the absolute accuracy of the forecasts is the question of the
practical value of a set of forecasts. In other words, are the forecasts any
better than what could be obtained by some other, relatively simple, method?
If this is not the case, the forecasts are not likely to be of much value irrespective of how close they come to the true values, since this simpler method
would still be equally accurate. If, however, the forecasts under study are
superior, i.e., more accurate, than alternative forecasts, they may be of real
value even though quite wide of the mark in an absolute sense.

Hence, in evaluating the so-called "relative accuracy" of a set of forecasts,
a yardstick is sought, that is, an alternative set of forecasts obtainable
quickly and with little effort. The yardstick generally used in such instances
is one of the "naive model" approaches, a model set up to predict the actual
movement on the basis of a simple extrapolation of the current level. The

---

[38] *Ibid.*, pp. 84–85.
[39] H. THEIL, *op. cit.*, Chapter 2.
[40] *Ibid.*, pp. 33–34.

simplest such model is the projection of the current level under the assumption of no change. Thus, if E_t and A_t are the expected and actual levels of shipments in quarter t, the naive model forecast for the next quarter, assuming no seasonal variation, is:

$$E_{t+1} = A_t \qquad (10.17)$$

The average error of the naive model forecast becomes:

$$\sum \left| \frac{A_{t+1} - A_t}{NA_{t+1}} \right| \qquad (10.18)$$

which is compared with the average error of the more extensive model to obtain a measure of comparative accuracy.[41]

More sophisticated "naive models" can be constructed by incorporating change into the model. Thus, the naive forecast may postulate the projection of the average quarterly change over the past year which would be, in the absence of seasonal variation:

$$E_{t+1} = A_t \left(1 + \frac{A_t - A_{t-4}}{4A_{t-4}} \right) \qquad (10.19)$$

In a similar manner, modified rates of change can be incorporated into the naive model. For the purpose of evaluating relative accuracy, it is important that any such rates be reasonably naive and that the model itself be a mechanical one; otherwise this approach loses its value.

10.4.3. Correlation Test

A supplementary means of evaluating relative accuracy lies in correlating the forecasted relative changes with the actual relative changes. Like the naive model approach, this test offers the advantage of eliminating the spurious accuracy so common in economic and marketing forecasts that is brought about by the serial correlation between successive levels of a series. In addition, this test investigates the possibility that the model forecasts may not be too accurate either in an absolute or comparative sense but may nevertheless provide useful information on impending change. Such would be the case if the forecasts were to contain substantial and consistent biases. To the extent that such a correlation is statistically significant, the forecasts are useful indicators of change. At the same time, because this test is invariant to additive transformations it can not indicate consistent under- or over-estimation, as is true, for example, of the measure U (equation 10.16).

---

[41] The procedure is illustrated in ROBERT FERBER, *The Railroad Shippers' Forecasts*, Studies in Business Expectations and Planning, No. 1, University of Illinois Bureau of Economic and Business Research, 1953, Chapter 3. Also *Employer Forecasts of Manpower Requirements*, Studies in Business Expectations and Planning, No. 3, 1958, Chapter 2.

10.4.4. Turning Points

Anticipation of turning points is the heart of the forecasting problem. For this reason, evaluating the ability of a set of forecasts to predict reversals of trend is an acid test of their value. Hence, this is a test of relative accuracy that deserves special attention in any given case. The test can be carried out in various ways. As a general rule, it may be preferable to work with frequency counts rather than with the actual data. Thus, the proportion of

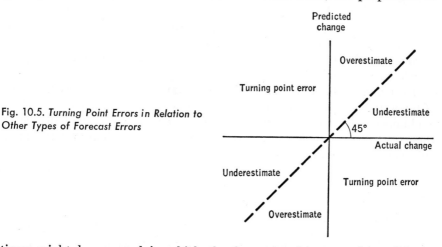

Fig. 10.5. *Turning Point Errors in Relation to Other Types of Forecast Errors*

times might be counted in which the forecasts: (*a*) correctly anticipate all reversals of current trend, the latter suitably defined, and (*b*) correctly anticipate turning points. The value of the forecasts for this purpose is then ascertained by comparing these frequency counts with the results of some naive model and/or with the extent to which they do better than what would be expected as a result of chance fluctuations.

In evaluating turning point errors, it is important to note that two types of errors are involved. A turning point may be erroneously predicted, or no turning point may be predicted when one takes place. Diagrammatically, we have:

		Prediction	
		Turn	*No turn*
Actual {	Turn	*a*	*c*
	No turn	*b*	*d*

This is brought out graphically in Fig. 10.5, which also shows the relation of turning point errors to other types of forecast errors. It might be noted that the term "turning point error" is used primarily in a statistical sense as referring to any forecasted direction of change that does not agree with the later observed direction of movement. Cyclical turning points in the economic sense represent a subset of this larger category.

Following Theil's procedure,[42] we may denote b as a Type I error and c as a Type II error. Quantitative measures of these errors can be set up as:

$$f_1 = \frac{b}{a+b}$$

$$f_2 = \frac{c}{c+d}$$

In general, the lower the value of f_i the better. Note, however, that these measures have to be considered in conjunction with each other. A shrewd forecaster can always evade, say, a Type I error by never predicting a turning point! A similar statement is true for Type II errors. There is some indication that in actual forecast surveys the two types of errors may be correlated with each other.[43]

In concluding this section, it might be mentioned that in practice a battery of these tests should be used on a set of forecasts so that a balanced picture is obtained of their predictive worth. By keeping track of the outcome of these tests through time, a firm basis is obtained for explaining discrepancies and improving the forecasting method.

PROBLEMS

1. *a*) Devise a naive model for predicting monthly retailers' stocks of shoes incorporating adjustments for both seasonal and erratic variation.

   b) Enumerate the assumptions required to sustain the validity of the model.

2. Devise a procedure for detecting and measuring biases in a quarterly survey of anticipated business sales.

3. Suppose the following forecasting model is proposed to you as objective, foolproof and as doing away with the problem of predicting independent variables:

   "If:
   Y is gross national product,
   C is consumption expenditures,
   G is government expenditures,
   I is investment outlays (including inventory change)."
   "Let:

   $$C = f(Y)$$
   $$G = g(Y)$$
   $$I = h(Y)$$

   Also, by definition:

   $$Y \equiv C + G + I$$

---

[42] H. THEIL, *op. cit.*, p. 29.
[43] *Ibid.*, pp. 116ff.

Hence, substituting for C, G, and I from the above:

$$Y = f(Y) + g(Y) + h(Y)$$

which is a single equation in one variable and hence yields a unique forecast for Y!"

Comment on the validity of this approach.

4. The data on which Table 10.1 is based are as follows (adding 1960):

Year	Energy generated from natural gas (in thousands of trillions of British thermal units)
1947	5.1
1948	5.7
1949	6.0
1950	6.9
1951	7.9
1952	8.7
1953	9.2
1954	9.6
1955	10.4
1956	11.0
1957	11.7
1958	12.1
1959	13.0
1960	13.7

a) Evaluate the absolute accuracy of prediction of trend equation (10.9) using all three approaches mentioned in Section 10.4.1. How do you explain such differences as are obtained from these methods?

b) Devise and carry out a test for evaluating the relative accuracy of the 1958–60 forecasts.

c) What information on predictive accuracy do the results of the correlation test provide? What weakness does the test have in this instance?

5. a) Discuss the pros and cons of using mathematical trends to predict U. S. gross national product in the year 2,000.

b) What measures of reliability would you use?

c) What qualifications would you attach to such a forecast?

6. For capital budgeting purposes, a concern mining zinc and lead wants to obtain a forecast of the demand for its products ten years hence.

a) What *type* of forecast would you recommend? Why?

b) What general *methods* might be considered? Which would you recommend, and why?

7. Under what circumstances would one be justified in combining f_1 and f_2 to obtain a single measure of turning point error? How would you set up such a measure?

8. To demonstrate the accuracy of its forecasts, a stock market service advertises that over the years its forecasts of gross national product have been "91% accurate," its forecasts of personal disposable income "93% accurate," etc. Comment.

SELECTED REFERENCES

Alternative Methods

The role of judgment in forecasting is discussed in considerable detail in Part 1 of *Economic Forecasting* by V L. BASSIE (New York: McGraw-Hill, 1958) and is illustrated in later parts of the book. A good general discussion of judgment forecasting applied to both business and economics will be found in Chapters 17–18 of *Business Forecasting* by ELMER BRATT (Homewood, Ill.: Richard D. Irwin, Inc., 1953).

The use of this approach in long-term forecasting is illustrated throughout the study by J. E. ROSENZWEIG, *The Demand for Aluminum: A Case Study in Long Range Forecasting* (Champaign, Ill.: University of Illinois, Bureau of Economic and Business Research, 1957).

A good discussion of the survey approach to short-term forecasting with emphasis on the European experience will be found in Parts 4 and 5 of *Economic Forecasts and Policy* by HANS THEIL. Chapter 7 of the book by BRATT provides a general discussion of the pros and cons of using surveys for this purpose. A similar discussion will be found in "Sales Forecasting by Sample Surveys" by ROBERT FERBER (*Journal of Marketing*, July, 1955, pp. 1–13).

The analytical approach to forecasting is discussed very clearly in Chapter 6 of *A Textbook of Econometrics* by L. R. KLEIN, focusing on the econometric aspects of forecasting and means of evaluating the results. *Experimental Short-term Forecasting Models* by P. J. VERDOORN and C. J. VAN EYK is devoted to the application of the analytical approach to short-term forecasting and presents several equation models based on this approach. A similar, though more general, exposition, with emphasis on policy problems, will be found in *Economic Policy: Principles and Design* by J. TINBERGEN. *An Econometric Model of the United States, 1929–1952*, by KLEIN and GOLDBERGER illustrates the application of the analytical approach to forecasting changes in the United States economy.

Appraisal of Forecasts

The publications by KLEIN and by VERDOORN and VAN EYK mentioned above provide good illustrations of the manner in which forecasts based on equation systems are evaluated. *An Appraisal of OBE-SEC Estimates of Plant and Equipment Expenditures, 1947–58*, published by the U. S. Bureau of the Budget, 1959, is a useful example of the appraisal of survey data. Another study in this area, focusing on means of appraising forecasts of consumer durables purchases, is *Consumer Expectations, Plans, and Purchases: A Progress Report*, by F. T. JUSTER (New York: National Bureau of Economic Research, 1959).

A thorough discussion of various approaches to evaluating business surveys will be found in Part 2 of the previously mentioned book by HANS THEIL, with applications of the methods given in subsequent parts of this book. The use of naive models and correlations as a basis for appraising businessmen's forecasts will be found in the following two publications by ROBERT FERBER: *The Railroad Shippers' Forecasts* (University of Illinois: Bureau of Economic and Business Research, 1953) and *Employers' Forecasts of Manpower Requirements: A Case Study* (University of Illinois: Bureau of Economic and Business Research, 1958).

Forecasts and Policy Decisions

An interesting though intricate approach to the role of forecasting in policy decisions will be found in Part 7 of the book by HANS THEIL. The same problem is discussed in a more general sense in the book by TINBERGEN, and on a more practical level in the books by BASSIE and BRATT.

11 | Coordinating Research Approaches: The Complete Marketing Audit

IN PRACTICE, business and economic problems can be quite complicated and their solution may entail the application of a variety of research approaches. Some of these are simple; others are intricate. Some are more common to economic research, some to marketing research, and some to other branches of the social and mathematical sciences. Individually, most of them have been covered in previous chapters. Accordingly, it would seem desirable in this final chapter to show how these various approaches may be brought together and used jointly to solve practical business problems.

The complete marketing audit serves as an ideal framework for such a presentation. As noted in Chapter 1, the marketing audit covers many practical problems involving numerous research techniques and methods. The principal problems and methods were outlined briefly in Sec. 1.3 and 1.4. A comprehensive discussion of the various stages of the marketing audit, therefore, will put the selection and coordination of research methods within a practical context. It will also show how research methods may be used in conjunction with one another, particularly how analysis of cross-section data and analysis of time-series data may supplement each other. Thus, this final chapter will illustrate the practical considerations entering into the selection and use of research methods, and will thereby supplement the material on the pros and cons of individual techniques provided in previous chapters.

11.1. THE SEVEN STEPS OF THE AUDIT

There are three main goals of the audit:

1. Establishing the firm's *effective position* in the market, as defined by present effective demand and the breakdown of this demand by the principal

486

partial markets. This goal is an unpretentious one. It aims only at describing quantitatively total sales and their distribution by different channels, areas and such relevant groupings of final consumers as are indicated by practical and theoretical considerations. (See Sec. 4.22.)

2. More ambitious is the determination of the *functional position* of the firm, i.e., finding the reasons for customer preference for one's own products rather than those of competitors. (See Sec. 1.3.)

3. The ultimate goal is to determine the firm's *optimal position* and the changes in the existing market mix required to attain that position. Optimal position is defined as that position where a change in one or more "instruments" (price, promotional effort, etc.) will not lead to an improvement in net profits or a better realization of one of the other targets for the period considered. Since the period considered normally refers to the future—the following year or the next five years—determining the optimal position implies, first, a forecast under the assumption that none of the instruments will be changed. Second, it implies a forecast of the consequences of certain policy changes, such as a change in prices, in the product line, or in the choice of distribution channels.

To be undertaken successfully, a complete audit consequently requires sound knowledge of the structure of the market for one's own products as well as for virtually identical and substitute products of competitors. Apart from that, in order to arrive at a reliable forecast, recent changes in the market need close analysis. In order to ascertain functional position from characteristics of the effective position and to infer from the latter policy changes required to attain an optimal position, a number of intermediate steps are clearly necessary. The following outline illustrates the *logical order* of the steps required:

I. *Design of the audit*

Market characteristics, targets and boundary conditions may differ considerably among firms. The design of the investigation will consequently not be the same for every firm.

II. *Establishing the effective position*

III. *Divergence analysis*

Closer analysis of actual sales will often reveal divergence between own sales and those of competitors in different markets. This may provide valuable clues for formulating provisional hypotheses on the functional position of the firm. One aim of this step, therefore, is to seek such differences. Another is to analyze competition. Particularly relevant are differences in the use of marketing instruments and the effect of these differences on the direction and volume of sales.

IV. *Development analysis*

The aim here is twofold. First, time-series analysis may be used to find the structural equation(s) governing demand for the whole market, and, wherever possible, to estimate the influence of the various instruments on market shares. This serves as a basis for deriving the forecasting equations required in step VII. A second, more qualitative, objective is to study the past development of marketing assets and marketing policies, changes in the "capabilities" of the firm, and an evaluation of the impact of such developments and changes on sales. Particularly worth noting is that the results of divergence analysis in some cases can be interpreted properly only in the perspective of development analysis, and that the results of the two should be compatible. A given distribution of sales by areas or by income classes in a saturated market may, for instance, lead to conclusions totally different from those in the case of a market still expanding rapidly.

V. *Diagnosis*

Diagnosis of current conditions covers a large number of research activities with different aims. Some have already been discussed in Sec. 1.2 and 10.2.1. In addition, time-series analysis might be required to evaluate the difference between the current and the "normal" level of some variables whenever basic changes in marketing policy are considered. Here diagnosis forms a bridge between the analysis of cross-sections and that of time series.

VI. *Defining the present functional position*

VII. *Determining the optimal position*

The two main lines of research pursued throughout these seven steps are, first, investigation of functional position and, second, preparation of the forecast, as illustrated by Fig. 11.1, which provides a general picture of the variety of research methods entering into the various stages of the audit.

In practice, these seven steps need not be scheduled in the order in which they are listed. Analysis of time series and of cross-section data may well coincide. Similarly, the activities of logically earlier stages are not independent of the results obtained in the following ones. As will be shown, a rigorous "feed back" of results is essential.

A summary view of the various research methods applicable to each of the successive stages of the audit is provided in Table 11.1. This table does not allow for feedback procedures, but focuses on the methods of primary use at each stage.

The audit can be performed either by the market research division of the enterprise itself, or by an independent research agency. In some respects, the latter might be preferable, since a check on existing marketing policies is involved. Similarly, an independent agency is in a better position to get unbiased data on dealer attitudes, etc. Usually, if the help of an independent agency is required, both the research division and the agency will work closely together. For purposes of illustration, however, it will be assumed in the following that the audit is undertaken entirely by an outside agency with no knowledge of previous investigations.

Two final remarks are in order before considering each stage in detail:

1. Important considerations with every audit are the costs incurred with different policy alternatives, whether production or selling costs. Here only the market side of the problem will be considered.

2. Sheer limitations of time make it often impossible to go as far with the audit as would have been justified by the money the firm is willing to spend

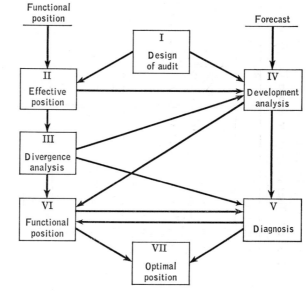

Fig. 11.1. *Outline of the Marketing Audit*

on a more thorough investigation. Particularly, if an audit is carried out for the first time with no basis of systematic past research, a *concentric approach* is indicated. According to this approach, all relevant aspects of marketing are given equal emphasis. In this way, a more equal distribution of information on the different aspects of the market and the efficiency of the instruments is obtained than would have been possible with a rigid sector-by-sector approach. A gradual deepening of information is thus postponed to later audits or, alternatively, it might be obtained by systematic research in between. The main advantage of this approach is that policy decisions need not be based upon detailed information about only one sector (say, channels or prices) while the most rudimentary information about other sectors is still non-existent.

Table 11.1

Research Methods That May Enter into a Complete Audit[1]

0 = Data referring largely to opinions, attitudes, etc.   X = Largely quantitative data.

STEPS OF THE AUDIT	OWN FIRM In-formal	HOUSEHOLDS Large Scale	HOUSEHOLDS Analytical	HOUSEHOLDS Small Scale	HOUSEHOLDS Sequential	ENTER-PRISES[3] Small Scale, Analyt., Sequent.	Classification Research	Input-Output Analysis	Motivation Research[4]	Experiment	MODEL CON-STRUCTION	Frequency Distributions	Cross-Classification	x² Test and Measures of Association	An. of Variance	Cross-Sections	Time-Series	Factor Analysis	FORE-CAST
1	*2*	*3*	*4*	*5*	*6*	*7*	*8*	*9*	*10*	*11*	*12*	*13*	*14*	*15*	*16*	*17*	*18*	*19*	*20*
I. Design of audit	0			0		0					X								
II. EFFECTIVE[2] POSITION		X	X	X			X	X				X	X						
III. Divergence[2] Analysis		X	X				X	X				X		X	X	X		X	
IV. Development[2] Analysis							X				X	X	X	X	X		X	X	
V. Diagnosis	0					0					X	X	X	X	X	X	X		X[5]
VI. FUNCTIONAL POSITION[2]	0		0	0		0	0		0		X	0	0	0	0	0	0	0	
VII. OPTIMAL POSITION	0				X	X		X		0	X								X

COLLECTING THE DATA — SURVEY METHODS WITH — QUANTITATIVE DATA — QUALITATIVE DATA
STATISTICAL ANALYSIS — REGRESSION ANALYSIS
MARKETS AND COMPETITORS — ATTITUDES AND INSTRUMENTS

[1] Feed-back streams are not indicated.
[2] Structural analysis.
[3] In the distributive trades and final users in the case of industrial selling.
[4] Including: depth questioning, attitude scaling, etc.
[5] "*Ex post*" forecasts only.

11.2. STEP I—DESIGN OF THE AUDIT

The planning stage of the audit does not differ essentially from that of other investigations (Chapter 2). Only, the scope of the investigation is much wider. As a consequence, the nature of the main problems to be investigated is more diffuse at the outset and possible lines of approach are less clear.

The main activities in this stage are:

1. *Ascertaining:*
    a) the firm's objectives (Sec. 1.3),
    b) its boundary conditions (Sec. 1.3),
    c) the main present problems seen by management and leading executives,
    d) its current "philosophies" and ideas about the functional position in the market.
2. Taking an *inventory* of available data: official statistics, data obtainable from internal records, etc.
3. Making a provisional *analysis* of underlying problems with the help of readily accessible internal and external data.
4. *Deciding* what tabulations, cross-classifications, structural constants, regression equations, etc., are needed to solve these problems, to define the company's functional position and to make the required forecasts.
5. *Specifying additional data* required for this purpose, together with the method of collecting it, including:
    a) surveys, both quantitative and qualitative,
    b) experiments,
    c) motivation research,
    d) regrouping existing statistical data (internal and external) for purposes of cross-section and time-series analysis.

The importance of (4) and (5) is self-evident. Some agencies therefore try to devote about one-third of the time available for the audit to this first, preparatory step. Faulty decisions on the kind of relations to be investigated and on the type of data to be collected result in a wrong start and unnecessary costs. Useful safeguards are incorporated in the next activities:

6. *Constructing a model* relating underlying problems (1-c and 3) to present conditions, objectives and boundary conditions of the firm. This model need not consist of a system of mathematical equations, but it ought to be such a clear statement of facts that, if desired, it could be translated into a set of mathematical relations. Thus, we have a check on whether the data to be collected are sufficient for solution of the problem. An important additional check is provided by points 7 and 8.

7. The *pre-test*, either a pilot survey or a "shadow" operation, covering data processing and statistical analysis (Sec. 2.3).
8. "Feed back" to management of:
    a) fields to be covered by the investigations,
    b) scope of the conclusions envisaged.

This procedure can test whether less patent, but possibly still intrinsic, relationships or aspects have been overlooked and whether the approach followed corresponds with needs as presently felt by management.

The research methods used with this step are mainly:

1. *Small, intensive, but informal, surveys* within the company. Respondents may range from directors and senior executives to salesmen and their supervisors.
2. *Model construction*, either in its narrow mathematical sense, or in its wider verbal, sense.
3. A *pilot survey* outside the firm to demarcate more closely the precise nature of a problem, or to verify a provisional hypothesis. Open-end questions and an informal survey with a few, say, 15 to 25 respondents, generally will serve best in this preliminary stage.

11.3. STEP II—ESTABLISHING THE EFFECTIVE POSITION

The aim of this step is to determine the extent and characteristics of effective demand: first, to provide the necessary data for the next step, divergence analysis; second, to provide a basis for evaluating the efficiency of the marketing instruments in the seventh and last step of the audit, where the desirability of a change in the marketing mix may be considered. Tabulation of sales by area, type of channel and different price brackets for own sales and that of competitors may serve as examples.

The main subjects to cover, therefore, are:

a) Total demand for the market as a whole.
b) Patterns of user demand for one's own product.
c) Patterns of demand for competing products.
d) Market characteristics related to efficiency of the instruments.

What market characteristics to select for intensive study depends on the exploratory analysis undertaken with the first step. Since the audit is repeated periodically, this year's effective position has to serve as a basis of comparison for the diagnosis of the next year's audit, and also for that of later audits. For this reason, a fixed program for collecting and analyzing relevant data is strongly recommended. Apart from this hard core, it may be found desirable with subsequent audits to collect other data on an *ad hoc* basis, as the nature of a firm's problems vacillate. Also, an audit, while in progress, will inevitably bring out new points that require investigation.

Activities implied by this step result in:

1. Estimates of *total demand for the market as a whole*. As suggested in Sec. 4.2.1, a dual approach from both the demand and supply sides of the market should be undertaken wherever possible.

2. *Univariate frequency distributions* by different attributes of total sales on the market under consideration. There are as many possibilities for a breakdown of total sales into market segments or *partial markets* (see Sec. 4.2.2) as there are attributes of the market itself. Relevant are the following four categories of attributes:

    a) *Sources of supply:* domestic production and imports. In each case a further breakdown by the more important competitors is necessary.

    b) *Characteristics of the product:* quality or type, price brackets and kind of use. The last attribute is relevant not only for industrial selling, but also for consumer goods.

    c) *Channels of distribution:* the whole composite flow from producer or importer to user. Representation by flow charts rather than by univariate tabulations may, therefore, appear preferable.[1] Frequency distributions of turnover by different types of retail outlets are, however, just as important. For distribution by size, cumulated frequency distributions as discussed in Sec. 3.1 are particularly useful as a starting point for further analysis.

    d) *Final demand:* of the plethora of attributes, the user's residence is no doubt most relevant for purposes of direct control. From an analytical point of view, however, a whole series of personal attributes such as income, sex, age, education, etc., may become an inevitable object of study where households are concerned. Likewise with industrial and institutional selling, apart from the geographical location of the user, such attributes as branch of industry, size of firm (whether measured by output or number of laborers), process of production, etc., may serve as a basis for a breakdown of partial markets.

Although a univariate frequency distribution of itself may not appear very flexible, there are nevertheless numerous possible transformations of the independent variable. As a consequence, there are just as many possibilities of tabulating "straight runs" with one and the same independent variable. Often, however, confusion arises over the nature of the transformed variable, particularly where working papers and internal reports are concerned. For reasons of efficiency, a systematic notation may prove helpful. If we define:

---

[1] See, for example, the diagrams in J. B. JEFFRYS, *The Distribution of Consumer Goods.* Cambridge University Press, 1950, p. 32; E. S. BRADFORD, *Marketing Research*, New York, McGraw-Hill, 1951, p. 79.

v = volume of total sales,
V = value of total sales,
p = average price,
u = total number of effective users,
N = total number of demand units (households, persons),

the tabulation of any of these characteristics, y, by any arbitrary independent variable, x, can be expressed as:

$$y_i(x_i) \tag{11.1}$$

where $i = 1, \ldots, k$, with k denoting the number of class intervals of x.

Note that (11.1) does not refer to a possible functional relationship between y and x. Wherever any confusion might arise, the expanded notation

$$y_i T(x_i) \tag{11.2}$$

should be used.

Finally, in order to distinguish tabulations of sample survey data from those referring to the total population, the former may be indicated with a prime:

$$v_i(x_i)' \quad \text{and} \quad v_i T(x_i)', \text{ respectively} \tag{11.3}$$

The following univariate distributions are commonly used in market research reports:

	Absolute distribution	Percentage distribution of total market
Volume of sales	$v_i(x_i)$	$\dfrac{v_i}{v}(x_i)$
Value of sales	$V_i(x_i)$	$\dfrac{V_i}{V}(x_i)$
Number of effective users	$u_i(x_i)$	$\dfrac{u_i}{u}(x_i)$

The more important transformations are:

Percentage of effective users	$\dfrac{u_i}{N_i}(x_i)$
Average use per demand unit	$\dfrac{v_i}{N_i}(x_i) \quad \text{or} \quad \dfrac{V_i}{N_i}(x_i)$
Average use per effective user	$\dfrac{v_i}{u_i}(x_i) \quad \text{or} \quad \dfrac{V_i}{u_i}(x_i)$
Average price paid	$p_i(x_i) \quad = \quad \dfrac{V_i}{v_i}(x_i)$

Average prices paid in different areas and average prices paid for products of competitors are particularly relevant to the audit. Equally relevant is the distribution of total sales by partial markets narrowly related to instrument variables, i.e.:

$$v_i(b_i), \qquad v_i(a_i) \qquad and \qquad v_i(d_i) \tag{11.4}$$

(sales breakdowns by groups of products, areas and distribution channels respectively), whereas the usefulness of $v_i(c_i)$, breakdown by own sales and those of competitors, hardly needs emphasis.

3. The third category of activities comprises the preparation of relevant *bivariate distributions* and such corresponding transformations as may be required. These cross-classifications represent second-order partial markets. They generally form the backbone of the audit. The more detailed information obtained in this manner serves two purposes:

a) For comparing characteristics of own sales with those of competitors in the corresponding first-order partial markets $v_j(x_j)$:

$$v_{ij}(c_i, x_j) \tag{11.5}$$

where $c_i(i = 1, \ldots, m)$ denotes the sources of supply; $i = 1$ that of the company itself; $i = 2, 3, \ldots, m$, that of competitors, where m may include the residual group of relatively less important ones; x_j represents any other attributes—areas, income classes, prices, etc. Relative distributions are denoted by:

$$\frac{v_{ij}}{v_i}(c_i, x_j), \qquad \frac{v_{ij}}{v_j}(c_i, x_j) \qquad and \qquad \frac{v_{ij}}{v}(c_i, x_j) \tag{11.6}$$

depending on whether v_{ij} is taken as a percentage of the corresponding row total:[2]

$$v_i = \sum_j v_{ij} \tag{11.7}$$

or as a percentage of the corresponding column total:

$$v_j = \sum_i v_{ij} \tag{11.8}$$

or, finally, as a percentage of the total market:

$$v = \sum_i \sum_j v_{ij} \tag{11.9}$$

b) For more refined analysis, particularly to verify relationships suggested by a univariate distribution. As is well known, a univariate distribution may be dangerously misleading when interpreted as representing the net effect of the independent on the dependent variable.[3]

---

[2] Compare the analogous notation used with input-output analysis.
[3] For an amusing example, see J. H. LORIE and H. V. ROBERTS, *Basic Methods of Marketing Research,* p. 62.

The situation is analogous to that of simple regression. Just as multiple regression may prove a superior tool for isolating net effects, joint distributions obtained by cross-classification of two attributes may lead to more correct information.

To some extent cross-classifications are a much more flexible tool of investigation since no specific assumptions about the form of the relationship are required. An interesting example is provided by Lazarsfeld. According to the univariate, or marginal, distribution by age in Table 11.2, radio listening to classical music programs is not appreciably different among the young and the old. Univariate tabulation by education shows, on the contrary, a considerable difference between the groups with low and high education. The most revealing fact, however, is brought to light by two counter trends, viz., the tendency of u/N to *decrease* with age with the lower-educated, but to *increase* with the higher-educated. It is this counter tendency that could not have been found with ordinary multiple regression.

Table 11.2

PROPORTION OF LISTENERS TO CLASSICAL MUSIC (u) BY AGE (y) AND EDUCATION (x)[a]

$$\frac{u_{ij}}{N_{ij}} \; (y_i, x_j)$$

AGE LEVEL	EDUCATION (x_j)		TOTAL
	Low	High	$\frac{u_i}{N_i} \; (y_i)$
Young	28 (400)	32 (600)	30 (1000)
Old	19 (900)	52 (400)	29 (1300)
Total $\frac{u_j}{N_j} \; (x_j)$	22 (1300)	40 (1000)	29 (2300)

[a] The number of observations (N_{ij}) is shown in parentheses.

Source: PAUL F. LAZARSFELD, "Interpretation of Statistical Relations as a Research Operation" in *The Language of Social Research* (ed. by Lazarsfeld and Rosenberg, 1955), p. 115.

Well-known with cross-classifications is the impossibility of reconstructing the joint distribution of two attributes if only the two marginal distributions are known.[4] Without further data or assumptions, the joint distribution cannot be established even in the case of the double dichotomous (2×2) classification. In the latter case, however, some useful inferences may often be obtained about the possible *ranges* of values of the four elements.

---

[4] See, for example, W. A. WALLIS and H. V. ROBERTS, *Statistics: A New Approach*, Sec. 6.4.1.

The readership survey data in Table 11.3 illustrate this approach. The percentage of regular readers of The Ladies' Home Journal falls steeply as both economic status and level of education decline. Looking only at the readership percentages by class, i.e., $\frac{u_i}{N_i}$ (y_i) and $\frac{u_j}{N_j}$ (x_j), one might ask what percentage of all regular readers belongs to the upper two status groups

Table 11.3

REGULAR READERS (u) AMONG WOMEN, AGED 16–35 (N), OF LADIES' HOME JOURNAL, BY ECONOMIC STATUS (y) AND EDUCATION (x), 1948

ECONOMIC STATUS					EDUCATION				
y_i	u_i/N_i	N_i	u_i	$u_i{}^a$	x_j	u_j/N_j	N_j	u_j	$u_j{}^a$
1	5.9	2,054	121 ⎫		1 8th grade &	4.7	2,006	94 ⎫	
2	12.4	2,055	255 ⎬	750	less			⎬	1,125
3	17.9	2,055	368 ⎭		2 High-school	16.4	6,227	1,021 ⎭	
4	20.8	2,055	427 ⎫						
5	24.5	2,055	503 ⎭	935	3 College	28.2	1,979	558	560
TOTAL		10,274	1,676	1,685	TOTAL		10,212	1,673	1,685

^{a} Combined classes are corrected for non-response and rounding-off.

Source: *Young Women and Magazines: A Survey*, by ELMO ROPER, January, 1948, pp. 11 and 12.

$(y_4$ and $y_5)$ and to the lower education groups $(x_1$ and $x_2)$. Computing the absolute values of u_i and u_j and combining the five status and three education groups into two groups for each attribute provide the marginal distributions of the dichotomous joint classification at the left side of Table 11.4. The relative distribution is given at the right side.

Table 11.4

DOUBLE DICHOTOMY OF REGULAR READERS OF LADIES' HOME JOURNAL

	$u_{ij}(y_i,x_j)$				$\dfrac{u_{ij}}{u}$ (y_i,x_j)		
Economic status	EDUCATION (x_j)				EDUCATION (x_j)		u_i
(y_i)	*Non-college*	*College*	u_i	y_i	*Non-college*	*College*	$\overline{u}$
	I	II			I	II	
I Low	u_{11}	u_{12}	750	I	$.67 - \dfrac{u_{21}}{u}$	$\dfrac{u_{21}}{u} - .22$	.45
II High	u_{21}	u_{22}	935	II	$\dfrac{u_{21}}{u}$	$.55 - \dfrac{u_{21}}{u}$	.55
u_j	1,125	560	1,685	u_j/u	.67	.33	1.00

As is easily seen, any of the elements of a dichotomous cross-classification can be written as a linear function of the marginal frequencies and a specific value, arbitrarily chosen, for *one* other element. In the choice of this value we are, however, not perfectly free. Limiting conditions arise since none of the elements can be negative. Thus, if we select u_{21}/u, three conditions can be imposed on the value of this element, as follows:

i) $u_{21}/u \geq 0$,   or $.67 - u_{21}/u \geq 0$ and $u_{21}/u \leq .67$.
ii) $u_{22}/u \geq 0$,   or $.55 - u_{21}/u \geq 0$ and $u_{21}/u \leq .55$.

Of these two conditions, only (ii) is "active," for given (ii), the first condition becomes superfluous.

iii) $u_{21}/u \geq 0$,   or $u_{21}/u - .22 \geq 0$ and $u_{21}/u \geq .22$.

Consequently our choice of u_{21}/u has to satisfy the condition:

$$.22 \leq u_{21}/u \leq .55. \tag{11.10}$$

To either of these extreme values of u_{21}/u corresponds a complete set of "expected" values for the other elements, as shown by Table 11.5. Hypothesis 1 ($u_{21}/u = .22$) corresponds with the maximum *positive* correlation between present economic status and education compatible with the marginal distributions. As a matter of fact, by this hypothesis none of the women having finished college would be classified in the lower economic status group.

Table 11.5

EXPECTED JOINT DISTRIBUTION OF $\dfrac{u_{ij}}{u}$ (y_i, x_j)

UNDER THREE ALTERNATIVE HYPOTHESES

	HYPOTHESIS 1 Maximal *positive* correlation OF x WITH y		HYPOTHESIS 2 x AND y PERFECTLY UNCORRELATED		HYPOTHESIS 3 Maximal *negative* correlation OF x WITH y		
			Education (x_j)				u_i
Status (y_i)	Non-College	College	Non-College	College	Non-College	College	$\overline{u}$
	I	II	I	II	I	II	
I Low	.45	0	.30	.15	.12	.33	.45
II High	.22	.33	.37	.18	.55	0	.55
u_j/u	.67	.33	.67	.33	.67	.33	1.00

On the other hand, hypothesis 3, assuming maximum *negative* correlation, does not classify any college woman in the higher economic status. An intermediate position is represented by the second hypothesis, by which education is assumed perfectly uncorrelated with economic status. (How?) Since a positive correlation between present status and education seems more realistic than a negative one, the unknown of our problem—the share of high-status–non-college women in the regular readership of the magazine—must be somewhere between 22 and 37 per cent. Allowing for sampling fluctuations, these margins may be set at approximately $\frac{1}{5}$ and $\frac{2}{5}$.

As a rule, it is not desirable to include more than two independent attributes in the same cross-classification. A breakdown by a third attribute within the separate cells is, of course, possible. Tables of this kind are often prepared for purposes of enumeration. With analytical work, however, they tend to obscure rather than to clarify any underlying tendencies by sheer force of the number of figures presented. Hence, the influence of a third attribute is best analyzed or—as the case may be—eliminated by either of the two following methods:

1. *Transformation of the dependent variable,* a procedure illustrated in the foregoing. Thus, market shares instead of absolute sales can be compared in a two-way tabulation. The use of ratios as the independent variable may, however, imply the introduction of *an a priori* coefficient that may not be justified (see Sec. 8.1).

2. Preparation of *three simple cross-classifications* (instead of one elaborate table) by any of the three pairs of attributes. In sales control, for instance, sales by area may be representative of the efficiency of the salesmen; sales by item of the product line may be important for margin control; whereas sales by kind of channel may indicate the adequacy of present distribution policies. A quick survey of the present effective position is obtained by cross-tabulating total sales with any of these pairs of attributes:

$$v_{ij}(a_i,b_j) \qquad v_{ik}(a_i,d_k) \qquad v_{jk}(b_j,d_k) \qquad (11.11)$$

In this way the activity of salesmen by both product line and type of channel is easily evaluated; similarly, the relative importance of a certain channel by different areas or by type of product is easily surveyed. The main advantage of this method of tabulation is that the efficiency of a salesman or channel, as represented by effective sales, can be compared immediately with that of other salesmen or channels. Systematic differences will therefore appear more clearly than with complicated tabulations.

11.3.1. Research Methods

Since at this stage the activities still are of an enumerative rather than of an analytical character, the corresponding research methods are limited to the following three categories:

1. *Regrouping of available statistical data.* From a theoretical point of view, the research concerned may be considered rather pedestrian. Nevertheless, selecting, regrouping, reweighting and, wherever necessary, correcting primary statistical data to fit the data to the requirements of a specific problem often require a considerable amount of practical statistical knowledge, ingenuity and judgment. *Classification research,*

aimed at determining the type and size of establishments in all branches of industry which are potential users of the product, may well serve as an example in the field of industrial and institutional selling.[5] A main difficulty here, as well as more generally with end-use analysis (see Sec. 6.4), is the fact that definitions of products and branches of industry as used by, for instance, the Census of Manufactures, reports of trade associations and the customary classification of the company itself do not always coincide. The definitions may overlap and/or the class limits used by these respective sources may differ. The same difficulties are encountered when input-output analysis is used to evaluate market potentials with different branches of industry.

Careful screening and processing of the basic data is therefore a necessary condition for mutually consistent and reliable results of the audit.

2. Analyzing *empirical univariate frequency distributions* and estimating the coefficients of the corresponding theoretical distributions. The latter may become relevant, for example, if the existing age distribution of durable consumer goods or equipment is required for estimating replacement demand (Sec. 4.2). Other examples are seeking the distribution of family income or that of retailers by amount of sales. Theoretical distributions may serve in such cases either as a means of characterizing a given distribution or as a means of obtaining the parameters to describe the distribution. Theoretical distributions also may prove useful for interpolation if shifts in given class intervals of an empirical distribution are considered necessary.

3. *Collecting data by survey methods.* However abundant official statistics of a certain product or branch of industry may be, more often than not they prove inadequate for closely delineating the effective position of a firm. In those cases a survey is required to provide the necessary complementary data.

Within the framework of a complete audit, a survey may become a multi-purpose operation. As shown by Table 11.1, surveys may be needed not only to ascertain the effective position, but also to get data on differences between own markets and those of competitors (Step III), and on opinions, attitudes, etc. (Step VI). Although there is the possibility of fulfilling two or more objectives with one survey, the investigator may find himself at cross-purposes. Thus, a store audit of retailers may provide data on total effective demand and its distribution by competitors and types of retail outlet. However, it leaves us in the dark on brand preference by type of final consumer, their reasons, attitudes, etc. Conversely, a survey of households may provide adequate data on consumers' reasons and attitudes, but none about dis-

---

[5] See L. O. BROWN, *Marketing and Distribution Research*, New York, Third Edition, 1955, p. 516.

tributors. Also, depending upon the product, it may prove an insufficient base for determining total demand, where estimates of quantities bought per effective user are difficult to obtain.

Choosing the type of survey or combination of surveys to be made may therefore become a major point of strategy. This also holds for sample design. One aim at the present stage of the audit is to gauge total demand as accurately as possible. The other is to prepare the ground for the next step by relating sales to the different, relevant, market characteristics. While the first purpose is preponderantly *aggregative*, with interest focused mainly on how much is being sold or used by the population as a whole, the second purpose may be called *analytical* because it studies relationships within the population rather than merely describing one or more characteristics.

Sample design will differ according to the relative importance attributed to each purpose. With a purely aggregative survey, accuracy of the final result is best served by applying the principles of optimal allocation (Sec. 5.5.4). With analytical studies, however, the sample allocation will try to minimize in one way or another the standard errors of the differences between the means of the relevant pairs of strata.

If only two strata are considered, and unit costs are the same in both, the optimal ratio for the observations to be taken from each stratum can be shown to depend exclusively on the standard deviations concerned, if we wish to minimize the variance of the difference between strata means:[6]

$$\frac{n_1}{n_2} = \frac{\sigma_1}{\sigma_2}$$

The main differences between this kind of allocation and that required for purposes of aggregation, for instance, with optimal allocation, is the fact that strata sizes (the N_i's of equations 5.17 and 5.18) cannot be reckoned with. Thus, presupposing equal within-strata variances, the analytical approach requires equal numbers of observations from each stratum. Since in practice the sizes of the population strata differ considerably, the analytical sample is usually sub-optimal.

The audit, however, usually requires both points of view to be covered. The customary solution is a fairly large sample with allocation by strata being set in such a way that neither the analytical nor the aggregative point of view is unduly impaired. Unfortunately, considerable sample redesigning is often unavoidable in order to obtain a satisfactory solution.[7]

On the other hand, if sufficient *a priori* information about total demand is available, a purely analytical design may prove preferable. A carefully designed small-scale survey may then be sufficient if only a few strata are to be investigated.

---

[6] See W. G. Cochran, *Sampling Techniques*, Sec. 5.22.
[7] For a good example of a related approach, see W. E. Deming, *Some Theory of Sampling*, pp. 233–238.

Small-scale surveys are likewise best for determining the effective position if the unit cost per observation is relatively high, such as in determining average amounts consumed or bought by effective users. The most efficient method then is often a combination of surveys. One small-scale survey assesses the characteristic with the higher unit costs (inventories, average use per user, etc.), while a large-scale survey is used for information available at the lower cost (such as the percentage of effective users in the total population). This procedure, a particular case of "double sampling," is sometimes the only means of estimating total demand with reasonable precision.

11.4. STEP III—DIVERGENCE ANALYSIS

Closer study of the firm's effective position in the several partial markets is the purpose of divergence analysis. This study serves a twofold purpose: continuing control of sales, and exploration of the firm's functional position. In the context of the audit, the second purpose is the more interesting of the two. To be sure, study of objective market characteristics is by no means the only source of information on the functional position. Major indications are often obtained from opinion or attitude surveys of distributors or users themselves, i.e., by the direct approach (Sec. 11.7). Nevertheless, since sales control requires periodic review of the effective position anyway, this indirect approach is usually the starting point for studying functional position.

This position is defined as the role played by one's own product as compared with that of competing products. To throw light on this, divergence analysis has to proceed in a roundabout way. First, objective market characteristics associated with total demand are determined. After that, a search is made for characteristics associated with major divergences between the pattern of total demand and own product demand. The reason behind this roundabout procedure is that wherever large divergences are associated with a certain objective characteristic, such as age or city-size, that characteristic may well provide a clue to the reasons for differences in customer preference.

Technically, answers to two critical questions are sought by divergence analysis:

1. On *total demand:* What characteristics of first- or second-order partial markets show the largest between-class variances?
2. On *own product:* What characteristics are associated with the largest divergences between own and total sales?

11.4.1. Research Techniques for Analyzing Total Demand

A variety of methods may be used to determine what characteristics are most closely associated with demand. With sample data, not only the degree of association as reflected, for instance, by the coefficient of correlation is relevant, but also the probability that this association exists in the universe. If the dependent attribute investigated is a discontinuous variable, such as in comparing users and non-users, *chi-square* analysis is the appropriate tool. If, on the contrary, the attribute measured refers to such continuous characteristics as quantities bought, money amounts spent or prices paid, *variance analysis* is applicable. (See Sec. 3.3 and 3.4.) Compared with chi-square, it has the advantage of providing an estimate of the part of the total variance due to the explanatory characteristic.

The combined influence of two or more characteristics can also be found with the help of variance analysis, whether the dependent attribute is continuous or not. The procedure required to determine what combination of characteristics shows the lowest residual variance is the same as that used to obtain efficient sample stratification, as illustrated in Sec. 5.5.

Although variance analysis yields estimates of the relative importance of each of the characteristics found significant, it does not show to what extent a given change in one—say, a one per cent increase in average income— affects total demand. For this purpose, regression analysis has to be used. The application of multiple regression may often result in fairly detailed behavior-equations of the type of equation (8.61), describing the pattern of demand for several consumer groups as observed during the survey period. As a matter of fact, the very nature of the regression equation makes it unavoidable that the influence of differences in age, income, family-size, etc., is represented in a simplified way, and that sometimes certain important interactions between variables are neglected. Nevertheless, quantification of the average influence of different factors on total demand may provide a useful basis for evaluating peculiarities of demand for one's own product. This type of analysis is also important for the study of the prevailing relationships between different instruments on a given market.

An example of this procedure is illustrated by Fig. 11.2, showing the relationship between price and "quality" for books in the field of mathematical economics, econometrics, and market research. The quality characteristic selected is the number of pages. The price is the list price. The sample—using this term loosely—consists of all books in this field listed in the "new title" sections of issues of the *American Economic Review*, *Econometrica*, and the *Journal of Marketing*, for 1949 through 1951.

The relationship found is a linear one:[8]

$$p' = 1.63 + .010b \qquad (R = .862) \qquad (11.12)$$
$$(.00077)$$

where p' denotes the estimated list price in dollars and b the number of pages. The standard error of the coefficient is shown in parentheses.

---

[8] Three extreme observations have been discarded from this analysis.

This simple analysis leads to two conclusions:

1. Considering (11.12) as a behavior-equation of price-setters, it suggests that publishers in this particular field usually charged a fixed sum of about $1.63 for the cover and, in addition, an amount of one cent per page.

2. Drawing two straight lines at a distance of $\pm \sigma_u$ from the regression line, according to theoretical considerations about $16\frac{1}{2}$ per cent of all observations should lie above the upper line and another $16\frac{1}{2}$ per cent below the lower

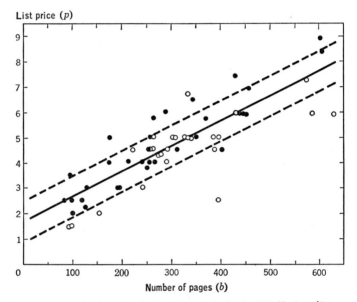

List price (p)

Number of pages (b)

Fig. 11.2. *Regression Analysis Applied to Second-Order Partial Markets (Price and quality of books on quantitative economics published in the U. S. 1949–1951)*

$p' = 1.63 + .010 \, (1 \pm .077)b$
$R = .862; \sigma_u = .80$
$p' = $ estimated list price in dollars
$b = $ number of pages
$N = 60$

Books of one group of publishers (university presses and Wiley) are plotted as solid dots.

one. This provides one indication whether the price of one's own products will be considered by the public as:

expensive: $p > p' + \sigma_u$ or
medium: $p' - \sigma_u > p > p'' + \sigma_u$ or
cheap: $p < p' - \sigma_u$

The logic behind this classification is that, if one's price is, for instance, higher than $(p' + \sigma_u')$, the product belongs to the highest-priced $16\frac{1}{2}$ per cent of the articles offered at the market concerned. Deviant case analysis may further reveal the particular nature of the observations outside the $2\sigma_u$ limit, and this again may provide a valuable clue to one's own functional position as well as that of competitors.

11.4.2. Research Techniques for Analyzing Divergences

A simple exploratory approach is the computation of market shares for those first-order partial markets for which the effective position has been established and for which corresponding data for total demand are available. Denoting total demand with a right-hand subscript T, market shares can be defined by any of the three following ratios, according to whether the number of effective users, volume sales or value sales is chosen as a yardstick:

$$h_i = \frac{u_i}{u_{T_i}} \tag{11.13}$$

$$s_i = \frac{v_i}{v_{T_i}} \tag{11.14}$$

and

$$S_i = \frac{V_i}{V_{T_i}} \tag{11.15}$$

The association of these shares with a given characteristic can be neutral or show differences from market to market. In the case of a continuous variable, or of an attribute that can be ranked, for instance, by education, the differences can be either systematic or erratic. Finally, with any of these three types of association, extreme values may easily occur, particularly with small samples.

In order to facilitate comparisons with shares of other products, or shares of competitors in the same markets as well as the computation of measures of association, standardized shares are computed by dividing the overall share into the shares on the partial markets:

Overall share: $\qquad\qquad \bar{s} = v/v_T$ $\qquad\qquad\qquad$ (11.16)

Standardized share: $\qquad\quad \bar{s}_i = s_i/\bar{s}$ $\qquad\qquad\qquad$ (11.17)

Index of divergence: $\qquad \delta_s(x) = \sqrt{\dfrac{\Sigma(\bar{s}_i - 1)^2}{k}}$ $\qquad\quad$ (11.18)

where k denotes the number of class-intervals of x ($i = 1, \ldots, k$). The statistic δ_s differs from the ordinary standard deviation in so far as the deviations are taken from unity instead of from the unweighted average of the k observations for $\bar{s}_i$, whereas $(k - 1)$ has been replaced by k.

Examples of different kinds of associations of s_i with the continuous characteristic x_i are shown in Table 11.6, together with the corresponding values of δ_s. Starting from the univariate tabulation of $\bar{s}$ (or of $\bar{S}$ or $\bar{k}$), the investigation may be focused either on finding systematic associations or on the analysis of extreme values.

In examining systematic associations, differences in divergence are often difficult to determine. Here the statistic δ_s may serve as a first approximation. With two or more tabulations with a different number of class intervals (k), it should be remembered that, besides a systematic component, δ_s^2 is also subject to sampling fluctuations. Whereas the variance due to the systematic component does not necessarily increase with k, the sampling variation does increase proportionately to ($k - 1$). For this reason, δ_s is biased in favor of tabulations with more class intervals.

Table 11.6

ASSOCIATION OF STANDARDIZED SHARE WITH A CONTINUOUS MARKET CHARACTERISTIC

Type of Divergence	x_1	x_2	$\bar{s}_i(x_i)$ x_3	x_4	x_5	$\delta_s(x)$ Index of Divergence
Neutral	1.11	.95	1.09	.83	1.13	.12
Systematic	.79	1.25	1.32	1.05	.80	.22
Erratic	.40	1.60	.30	.90	2.00	.67
Showing extremes	.82	.75	1.95	.63	.81	.48

After an attribute has passed this first selection, analysis of variance may be used to determine the extent of sampling fluctuations. This analysis, however, should be applied to the means of the original data by class interval, for both total and own product demand. After that, investigation is needed of what combinations of two or more characteristics serves to increase the systematic part of the total variance between shares on second- or higher-order partial markets. The aim of this step is not to reduce residual variance of the shares at all costs, but to maximize the absolute value of the systematic or "explained" part of total variance.

To give an example, cross-tabulation of market shares of, say, an electrical appliance, by age of housewife and geographic area may lead easily to small between-class differences and hence to a negligible residual variance, while the influence of either characteristic alone may be insignificant. Regrouping the same product by occupation and city-size, however, may well show a significant influence for these characteristics, although the residual variance has been appreciably increased.

Proceeding along these lines, tentative hypotheses on factors affecting brand preference and on functional position may be formulated. Wherever the relationships allow for the application of linear regression, the effects of specific factors on market shares should be quantified.

If investigation of systematic association is inconclusive—when, for instance, the residual variance remains unduly large—*deviant case* analysis applied to extreme values may be a last resort. The isolated extreme value, 1.95 in Table 11.6, might easily suggest that with consumers of characteristic x_3, important "non-x" influences might have affected sales. If the number of original observations pertaining to x_3 is sufficiently large to make it improbable that 1.95 is exclusively a result of sampling fluctuations, a closer analysis of the "group" x_3 seems justified. However, before reaching sweeping conclusions, it is necessary to verify whether the new factor does not affect sales equally in the classes $x_i(i \neq 3)$.

Although seldom applied in this field, *factor analysis* (see Sec. 3.6), too, may be of heuristic value, particularly where the number of possible factors that might affect sales is numerous and highly intercorrelated. Tabulating both own sales and total sales together with all possible market characteristics by, for instance, a large number of geographic areas, the "common factors" of all these variables can be determined. Similarly, the factor-loadings of v and v_T are established. If, for any factor, v_T shows a very different loading from that shown by v, this may point to a certain, as yet unidentified, basic factor influencing v_T more than v, or vice versa.

For the present purpose, the method of "principal components"[9] is to be preferred, as it allows factors to be calculated from the variables as well as the total influence of any factor on any given observation (in this case, any geographic area). This method makes it, therefore, easier to trace the total relative impact of a given variable on v and v_T. Factor analysis has the advantage that the combined influence of the most widely different variables can be studied. To take our present example: next to average income, family-size, age and other consumer attributes, characteristics of selling effort such as advertising appropriations by area and number of salesmen's calls, as well as data on retail outlets, and climatic factors, can be taken care of simultaneously. The only disadvantage of this flexibility is the fact that the common factors (principal components) are extremely dependent on the character of the series included in the analysis.

11.4.3. Summary of Research Techniques

As is clear from the summary Table 11.5, almost any technique available in the well-provided storehouse of mathematical statistics may serve at one time or another either to measure divergences between own product and total sales, or to evaluate their statistical probability, or to quantify the intensity and direction of the underlying relationships.

---

[9] K. J. HOLZINGER and H. H. HARMAN, *Factor Analysis* (Chicago, Illinois: The University of Chicago Press, 1948), and particularly, GIRSHICK's article, "Principal Components" in the *Journal of the American Statistical Association*, 1936, pp. 519–528.

Table 11.7

ANALYTICAL OBJECTIVES AND PREFERRED METHODS IN DIVERGENCE ANALYSIS

Specific objective	Resources	Precision of findings required?	POSSIBLE ANALYTICAL TOOL					Comments
			Measures of correlation, association	Chi-square[a]	Variance, covariance analysis[a]	Regression analysis	Factor analysis and principal components	
Determine if particular characteristic affects sales	Restricted	Yes		X				Scatter diagrams generally quickest but results can be unreliable.
		No	X					
Estimate degree of relationship	Ample	Yes or no						Resources may not be ample if many variables are involved.
	Restricted	Yes			X	X		
		No	X					Variance analysis preferable if much interaction among independent variables or if much market segmentation is desired.
	Ample	Yes or no			X	X		
Estimate direction and magnitude of one or more effects	Restricted	Yes or no						An electronic computer may be required. Primarily useful from a qualitative point of view.
	Ample	Yes or no				X		
Extracting uncorrelated factors affecting sales	Ample	Yes or no					X	

[a] Note that these are probabilistic approaches strictly valid only when the data have been obtained by probability sampling and satisfy independence criteria.

To bring together and demonstrate the different possibilities available for practical research, Table 11.7 cross-tabulates each of these techniques with various analytical objectives, precision of findings and resources required.

11.5. STEP IV—DEVELOPMENT ANALYSIS

By superimposing time as a separate dimension onto the results of divergence analysis, development analysis becomes the second pillar of structural research. On the one hand, this step concerns quantitative aspects, such as the systematic relationships governing demand over time. On the other hand, it calls for a closer analysis of the firm's past policies and capabilities against the background of the systematic demand relations just mentioned, which may reveal valuable information of a more qualitative nature. Both the quantitative and qualitative information thus obtained are indispensable for complementing divergence analysis and checking conclusions drawn from it. Development analysis, therefore, may help to clarify the reasons for the firm's present effective and functional position and may serve as a guide for formulating future policies.

11.5.1. Systematic Relationships

Ideally, a complete model ought to be available to portray the historical development of the firm's own sales and to lead to reliable estimates of future sales. Examples of the type of models required have already been mentioned in foregoing chapters.[10]

As discussed in Sec. 8.1, where total demand can be approximated without serious bias by a single equation approach, a fairly simple model may suffice. Two approaches are possible and should be undertaken at the same time: global analysis and analysis by partial markets.

With global analysis the different items of the product line are combined into fairly homogeneous groups. The definition of each of these groups should correspond as closely as possible with existing indices of consumption (or production) to allow for time-series estimates of corresponding aggregate demand. For each group a multi-stage explanation is sought by explaining first, total demand for the group of products studied: $v_T = \sum_i v_i$, where $i = 1$,

. . . , m denotes the different sources of supply—own firm and competitors. Second, demand for one's own product (v) is explained as a function of total demand.

A set of two equations may illustrate the procedure for a consumption

---

[10] See, for instance, Sec. 7.6.3.4, Sec. 8.6 and Chapter 9.

good. The equation chosen for total demand is as simple as possible, since different possible specifications have already been discussed in Chapter 8.

$$v_T = \alpha_1 y^{\beta_1} \left(\frac{p_T}{q}\right)^{\epsilon_1} e^{\rho_1 t} \tag{11.19}$$

$$v = \alpha_2 v_T^{\beta_2} \left(\frac{p}{p_T}\right)^{\epsilon_2} e^{\rho_2 t} \tag{11.20}$$

where: y = deflated disposable income
q = cost of living
p_T = average price of v_T
p = price of v
ϵ_2 = the approximate price-substitution-elasticity with regard to competitors.[11]

Substituting the right-hand side of (11.19) for v_T into (11.20) we find:

$$v = \gamma y^{\beta_1 \beta_2} \frac{p^{\epsilon_2}}{p_T^{\epsilon_2 - \beta_2 \epsilon_1} q^{\beta_2 \epsilon_1}} e^{(\beta_2 \rho_1 + \rho_2)t} \tag{11.21}$$

where: $\gamma = \alpha_2 \alpha_1^{\beta_2}$

Alternatively, it might have been possible to estimate v directly from y and q. The analytical advantage of this multi-stage approach is that differences in the demand-structure for v and v_T are shown by introducing explicitly β_2, ϵ_2 and ρ_2. A set of equations like (11.19) and (11.20) with appropriate specifications represents an analytical forecast, as required by the last step of the audit.

Apart from this, wherever β_2 differs significantly from unity and ρ_2 differs significantly from zero, it is the aim of development analysis to reveal the underlying causes and their dependence on marketing policies pursued in the past. Product or distribution channel policies may, for instance, be at the root of a more (or less) than average sensitivity to cyclical change. Particularly since the extrapolation of a residual trend inevitably remains a weak point with every forecast, the reasons for a significant value of ρ_2 need to be investigated. As noted in Sec. 8.1, those components of a trend that can be quantified should be introduced explicitly in the demand equation as so many explanatory variables. In some cases qualitative characteristics of the product can be quantified, as may be true, for instance, of the ratio of own advertising to that of competitors. As experience shows, experiments in this direction can prove worthwhile.[12]

---

[11] Assuming $v_T = v_1 + v_2$, and p_T to be the geometric mean of p_1 and p_2, it is easily shown that:

$$\frac{d \log v_1/v_T}{d \log p_1/p_T} = \frac{d \log v_1/v_2}{d \log p_1/p_2}$$

[12] See, for instance, Sec. 8.5 and Fig. 4.1.

In explaining the residual trend, $e^{\rho_2 t}$, the global approach converges with the *analysis by partial markets*. Here the main aim is to study long-term changes (periods of 5 years or more) in sales.[13] What first- and second-order partial markets and what attributes are relevant to between-class differences are already known from divergence analysis. Comparison of the corresponding univariate and bivariate frequency distributions—such as breakdown by areas and types of channel for successive intervals of 5 or 10 years—brings out shifts in the pattern of sales in the intervening periods.

Methods of analyzing change within a given bivariate distribution are numerous and the kind of information to be obtained multitudinous. Some numerical examples are given in Table 11.8. The first two matrices present a hypothetical distribution of sales cross-classified by three areas and three different channels of distribution, the first matrix referring to the sales in the base year and the second matrix to sales in a recent year. Matrices (3) and (4) present corresponding percentage distributions of these sales, the base being in each case the total sales in the particular year. Matrices (5) and (6) refer to the rate of change of sales in the separate cells. The relative contribution of each cell to total change is shown in (7), while the resulting shifts in relative importance are given by (8).

This example also illustrates the inadequacy of univariate distributions for studying the influence of a given attribute. In the present case, the marginal distribution by channels conceals altogether the sharp decline in relative importance of the third channel in the second area, as shown by (6) and (8). Whether or not this decline is responsible for the second area lagging behind the company average ($_tv/_ov = 100$) is difficult to say from this tabulation alone. The factors affecting total demand there might have been less favorable than elsewhere.

A more refined analysis, therefore, would require correction for differences in market saturation, in disposable income, in relative prices, etc.

A method of determining the residual trend of own sales in a partial market is to estimate changes in market share with the help of store-audit or other survey data. Defining the share for a first-order partial market as:

$$_tS_i = \frac{_tv_i}{_tv_{T.i}} \tag{11.22}$$

where $v_{T.i}$ denotes total demand in the market i, it is possible to estimate the residual trend from a formula of the type of (11.20), if estimates of the parameters are available.

Writing for simplicity's sake:

$$_tP_i = \frac{_tp_i}{_tp_{Ti}}$$

---

[13] Short-term changes, on the contrary, are the object of the diagnosis.

Table 11.8
ANALYSIS OF CHANGE OF SECOND-ORDER PARTIAL MARKETS*

I. Absolute distribution

1) $_0v_{ij}$

Area (a_i)	CHANNELS (d_j)			v_i
	1	**2**	**3**	
1	20	50	80	150
2	30	50	120	200
3	50	100	100	250
v_j	100	200	300	600

2) $_tv_{ij}$

Area (a_i)	CHANNELS (d_j)			v_i
	1	**2**	**3**	
1	70	140	210	420
2	50	100	150	300
3	80	160	240	480
v_j	200	400	600	1200

II. Relative distributions

3) $\dfrac{_0v_{ij}}{_0v} \times 100$

	1	2	3	$\dfrac{_0v_i}{_0v}$
1	3	8	13	24
2	5	8	20	33
3	9	17	17	43
$\dfrac{_0v_j}{_0v}$	17	33	50	100

4) $\dfrac{_tv_{ij}}{_tv} \times 100$

	1	2	3	$\dfrac{_tv_i}{_tv}$
1	6	12	17	35
2	4	8	13	25
3	7	13	20	40
$\dfrac{_tv_j}{_tv}$	17	33	50	100

III. Absolute changes

5) Δv_{ij}

	1	2	3	Δv_i
1	50	90	130	270
2	20	50	30	100
3	30	60	140	230
Δv_j	100	200	300	600

IV. Relative changes

6) $(_tv_{ij}/_0v_{ij}) - 1$

	1	2	3	$(_tv_i/_0v_i) - 1$
1	2.50	1.80	1.60	1.80
2	.67	1.00	.25	.50
3	.60	.60	1.40	.92
$(_tv_j/_0v_j) - 1$	1.00	1.00	1.00	1.00

V. Percentages of total change

7) $\Delta v_{ij}/\Delta v \times 100$

	1	2	3	$\Delta v_i/\Delta v$
1	9	15	22	46
2	3	8	5	16
3	5	10	23	38
$\Delta v_j/\Delta v$	17	33	50	100

VI. Shifts in relative importance

8) $\Delta(v_{ij}/v) \times 100$

	1	2	3	$\Delta(v_i/v)$
1	3	4	4	11
2	−1	0	−7	− 8
3	−2	−4	3	− 3
$\Delta(v_j/v)$	0	0	0	0

* Time is indicated by left-hand subscript.

our formula for the *corrected share index* becomes:

$$\frac{{}_tS_{ij}}{{}_oS_i}\left(\frac{{}_tv_{T.i}}{{}_ov_{T.i}}\right)^{1-\beta_{2.i}}\left(\frac{{}_tP_i}{{}_oP_i}\right)^{-\epsilon_{2.i}} = e^{\rho_2 it} \tag{11.23}$$

Thus corrected for differences in income and prices, the remainder of the share index represents essentially the residual trend of the company's effective position in the market.

It is important to note that the elasticities β_2 and ϵ_2 are not necessarily the same for all partial markets. As pointed out in Sec. 4.2, income elasticities, for instance, vary with the level of income and hence may differ between population groups, areas, etc. Differences in residual trend, however, if computed for partial markets, will often tend to surpass income effects. Consequently, a rough approximation of the expected differences in elasticity will be sufficient for many practical purposes.

Estimates derived along these lines will show the residual trend for the more important partial markets. They may also throw light on the component of the "overall trend," $e^{\rho_2 t}$, in equation (11.20).

A less exact method where no share-estimates are available consists in estimating the total trend from an adapted version of (11.21), the *corrected sales index*:

$$\frac{{}_tv_i}{{}_ov_i}\left(\frac{{}_ty_i}{{}_oy_i}\right)^{-\beta_{1.i}\beta_{2.i}}\left(\frac{{}_tP_i}{{}_oP_i}\right)^{-\epsilon_{2.i}}\left(\frac{{}_tQ_i}{{}_oQ_i}\right)^{-\beta_{2.i}\epsilon_{1.i}} = e^{(\beta_{2.i}\rho_{1.i}+\rho_{2.i})t} \tag{11.24}$$

where
$$Q = \frac{p_T}{q}$$

In this case inferences of differences in $\rho_{2.i}$ are possible only on the assumption that $\beta_{2.i}\,\rho_{1.i}$ is a constant for all markets concerned.

A last possibility is to relate the sales index for a given partial market not to prevailing demand factors but to an index of aggregate company sales. This yardstick of relative sales increase:

$$\frac{{}_tv_i}{{}_ov_i}\Big/\frac{{}_ov}{{}_tv} \tag{11.25}$$

may well serve as a *standardized company index* for the markets concerned. Its principal merit is that it is easily computed from internal records. Also it is easier to analyze second-order partial markets since no external data are required. However, conclusions about a gain in position relative to competitors are only possible as long as differences among markets in demand factors and in relative prices can be neglected. Nevertheless, even where this condition is not fulfilled, deviations in some markets from the company average may not be attributable to general factors. If sales volume is not too small, such elements, when subjected to deviant case analysis, may help explain the overall trend in sales.

11.5.2. Forecasting Relations

Apart from explaining past sales growth, quantitative analysis in this step is also directed at deriving *forecasting equations*. Here again, a choice has to be made for each group of products on whether a global or a detailed approach will be followed.

Since statistical information at the level of national aggregates is, as a rule, more reliable and complete than information on partial markets, the global approach allows more adequate specification of the demand equation. On the other hand, if both the following conditions hold:

i) the parameters differ widely among partial markets,
ii) the explanatory variables show different patterns during the business cycle or with regard to long term growth,

the advantages of a more precise estimate of the influence of the more important variables may well outweigh the gains of more correct specification. A clear example is found in the case of industrial selling. End-use analysis may be used then to identify which branches of industry use the product as well as the type of final customers of each of these industries. Since the equations governing output for each of these industries may be different and, moreover, the rate of change of the same explanatory variable may differ from market to market, a detailed approach by partial markets might be indicated. (See for example, Chapter 4, Table 4.9 and Sec. 6.4.)

11.5.3. Systematic Review

The qualitative counterpart of quantitative analysis of the firm's life history is a systematic review of its capabilities and policies. Initially, the firm has to be considered as a whole, and its policies have to be treated as so many unknowns (rather than as data, as is usual with demand analysis) to be explained from (a) development of the firm's capabilities and (b) changes in supply and demand. By reviewing these factors, policy shifts manifest themselves as responses to changes in these basic conditions, and hence evaluation may be possible. Also, changes in policy may help to explain deviations by partial markets as well as differences in residual trends between such markets. Finally, this review when supported by the necessary quantitative data, as just discussed, may throw light upon the adequacy of existing policies.

The review of policies covers, among other matters, changes in:

1. *Product-line* and in emphasis on different aspects of *quality*.
2. *Promotional effort*, such as number of salesmen and selling techniques used, advertising and service. Changes in emphasis in different partial

markets are extremely important for explaining rates of penetration hitherto achieved.

3. *Prices*, discounts, etc.
4. *Distribution channel* policies.
5. *Organization* for marketing, e.g., the degree of centralization.

A meaningful review is only possible if it also considers marketing policies pursued by competitors.

Similar considerations hold for the review of capabilities.[14] The main aspects to be covered there are changes in:

1. *Capacity of productive equipment* and qualitative developments.
2. *Capabilities of management* in the fields of marketing and production.
3. *Technical knowledge* and the role of research with regard to new products, new uses of existing products as well as customer research in general.
4. *Costs* of producing and selling the major items of the assortment.
5. *Financial* possibilities.

Each of these capabilities may once have set an effective boundary to marketing policies and thus led to policies that ought to have been considered as sub-optimal without such a restraint. Moreover, gradual shifts in the limits imposed by these capabilities may have been the cause of systematic policy changes. Such shifts may have had decisive effect on existing "marketing assets" and consequently on the present functional position. However, no specific generalization of this kind should be considered unless supported by corresponding shifts in sales in the partial markets concerned.

11.5.4. Research Methods

Research methods required by development analysis coincide with those of divergence analysis where the study of cross-tabulations is concerned. Also, the same significance tests may play an important role in the probabilistic evaluation of differences between partial markets at different points of time.

New for the study of development, however, is the application of regression analysis and model systems for estimating demand functions from time-series data. Here, the whole arsenal of methods discussed in Chapters 7–9 is at the investigator's disposal.

Finally, the study and evaluation of policy changes may require much patient research, both by studying internal records and interviewing within the company. The difficulties are the same as those encountered when

---

[14] See R. S. ALEXANDER, J. S. CROSS and R. M. CUNNINGHAM, *Industrial Marketing.* Homewood: Richard D. Irwin, Inc., 1956, pp. 60–67.

preparing case-studies from actual situations. Apart from this, verifying conclusions on the impact of a certain factor or decision may call for construction of a model especially adapted to represent interactions between variables of the then-prevailing situation.

11.6. STEP V—THE DIAGNOSIS

11.6.1. The Global Approach

As a result of development analysis, we now have one estimator equation explaining the development over time of total demand and another one that relates own sales to that demand. However, it would be a serious mistake to forecast sales with these equations without further checks.

One check is to compare total demand for own sales for the last two or three years with the expected values as obtained by an *"ex post* forecast" from the estimator equations. A rigorous analysis of the differences between the actual and the expected values may reveal that, for example:

1. Adjustments of the coefficients of the estimator equations are necessary, either because of a change in the basic structure of demand or as the result of an erroneous specification of the equation (see Sec. 4.1, 10.2.1 and Chapter 8).
2. Variables neglected in the estimator equations have gained in importance, or altogether new variables have started to dominate the picture like, for instance, the introduction of substitute products.
3. Incidental factors have been active, e.g., bottlenecks, temporary government measures, climatic factors, etc.

Taking into account probable changes in relevant variables during the forecasting period, one then has to decide whether to make the forecast with the estimator equation in its original form, or whether feed-back with the previous step is required to re-estimate the parameters, to add a new variable, or to change the mathematical form of the equation. In either case, however, it may be found desirable to add an additional constant to cope with specific influences that are expected for the forecasting period but that cannot be described appropriately by the variables of the estimator equation. Here particularly, discontinuance of incidental factors that have affected demand in the base year should be considered. Procedures to be followed have been covered in Sec. 10.2.

11.6.2. Diagnosis and Sales Control

Testing the global equations and adapting them to present conditions is one aim of the diagnosis. Another aim follows from the fact that a sales forecast is essentially a sales plan and, hence, normally entails changes in the marketing instruments if it is to be optimal in the sense of approximating as closely as possible the company's objectives without surpassing the boundary conditions. The diagnosis, therefore, has to provide the necessary information about the present efficiency of the instruments to pave the way for the last step of the audit: determining the optimal position. For this reason the diagnosis is an essential part of sales control and many of its activities are concerned with a systematic evaluation of such sales data as are already available.[15]

The main advantage of an equation like (11.19) or (11.20) is, therefore, the possibility of separating the influence of factors affecting total demand from those affecting own sales, in order to isolate the influence of changes in the instrument variables during the period under consideration. To highlight the efficiency of the instruments, more detailed analysis is inevitable. This will be pursued along three different lines, as discussed in the following sections.

11.6.3. Time-Series Analysis of Monthly and Quarterly Data

The use of annual figures exclusively may easily suppress valuable information on the precise moment at which a certain change did occur. Monthly data appropriately adjusted for seasonal variation, differences in working days, etc., help, therefore, to pinpoint the date of a turning point or shift in the level of sales. This may greatly enhance the identification of the responsible factors and consequently eliminate erroneous hypotheses on probable causes.

11.6.4. Analysis by Partial Markets

The procedure here is analogous to the one described in Section 11.5.1 with the difference that the time span covered is much shorter and short-term changes, rather than structural shifts, are the aim of the analysis.

1. In order to evaluate their efficiency, breakdowns of instruments are desirable into second-order partial markets such as the following:

a) products and areas
b) areas and channels of distribution
c̀) channels and products

Where changes in relative prices have occurred, cross-tabulations with prices should be analyzed. The use of the uncorrected sales index or the standardized company index may facilitate a quick survey of strong and weak points in recent developments.

---

[15] See, for instance, D. M. Phelps, *Sales Management*, 1951, Part VII.

2. For those relevant market segments where market shares can be obtained by store audits, consumer surveys, etc., a more refined appraisal of marketing policies becomes possible.

3. Here again, an analysis by monthly data for the more important partial markets is useful. Since seasonal adjustments for too many series hardly pay, the simpler device of Z-charts is recommended. They are an efficient means of quickly analyzing and mutually comparing a large number of series. Moreover, they allow for a simple comparison with budgeted sales for the separate items of the product-line, sales quota per area, etc., and are often prepared by sales departments for continuing control of sales.[16]

4. Findings obtained by partial markets need to be reconciled with the results of the global analysis of total demand and own sales. Otherwise, detailed analysis may lead to exaggerated conclusions on the effectiveness or deficiency of own instruments or the activities of competitors. Reconciliation of the two approaches is therefore a "must" for a balanced view of present conditions.

5. Finally, detailed analysis may point to new sales opportunities hitherto overlooked. Lack of growth in otherwise rapidly expanding areas is one example.

11.6.5. Attitude Surveys

Working on the hypothesis that changes in buying habits are accompanied and often preceded by changes in attitudes,[17] the researcher can get valuable information by asking consumers a set of simple questions like:

"What brand or brands of . . . . are you now using?"

"What brands have you used in the past?"

"What brand are you planning to buy next time?"

"What other brands have you heard of?"

"Which of these brands in your opinion rates first? Second? Third?"

Such a survey may serve various purposes. First, if repeated periodically, it indicates changes in use and preference for own and competing brands. Thus, it serves as a check on assumptions of the relative impact of those factors that influence total demand and those that are specific for the brand under consideration. Second, if the sample is sufficiently large and appropriately stratified, it may help to pinpoint those users who account for recent changes in sales. Third, changes in rating and in the percentage of people planning to buy the brand may presage a change in relative position in the near future. A closer analysis by means of cross-tabulations of such changes

---

[16] See, for instance, PAUL H. NYSTROM, *Marketing Handbook*, New York, Ronald Press, 1951, pp. 1292–1293.

[17] See, for instance, GEORGE H. BROWN, "Measuring Consumer Attitudes Towards Products," *Journal of Marketing*, April, 1950, pp. 691–698.

in attitude may show, at an early stage, weaknesses of a certain instrument—whether price, quality, advertising or dealers' activity—in prevailing competitive conditions.

A major use for this type of survey is determining the effectiveness of a specific advertising campaign. Assume that advertising takes place in media A and B; in a survey using the principle of the *double control group*, four groups are interviewed:

(1) before the campaign:	i) Readers of both A and B
	ii) Non-readers of neither A nor B
(2) after the campaign:	i) Readers of both A and B
	ii) Non-readers of neither A nor B

In this way, the survey has the advantage of separating the effects of advertising from other factors influencing demand for one's own product.

The relative merits of survey methods for the forecast proper have been reviewed already in Sec. 10.1.2. As far as the diagnosis is concerned, survey results are used as a means of analyzing present conditions rather than as a forecasting tool, though the same survey may serve both ends.

11.6.6. Research Methods

New with the present step is *time-series analysis* as applied to short-term changes. Hence, seasonal adjustment and mechanical extrapolation of trends enter the picture. Further, demand analysis with emphasis on dynamic specification may become an important tool of analysis. The same holds for short-term price-substitution relationships allowing for competing supply and related products (see Sec. 8.3 and 8.5). Apart from this, significance tests with the help of tolerance intervals may be used to test the applicability of forecasting equations (Sec. 10.2.1.1).

In the field of *sample surveys*, the analytical survey may be used to study differences in sales among groups of customers. Similarly, brand-awareness studies, product-acceptance tests, etc., help to diagnose current changes in the pattern of demand.

11.7. STEP VI—DEFINING THE PRESENT FUNCTIONAL POSITION

11.7.1. Definitions

The concept of functional position is perhaps the most useful analytical tool for evaluating the efficiency of the marketing mix. The functional position of a firm's product is defined as the role played by that product in the markets studied, as distinguished from the role played by the products of competitors. The type of reasoning involved may be illustrated as follows:

Assume sales to have been at an annual rate of, say, $10 million.

This shows clearly the existence of a certain preference by users for this product over those of competitors: without any, or at least equal, preferences, sales would have been zero.

It follows that our product performs a certain function for customers' needs and requirements that could not have been performed as well by competing products.

The relation between the company and the customer is governed almost exclusively by the specific use the company has made of its marketing instruments. Consequently, unless preferences for products of different suppliers happen to be perfectly equal, the customers' preferences are based on some specific differences between the company's marketing mix and that of competitors.

It stands to reason that the marketing mix of different producers may show many differences, even where similar products are concerned. *A priori*, we may expect both relevant and non-relevant differences.

The major concern in defining the company's functional position is, therefore, to explain customers' preferences in terms of differences in the use of instruments. The case where preferences are equal and no relevant differences in instruments exist may be denoted as an *amorphous functional position*, with the distribution of sales among competitors determined largely by chance.

This situation, however, applies usually only to a customer preferring a limited number of suppliers equally; his rating of the products of all other suppliers in the same market may be definitely different. Although two or more producers may share the same functional position with regard to a certain group of customers, this common position will be different from those held by other competitors. Hence, here again differences in instruments are necessarily relevant.

11.7.2. The Indirect Approach

The explanation of preferences in terms of instruments may proceed either by indirect or by direct inference. As is usual with market research, the two methods may often be used together, to complement and check each other.

With the indirect method the results of divergence analysis, development analysis and the diagnosis serve as a starting point. The full emphasis, however, is now on the differences in the marketing mix compared with those of competitors. For each separate instrument the possible effects of such differences on demand are analyzed successively. Any tangible differences thought relevant should be verified and borne out by divergence analysis.

In the simpler cases, indirect inference may point to gaps in the lower, intermediate or upper brackets of the price or quality range of competitors, or in the service offered by them. Illustrative is the cash-and-carry grocery wholesaler compared with the wagon distributor. In the first case, rock-bottom prices and a full line are offered with just about no service. In the second, full service is given, particularly in delivering at the shop; credit policies are liberal, and piecemeal orders are accepted, but the line is restricted to a small number of fast moving, high-margin items. The functional position of each type of wholesaler is reflected by his group of customers. The cash-and-carry wholesaler primarily serves the larger, independent grocery that owns a truck and whose liquidity is not a restraint on buying policies. Representative of the wagon distributor's customers are the Mama and Papa stores "which are typified by a small investment and little or no facilities for providing their own transportation."[18]

More often than not, discontinuities in the use of instruments are less apparent, and the explanation of preferences by a "fill the gap" theory is impracticable. Particularly with homogeneous oligopoly,[19] small differences in quality combined with differences in advertising themes and channel policies will account for differences in preferences among customers. Nevertheless, a careful analysis of ultimate users may reveal significant differences in market shares.

At this stage, systematic feed-back with divergence and development analysis becomes highly important. For, in order to evaluate the efficiency of the instruments, it is vital that differences in market share between different groups of users, such as age classes, social groups, city size, are not considered simply as "given," but can be related to the specific use (or non-use) of one or more instruments. Combining the information obtained with the successive steps of the audit will probably point to the desirability of a new analysis of market segments hitherto neglected in the investigation.

In defining the functional position and evaluating the efficiency of the instruments, it should be noted that the customer regards the marketing mix as a whole—quality, price, service, channels where to buy the product, etc. For this reason the functional position is often not merely the total of loosely related demand and instrument characteristics, since a whole can be more, and perhaps even something else, than the sum of its constituent parts. In industrial selling, for instance, technical know-how coupled with an extensive product line covering alternative devices, good service and integrity of advice make, as it were, for a new dimension, i.e., the guarantee that the product supplied will be the best obtainable to fit the customers' needs.

---

[18] See R. CASSADY and W. L. JONES, *The Changing Competitive Structure in the Wholesale Grocery Trade: A Case Study of the Los Angeles Market, 1920–1946* (Berkeley and Los Angeles: University of California Press, 1949).

[19] Compare JOEL DEAN, *Managerial Economics* (New York: Prentice Hall, 1951), p. 427ff.

Neither product line, integrity, nor service alone could provide this guarantee. It is the combination that matters.

Consequently, the functional position as a whole has to be taken into account in evaluating the effect of a given instrument on the demand for the company's product. Reverting to a former example: a liberal credit policy generally need not be essential in the grocery wholesale trade. In the case of wagon distribution, however, interpreted in the light of the particular kind of customers served, it becomes a necessary condition for the distributor's functional position.

11.7.3. The Direct Approach

Rather than relying on objective but circumstantial evidence from quantitative analysis by market shares and partial markets, the direct method aims at extracting information from the customer himself. Since we are interested in the reasons why he buys our own instead of competing products, asking the customer seems like a logical thing to do. Nevertheless, from a practical point of view, precedence should be given to quantitative analysis. First of all, results obtained in this way might well point unambiguously to a definite functional position and make attitude surveys redundant. Second, quantitative analysis by partial markets yields, as a rule, valuable information about buyer characteristics. Since stratification of such surveys is highly desirable, data obtained from quantitative analysis can contribute substantially to ensuring efficiency of stratification. This holds particularly where the analysis by partial markets points to the desirability of a survey to investigate systematic differences in attitude between different groups of buyers. Finally, prior quantitative analysis often will point to a specific problem that requires solution by an attitude study. Reversal of the sequence of the two types of investigation may leave this problem untouched.

In order to interpret preferences in terms of instruments, the purchase of, say, brand A instead of B, C, or D may be interpreted as the result of a *decision situation*. Three major categories of factors determine the outcome of this situation and are at the same time relevant for an appraisal of the marketing instruments:

1. *The product.* Pertinent are not only the attributes (quality, price, etc.) of brand A but also those of available competing brands and of substitute products.

2. *The available information* about the product, including analysis by sources of information, their sequence in time and impact on buying decisions. Principal sources to be distinguished with consumer goods are:

    a) previous experience with the product,
    b) advertising media,
    c) point-of-purchase advertising,

d) advice of friends,

e) advice of retailer, etc.

The relative importance of the several sources of information differs not only with the nature of the product and the promotional effort spent on the brand considered but also with the nature of the particular group of buyers. With industrial selling, for instance, manufacturers' catalogues, salesmen's calls and directories are perhaps the more important sources of initial information.

3. *The user.*[20] Selecting among alternative brands or substitutes is restricted by availability and by knowledge of the alternatives. The decision among the remaining alternatives, of which there are usually many, is controlled largely by three sets of factors:

a) The *needs* of the user,

b) His *values* (motives, ideologies),

c) *Obstacles* to overcome.

The effects of the user's prevailing value system are superimposed upon his basic needs. In turn, the value system consists of a number of different frames of reference. For practical purposes, this often loosely-used term, "frame of reference," can best be regarded as the total of all images, feelings and value-judgments associated with a certain concept. In the case of food consumption, for instance, at least four such concepts—or more specifically, values—with their accompanying frames of reference may be used to evaluate a certain product:

expense

health

taste

status

Like information, the relative strength of these different frames of reference is not the same for various groups of people and will also vary for different products. For interpreting the preference of a certain group for brand *A* in terms of instruments, it is important to know, first, for the product as such: (1) What values are most frequently associated with the product? (2) What is the relative weight of each value with various groups? (3) How is the specific product linked with these values?

With regard to the last question, a distinction has to be drawn between

---

[20] This subsection is based primarily on the approach of KURT LEWIN. See particularly his *Field Theory in Social Science* (London: Tavistock Publications, 1952), Ch. VIII, pp. 170–188. Also, "Group Decision and Social Change" in T. M. NEWCOMB and E. L. HARTLEY, *Readings in Social Psychology* (New York: Henry Holt, 1947), pp. 330–344; also J. CLAWSON, "Lewin's Vector Psychology and the Analysis of Motives in Marketing," in R. Cox and W. ALDERSON, *Theory in Marketing* (Chicago, Ill.: Richard D. Irwin, 1950), pp. 41–65.

the relative weight of each value and the position of the product in the frame of reference of that value. Pheasant, for example, may be mentioned in a survey as a dish for "company" dinner, and hence possess a high position in the "company," or "fuss," frame of reference. But in the "nutrition" or "health" frame of reference it may occupy a decidedly lower position.

Obstacles to overcome need not be related systematically to the product or brand or to the user. Obstacles may intervene because the brand is not easily or readily available. Slow delivery times are an example in the case of industrial selling. An insufficient number of retail outlets handling the product or the product being frequently out of stock are examples in the case of consumer goods. Inadequate service would also fall under this heading.

Analysis of these preferences, first for the product and after that for the brand, facilitates identification of differences in the use of instruments that are responsible for variations in buying habits among groups of users. In addition, since the relative weights of the relevant frames of reference usually are related narrowly to certain objective consumer characteristics— income, religion, social status, sex, age, race, etc.—this procedure often allows for results obtained from a small scale survey to be "extrapolated" to other groups.

Nevertheless, this type of analysis inevitably becomes rather complicated as soon as preferences are associated exclusively with small differences in quality, packaging, etc. Then the position of two competing brands in the several frames of reference may be about equal, although some groups prefer A and others B. In order to pinpoint the influence of instruments under these circumstances, it may be necessary to carry out the analysis with more narrowly defined frames of reference. "Ease of handling," for example, as a frame of reference for electrical appliances may be reduced to a number of separate frames of reference each of which conveys a definitive value judgment:

    a) speed of operation,
    b) technical skill,
    c) physical effort,
    d) psychological effort, etc.

11.7.4. The Role of Information

Neither the relative weight nor the contents of a given frame of reference need necessarily remain constant over time. Emphasis upon nutritional food during World War II may have increased the relative weight of the "health" frame of reference. Likewise, the position of a product is liable to change. Before the war, fowl occupied a high position with the lower-income classes mainly in the "company" frame of reference. It was almost never mentioned as a dish to have when short of money, or as a healthful or filling food. Due to lack of supply of other meats during the war years, its suitability as a filling food increased considerably and so did its position in the "health" frame of reference.[21]

Generally, changes of position in the relevant frames of reference are to be expected as a result of changes in basic needs, or in the supply of the product or of its substitutes, while overall changes in attitude or habits also may play a dominant role.

Table 11.9

RELATIVE FREQUENCY OF SOURCES OF INFORMATION: TWO EXAMPLES

INDUSTRIAL BUYING[a]			MOVIE PICTURE ATTENDANCE				
	FREQUENCY AS A FIRST SOURCE			SEQUENCE OF INFLUENCE IN TIME[e]			
				First	*Second*	*Third*	
Source	*Per cent*	*Number*	*Source*	*per cent*	*per cent*	*per cent*	*Base*
Previous experience	61	318	Personal contact	44	37	19	190
Directory[b]	9	45	Theater marquees	12	29	59	61
Catalogue[c]	9	45	Previews	48	29	23	114
Salesman	8	42	Newspapers	22	51	27	295
Advertisement	5	27	Magazines	52	26	22	139
Recommendation	4	20	Books	64	3	33	36
Other sources[d]	3	16					
No answer	1	7					
TOTAL	100%	512					

[a] Non-routine purchases of equipment and components, excluding replacement parts.
[b] Trade and telephone directories, etc.   [c] Individually bound and bound collections.
[d] Show or exhibition; saw or heard about it at another plant; reciprocity, etc.
[e] Thus, of 295 mentions of newspapers as a source of movie-going, 22% placed it first, 51% second, and 27% third.
Sources: *N.I.A.A.*: *Survey of Industrial Buying Practices*, New York, 1949, p. 33, Table 4. E. KATZ and P. F. LAZARSFELD, *Personal Influence* (Glencoe, Illinois: The Free Press, 1955), p. 193, Table 9.

Important to the definition of the functional position of a brand is the role played by the information at the disposal of the user. As pointed out by Lazarsfeld, "the actual purchase is the end-point of a long-continued process. Back of this final response lies the history of desires and attitudes which now dominate conduct."[22] In this process, new information may affect a product's or brand's position in a given frame of reference. Although additional information may result in a changed attitude, it is essential to note that the effect might have been zero or even opposite without the information obtained at an earlier date. Consequently, the functional position, as determined by the consumer's value system today, may be determined to a large extent by the available information and the time-sequence of its receipt. Two examples illustrating the differences in the relative frequency of various sources of information are given in Table 11.9. The first example refers to industrial

---

[21] K. LEWIN, *Field Theory in Social Science*, pp. 181, 185.
[22] P. F. LAZARSFELD and M. ROSENBERG, *The Language of Social Research* (Glencoe, Ill.: The Free Press), 1955, Sec. V, p. 396.

buying, the second to a consumption good in the service sector. As follows from the foregoing, the first information received need not necessarily be the most effective in determining the attitude of buyers. Possibilities of establishing the relative effectiveness of different sources of information are discussed by Katz and Lazarsfeld.[23] Emphasis on personal contact and on its influence in shaping preferences is well brought out by the same authors.[24]

11.7.5. Brand Loyalty: Deviant Case Analysis

Two other approaches to the functional position may be mentioned briefly.

The first starts from the concept of *brand loyalty*, an appropriate definition of the concept being:[25] "the probability that the user, when needing the product again, will buy the brand last used." Tabulating buyers by degree of brand loyalty, say, by three groups, may throw light on the functional position of the brand. According to the share of total sales going to high- and low-loyalty buyers, the functional position with regard to users may be characterized as either a *fixed* functional position or a *loose* functional position, with intermediate shades between these two extremes. Although high-loyalty buyers are the most interesting for determining the role played by the product, the objects of competition are generally the medium- and low-loyalty buyers, since promotional effort is most effectively aimed at increasing brand loyalty of these groups. Knowledge of the characteristics and reasons for brand preference of medium- and low-loyalty buyers is therefore particularly important for evaluating the adequacy of the present marketing mix.

This is not to say that a loose functional position always should be, or even could be, transformed into a fixed functional position. Servicing occasional or incidental buyers may well be a proper role for a certain product or brand. Door-to-door selling of encyclopedias (with necessarily zero brand loyalty), or some kind of subcontracting and repair shop are examples.

The other approach starts from the diagnosis and aims at comparing those partial markets where market shares have recently shown opposite or at least widely different trends. Apart from such differences being due to chance, *deviant case analysis* applied to the attitudes of sampled consumers often may

---

[23] E. Katz and P. F. Lazarsfeld, *Personal Influence: The Part Played by People in the Flow of Mass Communications* (Glencoe, Ill.: The Free Press, 1955), Part 2, Section II, p. 162ff.

[24] See in this context also F. S. Bourne, "Group Influence in Marketing and Public Relations," in R. Likert and S. P. Hayes, *Some Applications of Behavioral Research*, UNESCO, 1957, Ch. VI, pp. 257–258.

[25] P. J. Verdoorn, *De Eigen Markt der Onderneming* (Leiden: Stenfert Kroese, 1952), pp. 10 and 11. For an interesting approach implying the use of Markoff Chains, see W. Alderson, "Measuring the Sales Effectiveness of Advertising—A Progress Report," in *How Can Advertising be Better Evaluated in Today's Economy? Proceedings of the Fourth Annual Conference of the Advertising Research Foundation*, New York, 1958, pp. 98–99.

indicate a systematic change in the efficiency of a certain instrument, hitherto hidden by other factors.

11.7.6. Defining the Functional Position

The different sorts of information obtained so far with the audit are summarized in Table 11.10. Three types of information are shown:

Table 11.10

TYPE OF INFORMATION OBTAINED FROM AUDIT

STEP		CHARACTERISTICS OF USERS		INSTRUMENT VARIABLES *Own and Competitors*
		Objective	*Attitudes*	
3	Divergence analysis	+		(+)
4	Development analysis	+		+
5	Diagnosis	+	(+)	+
6	Functional position		+	+

1. Association of sales with *objective characteristics* of users—such as income, geographic areas, etc.

2. *Attitudes of users* toward products, the diagnosis being interested primarily in recent changes of brand awareness.

3. Association of sales with *instrument variables*. With divergence analysis, results pertaining to instruments emerge naturally insofar as consumer characteristics may be related to instrument variables—sales by areas, average prices paid, type of channel, etc. The main results, however, are obtained in the later stages, 4, 5, and 6.

Apart from this, time enters the picture with Steps 4 and 5. Hence, we are also in a position to separate general factors affecting demand from the factors peculiar to the development of the firm.

Information on each of these three categories may have led at almost any step to a suggestion regarding the functional position. Our attitude thus far has been to accept these suggestions as so many working hypotheses. Although the information secured in a certain step or in one category is, as a rule, not statistically independent from information collected in another step or in another category, the working hypotheses have, at least, the advantage of being the result of different methods of analysis. The claim of independency may therefore be justified from a methodological point of view.

In order to arrive at a final formulation of the firm's functional position, the working hypotheses have to be compared to see where they converge and complement one another, or where they appear mutually incompatible. In the latter case, one of the opposing hypotheses may be incorrect, or may be based upon inadequate data or on inadequate processing. If data and data-processing are sufficiently reliable, the logical solution for the problem of opposing hypotheses is to find an alternative interpretation that fits the same sets of data and leads to a single and more general hypothesis.

One point sometimes overlooked is the simple fact that different buyers may buy the same brand or make for different reasons. A certain breakfast cereal, for instance, may be preferred because the children like it, or because of its comparative ease of preparation. Formulation of the functional position should accordingly be sufficiently flexible to cover a plurality of reasons. On the other hand, many a hypothesis will be discarded at a later stage as redundant if it does not contribute to the explanation of why users prefer A against B, C or D. What the present problem requires is, ultimately, a *differential explanation* and not a set of exhaustive theories covering all aspects of buying behavior.[26]

The final formulation of the functional position should satisfy four conditions:

1. It should be based on a differential explanation.
2. In order to be pragmatic, the functions performed should be formulated in such a way as to relate them immediately to instrument variables.
3. It should be sufficiently flexible to cover a plurality of functions.
4. The explanation of the preferences should be compatible with available data on objective consumer characteristics.

The importance of the last condition need hardly be emphasized. Brand attitudes are basically related to instruments, and the weights of the different frames of references underlying these attitudes are in most cases associated with objective characteristics. For this reason, from whatever category of data a working hypothesis has been derived, the twofold relationship of attitudes with frames of reference and of attitudes with instruments often permits a valuable check.

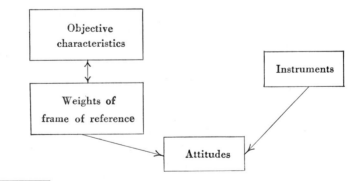

---

[26] This subject is covered more generally by A. KORNHAUSER and P. F. LAZARSFELD in LAZARSFELD and ROSENBERG, *op. cit.*, pp. 398–402.

Let us assume, for purpose of illustration, that a study of competitive prices has suggested a simple "fill the gap" theory, our brand supposedly filling a need for products in the next-to-the-lowest price interval. In such a case, we need not be satisfied with the single check that, for instance, in the attitude study, "price" has frequently been mentioned as important. We may also require that divergence analysis show our market share to be highest with those groups where the relative weight of the "expense" frame of reference is such that consumers are willing to sacrifice whatever "convenience" or "status" value might go with higher-priced brands.

Similarly, as long as quality has not been mentioned as a particularly important factor, we are justified in expecting that a relative change in our own price in the past was accompanied with a sizeable opposite change in our share in the market. Prices being assumed a major, if not the only, determinant of preference, this hypothesis clearly requires a high price-substitution effect on demand. Thus, development analysis may serve as a final check.

11.7.7. Research Methods

The *indirect approach* to the functional position consists of interpreting and combining such objective characteristics of markets and buyers as have been brought to light by earlier stages of the audit. Renewed analysis of partial markets or time series may become necessary before accepting a certain hypothesis. As mentioned already, frequent feed-back of information is characteristic of the audit.

What actually matters in this stage of interpreting a large quantity of loosely related facts is, rather than specific research techniques, an open mind and an unbiased attitude, allowing the figures to speak for themselves. Serendipity, the art of "spotting and exploiting good things encountered accidentally while searching for something else"[27] is as valuable with data-interpretation as it is elsewhere.

The *direct approach* is one of the most fertile fields for opinion and motivation research. Techniques available differ considerably in the information obtainable and in the intensity or "depth" of the investigation. In effect, four types of data are sought from the respondent. Apart from the usual objective characteristics asked in any case, they are:

1. The *behavior patterns* of users toward the product. These patterns refer not only to the complete buying act—the planning and preparation of the purchase, the way the latter is effectuated, etc.—but also to the use made of the product. For the same product, the behavior pattern may vary with different groups and with the particular type of use.

---

[27] W. A. WALLIS and H. V. ROBERTS, *Statistics: A New Approach*, p. 9.

2. The main *frames of reference* that determine the respondent's attitude toward the product in general, and his specific attitudes toward the brands A, B, C, ...
3. The *information* about the product available to respondents, sources and, possibly, the time-sequence in which it became available.
4. The experience of the respondent in the *buying situation*, obstacles overcome, etc.

If there are no previous attitude studies on the same product, the variety of data that might throw light on the functional position requires a concentric approach to cover the field evenly. The usual thing to do, therefore, is to start with an *unstructured interview* with a restricted number of respondents.

Questions on (2) and (3) will be largely open end, formulated by the interviewer according to the particular requirements of the situation. Wherever possible, replies are recorded in the respondent's own words. The instructions will mainly indicate, therefore, what points to cover and what types of probing to use. Questions raised by the indirect approach may have indicated what additional information might be useful. However, since independence of information is desired, it is important that specific questions covering these particular subjects not influence spontaneous answers to general questions. Starting with a question on some aspect of quality, for instance, might "load" the answers to following questions. Generally, a small pilot survey of about 10 or 20 observations is desirable as a start.

For the second type of data, information about the product and its sources, a formal structured questionnaire is usually to be preferred.

A differential analysis of brand attitudes and preferences may result either in a clear unambiguous picture of the role played by brand A as compared with B, C, D, . . . , or it may not. One check is the consistency of the preferences with other "interlocking" information obtained with the same questionnaire; another internal check is consistency with objective characteristics of the respondent's background.[28] If the picture thus obtained is acceptable, it has to be checked for external consistency, i.e., compatibility with results from the indirect approach. In many cases results obtained with this kind of small-scale survey may still remain unsatisfactory even when the tests mentioned have been passed successfully. For, although we know now how the mechanism works, and what reasons and factors affect brand preference, we are still uncertain as to:

a) the relative frequency of specific reasons and factors in the total population,
b) whether the same mechanism works with different groups in the same way.

---

[28] See, for instance, A. B. BLANKENSHIP, *Consumer and Opinion Research*, p. 211.

The second step in the case of a successful exploratory survey, therefore, is a large-scale survey with a *structured questionnaire,* using wherever possible multiple-choice questions.

In order to obtain insight into the intensity of the attitudes or preferences studied, *graded questions* or numerical scales can be used, as discussed in Chapter 6. Cross-tabulations of the answers with continuous, objective characteristics of respondents may lead to interesting conclusions.

In those cases where a certain attitude is of crucial importance for the explanation of preference, Gallup's so-called *quintamensional design* may prove very useful, particularly on large-scale surveys.[29] This design consists of five questions aimed at securing an all-round appraisal of a respondent's opinion on a given subject. First, awareness of the subject is ascertained by asking an open-end question. A second open-end question seeks his attitude toward the critical issue, followed by a two-way (or perhaps multiple-choice) question on specific issues. The reasons behind the answer to this two-way question are uncovered by a fourth question that is again open-end. The fifth question, finally, is a graded one and asks the respondent how strongly he feels about the issue.

In general, the unstructured small-scale survey will have brought out the main relevant answer patterns to be expected. This considerably facilitates a survey of the possible frames of reference associated in the respondent's mind with a certain question. The variety of frames of reference from which the respondent may select his answer can be restricted appreciably by wording the question appropriately. In this way much can be done to establish unidimensionality of the answer. Nevertheless, particularly where intensity measures are concerned, independence of question-wording remains highly desirable. It is in this respect that scalogram analysis, as discussed in Sec. 6.3, is so useful: it guarantees unidimensionality and is able to locate the neutral position of attitude.

In many cases, particularly with homogeneous oligopoly (a small number of large firms producing an identical product), one cannot get an unambiguous picture of the reasons behind brand preference from the unstructured interviews. Before inferring an amorphous functional position, it is worth while to consider more intensive approaches. The one to follow depends largely on the indications provided by the survey or the indirect approach of frames of reference or objective factors possibly at the root of brand preference. If, for instance, such indications point to the possible relevance of quality aspects, organizing group discussions among users may sometimes help bring out attitudes more pointedly than is possible by questioning users separately. In a case where a better insight was needed into attitudes toward

---

[29] GEORGE GALLUP, "The Quintamensional Plan of Question Design," *Public Opinion Quarterly,* Fall 1947, pp. 385–393.

style, shape or finishing of work-clothing, bringing the factory workers together in the canteen and letting them discuss the subject proved effective.[30]

If the issue remains obscure, *depth questioning* may be applied again to the whole range of factors that might affect preferences, this time more minutely. Conducted along general lines, the depth interview enhances the chance of pinpointing frames of reference and factors that determine brand choice. If the "reason why" still remains hidden, more specialized *projective techniques*, as discussed in Sec. 6.5, may yield positive results. This holds particularly in those cases where respondents are either *unwilling* to tell the reasons, although they know them, or are *unable* to do so, as when users are themselves not aware of them for psychological reasons. Projective techniques, however, are inevitably of little value as long as the actual reason remains unrelated to the respondent's conscious or subconscious value system. Here the solution of the problem lies with an indirect approach rather than with psychological analysis.

11.8.   STEP VII—DETERMINING THE OPTIMAL POSITION

As with the making of gold in the Middle Ages, determining optimal positions is today's *magnum opus*. With regard to the marketing audit, this implies looking for the functional position that satisfies the given criteria within the framework of the firm's capabilities and any other boundary conditions that may arise from its specific objectives. (See Sec. 1.3.)

11.8.1.   The Forecast Proper

The audit is essentially forward looking. The best functional position, therefore, must refer to a future period that will ordinarily coincide with a sales plan covering the next one, two, or three years. Accordingly, the backbone of this step is the forecast proper, showing the expected course of sales and profits if the marketing mix were unchanged. By taking into account the instrument variables required to gear the existing functional position to the optimal one, the sales plan for the future period is obtained. The dependence of the present step upon the results of the foregoing ones, as illustrated by Fig. 11.3, hardly needs comment. Different techniques available for making forecasts have already been discussed in Chapter 10. In the case of the audit, an analytical forecast based on a multi-stage approach as discussed in Sec. 11.5,

$$\begin{array}{ccc} \textit{National} & \rightarrow & \textit{Total demand} & \rightarrow & \textit{Demand for} \\ \textit{aggregates} & & \textit{for product} & & \textit{brand A} \end{array}$$

---

[30] *Business Week*, March 27, 1954.

recommends itself strongly since factors affecting total demand can be distinguished from the effects of instruments and other factors distinctive to brand A. Apart from providing insight into the quantitative impact of the factors governing future trends and hence providing a plausibility check on the final result, this procedure considerably facilitates the construction of alternative forecasts and plans. (See below, Sec. 11.8.5.)

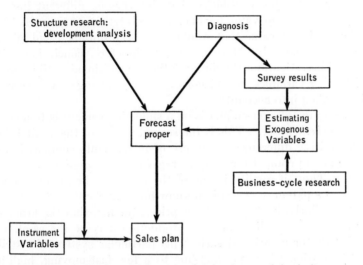

Fig. 11.3. *The Forecast Proper and Other Stages of the Audit*

Even at this forecasting stage, as noted in Sec. 11.5, a detailed approach is desirable besides the global approach and in many cases is indispensable.

11.8.2. Audits of Instruments

The shift from the present to the optimal functional position must be made by a change in the instrument variables. For this reason, a thorough investigation of the instruments, as hitherto used, is necessary. Although much information—such as retail coverage by area, influence of relative prices on the market share, or that of advertising on brand awareness—might have become available in previous stages, a final evaluation is possible only after the functional position has been analyzed. For it is only then that the role of a certain instrument can be properly studied in relation to the other instruments and their combined effect on consumer preferences.

The evaluation has two different aspects. First is the *efficiency aspect*. For this purpose, such techniques from advertising and distribution research as studies of salesmen's efficiency and of selling methods are available. These specialized techniques, however, are beyond the scope of this book. In many cases also, model systems like those used in operations research may be successfully applied to establish optima with one or more instruments. The optima thus obtained are mostly partial optima, with use of all other instruments assumed constant. Usually, this assumption will be justified. Even where simultaneous changes in instruments are considered, they need not necessarily invalidate conclusions about the instrument studied. Nevertheless, there remains the possibility that, by varying different instruments together, the optimum value for one, say, advertising, turns out higher or lower than the best value that would have been obtained had advertising been studied separately. More generally, therefore, conclusions obtained with partial investigations remain essentially conditional until interdependence with other variables and the consequences of changes in those variables have been taken into account.

One way to avoid over-emphasis on a single instrument is to analyze the ultimate *marketing assets*. This is the second aspect of the audit by instrument. A positive difference in the use of instruments compared with the marketing mix of competitors may be regarded as representative of an ultimate asset. Thus, if quality is one of the causes of brand preference, the possession of a patent or specialized know-how may be the ultimate marketing asset. Similarly, in the case of low prices, the fact that the firm's output is organized along the lines of mass-production may be the asset. For the wagon distributor mentioned earlier, his particular system of distribution and the limitation of his product-line to a few fast-moving, high-margin items are assets. By this reasoning, it will be noted, the line of thought is the reverse of the customary one, where customer preference or the firm's goodwill is itself considered an asset.[31]

What matters from the present point of view is to trace the reasons for the "asset" goodwill to its ultimate causes. For if a difference in the use of instruments is the cause of preference, the firm might well have certain relative advantages over competitors. Patents, mass-production, the wagon distributor's trucks, or a successful advertising theme are examples. The audit by instrument should, therefore, investigate what assets are associated with specific instruments and whether they are already used to their optimal extent. To take a simple example: the quality of a certain make might have two main features, a and b. Assume that the former is, say, technical advantages due to the firm holding a license, and is the reason for existing brand preference; and the latter is design and limits demand to a restricted group of buyers. In this case, it is clear that the use made of the license as an ultimate asset is suboptimal if a change in design and greater emphasis in advertising and selling on the product's technical advantages could broaden the market.

---

[31] See, L. HURWICZ, "Theory of the Firm and Investment," *Econometrica*, April 1946, pp. 109–137.

Ideally, a study of either aspect, efficiency or assets, would lead to the same results. Since the study of assets is focused more exclusively on the reasons behind preferences, and hence on the functional position as a whole, the two approaches tend to be complementary rather than overlapping.

11.8.3. Conditions for "Overall" Equilibrium Among Instruments

Starting from the formal theoretical point of view, an optimal position may be said to be obtained when improvement in net profits is not possible either by a change in one of the instruments or by any other combination. Abstracting from discontinuities and boundary conditions, this *optimum rule* can be made more concrete by means of a simple two-equation model expressing demand for the firm's product as an arbitrary function of price and unit-costs, and profits as the difference between gross-revenue from sales and total costs.

$$v = v(p,b,r,u),\tag{11.26}$$

and

$$Z = v(p - k - b - r - u) - C\tag{11.27}$$

where:

v = volume of output,
Z = net profits,
p = price,
k = variable cost of producing one unit of the "standard" or minimum quality,
b = additional unit costs of improving quality,
r = unit cost of advertising,
u = unit cost of the sales force,
C = constant cost.

As is shown in the Supplement to this chapter, the optimum-rule requires that:

$$\frac{\partial v}{\partial b} = \frac{\partial v}{\partial r} = \frac{\partial v}{\partial u} = -\frac{\partial v}{\partial p} = \frac{v}{p - b - k}\tag{11.28}$$

This condition implies that in an optimum position the additional sales obtained by a small increase in unit costs are the same for all non-price instruments and at the same time equal to the additional sales accompanying a corresponding decrease in unit prices.

The *rule of choice* discussed in the Supplement to Chapter 1 is easily derived from this formulation of the optimum rule. An increase in b is preferred over an increase in, say, r and over a decrease in p, as long as:

$$\frac{\partial v}{\partial r} < \frac{\partial v}{\partial b} > -\frac{\partial v}{\partial p}\tag{11.29}$$

The equality of marginal sales for the several instruments by the optimum rule also leads to interesting conclusions about the optimal *level* of the price and the unit costs of the other instruments. As shown in the Supplement to this chapter, for each instrument this optimal level is dependent on both the variable unit costs of producing the minimum quality and on the elasticities of the demand function:

$$b = \frac{-\epsilon_{vb}}{\epsilon_{vp} + \epsilon_{vb} + \epsilon_{vr} + \epsilon_{vu} + 1} k$$

$$r = \frac{-\epsilon_{vr}}{\epsilon_{vp} + \epsilon_{vb} + \epsilon_{vr} + \epsilon_{vu} + 1} k \qquad (11.30)$$

$$\cdots \cdots \cdots \cdots \cdots \cdots \cdots \cdots$$

$$p = \frac{\epsilon_{vp}}{\epsilon_{vp} + \epsilon_{vb} + \epsilon_{vr} + \epsilon_{vu} + 1} k$$

It follows from (11.30) that the ratio between the optimal levels for any two instruments is determined exclusively by the ratio between the demand elasticities of the two instruments concerned. The optimal ratios of the unit costs of, for instance, quality or advertising with respect to price, is given by:

$$\frac{b}{p} = -\frac{\epsilon_{vb}}{\epsilon_{vp}} \quad \text{and} \quad \frac{r}{p} = -\frac{\epsilon_{vr}}{\epsilon_{vp}} \qquad (11.31)$$

These ratios with respect to price also represent the share of total expenditure on an instrument out of gross revenue from sales. *In the optimum position, therefore, this share is determined for each instrument by the ratio of its own elasticity to the price-volume elasticity of demand—the "parity rule."*

However elegant from a theoretical point of view, the specific formulations of the optimum rule given by equations (11.30) and (11.31) cannot be applied in practice without qualification.

First, in the form given by (11.30) and (11.31), the rule is subject to the condition that a maximum for Z exists. Generally, therefore, the sum of the demand elasticities in the denominator of the right-hand side of (11.30) should be smaller than *minus* one.[32] Nevertheless, if this condition is not fulfilled (as for a monopoly faced with inelastic demand), the optimal ratio between two arbitrary, non-price, instruments remains determined by the ratio between the corresponding elasticities of demand.

Second, the elasticities appearing in (11.30) and (11.31) are variable magnitudes. For this, there are several reasons:

1. Beyond a certain point, every instrument is subject to *decreasing marginal sales.* Consequently, increased intensity of use necessarily leads to a decline in the numerical value of the elasticities (compare in this context Fig. 4.1 and the "maximum rule" given in the Supplement to Chapter 1).

---

[32] See the Supplement to this chapter.

2. Apart from this, the net effect of a given instrument is sometimes largely determined by existing marketing opportunities. Thus, a given strategy may be effective under certain conditions but ineffective under others. Cyclical conditions or marketing policies of competitors are examples.

3. Most important, perhaps, is the *multidimensionality* of every instrument. Price changes, for instance, may refer to list price or to one or more forms of discounts. Again, changes in advertising appropriations may be effected not only by altering the frequency or size of advertisements, but also by another choice of media, of geographic areas covered, of an advertising theme, etc. For these reasons, marginal sales are not independent of the specific way in which an instrument is changed.

The elasticities, therefore, cannot be considered as constants, nor are there fixed optimal values of the ratios, $\dfrac{b}{p}, \dfrac{r}{p}$ and $\dfrac{u}{p}$ for all times and purposes. Formula (11.31), accordingly, provides no support for the prevailing custom of fixing the advertising budget at a constant percentage of sales.[33]

Nevertheless, if elasticity estimates are available, the parity rule may give a preliminary indication of whether the marketing mix is in accordance with the marginal efficiency of the instruments. For purposes of extrapolation, this assumes that the numerous external factors—cyclical conditions, marketing methods used by competitors, etc.—remain essentially unchanged, and that the specific use of the instruments remains the same as before. Another advantage of these formulas is that they warn against undue emphasis on any single instrument.

11.8.4. Selecting the Optimal Position

One method of dealing with multidimensionality of instruments and of changes in concrete opportunities is the *oasis and desert map*, as discussed in the Supplement to Chapter 1. This method also allows explicit account to be taken of discontinuities and boundary conditions. An approach along these lines is essentially the practical counterpart of the purely formal approach presented in the foregoing section. A straightforward forecast on the basis of the existing marketing mix represents one point on the oasis and desert map. Suggestions for improving net profits derived from either the diagnosis or the audits by instrument represent so many alternative points. Other points may be added by interpolation or extrapolation of systematic relationships between instrument variables, demand and total cost.

Every point represents one marketing mix and hence a certain functional position. But one and the same functional position may be represented by a

---

[33] See R. W. JASTRAM, "Advertising Outlays Under Oligopoly," *Review of Economics and Statistics*, May, 1949, pp. 106–109; and "The Development of Advertising Appropriation Policy," *Journal of Business of the University of Chicago*, July, 1950, p. 158

whole set of points. For some points the marketing mix, then, is better adapted to the corresponding functional position than for others. The important thing in selecting the optimal position is to determine the minimum cost curves for each of the possible functional positions that will be investigated. The rationale behind this procedure is that a change in the marketing mix may well imply a change in customers and in reasons for brand preference. Translating changes in instruments into shifts of functional position allows one to look behind the numerical results of a mechanical extrapolation, and guarantees that a change of instruments will not inadvertently impair existing preferences of one group of buyers without compensating for this loss by increased preference of other groups.

As noted in Sec. 1.3, the best sequence for the present analysis is:

a) to investigate whether better use of the *existing* functional position is possible,

b) to investigate whether either expansion or radical change might be indicated.

This sequence has the definite advantage that no possibility for minor changes of equal profitability is overlooked before recommendations for a major change are made. At the same time, it assures that the already existing marketing assets are fully utilized. In this way, continuity in marketing policies can be maintained, while the costs of reorganization that are easily overlooked and that usually accompany a major change will not be incurred without good reason.

The ultimate choice among a given number of possibilities depends to a large extent on the analysis of the objectives, boundary conditions and the management's present problems, as undertaken with the first step. Here again, the sequence just indicated has a certain advantage, for the smaller the change in functional position, the smaller becomes the risk that one of the boundary conditions will be violated.

11.8.5. Presenting the Results

With a complete audit conducted along these lines, each instrument of the marketing mix has to fulfill one or more objectives. Particularly where changes in the instrument variables are recommended, three requirements are imposed on the audit:[34]

1. The objectives of the instruments must be *defined* one by one. Thus, a price reduction may be undertaken in order to stimulate primary demand, to meet competition, or to improve the attitude of distributors.

---

[34] The main argument of this section is taken from P. J. VERDOORN, "Advertising Effectiveness and the Task-Setting Budget," *The Quarterly Journal of the Advertising Association*, November, 1955, pp. 4–11.

2. The objectives must be *measurable* as far as possible. Otherwise the required size of the change in instruments cannot be estimated, nor can results be checked. In the case of advertising, for instance, it is not sufficient to say that the campaign is to increase brand familiarity. Rather it should be stated that brand familiarity has to increase, say, from 40 per cent to 60 per cent. If the objective is to stimulate sales in the East, the required expansion must be expressed as a target percentage of existing sales in Eastern districts, and so on.
3. The third requirement concerns next year's audit rather than the present one, i.e., the *check* on whether the objectives have been attained. As mentioned already, this check is specifically the task of the diagnosis.

The objectives thus defined may refer either to an improvement of the functional position or to more efficient use of the instruments, i.e., reduction of unit costs, while maintaining the present position. Here it should be noted that a given objective is not necessarily associated with the use of one instrument only. To give some examples:

1. Improving good will among retailers may mean a specific target for the salesmen, for advertising, or both; and perhaps also for pricing policy, possibly reviewing discounts.
2. Meeting competition may imply price reductions with advertising performing a tactical role, or the whole emphasis may be placed on the strategic function of advertising.
3. Increasing consumer familiarity with qualitative advantages of the product may entail emphasis either on the strategic function of advertising or on the sales force effectuating a change in dealer's attitudes.

The allocation of tasks among the different instruments is governed by the relative efficiency of the instruments with regard to the objectives as well as by the existence of boundary conditions. The allocation of tasks in the case of advertising is illustrated in Fig. 11.4. The dotted semi-circular line beginning at the marketing audit represents the development and the follow-up of targets. Via the analysis of the functional position, a distribution of tasks is obtained between the different instruments, shown as squares. For advertising these tasks are shown separately by the small circles: 1, 2 and 3. The decision to allocate these tasks to advertising is based upon cost estimates for each as compared with the costs that would have been incurred by attributing the tasks to other instruments.

As shown in the diagram, the required cost estimates in the case of advertising are obtained from experience in previous campaigns. This experience is represented by the outer, dark ring in the diagram within which the entire advertising policy is set, so to speak. By reference to these cost estimates it is possible to consider how far advertising is the appropriate instrument for achieving a certain objective.

One point emphasized by this diagram is the dependence of the audit on a systematic evaluation of the instruments in earlier periods. To the extent that experience is accumulated, the outer circle in the diagram becomes heavier and the accuracy of the estimates is accordingly increased.

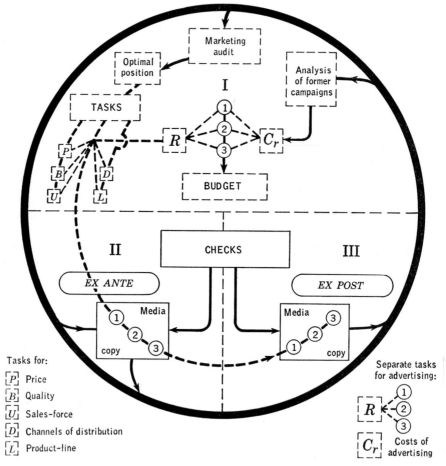

Fig. 11.4. The Advertising Budget

Source: P. J. Verdoorn, *op. cit.*

Nevertheless, it is clear that, however large the accumulated experience, marketing research will never be able to reduce to zero uncertainty that accompanies almost every policy decision. Where major policy decisions are concerned, conditions are never such that we could program the problem and feed into a computer the data as well as the formulas that represent the pattern of the solution. A subjective element of judgment inevitably remains. As mentioned in Sec. 1.2, the task of the researcher is essentially an advisory one, and in the case of marketing research the final decision remains with the senior executives.

The only thing the audit can do, therefore, is to pinpoint uncertainty as clearly as possible. This may be the case for either the forecast proper or the choice of the optimal policy. Uncertainty about the forecast may lead to the presentation of one or more *data alternatives*, while uncertainty about optimal policy makes *policy alternatives* desirable. (For an explanation of these two kinds of alternatives, see Sec. 10.3.) A cross-tabulation of the main forecasts, i.e.:

> total volume of sales,
> total money sales,
> market share,
> sales expense budget,
> capital requirements,

according to the data alternatives and policy alternatives, shows for each policy the expected values of these variables under different external conditions. Compared with an unconditional forecast, this method of presenting the results of the audit has the advantage of making explicit the impact of uncertainty with regard to the external factors on each of the different policy alternatives.

In order not to have too many alternatives and, hence, to confuse the main issues, it is desirable to combine these assumptions into one alternative for external variables that can be regarded as pessimistic, and those that can be regarded as optimistic into another. In this way, three main data alternatives are obtained: one representing the influence of possible unfavorable cyclical conditions and demand factors, one representing the most probable development and, finally, an alternative for relatively favorable conditions. In this way, the probable range of the impact of future developments on the results and requirements of a given policy can be evaluated.

11.8.6. Research Methods

In this final stage of the audit the main emphasis is on forecasting and problems of variation. Although not always necessary, model systems can prove useful for both purposes, though the model to be used will be different in each case.

For the forecast proper, the business cycle type of model is indicated where national aggregates determine total demand for the product under consideration. If estimates of total demand are available, a single demand equation may suffice to estimate either effective total demand or market prices. Two conditions, however, must be fulfilled. First, for short-term forecasting, supply must be independent of prices, or vice versa. Second, the value added to the product must not affect total demand appreciably on the income side. If these conditions are not fulfilled, model systems must be applied (see Sections 4.3 and 9.1).

The same conditions hold for durables, where the influence of average age (or the age distribution) on replacement demand must be evaluated. They may be necessary too where the impact of inventory fluctuation on either demand or supply has to be taken into account.

End-use analysis by *input-output models* is often indispensable for appraising trends in different segments of industry. It is the appropriate tool, therefore, for forecasting demand for raw materials and semi-manufactured goods, wherever demand is dependent on a variety of final products.

Models along the lines of *operations research* are suitable for determining in what dimensions and what intensity a given instrument should be used. They are applicable, too, for establishing the optimal allocation of tasks and expenditures between instruments, and hence may make a valuable contribution toward the selection of policy alternatives. Particularly where boundary conditions are applicable, *linear programming* may help find a correct solution.

Likewise, experiments may be used to decide among different policy alternatives. Sometimes, however, their use will be restricted to the audit by instrument, in order to check the relative efficiency of the actual or—as the case may be—the possible use of an instrument. In other cases, experiments facilitate the final choice between secondary aspects of quality or of another instrument, with the main lines of the marketing mix as a whole already set. One particular form of experiment, the test market, is often used as a final check on the marketing mix as a whole, after the production of a new quality has been started on a pilot scale, the advertising campaign in a preliminary form has already been launched in the test area, and distributors' discounts and list prices have been tentatively fixed. This form of experiment belongs strictly to the execution of the sales plan rather than to the audit itself.

Survey methods, finally, again enter into this closing stage. First is the *informal survey* with executives and personnel of the company, since the results obtained are often in need of verification. Also, feed-back with the first step is desirable, in order to check whether the results obtained will contribute to the solution of present problems. Second, wherever available data obtained from former steps are insufficient to allow a choice between two mutually exclusive policy alternatives, *sequential sampling* may be a fast and efficient method of collecting the required additional information.

Derivation of the Optimal Values of Instrument Variables

The proof of equations (11.30) and (11.31) is easiest for the two-instruments case. Using the same symbols as in Sec. 11.8.4, the system is reduced to:

$$v = v(p,b) \tag{1}$$
$$Z = v(p - k - b) - C \tag{2}$$

The optimum position requires that a change in unit costs or price shall not affect net profits. This requires that:

$$\frac{\partial Z}{\partial b} = -\frac{\partial Z}{\partial p} = 0 \tag{3}$$

Differentiating (2) with respect to b and p we find:

$$\frac{\partial Z}{\partial b} = (p - b - k)\frac{\partial v}{\partial b} - v \quad \text{and} \quad -\frac{\partial Z}{\partial p} = -(p - b - k)\frac{\partial v}{\partial p} - v \tag{4}$$

Substitution of the right-hand side of (4) into (3) gives, after rearrangement:

$$\frac{\partial v}{\partial b} = -\frac{\partial v}{\partial p} = \frac{v}{p - b - k} \tag{5}$$

Hence, the optimum position has to satisfy two conditions:

$$\frac{\partial v}{\partial b} = \frac{v}{p - k - b} \quad \text{and} \quad \frac{\partial v}{\partial p} = \frac{-v}{p - k - b} \tag{6}$$

By definition:

$$\frac{\partial v}{\partial b} = \epsilon_{vb}\frac{v}{b} \quad \text{and} \quad \frac{\partial v}{\partial p} = \epsilon_{vp}\frac{v}{p} \tag{7}$$

Substitution of the right-hand sides of the set (7) in set (6) results in:

$$\frac{\epsilon_{vb}}{b} = \frac{1}{p - k - b} \quad \text{and} \quad -\frac{\epsilon_{vp}}{p} = \frac{1}{p - k - b} \tag{8}$$

In the present case we have, therefore, two equations from which to solve for the optimal values of the two instrument variables. As is easily seen, this method of solution remains valid for any arbitrary number of instruments. Solving the set (8) for b and p, we find:

$$b = \frac{-\epsilon_{vb}}{\epsilon_{vb} + \epsilon_{vp} + 1} k \tag{9}$$

$$p = \frac{\epsilon_{vp}}{\epsilon_{vb} + \epsilon_{vp} + 1} k \tag{10}$$

Dividing (10) into (9) the *parity rule* is easily deduced:

$$\frac{b}{p} = -\frac{\epsilon_{vb}}{\epsilon_{vp}} \tag{11}$$

Equations (9) through (11) are meaningful only if:[35]

$$\epsilon_{vb} + \epsilon_{vp} < -1 \tag{12}$$

The same approach is applicable to those cases where one of the instruments, such as price, is "pegged" independently of the other instruments. Introducing r (the unit cost of advertising) as a third instrument variable, the demand and profit equations (1) and (3) are replaced by:

$$v = v(b,r) \tag{13}$$
$$Z = v(p - k - b - r) - C \tag{14}$$

In this case the optimal values for b and r are given by:

$$b = \frac{\epsilon_{vb}}{\epsilon_{vb} + \epsilon_{vr} + 1} (p - k) \tag{15}$$

$$r = \frac{\epsilon_{vr}}{\epsilon_{vb} + \epsilon_{vr} + 1} (p - k) \tag{16}$$

In the case of "pegged" prices, the parity rule still applies to the non-price instruments:

$$\frac{b}{r} = \frac{\epsilon_{vb}}{\epsilon_{vr}} \tag{17}$$

whereas the optimal ratio with respect to any arbitrary price is given by:

$$\frac{b}{p} = \frac{\epsilon_{vb}}{\epsilon_{vb} + \epsilon_{vr} + 1} \frac{(p - k)}{p} \tag{18}$$

$$\frac{r}{p} = \frac{\epsilon_{vr}}{\epsilon_{vb} + \epsilon_{vr} + 1} \frac{(p - k)}{p} \tag{19}$$

---

[35] Equations such as (9) and (10) are the *first-order conditions*. They must be satisfied if Z is to attain an extreme value. Whether this extreme represents a maximum must be inferred from the *second-order conditions*. If the latter are inconclusive, as in the present case, no general conclusion is possible. Each individual case must be studied separately. As is easily verified, the present system has no maximum when the demand curve (1) is assumed to be linear. The assumption of an exponential demand function with constant exponents, however, leads to second-order conditions that are fulfilled if equation (12) is satisfied.

PROBLEMS

1. *a*) Discuss the difference between divergence analysis and development analysis as applied to a marketing audit of a chain of 8 supermarkets spread over five cities.
   b) What analytical methods might be used in each case?

2. Illustrate the operation of the feed-back principle by applying Fig. 11.1 to the preceding example.

3. Discuss the pros and cons of having a marketing audit of an aluminum fabricator carried out by a consultant with no previous experience in this area.

4. What distinctive problems are likely to be encountered in planning an audit of a holding company, such as Textron Inc., made up of different divisions with each making different products, headed by its own president and operating more or less autonomously?

5. Design an audit for a college textbook publisher that has been in business for just five years and is anxious to increase his market share. Outline a provisional model for such an audit and indicate what sort of pretests or surveys might be undertaken at this stage.

6. Outline the type and sequence of surveys that might be undertaken in an audit of the textbook publisher, listing the objectives of each.

7. What sort of partial markets might be considered in an audit of a department store? Assign symbols to the characteristics selected and, using the notation system outlined in Sec. 11.3, specify what tabulations and cross-tabulations should be made in analyzing sales of (*a*) different items of men's clothing; (*b*) different appliances.

8. Which statistical method of analysis would you select for each of the following problems, and why:
   a) To select the most efficient stratifying characteristics in a survey of people's preference for brick as a building material.
   b) To determine why some people buy stock and others at the same income level deposit all their savings in a savings account.
   c) To measure the net effect of different socio-economic characteristics on likelihood of purchasing an adult encyclopedia.
   d) To identify what types of factors influence people to vacation overseas.
   e) To measure the effect of traffic on value of residential properties, from survey data.
   f) To estimate the price elasticity of demand for TV sets, from time-series data.

9. Prepare a proposal for a marketing audit of your local transportation system outlining:
   a) the objectives

b) how each of the steps is to be carried out

c) research methods to be used

d) nature and extent of feed-back

10. Set up hypotheses as a basis for applying the global approach to explaining fluctuations in demand for Company A's cement output, Company A being a large producer in the Northeast.

11. What might the role of the audit method be in an analysis of the market for home appliances?

12. What marketing "instruments" are likely to be available to a wheat farmer? How might he go about evaluating the efficiency of these "instruments"?

13. Discuss the application of the "parity rule" to deriving the optimal position for a baking company with reference to:

a) what data are needed and how they might be collected

b) determining the applicability of the "rule" to the particular situation.

SELECTED REFERENCES

Since this chapter attempts to bring together the material that has been covered in the preceding parts of the book, it is difficult to cite references that are distinctive to the subject matter of the chapter and that have not been cited already. Indeed, from a logical point of view, the appropriate references would nearly be all of those cited in the footnotes to the previous chapters as well as those cited at the end of those chapters. For this reason, no systematic listing of references will be attempted in this chapter, as has been done previously. Rather, a few general remarks will be offered on the type of reading material that might be consulted in connection with the marketing audit.

A good practical and theoretical knowledge of marketing and of the use of each of the separate instruments is, of course, indispensable for the understanding of the firm's marketing problems and, hence, for the planning of the audit. In the context of the audit, *Marketing Management, Analysis and Decision*, by J. A. HOWARD (Homewood, Illinois: Irwin, 1957) might best serve as an all around introduction.

A wealth of practical and theoretical detail is to be found in D. M. PHELPS, *Sales Management, Procedures and Policies* (Chicago, Illinois: Irwin, 1951), and in *Marketing Handbook* by P. H. NYSTROM (New York: Ronald Press, 1951). Extremely valuable for the overall picture and where price-line, product-line and advertising policies are concerned, is JOEL DEAN, *Managerial Economics* (Englewood Cliffs, New Jersey: Prentice-Hall, 1951). Important also for the overall picture is the book by HANS BREMS, *Product Equilibrium in Monopolistic Competition* (Cambridge, Mass.: Harvard University Press, 1951), where special emphasis is given to quality as a marketing instrument.

With regard to the research approaches to be followed, many of the marketing research texts provide a good general picture of the type of problems that are encountered at various stages of the marketing audit, though the problems are not identified in this manner. In particular, *Marketing Research* by RICHARD D. CRISP (New York: McGraw-Hill Book Co., 1957) provides in Parts 4 and 5 some excellent examples of the types of practical problems that are encountered and of means of dealing with them. The book illustrates how many problems can be solved without recourse to sophisticated techniques. A previously mentioned book by HANS ZEISEL, *Say it with Figures*, provides many more good examples on how research problems can often be solved by a relatively simple approach.

The possibilities of applying regression techniques for purposes of marketing to partial markets of higher order are well illustrated by the book of DONALD COWAN, *Sales Analysis from the Management Point of View* (Chicago, Ill.: Chicago University Press, 1938). This book, unfortunately out of print long ago, is also noteworthy for its attempt to determine the impact of competition by geographic area. Some, now classical, examples of the application of different approaches with the help of regression analysis are to be found in CHARLES ROOS' *Dynamic Economics* (Bloomington, Ind.: Principia Press, 1934).

A great variety of other techniques is presented in *The Language of Social Research* edited by P. F. LAZARSFELD and M. ROSENBERG (Glencoe, Ill.: The Free Press, 1955). Many of these techniques are designed to deal with data of a qualitative nature. Particularly useful for problems related to the "why" in market research is *Motivation and Market Behavior* edited by ROBERT FERBER and H. G. WALES (Homewood, Ill.: Irwin, 1959), which illustrates how different techniques from such areas as economics, sociology and psychology can be exploited for this purpose. Where consumer preferences are concerned, the more basic works in psychology are appropriate, those dealing with "Gestaltpsychologie" being, perhaps, the best suited to a general approach. Chapter VIII of KURT LEWIN's *Field Theory in the Social Sciences* (London: Tavistock Publications, 1952) and the contribution by JOSEPH CLAWSON, "Lewin's Vector Psychology and the Analysis of Motives in Marketing" in R. Cox and W. ALDERSON, *Theory in Marketing* (Chicago, Ill.: Irwin, 1950) are useful introductions.

Specific references to the marketing audit, finally, are to be found in the article by WROE ALDERSON, "The Marketing Audit and the Ad Budget" in the December, 1947, issue of *Industrial Marketing*, and in "An Audit of Marketing Methods and Channels" in *Cost and Profit Outlook* (Philadelphia: Alderson and Sessions, superseded by Alderson Associates, October, 1954), in P. J. VERDOORN, "Marketing from the Producer's Point of View," *Journal of Marketing*, pp. 221–235, and in "Advertising Effectiveness and the Task-setting Budget" (*The Quarterly Journal of the Advertising Association*, August, 1955, pp. 22–28, and November, 1955, pp. 4–11) by the same author.

Appendix | Selected Statistical Tables

Table A1
AREAS UNDER THE NORMAL CURVE*

The values in the body of the table indicate the proportion of the area under either tail of the normal curve lying beyond the ordinate, x/σ.

x/σ	.00	.01	.02	.03	.04	.05	.06	.07	.08	.09
0.0	00000	00399	00798	01197	01595	01994	02392	02790	03188	03586
0.1	03983	04380	04776	05172	05567	05962	06356	06749	07142	07535
0.2	07926	08317	08706	09095	09483	09871	10257	10642	11026	11409
0.3	11791	12172	12552	12930	13307	13683	14058	14431	14803	15173
0.4	15554	15910	16276	16640	17003	17364	17724	18082	18439	18793
0.5	19146	19497	19847	20194	20450	20884	21226	21566	21904	22240
0.6	22575	22907	23237	23565	23891	24215	24537	24857	25175	25490
0.7	25804	26115	26424	26730	27035	27337	27637	27935	28230	28524
0.8	28814	29103	29389	29673	29955	30234	30511	30785	31057	31327
0.9	31594	31859	32121	32381	32639	32894	33147	33398	33646	33891
1.0	34134	34375	34614	34850	35083	35313	35543	35769	35993	36214
1.1	36433	36650	36864	37076	37286	37493	37698	37900	38100	38298
1.2	38493	38686	38877	39065	39251	39435	39617	39796	39973	40147
1.3	40320	40490	40658	40824	40988	41149	41308	41466	41621	41774
1.4	41924	42073	42220	42364	42507	42647	42786	42922	43056	43189
1.5	43319	43448	43574	43699	43822	43943	44062	44179	44295	44408
1.6	44520	44630	44738	44845	44950	45053	45154	45254	45352	45449
1.7	45543	45637	45728	45818	45907	45994	46080	46164	46246	46327
1.8	46407	46485	46562	46638	46712	46784	46856	46926	46995	47062
1.9	47128	47193	47257	47320	47381	47441	47500	47558	47615	47670
2.0	47725	47778	47831	47882	47932	47982	48030	48077	48124	48169
2.1	48214	48257	48300	48341	48382	48422	48461	48500	48537	48574
2.2	48610	48645	48679	48713	48745	48778	48809	48840	48870	48899
2.3	48928	48956	48983	49010	49036	49061	49086	49111	49134	49158
2.4	49180	49202	49224	49245	49266	49286	49305	49324	49343	49361

549

Table A1—(Cont.)

AREAS UNDER THE NORMAL CURVE*

x/σ	.00	.01	.02	.03	.04	.05	.06	.07	.08	.09
2.5	49379	49396	49413	49430	49446	49461	49477	49492	49506	49520
2.6	49534	49547	49560	49573	49585	49598	49609	49621	49632	49643
2.7	49653	49664	49674	49683	49693	49702	49711	49720	49728	49736
2.8	49744	49752	49760	49767	49774	49781	49788	49795	49801	49807
2.9	49813	49819	49825	49831	49836	49841	49846	49851	49856	49861
3.0	49865									
3.5	4997674									
4.0	4999683									
4.5	4999966									
5.0	4999997133									

* WAUGH, A. E., *Laboratory Manual and Problems for Elements of Statistical Method*, Table A1, as adapted from F. C. KENT, *Elements of Statistics*, McGraw-Hill Book Company, Inc., New York, 1924. Copied through the courtesy of Professor WAUGH and of McGraw-Hill.

Table A2

TABLE OF t*

The value at the head of each column indicates the probability of obtaining a value of t outside the range $\pm t$, for different degrees of freedom, purely as a result of random sampling variations. For example, with 10 degrees of freedom, a value of t exceeding plus or minus 2.228 would be expected to occur 5 times out of 100 purely as a result of chance.

n	$P = 0.9$	0.8	0.7	0.6	0.5	0.4	0.3	0.2	0.1	0.05	0.02	0.01
1	0.158	0.325	0.510	0.727	1.000	1.376	1.963	3.078	6.314	12.706	31.821	63.657
2	0.142	0.289	0.445	0.617	0.816	1.061	1.386	1.886	2.920	4.303	6.965	9.925
3	0.137	0.277	0.424	0.584	0.765	0.978	1.250	1.638	2.353	3.182	4.541	5.841
4	0.134	0.271	0.414	0.569	0.741	0.941	1.190	1.533	2.132	2.776	3.747	4.604
5	0.132	0.267	0.408	0.559	0.727	0.920	1.156	1.476	2.015	2.571	3.365	4.032
6	0.131	0.265	0.404	0.553	0.718	0.906	1.134	1.440	1.943	2.447	3.143	3.707
7	0.130	0.263	0.402	0.549	0.711	0.896	1.119	1.415	1.895	2.365	2.998	3.499
8	0.130	0.262	0.399	0.546	0.706	0.889	1.108	1.397	1.860	2.306	2.896	3.355
9	0.129	0.261	0.398	0.543	0.703	0.883	1.100	1.383	1.833	2.262	2.821	3.250
10	0.129	0.260	0.397	0.542	0.700	0.879	1.093	1.372	1.812	2.228	2.764	3.169
11	0.129	0.260	0.396	0.540	0.697	0.876	1.088	1.363	1.796	2.201	2.718	3.106
12	0.128	0.259	0.395	0.539	0.695	0.873	1.083	1.356	1.782	2.179	2.681	3.055
13	0.128	0.259	0.394	0.538	0.694	0.870	1.079	1.350	1.771	2.160	2.650	3.012
14	0.128	0.258	0.393	0.537	0.692	0.868	1.076	1.345	1.761	2.145	2.624	2.977
15	0.128	0.258	0.393	0.536	0.691	0.866	1.074	1.341	1.753	2.131	2.602	2.947
16	0.128	0.258	0.392	0.535	0.690	0.865	1.071	1.337	1.746	2.120	2.583	2.921
17	0.128	0.257	0.392	0.534	0.689	0.863	1.069	1.333	1.740	2.110	2.567	2.898
18	0.127	0.257	0.392	0.534	0.688	0.862	1.067	1.330	1.734	2.101	2.552	2.878
19	0.127	0.257	0.391	0.533	0.688	0.861	1.066	1.328	1.729	2.093	2.539	2.861
20	0.127	0.257	0.391	0.533	0.687	0.860	1.064	1.325	1.725	2.086	2.528	2.845
21	0.127	0.257	0.391	0.532	0.686	0.859	1.063	1.323	1.721	2.080	2.518	2.831
22	0.127	0.256	0.390	0.532	0.686	0.858	1.061	1.321	1.717	2.074	2.508	2.819
23	0.127	0.256	0.390	0.532	0.685	0.858	1.060	1.319	1.714	2.069	2.500	2.807
24	0.127	0.256	0.390	0.531	0.685	0.857	1.059	1.318	1.711	2.064	2.492	2.797
25	0.127	0.256	0.390	0.531	0.684	0.856	1.058	1.316	1.708	2.060	2.485	2.787
26	0.127	0.256	0.390	0.531	0.684	0.856	1.058	1.315	1.706	2.056	2.479	2.779
27	0.127	0.256	0.389	0.531	0.684	0.855	1.057	1.314	1.703	2.052	2.473	2.771
28	0.127	0.256	0.389	0.530	0.683	0.855	1.056	1.313	1.701	2.048	2.467	2.763
29	0.127	0.256	0.389	0.530	0.683	0.854	1.055	1.311	1.699	2.045	2.462	2.756
30	0.127	0.256	0.389	0.530	0.683	0.854	1.055	1.310	1.697	2.042	2.457	2.750
∞	0.12566	0.25335	0.38532	0.52440	0.67449	0.84162	1.03643	1.28155	1.64485	1.95996	2.32634	2.57582

* Reprinted from Table IV of R. A. FISHER, *Statistical Methods for Research Workers*, Oliver & Boyd, Ltd., Edinburgh and London, 1936, by permission of the author and publishers.

Table A3
VALUES OF CHI SQUARE (χ^2)*

n†	$P = 0.99$	0.98	0.95	0.90	0.80	0.70	0.50	0.30	0.20	0.10	0.05	0.02	0.01
1	0.000157	0.000628	0.00393	0.0158	0.0642	0.148	0.455	1.074	1.642	2.706	3.841	5.412	6.635
2	0.0201	0.0404	0.103	0.211	0.446	0.713	1.386	2.408	3.219	4.605	5.991	7.824	9.210
3	0.115	0.185	0.352	0.584	1.005	1.424	2.366	3.665	4.642	6.251	7.815	9.837	11.345
4	0.297	0.429	0.711	1.064	1.649	2.195	3.357	4.878	5.989	7.779	9.488	11.668	13.277
5	0.554	0.752	1.145	1.610	2.343	3.000	4.351	6.064	7.289	9.236	11.070	13.388	15.086
6	0.872	1.134	1.635	2.204	3.070	3.828	5.348	7.231	8.558	10.645	12.592	15.033	16.812
7	1.239	1.564	2.167	2.833	3.822	4.671	6.346	8.383	9.803	12.017	14.067	16.622	18.475
8	1.646	2.032	2.733	3.490	4.594	5.527	7.344	9.524	11.030	13.362	15.507	18.168	20.090
8	2.088	2.532	3.325	4.168	5.380	6.393	8.343	10.656	12.242	14.684	16.919	19.679	21.666
10	2.558	3.059	3.940	4.865	6.179	7.267	9.342	11.781	13.442	15.987	18.307	21.161	23.209
11	3.053	3.609	4.575	5.578	6.989	8.148	10.341	12.899	14.631	17.275	19.675	22.618	24.725
12	3.571	4.178	5.226	6.304	7.807	9.034	11.340	14.011	15.812	18.549	21.026	24.054	26.217
13	4.107	4.765	5.892	7.042	8.634	9.926	12.340	15.119	16.985	19.812	22.362	25.472	27.688
14	4.660	5.368	6.571	7.790	9.467	10.821	13.339	16.222	18.151	21.064	23.685	26.873	29.141
15	5.229	5.985	7.261	8.547	10.307	11.721	14.339	17.322	19.311	22.307	24.996	28.259	30.578
16	5.812	6.614	7.962	9.312	11.152	12.624	15.338	18.418	20.465	23.542	26.296	29.633	32.000
17	6.408	7.255	8.672	10.085	12.002	13.531	16.338	19.511	21.615	24.769	27.587	30.995	33.409
18	7.015	7.906	9.390	10.865	12.857	14.440	17.338	20.601	22.760	25.989	28.869	32.346	34.805
19	7.633	8.567	10.117	11.651	13.716	15.352	18.338	21.689	23.900	27.204	30.144	33.687	36.191
20	8.260	9.237	10.851	12.443	14.578	16.266	19.337	22.775	25.038	28.412	31.410	35.020	37.566
21	8.897	9.915	11.591	13.240	15.445	17.182	20.337	23.858	26.171	29.615	32.671	36.343	38.932
22	9.542	10.600	12.338	14.041	16.314	18.101	21.337	24.939	27.301	30.813	33.924	37.659	40.289
23	10.196	11.293	13.091	14.848	17.187	19.021	22.337	26.018	28.429	32.007	35.172	38.968	41.638
24	10.856	11.992	13.848	15.659	18.062	19.943	23.337	27.096	29.553	33.196	36.415	40.270	42.980
25	11.524	12.697	14.611	16.473	18.940	20.867	24.337	28.172	30.675	34.382	37.652	41.566	44.314
26	12.198	13.409	15.379	17.292	19.820	21.792	25.336	29.246	31.795	35.563	38.885	42.856	45.642
27	12.879	14.125	16.151	18.114	20.703	22.719	26.336	30.319	32.912	36.741	40.113	44.140	46.963
28	13.565	14.847	16.928	18.939	21.588	23.647	27.336	31.391	34.027	37.916	41.337	45.419	48.278
29	14.256	15.574	17.708	19.768	22.475	24.577	28.336	32.461	35.139	39.087	42.557	46.693	49.588
30	14.953	16.306	18.493	20.599	23.364	25.508	29.336	33.530	36.250	40.256	43.773	47.962	50.892

* Reprinted from Table III of R. A. FISHER, *Statistical Methods for Research Workers*, Oliver & Boyd, Ltd., Edinburgh and London, 1936, by permission of the author and publishers.

† For larger values of n, the expression $\sqrt{2\chi^2} - \sqrt{2n - 1}$ may be used as a normal deviate with unit variance.

Table A4

5 AND 1 PER CENT SIGNIFICANCE POINTS OF F*

(5 per cent points are in roman type; 1 per cent points are in boldface type)

n_1 DEGREES OF FREEDOM (FOR GREATER MEAN SQUARE)

Each cell shows: 5 per cent point / **1 per cent point**

n_2	1	2	3	4	5	6	7	8	9	10	11	12	14	16	20	24	30	40	50	75	100	200	500	∞
1	161 / 4,052	200 / 4,999	216 / 5,403	225 / 5,625	230 / 5,764	234 / 5,859	237 / 5,928	239 / 5,981	241 / 6,022	242 / 6,056	243 / 6,082	244 / 6,106	245 / 6,142	246 / 6,169	248 / 6,208	249 / 6,234	250 / 6,258	251 / 6,286	252 / 6,302	253 / 6,323	253 / 6,334	254 / 6,352	254 / 6,361	254 / 6,366
2	18.51 / 98.49	19.00 / 99.00	19.16 / 99.17	19.25 / 99.25	19.30 / 99.30	19.33 / 99.33	19.36 / 99.34	19.37 / 99.36	19.38 / 99.38	19.39 / 99.40	19.40 / 99.41	19.41 / 99.42	19.42 / 99.43	19.43 / 99.44	19.44 / 99.45	19.45 / 99.46	19.46 / 99.47	19.47 / 99.48	19.47 / 99.48	19.48 / 99.49	19.49 / 99.49	19.49 / 99.49	19.50 / 99.50	19.50 / 99.50
3	10.13 / 34.12	9.55 / 30.82	9.28 / 29.46	9.12 / 28.71	9.01 / 28.24	8.94 / 27.91	8.88 / 27.67	8.84 / 27.49	8.81 / 27.34	8.78 / 27.23	8.76 / 27.13	8.74 / 27.05	8.71 / 26.92	8.69 / 26.83	8.66 / 26.69	8.64 / 26.60	8.62 / 26.50	8.60 / 26.41	8.58 / 26.35	8.57 / 26.27	8.56 / 26.23	8.54 / 26.18	8.54 / 26.14	8.53 / 26.12
4	7.71 / 21.20	6.94 / 18.00	6.59 / 16.69	6.39 / 15.98	6.26 / 15.52	6.16 / 15.21	6.09 / 14.98	6.04 / 14.80	6.00 / 14.66	5.96 / 14.54	5.93 / 14.45	5.91 / 14.37	5.87 / 14.24	5.84 / 14.15	5.80 / 14.02	5.77 / 13.93	5.74 / 13.83	5.71 / 13.74	5.70 / 13.69	5.68 / 13.61	5.66 / 13.57	5.65 / 13.52	5.64 / 13.48	5.63 / 13.46
5	6.61 / 16.26	5.79 / 13.27	5.41 / 12.06	5.19 / 11.39	5.05 / 10.97	4.95 / 10.67	4.88 / 10.45	4.82 / 10.27	4.78 / 10.15	4.74 / 10.05	4.70 / 9.96	4.68 / 9.89	4.64 / 9.77	4.60 / 9.68	4.56 / 9.55	4.53 / 9.47	4.50 / 9.38	4.46 / 9.29	4.44 / 9.24	4.42 / 9.17	4.40 / 9.13	4.38 / 9.07	4.37 / 9.04	4.36 / 9.02
6	5.99 / 13.74	5.14 / 10.92	4.76 / 9.78	4.53 / 9.15	4.39 / 8.75	4.28 / 8.47	4.21 / 8.26	4.15 / 8.10	4.10 / 7.98	4.06 / 7.87	4.03 / 7.79	4.00 / 7.72	3.96 / 7.60	3.92 / 7.52	3.87 / 7.39	3.84 / 7.31	3.81 / 7.23	3.77 / 7.14	3.75 / 7.09	3.72 / 7.02	3.71 / 6.99	3.69 / 6.94	3.68 / 6.90	3.67 / 6.88
7	5.59 / 12.25	4.74 / 9.55	4.35 / 8.45	4.12 / 7.85	3.97 / 7.46	3.87 / 7.19	3.79 / 7.00	3.73 / 6.84	3.68 / 6.71	3.63 / 6.62	3.60 / 6.54	3.57 / 6.47	3.52 / 6.35	3.49 / 6.27	3.44 / 6.15	3.41 / 6.07	3.38 / 5.98	3.34 / 5.90	3.32 / 5.85	3.29 / 5.78	3.28 / 5.75	3.25 / 5.70	3.24 / 5.67	3.23 / 5.65
8	5.32 / 11.26	4.46 / 8.65	4.07 / 7.59	3.84 / 7.01	3.69 / 6.63	3.58 / 6.37	3.50 / 6.19	3.44 / 6.03	3.39 / 5.91	3.34 / 5.82	3.31 / 5.74	3.28 / 5.67	3.23 / 5.56	3.20 / 5.48	3.15 / 5.36	3.12 / 5.28	3.08 / 5.20	3.05 / 5.11	3.03 / 5.06	3.00 / 5.00	2.98 / 4.96	2.96 / 4.91	2.94 / 4.88	2.93 / 4.86
9	5.12 / 10.56	4.26 / 8.02	3.86 / 6.99	3.63 / 6.42	3.48 / 6.06	3.37 / 5.80	3.29 / 5.62	3.23 / 5.47	3.18 / 5.35	3.13 / 5.26	3.10 / 5.18	3.07 / 5.11	3.02 / 5.00	2.98 / 4.92	2.93 / 4.80	2.90 / 4.73	2.86 / 4.64	2.82 / 4.56	2.80 / 4.51	2.77 / 4.45	2.76 / 4.41	2.73 / 4.36	2.72 / 4.33	2.71 / 4.31
10	4.96 / 10.04	4.10 / 7.56	3.71 / 6.55	3.48 / 5.99	3.33 / 5.64	3.22 / 5.39	3.14 / 5.21	3.07 / 5.06	3.02 / 4.95	2.97 / 4.85	2.94 / 4.78	2.91 / 4.71	2.86 / 4.60	2.82 / 4.52	2.77 / 4.41	2.74 / 4.33	2.70 / 4.25	2.67 / 4.17	2.64 / 4.12	2.61 / 4.05	2.59 / 4.01	2.56 / 3.96	2.55 / 3.93	2.54 / 3.91
11	4.84 / 9.65	3.98 / 7.20	3.59 / 6.22	3.36 / 5.67	3.20 / 5.32	3.09 / 5.07	3.01 / 4.88	2.95 / 4.74	2.90 / 4.63	2.86 / 4.54	2.82 / 4.46	2.79 / 4.40	2.74 / 4.29	2.70 / 4.21	2.65 / 4.10	2.61 / 4.02	2.57 / 3.94	2.53 / 3.86	2.50 / 3.80	2.47 / 3.74	2.45 / 3.70	2.42 / 3.66	2.41 / 3.62	2.40 / 3.60
12	4.75 / 9.33	3.88 / 6.93	3.49 / 5.95	3.26 / 5.41	3.11 / 5.06	3.00 / 4.82	2.92 / 4.65	2.85 / 4.50	2.80 / 4.39	2.76 / 4.30	2.72 / 4.22	2.69 / 4.16	2.64 / 4.05	2.60 / 3.98	2.54 / 3.86	2.50 / 3.78	2.46 / 3.70	2.42 / 3.61	2.40 / 3.56	2.36 / 3.49	2.35 / 3.46	2.32 / 3.41	2.31 / 3.38	2.30 / 3.36

552

The following is a rotated (landscape) numerical table. The figures 13–25 along both long edges are the row labels (shown at left and repeated at right). Each cell contains two stacked values (upper value over lower value). There are 24 unlabeled data columns per row.

Row	1	2	3	4	5	6	7	8	9	10	11	12	13	14	15	16	17	18	19	20	21	22	23	24
13	2.21/3.16	2.22/3.18	2.24/3.21	2.26/3.27	2.28/3.30	2.32/3.37	2.34/3.42	2.38/3.51	2.42/3.59	2.46/3.67	2.51/3.78	2.55/3.85	2.60/3.96	2.63/4.02	2.67/4.10	2.72/4.19	2.77/4.30	2.84/4.44	2.92/4.62	3.02/4.86	3.18/5.20	3.41/5.74	3.80/6.70	4.67/9.07
14	2.13/3.00	2.14/3.02	2.16/3.06	2.19/3.11	2.21/3.14	2.24/3.21	2.27/3.26	2.31/3.34	2.35/3.43	2.39/3.51	2.44/3.62	2.48/3.70	2.53/3.80	2.56/3.86	2.60/3.94	2.65/4.03	2.70/4.14	2.77/4.28	2.85/4.46	2.96/4.69	3.11/5.03	3.34/5.56	3.74/6.51	4.60/8.86
15	2.07/2.87	2.08/2.89	2.10/2.92	2.12/2.97	2.15/3.00	2.18/3.07	2.21/3.12	2.25/3.20	2.29/3.29	2.33/3.36	2.39/3.48	2.43/3.56	2.48/3.67	2.51/3.73	2.55/3.80	2.59/3.89	2.64/4.00	2.70/4.14	2.79/4.32	2.90/4.56	3.06/4.89	3.29/5.42	3.68/6.36	4.54/8.68
16	2.01/2.75	2.02/2.77	2.04/2.80	2.07/2.86	2.09/2.89	2.13/2.96	2.16/3.01	2.20/3.10	2.24/3.18	2.28/3.25	2.33/3.37	2.37/3.45	2.42/3.55	2.45/3.61	2.49/3.69	2.54/3.78	2.59/3.89	2.66/4.03	2.74/4.20	2.85/4.44	3.01/4.77	3.24/5.29	3.63/6.23	4.49/8.53
17	1.96/2.65	1.97/2.67	1.99/2.70	2.02/2.76	2.04/2.79	2.08/2.86	2.11/2.92	2.15/3.00	2.19/3.08	2.23/3.16	2.29/3.27	2.33/3.35	2.38/3.45	2.41/3.52	2.45/3.59	2.50/3.68	2.55/3.79	2.62/3.93	2.70/4.10	2.81/4.34	2.96/4.67	3.20/5.18	3.59/6.11	4.45/8.40
18	1.92/2.57	1.93/2.59	1.95/2.62	1.98/2.68	2.00/2.71	2.04/2.78	2.07/2.83	2.11/2.91	2.15/3.00	2.19/3.07	2.25/3.19	2.29/3.27	2.34/3.37	2.37/3.44	2.41/3.51	2.46/3.60	2.51/3.71	2.58/3.85	2.66/4.01	2.77/4.25	2.93/4.58	3.16/5.09	3.55/6.01	4.41/8.28
19	1.88/2.49	1.90/2.51	1.91/2.54	1.94/2.60	1.96/2.63	2.00/2.70	2.02/2.76	2.07/2.84	2.11/2.92	2.15/3.00	2.21/3.12	2.26/3.19	2.31/3.30	2.34/3.36	2.38/3.43	2.43/3.52	2.48/3.63	2.55/3.77	2.63/3.94	2.74/4.17	2.90/4.50	3.13/5.01	3.52/5.93	4.38/8.18
20	1.84/2.42	1.85/2.44	1.87/2.47	1.90/2.53	1.92/2.56	1.96/2.63	1.99/2.69	2.04/2.77	2.08/2.86	2.12/2.94	2.18/3.05	2.23/3.13	2.28/3.23	2.31/3.30	2.35/3.37	2.40/3.45	2.45/3.56	2.52/3.71	2.60/3.87	2.71/4.10	2.87/4.43	3.10/4.94	3.49/5.85	4.35/8.10
21	1.81/2.36	1.82/2.38	1.84/2.42	1.87/2.47	1.89/2.51	1.93/2.58	1.96/2.63	2.00/2.72	2.05/2.80	2.09/2.88	2.15/2.99	2.20/3.07	2.25/3.17	2.28/3.24	2.32/3.31	2.37/3.40	2.42/3.51	2.49/3.65	2.57/3.81	2.68/4.04	2.84/4.37	3.07/4.87	3.47/5.78	4.32/8.02
22	1.78/2.31	1.80/2.33	1.81/2.37	1.84/2.42	1.87/2.46	1.91/2.53	1.93/2.58	1.98/2.67	2.03/2.75	2.07/2.83	2.13/2.94	2.18/3.02	2.23/3.12	2.26/3.18	2.30/3.26	2.35/3.35	2.40/3.45	2.47/3.59	2.55/3.76	2.66/3.99	2.82/4.31	3.05/4.82	3.44/5.72	4.30/7.94
23	1.76/2.26	1.77/2.28	1.79/2.32	1.82/2.37	1.84/2.41	1.86/2.48	1.89/2.53	1.96/2.62	2.00/2.70	2.04/2.78	2.09/2.89	2.14/2.97	2.20/3.07	2.24/3.14	2.26/3.17	2.32/3.30	2.38/3.41	2.45/3.54	2.53/3.71	2.64/3.94	2.80/4.26	3.03/4.76	3.42/5.66	4.28/7.88
24	1.73/2.21	1.74/2.23	1.76/2.27	1.80/2.33	1.82/2.36	1.84/2.44	1.87/2.48	1.94/2.58	1.98/2.66	2.02/2.74	2.06/2.85	2.13/2.93	2.18/3.03	2.22/3.09	2.24/3.13	2.30/3.25	2.36/3.37	2.43/3.50	2.51/3.67	2.62/3.90	2.78/4.22	3.01/4.72	3.40/5.61	4.26/7.82
25	1.71/2.17	1.72/2.19	1.74/2.23	1.77/2.29	1.80/2.32	1.82/2.40	1.84/2.44	1.92/2.54	1.96/2.62	2.00/2.70	2.06/2.81	2.11/2.89	2.16/2.99	2.20/3.05	2.22/3.09	2.28/3.21	2.34/3.32	2.41/3.46	2.49/3.63	2.60/3.86	2.76/4.18	2.99/4.68	3.38/5.57	4.24/7.77

Table A4—(Cont.)

5 AND 1 PER CENT SIGNIFICANCE POINTS OF F*

(5 per cent points are in roman type; 1 per cent points are in boldface type)

n_1 DEGREES OF FREEDOM (FOR GREATER MEAN SQUARE)

n_2	1	2	3	4	5	6	7	8	9	10	11	12	14	16	20	24	30	40	50	75	100	200	500	∞
26	4.22 **7.72**	3.37 **5.53**	2.98 **4.64**	2.74 **4.14**	2.59 **3.82**	2.47 **3.59**	2.39 **3.42**	2.32 **3.29**	2.27 **3.17**	2.22 **3.09**	2.18 **3.02**	2.15 **2.96**	2.10 **2.86**	2.05 **2.77**	1.99 **2.66**	1.95 **2.58**	1.90 **2.50**	1.85 **2.41**	1.82 **2.36**	1.78 **2.28**	1.76 **2.25**	1.72 **2.19**	1.70 **2.15**	1.69 **2.13**
27	4.21 **7.68**	3.35 **5.49**	2.96 **4.60**	2.73 **4.11**	2.57 **3.79**	2.46 **3.56**	2.37 **3.39**	2.30 **3.26**	2.25 **3.14**	2.20 **3.06**	2.16 **2.98**	2.13 **2.93**	2.08 **2.83**	2.03 **2.74**	1.97 **2.63**	1.93 **2.55**	1.88 **2.47**	1.84 **2.38**	1.80 **2.33**	1.76 **2.25**	1.74 **2.21**	1.71 **2.16**	1.68 **2.12**	1.67 **2.10**
28	4.20 **7.64**	3.34 **5.45**	2.95 **4.57**	2.71 **4.07**	2.56 **3.76**	2.44 **3.53**	2.36 **3.36**	2.29 **3.23**	2.24 **3.11**	2.19 **3.03**	2.15 **2.95**	2.12 **2.90**	2.06 **2.80**	2.02 **2.71**	1.96 **2.60**	1.91 **2.52**	1.87 **2.44**	1.81 **2.35**	1.78 **2.30**	1.75 **2.22**	1.72 **2.18**	1.69 **2.13**	1.67 **2.09**	1.65 **2.06**
29	4.18 **7.60**	3.33 **5.42**	2.93 **4.54**	2.70 **4.04**	2.54 **3.73**	2.43 **3.50**	2.35 **3.33**	2.28 **3.20**	2.22 **3.08**	2.18 **3.00**	2.14 **2.92**	2.10 **2.87**	2.05 **2.77**	2.00 **2.68**	1.94 **2.57**	1.90 **2.49**	1.85 **2.41**	1.80 **2.32**	1.77 **2.27**	1.73 **2.19**	1.71 **2.15**	1.68 **2.10**	1.65 **2.06**	1.64 **2.03**
30	4.17 **7.56**	3.32 **5.39**	2.92 **4.51**	2.69 **4.02**	2.53 **3.70**	2.42 **3.47**	2.34 **3.30**	2.27 **3.17**	2.21 **3.06**	2.16 **2.98**	2.12 **2.90**	2.09 **2.84**	2.04 **2.74**	1.99 **2.66**	1.93 **2.55**	1.89 **2.47**	1.84 **2.38**	1.79 **2.29**	1.76 **2.24**	1.72 **2.16**	1.69 **2.13**	1.66 **2.07**	1.64 **2.03**	1.62 **2.01**
32	4.15 **7.50**	3.30 **5.34**	2.90 **4.46**	2.67 **3.97**	2.51 **3.66**	2.40 **3.42**	2.32 **3.25**	2.25 **3.12**	2.19 **3.01**	2.14 **2.94**	2.10 **2.86**	2.07 **2.80**	2.02 **2.70**	1.97 **2.62**	1.91 **2.51**	1.86 **2.42**	1.82 **2.34**	1.76 **2.25**	1.74 **2.20**	1.69 **2.12**	1.67 **2.08**	1.64 **2.02**	1.61 **1.98**	1.59 **1.96**
34	4.13 **7.44**	3.28 **5.29**	2.88 **4.42**	2.65 **3.93**	2.49 **3.61**	2.38 **3.38**	2.30 **3.21**	2.23 **3.08**	2.17 **2.97**	2.12 **2.89**	2.08 **2.82**	2.05 **2.76**	2.00 **2.66**	1.95 **2.58**	1.89 **2.47**	1.84 **2.38**	1.80 **2.30**	1.74 **2.21**	1.71 **2.15**	1.67 **2.08**	1.64 **2.04**	1.61 **1.98**	1.59 **1.94**	1.57 **1.91**
36	4.11 **7.39**	3.26 **5.25**	2.86 **4.38**	2.63 **3.89**	2.48 **3.58**	2.36 **3.35**	2.28 **3.18**	2.21 **3.04**	2.15 **2.94**	2.10 **2.86**	2.06 **2.78**	2.03 **2.72**	1.98 **2.62**	1.93 **2.54**	1.87 **2.43**	1.82 **2.35**	1.78 **2.26**	1.72 **2.17**	1.69 **2.12**	1.65 **2.04**	1.62 **2.00**	1.59 **1.94**	1.56 **1.90**	1.55 **1.87**
38	4.10 **7.35**	3.25 **5.21**	2.85 **4.34**	2.62 **3.86**	2.46 **3.54**	2.35 **3.32**	2.26 **3.15**	2.19 **3.02**	2.14 **2.91**	2.09 **2.82**	2.05 **2.75**	2.02 **2.69**	1.96 **2.59**	1.92 **2.51**	1.85 **2.40**	1.80 **2.32**	1.76 **2.22**	1.71 **2.14**	1.67 **2.08**	1.63 **2.00**	1.60 **1.97**	1.57 **1.90**	1.54 **1.86**	1.53 **1.84**
40	4.08 **7.31**	3.23 **5.18**	2.84 **4.31**	2.61 **3.83**	2.45 **3.51**	2.34 **3.29**	2.25 **3.12**	2.18 **2.99**	2.12 **2.88**	2.07 **2.80**	2.04 **2.73**	2.00 **2.66**	1.95 **2.56**	1.90 **2.49**	1.84 **2.37**	1.79 **2.29**	1.74 **2.20**	1.69 **2.11**	1.66 **2.05**	1.61 **1.97**	1.59 **1.94**	1.55 **1.88**	1.53 **1.84**	1.51 **1.81**
42	4.07 **7.27**	3.22 **5.15**	2.83 **4.29**	2.59 **3.80**	2.44 **3.49**	2.32 **3.26**	2.24 **3.10**	2.17 **2.96**	2.11 **2.86**	2.06 **2.77**	2.02 **2.70**	1.99 **2.64**	1.94 **2.54**	1.89 **2.46**	1.82 **2.35**	1.78 **2.26**	1.73 **2.17**	1.68 **2.08**	1.64 **2.02**	1.60 **1.94**	1.57 **1.91**	1.54 **1.85**	1.51 **1.80**	1.49 **1.78**
44	4.06 **7.24**	3.21 **5.12**	2.82 **4.26**	2.58 **3.78**	2.43 **3.46**	2.31 **3.24**	2.23 **3.07**	2.16 **2.94**	2.10 **2.84**	2.05 **2.75**	2.01 **2.68**	1.98 **2.62**	1.92 **2.52**	1.88 **2.44**	1.81 **2.32**	1.76 **2.24**	1.72 **2.15**	1.66 **2.06**	1.63 **2.00**	1.58 **1.92**	1.56 **1.88**	1.52 **1.82**	1.50 **1.78**	1.48 **1.75**

F-distribution critical values (5% roman type, 1% boldface type). Denominator degrees of freedom (df) shown at left; each cell lists the 5% point over the 1% point.

df	1	2	3	4	5	6	7	8	9	10	11	12	14	16	20	24	30	40	50	75	100	200	500	∞
46	4.05 / 7.21	3.20 / 5.10	2.81 / 4.24	2.57 / 3.76	2.42 / 3.44	2.30 / 3.22	2.22 / 3.05	2.14 / 2.92	2.09 / 2.82	2.04 / 2.73	2.00 / 2.66	1.97 / 2.60	1.91 / 2.50	1.87 / 2.42	1.80 / 2.30	1.75 / 2.22	1.71 / 2.13	1.65 / 2.04	1.62 / 1.98	1.57 / 1.90	1.54 / 1.86	1.51 / 1.80	1.48 / 1.76	1.46 / 1.72
48	4.04 / 7.19	3.19 / 5.08	2.80 / 4.22	2.56 / 3.74	2.41 / 3.42	2.30 / 3.20	2.21 / 3.04	2.14 / 2.90	2.08 / 2.80	2.03 / 2.71	1.99 / 2.64	1.96 / 2.58	1.90 / 2.48	1.86 / 2.40	1.79 / 2.28	1.74 / 2.20	1.70 / 2.11	1.64 / 2.02	1.61 / 1.96	1.56 / 1.88	1.53 / 1.84	1.50 / 1.78	1.47 / 1.73	1.45 / 1.70
50	4.03 / 7.17	3.18 / 5.06	2.79 / 4.20	2.56 / 3.72	2.40 / 3.41	2.29 / 3.18	2.20 / 3.02	2.13 / 2.88	2.07 / 2.78	2.02 / 2.70	1.98 / 2.62	1.95 / 2.56	1.90 / 2.46	1.85 / 2.39	1.78 / 2.26	1.74 / 2.18	1.69 / 2.10	1.63 / 2.00	1.60 / 1.94	1.55 / 1.86	1.52 / 1.82	1.48 / 1.76	1.46 / 1.71	1.44 / 1.68
55	4.02 / 7.12	3.17 / 5.01	2.78 / 4.16	2.54 / 3.68	2.38 / 3.37	2.27 / 3.15	2.18 / 2.98	2.11 / 2.85	2.05 / 2.75	2.00 / 2.66	1.97 / 2.59	1.93 / 2.53	1.88 / 2.43	1.83 / 2.35	1.76 / 2.23	1.72 / 2.15	1.67 / 2.06	1.61 / 1.96	1.58 / 1.90	1.52 / 1.82	1.50 / 1.78	1.46 / 1.71	1.43 / 1.66	1.41 / 1.64
60	4.00 / 7.08	3.15 / 4.98	2.76 / 4.13	2.52 / 3.65	2.37 / 3.34	2.25 / 3.12	2.17 / 2.95	2.10 / 2.82	2.04 / 2.72	1.99 / 2.63	1.95 / 2.56	1.92 / 2.50	1.86 / 2.40	1.81 / 2.32	1.75 / 2.20	1.70 / 2.12	1.65 / 2.03	1.59 / 1.93	1.56 / 1.87	1.50 / 1.79	1.48 / 1.74	1.44 / 1.68	1.41 / 1.63	1.39 / 1.60
65	3.99 / 7.04	3.14 / 4.95	2.75 / 4.10	2.51 / 3.62	2.36 / 3.31	2.24 / 3.09	2.15 / 2.93	2.08 / 2.79	2.02 / 2.70	1.98 / 2.61	1.94 / 2.54	1.90 / 2.47	1.85 / 2.37	1.80 / 2.30	1.73 / 2.18	1.68 / 2.09	1.63 / 2.00	1.57 / 1.90	1.54 / 1.84	1.49 / 1.76	1.46 / 1.71	1.42 / 1.64	1.39 / 1.60	1.37 / 1.56
70	3.98 / 7.01	3.13 / 4.92	2.74 / 4.08	2.50 / 3.60	2.35 / 3.29	2.23 / 3.07	2.14 / 2.91	2.07 / 2.77	2.01 / 2.67	1.97 / 2.59	1.93 / 2.51	1.89 / 2.45	1.84 / 2.35	1.79 / 2.28	1.72 / 2.15	1.67 / 2.07	1.62 / 1.98	1.56 / 1.88	1.53 / 1.82	1.47 / 1.74	1.45 / 1.69	1.40 / 1.62	1.37 / 1.56	1.35 / 1.53
80	3.96 / 6.96	3.11 / 4.88	2.72 / 4.04	2.48 / 3.56	2.33 / 3.25	2.21 / 3.04	2.12 / 2.87	2.05 / 2.74	1.99 / 2.64	1.95 / 2.55	1.91 / 2.48	1.88 / 2.41	1.82 / 2.32	1.77 / 2.24	1.70 / 2.11	1.65 / 2.03	1.60 / 1.94	1.54 / 1.84	1.51 / 1.78	1.45 / 1.70	1.42 / 1.65	1.38 / 1.57	1.35 / 1.52	1.32 / 1.49
100	3.94 / 6.90	3.09 / 4.82	2.70 / 3.98	2.46 / 3.51	2.30 / 3.20	2.19 / 2.99	2.10 / 2.82	2.03 / 2.69	1.97 / 2.59	1.92 / 2.51	1.88 / 2.43	1.85 / 2.36	1.79 / 2.26	1.75 / 2.19	1.68 / 2.06	1.63 / 1.98	1.57 / 1.89	1.51 / 1.79	1.48 / 1.73	1.42 / 1.64	1.39 / 1.59	1.34 / 1.51	1.30 / 1.46	1.28 / 1.43
125	3.92 / 6.84	3.07 / 4.78	2.68 / 3.94	2.44 / 3.47	2.29 / 3.17	2.17 / 2.95	2.08 / 2.79	2.01 / 2.65	1.95 / 2.56	1.90 / 2.47	1.86 / 2.40	1.83 / 2.33	1.77 / 2.23	1.72 / 2.15	1.65 / 2.03	1.60 / 1.94	1.55 / 1.85	1.49 / 1.75	1.45 / 1.68	1.39 / 1.59	1.36 / 1.54	1.31 / 1.46	1.27 / 1.40	1.25 / 1.37
150	3.91 / 6.81	3.06 / 4.75	2.67 / 3.91	2.43 / 3.44	2.27 / 3.14	2.16 / 2.92	2.07 / 2.76	2.00 / 2.62	1.94 / 2.53	1.89 / 2.44	1.85 / 2.37	1.82 / 2.30	1.76 / 2.20	1.71 / 2.12	1.64 / 2.00	1.59 / 1.91	1.54 / 1.83	1.47 / 1.72	1.44 / 1.66	1.37 / 1.56	1.34 / 1.51	1.29 / 1.43	1.25 / 1.37	1.22 / 1.33
200	3.89 / 6.76	3.04 / 4.71	2.65 / 3.88	2.41 / 3.41	2.26 / 3.11	2.14 / 2.90	2.05 / 2.73	1.98 / 2.60	1.92 / 2.50	1.87 / 2.41	1.83 / 2.34	1.80 / 2.28	1.74 / 2.17	1.69 / 2.09	1.62 / 1.97	1.57 / 1.88	1.52 / 1.79	1.45 / 1.69	1.42 / 1.62	1.35 / 1.53	1.32 / 1.48	1.26 / 1.39	1.22 / 1.33	1.19 / 1.28
400	3.86 / 6.70	3.02 / 4.66	2.62 / 3.83	2.39 / 3.36	2.23 / 3.06	2.12 / 2.85	2.03 / 2.69	1.96 / 2.55	1.90 / 2.46	1.85 / 2.37	1.81 / 2.29	1.78 / 2.23	1.72 / 2.12	1.67 / 2.04	1.60 / 1.92	1.54 / 1.84	1.49 / 1.74	1.42 / 1.64	1.38 / 1.57	1.32 / 1.47	1.28 / 1.42	1.22 / 1.32	1.16 / 1.24	1.13 / 1.19
1000	3.85 / 6.66	3.00 / 4.62	2.61 / 3.80	2.38 / 3.34	2.22 / 3.04	2.10 / 2.82	2.02 / 2.66	1.95 / 2.53	1.89 / 2.43	1.84 / 2.34	1.80 / 2.26	1.76 / 2.20	1.70 / 2.09	1.65 / 2.01	1.58 / 1.89	1.53 / 1.81	1.47 / 1.71	1.41 / 1.61	1.36 / 1.54	1.30 / 1.44	1.26 / 1.38	1.19 / 1.28	1.13 / 1.19	1.08 / 1.11
∞	3.84 / 6.64	2.99 / 4.60	2.60 / 3.78	2.37 / 3.32	2.21 / 3.02	2.09 / 2.80	2.01 / 2.64	1.94 / 2.51	1.88 / 2.41	1.83 / 2.32	1.79 / 2.24	1.75 / 2.18	1.69 / 2.07	1.64 / 1.99	1.57 / 1.87	1.52 / 1.79	1.46 / 1.69	1.40 / 1.59	1.35 / 1.52	1.28 / 1.41	1.24 / 1.36	1.17 / 1.25	1.11 / 1.15	1.00 / 1.00

555

* Reproduced through the courtesy of the author and the publisher from G. W. Snedecor, *Statistical Methods*, Collegiate Press, Inc., of Iowa State University, Ames, Iowa, 1946, Table 10.7.

Table A5

5 AND 1 PER CENT SIGNIFICANCE POINTS FOR THE RATIO OF THE MEAN-SQUARE SUCCESSIVE-DIFFERENCE TO THE VARIANCE*

At the given level of significance and the appropriate sample size (N), a computed K is indicative of positive serial correlation if it falls below the critical value of K, and is indicative of negative serial correlation if it exceeds the corresponding critical value of K'; if it falls between the two critical values, no evidence of serial correlation is present.

N	VALUES OF K		VALUES OF K'		N	VALUES OF K		VALUES OF K'	
	$P = 0.01$	$P = 0.05$	$P = 0.95$	$P = 0.99$		$P = 0.01$	$P = 0.05$	$P = 0.95$	$P = 0.99$
4	0.8341	1.0406	4.2927	4.4992	33	1.2667	1.4885	2.6365	2.8583
5	0.6724	1.0255	3.9745	4.3276	34	1.2761	1.4951	2.6262	2.8451
6	0.6738	1.0682	3.7318	4.1262	35	1.2852	1.5014	2.6163	2.8324
7	0.7163	1.0919	3.5748	3.9504	36	1.2940	1.5075	2.6068	2.8202
8	0.7575	1.1228	3.4486	3.8139	37	1.3025	1.5135	2.5977	2.8085
9	0.7974	1.1524	3.3476	3.7025	38	1.3108	1.5193	2.5889	2.7973
10	0.8353	1.1803	3.2642	3.6091	39	1.3188	1.5249	2.5804	2.7865
11	0.8706	1.2062	3.1938	3.5294	40	1.3266	1.5304	2.5722	2.7760
12	0.9033	1.2301	3.1335	3.4603	41	1.3342	1.5357	2.5643	2.7658
13	0.9336	1.2521	3.0812	3.3996	42	1.3415	1.5408	2.5567	2.7560
14	0.9618	1.2725	3.0352	3.3458	43	1.3486	1.5458	2.5494	2.7466
15	0.9880	1.2914	2.9943	3.2977	44	1.3554	1.5506	2.5424	2.7376
16	1.0124	1.3090	2.9577	3.2543	45	1.3620	1.5552	2.5357	2.7289
17	1.0352	1.3253	2.9247	3.2148	46	1.3684	1.5596	2.5293	2.7205
18	1.0566	1.3405	2.8948	3.1787	47	1.3745	1.5638	2.5232	2.7125
19	1.0766	1.3547	2.8675	3.1456	48	1.3802	1.5678	2.5173	2.7049
20	1.0954	1.3680	2.8425	3.1151	49	1.3856	1.5716	2.5117	2.6977
21	1.1131	1.3805	2.8195	3.0869	50	1.3907	1.5752	2.5064	2.6908
22	1.1298	1.3923	2.7982	3.0607	51	1.3957	1.5787	2.5013	2.6842
23	1.1456	1.4035	2.7784	3.0362	52	1.4007	1.5822	2.4963	2.6777
24	1.1606	1.4141	2.7599	3.0133	53	1.4057	1.5856	2.4914	2.6712
25	1.1748	1.4241	2.7426	2.9919	54	1.4107	1.5890	2.4866	2.6648
26	1.1883	1.4336	2.7264	2.9718	55	1.4156	1.5923	2.4819	2.6585
27	1.2012	1.4426	2.7112	2.9528	56	1.4203	1.5955	2.4773	2.6524
28	1.2135	1.4512	2.6969	2.9348	57	1.4249	1.5987	2.4728	2.6465
29	1.2252	1.4594	2.6834	2.9177	58	1.4294	1.6019	2.4684	2.6407
30	1.2363	1.4672	1.6707	2.9016	59	1.4339	1.6051	2.4640	2.6350
31	1.2469	1.4746	2.6587	2.8864	60	1.4384	1.6082	2.4596	2.6294
32	1.2570	1.4817	2.6473	2.8720					

* Adapted, with the kind permission of the editor, from B. I. HART, "Significance Levels for the Ratio of the Mean Square Successive Difference to the Variance," *Annals of Mathematical Statistics*, Vol. 13, No. 4, 1942, p. 446.

Table A6

MEAN VALUE OF RATIO SIGMA/RANGE AND 5 PER CENT, 2.5 PER CENT, AND 1 PER CENT SIGNIFICANCE POINTS*

[Estimate of σ in the population = $a_n \times$ range (or mean range)]

The values in the body of the table are in units of the range. The corresponding percentages indicate the proportion of the area under the particular curve lying beyond the values of the range. Thus, for $n = 6$, 5 per cent of the area under this distribution curve lies beyond 0.8 range. Confidence intervals are constructed accordingly. As an example, for a sample of eight observations, there would be 95 chances out of 100 that the interval, 0.709 range to 0.217 range, contains the true value of the standard deviation; or there would be 95 chances out of 100 that the true value of the standard deviation is not more than 0.625 times the observed range.

Size of Sample n	a_n	LOWER PERCENTAGE POINTS			UPPER PERCENTAGE POINTS		
		1.0	2.5	5.0	5.0	2.5	1.0
2	0.8862	0.275	0.315	0.361	11.111	25.000	50.000
3	0.5908	0.243	0.272	0.302	2.326	3.333	5.263
4	0.4857	0.227	0.251	0.275	1.316	1.695	2.326
5	0.4299	0.217	0.238	0.259	0.971	1.176	1.515
6	0.3946	0.210	0.229	0.248	0.800	0.943	1.149
7	0.3698	0.205	0.223	0.240	0.694	0.800	0.952
8	0.3512	0.200	0.217	0.233	0.625	0.709	0.833
9	0.3367	0.197	0.213	0.228	0.575	0.645	0.746
10	0.3249	0.194	0.209	0.224	0.538	0.599	0.680
11	0.3152	0.191	0.206	0.220	0.508	0.562	0.633
12	0.3069	0.189	0.203	0.216	0.483	0.532	0.595
13	0.2998	0.187	0.200	0.213	0.463	0.505	0.565
14	0.2935	0.185	0.198	0.211	0.446	0.485	0.538
15	0.2880	0.183	0.196	0.209	0.431	0.467	0.518
16	0.2831	0.182	0.195	0.206	0.418	0.454	0.498
17	0.2787	0.180	0.193	0.204	0.408	0.439	0.483
18	0.2747	0.179	0.192	0.203	0.398	0.427	0.467
19	0.2711	0.178	0.190	0.201	0.389	0.417	0.454
20	0.2677	0.177	0.189	0.200	0.380	0.408	0.444

* Adapted with the kind permission of Prof. E. S. PEARSON, editor of *Biometrika*, from E. S. PEARSON, "The Percentage Limits for the Distribution of the Range in Samples from a Normal Population," *Biometrika*, Vol. 24, 1932, pp. 404–417, and E. S. PEARSON, "The Probability Integral of the Range in Samples of n Observations from a Normal Population," *Biometrika*, Vol. 32, 1941–1942, pp. 301–308. The values at significance points are the reciprocals of the corresponding values, range/sigma, contained in Professor PEARSON's tables.

Table A7
RANDOM DIGITS (15,126–17,375)*

33591	59785	12833	98932	68064
58418	90331	55858	04015	21454
64446	51017	22280	75597	50227
72136	00303	38880	93327	49522
98626	82484	54610	07211	78610
58393	20225	05436	46172	88951
37346	51007	38032	36002	21080
70712	44236	96795	92351	92844
93585	09918	30983	44282	66849
09473	72923	16747	49802	50639
40229	34921	60405	06803	19332
39795	77221	10012	40798	33864
10288	57483	10881	58984	45136
75702	69428	34047	76224	45887
18129	93659	58389	19715	66259
17777	41004	47057	30688	07539
75195	62294	03371	11672	13089
09722	67635	12114	63055	09214
78800	86912	42076	50287	97998
94287	54751	36242	36557	85664
35997	30761	97081	09501	68887
88241	30402	12318	52430	40139
54382	73370	26184	14024	57444
77681	74946	02099	69091	19372
53148	26074	52293	65359	63971
27212	89889	46933	13364	33883
03867	03105	87912	29610	75108
79895	82633	19209	21548	35022
55256	69386	57453	70147	73538
75937	31113	07607	48037	71020
83389	80236	65972	74528	40888
37363	30345	79933	71058	34826
21960	95585	40374	13239	56162
49562	44137	46625	20031	08524
22666	27414	30980	74485	26480
55386	95918	92481	49234	62616
97725	69513	36950	63526	93824
04703	95851	90956	64424	95979
20077	65817	99523	73180	59978
21343	30031	18840	99260	21284
54021	29008	83672	53679	96395
71820	11033	20183	08804	29493
17709	94849	31771	23244	81585
08254	78963	95437	30231	59108
81351	70961	10255	60437	84576

Table A7—(Cont.)
RANDOM DIGITS (15,126–17,375)*

30665	43699	03593	29165	59990
09069	78653	90094	42735	82876
50593	14698	04737	72551	36417
49578	18100	59836	73221	91696
58388	40915	94507	32209	11548
36995	36202	07971	67001	62062
66348	87666	78055	44485	82955
45457	78252	98239	40000	75563
35406	59553	57852	07506	00009
09678	24538	52426	84852	83781
31604	55850	25644	44972	62275
05523	34355	75127	69797	71419
09458	29207	43632	32905	38513
74086	24077	21369	93541	75329
89299	30765	00348	01134	71581
78089	36887	65867	08595	47390
62067	41248	78667	95282	05622
18924	44409	45345	04972	52794
78656	18550	37171	13483	56058
68420	16483	26482	85964	71336
39182	51174	98146	42953	06606
26224	19972	13442	69662	76755
15737	00496	57764	52052	12835
51093	62290	38948	47473	16618
67799	28342	14551	44149	29854
23875	56766	01932	90063	31883
13701	95168	13169	42055	75609
37741	86434	22400	92732	99851
42479	47405	14055	75427	34464
76691	33263	62048	70917	97697
86707	18895	81790	71294	74832
92564	39987	02283	89970	28776
94648	05598	32171	28793	36746
29838	10664	28050	60122	13409
36368	17792	84792	76594	74110
09254	07510	51039	91683	84500
41486	58524	54508	20707	58504
90794	51934	03295	26582	16300
58558	84833	17105	46659	25003
52392	53546	70291	98846	67315
46095	19501	56181	85351	05023
09925	96974	34321	05454	12862
70550	42483	71204	99628	40642
50281	83708	27298	92651	95086
22767	26514	56322	78635	63731

* From *A Million Random Digits*, by the Rand Corporation, Santa Monica, California.

Table A8
LOGARITHMS TO THE BASE 10

	0	1	2	3	4	5	6	7	8	9
10	0000	0043	0086	0128	0170	0212	0253	0294	0334	0374
11	0414	0453	0492	0531	0569	0607	0645	0682	0719	0755
12	0792	0828	0864	0899	0934	0969	1004	1038	1072	1106
13	1139	1173	1206	1239	1271	1303	1335	1367	1399	1430
14	1461	1492	1523	1553	1584	1614	1644	1673	1703	1732
15	1761	1790	1818	1847	1875	1903	1931	1959	1987	2014
16	2041	2068	2095	2122	2148	2175	2201	2227	2253	2279
17	2304	2330	2355	2380	2405	2430	2455	2480	2504	2529
18	2553	2577	2601	2625	2648	2672	2695	2718	2742	2765
19	2788	2810	2833	2856	2878	2900	2923	2945	2967	2989
20	3010	3032	3054	3075	3096	3118	3139	3160	3181	3201
21	3222	3243	3263	3284	3304	3324	3345	3365	3385	3404
22	3424	3444	3464	3483	3502	3522	3541	3560	3579	3598
23	3617	3636	3655	3674	3692	3711	3729	3747	3766	3784
24	3802	3820	3838	3856	3874	3892	3909	3927	3945	3962
25	3979	3997	4014	4031	4048	4065	4082	4099	4116	4133
26	4150	4166	4183	4200	4216	4232	4249	4265	4281	4298
27	4314	4330	4346	4362	4378	4393	4409	4425	4440	4456
28	4472	4487	4502	4518	4533	4548	4564	4579	4594	4609
29	4624	4639	4654	4669	4683	4698	5713	4728	4742	4757
30	4771	4786	4800	4814	4829	4843	4857	4871	4886	4900
31	4914	4928	4942	4955	4969	4983	4997	5011	5024	5038
32	5051	5065	5079	5092	5105	5119	5132	5145	5159	5172
33	5185	5198	5211	5224	5237	5250	5263	5276	5289	5302
34	5315	5328	5340	5353	5366	5378	5391	5403	5416	5428
35	5441	5453	5465	5478	5490	5502	5514	5527	5539	5551
36	5563	5575	5587	5599	5611	5623	5635	5647	5658	5670
37	5682	5694	5705	5717	5729	5740	5752	5763	5775	5786
38	5798	5809	5821	5832	5843	5855	5866	5877	5888	5899
39	5911	5922	5933	5944	5955	5966	5977	5988	5999	6010
40	6021	6031	6042	6053	6064	6075	6085	6096	6107	6117
41	6128	6138	6149	6160	6170	6180	6191	6201	6212	6222
42	6232	6243	6253	6263	6274	6284	6294	6304	6314	6325
43	6335	6345	6355	6365	6375	6385	6395	6405	6415	6425
44	6435	6444	6454	6464	6474	6484	6493	6503	6513	6522
45	6532	6542	6551	6561	6571	6580	6590	6599	6609	6618
46	6628	6637	6646	6656	6665	6675	6684	6693	6702	6712
47	6721	6730	6739	6749	6758	6767	6776	6785	6794	6803
48	6812	6821	6830	6839	6848	6857	6866	6875	6884	6893
49	6902	6911	6920	6928	6937	6946	6955	6964	6972	6981
50	6990	6998	7007	7016	7024	7033	7042	7050	7059	7067
51	7076	7084	7093	7101	7110	7118	7126	7135	7143	7152
52	7160	7168	7177	7185	7193	7202	7210	7218	7226	7235
53	7243	7251	7259	7267	7275	7284	7292	7300	7308	7316
54	7324	7332	7340	7348	7356	7364	7372	7380	7388	7396

LOGARITHMS TO THE BASE 10

	0	1	2	3	4	5	6	7	8	9
55	7404	7412	7419	7427	7435	7443	7451	7459	7466	7474
56	7482	7490	7497	7505	7513	7520	7528	7536	7543	7551
57	7559	7566	7574	7582	7589	7597	7604	7612	7619	7627
58	7634	7642	7649	7657	7664	7672	7679	7686	7694	7701
59	7709	7716	7723	7731	7738	7745	7752	7760	7767	7774
60	7782	7789	7796	7803	7810	7818	7825	7832	7839	7846
61	7853	7860	7868	7875	7882	7889	7896	7903	7910	7917
62	7924	7931	7938	7945	7952	7959	7966	7973	7980	7987
63	7993	8000	8007	8014	8021	8028	8035	8041	8048	8055
64	8062	8069	8075	8082	8089	8096	8102	8109	8116	8122
65	8129	8136	8142	8149	8156	8162	8169	8176	8182	8189
66	8195	8202	8209	8215	8222	8228	8235	8241	8248	8254
67	8261	8267	8274	8280	8287	8293	8299	8306	8312	8319
68	8325	8331	8338	8344	8351	8357	8363	8370	8376	8382
69	8388	8395	8401	8407	8414	8420	8426	8423	8439	8445
70	8451	8457	8463	8470	8476	8482	8488	8494	8500	8506
71	8513	8519	8525	8531	8537	8543	8549	8555	8561	8567
72	8573	8579	8585	8591	8597	8603	8609	8615	8621	8627
73	8633	8639	8645	8651	8657	8663	8669	8675	8681	8686
74	8692	8698	8704	8710	8716	8722	8727	8733	8739	8745
75	8751	8756	8762	8768	8774	8779	8785	8791	8797	8802
76	8808	8814	8820	8825	8831	8837	8842	8848	8854	8859
77	8865	8871	8876	8882	8887	8893	8899	8904	8910	8915
78	8921	8927	8932	8938	8943	8949	8954	8960	8965	8971
79	8976	8982	8987	8993	8998	9004	9009	9015	9020	9025
80	9031	9036	9042	9047	9053	9058	9063	9069	9074	9079
81	9085	9090	9096	9101	9106	9112	9117	9122	9128	9133
82	9138	9143	9149	9154	9159	9165	9170	9175	9180	9186
83	9191	9196	9201	9206	9212	9217	9222	9227	9232	9238
84	9243	9248	9253	9258	9263	9269	9274	9279	9284	9289
85	9294	9299	9304	9309	9315	9320	9325	9330	9335	9340
86	9345	9350	9355	9360	9365	9370	9375	9380	9385	9390
87	9395	9400	9405	9410	9415	9420	9425	9430	9435	9440
88	9445	9450	9455	9460	9465	9469	9474	9479	9484	9489
89	9494	9499	9504	9509	9513	9518	9523	9528	9533	9538
90	9542	9547	9552	9557	9562	9566	9571	9576	9581	9586
91	9590	9595	9600	9605	9609	9614	9619	9624	9628	9633
92	9638	9643	9647	9652	9657	9661	9666	9671	9675	9680
93	9685	9689	9694	9699	9703	9708	9713	9717	9722	9727
94	9731	9736	9741	9745	9750	9754	9759	9763	9768	9773
95	9777	9782	9786	9791	9795	9800	9805	9809	9814	9818
96	9823	9827	9832	9835	9841	9845	9850	9854	9859	9863
97	9868	9872	9877	9881	9886	9890	9894	9899	9903	9908
98	9912	9917	9921	9926	9930	9934	9939	9943	9948	9952
99	9956	9961	9965	9969	9974	9978	9983	9987	9991	9996

Index